ORGANIZATION THEORY
A Strategic Approach

ORGANIZATION THEORY
A Strategic Approach

V. K. (VEEKAY) NARAYANAN
School of Business
UNIVERSITY OF KANSAS

RAGHU NATH
Katz Graduate School of Business
UNIVERSITY OF PITTSBURGH

Homewood, IL 60430
Boston, MA 02116

© RICHARD D. IRWIN, INC., 1993

Sponsoring editor: Craig Beytien
Project editor: Karen J. Nelson
Production manager: Ann Cassady
Art coordinator: Mark Malloy
Compositor: Carlisle Communications, Ltd.
Typeface: 10/12 Bembo
Printer: R. R. Donnelley & Sons Company
Marketing manager: Ron Bloecher

Library of Congress Cataloging-in-Publication Data

Narayanan, V. K. (Veekay)
    Organization theory : a strategic approach / V.K. (Veekay)
Narayanan, Raghu Nath.
        p.   cm.
    Includes bibliographical references.
    ISBN 0-256-08778-4
    1. Organization.   2. Management.   I. Raghu, Nath.   II. Title.
HD31.N25 1993
658.4′012—dc20   92–31180

Printed in the United States of America
1 2 3 4 5 6 7 8 9 0 DOC 9 8 7 6 5 4 3 2

To our parents
who inculcated in us the value of holistic thinking

V. K. Narayanan

V. K. (Veekay) Narayanan is currently Professor of Strategic Management and Associate Dean of Academic Affairs in the School of Business at the University of Kansas. He holds a bachelor's degree in mechanical engineering from the Indian Institute of Technology, Madras, a master of business administration degree from the Indian Institute of Management, Ahmedabad, and a Ph.D. in business from the Graduate School of Business at the University of Pittsburgh, Pennsylvania. He has had behavioral training with the National Training Laboratories, Bethel, Maine. He has taught at the University of Pittsburgh, the Graduate School of Management at Rutgers University, New Jersey, and the University of Kansas, where he was a Phillips Petroleum Fellow during 1984 to 1986.

Professor Narayanan teaches courses in Business Policy and Strategy, Organization Development, Strategy Implementation, Management of Technology, and Corporate Restructuring. *Organization Theory: A Strategic Approach* has been the basis of his innovative course on Strategy Implementation. He has published over 25 articles and book chapters and has made several professional presentations. His articles have appeared in professional journals such as *Academy of Management Review, Accounting, Organizations and Society, Industrial Relations, Journal of Applied Behavioral Science, Journal of Applied Psychology, Journal of Management, Journal of Management Studies, R&D Management,* and *Strategic Management Journal.* With Liam Fahey, he has authored *Macroenvironmental Analysis for Strategic Management.* Recently, he completed a monograph for NASA entitled "The Management History of the Space Station" (coauthored with Tom Lewin). He serves on the editorial board of *Organization Science.*

Veekay Narayanan has consulted with several organizations, both public and private. His clients have ranged from state government technology incubators to multinational corporations, from high-technology enterprises to banking and social service institutions.

Raghu Nath

Professor Raghu Nath is on the faculty of the Joseph M. Katz Graduate School of Business, University of Pittsburgh, where he has been Coordinator of the International Interest Group and Director of the Management Training Laboratory. He is the President of INSOHP, which specializes in organization change and systems development. He holds a bachelor of science degree (honors) in physics from the University of Delhi, a master of science degree in electrical engineering from the Indian Institute of Science in Bangalore, and a Ph.D. in industrial management from the Massachusetts Institute of Technology.

He has authored over 50 publications. His articles have appeared in such journals as *The Academy of Management Executive, The Academy of Management Review,* the *Accounting Review, California Management Review, Human Resource Planning Journal, Industrial Relations, Inter-American Journal of Psychology, International Journal of Social Science, Journal of Applied Behavioral Science, Journal of Applied Psychology, Journal of Educational Psychology, Journal of Systems Management, Kultura, Management International,* and *Psychiatric Communications.* He has served on the editorial boards of several professional journals and has been Chairman of the Organization Development (Eastern Region) and International divisions of the Academy of Management. His earlier book, entitled *Comparative Management: A Regional View,* has received wide acclaim and acceptance.

Dr. Nath has consulted with international organizations, governmental departments, and multinational corporations, among them the United Nations, the World Bank, the Departments of State and Navy, NASA, IBM, GE, Westinghouse, and Alcoa. His research interests and areas of consultation include comparative management, organization development and system design, management of strategic change, design of knowledge network, international corporate strategy, development of human resources, team management, interpersonal, and communication skills.

This book was conceived nearly 15 years ago, during discussions the authors were having on the state of organization theory. There were four major undercurrents in these discussions. First, we felt that there was an increasing convergence between the two fields of strategic planning and organization theory. Problems were beginning to surface during the implementation of strategies, forcing the relevance of organization theory into the consciousness of strategic planners. On the other hand, organization theorists were paying greater attention to the environment, partly because of heightened global competition and partly as a result of the increasing rate of environmental change. Second, we both felt that our experiences with teaching organization theory to managers were not satisfying since managers wondered what organization theory meant for them. The managers were smart and understood more than what the theory has to offer—that ultimately, organizations are mechanisms of control. Third, both of us were concerned that large-scale empirical works focusing on static correlational analyses were crowding out other forms of inquiry—both nomothetic and idiographic—that often yielded richer insights. We wondered whether in their ahistorical search for generalizations, the organization theorists have forgotten their rich heritage. Finally, we were disenchanted with (what we considered to be) the inadequate development of system theory by the organization theorist, especially the linkages among political, cultural, and informational elements of an organization. We continue to believe that an open system perspective is most useful for general managers who have to deal with strategic issues. Thus, the main rationale for writing this book was to take a strategic approach to organization theory, making organization theory more relevant to the interests of general managers, who we believe are—or certainly should be—concerned with strategic issues.

The original discussions focused on a paper that Raghu Nath had presented in 1964 to the Society for General Systems Research. The idea that grew out of these earlier discussions was to develop a short book (with no more than five chapters) that focused primarily on strategic planning and organization design and development, with systems and contingency theory as the foundation. Over the last 15 years, two events derailed our initial plans, changing substantially our thinking and writing of the book. First, Veekay Narayanan moved out of Pittsburgh to start his academic career at the University of Kansas. This meant that the writing of the book would have to be delayed, and in its place we continued our discussions. These discussions, which ranged from internationalization and environment to refining some ideas about politics, enriched this book. Second, many areas began to get greater attention from other organization theorists—strategy, politics, culture, and management information systems, to name a few. This meant that we had the help of many others in developing a strategic approach to organization theory. When these two events—our discussions and concurrent developments by others—came together, our book expanded to 15 chapters, three times our original target length. However, we believe the book is considerably more comprehensive than what we had originally planned.

Although we took a long time to bring the book to closure, and although the book itself has undergone major changes from our original conception, some ideas have remained the same over the course to its development. Four major themes deserve mention. First, although we have drawn on our extensive consulting experience over the last three decades in developing this book, the book itself is anchored in theory, because we believe that theory informs action and good theory leads to effective action. Although few academics will quarrel with this belief, it is, in our opinion, quite alien to the world of managers. We are not apologetic about presenting good theory to managers. Second, we strongly believe that organization theory is deeply rooted in historical context. More than anything else, the zeitgeist of the times greatly influences the development of a given organization theory. Therefore, in addition to the chapter on historical development in Part I, we have tried to include in the beginning of each chapter the historical antecedents of the theoretical or applied area that is being discussed in that chapter. Third, we believe that in order to develop a fuller understanding of a theory, it is absolutely essential to appreciate the assumptions underlying it. Every theory is an abstraction, and every theorist makes some assumptions that guide him or her as to what to abstract from reality. Yet, in organization theory, in our judgment, most books fail to address the assumptions explicitly. In this book, we have tried to be explicit about underlying philosophical assumptions, which in our view reflect the climate of the times. Finally, we have stuck to an open systems perspective as a unifying theme throughout the book. In Part I, we provide an overview of systems theory. We then use open systems language to provide necessary integration in Part II as we deal with each of the applied areas.

We owe an intellectual debt to a variety of scholars who have influenced our thinking and work over the years. First, Douglas McGregor's pioneering work on the human side of enterprise left an indelible mark on our minds. He was a philosopher theorist; his theory Y represented a cosmology rather than a theory. We have benefited greatly from his normative stance on the worth of human beings at work and especially his emphasis on cosmology. Second, we have not merely admired the intellectual prowess of J. W. Forrester but have learned about the dynamics of organizational systems and nonlinearity from his several works. Third, Ian Mitroff, while at Pittsburgh, reinforced the importance of assumptions in the many lectures he gave to his class, in which Veekay Narayanan was a student. Fourth, William R. King brought Veekay Narayanan into the field of strategic planning (away from operation research) and kindled his interest in environment.

Many others from the University of Pittsburgh and also from Rutgers GSM have influenced the development of the book in different ways. Veekay Narayanan developed our ideas on environmental analysis and politics in collaboration with Liam Fahey, while he had been at Pitt. James Craft and Robert Perloff provided valuable references on the topics of career development and evaluation research, respectively. David Blake, then Dean at Rutgers GSM, provided the needed motivation to Veekay Narayanan to continue with the book during his two-year stint there. He underscored that there is more to scholarship than journal articles. Rutgers' superb Organization and Management group, consisting of Hal Eastman, George Farris, Dick Hoffman, Nancy DiTomaso, Fariborz Damanpour, and Don McCabe, probably had greater faith in the book than the authors themselves.

We especially want to thank Professor Larry Cummings who, as a consulting editor, encouraged the development of this book. Several others helped us along the way. Professor Marilyn Taylor was kind enough to pilot test the chapters on strategic planning and organization design in her Business Policy class as early as 1986; as a result, these chapters had undergone major changes. Professor Rajesh Mirani contributed the section Historical Underpinnings in Chapter 10, Organization Information and Control.

We would like to express gratitude to our reviewers who were kind but tough, and their comments led us to restructure the book considerably. We are immensely grateful to them for their incisive and thoughtful feedback.

All writers need a good manager, and we were fortunate to have Craig S. Beytien. Although we continue to see the book as being in process, Craig's gentle but firm approach pushed us to bring the book to closure, this round.

Finally, and most importantly, we must mention our clients and students who try to implement esoteric theoretical ideas in real-life situations. Our clients have taught us the absolute necessity of implementing theory, that it is the interaction between theory and practice that generates insights for further development. Our students have always challenged us to make our assumptions explicit, and this has helped us to understand our own theory better.

Organizations have become a necessary part of modern life. They not only provide goods and services but have become an integral part of our lives. Most of us derive meaning from work. Whether we realize it or not, whether we like it or not, organizations shape our lives. It is imperative that they be managed well. Organization theory has much to offer to general managers, and we hope this book will help managers and students appreciate that.

V. K. Narayanan
Raghu Nath

C O N T E N T S   I N   B R I E F

CONTENTS

10   Organizational Information and Control Systems   350

11   Organization Development   388

C H A P T E R

1 INTRODUCTION

Chapter Outline

Organizations

In modern society, it is difficult, if not impossible, to imagine life without organizations. Let us look at a few scenarios to illustrate what role organizations play in sustaining our day-to-day living.

> Without utilities, there will be no power to light, warm, or cool our homes and offices. Without transportation companies and supermarkets, there will be little food available to most of the urban population. Without regulatory agencies, the air and water pollution in most urban areas would have a catastrophic impact on the health of the urban populace, particularly the young and the old.

In today's global village, many organizations across continents are involved in producing and marketing a single product such as a designer dress. For example, a cotton top by Ralph Lauren starts with cotton grown by an Egyptian farmer. It is spun into yarn by an English textile mill. Design is done by a French company, then the dress is sewn in a factory in Taiwan. It is imported by an import-export company in New York who sells it to a department or specialty store. In addition, several shipping, airline, and trucking companies are involved.

Organizations have become vital to the very fabric of modern society. It has, therefore, become necessary to understand organizations and learn about how to design and manage them. In this introductory chapter, we will try to discuss questions such as: What is an organization? How are organizations different from groups? How can organizations be classified into different types? Why are organizations important? How do we learn about organizations? What is organization theory? Are there different types of organization theories? Why should managers try to understand organization theory; that is, what is the practical utility of theories of organization? After discussing these questions, we will briefly outline key themes in the book. We will then describe a three-part plan for the book. Finally, we will offer a few guidelines as to how to read the book.

What Is an Organization?

Human organizations have existed from antiquity. In the beginning, aboriginal peoples had to organize to hunt for food and protect themselves from the elements.

The building of pyramids in Egypt must have required an enormous organizational effort. Indeed, the first large-scale organizations were Egyptian state monopolies, used for carrying out such projects as irrigation, canal building, and the construction of pyramids. At the top of the organization was the Pharaoh, who based his authority on divine right and delegated certain authority to his vizier. The vizier acted as prime minister, chief justice, and treasurer, and was directly responsible for an elaborate bureaucracy at the base of which were tens of thousands of slaves.

Another example of large-scale organizations in the preindustrial period is the Roman military organization. At the top of this organization was the Caesar, who was the commander-in-chief. Reporting to him were commanders of the various armies assigned to different regions of the Roman Empire. In most cases, the commander in charge of a given regional army also acted as the governor of the region. Each army unit was an elaborate bureaucracy at the base of which were thousands of soldiers.

Figure 1.1 graphically portrays the hierarchy of the Egyptian and Roman organizations. As can be seen from the figure, the Egyptian state monopolies had three top-management levels (Pharaoh, vizier, and persons in charge of irrigation, canal building, and pyramids), several middle- to first-management levels, and slaves at the bottom of the hierarchy. On the other hand, the Roman military organization has two top-management levels (Caesar and army commanders), several middle- to first-management levels, and soldiers at the bottom of the hierarchy. This is typical of large-scale organizations which usually have many levels of hierarchy comprising top management, middle management, first-line management, and workers (slaves and soldiers in the above two examples).

Organizations are also purposeful; that is, they have common goals. For example, an Egyptian state monopoly might have had as its primary goal the construction of pyramids. Similarly, the primary goal of the Roman military was to ensure the loyalty of various provinces (regions) to Rome

FIGURE 1.1

Egyptian and Roman hierarchies

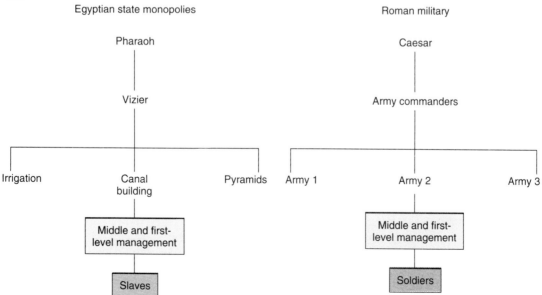

and protect them from foreign invasions. In order to achieve the common goals, each large-scale organization performs many complex tasks. For example, a pyramid-building Egyptian state monopoly would have engaged in mining stone from the quarries, transporting these stones to the construction site, then chiseling, installing, and polishing the stones. In addition, tasks related to site selection, preparation of the site, and providing access roads to each pyramid and to the pyramid city would have been performed.

> Thus, an organization can be defined as an arena where human beings come together to perform complex tasks so as to fulfill common goal(s).

How Are Organizations Different from Groups?

It is important to distinguish between groups and organizations. When two or more people get together for a common goal, they constitute a group. Groups have two levels: (1) individual level (since groups are made of individuals) and (2) group level. And when two or more groups get together for a common effort, it is an organization. While groups have two levels, organizations have at least three levels: individual, group, and organization. Thus, family and football teams are groups, whereas hospitals, universities, government agencies, and corporations are organizations. Egyptian state monopolies and the Roman military are organizations because each has at least three levels of hierarchy.

Types of Organizations

Organizations can be classified into different types according to their functions or goals, types of technology employed, ways to gain compliance, or the beneficiary of the organization. Probably the most easily utilized typology is based on the function performed or goal sought. Parsons[1] and Katz and Kahn[2] have developed this kind of typology.

According to Parsons, organizations that make things or products are classified as **production organizations,** whereas **political organizations** are concerned with ensuring that society as a whole achieves its objectives. **Integrative organizations** deal with the settling of conflict and seeing to it that the various parts of society fit together well. Finally **pattern maintenance organizations** are those that attempt to provide for the continuation of society by performing educational and cultural activities.

Katz and Kahn, like Parsons, also use functions performed or goals sought as the criteria to classify organizations. According to them, **production or economic organizations** exist to provide goods and services for society, whereas **pattern maintenance organizations** prepare people to enter other organizations smoothly and effectively. The **adaptive organization** creates knowledge and tests theories, while the **managerial or political organization** attempts to control resource use and authority. Table 1.1 summarizes these two classification systems.

Why Are Organizations Important?

There are several reasons why organizations are important entities. First, as discussed before, organizations are pervasive throughout the modern world. In fact, they have become vital to the existence of the modern society.

Second, people working alone can do simple tasks. It is only through working together in an organization that complex tasks can be performed. Thus, organizations extend the capacities of individuals acting alone. As societies develop, they face more complex tasks, hence, the importance of organizations tends to increase. Today, we can think of very little that can be done without organizing. In fact, even the simplest of societies today has a number of organizations. Thus, organizations have become a necessity for managing the complexity of today's world.

Third, when human effort is organized effectively, it results in higher productivity than would be possible with an unorganized collection of individuals. In other words, there is a synergistic effect created by people working together that enhances the final outcome. This is probably the most important reason that human activity needs to be organized and organizations have flourished and multiplied in recent times.

TABLE 1.1   **Types of Organizations**

Scholars	Types of Organizations	Example of Type
Talcot Parsons	Production	IBM
	Political	United Nations
	Integrative	Federal court system
	Pattern maintenance	Roman Catholic Church
Daniel Katz and Robert Kahn	Production or economic	General Motors, department store
	Pattern maintenance	School system
	Adaptive	Research and development organizations (e.g., Bell Labs)
	Management or political	Regulatory agencies (e.g., Food and Drug Administration)

Organization Theory

What Is Organization Theory?

The primary role of any **theory** is to provide a description as well as an explanation of some phenomenon. Therefore, a theory consists of principles that describe relationships observed in association with the phenomenon.[3] In other words, theory explains practice and helps to improve it.

Thus, organization theory can be thought of as a set of related concepts and principles that is used to describe and explain organizational phenomena. This means that organization theory can help us understand what organizations are, how they behave in a given environment, and how they might behave in a different set of circumstances.

All managers carry in their heads a theory of organizations even if they are not consciously aware of it. And they make decisions based on these theories. However, each theory is based on the experience of just one person. It may, therefore, apply to one manager's situation but cannot be generalized to other situations.

Organization theory, as we discuss it in this book, has developed as a result of systematic study of organizations. It has, therefore, general application to all types of organizations. It provides a way of thinking about organizations and a way of managing organizations.

How Is Organization Theory Different from Organization Behavior?

Before discussing how organization theory is generated, it is important to distinguish it from the field of **organization behavior.**

Organizational phenomena can be categorized into different levels—individual, group, intergroup, and organizational.

Organization behavior field primarily deals with individual and group levels and to some extent with intergroup levels. Therefore, it covers such individual level topics as motivation, perception, attitudes, decision making, job satisfaction, stress, and careers. At the group level, various topics are group function, group process, group performance, leadership, and team building. At the intergroup level, the areas of intergroup relationships, competition, and collaboration are usually covered.

Organization theory field, on the other hand, deals primarily with organization level phenomena such as organization change and growth, effectiveness, planning, design, development, politics, and culture. At the intergroup level, the topics covered are management of conflict between groups and/or organizational units.

As can be seen from the above, the intergroup level is where the two fields of organization behavior and organization theory intersect.

How Is Organization Theory Developed?

There are primarily two ways by which systematic knowledge about organizations is generated.

First is the experiential way. This is the way we learn about most things. This method usually requires three steps:

1. Experiencing organizational phenomena by working in an ongoing organization.
2. Reflecting on these experiences.
3. Making some systematic sense out of these reflections, which involves drawing inferences from the experiences and conceptualizing them into a coherent framework.

Some of the classic work in organization theory has been generated by this three-step process. *My Years with General Motors* by Alfred P. Sloan[4] is an excellent example of knowledge generated by the experiential method. In his book, Sloan reflects on years of his experience with General Motors and draws inferences about how to organize for effectiveness. Other examples are works by Chester Barnard,[5] Frederick Taylor,[6] Mooney and Reiley,[7] Mary Parker Follett,[8] and Henri Fayol.[9]

The second mode of generating knowledge about organizations is through scientific research. There are two kinds of basic research methods—exploratory and explanatory. The purpose of exploratory research is to discover what kind of relationships exist in ongoing organizations; that is, to generate hypotheses. On the other hand, the main objective of explanatory research is to test hypotheses. These hypotheses could be the outcome of exploratory research or derived from existing theories or hunches based on actual experiences in ongoing organizations. Box 1.1 provides a more detailed description of these two research methods.

Types of Organization Theories

Before 1960, management theory was in a state of chaos: There were lots of theories but no unifying framework. Each theory was unique and stood on its own. Since the organization field had borrowed from a variety of disciplines such as psychology, sociology, anthropology, economics, mathematics, and computer sciences, there were diverse perspectives that were quite distinct from each other. Though this created a chaotic situation, a major advantage of this diversity was that it resulted in a multidisciplinary approach to this field of inquiry. Thus, the organization theory field was enriched by contributions of scholars from diverse disciplines.

In the 60s, an open systems model was suggested as a possible integrating framework. In a presentation at the Society for General System Research, Nath[10] pointed out how an open system framework could provide an

---

Box 1.1

Research Methods

There are two types of research methods—exploratory studies and explanatory research.

Exploratory Studies

Exploratory studies often involve interviewing and/or observational methods. Some of the better studies in organizations have been based on observational techniques. The most frequently used method is participant observation, which was developed by anthropologists to study primitive societies. In this methodology, the researcher actually lives in an organization under disguised identity. For example, he or she may take up a regular job in an organization but not disclose his or her research intent. *Men Who Manage,* by Melvin Dalton (1959), is probably one of the best examples of this kind of research. Dalton took a position in a factory and studied day-to-day events in a systemic fashion. In this factory, the local managers had a grudge against the head office; thus, they all colluded to promote an incompetent manager to the general management position. However, the real power was wielded by these managers, who thwarted every move by headquarters. On a daily basis, Dalton recorded his observations of important events that took place in this factory. In doing so, he provided a rare insight into the political machinations of the managers who really managed the factory. Other studies of this ilk are those by William Foot Whyte, Chris Argyris, Selznick, and others. There have also been some very good studies using interviewing methodology. Two of these have been on the best-seller list in recent years: *GamesMen,* by Michael Macabey, and *In Search of Excellence* by Peters and Waterman. Macabey provided insight into the psyche and management style of the modern manager. Peters and Waterman, on the other hand, identified eight characteristics of successful organizations.

Explanatory Research

The last three decades have witnessed a flurry of explanatory research in organizations. The purpose of explanatory research is to test hypotheses. Empirical data are usually collected by administering valid and reliable questionnaires. Hypotheses are then tested using quantitative techniques. Contingency theory, which we shall discuss later in this book, is one of the major outcomes of this research. The contingency perspective in organization theory developed because hypotheses were confirmed in one context but not in others. As this evidence accumulated, it became clear that organization theory is context-related. This contingency viewpoint has been one of the major developments in organization theory in modern times.

integrating framework for various theories that existed at that time. Later, several scholars also proposed an open system framework (e.g., Katz and Kahn, 1966). Also, J. W. Forrester[11] proposed a methodology, namely industrial dynamics, to simulate management and organizational systems in terms of differential equations. Thus, he provided a quantitative approach to systems theories of organizations. As we discuss later in the system chapter, one of the basic tenets of open systems theory is that interactions among subsystems of the organization and between the organization and its environment are more important than either of these entities by themselves. In the 70s, contingency theory developed as an offshoot of systems theory as well as from empirical work in organizations.

Since the open systems theory provided the integrating framework, books in organization theory tried to pay lip service to this by including a chapter on systems theory in the beginning of the book and then discussing other topics independently of the systems theory. On the other hand, there were some books—for example, Gary Dessler[12]—that tried to use contingency theory as the integrating framework and did so successfully throughout the book.

An Integrating Framework

In *Organization Theory: A Strategic Approach,* we have outlined an integrating framework in Part I, based on an open systems model. This framework is then used to discuss various applied issues in Part II and the role of general management in Part III. This, in our view, is a major contribution of our book as well as its most unique feature.

The 70s and 80s saw the development of the strategic planning and policy area, which focuses on the interaction between the organization and its environment. Though organization theory books had discussed the environment from the contingency perspective, these discussions were rather abstract. On the other hand, strategic planning literature made a lot of headway in defining the environment in terms; that is, both its characteristics and its stakeholders. Therefore, we have tried to incorporate this strategic perspective into our book. We believe that this strategic approach is a very important addition to the field of organization theory.

To sum up, we have tried to provide an integrated framework comprised of an open systems model and a strategic perspective. We believe that this should enrich the field and, therefore, help students and managers to conduct a more thorough and coherent analysis of organizational level phenomena. This should also lead to recommendations that are more effective than a piecemeal approach to organizational problems.

How Is Organization Theory Useful?

It is important to study organization theory because it can answer such questions as: How should one describe and diagnose organizational phenomena? How should one organize? How should one bring about changes in organizations? And, how does one measure organizational effectiveness?

As depicted in Figure 1.2, organization theory should enable one to describe, understand, predict, and control organizational phenomena. Organizational phenomena can be divided into three levels—institutional,

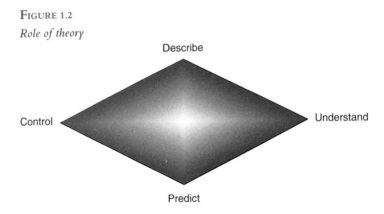

Figure 1.2
Role of theory

Describe

Control   Understand

Predict

Figure 1.3
Levels of organizational phenomena and role of the individual

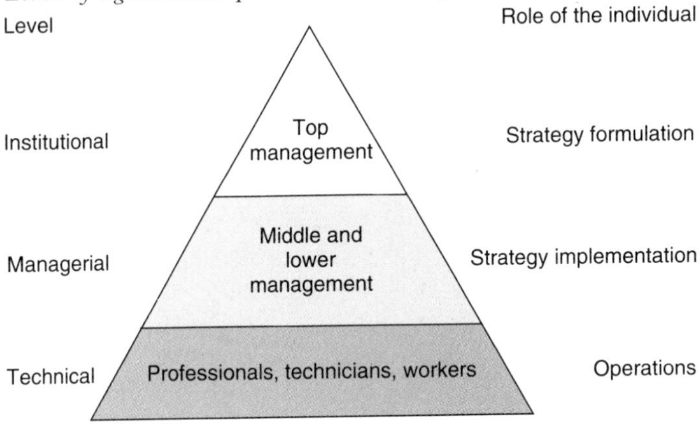

Level   Role of the individual

Institutional   Top management   Strategy formulation

Managerial   Middle and lower management   Strategy implementation

Technical   Professionals, technicians, workers   Operations

managerial, and technical. At each of these levels, there is a corresponding role for the individual. For example, at the institutional level, the role mostly involves strategy formulation. At the managerial level, which includes middle- and lower-level management, the role shifts to strategy implementation. Finally, at the technical level, which includes professionals and workers, the role becomes primarily operational; that is, carrying out the day-to-day tasks of the organization. Thus, the jobs at the technical level have primarily technical content, whereas jobs at the institutional level have mostly human and environmental content. At the managerial level, jobs involve primarily human and some technical content. The above is summarized in Figure 1.3.

What relevance has the organization theory for students of management and/or young professionals starting at the lower end of the organizational hierarchy? In addition to helping them to understand and interpret managerial actions, it should help them to plan their careers and increase their effectiveness. For example, an understanding of the role shift from the technical to managerial level may cause aspiring managers to plan their careers in a way that allows them to pay increasing attention to human skills rather than to concentrate solely on acquiring increased technical skills.

Key Themes in the Book

There are several key themes in the book.

Open versus Closed Systems

First, as discussed earlier, we regard organizations as *open rather than closed* systems. The major implication of this viewpoint is that we consider transactions between the organization and its environment as the most significant aspect of organizational phenomena. To emphasize this, we begin the action strategy cycle in Part II of the book with a chapter entitled "Environmental Analysis." Most organization theory books describe the environment in general terms. Instead, we provide a rather detailed treatment of how to describe, study, and analyze the organization's environment. Transactions between the organization and its environment are discussed in the chapters "Strategic Planning" and "Organization Design," as well as in other chapters of Part II whenever it is appropriate.

Human and Technical Elements

The second theme focuses on the human and technical components of organizational systems and the interaction between them. As discussed in Chapter 3, entitled "The Systems Model," organization comprises five subsystems—functional, informational, social, political, and cultural. Whereas functional and informational subsystems deal primarily with technical aspects, the other three subsystems deal primarily with human aspects of organizations.

As shown in Figure 1.4, technical elements push for *stability,* whereas human elements create *turbulence.* Since both elements are essential parts of the organization, and furthermore, they interact with each other, the role of general management is to *seek a balance* between the pull toward chaos and the need to preserve order. Also, each element requires a different way of managing. For example, the technical element requires a mechanistic (rigid) approach, while the human element can best be managed in an organic (flexible) way. The balancing act, therefore, requires accommodating conflicting ways of managing within a given organizational system. This creates perpetual conflict that needs to be recognized and managed.

FIGURE 1.4

Model of organization

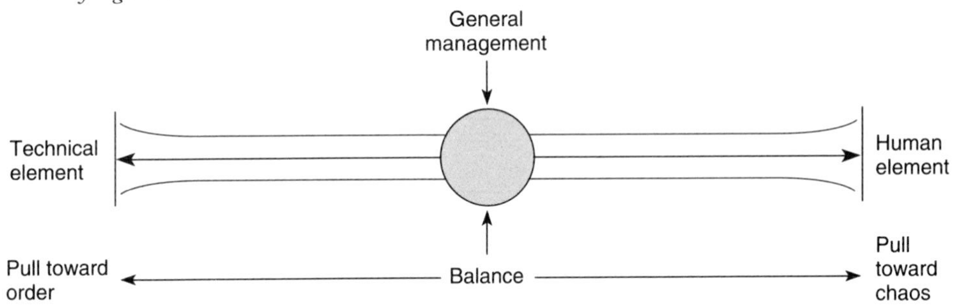

Ambiguity and Certainty

The third theme is *ambiguity versus certainty.* For example, at the managerial and institutional levels, one has to deal with human and environmental issues that involve a great deal of ambiguity and uncertainty. On the other hand, jobs at the technical level have a degree of certainty. In other words, strategy formulation involves a lot of ambiguity and uncertainty, whereas operational tasks are rather certain. Strategy implementation falls somewhere in between; that is, it has both certain and ambiguous elements. Yet all three levels of organizational phenomena need to be managed. And each requires different styles of management as well as skills. Effective organizations, therefore, have to manage this diversity of management styles and skills. This is another important aspect of general management's role.

Theory and Application

The fourth theme is the relationship between theory and its applications. As teachers of organizational theory, we have learned that business students and managers have difficulty understanding organization theory books when these books do not discuss application of theory to actual organizational and management problems. This is because both business students as well as managers are more application-oriented, while the books in the organization theory field tend to be theoretical and rather abstract. In fact, some of the best sellers in recent years have been management books such as *In Search of Excellence* by Peters and Waterman (1983). Our consulting experience also confirms that practicing managers are mostly interested in applications and care very little about theory.

In this book, we have tried to balance discussion of theory with its applications. Whereas Part I of the book is primarily theoretical with some examples of applications, Parts II and III are primarily application-oriented with some theoretical perspectives. In other words, we have tried to apply the open systems theory discussed in Part I to various action strategies in Parts II and III. Our experience in the use of materials from this book with both students and managers indicates that this approach excites their interest in the field.

Another way applications are built into the book is by providing examples from situations discussed in business periodicals. We believe that these illustrations try to make abstract theoretical principles more understandable. Finally, in the book of readings, a number of articles are included that are primarily application-oriented. They come from popular business periodicals rather than academic journals. Of course, a number of articles from academic journals are also included to provide the requisite balance between theory and practice.

Thus, the book provides a balanced coverage of theory and its application to various contexts. This balanced approach provides both rigor and usefulness. We strongly believe that cookbook-type, application-oriented books do disservice in the long run, while highly theoretically oriented books fail to reach an audience. The balanced coverage of theory and applications provides the appropriate and requisite mix for professional development of managers.

Global versus Domestic Perspectives

The fifth theme concerns global versus domestic perspectives. The framework implied in this book—the open systems model—is highly suitable for a global perspective. The open systems model emphasizes organization-environment interaction. As environments differ from nation to nation, organizational prescriptions must differ for these different environments.

Throughout the book, we have tried to integrate the available international and comparative material in relevant chapters. In contrast, other organization theory textbooks have a separate chapter on the international dimension. Since international studies in the organization area are of relatively recent origin, there are several gaps in our knowledge. These gaps have been discussed in the last chapter to highlight areas for future study and research.

To sum up, we have tried to integrate the international dimension throughout the book as well as to provide some fruitful directions for future study and research.

No Quick Fix

Finally, the sixth theme is that there are no quick fixes (Kilmann, 1989).[13] Managing organizations requires a systematic way of analyzing organizational phenomena, and developing and implementing an action plan. This requires long-range, systems-oriented perspectives rather than short-term, problem-oriented fixes.

The most fundamental difference between typical Japanese versus American management is that Japanese management has a long-range perspective while American management has a short-term orientation. The long-term perspective leads to sustained development and innovation over a period of time, while the short-term orientation results in pursuing management fads and in crisis management of perceived problems. This results in continuous improvement in Japanese organizations, which, over time, provides them with a great competitive advantage in the global marketplace.

Plan of the Book

After the introductory chapter, the book is divided into three parts. In Part I, we discuss the theoretical foundations of organization theory, whereas in Part II we deal with action strategies. In Part III, we describe the role of the general manager who is responsible for implementing various action strategies.

Part I

Part I is comprised of five chapters, as shown in Figure 1.5. The part starts with a chapter (Chapter 2) that broadly surveys the history of the development of management and organization theory. In this chapter, we

FIGURE 1.5

Part I: Theoretical foundations

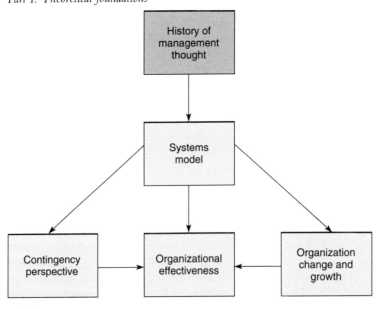

particularly focus on the underlying values and assumptions that guided the development of management and organizational principles in a given period.

Following this, Chapter 3 is devoted to the discussion of the open systems theory. First, we review various properties of open social systems. We then present our model of organizations as five interacting subsystems that in turn interact with the environment. We outline and discuss a company case to illustrate how interactions among subsystems generate most important aspects of organizational behavior. As indicated earlier, this chapter is the foundation for the rest of the book.

Chapter 4 discusses the contingency perspective in organizations. In this chapter, we explain how the contingency perspective flows from the open systems framework. While the systems theory provides a comprehensive framework for diagnosing organizations, the contingency perspective generates specific recommendations for a given situation. The systems framework is universally applicable, whereas the contingency perspective provides a way of applying this universal theory in specific contexts. On the one hand, most practicing managers argue that each organization is unique. On the other hand, universalist theorists claim that organizational phenomena are universally applicable. The contingency perspective provides a mid-range view by generating propositions that are applicable to a cluster of organizations.

Chapter 5 deals with issues of organization change and growth. Whereas the contingency chapter deals with static aspects, this chapter discusses dynamic aspects of organizations. We discuss various theories and models that are extant in the literature for dealing with these dynamic aspects. In this chapter, we also discuss the work of population ecologists who have tried to analyze the macro-macro level of organizational phenomena. In particular, these scholars have provided insight into how a population of organizations behaves over a period of time.

Chapter 6 discusses the issues related to organizational effectiveness. This is a very controversial topic, and there is no universally accepted definition of "organization effectiveness." Therefore, we present various viewpoints and suggest that the systems framework may provide an integrated approach to the discussion of this issue.

Part II

The focus in Part II is on action strategies for developing effective organizations. We discuss seven action strategies: environmental analysis, strategic planning, organization design, organizational information and control systems, organization development, organizational politics, and organizational culture. We would emphasize that all seven strategies are essential in a systemic approach to management of organizations. There are, of course, many Band-Aid℗ approaches that rely only on one or a few of these strategies.

These problem- or issue-oriented approaches may be useful in some situations; however, our experience indicates that organizational systems are holistic entities. Therefore, piecemeal interventions in them usually do not result in organizational effectiveness.

Chapter 7 in Part II discusses various approaches to environmental analysis. In this chapter, we expose the reader to various facets of the environment and describe how each facet can be analyzed.

Chapter 8 deals with strategic planning. Here, we describe various levels and models of strategic planning.

Chapter 9 describes various ways of designing organizations. In this chapter, we apply a contingency perspective to the design of organizations and discuss in a more specific and detailed way how various organizational elements can be designed in light of contingency recommendations.

Chapter 10 deals with the organizational information and control systems. Many scholars have argued that organizations are primarily information-processing entities. In this age of computers, it is impossible to ignore the informational aspects of organizations. Since information is a very important aspect of today's organizations, we have included an informational subsystem as one of the five subsystems of the organization. In this chapter we also discuss the related issue of organizational control.

Chapter 11 deals with organization development. As compared to the structural issues discussed in the design chapter, this chapter primarily focuses on the management of process issues in organizations. These issues deal with the underlying attitudes and climate that prevail in a given organization. If these issues are managed successfully, the major outcome is a strong commitment by organizational members to the objectives of the organization. It has become trite to say that American organizations suffer from mismanagement of organizational processes; therefore, member commitment in these organizations is rather low. In contrast, Japanese organizations have been highly successful in managing organizational processes and, therefore, obtaining a very strong commitment of their members. Thus, issues discussed in this chapter are central to the effectiveness of organizations. We explore in depth the philosophical underpinnings of organization development as well as describe various technologies and techniques. Above all, we strongly emphasize the notion of obtaining congruency between the underlying values of the organization and the interventions employed to manage its processes.

Chapter 12 discusses the concept of organizational culture. Unfortunately, this topic has been handled in a rather faddish way in the recent past. Culture is probably the most enduring aspect of a given organization. In our systems framework, culture undergirds the organization. In this sense, all aspects of the organization are impacted by the cultural subsystem. It is the invisible, informal part of the organization. Therefore, it is rather difficult to deal with culture. In this chapter, we not only discuss the concept of culture but also describe ways of diagnosing organizational culture.

The technology of managing culture is still developing and is in an experimental stage. We describe some of these technologies with a caveat that these are not proven technologies and one must use them with great caution. We fervently hope that, in the future, it will be possible to include in a book like this proven technologies to manage culture.

Chapter 13 deals with political aspects of the organization. As we point out in the beginning of the chapter, political processes have always existed within all organizations. Yet organization theorists have come to recognize these processes only recently. This is a rather new area in organization theory; we believe that the neglect of this issue has been the singular failure of organization theory. Our perspective is that political behavior occurs in every organization and, therefore, it is necessary to deal with political issues in organizations.

In this chapter, we particularly deal with the issue of management of conflict. We describe various strategies of dealing with conflict. We emphasize that conflict need not be dysfunctional. If managed properly, it could be a source of innovation and productivity. Left unmanaged, it can destroy organizations and careers.

Part III

This part has two chapters. Chapter 14 deals with the role of general management. Having described the seven-stage process model of managing organizations in Part II, it is important to look at the actor who is going to implement various recommendations generated in Part II of the book. In our view, this person has to be the general manager. Though some of the recommendations can be implemented by lower- and middle-level managers, it is only the general management that is likely to have the authority to implement the action strategies described in Part II.

Chapter 15 first summarizes previous chapters and then we try to speculate on what is likely to happen in the 90s. As a result of this speculation, we identify several major trends. Probably the most important of these trends is the internationalization of business.

We are living in a global environment and the business of business has become global in scope. Any organization that does not think in global terms is not likely to prosper in the future. This global perspective requires a different mindset than what has existed so far in many organizations. Particularly, many organizations in the United States, such as the steel and auto companies, that have ethnocentric viewpoints, have suffered in the internationally competitive environment of the 70s and 80s.

We hope that the organization theory field will become global in scope. Unfortunately, this is not so at the present time because our knowledge is rather limited. Most organization and management theory has been generated in the United States. Hence, these theories are ethnocentric. Therefore, we identify various gaps in organization theory from a global perspective and hope that scholars will turn their attention to filling these gaps.

Chapter Layout

Early in each chapter, we review historical, philosophical, and theoretical perspectives underlying the area under discussion. It is important for students to understand these basic assumptions early on so that they have a proper perspective regarding conceptual framework and/or prescriptions discussed in the chapter. Every theory or concept is an abstraction from reality. It is very important to understand what guided this process of abstracting reality. This develops a deeper understanding of the phenomena and an appreciation of the fact that what is being discussed is not the truth but an abstraction of that truth by some scholar or manager.

Following the historical, philosophical, and theoretical underpinnings, we discuss specific concepts, models, and frameworks relevant to the particular topical area. In the action strategy chapters in Part II, we discuss how these specific concepts or frameworks can guide decision making in organizations. In doing so, we summarize action strategy implications of these concepts.

Third, we illustrate the applicability of various concepts by focusing on specific tools or technologies or dealing with specific organizational problems and issues. In the action strategy chapters in Part II of the book, these tools and technologies are rather specific. Therefore, we point out in what situations application of these tools is appropriate. This is often illustrated by providing examples from our own experience as well as the experience of others.

We begin most chapters with either a critical incident or a case. This is followed by several questions that identify various subtopics and issues that are subsequently discussed in the chapter. These questions provide the reader with an advanced knowledge of what to expect from the chapter. After reading the chapter, it is fruitful for the reader to go back to these questions and try to answer them. This should help the reader to ascertain how much they learned from the chapter.

Several types of boxes are used throughout the various chapters. The first type elaborates on the work of key management scholars or executives. The second type provides details of a given research study. The third type pertains to an illustration and/or an example.

Each chapter may also include many tables that summarize salient dimensions pertaining to a topic or an issue being discussed in the chapter. On the other hand, some tables report results of research. Also, summaries are provided at the end of each section within a chapter.

At the end of each chapter, we provide a list of specialized terms used in the chapter. This is followed by a list of questions. Those marked with an asterisk are for advanced students and should be addressed after unmarked questions have been answered.

How to Read the Book

The book is intended for three types of students—the undergraduate, the graduate, and the executive.

In this section, we will first provide general guidelines as to how to read the book. Then, we will provide specific guidelines for undergraduate, graduate, and executive students.

During the first reading, it may be useful to skip all boxes and complex tables; that is, read only the text portion of the chapter. This should provide students with a broad (primarily conceptual) knowledge of the various topics covered in the chapter. The second reading of each chapter should include the complex tables as well as the boxes containing illustrations or examples. This second reading should facilitate application of conceptual knowledge to specific situations.

After the two readings, students should be able to understand the specialized terms listed at the end of the chapter. They should also be able to answer the questions posed in the beginning of the chapter, handle unmarked questions included at the end of the chapter, and analyze cases.

The above level of preparation should be adequate for undergraduate students, practicing managers, or managers attending short-term seminars and workshops.

Graduate Students

We believe that graduate students enrolled in M.B.A. or Ph.D. degree programs, as well as organizational consultants, need to go beyond the above cited level of preparation and understanding. They need to study materials in other boxes. This should help them to develop a deeper understanding of concepts and frameworks. This should also enable them to discuss advanced level questions marked with an asterisk at the end of each chapter.

Finally, the summaries provided at the end of each section within a given chapter should help students to review their learning. It should also help them to prepare for examinations.

Specialized Terms

Group
Organization
Levels of hierarchy
Types of organizations
Organization theory
Exploratory studies

Explanatory research
Organization behavior and
  organization theory
Institutional, managerial, and
  technical levels

Strategy formulation and
  implementation
Operational level activities and/or
  tasks

Role of top management
Open versus closed systems
Human and technical elements

Discussion Questions

1. What is an organization? How does an organization differ from a group?

2. What are different ways of classifying organizations? Be explicit about the criteria used in each classification scheme. Give some examples of each type.

3. Why are organizations important? What would happen if there were no organizations? Describe what modern society would look like without any organization.

4. What is organization theory? How is it different from the model implicit in any managerial action?

5. What is the usefulness of organization theory? Specifically, how can the understanding of organization theory help a young person who is joining an organization at the lower levels?

6. What is an open system? How is it different from a closed system?

7. How is theory related to its application? What would be the consequences of just learning organization theory without its applications?

8. Describe various elements of an open system. How are these elements related to each other? What is the role of general management in managing these elements? How does this role differ from the roles of lower- and middle-level managers?

★9. How is organization theory developed? Be specific about various research methods.

★10. It is often said that there are "no quick fixes" in organizations. Justify this statement with arguments and examples. What could be an alternate posture that management could take? What are some of the benefits as well as costs of taking the alternate posture?

End Notes

1. Talcott Parsons, *Structure and Process in Modern Society* (New York: Free Press, 1960), pp. 45–46.

★This is an advanced-level question.

2. Daniel Katz and Robert L. Kahn, *The Social Psychology of Organizations* (New York: John Wiley & Sons, 1978).

3. Robert Dubin, *Theory Building* (New York: Free Press, 1969).

4. Alfred P. Sloan, Jr., *My Years with General Motors* (Garden City, N.Y.: Doubleday, 1964).

5. Chester C. Barnard, *The Functions of the Executive* (Cambridge, Mass.: Harvard University Press, 1938).

6. Frederick W. Taylor, *The Principles of Scientific Management* (New York: Harper & Row, 1947).

7. James D. Mooney and Anthony C. Reilly, *Onward Industry* (New York: Harper & Row, 1939).

8. Mary Parker Follett, *Creative Experience* (London: Longmans, Green and Company, 1924).

9. Henri Fayol, *General and Industrial Management.* Trans. Constance Storrs (London: Sir Isaac Pitman and Sons, 1949).

10. R. Nath, "Research Problems in Organizational and Comparative Systems Analysis." A paper presented at the Society for General Systems Research Symposium held at the annual meeting of the American Association for the Advancement of Science, New York, September 1964.

11. Jay W. Forrester, *Industrial Dynamics* (New York: John Wiley & Sons, 1961).

12. Gary Dessler, *Organization and Management: A Contingency Approach* (Englewood Cliffs, N.J.: Prentice Hall, 1976).

13. R. H. Kilmann, Managing Beyond The Quick Fix (San Francisco: Jossey-Bass, 1989).

I THEORETICAL FOUNDATIONS

Part Outline

2 HISTORY OF ORGANIZATION AND MANAGEMENT THOUGHT

Chapter Outline

Each age produces a form of organization appropriate to its own tempo.
Alvin Toffler

Organization and management are as old as the human race. Indeed as we saw in the previous chapter, Romans and Egyptians had built up huge organizations to accomplish their goals. They were not, however, the only ones. The Chinese had given us, among other things, the first principles of strategy, whereas democracy flourished in Greece. Right through history, various civilizations had developed different forms of organization.

In this chapter, we summarize how organization and management thought has evolved over the years. It is our belief that to fully appreciate the various theories of organization and management, we need to place them in their appropriate historical context. There are two major reasons for this:

1. The problems of organizations are primarily those presented by the *environments* in which they operate. Environments generate (a) key uncertainties, (b) technological and market opportunities, (c) resources, and (d) constraints on behavior in the form of legal and cultural sanctions. Over time, environments change, and so do the problems facing organizations.

2. The solutions to the problems are *human* and *social* inventions. Hence, these solutions are at least partly influenced by the values and beliefs shared by human beings in a society. As beliefs and values have changed over time, so have the dominant solutions.

Taken together, these two reasons suggest that organization theories reflect the times in which they originated.

In this chapter, we will consider only the origins of modern concepts of organization. Fortunately for us, with a few exceptions, these origins can be traced to the developments that took place during this century in the United States. Therefore, we will focus primarily on the developments that took place in the United States.

This chapter is divided into three sections. First, we will summarize the beginnings of modern organization and management thought, presenting the classical theorists and the human relations critique of their theories. Second, we will enumerate the precursors of modern organization and management theory, which led to the conception of organizations as open systems. Third, we will mention the major theoretical works based on open systems notions. This section will be brief, since we will elaborate the open systems model in the remainder of the book. Finally, we will conclude with the key themes of modern organization theory that form the basis of the systems model presented in the next chapter.

Beginnings of Modern Organization and Management Thought

During the first half of the 20th century, the United States contributed a great deal to the understanding, refinement, and application of management practices. These contributions were facilitated by the sociocultural context in which they occurred.

In the half-century after the ratification of the Constitution, American business enterprises became increasingly specialized in commerce and production. The trend was particularly evident in commerce. Whereas in the 1790s the general merchant—the businessperson who dominated the economy of the colonial period—was the grand distributor, by the 1840s such tasks were being carried out by different types of specialized enterprises.[1] Banks, insurance companies, and common carriers had appeared. Economic expansion and business specialization increased the number of business enterprises in the economy.

The resulting expansion of the economy did not initially alter the internal operation or organization of these enterprises. In the 1790s the American business still relied on the commercial practices perfected earlier by British, Dutch, and Italian merchants. Such practices served well until the 1840s when newer technologies and markets that permitted mass production and distribution came into existence. Technological advances included the steamboat, the cotton gin, the iron plow, the telegraph, the electric motor, and the expansion of a railroad and canal network that opened new markets for producers.[2]

As newer technologies came into existence, they, in turn, necessitated the accumulation of resources for improving the efficiency of production. The increasing concentration of resources, or the rise of big business, witnessed the growth of a managerial class quite apart from ownership. Until the 1840s, the traditional enterprise remained all-pervasive in production as in commerce, since the volume of activity was not large enough and owners had no difficulty in administering their enterprise. The enterprise remained small and personal—in nearly all cases, it was a family affair; when it acquired a legal form, it was that of a partnership. With the rise of big business, this picture began to change. For example, the senior executives who made decisions concerning the railroad's basic policies and strategies included two quite different types of businesspeople: the manager who had made a lifetime career in railroad operation, and the entrepreneur or financier who had invested capital in the railroad. The full-time, salaried executives on a large railroad included the president, treasurer, general manager, and heads of the transportation and traffic departments. Of these, the last three were almost always career managers. The president and treasurer, on the other hand, were often major investors or their representatives.[3] The policies and strategies decided by these top managers required the approval of the board of directors, particularly its chairman. These board members, successful businesspeople in their own right who served on the board on a part-time basis, were almost always either large investors or spokesmen for investors. The institutional changes that helped create the managerial capitalism of the 20th century were as significant and as revolutionary as those that accompanied the rise of commercial capitalism half a millennium earlier.[4]

With the accumulation of resources came the need for *rationalization*. Rationalization was necessary, first because of the pressing need for efficiency, and second because the planning, organizing, and controlling then in existence were so crude as to be unsuited for the large-scale business enterprises of the day. The stage was set for the first glimmer of a systematic management theory.

We divide the beginnings of modern management thought into three stages: (1) classical theorists, (2) human relations school, and (3) early modernists.

Classical Theorists

As management began to change from a day-to-day brush fire type of operation to a more inclusive long-run approach, managers primarily concerned themselves with the problems of rationalization, efficiency, and control necessitated by mass production technologies and economic expansion. Leaders like Towne and Metcalfe began to develop and apply a unified system of management. In their search for rationalization, managers of industrial complexes began discussing their problems and reading papers before associations such as the American Society of Mechanical Engineers. It was a time of genesis in management thought. Into this generative air emerged the classical theorists.

We consider three groups of classical theorists: (1) the scientific management school, (2) administrative theorists, and (3) the bureaucratic school.

Scientific Management School

The major theme of scientific management was that work, especially blue-collar work, could be studied scientifically. To a large extent, Frederick Winslow Taylor is considered to be the father of the scientific management school. Taylor[5] believed that objective analysis of the data collected in the workplace could provide the basis of the "one best way" to organize work. Taylor, in his two major works, *Shop Management* and the *Principles of Scientific Management,* suggested a system consisting of four principles:

1. Develop a science for each element of a person's work, which replaces the old rule-of-thumb method.
2. Scientifically select and then train, teach, and develop the worker; in the past, workers chose their own work and trained themselves as best they could.

3. Heartily cooperate with the workers to assure that all the work is being done in accordance with the principles of the science that had been developed.

4. Divide the work and responsibility as equally as practicable between management and the workers.

These principles reflect the basic characteristics of scientific management. Taylor himself gave fruition to these principles through time and motion studies. Perhaps the crucial point suggested here is the idea that management need not be totally an art but could be placed on a scientific footing.

Taylor was not alone in this movement. Henry Gantt, a contemporary and associate of Taylor, devised a wage-incentive scheme and a production charting system that remains the basis for many modern production scheduling techniques. Frank and Lillian Gilbreth developed the principles of motion study: they discovered that by applying scientific methods of observation and analysis, a worker may be educated to be more efficient through redesign of the motions required to perform a job. Similarly, Dr. Hugo Munsterberg, a psychologist, ushered in the beginning of vocational guidance along scientific lines in industry through his experiments in developing tests for the selection of streetcar drivers. As a result of his efforts and writing, industrial psychology was well established by 1920 as one of the most important aspects of the new science of management.

In addition to calling for a scientific approach to management, Taylor noted that the application of scientific management should be accompanied by a "mental revolution" on the part of management. Taylor stressed the importance of worker-management harmony; he noted that the increased efficiency would lead to increased productivity and that the fruits of this increased productivity should be shared among management and workers. However, this aspect of Taylor's thinking was not realized to the degree that time and motion studies were.

Administrative Theorists

The scientific management school remained primarily at the level of the shop floor and did not address broader questions of organization design. With the exception of planning and supervising, managerial functions such as organizing, controlling, and staffing were not analyzed. Administrative theorists like Fayol, Urwick, Gulick, and Mooney and Reilly primarily devoted their attention to these larger organizational issues.

Henri Fayol was a Frenchman who had been the general manager of a coal and steel company. He developed his system of general management from the vantage point of an executive, and applied it to lower organizational levels. Fayolism was probably the earliest comprehensive statement of a general theory of management. Fayol's *Administration Industrielle et Generale* was first published in France in 1916; however, it was virtually ignored in the United States until published here in 1949 as *General and Industrial Management.*

Fayol observed that management was an activity common to all human undertakings, whether in the home, business, or government. All these undertakings required some degree of planning, organizing, commanding, coordinating, and controlling. Everyone would benefit from a general knowledge of management, given its universality. Fayol, therefore, presented a theory to serve as a model of instruction.[6]

Fayol began by dividing the total industrial undertaking into six independent activities: (1) technical, (2) commercial, (3) financial, (4) security, (5) accounting, and (6) managerial. Indicating that the last of these—the managerial activity—was by far the most important and deserved the most attention, Fayol developed this aspect further. He indicated that all management activity is made up of five components; *planning, organizing, commanding, coordinating,* and *controlling.* Finally, Fayol completed his theory by noting that to be effective, management should be founded on a set of principles. (See Box 2.1.)

Fayol's contribution was significant, though its impact was felt primarily in Europe. He was instrumental in promoting the idea that management is a separate body of knowledge. Further, he presented the first complete and comprehensive theory of management that could be applied to all endeavors.

During the 1920s and 1930s, a number of people primarily engaged in management and consulting practices set forth views similar to those of Fayol. In the United States, James Mooney and Alan Reilly coauthored *Onward Industry;* in Great Britain, Luther Gulick and Lyndall Urwick extended Fayol's work, coediting *Papers on the Science of Administration.*[7] All these writings popularized such principles as unity of command; span of control; the coordinative, scalar, functional, and staff principles; and fitting people to the organization structure.

Bureaucratic School

Meanwhile, in Germany, an intellectual by the name of Max Weber was developing a theory of bureaucracy. His work was not translated and published in America until 1947 and was unknown to the management theorists of the 1930s. Weber drew his models of organization from institutions such as the church, the government agency, and the military. He came from an affluent family and had wide-ranging interests in sociology, political science, economics, and religion.

Weber noted that the growth of large-scale organizations necessitated a formal set of procedures for administrators. Further, he noted that the capitalist market economy required that the official business of administration should be discharged precisely, unambiguously, continuously, and at maximum speed. Weber developed the notion of bureaucracy as the ideal form of organization. To him, bureaucracy was the most *efficient* form of organization. He described bureaucracy as having:

Box 2.1

Fayol's Management Principles

Fayol presents managerial theory by stating that to be effective, management should be founded upon and observe the following 14 principles:

1. Division of work (specialization belongs to the natural order).
2. Authority and responsibility (responsibility is a corollary with authority).
3. Discipline (discipline is what leaders make it).
4. Unity of command (men cannot bear dual command).
5. Unity of direction (one head and one plan for a group of activities having the same objectives).
6. Subordination of individual interest to the general interest.
7. Remuneration (fair, rewarding of effort, reasonable).
8. Centralization (centralization belongs to the natural order).
9. Scalar chain (line of authority, gangplank principle).
10. Order (a place for everyone and everyone in his place).
11. Equity (results from combination of kindliness and justice).
12. Stability of tenure of personnel (prosperous firms are stable).
13. Initiative (great source of strength for business).
14. Esprit de corps (union is strength).

Most of these principles need little elaboration, except number four: unity of command. Fayol was most emphatic about this principle, stating that each individual, whether manager or laborer, should have one and only one boss. In fact, he took Taylor to task for his idea of functional foremanship, whereby each worker might have as many as eight bosses.

Source: Adapted from Henri Fayol, *General and Industrial Management* (London: Sir Isaac Pitman and Sons, 1949).

1. A well-defined hierarchy of authority.
2. A division of work based on functional specialization.
3. A system of rules covering the rights and duties of position incumbents.
4. A system of procedures for dealing with work situations.
5. Impersonality of interpersonal relationships.
6. Selection for employment and promotion based on technical excellence.

Weber noted that such a form of organization compared with other organizations exactly as did the machine with nonmechanical modes of production—that is, technically superior in terms of precision, speed, unambiguity, and continuity.[8]

There were similarities between the ideas of the administrative theorists and those of Weber. The ideas of specialization, scalar chain, unity of command, and direction were common to all. Further, both described the objectives of their models in similar terms: Fayol referred to order and stability, while Weber emphasized discipline and reliability. However, there were some differences as well.

First, Weber was an intellectual, whereas the administrative theorists were practitioners. Thus Weberian models are typically used by scholars for predictive and explanatory purposes, whereas the principles of administrative theorists are primarily used by practitioners for organization design.

Second, there were differences among these writings in the degree to which they stressed the universal principles of management. To Weber, bureaucracy was ideal and, therefore, any deviations from this model would be associated with inefficiencies. Fayol was more tentative; he stressed the flexible nature of his principles.

Summary

How do we interpret the writings of classical theorists? Given the predominant need for rationalization of production systems after a period of resource accumulation, it is probably natural that the critical problem of management during this period was the realization of production *efficiencies.* Further, much of the labor force in the United States were immigrants, with low levels of education, skills, and income. The primary efficiencies to be reaped from mass production, therefore, hinged on *controlling* and training the work force. Third, the environments, primarily the markets, were highly competitive but fairly undifferentiated and highly *stable.* Finally, the mass production technology required stability in raw materials, labor, and production techniques. The problems of attaining *stability, control,* and *efficiency* were the central issues of management.

The solutions that emerged and the theories that developed during this period reflect dominant cultural assumptions. Table 2.1 presents the classical theories in a comparative light. Assumptions of the utilitarian-rational man and an individualist ethic seemed to have pervaded these theories. First, the assumption of rationality guided Taylor and his associates and their classical counterparts in their search for universal principles and the "one right way" of management. Second, most of the theorists tended to view the employee as an inert instrument: they assumed that people did not like work and that they acted rationally and required detailed guidance and clear job limits in order to perform adequately. Taylor's insistence on time studies and the administrative theorists' and Weber's insistence on precision, clarity, and reliability reflected these assumptions. This was understandable, given the needs of management and the nature of the labor force. However, the concept of man as a rational being and the myth of the individualistic ethic led the theorists to largely disregard the variables of human behavior in organizations other than the purely physiological. The central managerial

TABLE 2.1   **Classical Theorists in a Comparative Light**

Dimensions of Comparison	Scientific Management	Administrative Theorists	Bureaucracy
Common Elements			
1. Assumptions about human beings	Economic man. Inert instrument of management	Economic man. Inert instrument of management	Economic man. Inert instrument of management
2. Assumptions about environment	Closed systems view of organization (Assumptions implicit)	Closed systems view of organization (Assumptions implicit)	Closed systems, though Weber made his assumptions explicit
3. Orientation to management	Managers as elites. Control is key to efficiency	Managers as elites. Control is key to efficiency	Managers as elites. Control is key to efficiency
Unique Elements			
1. Focus	Individual: typically blue-collar worker	Organization: fitting individual to hierarchy	Organization prescribed by rules
2. Management concepts	Job design through time and motion studies	Organization structure, span of control, etc.	Organization structure. Designing hierarchy, rules, and regulations
3. Application	Applied widely; predecessor of industrial engineering	Applied by consultants	Primarily theoretical

strategy under these conditions became one of *control*. As rules became increasingly precise, they defined the minimum levels of acceptable behavior. When employees tended to avoid exceeding them, supervisors reacted by creating additional rules and procedures.

A second assumption imbedded in these theories is that *environments are stable*. Thus, most of the theories assume that markets are known and that production output somehow disappeared from the factory.

Human Relations Movement

In the United States, the period following the introduction of the scientific management and administrative theories witnessed drastic changes in the environment and in people's views of their own behavior. Economically, mechanization was rapidly replacing human effort. Administrative principles such as standardization, division of work, and specialization were widely emphasized at all organizational levels. Increasing division of work resulted in interdependencies and a need for tight coordination. Communications and transportation systems improved and this, in turn, brought people together on a scale larger than before.

At the same time, the population was rising, doubling between 1890 and 1930. The increasing mechanization and growth in population ran a collision course: unions and strikes began to appear in industrial communities. Threatened by the fear of losing their jobs, employees began to resist the application of time and motion studies. Unfortunately, the mental revolution that Taylor called for—a revolution that required splitting the spoils of scientific management between management and labor—did not take place. As a result, time and motion studies came to be looked on with suspicion by labor; at one point, they were even the subject of a congressional investigation.

These issues were further compounded by the closing of the American frontier.[9] The frontier served as a safety valve and contributed to a sense of optimism and growth during the 19th century, buttressing the spirit of individualism. With its closing, the proximity and dependency created by the industrial enterprise, technology, and population growth resulted in conflict. Things came to a head in 1933, as the country fell into a deep depression. Businesses were failing, unemployment was widespread, incomes were dropping, and national morale was low. The depression itself was taken as evidence of a breakdown in the economic assumptions of the day. Laissez-faire assumptions, which held that the market mechanism and price system would automatically adjust to an equilibrium point, were becoming suspect.

The individualistic ethic was giving way to a social ethic. People were not seen primarily as individuals in relentless pursuit of their goals, but as social animals who craved belonging. The social ethic expressed itself in a number of forms. First, government was becoming increasingly involved in economic matters to restrain the excesses of market mechanisms. President Theodore Roosevelt, for example, initiated a variety of suits based on the Sherman Act, which prohibited business organizations from mergers that enabled large organizations to drive out small competitors. Unions were encouraged. There were increasing attempts to establish a minimum wage. Second, in economic theory, John Maynard Keynes[10] gave expression to the skepticism about laissez-faire assumptions by putting forth a theory of government intervention in his book, *The General Theory of Employment, Interest and Money.*

These shifts in political, economic, and social ethics found their resonance in management theory. As early as 1924, Mary Parker Follet[11] had advocated the principle of integration in management. Throughout her life, Follet attempted to establish a management philosophy based on the grounds that any enduring society must be founded on a recognition of the motivating desires of the individual and group. Recognizing that a person on the job is motivated by the same forces that serve as motivation away from the job, Follet proposed that the basic problem of any organization was harmonizing and coordinating group effort to achieve the most efficient effort toward completing a task: hence, the principle of integration. Follet was a true management philosopher, who helped bridge the gap between the mechanistic approach of Taylor and the latter-day human relations school.

The era also witnessed an emergence of reaction against the scientific management school. As we noted earlier, the job design efforts of Frederick

Taylor were even the subject of a congressional investigation. However, no effective counterforce developed until 1938 when Chester Barnard,[12] a business executive with academic talents, published his book, *The Functions of the Executive,* presenting a fresh new theory of organizations. Barnard viewed organizations as cooperative systems, not as the products of mechanical engineering. He focused on decision-making processes in an organization and a person's limited power of choice, as opposed to the classical theorists' rational person. He stressed natural groups within the organization, upward communications, authority from below rather than above, and leaders who functioned as a cohesive force. Barnard's ideas were so rich that many of the later thinkers like Herbert Simon embraced these ideas. However, during the 1930s, it was his emphasis on *cooperative systems* that resonated with the times.

Hawthorne Studies

The social ethic found scientific expression in the Hawthorne Studies conducted at Western Electric's Hawthorne Works. The study was headed by Elton Mayo, then a Harvard professor, and his two research assistants, William Dixon and Fritz Roethlisberger. The study was sponsored by the National Research Council.

Initially, the study was designed to determine the effect of physical environment—specifically, illumination—on output. The story is well known. To quote Claude George[13]:

> A six-girl team started on their unique manufacturing career in April of 1927. As the account goes, the conditions of work were changed one at a time to study their effects on production, some of these changes being: rest periods of different length and number, shorter work days, shorter work weeks, soup or coffee at the morning coffee breaks, and so on. With each change the effect was consistent: output increased, and at the same time the girls felt less fatigued. Here was the proof Mayo needed to support his concept of the factors that influence industrial relationships.
>
> Briefly stated, Mayo's idea was that logical factors were far less important than emotional factors in determining productive efficiency. Furthermore, of all the human factors influencing employee behavior, the most powerful were those emanating from the worker's participation in social groups. Thus, Mayo concluded that work arrangements, in addition to meeting the objective requirements of production, must at the same time satisfy the employee's subjective requirement of social satisfaction at this work place. This concept was embodied in Mayo's book, *The Human Problems of an Industrial Civilization,* published in 1933.

The greatest contribution of the Hawthorne studies was, then, the discovery of the *social organization* of the workplace: workers in the factory constituted a culture of their own that could be observed and analyzed. Mayo noted that effective management required recognition of a person's subjective requirement of social satisfaction as well as the firm's requirement of productive output. Henceforth, management would be based on the sociological concept of group dynamics. As a result of Mayo's work, the corporate woods abound with social scientists trying to satisfy management's demand for the creation of a work situation conducive to long-run productivity.

Summary

In a large sense, the human relations school of management reflected the social ethic. More importantly, however, it was a reaction to the mechanistic, impersonal world inherent in the application of scientific management and administrative theories. Table 2.2 presents a summary comparison between human relations and classical theory. The human relationists retained the notion of universality of management, though they now saw the task of management as more complex: consisting of attention to the social aspects of the organization in addition to economic and production requirements. The school of thought was still operating under the assumption of a stable environment: Theorists were wont to assume that goals were given and not problematic and that anything that promoted harmony and efficiency was also good for society. They further assumed that the problems created by organizations were largely limited to the psychological

TABLE 2.2   **Human Relations Model and Classical Relations Theory Compared**

Dimension	Human Relations Model	Classical Management Theory
Socio-cultural milieu	Emerged in an era of social ethic, government involvement, and economic environment of depression	Arose in an era when the need to reap efficiencies of large-scale production had to be fulfilled in the presence of an immigrant work force of low levels of education
Assumptions about human beings	Social man	Economic man
Assumption about environment	Stable environment (Implicit assumptions)	Stable environment (Mostly implicit assumptions)
Central problem of management	Building cooperative systems for efficiency	Control for efficiency
Managerial solutions	Manipulate workers by building informal relations (e.g., giving attention)	Job and organization design
Approach to management solutions	Universal solutions are feasible	Universal solutions are feasible

consequences of poor interpersonal relations within them. Yet since the goals of the organizations were regarded as given, psychological health came to be defined in terms of its instrumentality for attaining the goals of management. As later critics would suggest, human relations thus came to be associated with manipulation.

The classical theorists and the human relationists need to be credited with leaving us one of the lasting legacies of contemporary organization and management thought: a dialectic that has continued to this day, both in theory and practice. Classical theorists embodied a rational conception of human beings whereas human relationists viewed people as social actors. These *alternative views* have ever since striven for supremacy in management thought. Contemporary approaches to organization and management display these differences, an issue to which we now turn.

Early Modernists

Efficiency considerations prevalent in previous periods enabled organizations to move into a stage in which organizations attempted to utilize slack resources to develop new products and new markets.[14] The movement was hampered by recession and the Second World War but the technological and managerial advances in the postwar era finally enabled the transition to occur.

The postwar era witnessed changes in technology, population demography, and institutional forms. On the technological side, many companies had been devoting attention and resources to research and development, with the objective of developing new products and better utilizing resources. This, in turn, accelerated the developments of technology. For example, at General Electric and Westinghouse, R&D resulted in the manufacture of plastics and alloys; automobile companies had begun to produce airplane engines, electrical equipment, and household appliances. Similarly, rubber companies began to market latex and plastic. At the same time, newer technologies and industries came to life. For example, television as a medium of communication emerged during the late 1940s. The science of electronics was born.

Population demography shifted in two distinct ways. First, after the turbulent beginnings of the union movement, the postwar era saw the increased strengthening of the union. The AFL-CIO, for example, under the strong leadership of George Meany, began to wield influence in industrial relations to a degree not witnessed before. Second, the educational level of the population was on the rise, spurred by government interventions such as the G.I. Bill. Together, these two forces led to a climate where workers were less inclined to take the dictates of management for granted.

The technological advances made by organizations, coupled with the diversification they undertook, led to such an increase in the number of products that coordination of product flows through several departments was rendered problematic and stretched the enduring capability of existing administrative structures. The decentralized structure was a response to this problem. As a result, an institutional innovation—the divisionalized structure—came into existence. The newer forms of organizations, especially the decentralized structure, necessitated that decision-making and problem-solving skills be disseminated at all levels of the managerial hierarchy. In order to harness the problem-solving potential of their employees, it was necessary for organizations to adopt democratic and participative processes.

This era of industrial innovations witnessed great excitement in management thought, with an explosion of writing taking place. These writings remain the harbingers of contemporary organization and management thought. We classify these developments into three categories: (1) human resource theorists, (2) the information and decision-making school, and (3) the political science school.

Human Resource Theorists

Extending the themes of human relationists, several researchers attempted to understand the functioning of the social system within the organization. There were two early influences on their stream of thought.

The first was the theory of motivation put forth by Abraham Maslow. His needs-hierarchy theory assumes that an individual's needs are organized in a hierarchy. As a given lower-level need is satisfied, the next higher-level need becomes the motivator. Maslow's need hierarchy consisted of physiological, safety and security, social esteem, and self-actualization needs as the higher-level needs. Maslow went beyond the human relations school as he suggested that human beings aspire not merely to social belonging but to higher-level needs such as autonomy, self-esteem, and self-actualization.

The second was the influence of Kurt Lewin. Lewin made his major contributions in the area of group dynamics. Though his work will be referred to in greater detail later, two of the seminal ideas that he brought to management thought deserve mention here. The first was the *field theoretic perspective* he brought to the study of social systems: the idea that environment had a significant influence on the behavior of an individual. The second was the notion of *action theory and research:* the idea that social scientists should focus not merely on the description of human activity, as human relationists would, but should engage in learning from active attempts to change social systems.

Lewin's influences are apparent in the writings of the latter-day human resource theorists: Rensis Likert, Doug McGregor, and Chris Argyris.[15] McGregor articulated these themes in his now famous *The Human Side of Enterprise,* where he identified two managerial strategies that he called Theory X and Theory Y. Theory X assumptions held that most people dislike work and responsibility; they are motivated primarily by lower-level needs, especially financial rewards. These assumptions led to a managerial strategy of control; that is, close supervision and sometimes coercion of employees to achieve organizational objectives. Theory Y assumptions held that human beings like work and responsibility; they are predisposed toward independence and, under appropriate conditions, would exercise self-control over their own performance. Managerial strategy under this set of assumptions was to design the appropriate environment to motivate employees toward superior work performance.

Argyris, writing from a different vantage point, noted that traditional organization structure, with its insistence on specialization, hierarchy, and control, ran counter to the adult striving of the individual. Thus, as individuals mature, they move toward increased independence and develop depth of interest, behavioral flexibility, and a longer time perspective. Further, they develop increased awareness of themselves and mature from the subordinate position of a child to that of independent adults. Argyris noted that the demands of traditional management ran counter to the needs of adults and, therefore, conflict between the organization and the individual was inevitable. Hence, integration of individual needs and organizational goals is a central managerial task.

Similar value premises are embedded in Rensis Likert's work. Likert noted that organizations may be classified along a continuum from System 1 to System 4, with System 1 characterized by classical management theory and System 4 by McGregor's Theory Y. Unlike Argyris, Likert paid attention to the role of work groups: to him, the work group was the primary building block in organizations. In System 4, the task of leadership shifts from close supervision to one of building effective work groups.

Human resource theorists continued the tradition of the Human Relations school through their focus on the social and human aspects of the organization. However, there were many differences between the two. First, the view of human beings held by the human resource theorists was that of autonomous beings who aspired to utilize their creative potential in addition to being social animals. Second, many human resource theorists were concerned with productivity in the workplace and the application of behavioral science concepts to enhance organizational effectiveness. Third, all of them advocated participative democracy as a way of functioning in modern day organizations.

Information and Decision-Making School

During this era, a number of scholars began to pursue the notion that managers are information processors, or more precisely *decision makers,* a view that led them to challenge the assumptions of rationality held by classical theorists. This school holds that senior executives face *unprogrammed* decision situations—decisions that are complex and poorly understood, unlike the programmed or routine situations confronting lower levels of organizations. In unprogrammed decisions, there is no obvious predetermined method for managers to use in their solutions.

Building on the earlier work of Chester Barnard, Herbert Simon developed this thesis in his now classic treatise, *Administrative Behavior.* In the typical decision situation faced by executives, Simon notes:

> There is no cut-and-dried method for handling the problem because it hasn't arisen before, or because its precise nature and structure are elusive or complex, or because it is so important that it deserves a custom-tailored treatment.[16]

In unprogrammed decision contexts, so this school argued, a most important part of the decision-making process is problem definition. Since alternatives and consequences are seldom known with clarity, managers "satisfice"; that is, they make choices to satisfy constraints, not to maximize objectives. Simon noted that under this characterization, executives behave in ways far removed from those depicted in classical management theory, which attributed rational behavior to human beings. Simon suggested two very important reasons: the role of values and cognitive limits on rationality.

1. *The role of values* emphasized the *subjective* elements of decision makers: in their choices, executives are guided by values not all of which are economic. Hence, the notion of an objectively definable "one best way" in choice situations is a caricature, not reality.
2. *Cognitive limits on rationality* emphasized that human beings are limited in their information processing capabilities; thus even if executives are intendedly rational, the inherent limits of humanness prevent them from being rational in the economic sense.[17]

Simon noted that decisions are made at all levels of the organization. At the lowest levels, work is routine or programmed—familiar stimuli are reacted to with predictable and organized responses. Organizations may, therefore, be portrayed as a set of hierarchical programs (established procedures) so that the higher-level programs do the work of designing or modifying the lower-level ones that perform the basic work. This view had some important anchors in the political perspective. To quote Charles Perrow:

> This view had some rather unusual implications. It is suggested that if managers were so limited, then they could be easily controlled. What was necessary was not to give direct orders (on the assumption that subordinates were idiots without expertise) or to leave them to their own devices (on the assumption that they were supermen who would somehow know what was best for the organization, how to coordinate with all the other supermen, how to anticipate market changes, etc.). It was necessary to control only the premises of their decisions. Left to themselves, with those premises set, they could be predicted to rely on precedent, keep things stable and smooth, and respond to signals that reinforce the behavior desired of them.[18]

As will be pointed out later, much of the contemporary development of organizational politics has anchors in this stream of work.

The information and decision-making school has had a significant influence not only on organization theory but on its practice. It focused attention on the design of information networks or systems within organizations to overcome the inherent limits on rationality with the help of information technology. Further, the idea that the managerial job itself is a higher-level program has led to the vast possibility that managerial work may be programmed. The fast developing science of artificial intelligence is a direct offshoot of these ideas.

Political Science School

The political science school that emerged during this era also attacked the rationality assumptions of classical theorists. At another level, it undermined the cooperative assumptions of the human relations school.

Political scientists interested in the study of organizations began to pay attention to the influence of environments on organizations. Partly because the early focus of these theorists was on public agencies, the authors of these schools were concerned with conflict. In the world of political parties, pressure groups, and legislative bodies, conflict was not only pervasive, it was also functional.

Philip Selznick,[19] in his study of *TVA and the Grass Roots,* noted differences in goals leading to conflict among various subgroups; further, unlike the administrative theorists, he discovered hidden power bases of the lower-level employees, thus further demolishing the conception of the worker as an inert instrument.

There was increasing recognition of the fact that the goals of an organization are problematic; that sometimes organizations pursued conflicting goals. Goals were, of course, not what they seemed to be: The important ones were quite unofficial, with history playing a big role. Assuming profit as the preeminent goal explained almost nothing about a firm's behavior. Given the problematic view of goals, conflict was considered to be legitimate—under certain conditions. This replaced the idea underlying the classical theorists and the human relations schools that organizations are by nature cooperative systems.

Summary

Where do the early modernists stand? Refer to Table 2.3 for a comparative summary. The increasing dynamism of the environment and the problems of management this presented led to the rejection of classical theorists and their solutions as the *sole* prescription for managing organizations. As shown in Table 2.3, scholars began to advance differing visions of humans and their behavior. At one end of the spectrum, the human relations assumptions were being replaced by a grander set of assumptions proposed by human resource theorists. At another end, however, we began to discover the limitations of individuals in terms of their cognitive rationality. At the

TABLE 2.3   **Early Modernists Compared**

Elements of Comparison	Human Resource Theorists	Information and Decision-Making School	Political School
1. Focus	Primarily individual and groups in organizations	Executives as individual decision makers	Organizational systems
2. Assumptions about human beings	Autonomous human beings displaying potential for growth and self-actualization	Human beings are driven by values but limited in cognitive abilities	Human beings seeking power (implicit)
3. Assumptions about environment	Individual behavior is affected by environment	Executives function in unprogrammed ambiguous and ill-structured situations	Unstable environments leading to changing goals
4. Assumptions about organization	Organizations stifle individual growth and this leads to ineffectiveness	Organizations are networks of decision centers	Organizations are conflict-filled
5. Central problem of management	Integrating individual needs with organizational goals; building work teams	Design of decision premises	Managing conflict
6. Common theme		Universal solutions are not valid	

level of organizations, the stability and consistency assumptions of administrative theorists and cooperative systems notions of human relationists gave way to a version wherein organizations are seen as conflict-filled, pursuing inconsistent goals with inherent conflict between individual and organization. Environments are not all stable; sometimes they are seen as problematic, changing, and uncertain. Management theorists began to discover their ignorance and discarded the simplistic and safe prescriptions of the classical theorists.

One theme, however, remained: Organizations *are dynamic open systems* in interaction with the environment. As the growth of the field has forced ever more variables into our consciousness, flat claims of predictive power have declined. As Perrow succinctly notes:

> The systems view is intuitively simple. Everything is related to everything else, though in uneven degrees of tension and reciprocity. Every unit, organization, department, or work group takes in resources, transforms psychological, sociological, and cultural aspects of these units which interact. The systems view was explicit in the institutional work, since they tried to study whole organizations; it became explicit in the human relations school, because they were so concerned with the interactions of people. The political science and technology viewpoints also had to come to this realization, since they deal with parts affecting each other (sales affecting production; technology affecting structure).[20]

As we move into the contemporary era, these ideas play a central role in management thought, a point to which we now turn.

Contemporary Organization and Management Thought

In the United States, the 60s was a decade of unprecedented affluence. Optimism prevailed throughout the nation. The mood of the age was summed up by John F. Kennedy in his inaugural address when he said:

> Let the word go forth from this time and place, to friend and foe alike, that the torch has been passed to a new generation of Americans—born in this century, tempered by war, disciplined by bitter peace, proud of our ancient heritage—and unwilling to witness or permit the slow undoing of those human rights to which this nation has always been committed, and to which we are committed today at home and around the world.
>
> Let every nation know, whether it wishes us well or ill, that we shall pay any price, bear any burden, meet any hardship, support any friend, oppose any foe to assure the survival and the success of liberty.[21]

In many ways, those were times filled with great hopes for the future. There was confidence in the health of the economy and the capabilities of the United States. Most institutions were proud of their past accomplishments and planned to do better in the future. Not only did World War II show the resilience of the productive capacity of the American economy, but the Marshall Plan that followed indicated bold action to build Europe from the devastation of World War II. Since America was helping Europe to rebuild its institutions and organizations, its advice was sought all over the world and its economy and industrial ingenuity were envied by the rest of the world. American corporations continued to occupy this position of preeminence until recent times. As late as 1970, the famous French journalist Servan-Schreiber praised the effectiveness and power of American corporations and entreated French corporations to learn management know-how from their American counterparts.[22]

The 60s was also a period of social upheaval. A liberal, highly educated segment of the population had emerged that began to question the inherent values of organizations anchored in classical models. On the technological front, television had become a permanent feature of American living, enabling rapid transmission of information in a manner not possible by the printed word. At another level, though not visible to many, the economy shifted to what Daniel Bell[23] termed the post industrial society with service sectors becoming important in terms of employment. Computers were coming of age, and the information revolution was beginning.

Organizationally, this rapid economic expansion manifested itself in more diverse, interwoven markets, the use of advanced technologies, the widespread use of specialists, and larger, more complex organizational structures.[24] Managers were occupying positions of influence, leading to a great demand for professional managers. Further, beginning in the late 1950s, two reports—one commissioned by the Ford Foundation, one by the Carnegie Corporation—provided the impetus to replace management education based on worn-out precepts with education based on scientific inquiry. This led to an acceleration of research and writing in this area, a phenomenon we witness even today. Management schools were coming of age.

However, a deeper and more serious study of the 60s would indicate that fissures were already beginning to appear in the whole fabric of U.S. society and its organizations and institutions. The Bay of Pigs incident taught a very humiliating lesson to the young President and his Boston advisers. As analyzed by Jack Anderson in a feature article on J. F. Kennedy in the Sunday Press, Kennedy had already started questioning the organizational effectiveness of the CIA and Department of Defense, the latter being the largest organization in the U.S. government. The world was changing in very significant ways, and organizations like DOD that had performed very well during World War II and in the subsequent decade were already becoming ineffective in terms of either projecting and/or planning to meet the needs of the future. As Anderson pointed out, "It was on the advice of the DOD Generals that Lyndon Johnson plunged the U.S. into a most disastrous war in Asia that finally resulted in a massive breakdown in the very fabric of the American society and destroyed confidence in its governmental apparatus." This process of loss of confidence continued after the departure of Lyndon Johnson and climaxed during the Nixon presidency during Watergate. We witnessed a great transition during that decade from a position of optimism and great confidence in our institutions to the building of organizations like the Nixon White House, which was out of tune with the values and needs of the American society and the world.

A similar set of forces was at work in the private sector, particularly in the industrial corporate structure. Following World War II, a number of social scientists such as Riesman, McGregor, Likert, Bennis, Argyris, Emery, and Trist had started predicting profound changes in the nature of the environment facing our industrial organizations.[25] Some of them had already started predicting the eclipse of the current organizational system of bureaucracy because it could not meet the developing changes in the society and the environment. In spite of the early warning by the social scientists, it was clear that organizations were going to follow their past practices and organizational structures because those had proven to be very successful in the past. Just like DOD, most of the industrial organizations stayed confident and, therefore, not only maintained their present policies and structures, but in many cases strengthened them. This was reflected in another development. Many of the early experiments in industrial democracy, spurred on by the writings and consulting of human resource theorists, met with mixed success.

Contingency Theory

The first set of writings in this period mirror this context. By now, the metaphor of the organization as an open system—a legacy left by early modernists—had become an accepted one for guiding management thinking. Contingency theorists attempted a reconciliation between the rational-classical schools on the one hand and human resource theorists on the other, suggesting that factors external to an organization—an organization's environment—determined which management practices are appropriate. Paul Lawrence and Jay Lorsch, authors of the landmark piece *Organization and Environment,* argued:

> During the past few years there has been evident a new trend in the study of organizational phenomena. Underlying this new approach is the idea that the internal functioning of organizations must be consistent with the demands of the organization's task, technology, or external environment, and the need of its members if the organization is to be effective. Rather than searching for the panacea of the one best way to organize under all conditions, investigators have more and more tended to examine the functioning of organizations in relation to the needs of their particular members and the external pressures facing them. Basically, this approach seems to be leading to the development of a "contingency" theory of organization with the appropriate internal states and processes of the organization contingent upon external requirements and member needs.[26]

In addition to its intuitive appeal, contingency theory seemed to be able to explain the existing order of things: different industrial organizations displayed different structures; some were organized along classical lines, whereas others promoted participative mechanisms.

On the whole, contingency theorists were interested in prescriptions. They sought management approaches—especially organization structures—that were appropriate for different circumstances. Contingency theorists placed great emphasis on *congruence as the key to effectiveness;* if the elements of an organization fit among themselves and with the environment, then the organization should prosper. Management had some degree of control over the destiny of corporations; its task was building congruence.

The economic expansion of the 60s, and the increasing optimism associated with it, gave way in the 70s. A number of events shaped the course of the economy:

1. The oil embargo of the 1970s, initiated by OPEC countries, led to an energy crisis that in turn led to a recession.
2. The delayed effects of government programs initiated in the 60s, both social and military, began to have an impact on economic growth, interest rates, and inflation.
3. Public institutions and officials became the object of suspicion in the era of "post-Watergate" morality.

4. Foreign competitors, especially the Japanese, were making inroads into the American economy.

The recent plight of the steel industry is in many ways a direct result of the phenomena described above, where the whole industry, within a decade, fell from its position of world leadership to losing jobs and business at an unprecedented rate. A study conducted in Pittsburgh indicated that, due to the difficulties experienced by the steel industry, the Pittsburgh area alone had lost 17,000 jobs and a potential business of about a quarter of a billion dollars during the 1973–77 period.

Organizationally, this meant adjusting to an altered environment. Unlike the benign environments of the 60s, firms had to cope with resource scarcities, hostile competitors, and sometimes a not-too-cooperative government. In addition, organizations began to experience pressure from environmental agents—organized consumers, community action, environmental, and even employee groups—to a degree they had never experienced before. At another level, foreign competition and the emergence of a global economy enhanced the turbulence of environments and necessitated different ways of organizing.

As the environment became powerful, theorists began to portray the dependence of organizations on the environment. Two major theories were proposed: (1) resource dependence theory and (2) population ecology theory.

Resource Dependence Theory

Working from a political perspective and building on the earlier works of Simon and his colleagues, Jeffrey Pfeffer and Gerald Salancik put forth their thesis in the celebrated work, *The External Control of Organizations:* Organizations are dependent on the environment for critical resources, and a key managerial task is the amelioration of this dependence and hence, the acquisition of resources. They note:

> We have described how organizations cope with the uncertainty created by interdependence by managing interdependence through interorganizational coordination. By law, collusion, merger, cooptation, and other strategies, organizations seek to avoid uncertainty arising from their need to acquire and maintain resources.[27]

Political actions are, hence, not only inevitable but necessary for effective managerial functioning.

Population Ecology Theory

Unlike Pfeffer and Salancik, a second group of scholars viewed environments as all-powerful in determining the fate of organizations. Drawing their inspiration from the work of Charles Darwin, this group presented a *population ecology* model that portrayed successful organizations as the fittest in a competitive game whose rules are determined by the environment. In his influential work, *Organizations and Environments,* published in 1979, Howard Aldrich, advocate of the population ecology model, commented:

> The population ecology model of organizational change is taken from a model well-developed in biological ecology and is one that is currently enjoying increasing uses in social sciences. . . .
>
> ★★★★★
>
> the population ecology model differs from traditional explanations of organizational change . . . it focuses on the nature and distribution of resources in organizations' environments as the *central* force in change, rather than on internal leadership or participation in decision making (emphasis ours).[28]

Predictably, population ecologists addressed the processes of environmental selection, although to date they have only been able to demonstrate the applicability of their model to small organizations.

While environments were being described as being powerful by the above theorists, some others were curious as to why many Japanese corporations, and indeed even many U.S. corporations, were persistently successful. Their investigations led them back to the human side of the enterprise. Organizations are cultural systems, the soft side matters, and strong cultures inevitably turn in persistently stellar performance. For example, William Ouchi, after an intense study of Japanese and U.S. corporations, discovered common cultural traits among successful firms in both countries.[29]

Although we have learned much during this century, we can look forward to considerably more experimentation and learning as we enter the 21st century. As the environment changes and as managers and management scholars invent new solutions to the problems generated by changing environments, organization theory will be further elaborated and enriched.

Summary

In the past two decades we have seen many open systems models of organizations. One version, the contingency theory, viewed managers as shaping their organization's adaptation to its environment through redesign of its structures. Resource dependence theorists focused on resource flows and enumerated the methods of gaining resources from the environment. Population ecologists explained the failure of organizations. For a while, theorists who attended to the technical elements of organizations seemed to have dominated organization theory. However, during the 80s, the internal human elements received renewed attention, and organization culture was discovered.

We will deal with these and other related works in greater detail in the ensuing chapters.

Conclusions

Much of our knowledge about organization and management has so far originated in the United States. Over the years, our thinking about management and organizations has evolved partly as a result of the changing environments faced by organizations in the United States. Based on this evolution of thought, we may make three broad observations:

1. The closed systems view of the classical theorists and the human relations school has been rejected in modern management thought in favor of an open systems view. Put another way, we can confidently assert that the debate between closed and open systems views of organizations has been settled in favor of the open systems theorists.

2. At least for the present, we have to live with two seemingly contradictory tendencies in organizations. One is a tendency toward order highlighted by the group of scholars who have emphasized the *rational* elements of organizations. The other is a tendency toward turbulence documented by the scholars who have emphasized the *subjective* aspects of organizations. The debate between these two groups, which has dotted the historical landscape of management theory, has not been settled in favor of one or the other.

3. The open systems view has highlighted different *aspects* of management, which will be elaborated on further in the future, as experience with theory and action is reflected on and debated by both scholars and practicing managers.

These three themes—that (1) organizations are open systems, (2) they incorporate human and technical elements, and (3) they consist of various facets—underlie the systems model we describe in the next chapter. The systems model will elaborate on how two technical elements—functional and informational—and three human elements—social, political, and cultural—interact among themselves and with the environment.

Specialized Terms

Classical theorists
  • The scientific management school
  • Administrative theorists
  • Bureaucracy
Human relations movement
  • Hawthorne studies
Human resource theorists

Information and decision-making school
Political science school
Open versus closed system
Contingency theorists
Resource dependence
Population ecology

Discussion Questions

Theoretical

1. An organization theorist recently remarked, "Scientific laws are ahistorical. Therefore, knowing the history of management thought is useless for organization scientists." Discuss the comment with respect to the chapter.

2. What were the major principles of management advocated by the scientific management school? Administrative theorists? Weber?

3. Compare and contrast the human relations school with human resource theorists.

4. What was the significance of the Hawthorne studies?

5. Describe the differences between programmed and unprogrammed decision making. What is the relationship between information and power as suggested by Simon?

6. Why does the political science school maintain that goals are problematic?

★7. What are the major differences between administrative theorists and Weber?

★8. Compare and contrast resource dependence theorists and population ecologists.

Applied

1. You have been approached by a manager to help him solve a problem. How would you approach the problem from the viewpoint of: 1) an open systems theorist; 2) the scientific management school; 3) a contingency theorist.

2. You have been invited to give a talk to a Chamber of Commerce about your views of organization theory. Prepare a talk outlining what organization theory can contribute to effective management.

End Notes

1. Alfred D. Chandler, Jr., *The Visible Hand: The Managerial Revolution in American Business* (Cambridge, Mass.: Belknap Press of the Harvard University Press, 1977), p. 15.
2. Chandler, Jr., *The Visible Hand,* p. 16.
3. Chandler, Jr., *The Visible Hand,* p. 145.
4. Chandler, Jr., *The Visible Hand,* p. 145.

★This is an advanced-level question.

5. Frederick W. Taylor, *Shop Management* (New York: Harper & Row, 1903). Frederick W. Taylor, *The Principles of Scientific Management* (New York: Harper & Row, 1911).

6. Henri Fayol, *General and Industrial Management,* trans. Constance Storrs (London: Sir Isaac Pitman and Sons, 1949).

7. James D. Mooney and Allan C. Reilly, *Onward Industry* (New York: Harper & Row, 1939). Luther Gulick and Lyndall Urwick, eds., *Papers on the Science of Administration* (New York: Institute of Public Administration, Columbia University, 1937).

8. Max Weber, *Essays in Sociology,* trans. and ed. by H. H. Gerth and C. W. Mills (New York: Oxford University Press, 1946).

9. William G. Scott, *Organization Theory* (Homewood, Ill.: Richard D. Irwin, 1967), p. 52.

10. John Maynard Keynes, *The General Theory of Employment, Interest and Money* (New York: Harcourt, Brace and World, 1964).

11. Mary Parker Follet, *Creative Experience* (London: Longmans, Green and Company, 1924).

12. Chester Barnard, *The Functions of the Executive* (Cambridge, Mass.: Harvard University Press, 1938).

13. Claude S. George, Jr., *The History of Management Thought* (Englewood Cliffs, N.J.: Prentice Hall, 1968), p. 129.

14. Alfred D. Chandler, Jr., *Strategy and Structure* (Cambridge, Mass.: MIT Press, 1962), pp. 19–51.

15. Chris Argyris, *Integrating the Individual and the Organization* (New York: John Wiley and Sons, 1964). Rensis Likert, *New Patterns of Management* (New York: McGraw-Hill, 1961). Douglas McGregor, *The Human Side of Enterprise* (New York: McGraw-Hill, 1960).

16. Herbert Simon, *Administrative Behavior* (New York: Free Press, 1957).

17. Simon, *Administrative Behavior.*

18. Charles Perrow, "The Short and Glorious History of Organization Theory," *Organizational Dynamics* 2 (1973), pp. 2–15.

19. Philip Selznick, *TVA and the Grass Roots* (Berkeley: University of California Press, 1949).

20. Charles Perrow, "The Short and Glorious History of Organization Theory."

21. John F. Kennedy, Presidential Inaugural Speech delivered in 1961.

22. Jean Servan-Schreiber, *The American Challenge* (New York: Atheneum Publishers, 1968).

23. Daniel Bell, *The Coming of Post Industrial Society: A Venture in Social Forecasting* (New York: Basic Books, 1973).

24. Gary Dessler, *Organization and Management: A Contingency Approach* (Englewood Cliffs, N.J.: Prentice Hall, 1976), p. 46.

25. Chris Argyris, *Integrating the Individual and the Organization.* Warren G. Bennis, "Organization Development and the Fate of Bureaucracy," invited address delivered before the Division of Industrial and Business Psychology, American Psychological Association, on September 5, 1964. Fred E. Emery and Eric L. Trist. "The Causal Texture of Organizational Environments," *Human Relations* 18 (August 1963), pp. 20–26. Douglas McGregor, *The Human Side of Enterprise.* David Riesman, Nathan Glazer, and Reuel Denney,

    The Lonely Crowd: A Study of Changing American Character (New Haven, Conn.: Yale University Press, 1950).

26. Paul R. Lawrence and Jay W. Lorsch, eds., *Studies in Organization Design* (Homewood, Ill.: Richard D. Irwin and The Dorsey Press, 1970), p. 1. and *Organization and Environment.* (Boston: Division of Research, Graduate School of Business Administration, Harvard University, 1967).

27. Jeffrey Pfeffer and Gerald Salancik, *The External Control of Organizations* (New York: Harper & Row, 1978).

28. Howard Aldrich, *Organizations and Environments* (Englewood Cliffs, N.J.: Prentice Hall, 1979), pp. 54–55.

29. William Ouchi, *Theory Z* (New York: Basic Books, 1979).

References

Emerson, Harrington. *Efficiency as a Basis for Operation and Wages.* New York: The Engineering Magazine Co., 1911.

Gantt, Henry L. *Industrial Leadership.* New Haven, Conn.: Yale University Press, 1916.

Gilbreth, Frank B., and Lillian M. Gilbreth. *Applied Motion Study.* New York: Sturgis & Walton Company, 1917.

Lewin, Kurt. *Field Theory and Social Science.* New York: Harper & Row, 1951.

Maslow, Abraham H. *Motivation and Personality.* 2nd ed. New York: Harper & Row, 1970.

Mayo, George Elton. *The Human Problems of an Industrial Civilization.* Boston: Division of Research, Harvard Business School, 1933.

Munsterberg, Hugo. *Psychology and Industrial Efficiency.* Boston: Houghton Mifflin, 1913.

3 The Systems Model

Chapter Outline

The Dashman Company was a large concern making many types of equipment for the armed forces of the United States. It had 20 modern plants, located in the central part of the country, whose purchasing procedures had never been completely coordinated. In fact, the head office of the company had encouraged the plant managers to operate with their staffs as separate independent units in most matters. During the war, when it began to appear that the company would face increasing difficulty in securing certain essential raw materials, Manson, the company's president, appointed Post, an experienced purchasing executive from another company, as vice president in charge of purchasing, a position especially created for him. Manson gave Post wide latitude in organizing his job, and he assigned Larson as Post's assistant. Larson had served the company in a variety of capacities for many years, and knew most of the plant executives personally. Post's appointment was announced through the usual formal company channels, including a notice in the house organ published by the company.

One of Post's first decisions was to begin immediately to centralize the company's purchasing procedure. As a first step he decided that he would require each of the executives who handled purchasing in the individual plants to clear with the head office all purchase contracts made in excess of $50,000. He felt that if the head office was to do any coordinating in a way that would be helpful to each plant and to the company as a whole, he must be notified of contracts that were being prepared at least a week before they were to be signed. He talked this latter proposal over with Manson, who presented it to his board of directors. The board approved the plan.

Although the company made purchases throughout the year, the beginning of its peak buying season was only three weeks away at the time this new plan was adopted. During this period, contracts totaling millions of dollars would be placed. Post prepared a letter to be sent to the 20 purchasing executives of the company. The letter follows.

Dear _____:

The board of directors of our company has recently authorized a change in our purchasing procedures. Hereafter, each of the purchasing executives in the several plants of the company will notify the vice president in charge of purchasing of all contracts in excess of $50,000 that they are negotiating at least a week in advance of the date on which they are to be signed.

I am sure you will understand that this step is necessary to coordinate the purchasing requirements of the company in these times when we are facing increasing difficulty in securing essential supplies. This procedure should give us in the central office the information we need to see that each plant secures the optimum supply of materials. In this way the interests of each plant and of the company as a whole will best be served.

Yours very truly,

Post showed the letter to Larson and invited his comments. Larson said that he thought the letter an excellent one but suggested that, since Post had not met more than a few of the purchasing executives, he might like to visit all of them and take the matter up with each of them personally. Post dismissed the idea at once because, he said, he had so many things to do at the head office that he could not get away for a trip. Consequently, he had the letters sent out over his signature.

During the two following weeks, replies came in from all except a few plants. Although a few executives wrote at greater length, the following reply was typical.

Dear Mr. Post:

Your recent communication in regard to notifying the head office a week in advance of our intention to sign contracts has been received. This suggestion seems a most practical one. We want to assure you that you can count on our cooperation.

Yours very truly,

During the next six weeks, the head office received no notices from any plant that contracts were being negotiated. Executives in other departments who made frequent trips to the plants reported that the plants were busy and the usual routines for that time of year were being followed.[1]

How would we explain what happened in the case of the Dashman Company? Why is the change in the purchasing policy and the organizational structure not working as intended? What was Post's view of his job and his organization when he initiated the memo? Which model of organization is appropriate for describing and understanding organizations? In this chapter, we will present an open systems model of organizations. Using this model, toward the end of the chapter we will try to develop a comprehensive diagnosis of the Dashman Company case.

As we have shown in the previous chapter, over the years, organization theorists have concluded that the open systems model—sometimes referred to simply as the systems model—is an appropriate way of describing organizations. Hence, this chapter is devoted to explicating an open systems model of organizations. Before we do so, let us first define what we mean by a system.

System

The notion of a system is that of a set of elements interrelated in a specific manner. Henderson, one of the earlier proponents of the idea of a system, pointed out that "the interdependence of the variables in a system is one of the widest inductions (inferences) from experience that we possess, or we may alternately regard it as the definition of the system."[2] Formally, we use the following definitions:

The kind of systems we are interested in may be defined as a complex of components (elements) directly or indirectly related in a causal network, such that each component is related to at least some others in a more or less stable way within any period of time. The components may be relatively simple and stable, or complex and changing.

The *entities* of a system are things of which the system is composed. For example, the entities of an organizational system are groups, organized and unorganized, and individuals.

The *components* of a system, also called *elements* or *variables,* are the characteristic qualities, or states, of the entities in the system, and not the entities themselves. These elements may be objectives, structures, processes, acts, needs, roles, norms of conduct, or other psychological states of individuals, groups, or organizations; but they may not be the individuals or organizations themselves. Furthermore, these components must exist in conceptually measurable variation, that is, they must be capable, at a minimum, of taking two or more alternative states that are distinguishable.

For example, a wristwatch consists of a myriad of parts—dial, springs, case, and so on—that are the entities that constitute the system. In addition, these parts are assembled—*organized*—in a specific manner. Any collection of these parts is not sufficient in and of itself to tell time; rather it is the unique assembly—the unique organization of the parts—that makes it a watch. In other words, the parts are interrelated in a unique manner to tell us the time of day.

Modern systems theory has sought to discover the principles that govern various types of systems. In recent years, especially the last two decades, there has been an acceleration in the application of the concepts of modern systems theory to various disciplines within the social sciences, particularly in the field of organization studies. This can be seen from the increasing number of articles and books that have been appearing in the market lately.

The model for organizational analysis delineated in this chapter is anchored in modern systems theory. It provides the integrating framework for the discussion of approaches to organizing and management pursued in later chapters. Given the centrality of the model, we will trace its origins, sketch the underlying perspective, and introduce key concepts before describing the model.

The scheme of the chapter is as follows: First, we trace the philosophical, historical, and theoretical underpinnings of modern systems theory and its application to organization studies. Second, we will discuss some of the key concepts of modern systems theory. Third, we will present and explain our model for the study of organizations based on modern systems theory. Fourth, we will describe emergent behaviors and illustrate how the model can be used to understand the dynamics that emerged in the Dashman Company. Fifth, we will indicate the different ways in which we will utilize the systems model throughout the book. Finally, we will consider some of the values underlying the systems perspective.

Underpinnings

Philosophical Underpinnings

Modern systems theory, though receiving a great boost in its development during World War II, can best be seen as the culmination of a broad shift in scientific perspective taking place over the last few centuries. This shift may best be described as one from an atomistic, mechanistic conception of the world to one that emphasizes holistic organic aspects.

The atomistic conception held that the world, or for that matter any entity, can be explained by understanding its parts; hence, people sought to take the world apart, to analyze its contents and their experiences of them down to indivisible parts: atoms, chemical elements, instincts, elementary perceptions, and so on. This conception was reflected in the organization of science: it took itself apart, dividing itself into narrower and narrower disciplines; each discipline represented a way of looking at a different aspect of the same world. Second, the mechanistic conception upheld the notion of strict causality: The world was held together by causal laws that are immutable, though difficult to understand. Understanding the laws would enable one to predict the behavior of any entity subject to certain external forces: The entity itself is seen as passive, without any will to make choices of its own. Thus, each scientific discipline posited its own set of causal laws to explain the phenomena falling within its domain of interest. Third, the causal laws could be unearthed by an observer and the act of observation would not have any significant effect on the phenomena under investigation. Thus, scientists were called on to be objective and dispassionate, as these qualities—objectivity and disinterest—were necessary to arrive at true causal laws. The atomistic conception was (and in certain disciplines, continues to be) the dominant cosmology during the 19th century and reflected the successes of the Newtonian physics it represented.

Under the systems conception, a system is a whole that cannot be taken apart without the loss of its essential characteristics; hence, it must be studied as a whole. This shifted the study focus to the way the parts interrelate to each other—their organization—in addition to the study of the parts themselves. The systems theorist, instead of explaining the whole in terms of the parts, explains the parts in terms of the whole. This conception was reflected in a different organization of science whereby science began to study phenomena as a whole: interdisciplines such as cybernetics, operations research, and environmental sciences began to emerge in the latter half of the 20th century.[3] Unlike earlier scientific disciplines, which sought to separate themselves from each other and to subdivide, the new interdisciplines seek to enlarge themselves, to combine so as to take account of more and more aspects of reality. The ultimate aim is unification of the sciences. Although the holistic conception remains the single most distinguishing characteristic of systems theory, two other points of departure from the atomistic conception also need to be pointed out. Systems theorists do not adhere to the dictates of strict causality; emergent behaviors are admissible under this scheme: Behaviors of entities due to the interaction of their parts are partly—*not fully*—predictable from initial conditions. Secondly, although the systems theorists believe observations do not change the phenomenon in a large number of instances, they disavow that such an assertion is valid under *all* conditions. Especially in the social sciences, just as in quantum physics, the assertion of the independence of the observer from the phenomenon being observed is suspect.

The differences between the two conceptions are presented in Table 3.1.

The two alternative conceptions—the atomistic and the holistic (or systems)—have striven for dominance over the centuries; however, it was only after World War II that systems theory began to be accepted in the social sciences. Of course, by now, Newtonian mechanics was replaced by—or at least was seen as a first approximation to—relativistic and quantum theoretic notions in the realm of physics: The atomic explosions at Hiroshima and Nagasaki provided the world with the first glimpse of the physical effects of the newer physical science theories.

In addition, a number of events contributed to the acceptance of the systems theory. First, the era witnessed a number of scholarly treatises anchored in systems notions and the emergence of applied fields that relied on these notions (at least in a primitive sense). Thus, Ludwig von Berta-lanffy, a biologist, presented his now classic *General Systems Theory,* which presented the outlines of a theoretical framework to unify the sciences. Similarly, Norbert Wiener presented his cybernetic models of communication, whereas Ross Ashby postulated his notions of the design of intelligent

TABLE 3.1   **Differences between Atomistic and Holistic Conceptions**

	Conception of the World	
Dimension	*Atomistic*	*Holistic*
Orientation	An entity can be understood solely in terms of its parts	An entity can be fully understood only in terms of both the organization of its parts and the parts themselves
Organization of science	Increasing differentiation	Unification of highly differentiated scientific disciplines
Orientation toward causality	Strict causality Entity is passive	Admits emergent behavior
Relationship of observer to phenomenon observed	Independent	Not necessarily independent

machines—both anchored in systems ideas. The era also witnessed the emergence of such interdisciplines as operations research. Second, disenchanted with the increasing fragmentation of knowledge created by the mechanistic conception of the world, a number of scientists formed the *American Association for the Advancement of Science,* a society dedicated to the pursuit of general systems notions and for the unification of science. Third, a number of dedicated scholars such as economist Kenneth Boulding began to pursue and articulate systems theoretic notions. As a consequence, the systems conception began to gain currency in scholarly circles.[4]

It must be noted that systems theory does not constitute a rejection of traditional scientific disciplines. It supplements them with a new way of thinking. Many believe that this new way of thinking is better suited than traditional approaches to the study of contemporary management problems.

Historical Underpinnings

In addition to the intellectual ferment created by general systems theory, several historical trends facilitated the acceptance and upsurge of the application of systems theory in organizational studies. First and foremost is the complexity of organizations compared to physical and biological systems. That modern organizations are complex is too widely accepted to merit comment here. As we have seen in the previous chapter, this complexity has been on the increase. Modern organizations have thousands of interacting variables, whereas physical systems may involve only a few (variables): This, in itself, facilitated the acceptance of systems notions.

Secondly, as was noted in the previous chapter, there has been a failure of approaches based on a single discipline. For example, classical theorists like Frederick Taylor failed to take into account the unanticipated consequences of their rational models. Scientific management advocates developed excellent standards and models but ran into problems in implementing them, and the human relations school went out of vogue because this group of scholars emphasized social and psychological factors to the exclusion of economic and technical factors. As a result, there has been a growing realization on the part of organization theorists that they should employ a multidisciplinary approach to the study of organizations. Systems theory offered probably the best avenue for employing such an approach.

Third, there had been a growing use of computers by industry after World War II. Also, the era witnessed the increasing application of systems analysis to many areas of organizations. Large numbers of staff people had been trained in systems analysis, working in such areas as operations research, management science, and information systems. This, in turn, led to wide acceptance of systems notions.

Finally, there were a number of forerunners to contemporary systems theories of organizations that anticipated the later theories and reflected conceptions of organizations similar to them. For example, in sociology,

Talcott Parsons and his students saw our society as integrated by a common set of values and were interested in how various parts of the society contributed to these values and were affected by them. Similarly, in psychology, Gordon Allport called attention to the fact that social systems are contrived entities and hence are different from physical and biological systems; further, he suggested the replacement of traditional causal logic (a key component of the atomistic conception) with a logic that focused on ongoing system processes. George Homans, in his study of groups, presented one of the early attempts to adopt a systems perspective. In the United Kingdom, specific formulation of organizations as sociotechnical systems had been accomplished in the early 50s and application of such theoretical ideas had led to the modern day concepts of autonomous work group designs.[5]

In retrospect, the socioeconomic and intellectual milieu of the times facilitated the acceptance of the systems view of organizations. The latter half of the decade of the 60s witnessed the early accomplishments of scholars applying systems concepts to the study of organizations; to this we now turn.

Theoretical Underpinnings

In the United States, a large number of scholars contributed to the acceptance of the systems view of organizations. We will refer to many of them in later chapters in terms of the specific contributions they made to our understanding of organizations. At this point, we will focus on some of the seminal attempts to portray organizations as open systems in a comprehensive manner.

Daniel Katz and Robert Kahn of the University of Michigan were two of the earliest scholars who championed the cause of open systems theory in organizational studies. *The Social Psychology of Organizations,* which they coauthored in the mid-60s, presented the first open systems view of organizations from a social psychological perspective. Their primary focus was on social structure, and their approach emphasized two aspects of social behavior patterns: interdependent behavior, so that movement in one part leads to movement in other parts; and openness to environmental inputs, so that organizations are continually in a state of flux.

> In our attempts to extend the description and explanation of organizational processes we have shifted from an earlier emphasis on traditional concepts of individual psychology and interpersonal relations to system constructs. The interdependent behavior of many people in their supportive and complementary actions takes on a form or structure which needs to be conceptualized at a more appropriate collective level. Classical organization theory we found unsatisfactory because of its implicit assumptions about the closed character of the social structures. The development of open-system theory, on the other hand, furnished a much more dynamic and adequate framework.[6] (See Box 3.1.)

Box 3.1

Katz and Kahn's Open Systems Model

Daniel Katz and Robert Kahn's characterization of organizations is elaborate. For simplicity in presentation, we summarize the four key components they delineated; (1) nature of social systems, (2) components, (3) description of the subsystems, and (4) relationship to the environment.

Nature of Social Systems: Katz and Kahn note that social systems are contrived: People invent complex patterns of behavior and design social structures by enacting those patterns of behavior. Psychological rather than biological forces provide cohesion to the systems; thus, social systems are more complex than biological organisms. Thus, the attitudes, perceptions, beliefs, motivations, habits, and expectations of human beings play a very important role. The patterns are stable: They are maintained in spite of the turnover of individuals.

Components: The components of the social system are: (1) the *role behavior* of members, (2) the *norms* prescribing and sanctioning these behaviors, and (3) the *values* in which these behaviors are embedded. These three furnish the bases of integration of social systems. Roles provide integration for the functional interdependence; norms provide an additional cohesive force. For example, the worker not only plays a part in the interdependent chain

of activities, but accepts the norms about doing a satisfactory job. Finally, values provide cohesion in the objectives of the system.

Description of Subsystems: Katz and Kahn identify five types of subsystems: (1) production subsystems concerned with the work that gets done; (2) supportive subsystems of procurement, disposal, and institutional relations; (3) maintenance subsystems for tying people into their functional roles; (4) adaptive subsystems concerned with organizational change; and (5) managerial subsystems for the direction, adjudication, and control of the many subsystems and the structure.

Relationship to Environment: Katz and Kahn assert that organizational functioning must be studied in relation to the environment. Thus, social systems as open systems are dependent on other social systems; their characterization as subsystems, systems, or suprasystems is relative to their degree of autonomy in carrying out their functions. From a societal point of view, the organization is a subsystem of one or more larger systems, and its linkage or integration with these systems affects its mode of operation and its level of activity.

Source: Adapted from Daniel N. Katz and Robert L. Kahn, *The Social Psychology of Organizations.* New York: John Wiley, 1978.

A second major effort to model formal organizations as open systems is represented in Rocco Carzo and John Yanouzas, *Formal Organizations: A Systems Approach.* Primarily addressing public agencies, these authors focused on the purposive and orderly behavior of people in organizations and presented a diagnostic framework for analysis of organizations (see Box 3.2). Thus, unlike the dynamic treatment of Katz and Kahn, here the

---

Box 3.2

Carzo and Yanouzas's Systems Approach to Formal Organizations

Rocco Carzo and John Yanouzas suggested that formal organizations are composed of three subsystems: technical, social, and power. They noted that each subsystem is identified by certain objectives, processes, roles, structures, and norms of conduct.

Technical subsystem: refers to the deliberate employment and arrangement of people and capital to perform tasks required by formal organizations. Technical structure refers to the arrangement of jobs in relationship to each other. Processes refer to decision, communication, and action. Authority is related to the job and delegated from above. Individuals play roles according to their job requirements, and derive status from their ability to meet job requirements.

Social subsystem: arises spontaneously from social interactions and shared values of people placed in contact with each other. Structure refers to patterns of friendship relations. Processes are interactions, sentiments, and activity. Informal authority is derived from those who are its subjects. Individuals play roles according to sentiments, beliefs, attitudes, and social mores and hold status because of the sentiments of others in the system.

Power subsystem: arises as people use the various sources of power to acquire things that are judged valuable by others and successfully implement decisions. Structure refers to differentiation based on behavioral areas controlled. Key processes are decision implementation and order maintenance. Various sources of power exist: Official positions, location, coalitions, and so on. Individuals play opportunistic roles, and hold status because of the degree of success attained in implementing their decisions.

Carzo and Yanouzas note that distinctions made among these subsystems, while necessary for discussion, are not clearly identifiable in fact. The three subsystems are intertwined by overlapping relations. For example, some power relations are coincident with technical relations, as when the holder of administrative authority—a technical subsystem variable—successfully employs the sanctions at his or her disposal to influence the behavior of subordinates. Social relations may also intersect technical relations when, for example, business is conducted at a social gathering.

Source: Adapted from Rocco Carzo, Jr., and John N. Yanouzas. *Formal Organizations: A Systems Approach.* Homewood, Ill.: Richard D. Irwin, 1967.

emphasis was on explaining the regularities of behavior found in organizations, and not on explaining organizational change.[7]

Systems theory also received a boost from scholars working in such fields as operations research and system simulation. For example, Jay Forrester developed the industrial dynamics model in the late 50s, which provided a methodology (and several applications) for modeling organizations (see Box 3.3). The mathematical intricacy of the modeling procedures precluded inclusion of social and human variables at the time of its invention;

Box 3.3

Jay W. Forrester

The work of Jay Forrester, an engineer and computer sciences expert, led to the emergence of the new field of systems dynamics. Born July 14, 1918, in Anselmo, Nebraska, Professor Forrester holds a B.S. from the University of Nebraska (1939); an M.S. from Massachusetts Institute of Technology (1945); and honorary doctoral degrees from the University of Nebraska, Newark College of Engineering, University of Notre Dame, Boston University, and Union College. He has received numerous awards and honors, including induction into the National Inventors Hall of Fame in 1979. He holds patents in the servomechanism and digital computer fields.

Jay Forrester has spent his career at the Massachusetts Institute of Technology (MIT), Cambridge, where he was cofounder of the Servomechanisms Laboratory in 1940. From 1940 through 1946, he developed servomechanisms for radar and gun mounts. He was director of the Digital Computer Laboratory from 1946 through 1951 and head of the Digital Computer Division, Lincoln Laboratory, from 1952 through 1956. From 1956 through 1972, Forrester was professor of management at MIT's Alfred P. Sloan School of Management. Since 1972, he has served as Germeshausen Professor of Management and director of the system dynamics program at MIT.

In addition to being a contributor of technical papers on digital computers and articles on industrial management to professional journals, Professor Forrester has published several books through the MIT Press, including: *Industrial Dynamics,* 1961; *Principles of Systems,* 1968; *Urban Dynamics,* 1969; *World Dynamics,* 1971, 2nd edition, 1973; and *Collected Papers,* 1975.

While head of the Digital Computer Laboratory at MIT from 1946 through 1951, Forrester was responsible for the design and construction of the Whirlwind I, one of the first high-speed computers. He invented and holds the patent on what was for many years the standard memory device for digital computers—"random-access, coincident-current magnetic storage." He was further responsible for the most extensive early application of digital computer technology through his guidance, as head of the digital computer division of MIT's Lincoln Laboratory, of the planning and technical design of the U.S. Air Force's Semi-Automatic Ground Environment (SAGE) system for continental air defense.

The field of systems dynamics emerged through Jay Forrester's application of his computer sciences and engineering background to the development of computer modeling and analysis of social systems during his tenure at the Alfred P. Sloan School of Management. He and his associates developed a comprehensive simulation model for examining the forces underlying inflation, unemployment, energy shortages, foreign exchange rates, mobility of the population, and tax policy. Recent papers describe his early work in this field. Forrester believes that by incorporating microeconomic structures at the level of industrial firms and macroeconomic structures at the national level, implications can be explored for the full range of policies that create behavior and cause difficulties in the socio-economic system.

Source: Adapted from *Contemporary Authors,* New Revision Series, vol. 1, edited by Ann Evory. Copyright © 1981 by Gale Research, Inc. Reprinted by permission of the publisher.

in later years, such intricacy has prevented the diffusion of this approach into the social sciences.

Summary

Systems theorists believe that anything that is composed of many parts can be understood only as a whole and not simply by understanding its parts. Organization theorists have come to accept this view because of several reasons: the rising complexity of modern day organizations, failure of other approaches that were described in the last chapter, the accelerating use of computers, and the increasing use of systems concepts in other social science disciplines such as sociology and psychology. In the 1960s, three major works laid the foundations of the open systems model of organizations. Katz and Kahn formulated an open systems model to describe the evolution of organizations; Carzo and Yanouzas described the stable behavior patterns of public agencies; and operations researchers provided simulation models of industrial systems. All these and later works shared some essential concepts of modern systems theory; we will now describe the concepts.

Some Essential Concepts in Modern Systems Theory

In order to explicate our view of organizations as open social systems, we describe eight key concepts that are used throughout this book:
   1. open systems
   2. static versus dynamic equilibrium
   3. interdependence
   4. feedback
   5. stability and change
   6. equifinality and multifinality
   7. levels
   8. subsystems
Let us define each of them.

Open Systems

In the case of a closed system, the environment has no impact on the system. In real life, however, organizational systems (social and/or industrial) are "open" systems in which there is continual interaction with the environment. These systems have highly flexible structures and within them some process is continually going on. Thus, the distinction between system boundaries and the environment is an arbitrary matter for open systems; the boundaries are dependent on the purpose of the observer.

Static versus Dynamic Equilibrium

Both the system and the conditions for its equilibrium can be approached from the static as well as dynamic viewpoints. Static aspects are concerned with time invariant phenomena; that is, those aspects that do not vary with time. On the other hand, dynamic aspects deal with time-varying interactions.

In a static equilibrium, the components of a system are in such a relationship to each other that all tend to remain constant in value. A temporary disturbance in the magnitude of one component causes changes in other magnitudes such that the final result of the interaction is a return to the initial values. We will note that systems in static equilibrium are generally closed systems.

The process through which an open system reaches a state of equilibrium at a particular point in time from a state of disequilibrium induced by external disturbance and/or parameter changes is called *dynamic*. In such a case, parameters are not constant but changing, and a permanent change in the parameter results in a corresponding change in the magnitudes of other components of the system.

However, a point of caution should be introduced here in applying the concept of equilibrium to open systems. Open systems are in continual interaction with the environment, which is constantly changing. The typical response of open systems to environmental intrusion is elaboration or change of their structure to a higher or more complex level. Thus, open systems are constantly changing and elaborating their structure. The particular kinds of more or less stable interrelationships among components that become established *at any time* constitute the particular structure of the system *at that time,* thus achieving a kind of "whole" with some degree of continuity and boundary. And it is only in this sense that one can speak of dynamic equilibrium in the case of open systems.

Let us now illustrate these concepts of static and dynamic equilibrium with an example. Imagine, for a moment, a school of business whose only goal is to turn out a certain number of students a year. Let us also grant that this hypothetical school has been able to acquire faculty and facilities that neither age nor depreciate. Furthermore, the faculty has designed a set of courses and examination systems that they teach and administer without change. Also assume the school has been able to devise a master selection procedure that brings in a specified number of students of required skills, aptitudes, and intellectual abilities and that this remains constant from year to year. And further, let us assume that outside pressures on the school and its administration do not change with time. If such an institution ever existed, it would be an example of a static system. And one can study and determine the conditions of static equilibrium for each of its subsystems as well as for the total system.

Of course, one must argue that such an institution could not exist. That is precisely the case because change in any entity and/or component of the system—student body, faculty, outside pressures, goals, and the like—will start the dynamics of the system. Because of the interlocking nature of the components, a change initiated in one component will have an effect on other components. If the disturbance that initiated change in the system is a drastic one, such as a 10 percent increase in the student body, the system will adjust to a new static level after the effects of the disturbance have worked through the system. On the other hand, if the disturbance is of a persistent nature (a yearly intake of a certain number of faculty), the system may never come to a static equilibrium but continue changing to new levels at a predictable rate. That is the case of dynamic equilibrium.

Interdependence

One of the most important concepts in systems theory is that a system consists of interdependent elements. This implies that significant problems are those that arise as a result of interactions among the elements, not ones that are attributable to a given element. In other words, one can expect that the interconnections and interactions between the components of the system are often more important than the separate components themselves.

Feedback

Organizations, by definition, are collections of people (or people and machines) brought together to achieve certain goals or objectives. It is this concept of "purposive" or goal-seeking behavior that separates organizations (complex adaptive systems) from pure physical systems. Therefore, we characterize organizations as *purposive systems*. It is generally agreed among system theorists that a principle underlying the purposive or goal-seeking behaviors is embodied in the concept of feedback. Feedback-controlled systems are referred to as goal *directed*, not merely goal *oriented*, since it is the deviation from the goal state itself that directs the behavior of the system, rather than some predetermined internal mechanism that aims blindly.

> The concept of feedback can be broadly defined as a process that starts with detection of any deviation of the system's internal states and/or overt behavior from goal states defined in terms of the criterion variables and feeds back this "mismatch" information or deviation into the system's behavior-directing centers such that this feedback reduces (in the case of negative feedback) or increases (in the case of positive feedback) the deviation of the system from its goal states or criterion limits.

A simple illustration of the feedback concept is the single-loop servomechanism shown in Figure 3.1.

FIGURE 3.1

Single-loop Servomechanism

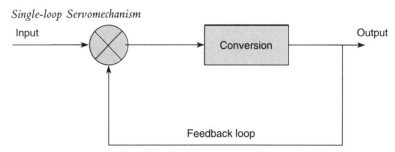

Stability and Change

Organizational systems experience processes of both stability and change. Some processes in the system-environment exchange tend to preserve or maintain a system's given form, organization, or state. Homeostatic processes in organisms, and ritual in sociocultural systems, are examples of processes that induce stability.

On the other hand, some processes tend to elaborate or change a system's given form, structure, or state. Biological evolution, learning, societal development, and organizational growth are examples of such processes.

Equifinality and Multifinality

The classical principle of causality held that similar conditions produce similar effects, and consequently, dissimilar results are due to dissimilar conditions. The concept of equifinality implies that a final state may be reached by any number of different developmental routes. According to the concept of multifinality, similar conditions may lead to dissimilar end states. Thus, two organizations developing in very similar environments may end up very differently.

Levels

Complex systems consist of several levels that are related hierarchically. We say hierarchically because the higher levels *include* lower levels. For example, organizations consist of individuals, groups, departments, and divisions. Yet, a division consists of several departments, a department may consist of many groups, and a group may consist of several individuals.

Subsystems

Subsystems, like levels, are parts of a system. Each subsystem is a collection of related entities and components. For example, entities of the social subsystem are people and some of the components are sentiments, feelings, and needs.

There are many different types of systems, organizations being only one type. Systems, of course, differ in complexity. Needless to say, organizations—the focus of our attention—are systems at a very high level of complexity.

A famous systems theorist by the name of Kenneth Boulding used the concept of levels to describe the complexity of systems. He identified nine levels of increasing complexity—from a very simple framework structure (for example, a solar system) to very complex human and social systems—that is, organizations. (See Box 3.4.)

Boulding's hierarchy suggests that even with the high level of complexity, organizations will display some simple properties that are characteristic of lower level systems. For example, the plant settings and physical layout of an organization are relatively unchanging and hence not dynamic (framework level). However, organizations do possess highly complex properties such as the ability to choose environments, existence of shared culture, and the like.

Having discussed some of the key concepts of open systems theory, it is now possible to sketch the correspondence between the philosophic orientation of systems theory and various concepts delineated above. Our definition of the system as a complex of interrelated components underscores the philosophic assumption that to understand an entity, we need to know not only the parts but also the organization (or interrelationship) of the parts. The focus on interdependence among levels and subsystems provides a way of gaining an understanding of the system but also highlights the necessity of bringing a multidisciplinary orientation to the study of organizations. The systems theoretic notions of multifinality and equifinality render invalid the prediction of system behavior based only on antecedent conditions. Together, these characteristics depart from the notions of strict causality found in the physical sciences. Finally, we note that how one draws the boundaries of the system is arbitrary and, to some extent, dependent on one's perspective—a fact that underscores the relationship between the observer and the phenomenon observed. Table 3.2 sketches how the philosophic underpinnings of systems theory get reflected in the concepts that we have presented.

Summary

In summary, from the systems point of view, organizations have several properties. They consist of at least three levels (individuals, groups, and total organization), and several subsystems that are interdependent. Organizations continually interact with their environments. They experience both stability-inducing and change-inducing processes. Organizations are

---

Box 3.4

Boulding's Hierarchy of System Complexity

Boulding identifies nine levels of complexity. These levels are:

Level 1: Frameworks. Only static structural properties are represented in frameworks, as in the descriptions of human anatomy, or the cataloging system used by libraries.

Level 2: Clockworks. Noncontingent dynamic properties are represented in clockwork systems. Unlike level 1, the state of a level 2 system changes over time.

Level 3: Control systems. Control system models describe regulation of system behavior according to an externally prescribed target or criterion, as in thermostats. The crucial difference from level 2 is the flow of information within the system between regulator and operator, and in fact the functional differentiation between operation and regulation.

Level 4: Open systems. Whereas a control system tends toward the equilibrium target provided to it and, therefore, produces uniformity, an open system maintains its internal differentiation. Open systems are maintained by the requisite variety in the environment, such as the flames of a fire.

Level 5: Blueprinted growth systems. These systems reproduce not through a process of duplication but by producing seeds or eggs that contain preprogrammed instructions for development, such as the egg-chicken system. In this sense, they differ from level 4 systems, since the latter reproduce through duplication.

Level 6: Internal image systems. The essential characteristic of level 6 systems is a *detailed* awareness of the environment acquired through differentiated information receptors and organized into a knowledge structure. The previous levels incorporate only primitive mechanisms for absorbing and processing information.

Level 7: Symbol-processing systems. Systems at these levels exhibit not only detailed awareness of the environment but of *self-consciousness*. This additional property is correlated with the ability to generalize or abstract information into ideas and symbols that stand for them. These systems are self-conscious language users; for example, individual human beings.

Level 8: Multicephalous systems. These are literally systems with several brains, or as Boulding notes, a collection of individuals acting in concert. These systems have elaborate shared systems of meaning—for example, systems of law or culture—that no individual human being seems to have. All human organizations are level 8 phenomena.

Level 9: Systems of unknown complexity. Boulding's ninth level is created to reflect the possibility that some new level of system complexity not yet imagined may emerge.

Boulding notes two characteristics of this hierarchy. First, the adjacent levels in the hierarchy differ in complexity not merely in their degree of diversity or variability but in the *appearance of wholly new system properties.* Thus, the difference between level 6 and level 7 is the appearance of the property of self-consciousness. Second, Boulding asserts that the hierarchy is *cumulative:* each level incorporates all the properties of all lower levels.

Source: Adapted from Kenneth E. Boulding, "General Systems Theory: The Skeleton of Science," *Management Science* 2 (April 1956), pp. 197–208.

TABLE 3.2   **Some Relationships between Systems Concepts and Philosophic Orientation of Systems Theory**

Dimension	Holistic Conception	Specific Systems Concepts
Orientation	An entity can be fully understood only in terms of both the parts and their organization	System
Organization of science	Unification of highly differentiated scientific disciplines	Interdependence among levels and subsystems
Orientation towards causality	Emergent behavior	Unintended consequences
Relationship of observer to phenomenon observed	Not necessarily independent	Arbitrary nature of boundaries

goal directed, with many pathways available to them to achieve their desired goals.

A Systems Model of Organization

Having discussed some of the essential concepts in modern systems theory, in this section we will outline the details of a model of organization based on these concepts. The model will serve two functions: first, it will provide a framework for organizational analysis and diagnosis; second, it will serve as the organizing framework for the discussion of action strategies as well as our exposition of the roles of a general manager. But to begin, it is necessary to summarize some of the assumptions that guided us in the construction of the model.

Assumptions Underlying the Model

The model is anchored in four crucial assumptions pertaining to the character of organizations:

1. An organization is considered to be a highly complex system that shares the eight properties enumerated in the previous section. The boundary of the organizational system is stable at a given point in time, but changes over time.
2. An organization is assumed to have multiple inputs and outputs and, given its open systems character, is in continual interaction with the environment.

3. The organizational system is divided into five (internal) subsystems. These subsystems are not independent of one another and there is a certain degree of overlap among them.

4. There are linkages between subsystems, in addition to linkages between the organization and its environment. Thus, there is a high degree of interdependence among the subsystems.

Figure 3.2 outlines the broad structure of our open systems model of an organization. We will now describe the key aspects of the model.

Environment

Each organization is embedded in an environment. The environment may be a town, a state, a nation, or the world, depending on the scope of operations of the organization. For example, for a large national organization, it is the entire nation; for a multinational organization like General Electric, or the United Nations, it may be the whole world.

Inputs and Outputs

The type of inputs and outputs vary depending on the nature as well as the scope of the organization. Some of the typical inputs and outputs are employee labor, finances, logistics (the physical flow of goods and services), and information. Of course, organizations vary depending on what their primary inputs and outputs are. Primary inputs for an industrial company are orders and raw materials, whereas it is students for universities, and patients for hospitals. Similarly the primary output of an industrial company

FIGURE 3.2

Outline of the Proposed Model of Organization

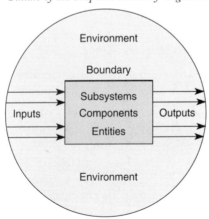

is finished goods, whereas it is trained students for the university, and cured patients for the hospitals.

Subsystems

As indicated earlier, the organizational system is composed of five somewhat overlapping subsystems. These subsystems are shown in Figure 3.3.

Functional Subsystem

This subsystem is concerned with the formal definitions of jobs, their relationships to each other (i.e., the job structure), formal or legitimate authority structure of the organization, written policies, procedures, rules, formal reward and incentive systems, and functional specialization and coordination. This subsystem is, thus, comprised of the traditional aspects of management and organization theory. Important problems and issues in this subsystem are job specification and specialization, coordination and control, design of authority structure, and rules and policies to enforce such a design. The activities within this subsystem are of the instrumental (task-related) type, and roles are of a technical nature.

FIGURE 3.3

Subsystems of the Organizational System

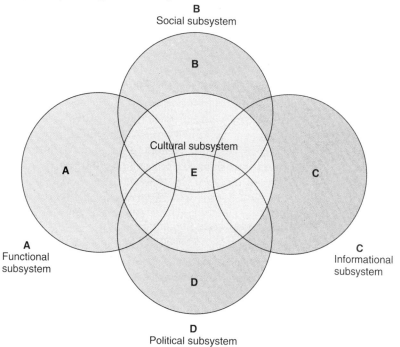

This area has been the province of classical organization theorists like Max Weber, administrative theorists like Luther Gulick and Lyndall Urwick, and industrial engineers like Frederick Taylor.

The components (or variables) of this subsystem are authority, status, rank, span of control, instrumental (task) role or job description, authority structure, and other economic variables such as profits. The entities are people and, in cases of industrial organizations, technical inputs such as capital, equipment, and raw materials.

Social Subsystem

This subsystem arises from the social interaction of people within organizations. The functional subsystem specifies functional roles for individuals in the organization. In the performance of these roles, people interact and develop sentiments toward each other such as liking, disliking, respect, or attraction. Social relations become differentiated, social structure is elaborated, social norms develop to maintain this structure, an informal communication network develops, and individuals are required to play their social roles in addition to their task (instrumental or technical) roles.

This area has been the field of activity of the social scientists, particularly the industrial, social, and organizational psychologists.

Components (or variables) of this subsystem are noninstrumental or social activities, sentiments, feelings, needs, attitudes, social structure, informal communication channels, friendship links, esteem, and so on. The entities of this subsystem are primarily people.

Informational Subsystem

The main activity within this subsystem is the transmission of information, which takes place through both *formal* and *informal* channels. The formal communication process involves the collection, processing, and transmission of information from one point to another in the organization. For example, data about spending is gathered from the various units of the organization and transformed into various reports; or data is gathered about consumer behavior, competitors, and economic conditions, and transformed into sales forecasts. The informal channels include rumor mills, gripe sessions, and, in general, channels that are not prescribed formally.

This subsystem serves primarily the needs of the functional subsystem and to some extent those of the social, cultural, and political subsystems. In order to coordinate and control task activities, information is needed by those charged with coordination and control.

It could be argued that the informational subsystem should be a part of the functional subsystem. We have chosen to make it a separate subsystem because recent advances in information and computer technology have made this field quite distinct and different from the activities of the functional subsystem. Of course, there is and will always remain a considerable overlap between the informational and the functional subsystems.

The informational subsystem deals primarily with the cognitive aspects of organizations. The issues within this subsystem are delays in information processing, accuracy and quality of the information, design of collecting and transmitting channels, selection of media for transmission, and so on. As indicated earlier, this area has felt the maximum impact of the recent advances in technology.

Scholars who are active in this field come from various disciplines: information theory, engineering, cybernetics, computer sciences, organization communications, organization theory, and other social sciences.

The components (variables) of this subsystem are written documents, type of media, number of channels, quantity and quality of information, and network characteristics such as noise and filters. The entities are people and technical inputs such as computing equipment.

Political Subsystem

This subsystem deals with power relations and the coalitions and alliances of participants. There are coalitions and alliances in the form of groups within the social subsystems, but these are formed to satisfy social needs (affiliation and affection) of the members. On the other hand, people form political coalitions and alliances to satisfy their power needs (need for control, prestige, etc.). Also, there are alliances within the functional subsystem based on authority relationships such as departmental committees, coordinating committees, and executive committees. But authority is only one aspect of power; power in its generic sense refers to a condition or ability whereby one can induce others to produce an intended result. There are many sources of power: formal position or rank (authority), job importance, location, expertise, interest, tenure, coalition membership, esteem, external relationships, and even personal attributes. As the people who hold these means engage in power plays and gain success in the use of power, the power structure becomes elaborated. Thus are developed relatively stable coalitions and alliances, holding varying degrees of power. These coalitions in turn engage in bargaining, compromise, and threats to expand their autonomy. They also come to play an important part in the evolution and formulation of organizational goals.

Scholars working in this area have primarily come from the social sciences: particularly political science, labor and industrial relations, organization theory, sociology, and to some extent social psychology. There has also been work done by mathematicians, particularly game theorists.

The components of this subsystem are sources of power, bargaining skills, conflict, scarce resources, goals, need for control, and so forth. The entities are primarily people.

Cultural Subsystem

The cultural subsystem represents the relatively enduring aspects of an organization—deeply held assumptions, norms, values, and beliefs—that are shared among organizational participants. As members engage in day-to-day activities, they begin to construct shared views of reality; including key members' view of the relationship to the environment, the linguistic and behavioral rules that define what is real and what is not, what constitutes the right way for people to interact with each other, and what are the right things for the organization and the members to do. Over time, these shared aspects are transmitted to newer members through the socialization process. Members begin to accept the culture as a given and as a result, the cultural variables become inaccessible to public scrutiny and examination. To some extent, therefore, the cultural subsystem represents the unarticulated and invisible aspects of the organization. The cultural subsystem thus becomes a sort of organizational unconscious; it serves to tie the various other subsystems together and provides an identity to the organization.

Scholars working in this area have come primarily from the social sciences, especially anthropology, psychoanalysis, and social psychology. Organizational anthropology is evolving as a new branch of inquiry in the organizational sciences, as the importance of the cultural subsystem is increasingly recognized.

The components of this subsystem are artifacts, beliefs, norms, values, and premises. The entities are primarily people.

The key characteristics of each of the five subsystems are summarized in Table 3.3.

We make two observations about our formulation of organizations as five interacting subsystems:

1. This formulation includes *both technical and human elements* as part of any organization. The functional subsystem, and to some extent the informational subsystem, represent the technical elements, whereas the social, political, and cultural subsystems represent the human elements of an organization. Thus the functional and informational subsystems emphasize rationality and order while the political, social, and cultural subsystems represent the turbulent side of an organization.

2. Different subsystems not only focus on different elements of an organization, but *operate under different, sometimes contradictory, assumptions.* For example, the social subsystem emphasizes harmony, whereas the political subsystem emphasizes power plays.

Given the interdependence among subsystems, their interactions lead to processes, a topic to which we now turn.

Structures and Processes

We have so far primarily discussed structures within the five subsystems. We discussed the job (task) structure within the functional subsystem, informal

TABLE 3.3   **Characteristics of the Five Subsystems of an Organization**

Characteristics	Functional Subsystem	Social Subsystem	Political Subsystem	Informational Subsystem	Cultural Subsystem
Focus	Formal organization; deliberate definition of jobs and authority structure	Social interaction of people within organization	Power relations among individuals and groups	Information systems; the structure of data transmission	Enduring and unarticulated aspects of organization
Components	Authority, status, span of control, job description, structure, policies, procedures and rules	Social activities sentiments, feelings, needs, attitudes	Power, conflict, coalitions, cliques, scarce resources	Written documents, media, channels, network, filters	Shared assumptions, norms, values, beliefs, and myths
Management task	Organization design	Organization development	Governance	Design of information	Nurturing culture
Structure	Arrangement of jobs in relation to each other	Social structure	Power structure, coalitions	Information structure	Structure of myths and cultural components
Process	Decision making, conversion	Interaction, informal communication	Politics, conflicts	Collection, coding, and transmission of data	Transmission, socialization
Individual roles	Performer of tasks	Social being	Opportunist	Information processor	Carriers of culture, "heroes"
Underlying norms	Efficiency	Harmony	Pragmatism and expediency	Accuracy	Conformity with central values
Examples of contributing disciplines	Classical organization theories	Industrial, social, and organizational psychology	Political science, industrial relations, sociology, organization theory	Information theory, cybernetics, computer sciences	Anthropology, psychoanalysis, organization theory

communication and social-relational structures within the social subsystem, the communication structure within the informational subsystem, power coalition structures within the political subsystem, and the structure of assumptions, values, and beliefs in the cultural subsystem. These structures are relatively stable.

A major part of the dynamics of the organizational system—other than those induced by rare events or shocks—is accounted for by its processes.

There are at least three major processes in organizational systems: (1) problem solving and decision making, (2) communication, and (3) conversion processes.

1. Probably the most important is the problem-solving and decision-making process, which consists of goal formation or objective setting, planning, executing or implementing, and controlling or evaluating.
2. Closely linked with the first is the communication process which involves collection, processing, and transmission of information as well as decisions.
3. By no means the least important is the manufacturing or conversion process, which transforms inputs (raw materials, students, or patients) into value-added outputs (finished products, graduates, or cured patients).

Internal and External Linkages

As stated earlier, there are many linkages among the five subsystems as well as between the environment and the organizational system.

Linkages with the environment have already been discussed in the form of inputs and outputs. Some of the inputs such as people are linked with all of the five subsystems, whereas other inputs have primary linkage with only one or two subsystems. For example, cultural values and social norms have primary linkage to the cultural subsystem, and to some extent with the political and social subsystems, whereas information technology has its primary linkage with the informational subsystem.

Since the subsystems are interdependent and also have a significant amount of overlap, there are important linkages among them (see Figure 3.4). For example, decisions as to what type of information is needed flow from the functional subsystem to the informational subsystem, and information flows back from the informational to the functional subsystem. Box 3.5 presents some examples of these interrelationships between subsystems, taken two at a time. These linkages obscure the distinctions among the five subsystems: just as we noted in the case of the boundary of an organization, subsystems are not always clearly identifiable.

The linkages among the subsystems underscore the holistic nature of an organization. The examples in Box 3.5 present the stable linkages among subsystems in the respective organizations. The interdependence notion also suggests that if changes are initiated in one subsystem, there will be repercussions in other subsystems. Such changes start the dynamics within a system, unleashing forces that may counteract the initiated changes or move the system in ways not originally intended. The above ideas are captured in two related ideas: emergent behaviors and unintended consequences.

FIGURE 3.4

Linkages between Subsystems

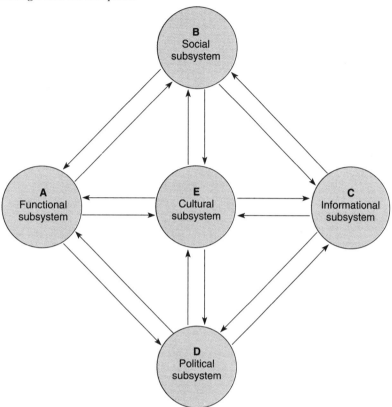

Emergent Behaviors and Unintended Consequences

Key organizational decision makers, in their pursuit of system-level (or their own) goals often specify prescribed forms of behavior in organizations. Very often the behaviors prescribed are in the functional subsystem: job specifications, standards of behavior, and the like. However, as we have noted, the functional subsystem influences, and is influenced by, other subsystems. What happens, in effect, is that the various subsystems interact, and through interaction new patterns of behavior emerge that are separate from, but related to, the ways of behaving and thinking that are specified initially. This new behavior is called *emergent behavior.*

What emerges from the interplay of forces will most probably represent compromises among the several interest groups participating in organizations. The mutual dependence of organizational subsystems dictates that no one group can attain its goals without the cooperation of other groups participating in the accomplishment of organizational objectives. Since all

---
Box 3.5

Examples of Linkages among Subsystems

We list a number of examples of linkages observed among subsystems. These are neither hypotheses nor universal truths: They are specific to the organizations mentioned. Since organizations obey the properties of multifinality and equifinality, specific linkages described here need not be observed in other organizations. We have developed our examples from published literature wherever possible; in some cases, we have reinterpreted the literature in our own terms.

1. *Functional-social subsystems:* Cohesive groups develop norms of acceptable output. In some organizations group norms restrict productivity; thus, skilled employees are prevented from operating at their peak levels (Seashore, 1954).

2. *Functional-informational subsystems:* Managers charged with production and marketing decisions typically respond to the available information (Forrester, 1967); organizations install management information systems to provide them with data as current as possible to improve organizational

productivity (King and Cleland, 1978).

3. *Functional-political subsystems:* The power of various departments in an organization often determines the level of financial resources flowing into the department. This has been observed in the budgeting practices of the universities of Illinois and California (Pfeffer and Salancik, 1978).

4. *Functional-cultural subsystems:* Cultural factors influence the performance of functional subsystems and the decisions made in them. "Prospector" cultures place a lot of emphasis upon innovation and try out new ways of doing things, whereas "defenders" are reluctant to bring about changes in their operations (Miles and Snow, 1978). Organizational cultures often get characterized by the dominant function: for example, IBM is often regarded as being dominated by a marketing culture.

---

groups cannot attain goals to their total satisfaction, and no one group can attain value to the exclusion of others, compromise becomes inevitable. Emergent behavior is a reflection of this compromise. As Carzo and Yanouzas note:

> The compromise among forces allows an explanation of a seeming paradox in formal organizations. People in organizations have, thus far, been characterized as behaving and thinking in ways that are different from, or in addition to, the ways in which they are supposed to behave and think. However, virtually all available evidence indicates that actual behavior in formal organizations is orderly and purposeful; that is, actual organizational behavior generally supports and is directed toward the objective of the formal organization. The fact that

Box 3.5 continued

5. *Social-informational subsystems:* Social networks facilitate diffusion of information and innovations through mechanisms such as rumor (Allport, 1941). Similarly, group-think often results in suppression of information contrary to the group's beliefs (Janis, 1977).

6. *Social-political subsystems:* Patterns of patronage develop in organizations where a powerful sponsor favors friends in terms of contract awards or personnel appointments, as in the case of the late Mayor Richard J. Daley of Chicago. Of course, such mentors and sponsors are often regarded as important to an individual's career advancement (Royko, 1971).

7. *Social-cultural subsystems:* Cultures often influence the forms of social behavior that are acceptable in an organization (Kretch et al., 1964). For example, Japanese organizations place a lot of emphasis upon face-saving, to preserve social harmony; as a result,they are often reluctant to say

no but communicate the intent by postponement or inaction.

8. *Informational-political subsystems:* Informational and political subsystems are closely intertwined. Political actions shape decision premises (Simon, 1947), setting decision agendas, the kinds of information sought, and lead to information suppression and even distortion (Narayanan and Fahey, 1982). Access to information often gives individuals power.

9. *Cultural-informational subsystems:* Some organizational cultures influence the kinds of information sought and even allow for public discussion. Many organizations disallow discussion of negative and threatening issues (Argyris, 1985).

10. *Cultural-political subsystems:* Violations of cultural dictates often lead to symbolic actions on the part of powerful leaders, often in excess of the degree of violations in order to drive home the importance of the dictate.

actual organizational behavior is orderly and purposeful but generally different from formally prescribed behavior is not really a paradox, because organizational objectives change through the process of action and reaction among the parts of the system; and as objectives evolve to reflect the needs of the participants, organizational behavior will become oriented towards these goals.[8]

Actions initiated by key decision makers often have ramifications beyond the immediate goals they are pursuing, some of which will not be intended in the first place. Decision making involves a weighing of consequences of alternative courses of action: Here, the consequences of the chosen action alternative are intended. In organizations, several subsystem forces interact; actions taken in one subsystem have repercussions in others. Thus, what ensues is emergent behavior. Emergent behaviors have consequences not originally intended; these consequences are termed *unintended consequences.*

We can identify at least two sources of unintended consequences: (1) limiting function of goals; and (2) interaction among subsystems.

Limiting Function of the Goals

The aim of an action tends to limit the perception of its ramified consequences. Further, not all consequences are relevant to the aim. The necessity to "keep your eye on the ball," which demands the construction of a rational system explicitly relating means and ends, will restrain the actor from taking account of consequences that indirectly shape the means and ends of policy. This source of unintended consequences will never be extinguished: There will always be a minimum residue of unintended consequences.

Interaction among Various Subsystems

A second source of unintended consequences is the interaction of various subsystems and the resultant compromises. As we noted earlier, any chosen course of action sets in motion the dynamics of the system. The course of action or policy change requires key decision makers to translate such plans and policies into action through day-to-day decisions relevant to actual problems. In doing so, they create precedents, alliances, effective symbols, and personal loyalties. Such linkages transform an organization from an inert and manipulable instrument into one that is resistant to treatment as a means to some external goal. Stated differently, changes in a functional subsystem—usually the product of a rational calculus—get modified and transformed by forces generated in other subsystems. The ensuing consequences are often unintended by the decision makers. Unintended consequences severely limit the realm in which rational adjustment of means and ends can be accomplished in organizations. In other words, accomplishment of goals by sole attention to the functional subsystem is possible only in a very limited set of circumstances.

Dashman Company

Let us now return to Dashman Company, the example with which we started this chapter. You may want to reread the case and describe the organization dynamics using systems concepts. We will summarize the case using the systems model.

> *Environment.* The major factor in the environment that concerned the president was the perceived shortage of raw materials. The war was expected to create such shortages. This meant that the raw material inputs would shrink, which, of course, would have been disastrous for the normal functioning of the company.
>
> *Functional subsystem.* Before Manson took action, Dashman's functional subsystem may be represented by the organization chart shown in Figure 3.5A, It consisted of the board of directors, the

FIGURE 3.5

Dashman Company

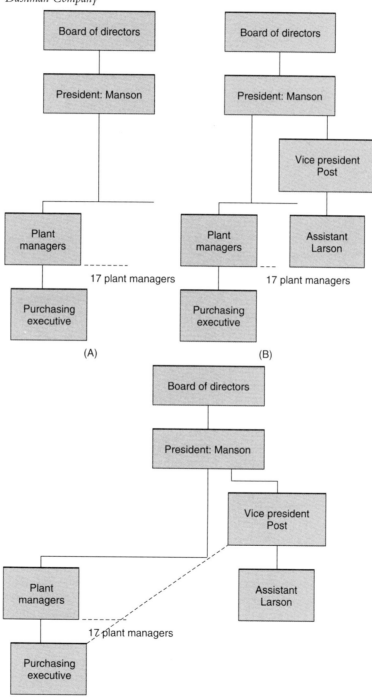

(A)

(B)

(C)

president, and the 20 plant managers who reported to the president. Decision making with respect to purchasing was decentralized; that is, each plant did its own purchasing with the help of a purchasing executive. Coordination among plants was minimal or nonexistent. After Manson brought in Post, the organization chart looked as in Figure 3.5B. Post wanted to centralize purchasing, and therefore his view of the right organization perhaps looked like Figure 3.5C.

Social subsystem. We do not have a great deal of data about the social subsystem. However, we may infer that Larson, Post's assistant, was probably well liked by the people in the organization. We may also infer that some of the other corporate executives also had informal social ties with the plant executives.

Cultural subsystem. We know that before Post's arrival, Dashman had developed a culture of plant autonomy over the years. It was a norm that the corporate office left the plants alone with respect to their operations. "You don't meddle with us, we don't meddle with you." Such norms would never have been written down in any memos or documents within the organization, but Post's memo was contrary to the *unwritten* norms in the organization.

Informational subsystem. Both informal and formal communications were active in Dashman. Post's appointment and his attempt at centralization were all communicated through **formal** channels. On the other hand, the visiting corporate executives brought the news of plant operations through **informal** conversations they had at the plants.

Political subsystem. Both Post and Manson had power because of their formal positions. The plant managers had considerable power because of their plant-related knowledge. Before Post, the political subsystem was dormant. Post's memo changed all that since it did not actually have any impact on the plants, suggesting that plant executives decided to flout their new superior's instructions or possibly that they decided to circumvent them by splitting their purchases so that none exceeded the $50,000 limit.

Before we deal with the question of how Post should have proceeded, we want to emphasize two fundamental points made by systems theorists.

First, since the various subsystems are *interdependent,* a change in one subsystem triggers dynamics in other subsystems. Here, a change in a functional subsystem that ran counter to the organization's culture of autonomy triggered the political dynamics such that a superior's order was either flouted or circumvented. Thus, political dynamics nullified the attempt to centralize the purchasing function, and the plants continued to do what they had historically done. In this case, the internal organizational subsystem reverted to stability; the attempted change was, thus, a failure.

Second, the case also underscores the concept of *emergent behavior* in an organization. Since Post's order was violated and the political subsystem was activated, Post's credibility as an executive was destroyed. He might take action to restore his authority. This might even include firing plant executives. Neither loss of credibility nor further actions to restore credibility could have been intended by Post when he undertook actions to centralize the purchasing function.

It is clear that Post defined his job primarily in terms of his role in the functional subsystem. According to this logic, since he was the superior, the subordinates, the plant purchasing executives, would follow his instructions. Indeed, he chose to ignore Larson's suggestion that he should personally visit with the plant executives before taking any action. Had he acted on Larson's suggestion, perhaps he would have understood that Dashman had a culture of plant autonomy, centralization ran counter to the culture, and hence, either

1. other culturally consistent solutions might have to be forged to solve the perceived shortage of raw materials, or

2. considerable resistance would have to be overcome, from both plant purchasing executives and their present bosses, the plant managers.

Put another way, the systems model that we have presented in this chapter suggests that *an appropriate diagnosis should include not merely the functional subsystem, but other subsystems as well.* It is, therefore, essential to analyze the total system so as to develop an understanding of various issues (problems) that would need to be addressed. A partial analysis is likely to lead to the wrong diagnosis.

We should make one final point. *The situation at the end of the case is different from the time when Post first took up his job with the Dashman Company.* As we have noted, the political subsystem became active and a superior's order was flouted. Therefore, now the organization would have to deal with this political reality in addition to dealing with the original problem of ensuring the supply of raw materials. Thus, Mr. Post has to reestablish his credibility as an executive or he will lose his effectiveness in this organization. Hence, the action plan now needs to be different from what would have been appropriate when Post first came on line.

A word of caution: The systems concept emphasizes the idea that policy changes are almost always associated with a residue of unintended consequences. It would be incorrect to place a fatalistic interpretation on this observation: If you cannot avoid them, then why bother? From the systems perspective, although unanticipated consequences cannot be eliminated, they may be minimized to the extent that policy changes and attendant weighing of the alternatives are anchored in a holistic understanding of the system. In this sense, the systems theorist works toward increased understanding of the system's behavior, and at the same time admits unexpected events, behaviors, and even surprises in organizational functioning.

Summary

In this section, we presented the systems model that will serve as the framework for the entire book. We described organizations as open systems with multiple inputs and outputs. Internally, the organization is composed of five subsystems: functional, social, informational, political, and cultural. We identified three major processes: problem solving and decision making, communication, and conversion. The subsystems are interlinked among themselves and with the environment. Although the functional and the informational subsystems (formal aspects) of an organization can be prescribed, the human elements of the organization, especially the social and political subsystems, display emergent properties, and cannot be fully prespecified. This is but another way of saying that the human elements in an organization tend to pull the organization toward turbulence. Consequently, any formal action taken by managers is likely to have unintended consequences.

Some Applications of the Systems Model

Having presented the major characteristics of the systems model, we will indicate five different ways in which we will utilize the model in this book: (1) to classify the work done in contemporary management literature; (2) to study specific organizational phenomena; (3) to organize major approaches to the management of organizations; (4) as an analytic framework for studying specific organizations; and (5) as a paradigm for the study of organizational change.

Classification of Management Literature

The concepts of environment, system, the five interdependent subsystems, and the linkages among them provide a logically coherent and comprehensive scheme for classifying the contemporary management literature. Reviewing the evolution of contemporary management thought from the previous chapter, we note that the classical management school primarily focused on the functional subsystem, whereas the human relations theorists addressed the social subsystem; neither paid attention to the environment. Human resource theorists showed some concern for the environment at the individual level, but focused primarily on the social subsystem and secondarily on the cultural subsystem at the organizational level. Information theorists and political scientists address their respective subsystems; strategy scholars focus on the linkages between the organization and its environment; and the emerging field of organizational anthropology is exclusively devoted to the cultural subsystem. The ensuing chapters will devote attention to several other scholars; the systems model will be useful in classifying them as well.

Study of Specific Organizational Phenomena

Specific organizational phenomena such as resistance to change or organizational conflict can be discussed from the vantage point of the systems model. Consider Hagg et al.'s now classic study of protest absorption. These authors note:

> [Reviewing them,] we have seen how in phase one a protest is initiated in the Social Subsystem. Phase two contains the open conflict of hierarchical power and the emerging protest enclave (Political Subsystem). The functional structure of the organization is then permanently changed in phase three when the protest is absorbed. The protest absorption was the vehicle by which a change in the Social Subsystem was transmitted (via Political Subsystem) to the Functional Subsystem, thereby altering it.[9]

Hagg et al., therefore, identify protest absorption phenomena primarily as an interaction of functional and social subsystems. We will discuss many organizational phenomena later in a similar manner, using the systems model as a frame of reference.

Organizing Approaches to Management

A number of approaches to management are evident in the contemporary literature as well as in practice. For example, such practices as strategic planning, organization design, and organization development are prevalent in many organizations. Although these approaches are related, they vary in terms of the relative emphasis they place on the environment and the various subsystems in an organization. The second section of this book details the salient approaches to management. Just as we do in the case of various theories of organization, we anchor the discussion of management approaches in the systems model.

Analytic Framework

One of the more important uses of the model is to describe and understand the behavior of specific organizational systems. The systems model suggests that a comprehensive understanding of an organization requires detailing its environment and all the five subsystems as well as interactions between the system and its environment on the one hand and various subsystems on the other. The model presented here thus provides a comprehensive framework for diagnosis of specific organizations. As we will elaborate in the next chapter, such a diagnosis is a necessary prerequisite to effective managerial action.

Paradigm for the Study of Organizational Change

Finally, in our view, the most important application of the model is to provide a paradigm for the study of organizational change. Change in organizations occurs within the context of a very dynamic process. It may be initiated in any one of the subsystems, but it almost always ends up involving the total organization because of the interdependency between various parts (subsystems) of the system. The planning of change has to take account of the implications for the total system if the change is to be successfully carried out. If this is not done, the organization might find itself caught by surprise. And since it will not be prepared to deal with these systemwide effects, the change program ends up a failure or only a partial success. Consider the following example:

> Benecki and French, using the paradigm suggested in the model, analyzed the changes occurring in a large department store as a result of the computerization of the accounts receivable area. They found that the organization, during the planning stage of the feasibility, saw change only in terms of the informational subsystem. Thus, the organization failed to see the implications for the other subsystems. As Benecki and French show, the computerization showed effects in three of the other subsystems of the organization, though it was initiated in the informational subsystem. In fact, they found that within two years after the introduction of computerization, the functional subsystem relating to the accounting department had almost completely changed. This change was in both structure and personnel. Levels of organization had been reduced from five to four, but there were two new staff positions attached to the second level from the top. In terms of personnel, all staff were replaced by new employees except the controller. Almost the entire old team had left the department, and in many cases, the organization. Thus, the organization had lost a number of its key personnel—an unintended consequence, in this case, because the organization failed to foresee and plan for the effects of the computerization on the other subsystems.[10]

To be effective, the planning of change in organizations must not be confined to the target subsystem but must account for total system dynamics.

Underlying Values and Assumptions

Before we deal with specific implications of the systems model for managers, it is useful to recapitulate some of its underlying values. We do this in accordance with our axiom (postulated in the previous chapter) that management theories are socioculturally and historically determined, and hence an appreciation of the world views underlying them is imperative for their proper application. Three key values—openness, holism, and uniqueness—and three assumptions—pattern recognition, synthesis and elaboration, and range of feasible alternatives—underlie the systems model.

Openness

The systems model upholds the value of openness to the environment: organizations have to be viewed as subsystems of a larger entity—the society—

an idea promoted by Parsonians. Or, put another way, to survive in the long run, organizations will have to adapt to their environments to serve some relevant function in society.

Holism

The model values understanding the organizations as a whole, and eschews atomistic conceptions or fragmented disciplinary approaches in the study of organizations. This predisposes systems theorists against accepting simple explanations for phenomena observed in organizations. The systems theorist views organizational phenomena as the result of a complex set of forces and searches for a comprehensive or relatively integrated and inclusive understanding of organizations.

Uniqueness

The systems model places a premium on understanding the uniqueness of organizations without disclaiming the utility of generalized theories. Such notions as multifinality explicitly recognize an organization's potential for autonomous behaviors; they also point out how organizations under similar starting conditions may distinguish themselves from one another by following different developmental paths. The systems model suggests that to bring about effective changes, a feel for the uniqueness of each organization is necessary.

Pattern Recognition

The model assumes that interactions among subsystems are probably more important than changes in one subsystem alone. Hence, one has to develop a feel for the dynamics of an organizational system. This requires recognition of patterns or cycles of events. Pattern recognition is akin to fitting the pieces of a jigsaw puzzle together: It is a messy process that is not easily reducible to a heuristic.

Synthesis and Elaboration

Organizational systems elaborate their structure as they grapple with the changing exigencies of circumstances. The general tendency of all organizations is to become complex.

Range of Feasible Alternatives

The systems model departs from much of conventional decision-making theory as it disavows the existence of a single "right" answer to important organizational problems. Multifinality and equifinality, which we referred to earlier, capture this idea. In one sense, the series of choices made by an organization— or to use a phrase coined by Herbert Simon, the pattern in its stream of decisions—determine its uniqueness. In another sense, this assumption underscores the potential of organizational systems to be autonomous.

Chapter Summary

In the last chapter, we noted that as management theory evolved over the years, we began to discard the simple explanations for organizational phenomena prevalent at the turn of the century. Organizations are complex phenomena that resist simplistic explanations. This insight facilitated the acceptance of systems thinking in organizations. Systems thinkers held that a system such as an organization can be understood only as a whole, not as the sum of its parts.

Organizations began to be conceptualized as open systems, in continual interaction with the environment; hence, their equilibrium was characterized as dynamic. Goal-directed organizations require feedback for taking corrective action if they deviate from prescribed goals. Organizations displayed stability and change; as we said in Chapter 1, the technical elements pull organizations toward order, whereas human elements create turbulence. Further, systems concepts emphasized interdependence, or the idea that the interaction among parts is more important than the individual parts themselves in explaining organizational dynamics. Finally, complex systems may be understood in terms of the interactions that take place among levels and subsystems.

These concepts are brought to life in our proposed systems model of organizations. The model considers an organization as an open system exchanging multiple inputs and outputs with the environment. The internal organization is composed of five interacting subsystems: functional, informational, social, political, and cultural. The functional and some of the formal informational subsystems represent the technical elements, whereas social, political, and cultural systems, and some informal elements of the informational subsystems represent the human side of the organization. The interactions among the elements were captured by three processes: decision making, communication, and conversion; in addition, we emphasized that interactions will generate unintended consequences to any formally prescribed change.

The systems model can be used to classify management theories and approaches to management. Indeed, in the second section of the book, when we deal with action strategies, we will utilize the systems model to illustrate the major focus of each action strategy. It can also be used to guide change (1) by conducting a comprehensive diagnosis (as Post should have done) and (2) for prescribing action plans.

The systems model is rooted in an ideology that emphasizes openness to the environment, holistic thinking, recognition of patterns, synthesis, appreciation of the uniqueness of an organization, and a departure from the search for single optimal solutions.

As we have noted, the systems model emphasizes stability as well as change. In the next chapter, we will focus on organization theorists who have studied how to stabilize an organization for optimal performance. Following that, we will take up the theme of organizational change.

Specialized Terms

Atomistic versus holistic
  conception
System
Static versus dynamic equilibrium
Linearity versus nonlinearity
Stability versus instability
Interdependence
Feedback
  • Negative
  • Positive
Equifinality
Multifinality
Boundary
Levels
Open versus closed systems

Environment
Inputs and outputs
Subsystems
  • Functional
  • Social
  • Political
  • Informational
  • Cultural
Processes
  • Decision making
  • Communication
  • Conversion
Emergent behavior
Unintended consequences
Subsystems

Discussion Questions

Theoretical

1. What are the major differences between mechanistic and holistic conceptions of the world?

2. What are some of the historical trends that led to the acceptance of systems thinking?

3. Discuss the major system concepts.

4. According to Boulding, at what level are organizations? Also identify systems at other levels.

5. Why is it difficult to determine the boundaries of an organization? How then is the concept of dynamic equilibrium useful?

6. Compare and contrast the functional, social, political, informational, and cultural subsystems.

7. How is the systems model useful in studying organizations?

★8. What implications flow from the systems model for managers?

9. What are the major values inherent in the systems perspective?

★10. Describe the major differences between (a) Katz and Kahn's model and (b) Carzo and Yanouzas'.

Applied

1. Discuss an automobile from the point of view of the systems theorist.

2. Describe your school, business, or university with the help of the systems model. Identify inputs, outputs, the environment, subsystems, structure, process, and their linkages.

★3. How will you describe the differences between General Electric and your university with the help of the systems model?

End Notes

1. Adapted from "The Dashman Company," in Paul Lawrence and John Seiler, *Organization Behavior: Cases, Concepts and Research Findings* (Homewood, Ill.: Richard D. Irwin, 1965), pp. 16–17.

2. L. Henderson, *Pareto's General Sociology* (Cambridge, Mass.: Harvard University Press, 1936), p. 80.

3. Russell L. Ackoff, "Foreword," in Schoderbek, Schoderbek, and Kefalas, *Management Systems* (Dallas, Tex.: Business Publications, Inc., 1980). See also Russell L. Ackoff, *Redesigning the Future: A Systems Approach to Social Problems* (New York: John Wiley & Sons, 1974).

4. W. Ross Ashby, *Design for a Brain*, 2nd ed. (London: Chapman and Hall, 1960). Ludwig von Bertalanffy, "General Systems Theory: General Systems," *Yearbook of the Society for General Systems Theory,* vol. 1 (1956), pp. 1–10. See also Ludwig von Bertaltanffy, *General Systems Theory: Foundations, Development, Applications* (New York: Braziller, 1967). Kenneth E. Boulding, "General Systems Theory: A Skeleton of Science," in *Management Systems*, 2nd ed., ed. P. P. Schoderbek (New York: John Wiley & Sons, 1971). Norbert Wiener, *The Human Use of Human Beings* (Boston: Houghton Mifflin, 1950).

5. G. W. Allport, "Trend in Motivational Theory," *American Journal of Orthopsychiatry* 23 (1953), pp. 107–19. George C. Homans, "Social Behavior as Exchange," *American Journal of Sociology* 63 (1958), pp. 597–606. Talcott Parsons, *Structure and Process in Modern Societies* (New York: Free Press, 1960). Eric L. Trist and K. W. Bamforth, "Some Social and

★This is an advanced-level question.

Psychological Consequences of Long Wall Method of Coal-Getting," *Human Relations* 4, pp. 3–38.
6. Daniel Katz and Robert L. Kahn, *The Social Psychology of Organizations*, 2nd ed. (New York: John Wiley & Sons, 1978), p. v.
7. Rocco Carzo, Jr., and John N. Yanouzas, *Formal Organizations: A Systems Approach* (Homewood, Ill.: Richard D. Irwin, 1967).
8. Ibid., p. 246.
9. D. Hagg, P. Kilkeary, T. Luekens, and D. Robertson, "Interaction of an Organization's Functional and Social Subsystems through Protest Absorption." Unpublished manuscript, Graduate School of Business, University of Pittsburgh, 1965.
10. W. T. Benecki and J. M. French, "The Impact of a Computer: A Study of Organizational Change." Unpublished manuscript, Graduate School of Business, University of Pittsburgh, 1965.

References

Allport, Gordon W. *The Person in Psychology.* Boston: Beacon Press, 1969.
Argyris, Chris. *Strategy, Change and Defensive Routines.* Boston: Pitman, 1985.
Forrester, Jay W. *Industrial Dynamics.* Cambridge, Mass.: MIT Press, 1961.
Janis, Irving. *Victims of Group Think.* Boston: Houghton Mifflin, 1972.
King, William R., and David I. Cleland. *Strategic Planning and Policy.* New York: Van Nostrand Reinhold, 1978.
Kretch, David, Richard S. Crutchfield, and Egerton L. Ballachey. *Individual in Society.* New York: McGraw-Hill, 1962.
Miles, Raymond E., and Charles C. Snow. *Organizational Stragtegy, Structure and Process.* New York: McGraw-Hill, 1978.
Narayanan, V. K., and Liam Fahey. "The Micro-Politics of Strategy Formulation." *Academy of Management Review* 7, no. 1 (1982), pp. 25–34.
Pfeffer, Jeffrey, and Gerald Salancik. *The External Control of Organizations.* New York: Harper & Row, 1978.
Royko, Mike. *Boss: Richard J. Daley of Chicago.* New York: E. P. Dutton, 1971.
Seashore, Stanley E. *Group Cohesiveness in the Industrial Work Group.* Ann Arbor, Mich.: Institute of Social Research, 1954.
Simon, Herbert A. *Administrative Behavior.* New York: Macmillan, 1947.

4 CONTINGENCY PERSPECTIVE ON ORGANIZATIONS

Chapter Outline

In any discussion of contemporary management thought, the contingency perspective will occupy a prominent place. The decade of the 70s witnessed a profusion of research investigating organizational phenomena from this perspective, and a number of writers formulated contingency theories of organizations. Although the initial enthusiasm has given way to more critical analyses, contingency remains one of the major themes currently taught in various courses in organization theory.

Contingency theorists strive to prescribe organizational designs and managerial actions most appropriate for specific situations. In management literature, the term contingency implies that one thing is related to another. It is an admission of the highly complex and interrelated character of organizational characteristics. As Kast and Rosenzweig note:

> The contingency view seeks to understand the interrelationships within and among subsystems as well as between the organization and its environment and to define patterns of relationships or configuration of variables. It emphasizes the multivariate nature of organizations and attempts to understand how organizations operate under varying conditions and in specific circumstances.[1]

Contingencies refer to factors in a situation confronting managers that will influence their actions. This is a simple idea and easy to understand. Therefore, unlike in the case of the systems model, we do not offer detailed explanations of the contingency perspective.

Our discussion of contingency perspective in this chapter will stress two major themes:

1. We will present the contingency perspective as an offshoot of systems theory, albeit an important one. As we noted in the previous chapter, systems theory was an attempt to synthesize the sciences in general. In contrast, contingency theorists only focus on organizations. *In this sense, the contingency perspective represents an application of systems theory to the study of organizations.* Thus, systems theory, along with the contingency perspective, constitutes an integrated framework for organizational analysis.

2. Since almost all decision making in organizations is contingent, *we consider contingency as a perspective, not a specific theory.* Although we will present the works of several contingency "theorists" we do not imply that contingency theorists have offered a complete theory of organizations. In fact, we will argue that the current state of theory is incomplete in many respects.

The scheme of the chapter is as follows: First, we trace the historical, philosophical, and theoretical underpinnings of the contingency perspective. Second, we discuss the central themes in contingency perspective and portray contingency perspective as an offshoot of the systems model. Third, we summarize the crucial contingencies that organization theorists have identified over the years. Fourth, we illustrate the applicability of the contingency perspective to organizational problems and its implications for managerial action. Fifth, we outline the role of culture as a contingency variable and trace its key implications for managerial action. Sixth, we present the key values underlying this perspective. Finally, we point out the incompleteness of the perspective, but also highlight its utility.

Underpinnings

Although contingency formulations in management literature are relatively recent, the notion of contingency is not new. It is the product of a historical evolution of thought and has strong philosophical underpinnings. Further, a confluence of sociohistorical forces seems to have contributed to its development in management theory. An appreciation of these forces will generally heighten the understanding of the contingency perspective.

Historical Underpinnings

Three major historical trends appear to have facilitated the acceptance of the contingency perspective in management literature. The first is the increasing complexity of environments faced by organizations. At the turn of the 20th century, when the systematic study of management began, organizations faced a relatively stable environment. Since the range of variation in organizational environments was limited, scholars looked inside the organization to discover effective managerial approaches. The early formulations of practitioners such as Frederick Taylor focused on finding the one best way of managing. However, after World War II, in the United States, where the major technological, organizational, and management-related developments took place, environments facing organizations became increasingly dynamic and complex. The shifts in environments posed problems for management that could not be solved within the framework of conventional managerial thought. The earlier best ways of solving the problems were not as effective as they used to be, and in some cases, were downright dysfunctional. As a result, the idea that there is one best way began to be discarded in favor of the view that the appropriate way of managing *depends upon the situation* faced by the organization.

Second, business schools, where management was taught, were themselves undergoing a major change. At the turn of the century, when Taylor advocated a scientific approach to management, it was widely believed that management was an art rather than a science. Business schools were then considered nothing more than trade schools that passed on craft knowledge to aspiring students; there was no science involved. When the economic expansion of the 50s and 60s brought in its wake an explosive demand for managers, business schools saw an opportunity to *professionalize management.*

This meant getting rid of their trade school image and bestowing on management education a prestige parallel to that of the legal, medical, and engineering professions.

Third, our conception of the relationship between social science and policy making had been undergoing a fundamental shift. Although Hugo Munsterburg's early psychological studies at the turn of the century on the manual and visual skills of individuals established the role that psychology could play in the selection of workers, the social sciences were seen less in a utilitarian role and more in a philosophic light; that is, they had no applicability. As the social sciences began to come of age, they began to gain legitimacy and recognition among scholars and practitioners. During the 50s, it became respectable to consider oneself a social scientist. For example, C. P. Snow christened social sciences the "third culture," the first two cultures being the physical sciences and the humanities.[2] This enhanced status of social scientists was reflected in another trend: They were increasingly being hired in consultative roles at the federal policy-making level. Just as physical scientists provided technological expertise, social scientists were to play a role in engineering social choices.

The three trends came together when business schools, in their efforts toward gaining legitimacy in scholarly circles, sought to exploit the potential of social sciences for utilitarian purposes as well as to explain the emerging management realities. In fact, when the Carnegie Commission recommended that business school curricula be put on a solid research foundation, it pointed to such social sciences as psychology and sociology (in addition to economics) as anchors of modern business education.

The resulting research activity did much to discredit the one best way of management. Formulation of earlier theorists like Max Weber and even Frederick Taylor were open to criticism as armchair speculations, since they were based only on one man's observations, however astute, and not on any systematic research. As research unearthed counterexamples to popular management ideas, the *tentativeness* of the theories began to be clearly understood. This further assisted movement *away* from a universal posture and toward a contingent one. This last point is significant because *empiricism*—reliance on systematic research evidence—is what distinguishes current contingency theories from earlier versions of situational management taught in business schools such as the Harvard Business School.

Philosophical Underpinnings

In the history of social sciences, the contingency perspective represented a moderate position between two antagonistic stances. The *nomothetic* stance predisposed scientists to look for generalizations or find universal relations; the *idiographic* stance oriented the scientist to look for the particular. For example, in psychology, one could search for universal laws that hold for all individuals, or one could attempt to explore the uniqueness of an individual. Typically, the idiographic stance was pursued by clinicians—for example, psychoanalysts—whereas the nomothetic stance found favor with the scientific-minded—for example, industrial psychologists. Often, there have been acrimonious debates between the proponents of the two stances.

Partly as a response to this schismatic interpretation of sciences, some scholars also advocated the need for theories of the middle range. Such theories attempted to strike a compromise between the two polarized versions of science. As early as 1931, Lowell Julliard Carr had introduced the idea of situational analysis in sociology. In a similar vein, Kurt Lewin, the founder of social psychology, formulated the notion of a "psychological climate" to describe contextual factors. He argued that an individual's personality and the psychological climates jointly determined that person's behavior. Such "contingency theories" had always coexisted along with the two opposing camps described above.[3]

The historical evolution of management thought mirrored some of the philosophical tensions. Early organization theorists like Weber and management theorists like Taylor advocated a nomothetic or universalist stance. Weber maintained that bureaucracy represented the most efficient form of organization under all circumstances. Taylor was specifically looking for the one best way to improve employee productivity. Yet, in many schools of management, a clinical stance had been adopted for educating managers. For example, at Harvard Business School, the case method emphasized the unique aspects of every organization, maintaining that every organization needs to be analyzed in its own right, and that there are no panaceas for organizational illnesses.

Students of organization were awakened to the contingency perspective, with general systems theory gaining acceptance as a valid epistemological platform. The Janus-faced conception of scientific inquiry proposed by systems theory afforded a compromise between idiographic and nomothetic stances, with one face looking for generalizations, and the other for clinical validity. In fact, Paul Lawrence and Jay Lorsch, pioneers in contingency theory of organizations, acknowledge that their notions are really an outgrowth of systems theory.

The contingency perspective in organization studies was reflected in the kind of questions theorists framed about organizations. The universalists posed simple questions: What is the best solution? Is this method effective or not? Of course, they were interested in generalizations. The clinical approach focused on specific organizations (What will work here in *this* organization?) and eschewed generalizations. In contrast, contingency theorists attempted to understand the contexts in which different methods will be successful. They asked questions like: What are the alternative approaches? Under what conditions will each be successful? This meant searching not merely for solutions, but also for contexts in which solutions may be appropriate.

It is in the search for contexts that systems theory came to the rescue of management theorists. The characteristics of organizations proposed by the open systems model—their environmental dependence and the internal interdependence among their subsystems—provided a framework for describing organizational contexts and fueled many programs of research along contingency lines. The last two decades witnessed a proliferation of research findings, all of which unmasked the complexity of organizations and established the contingent nature of organizational phenomena.

Theoretical Underpinnings

We noted earlier that a number of theorists had advocated the need for a contingency perspective in studying organizational phenomena. In management-related disciplines, economists were among the first to advance contingency-type propositions. They categorized different market conditions—perfect competition, monopoly, oligopoly, and the like—and explicitly formulated how a firm's behavior varied in different markets. We have already pointed out how Lewin advanced the need for situational analysis in social psychology. Similarly, in sociology, Robert Merton championed the cause of middle-range theories, or theories that account for situational factors.

During the latter half of this century, management scholars advanced contingency propositions at several levels of analysis: individual, group, and organizational. At the *group level,* one of the earliest researchers adopting a contingency perspective was Frederick Fiedler. In 1951, he and his associates began an extensive program of research that focused on the situational nature of leadership effectiveness. Based on his research, Fiedler claimed that the leader style that maximized group performance depended on the nature of the group and the nature of the task. His theory suggested that under extreme conditions, autocratic leadership was needed, whereas under moderate conditions, a considerate leadership was appropriate. To quote Fiedler:

> In the very favorable conditions in which the leader has power, informal backing, and a relatively well-structured task, the group is ready to be directed, and the group members expect to be told what to do . . . In the relatively unfavorable situation, we would again expect that the task oriented leader will be more effective than will the considerate leader who is concerned with interpersonal relations (the group will fall apart without the leader's active intervention and control). . . . In situations which are only moderately favorable (or moderately unfavorable) for the leader, a considerate, relationship-oriented attitude seems to be most effective.[4]

Fiedler termed his theory the situational theory of leadership, to underscore the idea that there is no single leadership style that is best for all circumstances, and that what matters is the fit between leader style and circumstances. Although his theory has been subject to criticism, it represents one

---

Box 4.1

Fiedler's Contingency Theory of Leadership

Frederick Fiedler is currently a professor of management at the University of Washington. He is best known for his contingency theory of leadership, a theory he and his associates have developed and verified in many settings.

The origins of the theory date back to 1951, when Fiedler started a long program of research focusing on the situational characteristics of leadership. Fiedler was interested in finding out whether a leader who is lenient in evaluating his associates was more or less likely to have a high performing group than a task-oriented leader who is demanding. To measure the style of leadership, Fiedler developed a psychological instrument called the Least Preferred Coworker (LPC) scale. A considerate leader scored high, whereas a structuring leader scored low on the scale.

What Fiedler found was that no style of leadership was effective under all conditions. Rather, the effective leader style depended on the situation. Fiedler identified three dimensions of the situation:

Position Power, the degree to which the position itself enables the leader to get group members to comply with and accept his or her direction and leadership.

Task structure, whether the work group's task is routine and predictable.

Leader-Member Relations, the extent to which the leader gets along with his or her group members.

Fiedler claimed to have found that the appropriateness of leadership style for maximizing group performance is contingent on the favorableness of the group-task situation. As shown in the accompanying figure, strong leaders (low LPC) are effective when the situation is either very unfavorable or very favorable. In the middle ranges, a considerate leader (high LPC) is more effective.

Fiedler went on to comment that it is relatively difficult to change leader style. Therefore, he suggested that structuring the situation to fit the leader style is the pragmatic solution to enhancing group performance.

There have been a number of criticisms of Fiedler's work. Some researchers have tried to replicate Fiedler's findings in the laboratory,

---

of the early research efforts that adopted a contingency perspective. We have summarized Fiedler's work in Box 4.1.

Similarly, a contingency stance was adopted to study *organization-task fit.* For example, John Morse and Jay Lorsch tested the proposition that the fit between tasks and organizational characteristics would result in effectiveness. They used two types of effectiveness measures: higher performance and employees' sense of motivation. Morse and Lorsch studied four organizations. Two of these—Akron and Hartford container manufacturing plants— performed relatively routine and predictable tasks as they manufactured standard containers on the high-speed automated production lines. The other two—Stockton and Carmel laboratories—performed the relatively uncertain tasks of research and development in communications technology.

Akron and Stockton were high performers, whereas Hartford and Carmel were low performers. Morse and Lorsch found that the high

Box 4.1 continued

and obtained contradictory findings. Others have claimed that the LPC scale was not a reliable instrument.

Certainly, we do not present his theory as the final word on leadership; nor do we claim it is a reliable theory. However, at the time when it was put forward, the theory generated a considerable degree of interest. Perhaps more important to our purposes, this was one of the earlier theories based on the contingency perspective.

Fiedler's findings regarding effective leader style are illustrated in the following figure.

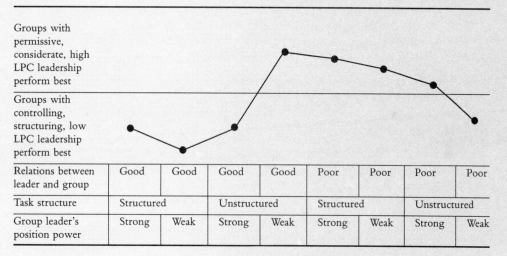

	Good	Good	Good	Good	Poor	Poor	Poor	Poor
Relations between leader and group	Good	Good	Good	Good	Poor	Poor	Poor	Poor
Task structure	Structured		Unstructured		Structured		Unstructured	
Group leader's position power	Strong	Weak	Strong	Weak	Strong	Weak	Strong	Weak

Source: Frederick E. Fiedler, "Engineer the Job to Fit the Manager," *Harvard Business Review* 45 (September–October 1965).

performing Akron and Stockton had very different management structures. Stockton had a low degree of structure, minimal flexible rules, and a participatory type of supervision, and provided a high degree of freedom to subordinates to choose and handle projects. Akron, on the other hand, was highly structured, had pervasive and stringent rules, employed directive supervision, and gave employees little freedom to choose and handle jobs. Further, Morse and Lorsch discovered that individuals in Akron and Stockton showed significantly more feelings of competence than did their counterparts in Hartford and Carmel. These researchers argued that the fit between organization and tasks led to higher performance and employees' sense of motivation. To quote:

> We found that the organization-task fit is simultaneously linked to and interdependent with both individual motivation and effective unit performance.[5]

Their work is summarized in Box 4.2.

Box 4.2

Morse and Lorsch Studies

Specifically adopting a contingency perspective, John Morse and Jay Lorsch, a team of researchers from the Harvard Business School, explored the question of fit between task, organization, and people. They noted that to answer this question, it is useful to recognize that individuals have a strong need to master the world around themselves, including the tasks they face in the work situation. The accumulated feelings of satisfaction that come from successfully mastering one's environment can be called a *sense of competence.*

Morse and Lorsch studied four organizations: Two of these performed the relatively certain task of manufacturing standardized containers on high-speed automated production lines. The other performed the relatively uncertain work of research and development in communications technology. In each category, there was one high performer and one low performer. Their study design is presented in the following table:

Characteristics	Predictable Manufacturing Task	Unpredictable R&D Task
Effective performer	Akron container plant	Stockton laboratory
Low performer	Hartford container plant	Carmel laboratory

The researchers grouped organizational characteristics into two sets of factors:

Formal Characteristics, which could be used to judge the fit between the kind of task being worked on and the formal practices of the organization.

Climate Characteristics, the subjective perceptions and orientations that had developed among individuals about their organizational setting.

Based on their data the researchers compared the four organizations, hypothesizing first of all that in high performing organizations, there will be a fit between the formal characteristics and the nature of the task. When this was found to be true, the researchers verified if there were differences in climate characteristics between the high-performing organization engaged in the manufacturing task and in the R&D task. This was also found to be true. These findings are displayed in tabular form below:

Differences in Formal Characteristics in High Performing Organizations

Characteristics	Akron	Stockton
(1) Pattern of formal relationships and duties as signified by organization charts and job manuals	Highly structured, precisely defined	Low degree of structure, less well defined
(2) Pattern of formal rules, procedures, control, and measurements systems	Pervasive, specific, uniform, comprehensive	Minimal, loose, flexible
(3) Time dimensions incorporated in formal practices	Short-term	Long-term
(4) Goal dimensions incorporated in formal practices	Manufacturing	Scientific

Box 4.2 continued

Differences in Climate Characteristics in High Performing Organizations

Characteristics	Akron	Stockton
(1) Structural orientation	Perceptions of tightly controlled behavior and a high degree of structure	Perceptions of a low degree of structure
(2) Distribution of influence	Perceptions of low total influence, concentrated at upper levels in the organization	Perceptions of high total influence more evenly spread out among all levels
(3) Character of superior-subordinate relations	Low freedom vis-à-vis superiors to choose and handle jobs Directive type of supervision	High freedom vis-à-vis superiors to choose and handle projects Participatory type of supervision
(4) Character of colleague relations	Perceptions of many similarities among colleagues, high degree of coordination of colleague effort	Perceptions of many differences among colleagues, relatively low degree of coordination of colleague effort
(5) Time orientation	Short-term	Long-term
(6) Goal orientation	Manufacturing	Scientific
(7) Top executive's "managerial style"	More concerned with task than people	More concerned with people than tasks

Finally, the researchers considered the competence motivation of the employees. For this, they devised a two-part test:

The first part asked respondents to write creative and imaginative stories in response to six ambiguous pictures.

The second asked respondents to write a creative and imaginative story about what they would be doing tomorrow in their job.

These are called *projective* tests because it is assumed that respondents project into their stories their own attitudes, thoughts, feelings, needs, and wants, all of which can be measured from the stories.

The results were indeed revealing. In the words of the researchers:

The results indicated that the individuals in Akron and Stockton showed significantly more feelings of competence than did their counterparts in the Hartford and Carmel organizations. We found that the organization-task fit is simultaneously linked to and interdependent with both individual motivation and effective unit performance.

Morse and Lorsch thus argued that managers must not only seek a fit between the organization and the task, but also *between task and people and between people and organization.*

Source: John J. Morse and Jay W. Lorsch, "Beyond Theory Y," *Harvard Business Review,* 48 (May–June 1970).

Contemporary discussions of the contingency perspective are based on the works of scholars who studied *organizational* level phenomena, especially organization structure. Three crucial contingencies were identified: (1) size, (2) environment, and (3) technology. We will summarize these works later in the chapter (see the Crucial Contingencies section) in somewhat greater detail, since they are crucial to organization theory.

Summary

Historically, three forces—the increasing complexity of the environment, the push toward professionalization of management education, and the increasing acceptance of social scientists in the policy-making process—led business schools to undertake rigorous research that discredited much of the prevailing management wisdom and led to the acceptance of the contingency perspective. Philosophically, the emergence of systems theory as a compromise between idiographic and nomothetic stances provided the needed inspiration to the development of the contingency perspective. Finally, several scholars adopted a contingency perspective at various levels of analysis—individual, group, and organizational.

Our focus in this book will primarily be at the organizational level, and we will deal with the relevant research extensively. We will do so to highlight the two themes identified in the introduction to this chapter:

1. how the contingency perspective is an operationalization of the systems model, and

2. why we consider this a perspective, not a theory.

In the next section, let us develop the first theme—the contingency perspective as an operationalization of the systems theory. We do so by identifying the key themes in contingency and then relating them to the systems model.

Key Themes and Linkage to Systems Concepts

Key Themes in Contingency Perspective

In this section, we will highlight three key themes in the contingency perspective. We will

1. describe the nature of contingency propositions,

2. discuss the process by which organization theorists arrive at contingency propositions, and

3. highlight the implications of the contingency perspective for managers.

1. Nature of Contingency Propositions

A contingency proposition is a statement that relates effectiveness to a set of contextual or situational factors and intraorganizational characteristics. It often takes the form:

If $X\{1,2,\ldots,i,\ldots\}$ *and* $Y\{1,2,\ldots,j\ldots\}$, then E. Where,
X_i refers to a contextual or situational factor
Y_j refers to an intraorganizational factor
E refers to effectiveness

We emphasize the word *and* in the above proposition because contingency propositions typically adopt from systems theory the notion of a fit: to the extent the contextual factors and intraorganizational characteristics are congruent, the effectiveness is enhanced. The purpose of theory and research is to specify the nature of this fit.

The criteria of effectiveness may vary depending on the interest of the researcher or manager: profits, job satisfaction, and so on. Contingency theorists do not advocate any specific criteria of effectiveness. Therefore, we will discuss the issue of organizational effectiveness in a later chapter where we will present a systems theoretic approach to organizational effectiveness.

We may illustrate the contingency proposition by means of a couple of examples. Fiedler's situational theory of leadership may be presented thus:

If $X1\{$leader–member relations$\}$ and $X2;$ $\{$task characteristics $\}$
and $Y\{$leader style$\}$, then $E;$ $\{$group performance$\}$.

Congruence exists when the considerate leader style exists in moderate circumstances (e.g., a weak leader with good relations with the group in an unstructured situation), as well as when the directive leader style exists in extreme conditions (e.g., a strong leader with good relations with his group in a structured task, or a weak leader with poor relations in an unstructured task). Fiedler focused on group performance as the criterion of effectiveness.

Or consider the contingency proposition implied in Morse and Lorsch's work:

If $X\{$predictability of task$\}$ *and* $Y\{$organization structure$\}$,
then $E\{$task accomplishment, employee sense of motivation$\}$.

Congruence exists when flexible organizational structures are present in unpredictable task situations or when rigid and formal structures exist in stable task environments. Morse and Lorsch focused on both task accomplishment and employee motivation as criteria of effectiveness.

A contingency proposition may be distinguished from the one implicit in the writings of universal theorists. The latter's propositions take the form:

If $X\{$intraorganizational factor or management practice$\}$, then
$E\{$effectiveness$\}$.

Thus, scientific management theorists would advocate time and motion studies as the X, whereas human relations people would argue for interpersonal relations. The concept of congruence does not exist in these theories.

2. Building Contingency Propositions

In one sense, the contingency perspective appears attractive because it is simple and *commonsensical*. The answer typically given by contingency theorists to the question, "What should be done?" is, "It depends on the context." This answer is intuitively appealing as it is more or less an accurate description of how individuals behave. Most of us, managers particularly, appreciate this because it easily validates our experiential reality.

The apparent simplicity is often deceptive. When practicing managers believe that their actions are based on context, they may not be acting from a contingency perspective in the sense in which management theorists conceive of the term. Most managers base their actions on the theories they have intuitively derived from their own experiences of the world. Although their own personal experiences are meaningful to the individuals concerned, conclusions based solely on them are not truly scientific. In contrast, when theorists suggest that action should be based on the context, they are invoking a set of conclusions that are *systematically* and *scientifically* arrived at.

Let us illustrate the above idea with an example. Consider the case of Winston Churchill. Churchill came to be the Prime Minister during World War II, at a time when Britain was in the throes of a devastating war with Germany. In those difficult times, he was able to infuse the nation with hope and keep alive the will to battle, partly relying on his great oratorical skills. Yet, when the war was over, Churchill was not reelected as the prime minister. One may suggest that Churchill's type of leader is effective for wartime and ineffective during peacetime. It is an interesting observation; in fact, many have advocated such a hypothesis. Few contingency theorists would elevate it to the level of a proposition on which managerial action can be prescribed. To be a contingency proposition, theorists would point out that one should have a clear conception of leadership and effectiveness. Further, one should be able to distinguish between wartime and peacetime. Finally, one should be able to observe a similar kind of relationship between leadership, peacetime/wartime, and effectiveness in other instances as well.

Just how, then, do theorists build contingency propositions? Broadly, we can identify four steps in building a contingency proposition.

First, theorists isolate the crucial determinants of the situation facing organizations. These determinants are alternately termed *contingencies*. As we have shown earlier, considerable research effort has been geared toward discovering the relevant contingencies. For example, Morse and Lorsch (whom we referred to earlier) isolated two sets of contingencies:

1. the predictability of the task environment and
2. a set of organizational practices, as discussed in Box 4.2.

Second, in pursuit of parsimony, *taxonomies* are developed to capture the multivariate complexity of organizational contexts and practices. Taxonomies are classification schemes anchored in empirical observations. They help to cluster organizations into different classes. Each class is so different from another as to be considered separately, and each organization within a class shares sufficient commonality with others in the same class as to be treated alike. In the Morse and Lorsch example, task variables are grouped to form two classes—predictable and unpredictable—whereas the organizational practices are grouped into rigid and flexible types.

Third, organizational effectiveness is hypothesized to be a derivative of contingency variables. Typically, contingency theorists specify effectiveness as a function of the *interaction* among contingency variables. Put another way, congruence among contingency variables leads to effectiveness: different combinations of contingency variables could alternately lead to effectiveness. Thus, Morse and Lorsch noted that both rigid and flexible structures could be effective; what matters is whether they are congruent with their tasks. Rigid structures are successful in predictable tasks, flexible types in unpredictable tasks. Conversely, rigid structures in unpredictable task environments and flexible types in predictable tasks environments are not effective.

Finally, such propositions are subjected to systematic and scientific *empirical* scrutiny before they are accepted as valid propositions.

In short, the simplicity of the contingency perspective is easily recognized, but only at the point of application can its complexity be clearly understood. To understand that "it depends" is easier than to understand how and on what "it" depends.

3. Action Implications from the Contingency Perspective

The pragmatic bias inherent in the contingency perspective is often attractive to managers as they confront the practical, day-to-day affairs of organizational life. However, as we noted earlier, contingency prescriptions do not grant license to managers in their action choices. Three managerial implications flowing from this perspective need to be underscored.

First, diagnosis becomes an important component of managerial decision making. Confronted with an organizational problem, managers are advised to understand what it is before they prescribe solutions. This data gathering and analysis function is often an enormously consuming task. It requires that managers suspend their judgment in the initial phases of decision, and let systematic empirical evidence inform their judgment.

Second, managers are exhorted to be rational actors in pursuit of organizational effectiveness. Their actions are expected to be deliberate, rationally ordered steps to accomplish the goals at hand. In this sense, thought precedes action; there is no room for play, fantasy, or pet solutions.

Third, the contingency perspective encourages managers to be flexible regarding organizational solutions. Managers have to be pragmatic rather than rule bound because the contingency perspective upholds the notion that there are no *absolutely* good or bad management styles or organizational practices.

Although the contingency perspective is simple to understand, its application requires managers to put aside their personal biases, transcend their historical conditioning, and let their thinking guide actions. These are demanding tasks, but contingency theorists would argue they are necessary for managers to be effective.

How do these themes emerge from the systems model? On the one hand, we have shown that major contingency scholars such as Lawrence and Lorsch have explicitly acknowledged their indebtedness to systems theory for their works. On the other, we can show the correspondence between some of the key themes and systems concepts, a point to which we now turn.

Linkage to Systems Concepts

There are several areas of correspondence between the contingency perspective and systems concepts.

First, the open systems model formalized the notion that all organizations are in interaction with their environments. In the contingency perspective, the environment is viewed as one of the key determinants of organizational effectiveness. Contingency theorists spend considerable effort in classifying the type of environment facing organizations and discovering the organizational characteristics suitable for different environmental classes. On this issue, we will discuss later in this chapter the contributions of Tom Burns and George Stalker; there have been others as well. Although the specifics of classification may vary from scholar to scholar, their objectives are the same: to understand how the environment affects organization.

Second, systems theory underscores the interdependence among subsystems. In the contingency perspective, the action prescriptions are designed not only to coalign the organization with the environment, but to align the internal elements as well. What is emphasized is not the characteristics of each element *per se,* but how these elements mesh together. This is what we had earlier referred to as interaction. Taxonomies facilitate this by creating clusters of variables; for example, the mechanistic and organic types of Burns and Stalker contain a number of internally consistent elements. It is the constellation of the elements, not merely the elements themselves, that is of concern to contingency theorists.

Third, the concept of equifinality in systems theory is analogous to the contingency notion that there is no single best solution. Further, even for a specific organization, the contingency perspective would suggest a range of possible solutions. The focus is on attaining balance or congruence; there may be a number of ways of attaining this.

Fourth, we noted that systems concepts are applicable at different levels. In a similar vein, the contingency perspective may be applied at different levels in an organization—individual, group, or organization. We illustrated this in our earlier discussion of Lorsch and Morse and of Fiedler.

Finally, feedback is a central concept in the systems model. This is dormant in the contingency perspective. We may note, however, that the process of data collection necessary for diagnosis is a form of instituting feedback in organizations.

TABLE 4.1   **Some Correspondence between Systems Concepts and Contingency Perspective**

Systems Concepts	Contingency Perspective
1. Open systems	Environment as a key determinant of organizational effectiveness; for example, to be an effective organization, design is contingent on the environment.
2. Interdependence among systems	Action contingent on interaction of contingency variables (environment is viewed as only one of the contingency variables).
3. Equifinality	There is a range of acceptable solutions (though there is no one best solution, some solutions are better than others).
4. Levels	Contingency perspective is applicable at various levels.
5. Feedback	Diagnosis intended to bring the subsystems into congruence with themselves and environment.

Just what, then, does the contingency perspective provide in addition to systems concepts? We noted that systems concepts provide an abstract diagnostic framework within which to describe organizational phenomena. Further, general systems theory is concerned with the identification of laws that cut across systems—be they physical, biological, or social systems. For example, one of the laws is the law of fit or congruence among systems and between the system and its environment. Contingency theorists utilize the diagnostic framework provided by systems theorists for specifically studying organizations. In the process, they attempt to draw on the general laws from systems theory to facilitate our understanding of organizations. Further, contingency theory is prescriptive—it attempts to specify just how and why organizations are effective. In this sense, the contingency perspective is largely an application of systems theory to organizational phenomena.

Summary

Table 4.1 summarizes our discussion of the correspondence between systems concepts and the contingency perspective.

Let us now return to the next theme: Why contingency relations are not completely worked out and why at this point we refer to a contingency perspective, not a contingency theory.

Crucial Contingencies in Organization Theory

Organization theorists have identified several contextual factors that influence the internal characteristics of organizations. We term these factors *contingencies*. As we mentioned in Theoretical Underpinnings, organization theorists have discovered three major contingencies over the years: (1) size, (2) environment, and (3) technology. We will discuss each one of these in turn.

Size

Organization theorists over the years have established a link between size (e.g., the total number of employees in an organization) and some of the internal characteristics of an organization. They drew their inspiration from Max Weber. Weber's ideal organization was *bureaucracy*. (Readers may want to return to Chapter 2 for a listing of the major characteristics of a bureaucracy.) To many organization theorists, bureaucratic characteristics are appropriate for large organizations.

In general, scholars interested in the influence of size on organizational characteristics focused on the bureaucratic dimensions of formalization, specialization, standardization, and centralization:

> *Formalization* pertains to the level of written documentation in the organization, including procedures, job descriptions, regulations, and policy manuals.
>
> *Specialization* is the degree to which organizational tasks are divided into separate jobs. As specialization increases, the range of work performed by employees is reduced.
>
> *Standardization* is the extent to which similar work activities are performed in a uniform manner. In a highly standard organization, jobs are prescribed in great detail, so employees in similar jobs are expected to perform their work in a uniform manner.
>
> *Centralization* refers to the locus of decision making in an organization. As centralization is higher, more decisions are made at the top, and lower levels are responsible for carrying out those decisions. As the decisions are made at lower levels in the hierarchy, the organization becomes decentralized.

The researchers were interested in questions such as: Should the organization be more bureaucratic as it grows larger? In what size organizations are bureaucratic characteristics more appropriate?

Organization theorists argued that as organizations grow larger in size, they have to control and coordinate the work of a larger number of employees; but personal surveillance of employee behavior becomes prohibitively expensive. Bureaucratization enables an organization to reduce the costs of coordination. Put another way, higher formalization, specialization, and standardization enable greater decentralization of decision making and are substitutes for personal surveillance as mechanisms of coordination. Thus, larger organizations are associated with higher levels of bureaucracy.

Over a hundred studies have elaborated these arguments through careful empirical work. In the process, these studies helped to explode some of the common myths about bureaucracy. See Box 4.3 for two of the myths and the evidence refuting them.

Size, therefore, influenced the level of bureaucracy in the organization.

Environment

The role of environment and its effect on organization structure is perhaps the most celebrated contingency proposition. The earliest of the works along these lines was that of Burns and Stalker, two British sociologists, who traced the linkages between patterns of management processes in companies and the rate of change in the environment—specifically, scientific techniques and markets.

Burns and Stalker discovered that when the external environment is *stable,* classical principles of management appear to be manifested in organizations. Organizations following classical principles, which they termed *mechanistic,* are characterized by rigid lines of authority, clear job specification, and a hierarchic structure of control, authority, and communication. In *dynamic* or changing environments, however, relatively flexible structures, which they termed *organic,* emerged. These structures were characterized by fluid lines of communication, unclear job descriptions, and control by expertise. The differences between mechanistic and organic systems are presented in Table 4.2.

As can be seen from the table, mechanistic and organic systems had significantly different internal characteristics. Thus, mechanistic systems resembled Weber's bureaucracy: they were highly formalized, standardized, specialized, and centralized. Organic systems deviated significantly from the bureaucratic type: they were not at all formalized, standardized, specialized, or centralized.

Since Burns and Stalker were interested in describing the naturally occurring linkages between structures and environments, they did not employ any specific measure of organizational effectiveness. Yet they ventured to suggest:

> When novelty and unfamiliarity in both market situation and technical information become the accepted order of things, a fundamentally different kind of management system becomes appropriate from that which applies to a relatively stable commercial and technical environment.[6]

Box 4.3

Size and Bureaucracy: Evidence from Empirical Research

The term *bureaucracy* evokes mixed feelings among us because we associate it with inefficiency, red tape, and, in general, many things we do not like in large organizations. The popular use of the term is different from the theoretical definition put forth by Weber; however, influential popular writers have satirized bureaucracy, propagating many myths about it. Empirical evidence generated by systematic scientific work has refuted many of these myths.

We cite two streams of work that have examined the relation between size and bureaucracy. The first suggests that as firms grow larger in size, bureaucratization leads to administrative efficiencies. The second suggests that increasing bureaucratization actually leads to higher performance as firms grow in size.

1. Bureaucracy and Administrative Efficiencies

One stream of research examined whether bureaucracy led to administrative efficiencies. Scholars studied the personnel configuration of administrative, clerical, and professional staff in school systems, churches, hospitals, employment agencies, and other business and voluntary agencies. These studies led to the conclusion that the ratio of top administration to total employment is actually smaller in large organizations. Organizations may experience administrative economies as they grow larger: They have larger departments, more regulations, and a greater division of labor. These mechanisms require less supervision from the top; the ratio of top administrators to workers is, thus, actually smaller in large organizations.

This work exploded a popular myth about bureaucracy popularized by many writers. For example, in 1957, C. Northcote Parkinson published an influential book, *Parkinson's Law,* which argued that work expands to fill the time available. The book was a satire intended to poke fun at the proliferating bureaucracy of large organizations. Parkinson argued that administrators were motivated to add more administrators for a variety of reasons, including the enhancement of their status through empire building. As an example, Parkinson cited the example of the British Admiralty, who during the period 1914–28, increased their officer corps by 78 percent, although both total navy personnel and the number of warships in use decreased significantly. Parkinson's book tended to portray large organizations as inefficient bureaucracies. *Systematic research did not support such satirical arguments about bureaucracy.*

2. Bureaucracy and Performance

A second popular criticism of bureaucracies is that they entangle employees and clients in red tape and are inherently inefficient. John Child specifically investigated the question of whether increasing bureaucratization leads to poor performance as expressed in profits and other economic indicators of performance. He surveyed *business* organizations in England, and measured their bureaucratic characteristics and their size in terms of employees. Child discovered that as the organizations grew larger, higher performance was associated with higher levels of bureaucracy. Thus, corporations that grew large and remained informal underperformed those that adopted bureaucratic characteristics. However, small organizations performed better if they were less bureaucratized. Thus, Child noted that

Box 4.3 continued

high-performing organizations acquired bureaucracy at a faster rate when they grew than
did the poor performers. With size should
come bureaucracy.

However, Child noted that this relationship
between the bureaucratic characteristics of an
organization and its performance is moderated
by the role of the environment in which the organization functioned. He noted that high-
performing corporations in dynamic environments acquired bureaucracy at a *slower* rate than
the high performers in stable industries. *In a dy-*

*namic environment, a balance must be met between
bureaucracy for size and responsiveness for change.*

Thus, as research on the relationship between
size and bureaucracy progressed, it also became
clear that size was not the sole factor that determined the most effective form of organization.
Other factors such as environment mattered.

Sources: John Child, "Parkinson's Progress: Accounting for
the Number of Specialists in Organizations," *Administrative
Science Quarterly* 18 (1973), pp. 328–48; John Child,
"Managerial and Organizational Factors Associated with
Company Performance—Part II: A Contingent Analysis,"
Journal of Management Studies 12 (1975), pp. 12–25.

TABLE 4.2   **Organic versus Mechanistic Systems**

Dimension	Organic	Mechanistic
1. Organizing principle	Integration	Specialization
2. Task definition	Fluid with concern on total situation	Clearly specified and limited
3. Coordination	Network structure	Formal hierarchy
4. Commitment	To the total organization	To the job
5. Communication	Lateral	Vertical
6. Content of communication	Information and counsel	Instructions and decisions from superiors
7. Knowledge	Widely dispersed through the organization	Presumed to be located at the top
8. Value	Commitment to task	Commitment to superiors
9. Prestige	Derived from expertise valid in environments outside the firm	Derived from knowledge internal to the firm

The two systems, organic and mechanistic, postulated by Burns and Stalker, may be compared along the
bureaucratic dimensions of formalization, specialization, standardization, and decentralization.

Bureaucratic Dimension	Organic	Mechanic
Formalization	Low	High
Specialization	Low	High
Standardization	Low	High
Decentralization	High	Low

Thus, mechanistic systems closely corresponded to the organizing principles of bureaucracy, whereas organic
systems departed significantly from them. Burns and Stalker were much more elaborate, and covered many more
dimensions of organizations than the four dimensions of bureaucracy.

Box 4.4

Burns and Stalker: Environment and Organization Structure

Tom Burns and G. M. Stalker, industrial sociologists from the United Kingdom, were the first to establish the linkage between organization structure and environment. They studied about 20 firms in the United Kingdom, primarily through extensive interviewing of key people.

The firms were drawn from a variety of industries. They included a rayon manufacturer, an electronic engineering firm, a number of Scottish electronics firms, and eight English firms operating in different segments of the electronics industry. The researchers were fascinated by the discovery that distinct sets of management practices had evolved in response to the differing rates of technological and market changes. Such changes, the authors believed, posed different demands on information processing in the organization.

For example, the rayon mill was situated in a stable environment and the nature of the production process required stability and long production runs. At all levels, decision making occurred within the framework of familiar expectations and beliefs, many of which could be formulated as a program. Fluctuations in demand did occur, but these were treated as exceptions, not the norm. The organization was run on the basis of plans: successively lower levels of hierarchy had more limited information, authority, and responsibility. Roles were clearly defined. Even the general manager's task was carried out within the framework of clearly defined procedures and regulations.

On the other hand, in the electrical engineering firm, every contract required some special units, and there was a constant flow of design improvements. The rate of technical improvements in the industry and hence in the internal structure of the firm was higher than in the case of the rayon firm. This led to a flexible structure. A number of plans were devised specifically to meet the contingencies, and clear lines of responsibility and functions were absent. Tasks were less clearly defined even at the lower levels, and personnel tended to regard their work as a contribution to the overall task of the firm. Committees were frequently employed to facilitate communication.

A summary of their study is presented in Box 4.4. According to Burns and Stalker, the type of organization structure is *contingent* upon the rate of environmental change.

Technology

The term technology means different things to different people. In organization theory, technology refers to the knowledge, tools, techniques, and actions required to transform inputs into outputs. Technology includes such things as machinery, employee skills, and work procedures. In the language of systems theory, technology drives the manufacturing or conversion process, and refers to throughput factors (refer to Figures 3.1 and 3.2).

Just how does technology influence the internal characteristics of an organization? The answer to this question was first provided by a research

Box 4.4 continued

Most of the electronics firms were operating in an even more uncertain environment. Consequently, no organization chart existed, and managers had great difficulty in saying who was at their own level in the firm. Individual jobs were defined as ambiguously as possible so that they could develop to fit the changing needs of a task. This ambiguity had problems; some personnel were uncomfortable with it.

The organization operating in the most uncertain environment was a newly created electronics firm. Here, tasks were defined almost entirely out of the interaction among individuals: superiors, colleagues, and subordinates.

From these findings, Burns and Stalker put forth the hypothesis that the organization structure and the management system are dependent on extrinsic factors: "These extrinsic factors are all, in our view, identifiable as different rates of technical or market change. By change, we mean the appearance of novelties: i.e., new scientific discoveries or technical inventions, and requirements for products of a kind not previously available or demanded."

Burns and Stalker distinguished between *organic* and *mechanistic* systems. We have presented the differences between the two in Table 4.2 in this chapter. Burns and Stalker hypothesized that mechanistic systems are natural in stable environments, whereas organic systems come to exist in uncertain environments.

Burns and Stalker thus opened up a new avenue of research about organizations. Their organic-mechanistic classification has come to stay in organization theory, and dominates discussion of organization-environment relations even today. Others such as Lawrence and Lorsch followed their lead. Even Woodward used their distinction in deriving conclusions about technology, even though her research predates Burns and Stalker's work. Of course, there have been recent criticisms of their work.[*] Nevertheless, the fact remains that with Burns and Stalker, *the open systems view of organizations* was firmly established.

––––––––
[*]Chris Argyris, *The Inner Contradictions of Rigorous Research* (New York: Elsevier, 1980). Argyris argues that much of the filed observations of organic systems provided by Burns and Stalker do not match their idealizations of such systems.

Source: Adapted from Tom Burns and George M. Stalker, *The Management of Innovation* (London: Tavistock, 1961).

team headed by Joan Woodward in South Essex, England. Woodward argued that technology is an important determinant of the management structure. She argued:

> Different technologies impose different kinds of demands on individuals and organizations, and those demands had to be met through an appropriate structure.[7]

Woodward defined technology as "the methods and processes of manufacture." Based on her research, Woodward classified technologies into three types:
1. unit and small-batch production,
2. large-batch and mass production, and
3. long-run process production.

Box 4.5

Woodward's Work on Management Structure and Technology

Joan Woodward is a British industrial sociologist. She and her research team began their studies in 1953 in South Essex, England, to understand the administrative practices of local firms. The prevailing wisdom at the time was contained in universal principles of management propagated by the classical theorists. Woodward wanted to gain firsthand experience of the practices of the firm.

The research team studied over 100 firms, which constituted 91 percent of all the firms that employed at least 100 employees. In each of these firms, the research team spent half a day collecting data on various aspects of management. Through interviews, observation, and analysis of company records, they obtained (1) information on the history, background, and objectives of the firm; (2) a description of the manufacturing processes and methods; (3) forms and practices through which the firm was organized and managed; and (4) measures of organizational performance such as stock price fluctuations, characteristics of the industry, and so on. Also, they were able to categorize the firms on Burns and Stalker's classification scheme: mechanistic or organic (refer to Table 4.2).

Initially, the data made no sense. The firms differed widely in terms of the classical principles: the number of managerial levels varied from 2 to 12, with a median of 4; span of control of the chief executive officer varied from 2 to 18 and that of the first-line supervisor from 10 to 90; and the ratio of direct to indirect labor varied from less than 1:1 to 10:1.

These variations in management practices prompted the research team to look for the causes of the management practices. The discoveries they made were disconcerting. First, the organizational practices did not correlate with the size or the nature of the industry. Thus many large firms had low levels of specialization. Even more surprisingly, some of the successful firms, 20 of them in fact, had little in common organizationally. No support was given to the "one best way of managing."

The researchers then sought some other way to make sense of the data. As Perrow would have us believe, Woodward discovered a pot of gold called *technology*. The final unused data that the team collected consisted of information related to technology. The researchers hit on the idea of classifying the firms into three categories according to the *complexity of technology*:

Unit and Small-Batch Production, which consisted of job shop operations that manufacture and assemble small orders to meet

---

In the first type, *unit and small-batch production,* each unit or batch of production is made to the customer's unique specifications, and the operations performed are nonrepetitive and noncomparable across batches. The movement of material from one machine to another depends on unique customer specifications.

In the second type, *large-batch and mass production,* mass produced units are more or less standardized, and the production steps are relatively predictable.

Box 4.5 continued

the specific orders of the customers. Since products are custom-made, they cannot be inventoried in any large amounts. This represented the lowest level of technology.

Large-Batch and Mass Production, characterized by long production runs of standardized parts. Since the products are standard and production runs are long, the output is typically inventoried. Automobiles and cotton mills operated this technology.

Continuous Production, the highest level of technology, represents mechanization and standardization one step beyond mass production. Examples include chemical plants and oil refining.

Woodward described some of the differences between production systems:

Moving along the scale . . . it becomes increasingly possible to exercise control of manufacturing operations. . . . Targets can be set and reached more effectively in continuous production than they can be in most up-to-date and efficient batch production firms.

There were systematic regularities in management practices across the three types of technology. The process technology had the highest number of levels, and from the CEO's point of view, the widest span of control. At the lower levels, the span of control varied in a

curvilinear fashion, with the job shops and process technologies having the lowest and the mass production the highest span of control. In addition, the research team noted:

There was a tendency for organic management systems to predominate in the production categories at the extremes of the technical scale, while mechanistic systems dominated the middle ranges. A clear-cut definition of duties and responsibilities was a characteristic of firms in the middle ranges, while a flexible organization with a high degree of delegation both of authority and of the responsibility for decision making, and a permissive and participating management, were characteristic of firms at the extreme.

What lent weight to Woodward's data were the comparisons she made between the structure-technology relationship and performance. An important conclusion was that many of the organizational characteristics of the successful firms were near the average of the production category. Below average firms tended to depart from the structural characteristics of their production type. *That management structure should be contingent on technology* was thus established, dispelling the universal theories of management.

Source: Adapted from Joan Woodward, *Industrial Organization: Theory and Practice* (London: Oxford University Press, 1965).

Sufficient production variations often exist to create some degree of unpredictability in production sequencing.

In the third type, *process technology,* the product is standardized and moves in a predictable, repetitive sequence from one step to another.

Woodward's study is summarized in Box 4.5.

TABLE 4.3   **Woodward's Findings**

Structural Characteristic	Unit Production	Mass Production	Continuous Process
Number of management levels	3	4	6
Supervisor span of control	23	48	15
Direct/indirect	9:1	4:1	1:1
Labor ratio: manager/total personnel	Low	Medium	High
Workers' skill level	High	Low	High
Formalized procedures	Low	High	Low
Centralization	Low	High	Low
Amount of verbal communication	High	Low	High
Amount of written communication	Low	High	Low
Overall structure	Organic	Mechanistic	Organic

Source: Joan Woodward, *Industrial Organization: Theory and Practice* (London: Oxford University Press, 1965), with permission.

According to Woodward, the three types represented an increasing sophistication of technology. Thus, unit and small-batch production represented lower levels of sophistication, whereas process production represented greater sophistication. Large-batch and mass production fell somewhere in between. The sophistication of technology is partly reflected in the decline in the ratio of direct labor to indirect labor as we move from the first type of technology to the third. In economists' terms, labor has been replaced by capital as we move from small-batch to process technology.

Woodward discovered systematic relationships between the sophistication of an organization's technology and its management structure. The three types of technology were associated with different management structures. The differences are presented in Table 4.3.

With respect to management structure, Woodward's studies concluded that the management structure reflected the sophistication of the technology. This meant at least three things:

1. As we move from unit to process production, the *number of hierarchical levels and the number of managerial personnel* in the total employee mix tended to *increase*.

2. At the level of the first-line supervisor—the person who is closest to the manufacturing employees—there existed a *curvilinear relationship between span of control and sophistication of technology.* This is partly because employees at the extreme ends of the technological spectrum—that is, in the first and third types of technology—tended to be highly skilled.

3. *Patterns of coordination also followed a curvilinear relationship.* Thus, both unit and process production necessitated an organic mode of

management, whereas mass production required a mechanistic type.

What lent weight to Woodward's conclusions are her findings with respect to the commercial success of the firms she studied. Based on such indices as profitability, market share, stock prices, and reputation, she classified firms as above average, average, and below average performers. Woodward noted that the above average performers had managerial structures close to those presented in Table 4.3, whereas below average performers deviated significantly from the prescriptions of the table. This led Woodward to suggest a *contingency* prescription:

> To be effective, the management structure should match the demands imposed by technology.

Most of Woodward's firms were small in size compared to present-day standards. Others who have followed Woodward's lead extended and modified her findings. Prominent among them is the work of a research team from the University of Aston in Birmingham (see Box 4.6 for details). The Aston group's data suggested that technology influenced only those structural variables centered on the *conversion* process or production work flow. In small organizations such as those Woodward studied, managers were close to the production work flow, and hence, the technological demands shaped management structure. However, as organizations become larger, management is no longer close to the work flow. Therefore, the Aston group suggested other variables such as size, ownership, or environment may be important to structural design. The congruency hypothesis remained, but was restricted in scope: to be effective, among other things, management structures close to production work flow should be congruent with the demands of technology.

Summary

Taken together, the early contingency theorists postulated that in effective organizations there is congruence between management structure on the one hand and technology, size, and environment on the other. Technology primarily affects features of the management structure close to production work flow. Size inevitably leads to greater bureaucracy. Dynamic environments push organizations to organic forms.

These early contingency theorists primarily focused on variables that we have associated with the **functional subsystem** in organizations. They had little to say about other subsystems—informational, social, or cultural—and hence, contingency relations provide an incomplete picture of an organization.

Box 4.6

Aston Group Studies

A research team from the University of Aston in Birmingham, England, extended the work of Woodward. David Hickson, Derek Pugh, and Diane C. Pheysey were some of the key members of the research team. The Aston group examined service firms in addition to manufacturing firms. They visited over 50 organizations to gather data about technology and structure.

The Aston group noted that Woodward did not include service firms in the sample she studied. Service firms were characterized by simultaneous production and consumption and by the fact that the product/service cannot be inventoried. An example would be airline transportation where passengers travel (consumption) just when pilots fly the airplane; the travel could not be "inventoried." This is quite unlike the batch and continuous production technologies of Woodward.

Since the Aston group included service firms, they had to measure technology slightly differently than did Woodward. The Aston group included three characteristics of technology pertinent to both service and manufacturing firms:

Automation of equipment represents the amount of activity performed by machine relative to that performed by human beings.

Work flow rigidity represents the degree to which the sequence of operations is tightly interconnected and unalterable.

Specificity of evaluation refers to the extent that work flow activity can be evaluated using precise, quantifiable measurements as opposed to subjective evaluations by managers.

The Aston group discovered that the three characteristics are closely related; hence, they coined a single technology variable called *work flow integration,* which is a summation of the three original variables.

Work flow integration scores were closely related to Woodward's scheme of classification of technology: As the sophistication of technology increased, so did work flow integration. Thus, unit and small-batch production technologies had low work flow integration scores, and continuous production technologies had high scores, with large-batch and mass production falling in between.

The Aston group discovered that service firms were lower on technology than manufacturing firms. They were characterized by less automation, less work flow rigidity, and less precise measurements than their manufacturing counterparts.

Like Woodward, the Aston group discovered that management structure was related to technology. As work flow integration increased, so did bureaucratic characteristics: extent of formalization, specialization, standardization of procedures, and decentralization. Also, the supervisory ratio decreased.

Major Finding

Unlike Woodward, who studied only small firms, the Aston group concluded that technology is only one factor influencing management structure. In fact, it may be less important than other variables such as size. The Aston group noted that technology affects those aspects of the management structure that are close to the work flow. In small organizations such as the ones studied by Woodward, the overall structure will be more influenced by technology. However, in large organizations, size becomes a critical factor in determining the level of bureaucracy. This was similar to what size theorists had argued.

Source: Adapted from David Hickson, Derek Pugh, and Diane C. Pheysey, "Operations Technology and Organization Structure: An Empirical Reappraisal," *Administrative Science Quarterly* 14 (1969), pp. 378–97.

Applicability to Organizational Problems

The contingency perspective postulates that there is no single best solution to organizational problems, but that some solutions are better than others. The processes that lead to the success of certain managerial practices are not random or completely dependent on chance, and in a given situation there are a limited number of alternatives that will be successful. The effectiveness of managerial action is contingent on the situation in which action is required.

In other words, given certain contingencies, one can specify some general approaches and practices that are more likely to be effective than others. Thus, the contingency perspective does not grant license to managers to do whatever pleases them. Theory limits the domain of action. In this sense, although there is no single best solution to an organizational problem, some solutions are better than others.

Let us illustrate how the contingency perspective can be applied to an organizational problem by means of a hypothetical example. Consider a manager who is troubled by the lack of employee productivity in his organization. He has three consultants to help him solve the problem. Two of them follow universal principles, whereas the third is a contingency theorist. One universalist follows Taylor and the theorists of the scientific management school. True to his beliefs, he advocates time and motion studies to discover the one best way of doing the jobs by breaking them down into finer and finer components. The other universalist follows the human relations school. She argues that repetitive jobs lead to boredom and neglect the social and belonging needs of individuals. Therefore, she suggests such methods as job enrichment and increased attention to employees by supervisors.

The contingency theorist starts with the proposition that congruence between individual and task leads to effectiveness. Stated specifically, effectiveness is likely to ensue (1) when tasks are routine *and* individuals have lower level needs, *or* (2) when the tasks are nonroutine *and* individuals have higher level needs. Armed with this proposition, the third consultant hypothesizes that effectiveness is low because there is a lack of congruence between individuals and tasks. He then collects data on the nature of the tasks (whether they are routine or nonroutine) and the nature of individuals (whether they are motivated by lower or higher level needs). The primary thrust of his recommendations is to bring about congruence between the two. There are a number of ways of accomplishing this. One alternative is to redesign the jobs. Thus, if individuals have higher order needs, techniques such as job enrichment that reduce repetitiveness of the tasks may be appropriate. Similarly, scientific management techniques may be employed to make tasks more routine if the individuals are primarily motivated by lower order needs. A second alternative is to change the nature of the individuals by appropriate selection methods or by educating them. Thus, for example, when the tasks are repetitive, individuals with higher order needs may be replaced by those with lower level needs. Contingency theorists would argue that either alternative may solve the productivity problem. However, the contingency theorist would suggest that scientific management techniques are not appropriate when tasks are nonroutine and individuals have higher order needs. In this sense, the contingency theorist fulfills the claim that there is no single best way of doing things, but that some are better than others.

Controllability and Time Frame of Action

Two further factors guide the choice of alternatives: controllability of factors and time horizons of decision making. At any given time not all contingencies are under the control of managers. For example, environments are not easily manipulable except perhaps for the top managers of very large corporations. By uncontrollable elements, we mean elements that, *during a given time frame,* are generally not manipulable or available for change. In the above example, if the manager concerned with employee productivity is a first-line supervisor in the production department, changes in personnel policies are not likely to be manipulable by him in the short run. Such changes may require the approval of the personnel department in consultation with top management and the union. Managers can only work with alternatives that focus on elements that are controllable by them. This restricts the domain of feasible alternatives. Of course, the domain of feasible action enlarges the higher up the manager is in the organizational hierarchy.

Controllability and time frame are often related. Let us illustrate this idea with the help of Woodward's studies. She posited the need to coalign management structure and technology. In an ongoing organization, production technology may not be easily changed in the short run because of the need to recoup the current investment in capital as well as the potential for disruptions in production caused by changeover. In such cases, if there is a misalignment between technology and management structure, it may be easier to vary management structure than technology. There is no reason to treat production technology as a given when managers are contemplating long-term decisions, as in the case of setting up a new factory. In that case, managers may be able to choose from a number of alternative production technologies. In general, the longer the time frame of decisions, the larger the number of factors under managerial control. We hasten to point out that controllability and time frame have not received systematic attention from contingency theorists.

Culture as a Contingency in the Global Context

As we indicated in the introductory chapter, organizations today are operating in the multinational or global context. We believe that culture is probably the most significant contingency variable in the multinational context; hence, it is very important for managers to understand the implications of culture as a contingency variable. In this section, however, we will adopt a speculative stance with respect to the role of culture since it has not been the focus of systematic attention from organization theorists.

There have been two major works that traced the role of culture on management systems. One, conducted by Geert Hofstede, drew data from over 40 countries and traced the impact of culture on work-related attitudes of employees. Hofstede was interested in the individual level of analysis, and hence, its relevance for organization structure and management systems is remote. We have therefore summarized his work in Box 4.7.

The other work, conducted by William Ouchi, traced the influence of culture on organization structure and management systems. Ouchi studied U.S. and Japanese organizations, identifying two different types of management systems: Type A and Type J. Type A organizations relied on formal rules and regulations, whereas Type J organizations are more informal and group-oriented. Thus, Type A organizations tend to be hierarchically organized; they centralize decision making, they have vertical communication patterns, and they tend to value things more than people. Type J organizations, on the other hand, are flatter; they encourage horizontal communications, and they tend to value people more than things. The differences between the two are presented in Table 4.4.

Ouchi discovered that Type A organizations are prevalent in the United States, whereas the Type J organization was the norm in Japanese firms. In Burns and Stalker's terms, Type A organizations tended to be mechanistic systems, whereas Type J organizations resembled organic systems.

Ouchi also discovered that there are several companies in the United States that have Type J systems. They exist because their executive groups invest a large amount of energy to maintain them in the J mode. Over time, however, they tend to acquire some of the characteristics of the Type A systems; hence, Ouchi called them Type Z organizations. A prime example of such an organization is IBM, which has several characteristics of the Type J system. For example, it cares about its human resources, has until recently tried to provide lifetime employment, and had a no-layoff policy. All of these are characteristics of the Type J organization. On the other hand, it also believes in individual responsibility rather than group responsibility and tends to reward people individually rather than in teams or groups. These are characteristics of Type A management systems. In order to maintain its Type J characteristics, IBM spends a lot of energy and resources. Part of this is accomplished by training and part by developing strong norms within the company.

Implications for Managers

What are the implications of cultural contingency for firms that are now operating in a highly competitive multinational or global environment?

Box 4.7

Hofstede's Work on Culture

Hofstede has completed one of the most comprehensive investigation of work-related values and culture. He surveyed managers from almost 50 nations. Using a combination of multivariate statistical analysis and theoretical reasoning, Hofstede was able to isolate four dimensions of culture:

1. Individualism/collectivism.
2. High/low power distance.
3. Strong/weak uncertainty avoidance.
4. Masculinity/femininity.

A brief description of each of these dimensions follows. The first dimension, individualism/collectivism, is concerned with the nature of the relationships between an individual and his or her fellow human beings. Some societies view individualism positively; other societies view it with contempt and disapproval. A society that values individualism is one in which the ties between individuals are very loose. Everyone is expected to watch after his or her own interests, and individuals are left with a great deal of freedom to choose their own directions and activities. In contrast, a society that values collectivism is one in which individuals are expected to have extended families, and everyone is expected to look after the interests of the other members of his or her ingroup.

What are the implications of this dimension for management practice? In countries where collectivism predominates, individuals tend to interpret their organizational relationships from a moral perspective, and the organization that transcends easy interpretation. There becomes a bond of responsibility that develops between the employee and his or her employer. Employees come to view their organization as their own; its successes become their successes and company failures become their

failures. In those countries in which individualism predominates, individuals are likely to interpret their relationship with organizations from a calculative and individualistic perspective. The employee's commitment to the organization is tenuous and exists only to the extent that the individual feels that it is to his or her distinct advantage. The individual employee develops little commitment to the organization or need to respond to its demands. To some degree, the individual places his or her personal interest above the organization.

Power distance is the second dimension, and it is associated with the means that a society uses to manage the fact that people are unequal. People are born unequal, and they differentially exploit their physical and mental attributes. Some societies let individuals' inequalities grow to such an extent that over time the inequalities lead to differences in wealth and power, and these differences in wealth and power become institutionalized by society. No longer is the inheritance of wealth and power justified on the basis of physical and intellectual qualifications. Rather, it becomes accepted that the inequalities among people are attributed to kinship and birth order. Personal accomplishment is no longer a necessary and sufficient requirement for the distribution of power and wealth. As a general observation, societies have developed different criteria for the allocation of resources, and consequently certain members of the society are more unequal than others. A society that tries to downplay the inequalities of power and wealth as much as possible is classified as a low power distance culture. A society that has institutionalized differences in wealth and power as justified and not to be challenged is classified as a high power distance culture.

Power distance can be observed in management and administrative processes of organi-

Box 4.7 continued

zations, too. Power distance is related to the degree of centralization of authority, leadership, and decision making. The strength of the relationship existing between the centralization of decision-making and autocratic leadership is rooted in the mental programming of the members of the society. For example, in organizations where superiors maintain high power distance, subordinates tend to emphasize dependence on their superiors. In this respect, superiors make decisions, and subordinates accept the decisions. In contrast, in low power distance societies, superiors maintain a lesser degree of power distance relative to their subordinates, and the subordinates prefer to participate in decisions that will affect the work performance.

Uncertainty avoidance is the third dimension, and it pertains to the means that a society uses to cope with the fact that time runs only in one direction. There is a past, there is a present, and there is a future, and societies deal with each time period differently. We live in a world in which the future is unknown, and uncertainty is associated with that condition of human existence. Some societies socialize their members into accepting that uncertainty is a fact of life and that there is little that one can do to alter that situation. Other societies socialize their members into trying to beat, influence, or control the future. A society that teaches its members to accept risk, to be tolerant, and to accept behavior different from their own can be classified as a weak uncertainty avoidance culture. In those societies that socialize their members into trying to beat the future, there is a tendency to try and control the future by rules and procedures, and to the greatest extent possible there is an attempt to achieve the predictable. There is an intolerance toward the unpredictable or toward behavior and opinions that deviate from societal norms.

From an organizational and managerial perspective, uncertainty avoidance influences the degree to which an organization attempts to cope with the need to structure its activities. In strong uncertainty avoidance societies, the establishment of work rules and regulations are examples of organizational procedures designed to cope with uncertainty, and management tends to be relatively task-oriented and essentially job-centered. When uncertainty avoidance is weak, there will be less emphasis on control, and employees are encouraged to accept ambiguity. There will be less attention and time devoted to the development of policies, practices, and procedures designed to restrict individual initiative.

Masculinity/femininity is the fourth dimension; it measures the division of roles between the sexes. Social role divisions are more or less arbitrary. The sexual role definitions of one society may vary significantly from those in another. Societies can be classified according to their inclination to minimize or maximize the social and sex-role divisions. Masculine societies stress such values as assertiveness, acquisition of money, and disregard for others. In a masculine-oriented society, the hero is considered to be a person who is a successful achiever and superman. In feminine societies, the dominant values for both men and women include such qualities as cooperation among people, conservation of the environment, the importance of the quality of life, and a belief that small is beautiful. The underdog attracts public approval, and individual brilliance is suspect.

Are there implications of this dimension for management? From an organizational perspective the masculinity/femininity construct seems to have a bearing on the importance that an individual attaches to earnings, recognition, achievement, and challenge. Thus an organization's reward system and management style will be affected by a society's orientation on this dimension.

The main finding to emerge from Hofstede's work is that organizations are heavily

Box 4.7 continued

culture bound. This not only affects people's behavior within organizations, but also influences the likelihood of successfully transporting theories of organization and management styles from one culture to another. Management and organizing are both culturally bound because they involve the manipulation of symbols that have meaning to the people involved. Meanings associated with these symbols derive from what an individual has learned from his or her family, school, work environment, and members of the society. As Hofstede

(1980) has written, "Management and organization are penetrated with culture from the beginning to the end." Through a better understanding and awareness of a culture's values and the attitudes expressed by its members, one can better understand and interpret the behavior of organizations and the nature and operation of management in a given cultural setting.

Source: Adapted from Geert Hofstede, *Culture's Consequences: National Differences in Thinking and Organizing* (Beverly Hills, Calif.: Sage Publications, 1980).

TABLE 4.4   **A Comparison of Type A and Type J Organizations**

Dimension	*Type A*	*Type J*
Nature of employment contract	Short-term	Long-term
Decision making	Individual	Consensual
Responsibility/authority	Individual	Collective
Nature of tasks	Segmented, specialized	Holistic
Speed of evaluation and promotion	Fast	Slow
Control	Explicit, formal	Implicit, informal

Source: Adapted from William G. Ouchi and A. M. Yaeger, "Type Z Organization: Stability in the Midst of Mobility," *Academy of Management Review,* 3 (1978), pp. 305–14.

Multinational corporations that operate in a number of nations with diverse cultures face the strategic problem of how to structure and manage their organizations. A universalist perspective—characteristic of classical management theorists—would argue that these organizations should develop a standard management approach that ought to be implemented in all countries where they operate. We will term this *global strategy.* Contingency theorists, on the other hand, would argue that firms should adjust their structures and systems to the particular requirements of each location where they operate. We will term this a *localized strategy.*

Real life is more complex than any theory would lead us to believe. Given the wide variety of environments and cultures multinational corporations face, it is not likely that they would be able to implement a standard organizational system wherever they operate. The localized strategy seems viable; however, this strategy may create complexities beyond the capability of the management. As a result, many organizations have developed a *global-localized strategy.* In such an approach, a global strategy is developed, based on inputs from various locations. However, during implementation, each strategy is adapted to the local conditions. Sony Corporation, for example, followed this approach in coming to New Stanton, Pennsylvania.

To sum up, cultural contingencies, although they have not been the focus of serious theoretical attention, may be significant in multinational contexts.

Central Underlying Values

The contingency perspective is guided by three values that merit mention: pragmatism, rational-empiricism, and congruence.

Pragmatism

The contingency perspective upholds pragmatic values: "What works is good." There is neither the methodological dogma of scientific management theorists nor the humanist concern for the welfare of individuals. The question of what "ought to be" is replaced by what "works." This feature of the contingency approach is, of course, consistent with the requirements of normal science as it is understood in management.

Rational-Empiricism

Given the pragmatic orientation, the perspective attaches a lot of importance to generating data about what is and what happens in organizations as a prelude to understanding and diagnosing organizational problems. Empiricism aids in rational decision making; that is, in deliberately choosing action to accomplish intended goals.

Congruence

The notion of congruence pervades the typical recommendations coming from this perspective. All contingency theories hold that lack of congruence leads to inefficiency and ineffectiveness. Congruence is discovered empirically, and the aim of rational decision making is to bring contingent variables into balance.

The contingency perspective is thus not value neutral, as some adherents have claimed. The theoretical position that there are no right or wrong ways of managing or organizing, that the classical principles of management should be discarded, and that situational diagnosis is everything seem to support the claim for such value neutrality. Nothing is farther from the truth. This point is underscored by Scott et al.:

> One . . . must not be led to the conclusion that the contingency approach is value-neutral, although the belief in this kind of normlessness is actually encouraged by writers in the field. . . . The contingency approach is not normless. . . . Instead, it is intensely conservative in that it relies upon and pursues established values. Contingency thinking is supposed to help managers achieve rationality, efficiency, growth, abundance, consensus, effectiveness, and whatever else managers require to increase the performance of organizations.[8]

We will again return to the issue of values and the role of the contingency theory in management in the next section, where we summarize the limitations and utility of the contingency perspective.

Limitation and Utility of Contingency Perspective

Having discussed the major ideas in the contingency perspective, we once again return to the second major theme that underlies our views of contingency; that is, the contingency perspective is incomplete but useful.

Limitations

The contingency theory is incomplete from three vantage points: theoretical, pragmatic, and philosophical.

Theoretically, we have already shown that contingency theorists have primarily addressed factors of management that we have (in the previous chapter) associated with the functional subsystem in organizations. Thus many significant variables in organizations—political, informational, social, and cultural factors—have not been systematically researched and integrated into contingency relations. Since organizational subsystems are interdependent, causality may actually reside in the unaddressed factors. Thus, even the specific relationships unearthed by researchers are subject to qualification as further research evidence is gathered.

Pragmatically, contingency theorists do not address the question of implementation, as they do not offer a theory of change. Political scientists have pointed out that in our pluralistic value system, implementation requires working with conflicting goals, building coalitions, and other political activities. Contingency theories are typically silent with respect to political factors. As a consequence, theorists can only point to effective organizational constellations, not *necessarily* how to get there from ineffective states.

Further, at the present state of development, the prescriptive value of contingency theories is confined to short-range organizational problems. The rational-empiricist philosophy predisposes contingency scholars to pick the best out of the available alternatives, "best" being contextually determined. This is fine-tuning within the status quo. There is little scope for invention, innovation, or creation of hitherto nonexistent alternatives under this scenario. Learning, play, fantasy, and experimentation as alternatives are ruled out in this rational frame of mind. This is fine as long as one does not confront discontinuities, where working within the confines of available alternatives is of no help. However, as Peter Drucker reminded us forcefully, discontinuities are the norm, not the exception, in the case of many strategic or nonroutine problems confronting modern day organizations. Contingency theorists have little to offer by way of solutions to strategic problems.

Philosophically, the pragmatism inherent in this perspective blinds one to the pervasive philosophical questions of what an organization should be, as well as human and political questions of justice and welfare. For example, contingency theorists sidestep the value issues raised by human resource theorists. Typically, contingency scholars adopt a contingent stance to the question of values, without recognizing the implicit values for which Scott criticized them. Thus, whereas human resource theorists would argue that all organizations should be designed to provide growth climates for individuals, contingency scholars point out instances where individuals are disdainful of such climates, partly as a result of a long process of past socialization. Further, when human resource theorists imply that organizations have some responsibility for educating individuals to realize their potential, contingency theorists point up instances where this is not possible given the economic and technological constraints facing the organization. Scott et al. argues this point well:

> The pragmatism of the contingency approach is . . . evidence of its micro orientation . . . The attention of the contingency approach is on the necessity of solving puzzles and putting out fires. The concern for the situation at hand stifles any motivation that theoreticians or practitioners might have for the broader effects of their ideas and decisions. . . . People are likely to be so occupied with the pressing problems of the moment, with each solution to these problems creating other pressing problems, that they will never get around to addressing the basic value question of "what ought to be." The microcosmic world of pragmatism is not a place where philosophy flourishes . . .

★ ★ ★ ★ ★

> [The] contingency approach is a valuable addition to the paradigmatic landscape as long as it is understood as a *tactical approach* to organizational puzzle solving. Its usefulness is on the level of routine organizational operation and short range planning. The danger of the contingency approach arises when it is elevated to

the status of a *strategic theory.* Then it becomes a theory of organizational change and a philosophy of organizational progress—two functions that it is ill-equipped to perform.[9]

Utility

Just what, then, is the utility of the contingency perspective? First, since almost all decision making in organizations is contingent, the contingency perspective is an accurate descriptor of what goes on in the real world. We repeat that attention to contingencies is necessary for managerial effectiveness. Hence, the contingency perspective is useful as an *orienting strategy* rather than as a set of interrelated propositions.[10] Thus, the general prescription of considering internal and external contingencies is indeed useful as long as we do not *limit* ourselves to the variables that have received empirical scrutiny.

Second, the avenues to effectiveness offered by specific theorists are a useful *short-term* guide to action. Much of the work in the last decade has focused on short-run phenomena, where many of the contingencies (for example, technology) were treated as uncontrollable factors. We noted earlier that two factors lay dormant in the recommendations of contingency theorists—controllability and time horizons. This need not be the case, but at the current state of development, Scott's assessment of the contingency perspective seems valid—it is most useful as a tactical guide to short-range actions.

In summary, the contingency perspective is useful if we treat it as an orienting strategy and augment it with a theory of change. We will cover the topic of organizational change in the next chapter.

Chapter Summary

Organizational theorists have so far isolated three major organizational contingencies: environment, technology, and size. The relationship of these three contingency variables to the nature of the management system is depicted in Figure 4.1.

Contingency theory suggests that if the environment is stable, the tasks routine (as in Woodward's assembly line), and the organization large, then organizations are effective if organized according to mechanistic principles. On the other hand, if the environment is dynamic, the tasks nonroutine, and the organization small, then organizations have to be organic to be effective.

In the two extreme cases outlined above, the contingency perspective provides clear prescriptions as to how to organize the system for effectiveness. There are, however, other combinations of these contingency variables

FIGURE 4.1

Summary of Crucial Contingencies

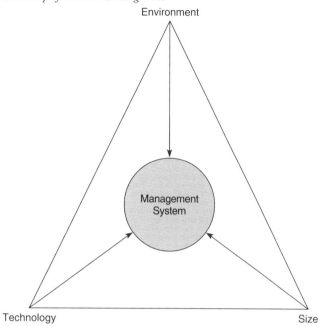

where the prescriptions from contingency theory are not as clear. For example, if the environment is dynamic, the tasks nonroutine, and the organization is large in size, there is no clear prescription coming from contingency theory.

Theorists would argue that where contingency variables are not congruent among themselves, managers need to develop a two-step plan. In the first step, contingency variables should be brought into congruency with each other; in the second step, a contingency prescription for an appropriate management system needs to be determined and implemented. This is more easily said than done. Many of the contingency variables may not be under the control of the manager. For example, the environment may not be under the control of the manager, hence, changing the environment from stable to dynamic or vice versa may not be feasible. When the contingency variables are not congruent among themselves, they will create conflicting demands on the management system. Such conflicts would need to be managed because they cannot be eliminated. Thus, managers in real-life situations have to deal with messy problems; prescriptions in these situations are rarely going to be clear-cut.

Specialized Terms

Empiricism
Ideographic versus nomothetic
Contingency
Taxonomies
Interaction
Crucial contingencies
  • Size
  • Technology
  • Environment
Bureaucratic dimensions
  • Formalization
  • Specialization
  • Standardization
  • Centralization
Organic versus mechanistic systems

Dynamic versus stable
  environment
Technology
  • Unit and small batch
  • Large batch and mass production
  • Process technology
Controllability
Time frame of action
Culture
Global versus localized strategy
Values
  • Pragmatism
  • Rational-empiricism
  • Congruence
Tactical versus strategic theory

Discussion Questions

Theoretical

1. How is the contingency perspective a middle ground between ideographic and nomothetic stances?

2. In a recent management conference, a prominent management theorist lamented, "Contingency theory is a sellout by discontented human resources theorists." Comment.

3. Distinguish between the situational theory of management and the contingency perspective.

4. What are the crucial organizational contingencies? How do they influence the organization?

5. What are the limits and utilities of the contingency perspective?

★6. Relate the influence of contingencies on the bureaucratic characteristics of organizations.

★7. Critically evaluate the claims of contingency theorists to strategic status.

Applied

1. You are faced with the problem of deciding on an appropriate structure for a subsidiary in Korea. Assume that you are not familiar

---

★This is an advanced-level question.

with how the business operates in Korea. Two management consultants have approached you. One has provided a detailed specific structure and has offered to train the overseas people to fit the structure. The other has outlined a process by which the structure will be arrived at. Both consultants have wide experience, and their proposed budgets are similar. Whom would you select? Why will your answer change if you are very knowledgeable about Korea?

End Notes

1. Fremont E. Kast and James Rosenzweig, *Contingency Views of Organization and Management* (Palo Alto, Calif.: Science Research Associates) Reproduced from their *Organization and Management* 4th ed. (New York: McGraw-Hill, 1985), pp. 17–18.
2. Charles Percy Snow, *The Two Cultures: And a Second Look* (Cambridge University Press), 1964.
3. See (1) Lowell Julliard Carr, *Situational Analysis: An Observational Approach to Introductory Sociology* (New York: Harper & Row, 1948); (2) Kurt Lewin, *Field Theory in Social Science* (New York: Harper & Row, 1951); (3) Robert K. Merton, *Social Theory and Social Structures*, rev. ed. (New York: Free Press, 1957).
4. Frederick E. Fiedler, "Engineer the Job to Fit the Manager," *Harvard Business Review* 45 (September-October 1965), p. 118.
5. John J. Morse and Jay W. Lorsch, "Beyond Theory Y," *Harvard Business Review* 48 (May-June 1970).
6. Tom Burns and George M. Stalker, *The Management of Innovation* (London: Tavistock, 1961).
7. Joan Woodward, *Industrial Organization: Theory and Practice* (London: Oxford University Press, 1965), p. vi. See also *Management and Technology* (London: Her Majesty's Stationary Office, 1958).
8. William G. Scott, Terence R. Mitchell, and Phillip Birnbaum, *Organization Theory: A Structural and Behavorial Analysis* (Homewood, Ill.: Richard D. Irwin, 1972), pp. 67–68.
9. Ibid., p. 67.
10. Claudia Bird Schoonhoven, "Problems with Contingency Theory: Testing Assumptions Hidden within the Language of Contingency 'Theory', *Administrative Science Quarterly* 26 (1981), pp. 349–377.

5 PERSPECTIVES ON ORGANIZATIONAL CHANGE

Chapter Outline

Facing lower enrollments, colleges are scrimping. But students and their future employers will gain from a new emphasis on teaching. And tuition hikes will slow.

Even the most prestigious colleges—Princeton, Stanford, Columbia, Cornell, and Johns Hopkins among them—have been struggling to balance their budgets. Princeton used to dispatch janitors twice a week to clean the bathrooms in dormitory suites. Now students scrub their own toilets (or don't, as the case may be).

Other cutbacks are more serious. In the face of swelling costs and diminishing enrollments, many universities are reducing staff, scaling back on student services, and shutting down academic departments.

Parents, watching their bank balances diminish with each semester's payment, have every right to wonder why colleges are suddenly so hard up. Indeed, tuition increased an average 9.3 percent a year during the 80s, twice the rise in the consumer price index. As the stock market boomed and alumni and corporations made record-breaking donations, endowments rose 213 percent.

Where did all the money go? Universities spent much of it *not* to educate students but rather to serve the parochial interests of professors and presidents.

Fortunately, academia's leaders are finally realizing that they must live within their means. Research, for one thing, has become uncontrollably expensive—even classics professors use costly computer technology. Smarter university administrators are catching on that they must conduct research in fewer fields so they can afford to provide a quality education.

In the process universities will become less universal. Says Columbia provost Jonathan Cole: "No university is capable of covering all areas of scholarship anymore." But this new vision of the university should not hamper America's pursuit of knowledge. Rather, if put fully into practice, it should yield significant advantages. Students—and their eventual employers—will benefit from a greater emphasis on teaching. The work of educating will be accomplished with less overlap among schools and less duplication of resources.[1]

Change is endemic to all organizations. Until recently, universities were considered immune to major changes. However, as the chapter introduction case above shows, even universities are experiencing phenomenal changes.

How do organizations change? Do they change because managers take action? Or do environments force them to change? Are there predictable stages in an organization's life, just as for individuals? In this chapter, we will sketch some answers to these questions provided by organization theorists. But first, let us clarify the focus of the chapter.

What Is Organizational Change?

When we talk about organizational change, we refer to changes that involve an entire organization or a major part of it. Undertaking a program of diversification, redesigning organization structure, filing for bankruptcy, installing a new information system, or changing organizational culture are examples of major organizational changes.

Organizations almost always experience change. Some changes are so small that we will not consider them organizational change. For example, in universities professors without tenure may be replaced, new students enroll every year, or new courses may be introduced; we will not consider these changes organizational change since they are so small as not to affect large segments of the university.

We may more clearly differentiate organizational changes from other changes using the concept of *levels,* a concept that we elaborated on in our chapter on the systems model. Thus, changes in organizations may take place at many different levels: individual, group, and organizational levels, and in organization–environment relations. Although these levels are inter-dependent, we focus only on organization–environment relations and organizational levels. This is so for three reasons:

1. The strategic focus within an organization is on organization-environment relations and organizational levels.
2. Organization–environment relations and organizational levels inevitably affect group and individual phenomena.
3. Historically, individual and group levels are dealt with in courses titled organizational behavior.

We adopted a similar stance in our discussion of the contingency perspective in the previous chapter, where we also focused primarily on the organizational level as well as on organization–environment relations.

However, there are three differences between the perspectives on change and the contingency perspective we described in the previous chapter:

1. The contingency perspective was oriented toward *prescriptions:* how to arrive at solutions to organizational problems. Unlike the contingency perspective, however, in this chapter we are concerned with *describing* the many ways in which organizations change.
2. Contingency theorists try to describe the organizational states *where performance is optimized.* Organizations do not always change for the better, that is, in the direction of optimal performance. Organizational change theorists try to unearth the *mechanisms by which organizations change, in the optimal direction or otherwise.*
3. Related to the above, contingency theorists prescribe how an organizational system may be stabilized; that is, when the elements of a system are congruent with key contingencies, the system achieves some degree of stability. Change theorists focus on how organizations change their structures and processes; they do not focus on the sources of stability within organizations.

In our chapter on the systems model, we elaborated on the concept of *unintended consequences* and *emergent behaviors;* almost all planned changes have unintended consequences. For example, universities have always used a professor's publications and research productivity as major criteria for evaluating performance. In turn, professors neglected teaching, and as the chapter introduction case notes, since research has become so expensive, universities are facing hard times. Certainly universities did not intend such a consequence of emphasizing research and publication over teaching. Organizations experience change in many ways, and planned changes are only one of them. Change theorists try to portray various aspects of organizational change, planned or otherwise. Unlike contingency theorists, they thus elaborate the notion of emergent behaviors.

Table 5.1 summarizes the operationalization of various systems concepts from the vantage point of organizational change. As can be seen from the table, change theorists view the environment as a source of change and thus emphasize the open systems character of an organization. Simultaneously, they highlight the interdependence of organizational elements by focusing on emergent behaviors created by the internal dynamics of organizations. Change theorists primarily address the organizational level and how changes at this level affect individuals and groups. Taken together, they describe many different mechanisms by which organizations change—with or without planning—and thus illustrate the notion of equifinality and multifinality.

In this chapter, we describe the major organizational change theorists. The scheme of the chapter is as follows: First, we will summarize some of the historical and philosophical underpinnings of the field. Second, we will describe the major theoretical frameworks in the field. Third, we will try to summarize implications of various change theories for managers. Finally, we will summarize and review the various theorists.

Underpinnings

Historical Underpinnings

Although organizations have always experienced change, scholars began to pay attention to the systematic study of organizational change only in the

TABLE 5.1   Systems Concepts and Organizational Change

Systems Concepts	Operationalization
Environment	Environment is a source of change
Interdependence	The internal dynamics create pressures for organizational change
Level	Organizational change affects individual and group levels
Equifinality/multifinality	There are many ways in which organizations change
Stability versus change	Focus on change
Emergent behavior	Planned and unplanned change

last two to three decades. Prior to 1950, almost all attention was on managerial behavior. As we have seen in the previous chapters, the role of the environment was neglected, and it was implicitly believed that managerial action was all that was needed to bring about organizational change. Scientific management, organization design, and human relations were all geared toward improving managerial effectiveness.

During the 1950s and 60s, the idea of *planned organizational change* received a boost from organization development and organization design scholars. Fueled by humanistic motives, scholars such as Douglas McGregor and Chris Argyris argued the case for organization development. They perceived the environment to be dynamic and turbulent, and based their call for organic systems on environmental demands. In the last chapter, we saw some of the prescriptions for planned change provided by contingency theorists who argued the case for organization design. These theorists, like the organization development scholars, pointed to environment as the reason for organization design. Thus, planned change approaches began to be assimilated within open systems concepts.

By the late 1960s, however, it became clear that organization development was not a panacea for organizational ills, and that the matrix designs promoted by some organization design scholars had not always succeeded. The hostile environments of the 1970s—the OPEC induced oil embargo, high inflation and interest rates, maturing markets—and the many failures of planned change efforts prompted scholars to question the efficacy of planned change approaches.

Thus, instead of focusing only on planned change, a new breed of theorists reframed the question: *What are the processes by which organizations change?* Planned change certainly is one process, but these scholars described other processes by which organizations changed. Consider:

Some described the predictable stages in the life of an organization—stages over which managers had little influence.

Others described failures and bankruptcies and saw the murderous hand of the environment in organizational deaths.

Partly stimulated by the success of Japanese organizations who copied the management practices of some of the best U.S. corporations, still other scholars described organizations changing through a process of imitation.

Some were interested in how organizations innovate; they focused on processes of innovation.

As the field of organizational change began to flourish, it became abundantly clear that planned change was only one mechanism of change, and that there were several processes of change in organizations.

Philosophical Underpinnings

Contemporary organizational change theorists are all *open system theorists.* They underscore the interdependence between organizations and environments on the one hand, and the internal interdependence among organizational subsystems on the other. Thus, they share somewhat similar philosophical assumptions.

There are, however, differences among change theories. These differences may be captured along two dimensions: (1) internal versus external, and (2) natural versus adaptive.

Internal versus external. Different scholars focus on different sources of change. Some describe organizational changes triggered by the environment (e.g., the market situation), whereas others focus on changes caused by internal tensions (e.g., problems of coordination).

Natural versus Adaptive. Natural system theorists focus on predictable patterns in organizational change. They describe changes that occur in organizations, whether engineered by managers or not. Managerial discretion is not important to them. Adaptive theorists describe the organization as shaping different responses to different pressures; they see managerial discretion as important.

The distinctions are portrayed in Figure 5.1

To illustrate the differences in emphasis, let us return to the example of universities cited in the beginning of this chapter. Some scholars will focus on population changes and economic downturns, forces over which universities have little control, as the sources of change for declining enrollments and the fiscal crises of universities (external-natural). Some will portray the changes as an inevitable process of aging (internal-natural). Others will focus on the failure of actions taken by universities to lobby the legislature to obtain

FIGURE 5.1

A typology of organizational change

SOURCE OF CHANGE

	Internal	External
Natural	Internal dynamics of organizations create life cycles	Environments induce changes outside managerial control
Adaptive	Managerial action brings about changes	Environments and managerial responses to them create change

TYPE OF CHANGE

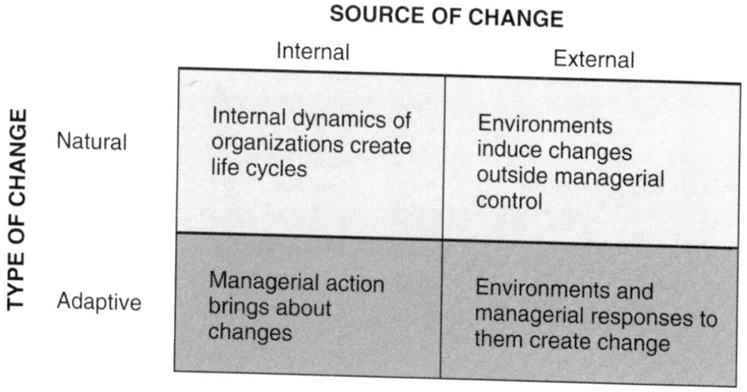

research dollars (external–adaptive), implicitly criticizing them for their in-effective management. Still others will focus on the role of great leaders in shaping the mission of universities (internal–adaptive). Diverse change theorists have thus focused on different sources of change in organizations.

In what follows, we will describe the major theories belonging to various groups.

Theoretical Frameworks

In this section, we discuss the major theoretical frameworks that describe the phenomenon of organizational change. We will summarize six theories: (1) population ecology model, (2) resource dependence theory, (3) institutional theory of imitation, (4) organizational life cycles, (5) process of innovation, and (6) planned change.

These theories invoke different philosophical assumptions about the sources and nature of change. Thus, the population ecology model focuses on the environment as the source of change and views change from a naturalistic perspective (external–natural). Both resource dependence and institutional theorists focus on the adaptive capabilities of the organization (external–adaptive). Organizational life cycle focuses on internal sources of change that occur naturally (internal–natural), whereas both innovation and planned change theorists focus on internal–adaptive processes (internal–adaptive). This is summarized in Figure 5.2.

Population Ecology Model

The population ecology model[2] of organizations is developed from theories of natural selection in biology. The biologist's theories try to explain why

FIGURE 5.2

Change theories arrayed according to change typology

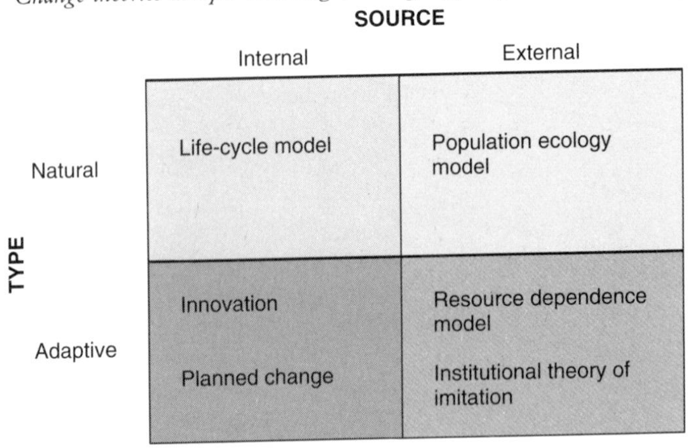

SOURCE

	Internal	External
Natural	Life-cycle model	Population ecology model
Adaptive	Innovation Planned change	Resource dependence model Institutional theory of imitation

(**TYPE** labels the vertical axis)

certain life forms appear and survive while others perish. The essential principle is that *the forms that are best fitted to the environment survive.*

Organization theorists following the footsteps of biologists make two major assumptions:

1. Organizations have limited capability to adapt to environmental change.
2. The processes of change are ultimately controlled by the environment.

These assumptions enabled population ecologists to adapt ideas from biology to explain organizational change.

Ecologists argue that organizations compete for resources that are controlled by environments. Who wins and who loses is determined by the environment. Change may occur through new organizations eliminating old ones or through the modification of existing organizations. Population ecologists explain *how* rather than *why* organizations survive. They are indifferent to the sources of change: The sources may be luck or chance on the one hand or managerial planning and organizational adaptation on the other.

Population ecologists propose a three-stage model for describing change: variation, selection, and retention. The model suggests that environmental pressures make the competition for resources the central force in organizational activities. The three stages of variation, selection, and retention explain how organizations are created, survive, or fail, and successful organizational practices are diffused throughout a population. The three-stage model is presented in Figure 5.3

Variation

Variation or differences within and between organizations is the first requirement for organizational change. Some variations occur through an organization's own attempts to generate alternatives and seek solutions to problems; however, error, chance, and luck are more likely sources of variations.

FIGURE 5.3

Population ecology model

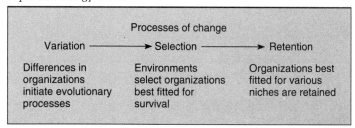

Ecologists point to two types of variation that create the possibility of external selection pressures affecting the direction of organization change:

1. There are variations between organizations in their overall form. Such variations are likely to be introduced into the organizational population whenever new organizations are created. For example, in recent years, new organizations have come into existence providing new services or new products. Other new organizations have sprung up making traditional products like steel using new technology.

2. Variation within organizations opens them to the potential for change. Growth is a common source of within-organization variation, as increasing complexity and control problems lead to fundamental changes in organizational practices.

When there are differences among organizations, some emerge as successful while others continue to lose and disappear. Thus, variation triggers selection, the second stage.

Selection

The selection of new organizational forms occurs as a result of environmental constraints. Organizations fitting environmental criteria are positively selected and survive while others either fail or change to match environmental requirements.

Environmental selection is described in terms of either the resources or the information made available to organizations:

Information: Changes in communication technology, improvements in methods of recording and storing information, the breakdown of barriers to information flow, and innovations that enhance people's understanding of the environment increase the likelihood of changes in organizational forms.

Resources: Organizations compete for environmental resources. Selection occurs through relative rather than absolute superiority in acquiring resources, and the effective organization is one that has achieved a relatively better position in an environment it shares with others.

Thus, as variations in organizational forms appear in environments, some forms find a niche and survive. This leads to the third stage.

Retention

Retention is the preservation of selected organizational forms. There are many such retained organizations: government, schools, churches, and automobile firms. The retained organizations may become a dominant part of the environment.

In summary, variation, selection, and retention constitute the three stages of organizational change. Variation among organizations initiates the process, selection by environmental criteria weeds out certain organizations, and retention mechanisms preserve the selected organizations.

In Box 5.1, we have summarized the recent plight of the retailing industry. As can be seen from the example, different retailers were pursuing different goals and activities. This has triggered competition for customers, and the selection criteria favor firms that are low on debt and spend heavily on growth. As a result, some famous retailers such as Bonwit Teller were forced to close most of their stores.

The population ecology model considers environmental selection to be of utmost importance in explaining organizational change. Returning to the

---

Box 5.1

Selection Criteria in Retailing

The wreckage in retailing has piled up so high that you need to check every week to see who's in and who's out of business. Once-proud names—B. Altman, Bonwit Teller, Garfinckel's—have closed most of their stores, victims of too much debt and too little management skill. The Federated-Allied stable, including Bloomingdale's, A&S, and Jordan Marsh, is operating in the fog of Chapter 11, unclear about the future. Industry experts and suppliers are casting nervous glances at Macy's, struggling under its own burden of debt and caught up in the profit-destroying cycle of endless price promotions.

At the same time, Home Depot, The Limited, Toys "Я" Us, Wal-Mart, the Gap, J. C. Penney, and Nordstrom are becoming the new rulers of retailing. They are succeeding by developing exciting merchandising programs, finding innovative uses for technology, and expanding smartly and aggressively. Debt for these market-share masters is a measly percentage of sales. That gives them the financial strength to weather the hits and misses of the industry without jeopardizing the business.

Retailing is thus becoming an industry of big winners and big losers. The reason is a matter of cruel economics. For strong retailers, those long-term investments trigger a beneficient cycle of moneymaking: As sales increase, operating costs as a percentage of those sales decline. That translates into lower prices for customers, which in turn boosts sales, and the cycle starts all over again. For strapped competitors, declining sales mean operating costs as a percentage of sales rise, making it more difficult to keep prices competitive or to offer the amenities that keep customers happy. Trying to remedy this problem by constantly putting goods on sale may move merchandise out the doors and up the cash flow, but it eats away at the bottom line, further compounding the problem.

As can be seen from this example, environmental selection criteria are favoring some retailers over others.

Source: Adapted from Susan Caminiti, "The New Champs of Retailing," *Fortune*, p. 85.

chapter introduction case about universities, ecologists will attribute the university's problems to shifting selection criteria. Universities' resource providers—the government, students, alumni—are demanding different things from universities. Thus, they are beginning to favor different types of universities, especially those that emphasize teaching in addition to research.

Ecologists are pessimistic about organizations' potential for change. They see change more frequently coming from newer organizations than from the modification of old ones.

The model is primarily applicable to small organizations. For them, environmental selection pressures are felt even in the short run. In fact, the failure rate of start-up organizations is quite high. However, the model is also applicable to large organizations, albeit in the long run. Even institutionalized organizations such as IBM are not permanent in the long run. The environment is always changing, and if the dominant organizational forms do not adapt to change, they will gradually disappear, having been replaced by other organizations.

The emphasis on selection obscures how organizations can adapt to environmental changes. External-adaptation theorists also focus on environment as the source of organizational change, but unlike the population ecologists, have described the processes by which organizations adapt to external changes. We consider two groups of theorists: (1) resource dependence theorists, and (2) institutional theorists.

Resource Dependence Theorists

Resource dependence theorists focus on an organization's ability to acquire resources from its environments as the key to its survival. Thus, as in the university example, in the beginning, organizational change is triggered by the changing resource situation—declining enrollments and dollars—a university faces vis-à-vis its environment. To quote the leading theorists:

> [The resource dependence theorists'] position is that organizations survive to the extent that they are effective. Their effectiveness derives from the management of demands, particularly the demands of interest groups upon which the organizations depend for resources and support . . . there are a number of ways of managing demands, including the obvious one of giving in to them.[3]

The resource dependence theory can be summarized by four major ideas: (1) the problem of resources, (2) the external control of organizations, (3) the strategies to cope with control, and (4) influence on internal organizational processes.[4]

The Problem of Resources

Organizations require resources to survive. Typically, to acquire resources, an organization must interact with others who control the resources. Thus, organizations are dependent on environments, which makes resource acquisition problematic and uncertain. Those who control the resources may be undependable, particularly when the resources are scarce. Since organizations prefer some stability to their operations, negotiating with others to ensure stable resource flows is the focus of much organizational action.

The External Control of Organizations
The environmental actors who control resources may be organizations, groups, or individuals. To the extent that they control critical resources, they are in a position to influence an organization. In this sense, we can talk about the external control of organizations. Some examples of the conditions that facilitate control are:

1. The possession of some resource by the environmental actor.
2. The importance of the resource to the organization.
3. The inability of the organization to obtain the resource elsewhere.
4. The organization's ability to take desired action.
5. The organization's lack of control over resources critical to the environmental actor.

Each of these conditions can be altered by the organization and the environmental actor. An organization can attempt to avoid these conditions, and thereby enhance its discretion. The environmental actor seeking control over the organization can act to make these conditions worse. Thus, organizations are involved in a dynamic sequence of actions and reactions leading to variations in control and discretion. This leads to the question of the strategies used by organizations to control or alter the above conditions.

Strategies to Manage Control
Organizations can employ several strategies to manage their environmental actors.

1. Organizations can comply with their environmental actors. However, organizations require some flexibility to adjust to contingencies as they develop; hence, compliance is not a satisfactory solution. Compliance perpetuates external control, and this makes future adjustments difficult.
2. Organizations avoid influence by others by restricting the flow of information about themselves and their activities, denying the legitimacy of demands made on them, diversifying their dependencies, and manipulating information to increase their own legitimacy.
3. Organizations can seek stability and certainty in resource flows by collective actions such as trade associations, joint ventures, and the like.

In addition to explaining these actions of organizations, resource dependencies also explain internal organizational phenomena.

Influence on Internal Organizational Processes

External control affects internal organizational processes primarily by altering the distribution of power and control in the organization. In turn, power affects succession to leadership positions in the organization. Thus, resource dependencies explain executive succession. The resource dependence theory is summarized in Figure 5.4.

Returning to our example of the universities, the most important resource—money—is controlled by students, alumni, and the government, which provides research grants. Recently, some major universities like Stanford and Harvard came under close scrutiny by the government for misspending research dollars. In fact, the president of Stanford, Paul Kennedy, stepped down in the wake of the scandals that erupted.

In summary, resource dependence theorists argue that an organization's changing resource situation explains the changes that it experiences—both the actions taken by the organization as well as its internal power distribution, including who gets selected to leadership positions. The effectiveness of the organization is dependent on its ability to acquire resources; in the extreme, if ineffective, it may not survive.

Institutional Theorists

Unlike resource dependence theorists, institutional theorists focus on *imitation* as a process by which organizations change. Figure 5.5 displays in graphic fashion the logic of imitation.

According to this theory, managers mimic other organizations in the same environment—that is, similar organizations in the industry that deal with similar customers, suppliers, and regulatory agencies.[5] Why do managers copy practices of other organizations? Mainly for two reasons:

FIGURE 5.4

Resource dependence model

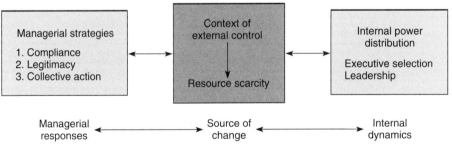

FIGURE 5.5

Institutional theory of imitation

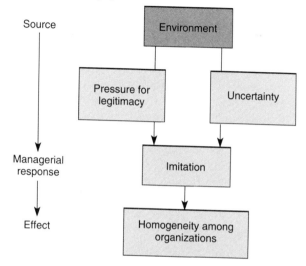

1. When managers confront uncertainty in their environment, they assume that other organizations face similar uncertainty. It makes sense to copy the practices of seemingly successful firms. Such copying serves to reduce uncertainty for managers.
2. Managers seek legitimacy from the environment. They do not want to be criticized by shareholders for being too different. Hence, once they detect that certain practices are in vogue, they copy these other practices.

What happens when organizations copy each other? First, organizations in the same environment begin to look alike. Thus, all airlines resemble one another, as do banks and television networks. Secondly, organizations experience fads and fashions as people do. Thus, acquisitions, downsizing, and flextime are all partly explained by organizations copying each other.

Both resource dependence and institutional theorists agree that organizations have some ability to adapt to changing environments; they thus differ from population ecology theorists. Consequently, their approach is applicable to a wide range of organizations even in the short run.

Organizational Life Cycle

Theorists belonging to this class adopt ideas from biology to answer the question: How do organizations grow? They seek sources of change internal to the organization. According to them, just as a newborn baby passes through a series of stages (such as infant, toddler, preschooler, or adolescent) before it becomes an adult, so do organizations pass through a number of stages.

Thus, a useful way to think about organizational growth and change is provided by the concept of *organizational life cycle*. The concept suggests that organizations are born, grow older, and eventually wither away. The internal characteristics of an organization—structure, leadership, administrative systems—follow a fairly predictable pattern through various stages in the life cycle. The stages are sequential and follow a natural progression; by implication, managers have little ability to alter the natural progression.

Larry Greiner has formulated the most popular life-cycle model in organization theory. The model is presented pictorially in Figure 5.6.

As shown in the figure, Greiner's model identifies five levels of growth in an organizational life cycle: birth, growth through direction, growth through delegation, growth through coordination, and growth through collaboration. Each stage is associated with a crisis. Greiner makes two points about the various stages:

1. Resolution of each crisis requires movement to the next level,
2. Decline can occur anywhere, and it is management's responsibility to prevent it if possible. We will now summarize each stage.

Birth

An organization is born when an entrepreneur, alone or with others, senses an opportunity for creating a product. The founders devote their energies

FIGURE 5.6

Greiner's model of organizational life cycle

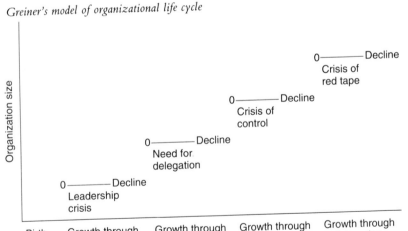

Adapted from: Larry E. Greiner, "Evolution and Revolution as Organizations Grow," *Harvard Business Review* 50 (July–August 1972), pp. 37–46.

to the technical activities of production and marketing. The organization is informal and nonbureaucratic and control is based on personal supervision.

As the organization grows, the number of employees increases, and administrative requirements mount. Many entrepreneurs do not want to worry about administrative details, spending time instead on production and marketing. This creates the first crisis, the crisis of leadership. To resolve this, the organization must move into the next phase: growth through strong direction.

Growth through Direction

If the leadership crisis is resolved, then strong leadership is obtained and the organization begins to develop clear goals and direction. Departments are established along with a hierarchy of authority, job assignments, and division of labor. The organization shifts to a mechanistic mode.

However, this leads to the next crisis, when employees discover that their autonomy is restricted by the formal structure of the organization. As growth continues, lower level personnel find their knowledge of problems to be superior to that of management. They want freedom to react quickly to customers, production problems, and other areas of performance. As long as top management tightly controls the organization, they will become overburdened with decisions they lack the expertise to make.

Growth through Delegation

Organizations solve the delegation crisis by moving onto the next stage of development, when managers let go of some authority and increase delegation at lower levels. Subordinates are now energized as they begin to exercise their newly acquired freedom in decision making.

As operations are increasingly delegated, top management risks the loss of control over operations. Conflicts erupt between various parts of the organization as decentralization leads to strong differences in goals of various departments.

Growth through Coordination

To solve the control crisis, top management installs formal planning practices, financial controls, and corporatewide controls to foster unity of goals in the decentralized organization. Vertical information systems may be installed and certain functions such as human resources may be recentralized. Managers at lower levels adapt to a new system where they are not free to run their own shows. They are now linked to the rest of the organization through an elaborate web of coordination mechanisms.

However, this, in turn, brings the next crisis: the organization gets bogged down in too much red tape. The proliferation of systems and programs may strangle middle level managers, who may begin to resent the staff people. Innovation may be stifled, and the organization may seem to be overbureaucratized.

Growth through Collaboration

Organizations solve the red tape crisis through a new sense of collaboration and teamwork. Managers develop skills for confronting problems and working together. Conflict resolution strategies assume greater importance because organizations cannot rely on formal coordination mechanisms. Teamwork is emphasized; formal systems may be simplified; temporary task forces may become common.

The collaborative organization may drain the energies of individuals because of too much ambiguity and the stress of team-based designs. This leads to further crises, which of course are yet to be identified. Table 5.2 summarizes the major differences among Greiner's steps.

Greiner's model depicts an organization moving through repeated cycles of delegation and control. In other words, as organizations grow, they swing between organic and mechanistic types. The simple fact of growth creates internal dynamics within organizations.

In Box 5.2, we have presented the problems faced by Sun Microsystems and the responses of the chief executive officer. The company faced a transition point, marked by a loss—the first time in history. Until then Microsystems had been run in an organic fashion, but lacked sufficient controls. It had thus swung too much in the organic direction. The CEO's response was to institute cost controls. The solution swung the organization in a mechanistic direction, but it seems to have worked for this company.

TABLE 5.2 Stages of Life Cycle

		Stage of Life Cycle			
Characteristic	Birth	Growth through Direction	Growth through Delegation	Growth through Coordination	Growth through Collaboration
Structure	Informal	Informal, but some procedures	Formal procedures but departmentalized	Formal procedures, departmentation, budgetary control	Teamwork within bureaucracy
Leadership style	Entrepreneurial	Directive	Delegative	Integrative	Participative Teams
Coordination mechanism	Personal, paternalistic	Personal and impersonal systems		Impersonal systems	
Systemic tendency	Organic	Mechanistic	Organic	Mechanistic	Organic
Crisis due to	Absence of administrative leadership	Control of employees	Inadequate coordination	Stifling of innovation	Psychological saturation

Adapted from: Larry E. Greiner, "Evolution and Revolution as Organizations Grow," *Harvard Business Review* 50 (July–August 1972), pp. 37–46.

Box 5.2

Sun Microsystems' Teething Troubles

Sun Microsystems' joyride was interrupted last year when it hit a $20 million quarterly loss, the first deficit in more than five years. With its hugely successful line of computer workstations for engineers, the eight-year-old high-tech *wunderkind* has grown at a rate of 114 percent. But a spate of problems appeared last year when Sun introduced a new series of products. Component shortages delayed delivery of the machines; a senior executive quit, citing differences over strategy; and a newly installed management information system malfunctioned, throwing Sun's accounting into disarray.

In growth-speak, Sun was suffering "product transition syndrome," an ailment that afflicts many young organizations as they try to broaden their scope. Chief executive Scott McNealy responded by imposing cost controls and streamlining Sun's organization, which had proliferated willy-nilly. The remedy worked: According to analysts' estimates, Sun finished its 1990 fiscal year in June with sales up 39 percent to $2.4 billion, and profits up 89 percent to $115 million.

Source: William E. Sheeline, "Avoiding Growth's Perils," *Fortune*, August 13, 1990, pp. 55–58.

Whereas Greiner's model views the stages of growth as predictable and indeed inevitable, the last set of models view managerial action as the key to bringing about organizational change. The source of change is key managers and hence internal, although the managers themselves may be responding to environmental pressures or bringing about change to realize their favored goals.

There are two major types of internal-adaptive models:
1. process of innovation, and
2. planned change.

The innovation process describes the ways by which an organization adopts new ideas—ideas that are new to itself, the industry, or the market. Innovation is thus a special class of change; the term *change* is broader in scope, as it refers to change in strategy, structure, and so on.

Process of Innovation

Models of innovation describe the key activities that have to be completed before a new idea is adopted by an organization. Key managers have to ensure that certain elements exist in organizations for adoption to occur.[6] If any of them is missing, the change process will fail. There are five required elements of the change process:

1. **Need.** The starting point for change is dissatisfaction with the existing state of affairs. Managers may be dissatisfied for two reasons: first, when they perceive a problem, such as customers complaining or losing market share; or second, when they sense an opportunity.

2. **Idea.** An idea may be a model, concept, or plan that can be implemented by an organization. Ideas may come from within an organization or from outside. Normally, an idea has to be matched with the need for it to be adopted.

3. **Adoption.** Adoption occurs when decision makers choose to go ahead with a proposed idea. For adoption to occur, some key managers have to approve of the idea.

4. **Implementation.** When organizational members actually use the idea, then adoption is complete. (This is a very important step, since without it, the previous steps are of no avail.)

5. **Resources.** Change does not happen on its own; it requires time and resources. When resources are withheld from the change process, the adoption process will very likely not flourish.

This process is presented in Figure 5.7.

A number of key points about the process are important. First, the need or idea may originate in the environment; however, managers must perceive the need or recognize the idea for organizational change to occur. Second, needs and ideas are listed simultaneously, since either may come first. Some change is driven by ideas, as in the case of many new technologies. Some others may be driven by severe need, as in the case of a cure for

FIGURE 5.7

Process of innovation adoption

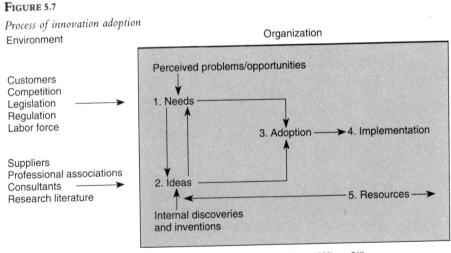

Source: Richard Daft, *Organization Theory* (St. Paul, Minn.: West Publishing, 1988), p. 269.

AIDS. Finally, resources are important at all stages in the process; if they are withheld, adoption may come to a halt.

Planned Change Processes

The second type of internal-adaptive model utilizes some of the ideas of innovation adoption in bringing about change in organizations. The change itself may not be based on new ideas. The second section of this book is devoted entirely to planned change approaches, and hence, we will not deal with them here.

Summary

There are various ways in which organizations change. The population ecology model captures how environments select certain organizational forms over others. The resource dependence model enumerates the strategies by which organizations can acquire scarce resources and thus ensure their effectiveness. Institutional theorists point to imitation as a means by which organizations cope with uncertainty. The life-cycle model describes certain inevitable patterns in the life of an organization. Both innovation and the planned change process describe how managers within an organization deliberately bring about new ideas and change in organizations. These differences are summarized in Table 5.3.

Implications for Managerial Action

As we have seen in this chapter, there are a large number of models that describe how organizations change. If we step back from the models and

TABLE 5.3   **Differences among Key Models**

	Model of Change				
Characteristic	Population Ecology	Resource Dependence	Institutional Theory	Life Cycle	Innovation
Type of change	Survival or failure	Effectiveness	Similarity among organizations	Aging of organization	Adoption of new idea
Source of change	Environment	Environmental actors	Other organizations	Internal dynamics	Managers
Mechanism of change	Selection	Dependence on external resources	Imitation	Natural causes	Managerial decisions

ask about their meaning for managerial action, several implications stand out:

1. Many changes in organizations take place without deliberate managerial action. Some changes are created by the environment, while some arise from the internal dynamics generated by the growth of an organization.

2. Thus, organizational effectiveness is not wholly attributable to managers; some of the successes and some of the failures are attributable to environmental and natural causes. The reverse is equally true: Managers may take the credit for some of the success and blame for some of the failures of an organization.

3. Managers need to pay attention to environmental selection criteria: When an organization does not meet these criteria, it should attempt to change. One aspect of this is the need for resources; managers must ensure the continued flow of resources from the environment.

4. Managers must also pay attention to the internal problems of their organizations, since an inability to resolve the problems may lead to organizational failure.

5. Imitation is an effective way of coping with uncertainty; there is nothing shameful about borrowing from another organization's success.

6. Planned change requires coupling of needs and ideas, resource support, and key management's approval.

Chapter Summary

Partly as a consequence of the failure of many planned change efforts—organization development and design—scholars began to formulate theoretical models of how organizations change. These change theorists, unlike contingency theorists, focus more on description than on prescribing managerial action. Although there are important differences among theories, they share the view that organizations are open systems.

Change theories may be distinguished along two dimensions: (1) source of change, whether external or internal; and (2) type of change, whether occurring naturally or coming about through managerial action.

Population ecologists view the environment as the source of change. They invoke a three-stage model of change: variation, selection, and retention. Thus, for the change to begin, there must be differences among organizations that are competing for the same pool of resources. In the presence of such variation, some organizations are preferred by the environment. The selected organizations are retained until the environment changes or new organizations are founded, which reintroduces variation.

Resource dependence theorists and institutional theorists also view the environment as the source of change, but focus on managerial action. Resource dependence theorists suggest that managers can ameliorate the dependence on the environment by (1) complying, (2) engaging in information control through lobbying and public relations, or (3) entering into collective action such as joint ventures or trade associations. Institutional theorists argue that managers imitate other successful organizations. Imitation leads to similarity among organizations in the same environment.

Life-cycle theorists describe the naturally occurring stages in the life of an organization. Greiner describes five stages: birth, growth through direction, growth through delegation, growth through coordination, and growth through collaboration. Greiner argues that organizations alternate between organic and mechanistic forms as they grow over time.

Both innovation and planned change theorists focus on managerial action to bring about change. Innovation focuses on ideas new to an organization, whereas planned change covers a broader range of actions. According to these theorists, change requires (1) coupling of felt need with a solution, (2) top management commitment, and (3) implementation—probably the most crucial stage. Resources are required in all stages.

By implication, change theorists conclude that managers need to take action both externally and internally, as well as monitor changes triggered by external and internal forces outside their control.

It is clear from the above discussion that there are many sources of change for an organization. It is also clear that since human beings have limited information-processing capability, managers may not be able to pay attention to all sources of change at any single point in time. Hence, any planned change approach requires them to focus on certain goals to the exclusion of others. This leads us to the question of organizational effectiveness; we will take this up in the next chapter.

Specialized Terms

Population ecology model
- Variation
- Selection
- Retention

Resource dependence model
Institutional theory
Organizational life cycle
Innovation

Discussion Questions

1. What is the population ecology model?
2. How does an organization craft responses to resource scarcity?
3. What are the problems that organizational growth brings about?
4. Sketch the process of innovation adoption.
5. What can managers learn from change theorists?
★6. Compare and contrast the various models of change.
★7. How may the process of planned change differ along the stages of organizational life cycle?

Applied
8. You are the new Chief Information Officer (CIO) of a large company hired to introduce computer-based information systems. How would you visualize the process of introduction?
★9. How will your responses to the above question change if you are the CIO of a (a) start-up firm, (b) medium-sized company?

End Notes

1. Deutschman, "Why Universities Are Shrinking," *Fortune,* September 24, 1990, pp. 104–8.
2. This section is drawn from Howard Aldrich, *Organizations and Environments* (Englewood-Cliffs, N.J.: Prentice Hall, 1979).
3. Jeffrey Pfeffer and Gerald R. Salancik, *The External Control of Organizations* (New York: Harper & Row, 1978), p. 2.
4. This section is based on Pfeffer and Salancik, *The External Control of Organizations.*
5. Paul J. DiMaggio and Walter W. Powell, "The Iron Cage Revisited: Institutional Isomorphism and Collective Rationality in Organizational Fields," *American Sociological Review* 48 (1983), pp. 147–60.
6. This section is drawn from (1) Richard Daft, "Bureaucratic versus Nonbureaucratic Structure in the Process of Innovation and Change," in *Perspectives in Organizational Sociology: Theory and Research,* ed. Samuel B. Bacharach (Greenwich, Conn.: JAI Press, 1982), pp. 129–66; and (2) Richard Daft, *Organization Theory and Design* (St. Paul, Minn.: West Publishing, 1988).

★This is an advanced-level question.

6 ORGANIZATIONAL EFFECTIVENESS

Chapter Outline

The ninth annual Corporate Reputations Survey that appeared in the 1990 *Fortune* 500 and *Fortune* Service 500 directories includes 306 companies in 32 industry groups. The survey polled more than 8,000 senior executives, outside directors, and financial analysts. They were asked to rate the largest companies—defined as those with sales of at least $500 million—in their own industry on eight attributes of reputation, using a scale of 0 (poor) to 10 (excellent). The attributes were quality of management; quality of products or services; innovativeness; long-term investment value; financial soundness; ability to attract, develop, and keep talented people; community and environmental responsibility; and wise use of corporate assets.

Companies are assigned to a group based on the industry or service that contributed most to their 1989 sales, and all made public filings of key financial information.

For the fifth year in a row, Merck, the world's largest maker of prescription drugs, earned the highest rating out of 306 major corporations. Runner-up Rubbermaid bounced back to the No. 2 slot after a one-year hiatus in third place. Some old friends rejoined the two champs at the top. Johnson & Johnson, last seen among the top 10 in 1986, rose four notches to No. 8. Boeing finally launched its new 777 and flew home to roost at No. 9, up from No. 11 last year. Eli Lilly, the only newcomer, leapfrogged 19 places to tie for 10th place with Liz Claiborne.

The Most Admired Companies

Rank			
This Year	*Last Year*	*Company*	*Score*
1	1	MERCK Pharmaceuticals	8.86
2	3	RUBBERMAID Rubber and plastics products	8.58
3	4	PROCTER & GAMBLE Soaps, cosmetics	8.42
4	6★	WAL-MART STORES Retailing	8.35
5	6★	PEPSICO Beverages	8.19
6	8	3M Scientific and photo equipment	8.12
7	12	JOHNSON & JOHNSON Pharmaceuticals	8.01
8	11	BOEING Aerospace	7.92
9	29	ELI LILLY Pharmaceuticals	7.90
10	13	LIZ CLAIBORNE Apparel	7.90

★Wal-Mart Stores and PepsiCo were tied in score last year.

The biggest surprise of the survey was Philip Morris's dizzying descent from No. 2 to No. 79. The reason: Having acquired Kraft in 1988, it has switched categories from tobacco to food, which now accounts for over 50% of sales. More than 8,000 top executives, directors, and security analysts are asked to rank companies in their industry group, and Philip Morris's new judges in the food business didn't think much of its best-known product—cigarettes. The director of one food company put it bluntly: "Anyone in the tobacco business must be severely downgraded." Another executive wrote, "I downgraded companies with political action committees, products that kill, and those insensitive to 'green' issues." Philip Morris's scores for product quality and community and environmental responsibility fell accordingly, accounting for most of its drop on the list.[1]

As illustrated in the chapter introduction case from *Fortune*, the business press frequently publishes scorecards of firms based on several criteria. In addition to the press, rating agencies, shareholders, employees, customers, government, and others make judgments about the effectiveness of organizations.

What is an effective organization? How do we measure the effectiveness of an organization? How do we conclude that a particular organization is effective? In this chapter, we will summarize the contributions of organization theory to our understanding of the concept of organizational effectiveness and its implications for management. But first, let us define the concept.

What Is Organizational Effectiveness?

In the broadest sense organizational effectiveness refers to human judgments about whether an organization is functioning satisfactorily. For managers, these judgments become the basis of initiating organizational change: When effectiveness is not satisfactory, changes are essential. Although this definition may seem obvious to many, we emphasize three major points implied by the definition.

First, in this chapter, we focus on the *organizational level* of analysis. Thus, effectiveness refers to an organization or a major segment of it, and does not refer to individual managers. For example, *Fortune* rated organizations, not specific managers in them. As we have seen in the previous chapter, among the many sources of change in organizations, only some are attributable to managers. Thus, an organization may be effective in spite of managerial action. Similarly, sometimes effective managerial action may be to dissolve an ineffective organization.

Second, conclusions about organizational effectiveness are ultimately *human* judgments. *Fortune,* for example, averaged the judgments of several executives nationwide to arrive at its ratings.[2] This idea is unique to organization theory. Unlike some other disciplines such as economics and finance, which emphasize "objective" measures such as profits and shareholder return, we consider organizational effectiveness ultimately to be a *subjective judgment.* Although the objective indices may be utilized, they are interpreted by human beings to arrive at their assessment of an organization.

Third, there are many groups of people making judgments about organizational effectiveness: shareholders, customers, competitors, employees, even government and the judiciary. These different groups invoke different criteria and make different judgments. Thus, when we focus on a specific organization, different groups of people may give us somewhat different responses to the question, "Is this organization effective?"

If organizational effectiveness is a subjective judgment that differs from individual to individual, why study it? For two major reasons. First, some criteria of effectiveness lie behind most managerial action. Thus, a theoretical understanding is useful to set goals and clarify the purpose of action. Second, managers need to be sensitive to the judgments made by *others* about their organization since the outsiders may have profound influence on their functioning.

Linkage to the Systems Model

There are four important connections between the concept of organizational effectiveness and the systems model:

1. The open systems model suggests that effectiveness of an organization is dependent on the nature of the relations it establishes with its environments as well as on the management of interdependencies within the organization.
2. Related to the above, agents both external and internal to the organization arrive at judgments about organizational effectiveness.
3. The systems model distinguishes between two types of effectiveness: (a) the negative feedback processes refer to the extent to which an organization achieves its goals; (b) *positive feedback* refers to the quality of the goals themselves.
4. Different subsystems within an organization—functional, social, political, cultural, and informational—emphasize different types of effectiveness criteria.

Table 6.1 summarizes these connections.

In the remainder of this chapter, we provide an overview of the concept of organizational effectiveness. First, we trace the historical developments and philosophical assumptions underlying the concept. Second, we sketch the major theoretical developments. Third, we describe the key managerial implications. Fourth, we provide a systems theoretic review and conclude with a summary.

TABLE 6.1 **Linkage to Systems Model**

Systems Concepts	Operationalization
Open systems	Environment and powerful external constituencies influence effectiveness criteria
Stability versus change	Organizations pursue multiple criteria of effectiveness over time
Levels	Different levels pursue different often conflicting criteria. Organizational level influences individual and group levels
Subsystems	Each subsystem espouses its own set of criteria

Underpinnings

Historical Underpinnings

Over the years, many ways of measuring organizational effectiveness have come into existence. In the beginning, most attempts were confined to profit-making institutions. The accounting principles codified the way by which annual statements may be prepared and audited by an independent agency—the accounting firm—so that shareholders may evaluate how the organization is doing. With the emergence of an active capital market in the United States, these statements were augmented by the stock price of the firm, widely available on a day-to-day basis, which by one theory contained all the economic information of a firm.[3]

Over the years, the performance data about a firm was augmented by other measures such as its inherent riskiness. For example, *Value Line,* a business publication, routinely publishes *Beta,* a measure of the riskiness of a firm's stock. Similarly, several rating agencies such as A. M. Best company began to provide credit ratings of companies, information that was useful to the lenders and bondholders of the company. These measures were economic and useful mainly to investors—shareholders or lenders.

In addition to the above measures, several other institutions were interested in the performance of an organization. Consider:

> During the 1960s and onward, government institutions became interested in the degree to which organizations met social objectives such as reducing the stress on the environment, hiring minorities, or conforming to fair employment practices.

> During the 1980s, the judiciary became increasingly interested in the behavior of investment banks, partly as result of the excesses of people like Michael Milliken, who were alleged to have violated insider trading laws.

> Similarly, consumer activism triggered publications such as *Consumer Digest,* which routinely evaluated firms' products from the point of view of the customers.

Box 6.1

Evaluation Research: A Brief History

Evaluation research is the systematic application of social research procedures in assessing the conceptualization and design, implementation, and utility of social intervention programs. In other words, evaluation research involves the use of social research methodologies to judge and improve the planning, monitoring, effectiveness, and efficiency of health, education, welfare, and other human service programs.

Although evaluation research emphasizes the application of social research procedures to the evaluation of social and human service programs, the approaches considered have utility in other spheres of activity as well. For example, the mass communication and advertising industries use fundamentally the same approaches in assessing media programs and marketing products; commercial and industrial corporations evaluate the procedures they use for selection and promotion of employees and organization of their work forces; political candidates develop their campaigns by evaluating the voter appeal of different strategies; consumer products are subjected to market testing; and administrators in both public and private sectors are continually assessing the clerical, fiscal, and interpersonal practices within their organizations.

Systematic, data-based evaluations are a relatively modern development, coinciding

with the growth and refinement of social research methods, as well as with ideological, political, and demographic changes that have occurred during this century. Actually, evaluation research can be traced back to the rise of the scientific enterprise during the 1600s. Thomas Hobbes and his contemporaries were concerned with numerical measures to be used in assessing social conditions and in identifying the causes of mortality, morbidity, and social disorganization.

In the modern era, commitment to the systematic evaluation of programs in such fields as education and public health can be traced to efforts at the turn of the century to provide literacy and occupational training by the most effective and economical means, and to reduce mortality and morbidity from infectious diseases. As far back as the 1930s, there were social scientists who advocated the application of rigorous social research methods to the assessment of programs.

From such beginnings in the 1930s and earlier, applied social research received considerable impetus. Its employment increased during World War II; Stouffer and his associates worked with the U.S. army to develop continual monitoring of soldier morale as well as to evaluate personnel and propaganda policies. The Office of War Information used sample

These agencies broadened the domains in which the performance of a firm was scrutinized.

During the last two decades, the concept of effectiveness was extended beyond economic institutions to include other agencies such as governments and sometimes major programs within them. This led to a set of activities called *evaluation research*. Evaluation researchers tried to discover, improve, and especially apply scientific methods to evaluate the effectiveness

Box 6.1 continued

surveys to measure civilian morale continually. At the same time, a host of smaller studies assessed the efficacy of price controls and campaigns to modify American eating habits. Similar social science efforts were mounted in Britain and elsewhere.

The period immediately following World War II saw the beginning of large-scale programs designed to meet needs for urban development and housing, technological and cultural education, occupational training, and preventive health activities. It was also during this time that major commitments were made to international programs for family planning, health and nutrition, and rural community development. Expenditures were huge, and consequently were accompanied by demands for "knowledge of results."

By the end of the 1950s, large-scale evaluation programs were commonplace. Social scientists were engaged in evaluations of delinquency prevention programs, felon rehabilitation projects, psychotherapeutic and psychopharmacological treatments, public housing programs, and community organization activities. Not only were such studies undertaken in the United States, Europe, and other industrialized countries, but in lesser developed nations as well: Increasingly, programs for family planning in Asia, nutrition and health care in Latin America, and agricultural and community development in Africa included

evaluation components. Knowledge of the methods of social research, including sample surveys and complex statistical procedures, became widespread. Computer technology made it possible to conduct large-scale studies and sophisticated statistical analyses.

While there is continuity in the development of the evaluation field, a qualitative change has occurred. Even as late as 1967, Suchman's definition of evaluation research as the application of social research techniques to the study of large-scale human service programs was a useful and sufficient delineation of the field. However, this definition fails to take into account the extensive influence on the evaluation enterprise of its consumers—policymakers, program planners, and administrators.

Evaluation research is more than the application of methods. It is also a *political* and *managerial* activity, an input into the complex mosaic from which policy decisions and allocations emerge for the planning, design, implementation, and continuation of programs to better the human condition. In this sense, evaluation research also needs to be seen as an integral part of the social policy and public administration movements.

Source: Peter H. Rossi and Howard E. Freeman, *Evaluation: A Systematic Approach* (Beverly Hills, CA: Sage Publishers, 1985).

of programs ranging from educational to political campaigns. See Box 6.1 for a summary of the history of evaluation research.

Just like evaluation research over the years, the concept of organizational effectiveness was extended beyond the economic interests of the investors to include the interests of many other groups affected by an organization. Indeed, the *Fortune* rating in the chapter introduction case is an example of how the concept of effectiveness is getting broader. Further, the concept is employed in an increasing variety of organizations—for example, noneconomic and regulatory organizations.

Philosophical Underpinnings

Two major ideas permeate our discussion of organizational effectiveness.

First, we distinguish between efficiency and effectiveness. At the turn of the century, scholars working from a closed systems perspective advanced the concept of efficiency, which pertained to the internal workings of an organization. Efficiency referred to the resource inputs utilized in producing a unit of output. It is often expressed as a ratio of output to input. Consider two organizations, A and B, both producing automobiles. If Organization A produces an automobile with less capital, raw material, and human inputs than Organization B, then A is more efficient than B.

When the open systems view of organizations gained prominence as a concept for guiding managerial action, efficiency was replaced by effectiveness. Open system theorists suggested that since the prime goal of an organization is adaptation to the environment, it is far more important to do things that are appropriate to the survival of an organization. Efficiency may be important in some cases, but not always. Efficiency pertains to doing things right, whereas effectiveness pertains to doing the right things.

Second, and related to our discussion of organizational change in the previous chapter, we view organizational effectiveness as a concept that guides managerial action, but not all types of change. Although organizations face many challenges at any particular point in time, managers choose to act on only some of them. Implicit in these actions is some criteria of organizational effectiveness. Planned change strategies thus pursue certain criteria of effectiveness.

However, not all change is guided by effectiveness criteria. It would be incorrect to suggest that environmental selection improves an organization. The selection process is value neutral and amoral; it is simply in the direction of ensuring greater fit between (surviving) organizational forms and environment. Nor would it be correct to say that life-cycle evolution is in the direction of increasing organizational effectiveness. Rather, as organizations move forward in their life cycle, they attain higher levels of complexity, not necessarily greater effectiveness.

Nonetheless, organizational effectiveness provides a major link between organization theory and planned change.

Theoretical Underpinnings

Over the past four decades, our understanding of effectiveness has improved, both because of clear theoretical reasoning as well as rigorous research. What criteria of effectiveness do organizations follow? What factors distinguish between effectiveness criteria?[4] These questions have fascinated many scholars in the past two decades. Their research has led us to be skeptical of much of the commonsense beliefs about organizations. Thus, although an unsophisticated onlooker may conclude that a specific organization pursues one particular goal or that its managers determine the effectiveness criteria, we now know these beliefs to be only partly true. Organizations pursue a complex web of effectiveness criteria, and many actors other than managers influence these criteria.

The idea that organizations pursue *multiple criteria* is now widely accepted in literature. Whenever managers are queried about their goals and criteria of effectiveness, they give us not one criterion but a list of criteria. One example of multiple criteria is the rating system used in the chapter opening case. Another is from a survey of U.S. business corporations. The 12 goals listed as being important to these companies are shown in Table 6.2.

These criteria differ along two major dimensions: (1) focus and (2) time perspective.

Focus

Various effectiveness criteria focus on different aspects of an organizational system's functioning: inputs, conversion process, and outputs. This has led to three different approaches to effectiveness: (1) system resource, (2) internal process, and (3) goal. Figure 6.1 displays the focus of each approach.

System resource approach: In this approach, the organization is effective to the degree that it can acquire scarce and valued resources from the environment. Examples: bargaining position with respect to

---

TABLE 6.2   **Corporate Goals**

Goal	Percent of Corporations
Profitability	89%
Growth	82
Market share	66
Social responsibility	65
Employee welfare	62
Product quality and service	60
Research and development	54
Diversification	51
Efficiency	50
Financial stability	49
Resource conservation	39
Management development	35

Source: Adapted from Y. K. Shetty, "New Look at Corporate Goals," *California Management Review* 22, no. 2 (1979), pp. 71–79.

environment (e.g., suppliers), flexibility, adaptability.

Internal process approach: In this approach, the effectiveness of an organization is judged by the degree to which it has a well-oiled internal process. Examples: morale, supervisory interest, quality of the decision-making process.

Goal approach: This consists of identifying an organization's goals and assessing how well the organization is attaining them. Examples: customer satisfaction, shareholder value.

Just as the focus of effectiveness criteria is different, so is the underlying time perspective.

Time Perspective

We have already pointed out in our discussion of the contingency perspective that the time frame over which managers contemplate action plans influences the choices available to them. Indeed, time considerations enter into the generation and application of effectiveness criteria. Thus, the effectiveness criteria may vary depending on whether a relatively shorter or longer time frame is adopted.

There are obviously conflicts among criteria that emphasize the long term on the one hand and the short term on the other. If current production, a short-run effectiveness criterion, is maximized at the expense of research and development investments in future products, an organization may ultimately find itself with an outmoded product and threatened for its very survival, a long-run criterion.[5] As shown in Box 6.2, in recent years, U.S. corporations have been criticized for their emphasis on short-run criteria.

Contingencies Affecting the Choice of Effectiveness Criteria

As we have noted earlier, planned change efforts involve some criteria of effectiveness. What contingencies determine the effectiveness criteria?

We can identify five major factors that influence the choice of organizational effectiveness criteria for managerial action at any point in time: (1)

FIGURE 6.1

Focus of organizational effectiveness

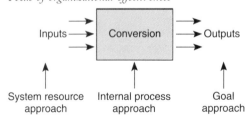

Box 6.2

Short-Run Orientation of U.S. Businesses

One of the attitudes that pervades U.S. business is the concentration by managers on the short time frame. This shortsighted attitude manifests itself in the investment approval system, in the ways in which international businesses are managed, in attitudes toward worker security and job enrichment, and in issues of quality. This attitude is also evident in the propensity of many U.S. managers to spend a significant portion of their time rearranging industrial assets. Finesse in legal and financial manipulating often yields greater short-term rewards than skill in increasing productivity.

The origins of the emphasis on a short-term view lie in the systems of evaluation in many U.S. companies. Perhaps the problem begins with the stock market, the banks, and the business press, all of which respond quarterly or even weekly to earnings and sales figures, and which find it difficult to evaluate short-term sacrifices undertaken for long-term returns.

Whatever the external reason, internal evaluation systems rarely look to long-term results. Managers who raise prices may be valued highly for the improved earnings they provide during their three-year tenure before

promotion, but their successors will suffer the consequences—loss of market share and long-term profitability.

Similarly, bonuses are often tied to yearly volume, cash flow, and/or profit targets. Managers sometimes engage in activities counterproductive to the long-term interests of the company in order to "meet their numbers." Such activities may include depleting inventories at the end of the year to improve ROIs or cash flows, relaxing quality standards to meet volume of production targets, or delaying needed expense investments to meet profit targets. These managers are not being irresponsible or dishonest; they are only adhering to the priorities set by the internal system of evaluation.

Systems for evaluating workers can also be shortsighted. Greater worker responsibility and participation require investments of time and energy in the short run, though they generally yield higher long-run benefits than systems based on discipline, fear, and distrust.

Source: Adapted from Ira C. Magaziner and Robert B. Reich, *Minding America's Business* (New York: Harcourt Brace Jovanovich, 1982), pp. 193–94.

managerial values, (2) stage of life cycle, (3) environment, (4) constituencies, and (5) types of organizations.

Managerial Values

Managers influence the choice of organizational effectiveness criteria because of their preference for doing things in particular ways.[6] Goals represent judgments of top managers: thus, Tom Watson was fanatical about customers at IBM, Ross Perot emphasized achievement at EDS, now a part of General Motors, and Jack Welch is pushing internationalization at General Electric.

The managerial values that influence the functioning of an organization may be described using two factors:

1. organizational focus.
2. organizational structure.

Organizational focus refers to whether the dominant values are internal or external to the organization. Internal focus reflects a management concern for the well-being and efficiency of employees, whereas an external orientation represents the well-being of an organization with respect to the environment.

Organization structure refers to whether stability or flexibility is the dominant structural consideration. Stability reflects a management preference for top-down control similar to the mechanistic structure, whereas flexibility represents a preference for adaptation and change similar to the organic structure.

Based on these two dimensions, organizations may be classified into four differing models of effectiveness. Each model reflects a different emphasis with respect to basic value dilemmas.

Open Systems Model

The open systems model reflects a combination of external focus and flexible structure. The primary goals are growth and resource acquisition. The organization accomplishes these goals through the subgoals of flexibility, readiness, and a positive external evaluation. The dominant value in this model is establishing a good relationship with the environment to acquire resources and grow in size. This model is similar in some ways to the system resource model described earlier.

Rational Goal Model

The rational goal model represents the values of structural control and external focus. The primary goals are productivity, efficiency, and profit. The organization wants to achieve output goals in a controlled way. Subgoals that facilitate these outcomes are internal planning and goal setting, which are rational management tools. The rational goal model is similar to the goal approach described earlier.

Internal Process Model

The internal process model reflects the values of internal focus and structural control. The primary outcome is a stable organizational setting that maintains itself in an orderly way. Organizations that are well established in the environment and simply want to maintain their current position would fit this model. Subgoals for this model include mechanisms for efficient communication, information management, and decision making.

Human Relations Model

The human relations model incorporates the values of an internal focus and a flexible structure. Here, the concern is on the development of human resources. Employees are given opportunities for autonomy and development. Management works toward the subgoals of cohesion, morale, and training opportunities. Organizations adopting this model are more concerned with employees than with the environment.

This discussion about the models is summarized in Figure 6.2.

Just as managers influence the choice of organizational effectiveness, so also does the life stage of an organization.

Stage of Life Cycle

We have seen in the previous chapter that as organizations grow, they pass through various life stages. Different managers come to dominate organizations in each life stage, since the organization swings back and forth between organic and mechanistic modes. Consequently, managerial preferences change over the life stages. For example, a preference for control is

FIGURE 6.2

Managerial values for effectiveness

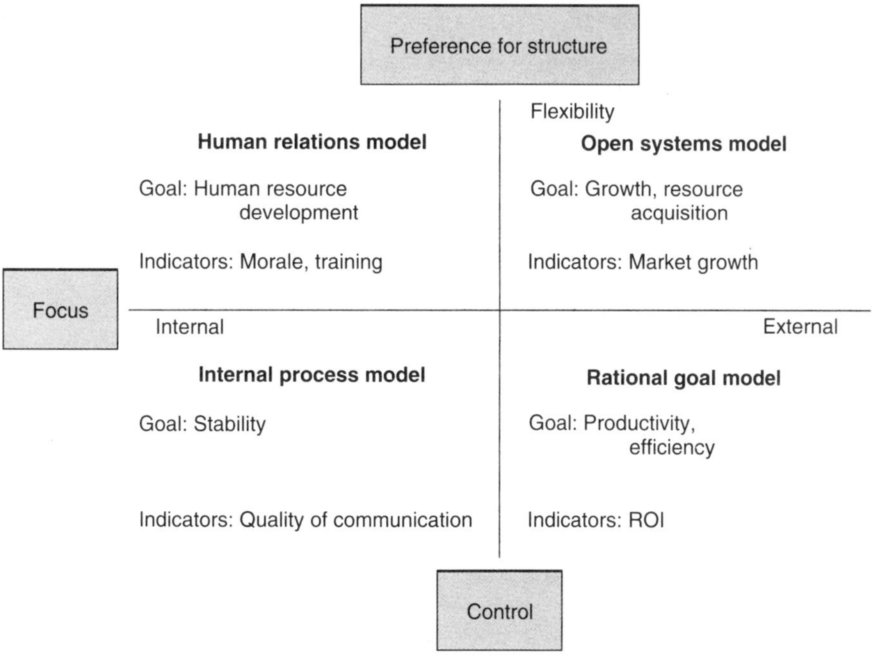

correlated with mechanistic modes, whereas a preference for flexibility takes the organization in the organic direction.

In the early stage of development, an organization is struggling to survive: Its major tasks are to develop an environmental niche and to acquire sufficient resources from the environment. The focus is thus external, and the organization may swing from a focus on flexibility to one on control. In the middle stages, when the organization is firmly established, the emphasis shifts to goals of efficiency and output levels. In the later stages of development, primary goals tend to deal with outputs and environmental relationships. Since the organization is well established, resource acquisition is taken for granted. It becomes concerned with its role in the environment and may focus on community and constituent satisfaction, along with efficiency, outputs, and profits. These ideas about the linkages between effectiveness and stage of development were tested in a field study described in Box 6.3.

As shown in the Box 6.3, the goals and effectiveness of the New York State Department of Mental Hygiene shifted over time.

Of course, this single case study does not provide conclusive evidence that our model of organizational life cycles and effectiveness applies to all new organizations. The case does provide, however, an *example* of the potential utility of this model for diagnosing and predicting organizational phenomena.

Environment

Although many constituencies are external to the environment, environmental conditions in addition may influence effectiveness criteria in two ways:

1. Environmental conditions may influence the *choice of criteria*. For example, when resources are scarce, organizational goals may define resource acquisition and efficiency criteria. Growth may be emphasized when resources can be easily acquired.
2. The time span over which effectiveness is measured may depend on environmental conditions. For example, in markets where product life cycles are short, return on investment may be measured over short periods of time, whereas in the pharmaceutical industry, with long delays, it may be defined over a 15- to 20-year horizon.

Constituencies

A third reason why organizations pursue different effectiveness criteria is because many individuals influence the choice of criteria. Discussion of effectiveness criteria ultimately leads to the question: who is being served by an organization? Indeed, organizations affect the lives of many groups of individuals: shareholders, customers, employees, creditors, suppliers, government regulators, and the host community, to name a few. All these groups of people make demands on the organization. They are called *stakeholders* or *constituencies*.

Different constituencies advocate different criteria of effectiveness. Indeed, there is little in common among the criteria employed by the various parties who assess organizational effectiveness. This was documented by Frank K. Friedlander and Hal Pickle in a study of small businesses in Texas (see Box 6.4).[7]

This research is significant in two ways. First, although the research was confined to the Texas small businesses, the ideas have greater appeal. Thus, many of the demands made on organizations may often be incompatible. Constituents of an organization may not have similar interests.

Second, the researcher's way of arriving at effectiveness deserves attention. The researchers assessed organization effectiveness in four steps: first they identified constituents, second their interests, then they operationalized the interests in measurable fashion, and finally they used a number of methods to measure the indicator. Our own suggested way of measuring effectiveness will include these steps. Indeed, organizations find it difficult to fulfill simultaneously the variety of demands made on them.

Since we cannot expect consensus among different constituencies concerning organizational effectiveness criteria, just how do various affected constituencies influence these criteria? Some of the constituencies are likely to be more satisfied than others with an organization—that is, their criteria are the ones to which the managers pay attention.

We make a simple statement: Managers will pay attention to the effectiveness criteria that are *important to powerful constituencies*. To understand how the process works, it is useful to classify effectiveness criteria along two dimensions:

1. Power of the constituency.
2. Importance to the constituency.

As shown in Figure 6.3, managers will tend to pay the greatest attention to criteria important to powerful constituencies, satisfice those less powerful, and ignore unimportant constituencies. If they ignore the powerful constituencies, they will be replaced by others who will pay attention to them. The story of Texas Air, presented in Box 6.5, illustrates this idea. Frank Lorenzo lost his empire because he antagonized some very powerful constituencies.

Types of Organizations

Do criteria of effectiveness differ among different types of organizations? In order to answer this question, we first draw a distinction between market and nonmarket organizations.

Box 6.3

New York State Department of Mental Hygiene

In order to explore further these hypothesized relationships between the stages of life-cycle development and changes in emphasis given to criteria of organizational effectiveness, two researchers, Robert Quinn and Kim Cameron decided to track an organization over time and to observe changes in its stages of development. Because the processes by which development occurs are also important, simply comparing different organizations in different stages of development is not appropriate. An organization had to be found in which observable changes in stage development occurred, and from which evidence for a change in the emphasis on effectiveness criteria could be produced.

The organization selected was a developmental center in the former New York State Department of Mental Hygiene. The events described here are from observations made over a three-year period, 1974–76. These observations are part of a "process research approach" in which interviews, observations, and archival techniques were employed.

The focal organization served children with developmental disorders and the handicapped of all ages in a six-county area. It included the development center and seven "teams," or subsystems, which operated in the six counties. A staff of over 800 and an operating budget of over $9 million were in place during the observation years.

The center was directed from its establishment in 1969 by a psychiatrist who was nationally known for his writings and for his work in the area of community mental health. He was a charismatic leader who tended to generate either extreme loyalty or opposition. While few of his associates felt indifferent towards him, both supporters and critics were in agreement that he was a near genius in conceptualizing innovative solutions to the problems of service delivery.

The director's past work and writings in community mental health had generated a series of prescriptions for the treatment of the mentally disabled. These prescriptions became the organizational ideology. Collectively, they were called the developmental treatment model. This model emphasized the broad participation of parents, consumers, and the community, as well as focusing on the development of independence and self-reliance by clients. This developmental ideology was on the cutting edge of the deinstitutionalization movement that was then sweeping the mental health profession.

The center was composed of seven teams and a support group. Although the teams were relatively autonomous, they followed a common set of guidelines. The teams were characterized by numerous disciplines (social work, child psychiatry, special education, pediatrics, psychology, rehabilitation counseling, etc.), and were staffed to maintain a balance among at least four areas: social-recreational, psychological, educational-vocational, and health care. For every professional hired, at least one person from

Box 6.3 continued

the community (with a bachelor's degree or less) also had to be hired.

The organizational structure was a reflection of the philosophy of its director. For example, the director had no office, but went where he believed he was needed, establishing a temporary base of operations. Strong emphasis was placed on openness, cooperation, creativity, and innovation. While the director reserved a veto power over group decisions, he seldom used it and most major decisions were arrived at through participative decision-making techniques. The physical plants of some teams were intentionally too small, because it was believed the overcrowding would encourage members to be in the community rather than in their offices. Dress standards and strict attention to seniority were not in operation. The chain of command was not easily identifiable, and there was a heavy emphasis on face-to-face communication rather than on formal written documents. The organic or ambiguous nature of the structure was illustrated by the fact that, despite attempts to do so, no one had been able to draw an organizational chart that satisfactorily reflected the functioning of the organization.

In the spring of 1975, one of the two major newspapers serving the area began to run an extensive expose of the entire Department of Mental Hygiene. Entitled "Wasted Dollars/Wasted Lives," the series included numerous devastating reports about bureaucratic inefficiency at the central office of the DMH and numerous descriptions about the bleakest as pects of life in institutions. Initially, the focal organization was mentioned only in summary statements. But beginning on May 9, 1975, the program became the primary point of focus in the series.

By July 19, it was reported that the director was asked by the Commissioner to take a six-week leave of absence in the midst of the DMH probe. The DMH investigations centered on administrative and personnel practices at the Center. On September 7, the results of the probe were made public. Findings criticized the director for failing to provide direction, a traditional organization structure, and other necessary controls. It also recommended the top-level administrative staff be relieved of their present duties.

When the probe was completed, the director was reinstated and given one year to address a list of problems. Most had to do with establishing clear lines of authority, clearly identifiable roles, following rules and regulations, and establishing mechanisms of accountability and control.

Not long after the year was over, the director left the state, and he was replaced with a "more administratively minded" director. Thereafter, many staff members left. By the end of the next year, there were few people working in jobs for which they were overqualified, the missionary zeal disappeared, and the Center began to function in a more controlled manner.

Source: Robert E. Quinn and Kim Cameron, "Organizational Life Cycles and Criteria of Effectiveness," *Management Science* 29 (1983), pp. 33–51.

Box 6.4

Friedlander and Pickle's Study

Two researchers, Frank Friedlander and Hal Pickle, wanted to verify that different people, groups, or organizations may have different criteria for evaluating an organization. Thus faced with conflicting demands, an organization must decide which groups to attend to and which to ignore. Favoring one group offends another.

To test their hunches, Friedlander and Pickle studied 97 small businesses in Texas. They identified several internal and external interest groups relevant to the Texas businesses, including owners, employees, customers, suppliers, creditors, the local community, and the federal government. For each group, the authors developed a measure of the organization's effectiveness on the group's criteria. For example, Friedlander and Pickle argued that owners were interested in profits, while employees were interested in their satisfaction with work.

Through a number of methods including direct questioning and the use of records, the researchers developed measures for assessing how effectively each organization was meeting the demands of various constituent groups.

When the indices of group satisfaction were correlated, Friedlander and Pickle discovered that the correlations were low, and even when positive, the correlations between some groups were greater than between others. For example, owner's satisfaction was significantly correlated with customers', employees', and community's satisfaction but not to any other group's. Similarly, creditors' satisfaction was correlated with customers' and the government's satisfaction.

Source: Adapted from Frank Friedlander and Hal Pickle, "Components of Effectiveness in Small Organizations," *Administrative Science Quarterly* 13 (1968), pp. 289–304.

Market organizations. A typical business or profit-making entity is a market organization. Here, the market provides a mechanism for linking the interests of organizational participants and external constituencies in such a manner that the former do not prosper unless they serve the interests of the latter.

Nonmarket organizations. Organizations such as government agencies operate from the outset in nonmarket environments. Thus, a major portion of their output is not directly or indirectly evaluated in any market external to the organization by means of voluntary quid pro quo transactions.

There are three major distinctions between these two types of organizations in terms of effectiveness criteria. First, the effectiveness of business enterprises is *directly* determined by their customers. If their interests are satisfied, they will continue to support the organization; if not, they will withhold their contributions, causing the organization to suffer and fail. In nonmarket organizations, there is no direct relationship between the services an agency provides and the income it receives.

FIGURE 6.3

Managerial strategies toward constituencies

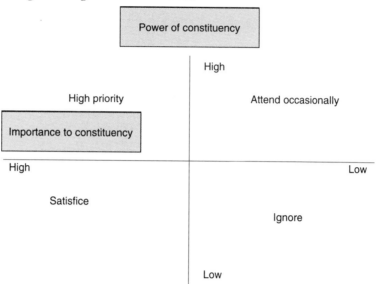

Second, nonmarket organizations are likely to lack *clear output goals.* Whether the goals are to provide for an adequate defense, to fight crime, or to provide education, it is difficult to assess how effective the performance is. Even the recipients of the service often cannot evaluate how good the service is. This is quite unlike the case of market organizations.

Third, and related to both of the above, the *linkage between inputs, internal process, and outputs* tends to be tighter in market organizations than in nonmarket organizations. In profit-making organizations, if the customers like the product, then inputs—especially capital—are likely to flow into the organization; this is not the case in nonmarket organizations.

Taken together, these differences suggest that it is far more difficult to demonstrate the effectiveness of nonmarket than market organizations. As governments have come under pressure from taxpayers to make every dollar count, new techniques have to be developed to ascertain the effectiveness of government agencies. The evaluation research we referred to in the Historical Underpinnings section of this chapter is an attempt to do that. In Box 6.6, we have described how one researcher operationalized the effectiveness of universities. Table 6.3 summarizes the differences between the two types of organizations.

In summary, managerial preferences, organizational life stage, environmental conditions, powerful constituencies, and types of organizations may influence the effectiveness criteria that shape an organization's functioning.

Box 6.5

Frank Lorenzo's Eastern Airlines

The case of Eastern Airlines clearly illustrates the need for both the classification and strategic assessment of key stakeholders. Hindsight provides us with an opportunity to analyze stakeholders far better than Eastern's management could at the time this situation occurred. Nonetheless, stakeholder analysis will also provide superior information and decision making if employed as situations arise. Frank Lorenzo's stormy relationship with the International Association of Machinists (IAM) certainly underscores the need for assessing and classifying key stakeholders.

In early 1989, Frank Lorenzo, chairman of Texas Air Corporation, was faced with the continuing problem of managing a turn around of financially troubled Eastern Airlines—a subsidiary of Texas Air. In addition, there existed a high probability that the IAM would strike. Lorenzo was no novice at such turnarounds, having brought Continental Airlines (another Texas Air subsidiary) back from bankruptcy less than six years earlier. That bankruptcy allowed Continental to free itself of union contracts resulting in a low-cost carrier able to complete with the nation's largest airlines.

To accomplish the turn around at Eastern, Lorenzo chose a retrenchment strategy similar to the one used at Continental, involving wage concessions from all employees. Even though Eastern's unionized pilots and flight attendants agreed to wage concessions after Texas Air acquired Eastern in 1986, the mechanics, baggage handlers, and other ground workers represented by the IAM had not. Eastern sought as much as a 40 percent wage reduction (approximately $178.6 million) from its baggage

handlers and mechanics; however, just before the 1989 strike deadline, Eastern reduced the wage concessions to 28 percent ($125 million). By the March 4, 1989, deadline, no agreement had been reached, so the IAM went on strike. Although the IAM attempted to spread the strike to other transportation industries, the federal courts prevented this maneuver.

Eastern planned to maintain its flight schedule throughout the machinists' strike by having management and other workers fill in for the 8,500 striking IAM workers. However, on March 7, 1989, the Air Line Pilots Association (ALPA) voted to support the IAM with a sympathy strike. By the fifth day of the strike, flights were reduced to 4 percent of the pre-strike level. Because of losses of $4 million per day, on March 9, 1989, Eastern filed for Chapter 11 bankruptcy.

One of Eastern's most important mixed-blessing stakeholders was the ALPA pilots who were flying before the strike. Even though the striking pilots' jobs were clearly in jeopardy, a majority refused to give in to Eastern's management. In fact, when Captain Jack Bavis, the chairman of ALPA, told the pilots that they needed to return to work in September 1989, the striking pilots replaced him with Captain Skip Copeland, who was more of a hardliner. However, in late November, President Bush vetoed legislation that would have set up a special commission to investigate the dispute. With no hope of gaining any concessions, the pilots and flight attendants voted to end their strike. By this time, however, few if any jobs remained open at the airline.

Although Eastern workers owned 25 percent of the company through an earlier settlement

Box 6.5 continued

under Frank Borman, Eastern missed the opportunity to collaborate with the pilots who were members of ALPA. For example if Eastern had offered a gain-sharing program in return for wage or work rule concessions, it might have prevented the pilots from joining the striking machinists. Four of Eastern's most important mixed-blessing-type stakeholders— creditors, the pilot union, the flight attendant union, and travel agents—became nonsupportive stakeholders.

During the early stages of bankruptcy, Lorenzo continued to sell or lease assets, including the Eastern shuttle and 21 Boeing 727s to Donald Trump for $365 million. The sale of the assets was to ensure that a downsized Eastern could survive bankruptcy and reduce the likelihood that striking employees would be able to force concessions from Eastern. During this time, the coalition of unions protested against the sale of these assets, claiming that Texas Air Corporation had already transferred assets from Eastern without paying fair market prices. Moreover, management claims that everything was going according to plan were clearly contradicted by the continuing strike. Consequently, Eastern's creditors became nonsupportive stakeholders who protested every attempt by Eastern to retain cash for operating expenses. Additionally, travel agents discouraged business travelers from booking reservations with Eastern before the strike and did not support the few remaining flights that Eastern could support after declaring bankruptcy. The indictment of Eastern for failing to perform mandatory maintenance on aircraft and falsifying related records alienated even nonbusiness travelers as Eastern struggled to retain market share in 1990.

As hindsight shows, the best defense against the IAM would have been to do whatever was necessary to keep the pilots and flight attendants from joining the strike. Instead, Lorenzo's retrenchment strategy unified the employees against him because he had greatly reduced the value of Eastern through asset sales. As the strike progressed and the company continued to lose money, the question of whether Eastern had any net worth became debatable. Employees recognized that any potential buyer of the airline would demand concessions. They were outraged as they realized that Lorenzo's tactics were designed to reduce their bargaining power. Lorenzo became the villain and striking employees were willing to abandon careers rather than concede to him. Hence, from the start, both the IAM and the ALPA determined that they would only settle for the transfer of Eastern's ownership and recruited buyers for the airline.

In summary, Eastern suffered tremendous losses and continued to lose money until its liquidation in 1991. The airline reported a 1989 operating loss of $852.3 million, and Eastern's market share shrunk from the seventh largest in the United States in early 1989 to the ninth largest by the end of 1989. Matters continued to worsen, and in April 1990, a bankruptcy judge wrested control of Eastern from Texas Air Corporation, appointing a trustee to manage the company. Ironically, as a result of the strike and its aftermath, Frank Lorenzo has resigned from Texas Air and is likely to walk away with $37 million.

Source: Grant T. Savage, Timothy W. Nix, Carlton J. Whitehead, and John D. Blair, "Strategies for Assessing and Managing Organizational Stakeholders," *The Executive* 5, no. 2 (May 1991), pp. 61–75.

Box 6.6

Evaluation of Universities

An instrument developed by Kim Cameron measures organizational effectiveness in institutions of higher education. The instrument relies on judgments of the degree to which the organization possesses characteristics indicative of effective organizations. Using the ratings of 610 faculty members and 707 administrators in 41 institutions, nine valid and reliable dimensions of organizational effectiveness were identified.

The nine dimensions and their definitions are:

1. Student educational satisfaction: The degree to which students are satisfied with their educational experiences at the institution.

2. Student academic development: The degree of academic attainment, growth, and progress of students and the academic opportunities provided by the institution.

3. Student career development: The degree of occupational development of students and the emphasis and opportunities for career development provided by the institution.

4. Student personal development: The degree of nonacademic, noncareer development (e.g., cultural, social) and the emphasis and opportunities for

personal development provided by the institution.

5. Faculty and administrator employment satisfaction: The satisfaction of faculty members and administrators with their employment.

6. Professional development and quality of the faculty: The degree of professional attainment and development of the faculty and the emphasis and opportunities for professional development provided by the institution.

7. System openness and community interaction: The emphasis placed on interaction with, adaptation to, and service in the external environment.

8. Ability to acquire resources: The ability of the institution to acquire resources such as good students and faculty and financial support.

9. Organizational health: The vitality and benevolence of the internal processes in the institution such as openness and trust, problem-solving adequacy, and shared information.

Source: Adapted from Kim Cameron, "The Relationship between Faculty Unionism and Organizational Effectiveness," *Academy of Management Journal* 25, no. 1 (1982), pp. 6–24.

Measuring Effectiveness

As we have seen in the previous section, criteria of organizational effectiveness depend on a number of contingencies. Even if we know the criteria of interest, some interesting problems need to be solved if we are to arrive at the assessment of an organization's effectiveness. Against what yardstick

---

TABLE 6.3   **Differences between Market and Nonmarket Organizations**

	Type of Organization	
Characteristics of Effectiveness Criteria	*Market*	*Nonmarket*
Clarity of goal	Clear	Unclear
Linkage between input and output	Direct	Indirect
Nature of coupling between inputs, process, and outputs	Tight	Weak
Ease of establishing criteria	Relatively easy	Relatively difficult

would we assess effectiveness? How do we operationalize the criteria in measurable fashion? Just as in the case of effectiveness criteria, the answers to these questions are not as straightforward as they may seem in the beginning. In this section, we will first discuss the key issues in measuring effectiveness and then sketch a method of arriving at the effectiveness of an organization.

Issues in Measuring Effectiveness

There are two major issues involved in measuring effectiveness, once effectiveness criteria are known. They pertain to:

1. standards
2. indicators

We will deal with each in turn.

Standards

We may perhaps judge a profit-making organization by some absolute measure of profitability: its goals are clear and measurable. But against what yardstick should one judge a university? Even worse, how should we judge unique organizations such as NASA or the Department of Defense? The problem of identifying standards is not easily solved.

The most influential model in determining the kind of standards to use was put forth by James Thompson and Arthur Tuden.[8] Thompson and Tuden identified two key dimensions that determine standards of effectiveness: (1) clarity of standards and (2) knowledge of cause-effect relations.

> *Clarity of standards:* whether the standards of desirability are relatively *clearly formulated or ambiguous.* To some extent, this is a measure of the degree to which the constituents are agreed on the goals of the organization.

> *Cause-effect relations:* whether constituents believe that they *do or do not* have complete knowledge about the links between action and results. This represents our knowledge base about organizational phenomena.

Based on these dimensions, we may identify four situations shown in Figure 6.4.

What are the appropriate standards of effectiveness for each situation? First, when standards are clear and cause-effect relations are known, then *efficiency* tests are appropriate. Such tests assess not merely whether a desired outcome was reached (e.g., level of sales) but whether it was done efficiently; that is, with a minimum of inputs (e.g., costs).

Second, if standards are clear, but the cause-effect relations are not known, then *instrumental* tests are suitable. These tests ascertain only whether the desired state was achieved and do not demand conservation of resources. Further, absolute performance standards are abdicated in favor of relative standards by comparing an organization to similar organizations or competitors. Thus, in the example in the chapter opening case, in addition to the overall assessments, *Fortune* provides a breakdown of the rankings of firms by industries. This way, a firm is compared to similar others, but not penalized for failing to accomplish the impossible.

Relative standards are becoming increasingly common in business, which traditionally used to rely on historical or absolute effectiveness measures. This is partly triggered by intense competition from Japanese firms, which has thrown historical standards developed in the United States into question, and partly because comparative data is available and accessible. Indeed, such relative organizational effectiveness measures have begun to affect how individual reward systems are designed. In Box 6.7, we have illustrated how some excellent companies such as IBM have moved on to relative standards as environments have become uncertain, and therefore cause-effect relations have become unclear.

FIGURE 6.4

Thompson's model

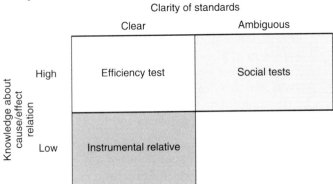

Source: James D. Thompson and Arthur Tuden, "Strategies, Structures, and Processes of Organizational Decision," in *Comparative Studies in Administration,* ed. J. D. Thompson et al. (Pittsburgh, Penn.: The University of Pittsburgh Press, 1959), pp. 195–216.

Box 6.7

Standards for Measuring Effectiveness

Last year, IBM built into its bonus formula sales growth relative to its industry. And this year, it is initiating a "best of breed" program, in which outside contractors are asking IBM customers which computer companies provide the highest degree of customer satisfaction. "Substantial parts of some executives' bonuses will depend on whether their customers rate IBM as the best," said Donald H. Edman, director of personnel programs.

More and more companies are adding a "look around" dimension—a check of how their results stack up in relation to those of other companies—to the traditional "look forward, look back" approach that based incentive pay solely on whether results had improved from the year before.

Comparative pay plans are still most prevalent in industries where competitive data was always readily accessible. Several airlines have long built published statistics on on-time arrivals into bonus plans. Electric utilities pay executives bonuses if they can attain costs per kilowatt hour that are below the industry average. Investment firms reward executives who outperform the market.

But now comparative pay plans are showing up in companies that have been whipsawed by economic or political fluctuations. One large oil and gas company now pays part of its executives' bonuses on the basis of growth in stock price and dividends vis-à-vis those of direct competitors. Several banks reward executives when returns on equity and assets are better than the industry norm, even when those returns are down precipitously from prior, healthier years.

Source: Claudia H. Deutsch, "Fitting the Bonus to the Performance," *New York Times*, May 5, 1991, section 3, p. 25.

Finally, when standards of desirability are themselves ambiguous, then we resort to *social* tests. Social tests are those validated by consensus or by authority. Their validity depends on how many or who endorses them. Social tests are based on such ceremonial awards as the Nobel Prize or Malcolm Baldridge Award for Quality, endorsements by important people, or the prestige of people and programs in external social circles. For example, the press (e.g., *Business Week* or *U.S. News & World Report*) routinely polls business school deans and academics to rank and compare business schools.

Indicators

As seen in the above examples, widely different indicators are employed to assess various facets of organizational effectiveness. We may broadly identify three types of indicators, those based on: (1) outcome, (2) process, and (3) structures.[9]

Outcome. Outcome indicators focus on specific characteristics of materials and objects on which an organization has performed some operation. Examples are changes in knowledge or attitudes of students in educational organizations, or changes in the health status of patients.

Process. Process indicators focus on the quality or quantity of activities carried on by organizations. Process measures assess effort, not outcome.

Structure. These indicators assess the capacity of an organization for effective performance. Manufacturing organizations can be assessed by the value and age of equipment; or schools can be assessed by the qualifications of the faculty, such as degrees earned, which form the basis of accreditation reviews and organizational certification systems.

Table 6.4 summarizes the advantages and disadvantages of each type of indicator.

As we have seen, in arriving at an assessment of an organization's effectiveness, we not only make choices about criteria, but about standards and indicators as well. Next, we describe the key activities involved in measuring effectiveness.

Steps Involved in Measuring Effectiveness

A four-step model of measuring effectiveness is portrayed in Figure 6.5.

TABLE 6.4   A Comparison of Different Types of Indicators

	Indicator Type		
Dimensions	*Outcomes*	*Process*	*Structural*
Focus	Outputs of an organization	Quantity or quality of activities carried on by an organization	Capacity for effective performance
Assumptions	Technology of conversion is well understood	Process leads to outcomes	The capacity is actually utilized
Problems	1. Comparison is problematic because inputs may be different 2. Time frame (short versus long) needs to be determined	Inspectors can be expensive	
Advantages	1. Easily understood 2. Sometimes less expensive	Directly assess performance values	Data not expensive
Disadvantages	Cannot easily apply to nonprofit organizations	May result in confusion of process over content	May stifle innovation
Examples	Change in the health status of individuals	Number of patients seen in the emergency room	Number of hospital beds

FIGURE 6.5

Steps in measuring effectiveness

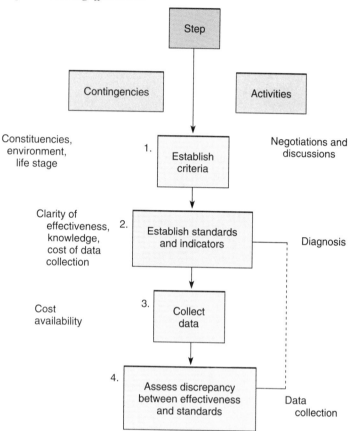

Step 1: Involves establishing criteria of effectiveness. Managers may consider specific contingencies such as stage of development, but this step involves identifying powerful constituencies, understanding their interests, and negotiations with them.

Step 2: Involves the choice of indicators and standards. As we have seen before, standards may be absolute, but are more likely to be relative or to be based on social tests. Similarly, there are a number of choices of indicators (see Table 6.4).

Step 3: Involves data collection around indicators. This may involve objective indices, surveys, and/or opinion polls, as necessary.

Step 4: Involves identifying any discrepancy between the state of effectiveness and the chosen standard, and determining if any action is actually necessary.

One final point: Some organizations engage in these steps systematically, whereas others follow the process intuitively. In either case, it is worth remembering that judgments are required in all the steps, and that this is not a routine exercise.

Managerial Implications

What do these ideas about effectiveness, developed by organization theorists, mean for managers? We may suggest four important points:

1. No manager can afford to pay attention only to a single criterion of effectiveness. At any point in time, organizations need to pursue *many criteria of effectiveness;* hence, managers need to learn how to set priorities, how to order effectiveness criteria sequentially, and in general live with deviations from optimal performance; that is, learn to satisfice.

2. Managers need to pay attention to their constituencies: shareholders, customers, employees, and others. Although managers have some leeway in the choice of effectiveness criteria, they survive to the extent they *serve their constituencies,* especially the more powerful ones.

3. Decisions with respect to effectiveness criteria are ultimately political decisions; that is, determined by the political subsystem of an organization consisting of individuals both internal and external to the organization. Managers need to *negotiate these criteria* through discussions with influential constituencies.

Yet planned changes in organizations require some effectiveness criteria to guide them. This means that the chosen criteria need to be defined in terms of measurable indicators, and data should be collected and analyzed.

Systems Theoretic Review

The concept of organizational effectiveness—as employed by contemporary organization theorists—is anchored in an open systems model of organizations. It is now widely understood that an organization has many stakeholders, both inside and outside, who make judgments about how well the organization is meeting its demands. There are thus many criteria of effectiveness; only some, such as profitability, can be measured in an objective and quantitative fashion.

Different internal subsystems pursue different effectiveness criteria. Thus, functional subsystem pursues primarily economic criteria (profitabil-

ity, return on investment, or shareholder value), social subsystem emphasizes morale and job satisfaction, informational subsystem focuses on speed
and accuracy of data, cultural subsystem emphasizes values, and political
subsystem focuses on feasibility. Just as in the case of stakeholders, different
subsystems pursue different criteria and they are often conflicting. An organization strikes a compromise among conflicting criteria. Typically, the
criteria relevant to the more powerful stakeholders obtain priority in this
process of compromise.

General managers, who are responsible for taking organizational level
action, become the arbiters of conflicting criteria. In this sense, all planned
organizational level changes are anchored in some effectiveness criteria.
Organizational effectiveness is thus a concept associated with planned
change; the concept is meaningless in the context of other changes.

Chapter Summary

Organizational effectiveness refers to human judgments about whether an
organization is functioning satisfactorily. Over the years, the concept of
organizational effectiveness was extended beyond the economic interests of
investors to include the interests of many other groups affected by an organization. It is a concept that guides planned change efforts, and is not
appropriate for other types of change.

Organizations pursue multiple criteria of effectiveness. The criteria differ in terms of (1) focus and (2) time frame. Thus, the criteria may focus on
inputs, process, or outputs. Similarly, the time frame over which the effectiveness is measured may vary from short- to long-term.

Several contingencies may influence organizational criteria. First, managerial preferences may determine whether the organization is internally or
externally focused and whether it adopts control or flexibility for designing
structures. Second, managerial preferences and hence the criteria of effectiveness will vary across the stages of the life cycle. Powerful constituencies
will have a strong influence on the choice of organizational effectiveness
criteria. Similarly, environmental conditions may also influence the criteria.
Finally, whereas profit-making organizations can use economic indicators,
in nonprofit organizations, the criteria tend to be qualitative and subjective.

Two major decisions have to be made in measuring effectiveness:
(1) standards and (2) indicators. There are three types of standards: efficiency tests (to be used when the goals are clear), instrumental tests, and
social tests (which are used when goals are unclear). Similarly, there are
three types of indicators: structure, process, and outcome.

Managers need to learn to negotiate the criteria of effectiveness, since
some notion of effectiveness guides planned change efforts. In the next

section of the book we summarize different planned change efforts, each addressing a different internal subsystem.

Specialized Terms

Evaluation research
Efficiency versus effectiveness
Focus of organizational
  effectiveness
  • System resource approach
  • Internal process approach
  • Goal approach
Managerial values
  • Open systems model
  • Rational goal model
  • Internal process model
  • Human relations model

Stage of life cycle
Constituencies
Market versus nonmarket
  organizations
Standards
  • Efficiency tests
  • Instrumental tests
  • Social tests
Indicators
  • Outcome
  • Process
  • Structure

Discussion Questions

1. Distinguish between efficiency and effectiveness.
2. Enumerate the traditional ways of measuring effectiveness.
3. Discuss the contingencies affecting the choice of effectiveness criteria.
4. What are the key decisions involved in measuring effectiveness criteria?
5. What are the three types of tests of effectiveness? When will you use them?
★6. Some criterion of effectiveness underlies managerial action. Discuss.
★7. Consider the types of change described in the previous chapter. What criterion of effectiveness underlies each type of change?

Applied
1. You have been invited to study the effectiveness of the Department of Health and Human Services in the federal government. How will you proceed?
2. You manage the research and development department of an electronics firm. How will you measure the effectiveness of your department? How will the process differ if you are the chief executive officer of the company?

★This is an advanced-level question.

End Notes

1. Alison L. Sprout, "America's Most Admired Corporations," *Fortune*, February 11, 1991, pp. 52–57.

2. Ibid. Such ratings as the one provided by *Fortune* may influence investors, customers, potential management recruits and employees, and even competitors.

3. This is typically referred to in finance literature as the *efficient market hypothesis*. See, for example, Fred Weston, Kwang S. Chung, and Susan E. Hoag, *Mergers, Restructuring and Corporate Control* (Englewood-Cliffs, N.J.: Prentice Hall, 1990).

4. Richard D. Scott, "Effectiveness of Organizational Effectiveness Studies," in *New Perspectives in Organizational Effectiveness* ed. Paul S. Goodman and Johannes M. Pennings (San Francisco: Jossey-Bass, 1977), pp. 63–95; and Richard D. Scott, Ann B. Flood, Wayne Ewy, and William H. Forrest, "Organizational Effectiveness and the Quality of Surgical Care in Hospitals," in *Environments and Organizations,* ed. Marshall Meyer (San Francisco: Jossey-Bass, 1978), pp. 290–305.

5. Richard M. Steers, "Problems in the Measurement of Organizational Effectiveness," *Administrative Science Quarterly* 20 (1975), pp. 546–58.

6. Robert E. Quinn and John Rohrbaugh, "A Spatial Model of Effectiveness Criteria: Toward a Competing Values Approach to Organizational Analysis," *Management Science* 29 (1983), pp. 363–77.

7. Frank Friedlander and Hal Pickle, "Components of Effectiveness in Small Organizations," *Administrative Science Quarterly* 13 (1968), pp. 289–304.

8. James D. Thompson and Arthur Tuden, "Strategies, Structures and Processes of Organizational Decision," in *Comparative Studies in Administration* ed. J. D. Thompson et al. (Pittsburgh, Penn.: The University of Pittsburgh Press, 1959), pp. 195–216. See also James D. Thompson, *Organizations in Action* (New York: McGraw-Hill, 1967).

9. Drawn from Avedis Donabedian," Evaluating the Quality of Health Care," *Milbank Memorial Fund Quarterly* (July 1966), part 2, pp. 166–206; Edward A. Suchman, *Evaluative Research* (New York: Russell Sage Foundation, 1967); Richard Scott, *Organizations: Rational, Natural and Open Systems*, 2nd ed. (Englewood-Cliffs, N.J.: Prentice Hall, 1987), pp. 322–33.

SUMMARY OF THEORETICAL FOUNDATIONS

We can now summarize the major lessons that we have learned during this century about the behavior of organizations. These lessons will serve as the foundation for the action strategies that will be discussed in the next section of the book.

1. *Organizations are open systems,* in continual interaction with their environments. They receive their inputs from the environments and organizational outputs, in turn, flow back to the environments. In addition, a number of constituencies have stake in the performance of organizations. Thus, in many ways, organizations and environments influence each other.

2. According to the systems model, *organizations are comprised of technical and human elements.* The technical elements are captured by the functional and informational subsystems, whereas social, cultural, and political subsystems embrace the human elements. To fully explain the internal dynamics of organizations, we need to include the interaction among subsystems as well as the forces in the environment. There are no simple explanations for organizational dynamics.

3. Although not always possible, *technical elements demand order and consistency.* Organization theorists have shown that when an organization's performance is high, its functional subsystem is congruent with the major contingencies such as environment, technology, and size of the organization.

4. *The major strategy for managing the technical elements is alignment,* i.e., to align them so that they are consistent among themselves and also with the environment. Although this is not always possible, the desirable alignments serve as ideal states toward which managers would like to move the organizational system.

5. *Organizational environments and the human elements within organizations create turbulence,* and lead to the dynamics of organizations. Turbulence, is as much natural to the organizations as order and consistency. Environments create turbulence by selecting out ill-fitted organizations, and by forcing organizations to adapt. Internal elements create turbulence by the processes of growth and or decline.

6. *The strategies for managing the environments include control of resource dependence and imitation,* in addition to adaptation.

7. *The strategies of managing the human elements in an organization embrace dynamic processes, including planned change.* The focus of management becomes continuous steering of the organization toward ideal alignment, although the ideal alignment itself will change over time due to environmental changes and internal dynamics of the organization.

8. *The managers are continually forced to make trade-offs* between the demands of consistency imposed by the technical elements and the pull of human elements toward turbulence. Such trade-offs are based on effectiveness criteria which reflect the interests of the more powerful constituencies of an organization.

What does this imply for managing organizations? First, as we have repeatedly noted, managers need to understand—*diagnose*—the organizational system, before they take action. Second, the strategies for managing the technical elements are somewhat different from managing the human elements. Finally, different strategies need to be interlinked, and this involves the choice of specific effectiveness criteria.

So far in this book we have focused on the theoretical foundations to the exclusion of action strategies. In the next section of the book, we will present the various actions strategies for managing an organization. We will describe the strategies for managing both the technical and human elements; we will also discuss how they can be interlinked.

II   ACTION STRATEGIES

Part Outline

Introduction

In the first section of the book, we described the major theoretical developments in organization theory. In this section, we will review the salient action strategies that have been developed by organization theorists. These strategies are grounded in theory; that is, the prescriptions that you will find are consistent with the theoretical predictions about effective managerial practice.

We have been selective in our choice of action strategies in two ways:

1. We have presented only those strategies that are anchored in organization theory. For example, we have not included the action strategies proposed in marketing, finance, manufacturing, and related areas.
2. We have focused only on macro level strategies—strategies for managing the total organization or major segments of it. Our focus is on general management, and general managers are typically responsible for macro level phenomena.

Since our focus is on general management, we deal exclusively with planned change; that is, changes initiated and implemented by managers. We will discuss two major groups of action strategies:

1. rational open system strategies
2. human system strategies

Figure II.1 presents an overview of action strategies.

Rational Open System Strategies

Rational open system strategies, or rational strategies for short, deal primarily with the technical elements of an organization. Most rational strategies:

1. Deal primarily with economic objectives. Shareholders are deemed to be the most powerful constituency. The managerial values espoused are either the rational goal or open system models (as defined in Chapter 6). The effectiveness criteria can more or less be quantified, although managers may differ in terms of the time frame of reference.
2. Focus on aligning an organization's functional subsystem with its environments, as well as on aligning its informational and functional subsystems.
3. Therefore provide the managers with descriptions of the ideal state to which they should strive.

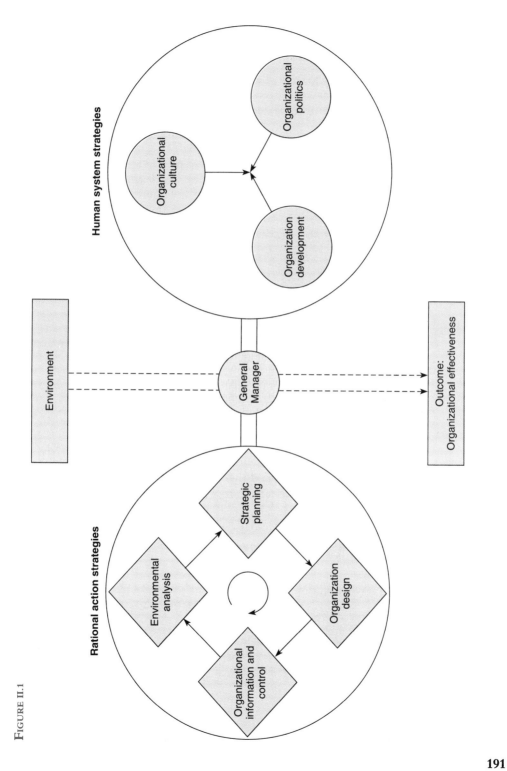

Figure II.1

Human system strategies

Organizational culture

Organizational politics

Organization development

Environment

General Manager

Outcome: Organizational effectiveness

Rational action strategies

Strategic planning

Environmental analysis

Organization design

Organizational information and control

We will discuss the rational strategy in four successive chapters:

1. "Organizational Environments" (Chapter 7) will deal with approaches to understanding and assessing organizational environments.
2. "Strategic Planning" (Chapter 8) will deal with methods to formulate strategies or ways of coping with the changes in the environment.
3. "Organization Design" (Chapter 9) will focus on developing organization structures to implement strategies.
4. "Organizational Information and Control Systems" (Chapter 10) will describe approaches to designing information and control systems to monitor implementation.

According to rational open system theorists, management of organizations consists of a *cycle of steps repeating itself,* starting with the analysis of the environment, developing ways of coping with the changes taking place in the environment, then devising organization structures to implement the strategies and monitoring the implementation through appropriate information and control systems.

Human System Strategies

Human system strategies focus on managing the social, political, and cultural subsystems in an organization. They:

1. Deal with a wide array of constituencies: employees, customers, and even resource providers. The constituencies vary from situation to situation. The effectiveness criteria are not always quantifiable, and therefore, instrumental tests and social tests of effectiveness are common.
2. Focus on developing the human organization—social subsystem or culture—or on dealing with power.
3. Therefore are not sequentially ordered as in the case of rational strategies.

We will discuss human system strategies in three successive chapters:

1. "Organization Development" (Chapter 11) will deal with approaches to develop the social subsystem of an organization.
2. "Organization Culture" (Chapter 12) will focus on methods to bring about cultural change.
3. "Organization Politics" (Chapter 13) will deal with conflict management, political strategies to manage environments, and industrial relations.

Human system strategies do not follow any prespecified sequence; they are evolutionary approaches to managing an organization.

As can be seen from the above, three characteristics set rational strategy apart from human system strategies:

1. The steps in rational strategy are preordered, and follow a *logical sequence* as shown in the figure. Unlike the rational strategy, human system approaches allow changes in the sequence of steps.

2. *Organization wide congruence or alignment* is ensured in rational strategy by ensuring that decisions in one step are congruent with the decisions in the prior steps. Thus strategic plans are to be congruent with the environment, organization structures are to be congruent with strategic plans, and the information and control systems are to be congruent with structures and plans.

3. Organizations go through *repeated cycles* of steps; any cycle starts with environmental analysis and ends with the design of information and control systems. Human system strategies do not assume repetition of cycles.

In organization theory, rational strategies are most fully developed, since they have had the longest history.

Two comments about our discussion of action strategies are in order. First, most action strategies reflect solutions forged by human beings, individually or collectively, to the problems confronting organizations at specific points in time. We expect our interest in specific strategies to change with times as new problems arise and need resolution. This does not obviate the need for understanding the current state of knowledge. There is no need to rediscover the strategies that have been refined over the years. Second, different action strategies are anchored in different assumptions. We will highlight the above two themes repeatedly by describing the historical and philosophical underpinnings of each strategy. Most of our discussion will of course focus on the action strategies themselves.

7 ORGANIZATIONAL ENVIRONMENTS

Chapter Outline

Overnight the markets in Eastern Europe have opened up. And money, talent, and other resources are being brought together to rescue a region that has suffered from political and economic stagnation. For example, the European Bank of Reconstruction and Development (EBRD) is reportedly raising $100 billion to finance the economic development of the region composed of Poland, Hungary, Czechoslovakia, Bulgaria, Romania, Yugoslavia, and the various Soviet Republics.

Along with capital, industrialists from all over the world are joining to develop the territory. Thus H. J. Heinz is considering setting up a food processing plant in Poland. The chief executive officer of Sprint recently visited the Soviet Republics to scout the market for telecommunications. EBRD is interested in cleaning up the polluted Baltic Sea and Danube River in conjunction with the World Bank and the European Investment Bank.[1]

Who would have thought, even a couple of years ago, that private business would be allowed to operate in Eastern Europe? As the chapter introduction case shows, the environment for business in Eastern Europe has changed almost overnight. What aspects of environment are important for organizational functioning? How, exactly, do environments influence an organization? How do we analyze environments so that we can take effective managerial action? These questions form the subject of discussion in this chapter.

In Section I, we demonstrated that in organization theory, open systems models have displaced the closed system models of organizations. By their very nature, all open system theories of organizations ascribe a central place to environments in explaining organizational phenomena. In this chapter, we will summarize organization theorists' ideas about environments.

This is not a mere theoretical discussion. In recent years, organizations have been devoting manpower, time, and financial resources to analyzing their environments. Professional societies have sprung up carrying names such as Strategic Issue Analysis, Society of Competitive Intelligence Professionals, and World Future Society. Their membership is composed of professionals who deal with various aspects of environments. Specialized university courses are now springing up carrying environment labels. In short, environmental analysis is fast becoming a profession and an identifiable subfield within management.

What Are Organizational Environments and Environmental Analysis?

Organizational environments refer to the *factors external to an organization* that influence its functioning and performance. The factors may range from behaviors of a firm's customers or competitors, characteristics of its industry, or even forces such as regulation or government intervention. Although the number of factors external to an organization may theoretically be infinite, organization theorists focus on those elements that help to explain or improve performance.

Environmental analysis refers to the process by which key decision makers develop an understanding of organizational environments—factors that may influence organizational functioning and performance currently or in the future. Environmental analysis has three basic goals:

1. To inform key decision makers about the *current* and *potential* changes taking place in the environment.
2. To provide *important intelligence* for strategic, top-level decision makers.
3. To challenge the assumptions widely held among decision makers so that they will be *sensitive* to opportunities, threats, and possibilities in the environment.

Environmental analysis shapes the *perceptions* of decision makers: how they view the environment, what they think are the routes to success, and in general the decision-making process in organizations. It involves gathering and analyzing information and drawing current and potential implications of changes in the environment. The focus of data collection is the *external* environment, *not what is going on within the organization.* Thus, environmental analysis does not focus primarily upon the informational subsystem within the organization.

Environmental analysis is expected to yield two benefits to organizations. The analysis:

1. Generates descriptions of current environmental changes, indicators of potential changes, and alternative descriptions of future changes. Such descriptions provide organizations *lead time* to identify, understand, and adapt to external issues.
2. Offers one mechanism for *organizational learning* by inducing top-level managers to think beyond their current operating concerns, forcing them to view the environment with an open mind.

There is a popular misconception that environmental analysis can foretell the future; hence, organizations doing it will not have to face surprises. No method or technique can realistically hope to accomplish that. Environmental analysis, however, seeks to specify which elements of environments are predictable, and to outline potentialities when the environments are not predictable. In this sense, it helps to reduce the frequency and extent of surprises that may confront an organization.

Linkage to the Systems Model

Environmental analysis ascribes central importance to environments in explaining organizational behavior. In this sense, it operationalizes the idea that organizations are *open systems:* The starting point of effective managerial action is the analysis of the environment.

In practice, environmental analysis has implications primarily for the functional subsystem of an organization. For example, environmental analysis enables an organization to understand its markets—which markets are growing or which ones are opening up. Hence, it helps an organization decide what products to sell in what markets. Since it focuses almost exclusively on the environment, the choice of organizational responses is outside its purview. Such responses—strategies and organization structure—are fashioned during strategic planning and organization design, which rely on the outputs of environmental analysis. Hence, environmental analysis is the starting point in rational approaches to managing organizations. This is schematically presented in Figure 7.1.

In this chapter, we summarize the role of environmental analysis in managing organizations. We start by describing the historical, philosophical, and theoretical underpinnings of the field. Next, we introduce the key ideas that form the basis of analysis. Third, we summarize the major models that have been developed to analyze various aspects of the environment. We conclude with a brief reference to its linkage to the systems model.

Underpinnings

Historical Underpinnings

In practice, organizations have always responded to environments. Whenever there has been a labor strike, price cut by competitors, or economic

FIGURE 7.1

Systems logic: Environmental analysis

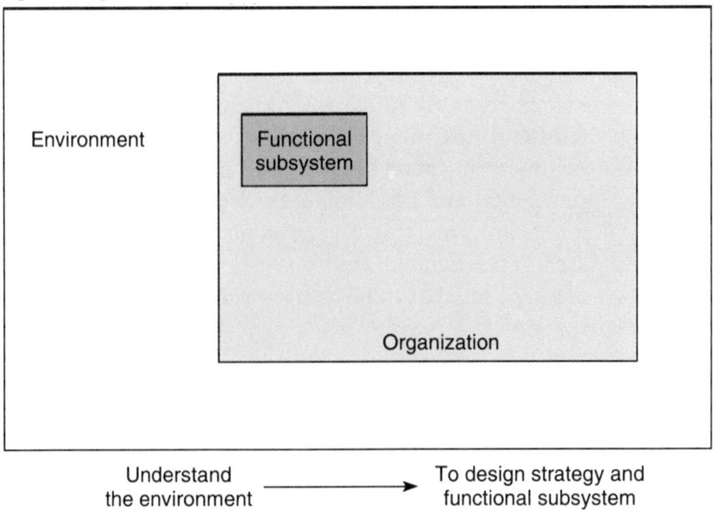

recession or boom, organizations have taken action to counteract the threat or exploit the opportunity. We would not say, however, that organizations analyzed their environments; in all the above cases, organizations were forced to respond after events in the environment had already taken place.

The earliest forms of analysis can be traced to marketing and finance departments within organizations. As early as 1950, marketing departments in leading edge organizations began to commit resources to market research: collecting and analyzing data about consumer needs and dislikes so that marketing strategies could be formulated on such information. Similarly, finance departments in many organizations, especially banks and major financial institutions, tracked economic indices such as interest rates for operational planning. Most of these efforts within an organization were not coordinated; environmental analysis as an organizationwide activity was then unknown.

During the 1960s, a group of intellectuals who called themselves futurists began to talk about the future. This group included mathematicians, economists, social scientists, and even journalists. Most of them were system thinkers who believed in the power of systems concepts to shed light on the probable evolution of advanced societies. Some of them began to build mathematical models of society. The most notable of these were the MIT project that culminated in the book *Limits to Growth,*[2] and the work of Mihajoo Mesarovic, also published as a book titled *Mankind at the Turning Point.*[3] These efforts had little impact on organizations since their immediate relevance was not clear to key decision makers.

During the 1970s when the first oil crisis hit the United States as a result of the OPEC-induced oil embargo, many organizations realized the need to look beyond market research and interest rates to effectively manage organizations. They hired social scientists and political scientists to advise them on what is taking place in the environment. In addition, many multinational organizations recognized that to function effectively abroad, they needed to interface with host governments, so they started creating a foreign affairs function within their organizations.

During the same period, many consulting organizations sprang up that provided information to organizations about the major trends in their environments. Like the systems thinkers, they adopted an integrated view of the environment. For example, John Naisbitt looking through myriad data sources and a large number of trends, suggested in his book *Megatrends* that the United States is experiencing 10 major trends.[4] (See Box 7.1.)

Most of the early environmental analysis efforts had attempted to predict the future. As organizations gained experience with such efforts, they also came to realize that the future was in many important ways difficult to predict. In some cases organizations could shape the future by their actions; for example, lobbying the government. And in some other cases, the environmental analysis provided them with insights into what is currently going on in their environments. They began to set up environmental

Box 7.1

Megatrends

In 1982, John Naisbitt published *Megatrends;* the book immediately became a national bestseller. The *Washington Post* called it a "field guide of the future," the *American School Board Journal* called it "a road map to the 21st century." What Naisbitt actually did was to present a new way of both looking at America's future and understanding the present.

To generate his findings Naisbitt applied a technique called *content analysis* to local newspaper articles drawn from various regions of the United States. He tracked events and behaviors reported in these newspapers over several years, deriving a scheme of classifying them and using the scheme to study newspaper reporting trends over time. For example, Naisbitt reported that during the 1960s, almost all of the space devoted to the general topic of discrimination was filled with concerns about racism. Then, beginning in 1969, that space began to be split between material about racism and material about sexism. Starting in 1977, both subjects began to yield to concerns about ageism. At that point, almost overnight, Congress outlawed mandatory retirement in the public sector and extended it from 65 to 70 years in the private sector. Concern about age discrimination has since been declining.

Naisbitt broke down the trends into 10 megatrends to characterize the transformation of U.S. society. He concluded:

1. We have shifted from an industrial society (one devoted to manufacturing goods) to an information society—one based on the creation and distribution of information.

2. We are moving in the dual directions of high tech/high touch, matching each new technology with a compensatory human response.

3. No longer do we have the luxury of operating within an isolated self-sufficient national economic system; we must now acknowledge that we are part of a global economy.

4. We are restructuring from a society run by short-time considerations and rewards in favor of dealing with things in much longer term time frames.

5. In cities and states, in small organizations and subdivisions, we have rediscovered the ability to act innovatively and to achieve results—from the bottom up.

6. We are shifting from institutional help to more self-reliance in all aspects of our lives.

7. We are discovering that the framework of representative democracy has become obsolete in an era of instantaneously shared information.

8. We are giving up our dependence on hierarchical structures in favor of informal networks; this will be especially important to the business community.

9. More Americans are living in the south and west, leaving behind the old industrial cities of the north.

10. From a narrow either/or society with a limited range of personal choices, we are exploding into a free-wheeling multiple option society.

In our terminology, Naisbitt conducted an analysis of the macroenvironment—his focus was on American society itself rather than any specific industry. He produced a provocative scan of the macroenvironment because his focus was on the present, not predicting the future. His scan was illuminating because it gave coherence to innumerable trends that we have been observing but have not been able to integrate into our understanding.

Source: Adapted from John Naisbitt. *Megatrends: Ten New Directions Transforming Our Lives.* (New York: Warner Books, 1984).

analysis units within their organizations or to look to consulting firms to provide them with an integrated view of the environment. This focus on integrating information about the different segments of the environment into a coherent pattern sets contemporary environmental analysis efforts apart from the early market research efforts.

Philosophical Underpinnings

Four major philosophical assumptions underlie the field of environmental analysis:

First, and perhaps most important, the environmental analysis field clearly signals the shift from a closed systems view of management to an open systems perspective. If organizations and environments are interdependent, then to be effective, management action should be based on a clear understanding of environments.

Second, and related to the above, environments should be understood in their own right, not merely from the vantage point of organizations. Important threats and opportunities in the environment can be appreciated only when management tries to learn about their environments rather than responding to crises or by listening to internally generated information.

Third, organizations have some degree of control over their environments. Thus, unlike some early contingency theorists, environmental analysts suggest that organizations may be able to create their environments, and that adaptation may not be the only way to manage the organization-environment interface.

Finally, since environments are complex, systems concepts are adopted to understand and analyze organizational environments. Thus, the environment is viewed as a system capable of being analyzed in much the same way as an organization.

Theoretical Underpinnings

As the open systems view of organizations came to dominate the field of organization studies, scholars began to systematically study environments and their relationships to organizations. How do environments evolve? What are the characteristics of environments currently facing organizations? How do organizations respond to them? How do managers analyze and understand their environments? In this section, we summarize the seminal works addressing each one of these questions.

Evolution of Environments

Scholars drawn from marketing were among the first researchers to model the evolution of the environment. They were interested in identifying predictable stages in sales growth of a new product from the time of its introduction. Drawing their ideas from diffusion models, they advanced the product life-cycle concept. (See Box 7.2.) According to the concept, the sales of a new product will follow an *S*-shape: Initially, sales will be slow, then they will grow very fast, and finally they will plateau and perhaps decline. Although the life-cycle model lacked empirical validity, it became a tool for market planning. Further, the model only focused on customers—a specific segment of environment—and was, therefore, not useful for generalized theory-building efforts.

Most credit Fred Emery and Eric Trist with the first comprehensive model of the evolution of the environment.[5] Based on their case study of a firm in the food canning market in the United Kingdom, Emery and Trist identified four types of environments. They called these ideal types of environments causal textures, approximations to which may be thought of as existing in the real world of most organizations. The four causal textures are as follows:

1. *Placid, randomized environment.* This type of environment is stable and unchanging. The elements of the environment are randomly distributed; there are no systematic relationships among them. Organizations can adapt as single and indeed quite small units. The best tactic for an organization in this environment is to learn by trial and error to do its best. Local (stand-alone) drug stores or small banks (before banking deregulation) in many rural areas of the United States faced this type of environment.

2. *Placid clustered environment.* In this environment, the resources are no longer randomly distributed but rather they are concentrated in some places. Thus, some positions in the environment are richer in resources than others. The environment is still stable, but because of resource concentration, location becomes an important factor in the survival of organizations. Survival becomes critically linked to an organization's knowledge of its environment. Optimal location becomes key to organizational success. Before the advent of Japanese competition, such giant corporations as U.S. Steel or GM faced this type of environment.

3. *Disturbed, reactive environment.* Here, not only are the resources concentrated, but the environment becomes unstable because there is more than one kind of organization. This leads to competition among the organizations. Now it becomes necessary to define the organizational objective not so much in terms of location as in terms of the power to be able to make and meet competitive challenges. Many industries where firms are locked in competitive battles face this type of environment.

4. *Turbulent environment.* This is a dynamic environment where the relations among the elements are changing and the rate at which these relationships change is high. Three trends contribute to the emergence of dynamic field forces: (a) the growth in the number

Box 7.2

Product Life-Cycle Concept

When an organization launches a new product, it hopes that the product will enjoy a long life so that the organization can earn a decent profit to cover all the effort and risk that went into developing it. Most firms know that sales of the new product will change with time, that is, the sales will exhibit a life cycle. Different market strategies are needed at various points in the cycle for the organization to register the best performance.

The product life cycle is an attempt to recognize *distinct stages* in the *sales history* of the product. Each stage presents distinct opportunities and problems with respect to marketing strategy and profit potential. By identifying the stage that a product is in, organizations can formulate better marketing plans.

So what does a typical product life cycle look like? Most discussions of product life cycle (PLC) portray the sales *history* of a typical product as following an S-shaped curve, as illustrated below. This curve is typically divided into four stages: *introduction, growth, maturity,* and *decline*. During introduction, sales and sales growth are low, since the product has just been introduced into the market; profits are nonexistent at this stage because of the heavy expenses of product introduction. During the growth stage, sales grow rapidly and profits correspondingly improve. When sales reach the maturity stage, the growth declines and profits stabilize. In the decline stage, sales show a strong downward drift and profits erode.

The product life-cycle concept is based on the theory of diffusion. When a new product is introduced, the company has to stimulate awareness, interest, trial, and purchase. This takes time, and only a few individuals will buy it. If the product is satisfying, larger numbers of buyers are drawn in. In turn, this causes more firms to market the product, and prices fall; consequently, still more buyers come in. Eventually, the growth rate decreases as the number of potential new buyers approaches zero. Sales then become steady at the replacement rate. Eventually, sales decline as superior new products displace the present one.

The product life-cycle concept has proven useful in market planning in the past when life cycles were relatively long (five to seven years). However, more recently, there has been a rapid decline in the length of product life cycles (to about three years); the concept's utility for planning in these cases is considerably lower.

The product life-cycle concept addresses only the behavior of customers and hence cannot be considered a comprehensive model of the environment. However, it is perhaps the first model of environmental evolution to appear in theory.

Source: Adapted from Philip Kotler, *Marketing Management: Analysis, Planning and Control* (Englewood Cliffs, N.J.: Prentice Hall, 1984).

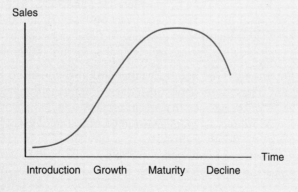

Box 7.3

Emery and Trist: Causal Texture of Organizational Environments

Fred Emery, an Australian, and Eric Trist, then in the United Kingdom, presented the first work on the evolution of organizational environments. They acknowledged that their ideas were drawn from cybernetics and information systems, both closely related to general systems theory.

Emery and Trist argued that although the open systems formulation (developed in 1950s) enabled us to look at exchange processes between organization and environment in a new light, it did not deal with those processes in the environment itself that are among the determining conditions of the exchanges. They argued that a comprehensive understanding of organizational behavior required some knowledge of four sets of elements: (1) processes within an organization, (2) exchanges from the organization to the environment, (3) from the environment to the organization, and (4) exchange processes within the environment itself. Their primary focus

was on the fourth set of elements, which they termed the "causal texture of organizational environments."

Emery and Trist argued that environments tend to become turbulent over time. They illustrated this tendency with a case study.

The case dealt with a company in the food-canning industry in the United Kingdom that belonged to a parent group. Its main product was canned vegetables, the firm had 65 percent of the market, which had been stable since before the war. The company persuaded the board to invest several million pounds to build an automated factory, to take advantage of the economies from long runs expected in the traditional market.

Meanwhile, a number of small canning firms appeared, not dealing with this product nor indeed with others in the company's range but with imported fruits. These firms arose because postwar controls had been removed from steel strip and tin and cheaper cans could now be obtained in any number. At the same time a larger market was developing in imported fruits. Since

---

of organizations in a disturbed reactive environment and the relationships among them, (b) the deepening of the interconnections between the economic sector and other sectors of the society, and (c) the increasing reliance on research and development to meet competitive challenges. In these environments, survival depends on efficient environmental scanning and monitoring.

Emery and Trist note that all environments tend to become turbulent over time. Thus, the general thrust of environmental evolution is toward increasing levels of turbulence, that is, uncertainty and complexity. (See Box 7.3.)

More recently, and working from an understanding of changes taking place in various industries over the 20th Century, Igor Ansoff also suggested that environmental turbulence has been increasing, although not all industries move in step with the trend.[6] Both Ansoff and Emery and Trist

Box 7.3 continued

this trade was seasonal, the firms were anxious to find a way of using their machinery and retaining their labor through the winter. They were able to do so through the development of quick-frozen foods: Since the quick-freezing process demanded great constancy at the growing end, something not possible beyond a certain point, large amounts of crops unsuitable for quick freezing but suitable for canning became available. The small canners now imported these cheap supplies.

Before the introduction of the quick-freezing form, the company's own canned product had been the premier brand. But its position in the product spectrum now changed. Affluent people could afford the quick-frozen form, and cheaper varieties of canned fruit also became available. At the same time, the number of supermarkets was increasing, and more and more large grocery chains came into existence that wanted to sell certain types of goods under their own house names. As the small canners provided an extremely cheap article, the retailers could undercut the manufacturer's branded product and within three years captured 50 percent of the market; previously, the retailers' varieties accounted for less than 1 percent of the market.

The changed texture of the environment was not recognized by an able but traditional management. They failed to appreciate that a number of outside events were becoming connected with each other in a way that was leading to irreversible general change.

Emery and Trist argued that the canning firm was operating somewhere between a placid clustered and disturbed reactive environment before events overtook the firm. What undermined the firm was not improper management of its organization-environment interface but processes taking place in the environment itself. Specifically, the development of quick-frozen foods, the removal of government controls, the appearance of small canners, and the changes in retail chains—all processes in the environment—came together to impoverish the market held by the firm.

Emery and Trist suggested that as environments become turbulent, such interconnections in the environment assume great significance. Consequently, monitoring the environment continually is a necessary prerequisite to survival.

Source: Fred E. Emery and Eric L. Trist. "The Causal Texture of Organizational Environments," *Human Relations* 18 (1965), pp. 21–32.

concur that to be effective, organizations should engage in environmental analysis in turbulent environments.

Characteristics of Environments

Over the years, scholars have refined the concepts by which environments may be described. Their schemes can best be understood by reference to two simple ideas:

1. As emphasized by Emery and Trist, in some environments organizations need more information than in others.
2. Organizations need to acquire resources from their environments.

To capture these two ideas, scholars have pursued two concepts: uncertainty and dependence.

Uncertainty.   Uncertainty refers to the condition wherein decision makers do not have sufficient information about environmental changes. The higher the uncertainty, the greater the risk of failure. Robert Duncan was among the first to detail the dimensions of uncertainty.[7] He argued that uncertainty may be captured along two dimensions: simple-complex and stable-dynamic.

The *simple-complex* dimension refers to the number of dissimilar elements that are relevant to the organization. In a simple environment, as few as two or three external elements influence the environment. The local (stand-alone) drugstore (in placid random environments) exemplifies a simple environment: It has to worry about suppliers, customers, and perhaps some competitors. On the other hand, universities interact with a large number of elements: government, professional and scientific associations, alumni, parents, foundations, athletic teams, and so on. In complex environments, there are large numbers of dissimilar elements.

The *stable-dynamic* dimension refers to whether the elements in the environment are unstable. In a stable environment, the elements remain the same over a protracted period of time. In dynamic conditions, the elements shift abruptly. The corner drugstore in rural areas typically faces a stable environment: suppliers and customers do not change rapidly. On the other hand, computer firms face a dynamic environment: new products regularly come on market, competitors frequently change their tactics, and customer tastes are also changing fast.

Duncan made two predictions about uncertainty facing an organization. He argued that:

1. Uncertainty is lowest when the environment is simple and stable, and highest when it is complex and dynamic; moderate uncertainty is experienced by firms in simple-dynamic and complex-stable environments. This is a relatively easy prediction.

2. The stable-dynamic dimension is more important in determining uncertainty. Complexity can be dealt with much more easily by managers than dynamism. Based on this argument, the simple-dynamic environment creates greater uncertainty than the complex-stable environment.

Duncan provided research evidence to support his contention, and the study is considered a classic. His scheme is presented in Figure 7.2 and is showcased in Box 7.4.

Resource Dependence.   Resource dependence is the second environmental characteristic that has attracted theoretical attention. The environment is the source of scarce and valued resources essential for organizational survival; both inputs and outputs are resources controlled by the environment. Thus

FIGURE 7.2

Duncan's typology of organizational environments

		Environmental Complexity	
		Simple	*Complex*
Environmental Change	Stable	1. *Small* number of *similar* external elements 2. Elements change *slowly* Example: Haircutting salons Low Uncertainty	1. *Large* number of *dissimilar* external elements 2. Elements change *slowly* Example: Universities Low-Moderate Uncertainty
	Dynamic	1. *Small* number of *similar* external elements 2. Elements change *frequently* Example: Fashion design High-Moderate Uncertainty	1. *Large* number of *dissimilar* external elements 2. Elements change *frequently* Example: Electronic firms High Uncertainty

Source: Adapted from Robert B. Duncan, "Characteristics of Perceived Environments and Perceived Environmental Uncertainty," *Administrative Science Quarterly,* 17 no. 3, 1972, pp. 313–27.

the environment provides raw materials, customers for firms' products, labor, and even capital. Organizations are dependent on the environment in varying degrees.

Resource dependence theorists (as we described earlier in Chapter 5) assume that most of the resources of an organization are controlled by other organizations. Hence, they focus primarily on relationships among organizations. Organizations seek to reduce resource scarcity by developing relationships with other organizations. This creates a dilemma for managers. On the one hand, they like to retain their freedom, but on the other hand, interorganizational links created to acquire resources restrict their freedom. Thus, interorganizational relationships represent a trade-off between resources and autonomy. Organizations that have abundant resources eschew developing new links to preserve their autonomy; organizations that need resources will give up their autonomy to acquire those resources.

Resource dependence theorists suggest several ways of acquiring resources that require influencing other organizations; they do not dwell as much on understanding the environmental characteristics as uncertainty theorists. Given their focus on influence attempts, resource dependence theorists adopt a *political perspective* on organizational environment relationships. The implications of this line of reasoning are often ignored in most conceptions of environmental analysis, which are based on the ideas from uncertainty theorists. The action implications of resource dependence theorists will be summarized in our chapter on organizational politics.

Box 7.4

Robert Duncan's Typology
of Organizational Environments

Robert Duncan, one of the leading scholars in organization theory, developed the typology of organizational environments in the early 1970s, based on the concept of uncertainty. He argued that uncertainty is composed of two dimensions: (1) complexity, and (2) dynamism. He tested his ideas in a major research project funded by the National Science Foundation.

Duncan studied 12 decision units in three manufacturing organizations and 10 decision units in three research and development organizations. A decision unit was defined as a formally specified work group within the organization under a superior with a formally defined set of responsibilities.

The environment was defined as the perceptions of individuals. To identify environmental components, research was carried out in a large industrial manufacturing organization. Nineteen individuals in various decision units in several functional areas were interviewed. From these interviews, a list of environmental components was constructed comprising a decision unit's: internal and external environment, as follows:

**Factors and Components
Comprising the Organization's
Internal and External Environment**

Internal Environment
(1) Organizational personnel component
    (A) Educational and technological
        background and skills

    (B) Previous technological and managerial
        skill
    (C) Individual member's involvement and
        commitment to attaining system's
        goals
    (D) Interpersonal behavior styles
    (E) Availability of manpower for
        utilization within the system
(2) Organizational, functional, and staff units
component
    (A) Technological characteristics of
        organizational units
    (B) Interdependence of organizational
        units in carrying out their objectives
    (C) Intraunit conflict among organizational,
        functional, and staff units
    (D) Interunit conflict among organizational,
        functional, and staff units
(3) Organizational level component
    (A) Organizational objectives and goals
    (B) Integrative process bringing together
        individuals and groups toward attaining
        organizational goals
    (C) Nature of the organization's product
        service

External Environment
(4) Customer component
    (A) Distributors of product or service
    (B) Actual users of product or service
(5) Suppliers component
    (A) New materials suppliers
    (B) Equipment suppliers
    (C) Product parts suppliers
    (D) Labor supply

Box 7.4 continued

(6) Competitor component
  (A) Competitors for suppliers
  (B) Competitors for customers
(7) Sociopolitical component
  (A) Government regulatory control over the industry
  (B) Public political attitude towards industry and its particular product
  (C) Relationship with trade unions with jurisdiction in the organization
(8) Technological component
  (A) Meeting new technological requirements of own industry and related industries in production of product or service
  (B) Improving and developing new products by implementing new technological advances in the industry

Based on the components, the 22 decision units were categorized into one of the two cells: (1) simple (e.g., lower level production unit) or (2) complex (e.g., programming and planning department). To classify the decision units on the stable-dynamic continuum, individuals in the unit were asked to rate the degree of change in each of the environmental components they identified as important, on a five-point scale ranging from never to very often.

Duncan tested his ideas about uncertainty on the decision units. He measured the perceived environmental uncertainty in each decision unit using questionnaires. He concluded:

1. It is the nature of an organization's environment rather than the kind of organization that is most important in explaining the degree of uncertainty experienced in decision making.

2. Decision units with static-simple environments perceive the least amount of uncertainty.

3. Decision units with dynamic complex environments experienced the greatest amount of uncertainty.

4. In the mixed situations, decision units with simple-dynamic environments experienced greater level of uncertainty than groups with complex-static environments, although the differences were not statistically significant. Other evidence, however, pointed to the conclusion that the static-dynamic dimension is a more important contributor to the perception of uncertainty.

Duncan also cautioned that the uncertainty and the degree of complexity and dynamism of the environment should not be considered as constant features in an organization. Rather, they are dependent on the perceptions of organization members and thus can vary in their incidence to the extent individuals vary in their perceptions. Some individuals may have a very high tolerance for ambiguity and uncertainty and may perceive situations as less uncertain than others with lower tolerances.

Source: Based on Robert Duncan, "Characteristics of Organizational Environments and Perceived Environmental Uncertainty," *Administrative Science Quarterly*, September 1972, pp. 313–327.

Organizational Responses to Environments

Organizations have a repertoire of mechanisms by which to respond and adapt to their environments. Generically, the responses may be classified into three types:

1. Choice of appropriate strategy
2. Internal structure and process
3. Mechanisms to anticipate and understand environments

Recently, Richard Daft[8] linked the type of organizational responses to the four environments identified by Duncan. Daft's synthesis is presented in Box 7.5. Daft argued that instead of focusing on one mechanism or the other, organizations adopt a configuration of mechanisms uniquely suited to different environmental settings. This is, of course, a specification of the systems theoretic principles outlined in Chapter 3.

Ever since the widespread acceptance of the open systems model, many scholars have pursued the contingent nature of organizational responses. In the ensuing chapters, we will discuss the role of strategy and design. In this chapter we will focus on the mechanisms to anticipate and understand environment.

Approaches to Environmental Analysis

Just how do managers and organizations develop an appreciation of the environment? Two groups of scholars have addressed this question.

Scanning Modes.   The earliest work was by Francis Aguilar[9], who developed a classification scheme for the modes of analysis undertaken by managers. He arrayed the modes on a continuum, from highly structured to highly unstructured, as shown in Figure 7.3.

Aguilar identified four modes: (1) undirected viewing, (2) conditioned viewing, (3) informal search, and (4) formal search.

Undirected viewing refers to a manager's exposure and perception of information that has no specific purpose. The sources and substance of information are highly varied, and typically much information is dropped from attention. Although this mode may appear sloppy, Aguilar noted that undirected viewing can be a valuable means to counteract the natural tendency to perceive and digest only information of immediate relevance.

Conditioned viewing involves a degree of purposefulness by the manager as he or she receives information. The manager has a set of concerns and is therefore receptive to certain types of information. This mode is reactive, that is, the manager does not actively seek information, but responds to available information.

Box 7.5

Daft's Contingency Model of Organizational Responses to Environmental Uncertainty

Richard Daft is an influential organization theorist who recently formulated a contingency framework for organizational responses to uncertainty. Daft built upon the work of Duncan, who had formulated four classes of environmental uncertainty. (Refer to Box 7.4 for Duncan's work.)

Daft argued that there are five types of organizational responses to environmental uncertainty:

1. *Environmental scanning roles*. These roles link and coordinate an organization with key elements in the external environment. The roles are to scan the environment, detect and bring into the organization information about changes in the environment, and send information into the environment that presents the organization in a favorable light. For example, a market research department scans and monitors trends in consumer tastes, and advertising people and salespeople represent the organization to customers.

2. *Imitation*. Daft argued that under high uncertainty, organizations mimic or imitate other organizations in the same environments. Managers in an organization experiencing great uncertainty assume that other organizations face similar uncertainty. These managers will copy the structure, management techniques, and strategies of other firms that appear successful. Such mimicking serves to reduce uncertainty for managers but it also means that organizations within an industry will tend to look alike over time. As an example, Daft noted that

retail establishments will tend to operate in a similar way, as will airlines, electronic firms, or banks.

3. *Planning*. Daft argued that under conditions of environmental uncertainty, planning and forecasting are necessary; but when the environment is stable, an organization can afford to concentrate on current operational problems and day-to-day efficiency.

4. *Organization structure*. Daft noted that the degree of specialization and coordination in an organization may also vary with environmental uncertainty. When the external environment is complex and rapidly changing, organizational departments become highly specialized to handle uncertainty in their external sector. As departments become specialized, the need for coordination also increases. Daft noted that organizations performed better when the levels of specialization and coordination match the level of uncertainty in the environment. Organizations that performed well in an uncertain environment had high levels of specialization and coordination, while those performing well in less uncertain environment had lower levels of each.

5. *Nature of control process*. Daft argued that the amount of formal structure imposed on employees decreases with environmental uncertainty. Building upon the work of Burns and Stalker (see Chapter 4), Daft distinguished between mechanistic and organic control processes. Mechanistic structures are likely to appear in relatively certain environments,

Box 7.5 continued

whereas organic structures appear in highly uncertain environments.

Daft's framework is presented in the following figure. We will make four comments about this framework.

1. Daft's five responses are similar to the three classes of responses we have set forth in the text. Thus, boundary-spanning roles are mechanisms to understand environments. Planning and forecasting are elements of the strategy formulation process in an organization. Finally, specialization, coordination, control process and imitation refer to the internal structure and process of organizations.

2. The five responses suggested by Daft are confined to the functional subsystem within an organization. As we suggest in Chapter 4, "Contingency Perspective on Organizations," this is true of most contingency frameworks in organization theory.

3. As Daft has argued, organizations need to formulate complex responses when confronted with increasing levels of uncertainty. Thus, as environments become more uncertain, organizations need to scan the environments more vividly, imitate more frequently, put greater emphasis on planning, evolve more departments and coordinate them more closely, and in general develop organic control processes.

4. Very much like Emery and Trist, Daft argued that conscious attention to environments is necessary as organizations face highly uncertain environments. In other words, the environmental analysis methods described in this chapter are less important for stable environments but essential in highly uncertain environments.

Environmental Complexity

		Simple	Complex
Environmental Change	Stable	1. Little scanning 2. Little imitation 3. Operating orientation 4. Few departments, little coordination 5. Mechanistic control	1. Some scanning 2. Some imitation 3. Some planning 4. Many departments, little coordination 5. Mechanistic control
	Dynamic	1. Some scanning 2. Quick imitation 3. Planning orientation 4. Few departments, some coordination 5. Organic control	1. Extensive scanning 2. Extensive imitation 3. Extensive planning 4. Many departments, extensive coordination 5. Organic control

Source: Adapted from Richard Daft, *Organization Theory and Design* (St. Paul, Minn.: West Publishing, 1989), p. 63.

FIGURE 7.3

Aguilar's modes of scanning

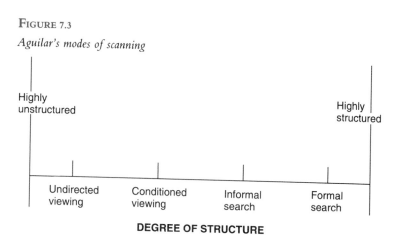

DEGREE OF STRUCTURE

Informal search involves a proactive orientation in searching for information; however, there is a limited and relatively unstructured effort to seek out information for a specific purpose.

Formal search is a highly proactive and structured mode deliberately undertaken to obtain information for specific purposes. Here, the emphasis is on formal procedures and methodologies for obtaining information.

Aguilar noted that in any mode, the source of information may be impersonal (e.g., data files or newspaper articles) or personal (interviews). Aguilar further noted that managers tend to favor personal over impersonal sources. His study is summarized in Box 7.6.

Scanning Systems.   Others following Aguilar's lead have focused on the organizational systems for analyzing the environment. In one study, Liam Fahey, William King and V. K. Narayanan[10] provided a typology of such systems: irregular, periodic and continuous.

In *irregular systems,* organizations conduct environmental analysis on an *ad hoc* basis for understanding specific events during crises or for immediate decisions.

In *periodic systems,* the analysis of environmental forces is periodically updated for strategic planning purposes.

In *continuous systems,* extensive environmental data is collected on an ongoing basis for spotting opportunities as well as solving problems. Here, the data is used for both short- and long-term decisions.

Especially in the case of large organizations, the authors argued that continuous systems are necessary for meaningful environmental analysis. Their study is summarized in Box 7.7.

Box 7.6

Aguilar and Modes of Scanning

Francis Aguilar was interested in investigating managerial practices related to information acquisition for strategic planning. He conducted a study of managers from 41 companies, most of them in the chemical industry dealing with industrial products.

Aguilar discovered three major facets of scanning from his study: (1) modes of scanning, (2) types of information, and (3) sources of information.

Modes of scanning. As discussed in the text, Aguilar discovered that modes of scanning can vary from an undirected, fortuitous, and subconscious observation to a purposeful, predetermined, and highly structured inspection. He classified the modes into four on a scale from unstructured to structured: undirected viewing, conditioned viewing, informal search, and formal search.

Kinds of information. Aguilar noted that the kinds of information managers sought can be classified into market, technical, acquisition leads, broad issues (general economic conditions, government actions, etc.), and other. Market information represented 58 percent of the first-choice responses in terms of relative importance, whereas technical information constituted only 18 percent. This was a surprise because in the chemical industry, technical information was expected to be of great importance.

Sources of information. Where do managers pick up their information? Aguilar identified two key dimensions along which to array sources: (1) inside versus outside sources, (2) personal versus impersonal sources. This led to four types of sources:

1. *Outside personal sources* such as customers, suppliers, business and professional associates, or bankers.

2. *Outside impersonal sources* such as trade publications, newspapers, tradeshows, or technical conferences.

3. *Inside personal sources* such as subordinates, peers, or superiors.

4. *Inside impersonal sources* such as reports, or notices.

Aguilar discovered that personal sources far exceed impersonal sources in importance (71 percent versus 29 percent). To a large extent, managers rely on face-to-face exchanges to obtain much of the information they find valuable.

Source: Adapted from Francis Joseph Aguilar, *Scanning the Business Environment* (New York: Macmillan 1967).

Summary

Historically, organizations began to practice comprehensive environmental analysis when they recognized that they could not confine their analysis to only economic environments. Organization theorists predicted that environments tend to become increasingly uncertain over time. Two factors contribute to uncertainty: complexity and dynamism; dynamism is the more important of the two. Organizations employ three major mechanisms to manage environmental uncertainty: (1) strategy, (2) internal structure and processes, and (3) mechanisms to anticipate and understand environments.

Box 7.7

Environmental Scanning Systems

What do organizations do to understand and analyze environments for long-term planning? This was the question that a group of researchers from the University of Pittsburgh under the leadership of William R. King posed in late 1970s. The group was intrigued by the reports that futurism was gaining a foothold in many large corporations; they wanted to know if the reports were true.

They adopted a two-pronged approach to answer the question. First, they conducted interviews with line managers in 12 large corporations to understand what their respective or-

ganizations did to analyze their environments. Seven of the large firms were capital intensive; five of them serving both industrial and consumer markets while the other four served only industrial markets. Second, they conducted a mail survey of professional futurists to assess the state of the art in environmental analysis.

The study resulted in a typology of environmental scanning systems: (1) irregular, (2) periodic, and (3) continuous. The major differences among them are presented in the following table.

Characteristic	Irregular	Periodic	Continuous
Reason for scanning	Crisis	Problem/issue	Spotting opportunity
Scope of scanning	Specific event	Selected events	Broad range of environments
Data	Past data for current decision	Past and current data for short-term decisions	Current and prospective for long term
Forecasts	Budgets	Sales oriented	Wide range of socioeconomic forecasts
Process	Ad hoc studies	Periodically updated studies	Structured data collection and analysis
Organization structure	Ad hoc teams	Various staff agencies	Environmental scanning unit

The researchers argued that as organizations confront increasingly complex environments, they have to adopt continuous scanning systems for effectively monitoring environments.

Source: Adapted from L. Fahey, W. R. King, and V. K. Narayanan, "Environmental Scanning and Forecasting in Strategic Planning—The State of the Art," *Long Range Planning,* February 1981, pp. 32–39.

Managers scan environments in a number of ways, from unstructured modes such as unconditioned and conditioned viewing to structured modes such as informal and formal searches. Similarly, organizations adopt different scanning systems: irregular, periodic, and continuous. Large organizations may require continuous environmental scanning systems.

Thus, theoretical work over the years has established that an understanding of environments is a necessary prerequisite to effective organizational responses. Further, organizational responses—strategy or structure—should be contingent on the picture of the environment developed by the organization. The emerging field of environmental analysis has provided a methodology for developing the picture of the environment necessary for formulating organizational responses. The central concepts and models that follow provide the focus of data collection and the analysis of concrete aspects of the environment.

Key Concepts

Environmental analysis focuses on developing a description of current and/or potential environments of an organization. Thus, it provides methods to answer two related questions: (1) What is our current environment? and (2) What are the potential environments we may face in the future? As noted in the introduction, environmental analysis does not address how an organization should respond to its current and future environments. Although, as shown in Box 7.5, we can consider the possible set of organizational responses to different environments, we will show how actual responses are developed in the ensuing chapters on strategic planning and organization design.

We introduce five concepts to summarize the frameworks for environmental analysis: (1) levels of environment, (2) constructs for describing environmental evolution, (3) process of analysis, (4) data sources and analysis, and (5) analysis mode.

Levels of Environment

To understand an organization's environment, it is useful to distinguish among three levels of environment: task environment, industry and competitive environment, and macroenvironment.

Task Environment
Task environment refers to the set of customers, suppliers, competitors, and environmental agencies such as trade associations *directly* related to the firm. Much of the day-to-day operations of a firm involve the task environment. The task environment is more or less *specific* to a firm. Thus, customers are sometimes loyal to a firm, suppliers may grant it preferred status, and so on.

Industry/Competitive Environment
This level refers to the industry composed of the firm and its competitors. This level of environment is shared by most competitors. It is therefore

broader than the task environment. Further, competitors' actions may change the relative position of the firm in the industry, for example, its market share.

Macroenvironment

Macroenvironment is the broadest level of environment and is sometimes referred to as the *general environment* or *political economy*. This level of environment affects almost all industries, although its impacts may be different across them; for example, inflation, interest rates, and antitrust laws affect a host of industries from financial services to personal computers.

Figure 7.4 graphically displays the levels of environment. As shown in the figure, macroenvironment affects the industry/competitive environment, which in turn affects the task environment.

The focus of the models of environment is either the industry/competitive or macroenvironment. In environmental analysis, the task environment is considered to be the output of strategic planning; that is, a choice relatively under the control of the firm. This choice is, however, guided by the analysis of the higher levels of environment: the industry and macroenvironments.

Constructs for Describing Environmental Evolution

Since both macro and industry environments tend to be dynamic, organizations may be interested in understanding how such environments are likely to change in the future. In environmental analysis, we distinguish between *closed* and *open* versions of environment.

Closed Environments

In closed environments, the probable future evolution of the environment is known, and the organization can do very little to change the course of that evolution. For example, the population of the United States older than 15 years of age in the year 2000 can be forecast with some degree of accuracy; any single firm can do little to change the magnitude of the population.

Open Environments

In open environments, the evolution of the environment is uncertain, and an organization can to some extent *by its own actions influence* the future evolution. For example, in some cases, organizations can lobby the government to change the regulations in an industry. The telecommunications industry became deregulated partly as a result of the lobbying efforts of MCI, which led to the breakup of the old AT&T.

The ways of analyzing and responding to these environments are different. When the evolution is predictable, an organization needs to predict it accurately. In a closed environment, the best an organization can do is to

FIGURE 7.4

Levels of environment

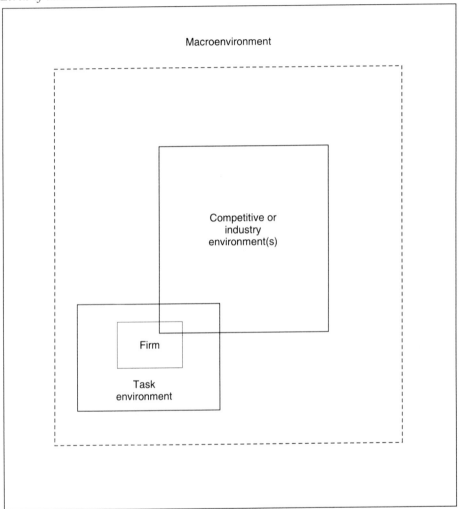

Macroenvironment

Competitive or
industry
environment(s)

Firm

Task
environment

gear up to *adapt* to the prediction. This it could do by redesigning its strategy or its internal characteristics such as structure. On the other hand, when evolution is unpredictable, an organization needs to chart out the feasible paths of evolution. Sometimes these alternative paths of evolution are termed *alternative futures*. An organization can design actions to influence which alternative future should more likely happen. Thus when the future is open to influence, an organization may be able to *create* its own environment.

Process of Analysis

Conceptually, the process of environmental analysis can be divided into four stages: scanning, monitoring, forecasting, and assessment.

Scanning

Scanning refers to the general surveillance of environmental elements to detect environmental change underway and to the identification of early signals of potential environmental change. In the former sense, scanning identifies surprises or strategic issues facing the firm that need immediate attention. In the latter sense, scanning identifies precursors of incipient environmental change for strategy formulation. Scanning is an ill-structured activity since the relevant data may show up in unexpected places. The data is likely to be ambiguous and sometimes vague and disconnected; hence, it has to be given meaning. There is thus a judgmental and intuitive quality to this stage. Scanning is crucial since the judgment made then significantly affects the quality of decision information.

Monitoring

Monitoring involves *systematically* tracking environmental trends and events unearthed during scanning. The activity involves confirming the hunches and intuitive judgments about ambiguous data made during scanning. The data search is focused and systematic. As monitoring progresses, the data becomes precise and focused. Some hunches will be discarded while others will emerge as potentially significant. At the end of monitoring stage, the firm has typically developed a specific description of environmental trends to be forecast.

Forecasting

Forecasting is concerned with developing projections of the direction, scope, speed, and intensity of environmental change. For example, when will a new technology arrive at the marketplace? What impact will a competitor's price reduction have? Forecasting involves first discovering the *forces* or the reasons driving the trends that have been established during monitoring. Secondly, the forces enable the analyst to forecast the pattern of evolution of the trends in the *future*. Finally, the implications of the forecasts—assumptions and projections—are drawn up during this stage.

Assessment

This stage involves identifying and evaluating how and why the current and forecasted environmental change affects the management of the organization. Thus, during this stage, the frame of reference moves from understanding the environment to deriving its implications for the organization.

The implications include strategy, structure, and relevant organizational characteristics.

The four stages are presented pictorially in Figure 7.5. In principle, the process is applicable to all levels of the environment. In practice, it is mostly used for macroenvironment and industry/competitor levels, since they are relatively distant from an organization. In the case of task environment, the process is less elaborate since the organization is already close to environmental elements and hence has a relatively clearer perception about them.

Data Collection and Analysis

The accuracy of the outputs of environmental analysis depends on the quality of the data gathered and the appropriateness of the forecasting techniques employed.

Data Gathering Methods

These may be characterized by (1) source of data, (2) nature of data, and (3) temporal dimension.

FIGURE 7.5

Process of scanning

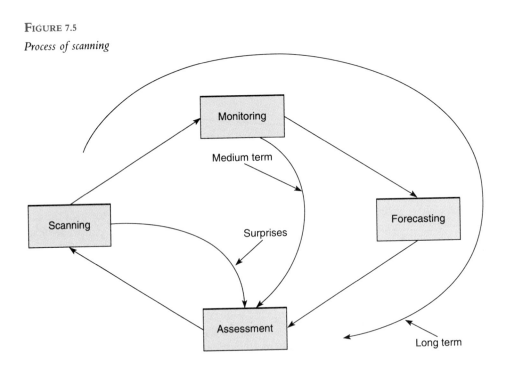

Source of data. Data sources may be either primary or secondary. Primary sources tend to be individuals, focus groups, expert panels, or random samples of populations, directly tapped by an organization for specific purposes and often not available to other organizations. Secondary sources are sources of data gathered by various agencies for wide dissemination (e.g., census tracks). Competitive informational advantages accrue to a firm from primary sources, but they are expensive. Therefore, most environmental analysis employs a combination of the two.

Nature of data. The data may be either *qualitative, quantitative,* or *inferential.* The first two are self-explanatory. Inferential refers to conclusions drawn from various data sources. Inferential data is filled with errors; however, in some cases, a firm will only have inferential data. For example, if a firm is interested in social value changes, it will have to rely on inferential data.

Temporal dimension. The temporal dimension refers to whether the data is collected on an ad hoc, periodic, or real-time basis. In the case of some environmental sectors, such as competitor reactions, it may have to collect data on a real-time (i.e., day-to-day) basis. For some others, such as population growth, a firm may only need to collect data on a periodic or ad hoc basis.

As noted earlier, quality of data influences the reliability of environmental analysis. Consequently, the design of the data collection should be done with care.

Forecasting Techniques

Broadly, there are three types of forecasting techniques: (1) deterministic, (2) adaptive, and (3) inventive.[11]

Deterministic. Deterministic techniques assume that the future is completely known from the past, provided the analyst has at hand a model of the underlying causes. Time series analysis and regression-based sales forecasting are examples. They are particularly appropriate for zones of predictability.

Adaptive. Adaptive techniques do not assume that the future is knowable; instead, they focus on creating alternative descriptions of how the future is unfolding. These techniques rely on abstractions of the world developed by the analysts. They are particularly useful for assessing the consequences of current decisions given a range of future environmental conditions. Scenarios, simulations, or what-if analyses are examples.

Inventive. Inventive techniques are especially useful for open versions of the future since they emphasize how the firm can redesign the future environment. They place a lot of emphasis on speculative or conjectural approaches to the environment.

Environmental analysis typically employs a number of techniques in combination, depending on the specific purpose.

Analysis Mode

Two distinct modes of analysis are typically adopted for environmental analysis: environment-centered and organization-centered.

Environment-Centered

In this mode, the organization engages in analysis to identify and examine plausible environments that may confront it. The objective is to understand the longer term dynamics in an environment without being unduly concerned about the implications for the organization. Naisbitt's book *Mega Trends* referred to in the Historical Underpinnings section earlier in this chapter is an example of this mode of analysis. This mode reduces the blinders that are heavily associated with an emphasis on organization.

Organization-Centered

In this mode, the ongoing business of the organization sets the stage for analysis. For example, which trends affect the markets, products, or technologies of the organization? This mode provides an efficient and well-focused analysis for strategy formulation. However, its narrow focus may result in many relevant trends not being captured in the analysis.

Historically, firms had employed the organization-centered approach almost to the exclusion of the other mode. We noted in the section on historical underpinnings how environmental analysis developed when organizations discovered the need to understand the environment in its own right. This means that they discovered the need to adopt an environment-centered mode. Table 7.1 describes the key differences between the two modes.

Indeed, the two modes are complementary. The environment-centered approach alone is not useful since the focus is on the environment, whereas an exclusive focus on the organization-centered mode, despite its immediate relevancy, may lead to missed opportunities. Further, when an organization is confronted with major environmental shifts, it is often forced to adopt an environment-centered mode. For example, in the wake of deregulation, telecommunication firms have discovered that old assumptions about the environment are no longer valid, and hence comprehensive environmental understanding is necessary for managing their organizations. In contrast, when the turbulence in the environment is low, it may be sufficient to engage in the organization-centered mode.

TABLE 7.1 **Differences between Modes of Analysis**

	Environment-Centered	*Organization-Centered*
Focus and scope	Unconstrained view of environment	View of environment constrained by conception of organization
Goal	Broad environmental analyses before considering the organization	Environmental analysis relevant to current organization
Time horizon	Typically 1–5 years, sometimes 5–10 years	Typically 1–3 years
Frequency	Periodic/irregular	Continuous/periodic
Strengths	Avoids organizational blinders	Efficient, well-focused analysis
	Identifies broader array of trends	Implications for organizational action
	Identifies trends earlier	

Source: Adapted from Liam Fahey and V. K. Narayanan, *Macroenvironmental Analysis for Strategic Management* (St. Paul, Minn.: West Publishing, 1986).

Summary

Organizational environments consist of three levels: task, industry/competitive, and macro levels. Organizations can to a great degree control their task environments during the strategic-planning process. Some elements of the other two levels evolve predictably, whereas other elements are influenced by an organization's actions. The process of environmental analysis consist of four steps: scanning, monitoring, forecasting, and assessment. There are a variety of data collection and forecasting techniques; environmental analysts employ a number of techniques in combination, depending on their specific purpose. Finally, there are two complementary modes of analysis: organization- and environment-centered.

Models for Environmental Analysis

Almost all functional areas in management—finance, marketing, human resources, or manufacturing—have evolved specific models for analyzing their respective environments. For example, finance specialists typically devote significant attention to the operation of capital markets, marketing specialists to customers, and human resource specialists to labor markets. To a large extent, most of these models focus on the level of environment that we defined earlier as the task level. As we also noted earlier (see Historical Underpinnings), these models are not truly integrative or comprehensive. In this chapter, we will not devote attention to them. Instead, we will present the major integrative models for analyzing macro and industry/competitive environments.

Macroenvironment

The macroenvironment, or the general environment, is the broadest level of environment and includes the various societal trends that affect almost all organizations. This level of environment is indeed complex, since it consists of so many elements. To deal with this complexity, Fahey and Narayanan developed a model in which they divided the macroenvironment into four meaningful segments: social, political and regulatory, technological, and economic. The model is presented pictorially in Figure 7.6.

Social

The social segment of the macroenvironment focuses on the shifting demographic patterns, variety of life styles, and social values prevalent or emerging in a society.

> *Demographics* refers to the size, age structure, geographic distribution, ethnic mix, and income distribution of the population in a society. These changes lie at the heart of many long-term changes in society. For example, the shift in age structure toward the elderly is at the root of concerns such as medical and insurance costs.
>
> *Life styles* are people's patterns of living in the world as expressed in household formation, work, education, consumption patterns (goods and services) and leisure activities. Life styles affect demand for goods and services. For example, the importance of women in

FIGURE 7.6

Model of macroenvironment

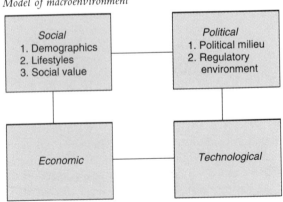

Source: Liam Fahey and V. K. Narayanan, *Macroenvironmental Analysis for Strategic Management* (St. Paul, Minn.: West Publishing, 1986).

automobile-purchasing decisions has led to the redesign of automobiles, different methods of advertising, and even more courteous behavior of salespersons.

Social values are a conception, explicit or implicit, distinctive of an individual or characteristic of a group, of the desirable which influences the selection from available means and ends of action.[12] Social value changes underlie the increasing concern with environment, activism among women and minorities, and similar societal trends.

Taken together the social segment focuses on the subjective elements in the environment that trigger many of the changes in other segments. For example, concern with the natural environment (a shift in social value) has created political and regulatory changes, redesign of consumer goods (e.g., recycling), and even technological developments such as antipollution equipment.

Political/Regulatory

Political and regulatory changes have increasingly been of concern to organizations. Especially in the last two decades in the United States these changes have been so extensive that hardly any facet of the management of large corporations has remained untouched. It is useful to separate the two components of this segment: political and regulatory.

Political milieu may be defined broadly as the arena in which different interest groups compete for attention and resources to advance their own values, interests, and goals. These groups seek power and influence so that their wishes may prevail. The milieu consists not only of the executive and legislative branches of the government but a vast array of interest groups in the society at large.

Regulatory environment consists of a body of laws and regulations that directly or indirectly affect the management of organizations *and* a set of institutions that administer, implement, enforce, and adjudicate laws and regulations, for example, federal and state agencies and the courts. The regulatory agencies use a variety of mechanisms to regulate: rate making, standard setting, instituting information disclosure requirements, and even economic incentives.

Taken together, the political and regulatory segment defines the acceptable and legal codes of behavior for organizations in a society.

Technological

Technology refers to the branch of knowledge that deals with industrial arts, applied science and engineering, and more broadly as the sum of ways in which a social group provides itself with the material objects of civilization. The technological segment embraces the institutions and activities involved in the creation of new knowledge (what is often referred to as science) and the translation of that knowledge into new products, processes, and materials.

Technological change is the most visible and pervasive form of change in society. It directly affects every aspect of society around us; for example, transportation modes, energy forms, communication, entertainment, health care, food, agriculture, and industry.

Technological changes can rejuvenate and obliterate existing industries or bring entirely new ones into existence. In addition, technological changes often bring about chain reactions or secondary consequences, transforming the institutions, life styles, and social structure of societies:

> Stone axes played important functions in Yir Yorunt life beyond that of cutting wood. The men owned stone axes, which were symbols of masculinity and respect for elders. When Christian missionaries distributed steel axes to men (a change in technology) women and children—apparently without discrimination!, the older men distrustful of the missionaries were less likely to accept the steel axes. Soon elders of the tribe, once highly respected, had to borrow steel axes from women and younger men. The previous status relationships were thoroughly upset (Bauer, 1969).[13]

As this quote suggests, sometimes seemingly minor technological changes can profoundly affect the functioning of a society.

Economic

By economic segment we refer to the nature and direction of the economy in which an organization operates. It includes the stock of physical and natural resources and the aggregation of all markets where goods and services are exchanged for payment. More specifically, economic activity is reflected in levels and patterns of industrial output, consumption, income, savings and investments, capital and labor availability, and price movements. Such indices as gross national product, inflation, interest and unemployment rates, foreign exchange fluctuations, concentration of wealth, and consumer price indices refer to various aspects of this segment.

Change is an enduring characteristic of the economic segment. The last two decades have witnessed such frequent economic change that economic uncertainty is now considered a fact of life.

The economic segment has perhaps the most direct impact on the functioning of most business organizations. It affects the level of demand, cost of operation, and access to capital. However, it may have a different impact on different industries. For example, demand for consumer durables may rise or fall with economic upturns and downturns, whereas some industries (e.g., beverage) may be immune to such fluctuations.

As shown in Figure 7.6, the macroenvironmental segments are interrelated. For example, changes in the economic segment may affect the political segment, technological change may affect social values, and so on. The linkages illustrate the theme that the macroenvironment can be understood only in an integrated fashion. Thus, every segment affects and is affected by other segments to varying degrees.

There are differences in the process of scanning, monitoring and forecasting among the environmental segments. Using the classification scheme for data sources and forecasting techniques, Table 7.2 displays the characteristics of the activities among the four segments. As shown in the table, quantitative data are available primarily for demographic and economic segments. In the case of technological change, although quantitative data are available at an aggregate level (e.g., R&D expenditure across all industries), data for managerial analysis need to be collected actively. For all the other segments, the data are qualitative and have to be specifically sought out.

The differences in data are reflected in the forecasting techniques employed in each segment. Except in the case of demographics and short-term economic forecasting, techniques require varying degrees of individual judgment. The techniques are not robust and the precision of their forecasts is variable. Put another way, many changes in the segments are uncertain.

The macroenvironment affects both industry/competitive and task levels of the environment. We will describe its linkages to industries after our discussion of the industry/competitive environment.

Industry/Competitive Environment

Michael Porter[14] has provided the most widely accepted and comprehensive model for analyzing the industry/competitive environment. Porter argued that the relatively enduring characteristics of an industry are perhaps the most important environment an organization should consider in the formulation of its strategies. This is so because the *collective* strength of the characteristics determine the ultimate profit potential of an industry.

According to Porter, the state of competition in an industry is determined by a set of five forces: (1) threat of entry, (2) power of suppliers, (3) power of buyers, (4) threat of substitution, and (5) intensity of rivalry. (See Figure 7.7.)

Threat of Entry

Porter notes that since new entrants into an industry bring new capacity, the desire to gain market share, and often substantial resources, they pose a threat to existing firms in the industry. The threat, according to Porter, is dependent on the *barriers to entry* present and on the reaction from existing. firms that the entrant can expect.

Just what constitutes barriers to entry? Porter identifies six potential entry barriers:

1. *Economies of scale.* If there are economies of scale in production, marketing, research and development, service, or any major *operation* of firms in an industry, then aspirants will have to enter

TABLE 7.2 Process of Environmental Analysis for Different Macroenvironmental Segments

Unique Features of Analysis	Demographics	Social Lifestyles	Social Values	Political Milieu	Regulatory	Technological	Economic
Activities **Scanning** Data availability	Abundance of quantitative data	Some quantitative data, qualitative data needs to be searched out	No standard measure available	Data available from personal sources, access may pose problems	Data available from primary and secondary sources	Data on national trends available, otherwise shrouded in secrecy	Abundant data on a weekly, monthly, and yearly basis
Key problem area	Organization and interpretation of data	Detection of new life-styles	Values have to be inferred in many cases	Data need to be elicited on real-time basis	Relatively detectable; discontinuities at the judicial level	Detection is difficult because of secrecy issues	Structural shifts difficult to detect
Monitoring Availability of indicators	Plentiful; available on ongoing basis	Indicators sometimes unique to life style; market research techniques needed	None. Have to be created for specific purposes	None. Have to be created for specific issues; key is tracking events	No standard measures	No standard measures. Specific performance parameters for specific changes. No timely availability	Wide array of standardized indicators, availability on real-time basis
Forecasting Theories of change	Models of population growth and shifts	None available for prediction	None available for application	None available	No theory of regulation	No theory of invention; some for diffusion of innovation	Several available for cyclical and seasonal change, e.g., Kondratief's cycle for long cycles

Unique Features of Analysis	Demographics	Social Lifestyles	Social Values	Political Milieu	Regulatory	Technological	Economic
General accuracy	Fairly high in the short run	Low for new lifestyle	Unknown	Variable; none for long term	Generally moderate	Generally moderate to low	Low in terms of magnitude of effects, high in terms of direction of effects
Assessment Primary impact[a]	Market potential, growth, regional concentration	Market segmentation, product differentiation	Creates discontinuities and unique pressures	Risk, creates discontinuities, stakeholders	Entry barriers, cost position diversification pattern, product requirements	Product substitution, product differentiation cost position, new industries for diversification	Demand, cost of doing business, availability of capital, acquisition, divestitures
Techniques	Transition matrices, log linear models	Focus groups, lifestyle profiling, diffusion matrices	Value profile, social pressures priority analysis, socio-political forecasting	Network analysis, political-risk analysis, socio-political forecasting	Network analysis, event-history analysis	Logistic curves, time independent comparison, Delphi, morphological method, relevance trees	Economic models, input-output matrices, simulation models, industrial dynamics time series analysis, trend extrapolation

a Selectively presented.

Source: V. K. Narayanan and Liam Fahey, "Macroenvironmental Analysis for Strategy Formulation," in *Strategic Planning and Management Handbook* ed. W. R. King and D. I. Cleland (New York: Van Nostrand Reinhold 1987), pp. 165-66.

229

FIGURE 7.7

Porter's model of industry

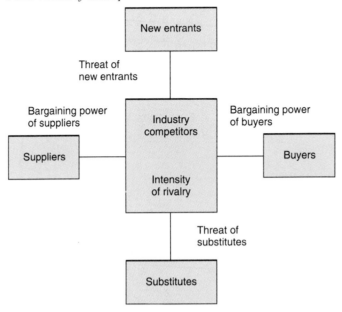

Source: Adapted from Michael Porter, *Competitive Strategy* (New York: Free Press, 1980).

on a large scale (thus requiring huge resources in the beginning) or accept a cost disadvantage.

2. *Product differentiation.* Brand identification creates a barrier by forcing entrants to spend heavily to overcome existing customer loyalty.

3. *Capital requirements.* The need to invest considerable financial resources in order to compete creates a barrier to entry, especially if the capital expenditures are for unrecoverable items such as advertising or R&D.

4. *Cost disadvantages independent of scale.* Existing companies may have advantages from the effects of the learning curve, proprietary technology, access to raw materials, favorable locations, and the like. Sometimes, cost disadvantages are legally enforced, as in the case of patents.

5. *Access to distribution channels.* "The more limited the wholesale or retail channels are and the more the existing competitors have these tied up, obviously the tougher the entry to that industry will be."[15]

6. *Government policy.* Sometimes government regulation may restrict industry through such actions as setting license requirements and limiting access to raw materials.

The entry barriers, together with the retaliation an aspiring new entrant expects from existing firms, determine the threat of entry. If the barriers are high and a newcomer expects sharp retaliation from existing firms, then it is less likely that newcomers will enter. Consequently, the industry is likely to be more profitable than another where there are low entry barriers and low threats of retaliation.

Bargaining Power of Suppliers and Buyers

Since the factors that constitute the power of suppliers and buyers are similar, we will discuss them together. Several factors determine the relative power position of buyers and suppliers vis-a-vis industry. The more significant ones are:

> *Concentration.* If their industries are dominated by a few firms, concentrated buyers/suppliers can exert great pressure on the industry.
>
> *Differentiation.* Differentiation is a source of power to the seller. Thus, if the suppliers offer a *unique* product, or if the industry offers an *undifferentiated* product, then firms in the industry may be in a disadvantageous position.
>
> *Switching costs.* If in switching from one supplier to another, the firm has to incur major costs (e.g., training from one computer system to another), the switching costs provide the suppliers leverage. Similarly, if buyers are locked in because of switching costs, then it gives the industry some power over them.
>
> *Credible threat of integration.* If either the buyer or supplier poses the threat of entering as competitors into the industry (i.e., forward or backward integration), then this serves as a check against the industry's ability to improve the terms on which it sells or buys.
>
> *Importance of the industry.* Suppliers and buyers have greater bargaining edge if the industry is not important to them.

If either suppliers or buyers are powerful relative to the firms in the industry, they can significantly lower the profitability by increasing costs of raw materials and other inputs (as in the case of suppliers) or forcing the firms to set lower prices, or offer higher quality or more service (as in the case of buyers).

Threat of Substitution

Substitute products limit the profit potential of an industry by placing a ceiling on the prices. To counteract the substitutes, an industry would have to upgrade the quality of the product or differentiate it. Porter notes that two types of substitutes are especially troublesome.

1. *Rapid improvement.* Substitutes where technological change is bringing rapid improvement in product features or reduction in costs.
2. *High-profit industries.* Substitutes produced by high-profit industries, who can afford to lower prices.

As we have pointed out in our discussion of the macroenvironment, technological change brings in substitutes often to the detriment of the industry.

Intensity of Rivalry

Rivalry is related to the presence of a number of factors:

> *Numerous competitors.* If the competitors are numerous or roughly equal in size, then rivalry is likely to be high.
>
> *Slow growth.* In slow growth industries, competition often fights for market share.
>
> *Undifferentiated products.* If the products are undifferentiated and have no switching costs, then rivalry is likely to be enhanced.
>
> *High fixed costs.* High costs encourage firms to cut prices so that there will be an increase in sales to cover the costs.
>
> *Exit barriers.* If there are barriers to exiting, such as specialized assets or management loyalty to a business, then firms are likely to persist even if they may be incurring losses.
>
> *Diversity among competitors.* If the competing firms have different personalities, intensity is likely to increase given very different ideas about how to compete.

Rivalry among competitors takes many forms: price cutting, new product introduction, advertising battles, and so on. Intense rivalry will most definitely lead to lower profitability for the industry.

Porter argues that the structure of the industry helps determine two key organizational responses. First, it enables firms to determine whether to enter, stay, or exit from the industry. Indeed, it is not reasonable to enter industries with poor profitability. Second, a firm's product-market strategy—how to compete—depends on matching its strengths to the opportunities and requirements of the industry structure.

For the purpose of environmental analysis, Porter's model serves two functions. First, the model of the five forces and the detailed characterization of each force provide a framework for collecting industry/competitive data. This data is widely available from a host of public sources: government publications, popular business periodicals, and the press. Second, since the model provides relatively clear implications, it facilitates strategy development (a topic we will take up in the next chapter).

Linkages between Models

As shown in Figure 7.8, the macro and industry/competitive environments are related, since macro-level forces influence industry structure. Thus, some of the forces driving industry change lie in the various macroenvironmental segments: social, political/regulatory, technological, and economic. We can sketch five important ways in which the macroenvironment influences industry.

FIGURE 7.8

Linkages between macro and industry environments

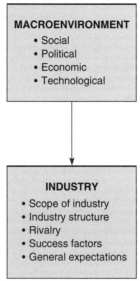

First, macro forces may influence the *scope of the industry* by opening up opportunities or stifling industry expansion. For example, regulatory changes in the telecommunications industry provided opportunities to computer firms to enter the industry—IBM entered through MCI. Similarly, personal computers have limited the scope of the personal calculator market.

Second, macro forces may affect each one of the *forces* identified by Porter. Demographic and life style changes may affect consumer tastes; technological change may create viable substitutes, lower the costs of doing business, and lower entry barriers; deregulation may intensify rivalry, and so on.

Third, macro forces may impact different groups of competitors differently, thus *shifting the nature of the rivalry*. For example, deregulation of the airlines in the late 1970s had an adverse impact on long-haul firms relative to shorter haul ones and led to the restructuring of routes.

Fourth, and related to the above, macro changes potentially affect the *key success factors* in an industry, or what it takes to be successful in it. For example, the gasoline shortage of the late 1970s caused motel chains to shift their locations from near the highways to near airports, since they feared loss of volume from infrequent highway usage. Location, a key success factor in the industry, was affected by the energy crisis of the 1970s.

Finally, macroenvironmental change potentially affects the *general expectation* about an industry and firms in it. Expectation is important because it influences the flow of capital into the industry and the stock price behavior of its firms. In Box 7.8 we have presented the structure of the U.S. airlines industry both before and after deregulation.

Box 7.8

Airline Industry

The birth of the U.S. airline industry followed the 1903 flight of the Wright brothers by 15 years. Commercial aviation had its beginnings in the delivery of mail when in 1918 the U.S. Post Office established the U.S. Aerial Mail Service, initially from Washington to New York. In the late 1920s, the goal of the U.S. Post Office was to establish transcontinental airmail service. By 1933, transcontinental routes were assigned to American, TWA, and United. Until 1978, the airline industry was regulated by the Civil Aeronautics Board (CAB), which had been established by the Civil Aeronautics Act of 1933.

The CAB dictated the terms of competitive rivalry within the airline industry until deregulation in 1980. The CAB controlled market entry and exit: in fact, in its 40-year history, the CAB never awarded a major route to a new airline. Exit also required complex, time-consuming CAB proceedings; consequently, mergers were the preferred means of exit. The industry was remarkably durable: All the 16 trunk carriers at the beginning of regulation in 1938 were represented either directly or via merger in the 11 trunk carriers existing at the end of regulation in 1978.

The CAB also regulated airfares on the basis of some percent of profitability to the airlines (de facto guaranteeing their profitability). As a result there was no price competition. Instead, airlines competed on service and schedule. The managements of airlines had little incentive to control costs; this, in turn, gave labor some power to extract higher wages.

In terms of Porter's framework, the airline industry before deregulation may be pictured thus:

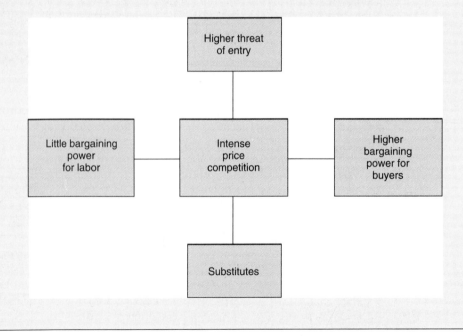

Box 7.8 continued

After deregulation in 1978, the picture changed drastically. Immediately after deregulation, a number of airlines entered the industry; the prices came down, and airline traffic increased. However, later, due to bankruptcies and mergers, the number of major airlines dwindled. There were a number of labor strikes, but few of them succeeded. Industry conditions had changed dramatically.

It was soon clear that there were other entry barriers. The lack of capacity in the air traffic control system and at major airports made it difficult for start-up airlines to enter certain major markets. The enormous capital investment in aircraft was also prohibitive, although it could be reduced through leasing rather than buying aircraft. Further, major airlines could price discriminate between regions; a start up airline, offering service to a limited geographic area, could not survive a fare war with a major carrier that subsidized its short-term losses with profits from less competitive markets.

Further, in the wake of increased price competition after deregulation, firms were interested in cost control since customers could not be sold on service alone. This reduced the power of the unions, and the strikes that followed did not lead to clear labor victories. The strikes, however, allowed the firms to increase the non-union labor and thus control labor costs.

In terms of Porter's framework, the airline industry could now be pictured thus:

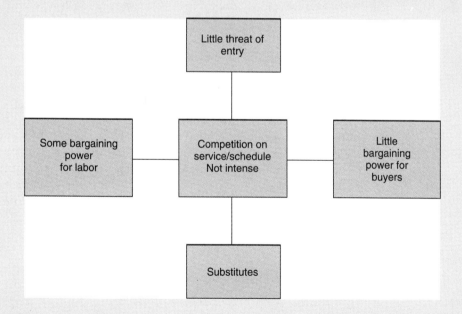

Many analysts note that long-run prospects for the surviving firms in the industry are good, although in the short run, when competitive battles are still being fought, the industry may experience some bad times.

In summary, although the two models capture different levels of environments, they are closely related. However, they have different levels of applicability, an issue to which we now turn.

Levels of Applicability

There are two contextual factors that influence the choice of the models of the environment: (1) the time frame for organizational response, and (2) the size of the firm.

Time Frame

Table 7.3 displays the relative importance of levels of environment for organizational responses. Simply stated, the longer the time frame of response, the more comprehensive the analysis should be. In the short run, the task environment dominates the responses of the firm. Macro and industry analyses are likely to be organization-centered and not comprehensive. In the medium term, when the industry level becomes important, comprehensive industry analysis is recommended, augmented by macro forces that drive industry changes. In the long run, macro forces assume great importance and an environment-centered approach is useful.

Size

A firm's size often dictates the amount of resources that are available for environmental analysis. Comprehensive macro and industry analyses may be affordable only by large and medium-large firms; smaller firms will probably have to be content with a task level focus augmented by selected macro and industry characteristics from an organization-centered perspective.

As the reader may have inferred from the discussion of the models, environmental analysis involves personnel, time, and costs of data collection and analysis; it could, therefore, be expensive. For the benefits of analysis to outweigh the costs, an appropriate level of analysis must be chosen. The two contextual factors—time frame of response and size of the firm—need to be considered in making the choice.

A Systems Theoretic Review

By now, it must be fairly clear that environmental analysis developed from the increasing recognition of the open systems character of modern-day organizations. The action frameworks emphasize the interdependence between an organization and its environment. Beyond this obvious point, the field borrows many of the central concepts from modern systems theory to study environments on the one hand and make assumptions about organizational behavior on the other. We will briefly discuss these two points.

TABLE 7.3   **Applicability of Environmental Models to Different Time Frames**

Time Frame	Focus		
	Task	*Industry*	*Macro*
Short term	High	Moderate	Low
Medium term	Moderate	High	Moderate
Long term	Low	Moderate	High

Source: Adapted from Liam Fahey and V. K. Narayanan, *Macroenvironmental Analysis for Strategic Management* (St. Paul, Minn.: West Publishing, 1986).

Systems Concepts to Study the Environment

The field conceives of the environment itself as a system of interconnected elements. What is seen as the environment of the organization from an organization-centered point of view is defined as the system for analysis. Consequently, some systems concepts are imported to the study of the environment itself. We may enumerate four of these concepts: levels, interdependence, instability, and nonlinearity.

1. The environment is seen as composed of *levels:* macro, industry/competitive, task environments, with the broader ones including the narrower ones.

2. Levels and the segments at each level are described as *highly interdependent.* For example, the segments of the macroenvironment are deemed to be interrelated, so, also, the forces in the industry/competitive environment. In addition, the levels themselves are interconnected: The macro level influences the industry/competitive level, and vice versa.

3. Many of the elements are changing, and hence, the environment itself is considered to be unstable.

4. It is believed that the linkages among the elements are deemed to be highly nonlinear. Environmental analysis suggests that nonlinearities become visible over a protracted period of time, not immediately.

Environmental analysis is thus conceptually anchored in the systems concepts for the very study of environments.

Assumptions about Organizations

Two distinct themes regarding organizational behavior underlie environmental analysis:

1. Environmental analysis underscores multiple forms of interdependence between an organization and its environment. In some cases, the interdependence forces an organization to adapt or become extinct, in some cases to change the environments in which it functions, in others to influence the course of environmental evolution, and in still others to create entirely new ones. The recognition of the potential to change and create environments is unique to the environmental analysis field.

2. Environmental analysis focuses on the cognitive processes that bring about organizational transformation, almost to the exclusion of political, social or cultural forces in the organization.

From the perspective of the systems model, environmental analysis has primary implications for the functional subsystem within the organization. If sufficient attention is paid to understanding the environment, then appropriate strategies, structures, and responses can be forged by the organization. In this sense, environmental analysis is the first step in the *rational* approaches to managing organizations. It provides the critical information for strategic planning and ensuing organization designs—approaches we will describe in the next two chapters.

Chapter Summary

The term organizational environment refers to the factors external to an organization which influence its functioning and performance. Environmental analysis is the process by which key decision makers develop an understanding of environmental factors that may influence organizational functioning and performance currently or in the future.

Various functional departments, such as marketing or finance departments in organizations, have always conducted the analysis of environmental segments relevant to their functions. However, environmental analysis as we know it came to be practiced when organizations discovered the need to develop an integrated view of their environments. It signalled the acceptance of open systems models, which underscored the need to understand the environments in their own right.

Organization theorists argue that environments evolve over four stages: (1) placid random, (2) placid clustered, (3) disturbed reactive, and (4) turbulent. Two features of environments are deemed to be important: uncertainty and resource dependence. Uncertainty itself was created by environmental complexity and dynamism. Organizations respond to environments through choice of strategy, internal structure and processes, and mechanisms to understand environments.

There are four different ways in which managers try to understand their environments. Some, such as undirected viewing, are highly unstructured; whereas others, such as formalized search, as the name implies, are highly structured. Still others, such as directed viewing and informal search, lie somewhere in between the continuum between highly structured and unstructured. Organizations usually set up mechanisms to understand and analyze their environments, these fall into three types: (1) irregular, (2) periodic, and (3) continuous.

Organization environments may be arranged according to three levels: task environment, industry/competitive environments, and macro environments. An organization has some control over its task environments whereas industry/competitive and macroenvironments are relatively less under its control. When the evolution of an environment is predictable and not under the control of an organization, we call it a closed environment; we call an environment open if the evolution is influenceable by an organization.

Environmental analysis proceeds in four steps: scanning, monitoring, forecasting, and assessment. The data may be derived from primary or secondary sources. There are three types of forecasting techniques: deterministic, adaptive, and inventive. Organizations typically adopt either an environment-centered or organization-centered approach to environmental analysis. The organization-centered approach is particularly useful for the short run whereas the environment-centered approach is almost always recommended for the long run.

Two models of environment have been developed to capture the (1) macro, and (2) industry/competitive environments respectively. Thus macroenvironment consists of social, economic, technological and political segments. Industry environment consists of five forces: barriers to entry, bargaining power of suppliers and buyers, threat of substitution, and intensity of rivalry. Changes in macroenvironments invariably affect some or all of the five forces in the industry environment.

Environmental analysis is the starting point in the rational approach to management. The outputs of the analysis form the basis of strategic planning, a topic we will describe in the next chapter. The characteristics of the environments and organizational strategies together determine appropriate organizational designs; therefore, we will deal with the design process after we have discussed strategic planning.

Specialized Terms

Megatrends
Types of environments
• Placid random

• Placid clustered
• Disturbed reactive
• Turbulent

Uncertainty
- Simple-complex
- Stable-dynamic

Modes of scanning
- Undirected viewing
- Conditioned viewing
- Informal search
- Formal search

Primary versus secondary source

Qualitative, quantitative, or
  inferential data

Social segment
- Demographics
- Life-styles
- Social values

Technological segment

Scanning systems
- Irregular systems
- Periodic systems
- Continuous systems

Task environment

Industry/competitive environment

Macroenvironment

Closed versus open

Alternative futures

Scanning

Monitoring

Forecasting

Assessment

Forecasting technique
- Deterministic
- Adaptive
- Inventive

Environment-centered versus
  organization-centered

Political segment

Economic segment

Barriers to entry

Bargaining power

Substitution

Discussion Questions

Theoretical

1. What are the objectives of environmental analysis? Why is environmental analysis the starting point in a rational open systems approach to managing organizations?

2. What are the stages in the evolution of an environment?

3. What are the key dimensions of an environment on which the responses must be based? What are the responses for different types of environments?

4. What are the stages in the analysis of an environment?

5. How do various levels of environment differ?

6. Enumerate the major differences between environment-centered versus organization-centered modes of analysis.

7. Outline a model for describing (1) the macroenvironment, and (2) the industry environment. Sketch the relationships between the two.

★8. Since all organizations are contained in their environments, the environment of an organization is a system of which the

---

★This is an advanced-level question.

organization is a subsystem. Comment. If this is true, what does it imply for understanding environments?

★9. What is the distinction between adaptation and the model of change implicit in the notion of alternate futures?

Applied

1. You have just taken over as the divisional manager of the electronics division of a major diversified corporation. What would you do to understand your environment?

2. A small business firm has approached you to help them understand their environment. How would you proceed?

End Notes

1. "Bankrolling the Rebirth of the East," *Business Week,* April 29, 1991, pp. 45–46.
2. Donnela H. Meadows et al., *Limits to Growth: A Report for the Club of Rome's Project on the Predicament of Mankind* (New York: Universe Books, 1972).
3. Mihajoo Eduard Mesarovic, *Mankind at the Turning Point: The Second Report to the Club of Rome* (New York: Dutton, 1974).
4. John Naisbitt, *Megatrends: Ten New Directions Transforming Our Lives* (New York: Warner Books, 1984).
5. Fred E. Emery and Eric L. Trist, "The Causal Texture of Organizational Environments," *Human Relations* 18 (1965), pp. 21–32.
6. Igor Ansoff, *Strategic Management* (New York: Halstead Press, 1981).
7. Robert B. Duncan, "Characteristics of Perceived Environments and Perceived Environmental Uncertainty," *Administrative Science Quarterly* 17, no. 3 (1972), pp. 313–27.
8. Richard L. Daft, *Organization Theory and Design,* 3rd ed. (St. Paul, Minn.: West Publishing, 1989).
9. Francis Aguilar, *Scanning the Business Environment* (New York: Macmillan, 1967).
10. Liam Fahey, William R. King, and V. K. Narayanan "Environmental Scanning and Forecasting in Strategic Planning—The State of the Art," *Long Range Planning,* February 1981, pp. 32–39.
11. Eric Jantsch, "Forecasting and the Systems Approach: A Frame of Reference," *Management Science* 19 (1973), pp. 1355–67.
12. Clyde Kluckohn, "Values and Value Orientation," in *Toward a General Theory of Action,* ed. T. Parsons and E. A. Shils (Cambridge Mass.: Harvard University Press, 1962), p. 395.
13. Ray A. Bauer, *Second Order Consequences* (Cambridge Mass.: MIT Press, 1969).
14. Michael E. Porter, *Competitive Strategy* (New York: Free Press, 1980).
15. Michael E. Porter, "How Competitive Forces Shape Strategy," *Harvard Business Review,* March/April 1979.

8 STRATEGIC PLANNING

Chapter Outline

Apple's John Sculley thinks that things have been rough. Since January 1990, the 14-year-old personal computer company has suffered flagging growth, an embarrassing turnover of top management, stiff competition from IBM-compatible PCs, and rock bottom employee morale. In October 1990 Apple was planning to revamp its popular Macintosh product line, rolling out three new systems priced to undercut IBM compatibles. One of the models, retailing for less than $1,000, made it from the drawing board to factory in under nine months, half the usual development time. Another, outfitted with a color monitor, will sell for under $2,500, half the price of current color Macs.

Selling computers at low prices represents a reversal of Apple's strategy. Since 1986, Sculley had been trying to shed the company's hobbyist image and tap into the lucrative market for office computers. To achieve his goal, Sculley focused on building ever more powerful Macs. The line included six models, ranging up to the Macintosh IIFX, which features fast processing, capacious memory, lavish color graphics, and sells for more than $10,000. This high-end, high-margin approach transformed Apple into one of the fastest growing and most profitable makers of PCs. Sales grew from $1.9 billion in 1986 to $5.3 billion in the fiscal year ending in September 1989. Profits rose to nearly half a billion dollars.

But in 1989, the strategy ran out of gas. Those same business customers who had clamored for more powerful Apple machines now complained that Macs were simply too expensive. Likewise, Apple's original customers—individuals, schools, and small businesses—were deserting to the clones. Finally, Microsoft Corp. unleashed a frontal assault, releasing Windows 3.0, a program that gives IBM compatibles a snazzier screen that rivals the famous friendly Mac.

Sculley has devised a two-pronged counterattack, in which he hopes lower prices and a broader product line will jump-start unit sales. By cutting Apple's notoriously fat operating margins, the strategy will profoundly alter the company's way of doing business. If it works, Apple will open up new markets for the aging Macintosh line and buy itself time to discover new technologies necessary to remain a PC leader. If it doesn't, Apple could end up an also ran in the industry it invented.[1]

The personal computer industry has been changing and the competition has been getting fiercer. In response to the industry situation, Apple was forced to reformulate its strategy. Instead of pursuing a strategy of differentiation—narrow product line, high-price premium quality personal computers—Apple decided to bet on a strategy of being a broad line player with lower prices, sacrificing operating margins.

How should an organization compete in an industry? How should it position its product? What should it do in terms of marketing—distribution, pricing, promotion, and the like? Which industries should it play in? In general, how should an organization fashion its strategy? These questions are typically raised and answered during the strategic planning process of an organization.

Over the last two decades, strategy and strategic planning have become business buzzwords: top managers determine strategic missions and objectives; divisional managers orchestrate product/market strategies; and functional managers formulate tactics for everything from marketing, research and development, and finance to manufacturing and human resources. Most large organizations have strategic planning departments; even small businesses are encouraged by venture capitalists and lending institutions to formulate a concrete business plan. Strategic planning is here to stay as a major approach to managing organizations.

What Is Strategic Planning?

Strategic planning refers to the process by which organizational goals and the means to achieve those goals are formulated and implemented. Thus, in practice, strategic planning addresses such questions as:

> What should the goals of the organization be—profit maximization, growth in revenues, being a market leader?
>
> By what means should the organization attain its goals? Should it divest some businesses or acquire new ones? What kind of customers should it cater to? How should it compete in the market: providing low-price or premium quality products?

As indicated by these questions, strategic planning primarily deals with the economic goals of the organization and the means or the strategy to attain the goals. An organization's strategy is reflected in the choice of industries in which the organization operates and the manner in which it competes in those industries. Apple, for example, has continued to operate in the personal computer industry, although as we saw in the beginning, it has decided to compete on price.

Proponents of strategic planning argue that the economic health of an organization is the prime requisite for its survival. To ensure this health, an organization's strategy should meet environmental threats and take advantage of environmental opportunities. If the strategy is out of step with the environment, no amount of changing individuals, structure, or reward systems will solve the problems of the organization. For example, in 1984, People Express Airlines was considered one of the best managed companies. Their employees were treated well; their customers were offered low prices and thus considered happy; People's president was invited to many management schools to give talks on the best way to manage. Yet just two years later, People Express folded. Many industry analysts noted that People had misjudged the nature of the environment, especially the hostile competition that was unleashed by deregulation of the airline industry.

Linkage to the Systems Model

Strategic planning is concerned with managing the match between an organization and its environments. Thus, in systems theory terms, strategic planning is concerned with the choice of desired outputs of the organization, and the coordination of inputs and the conversion process to achieve the desired outputs. The internal characteristics of the organization—structure, process, people, and so on—are viewed as tools to execute the strategy. The internal characteristics are, therefore, judged to be appropriate for an organization if they are consistent with the adopted strategy. Figure 8.1 displays the systems logic behind strategic planning.

Table 8.1 lists how the key systems concepts are operationalized in strategic planning. Perhaps no other management approach focuses on the organization-environment interface as explicitly or as comprehensively as strategic planning. Since strategic planning focuses primarily on industries, the environments are assumed to be competitive to varying degrees. Organizational boundaries are constantly shifting, sometimes by competitors' actions, and sometimes by the strategic decisions of top managers (corporate and business strategy decisions).

Strategic planning highlights two different ways by which organizations can manage their interface with environments: (1) the *choice of environment* and (2) *internal adaptation* by the firm. Thus, some facets of the environment—what we termed the *task environment* in the previous chapter—are deemed to be under the control of an organization. Thus, organizations have some discretion over the industries in which they should operate; organizations also have considerable discretion over the scope of business: products, customers, and regions.

Internal adaptation also receives attention, since strategies determine the direction in which to reorient a firm's internal operations. Strategy, thus, becomes the mechanism of managing internal and external interdependence. It sets the premises for organization design, as well as other internal characteristics.

In actuality, this approach primarily focuses on linking the functional subsystem of an organization with the environment, and sometimes addresses the internal dynamics related to the other subsystems. Thus, in

FIGURE 8.1

Systems logic behind strategic planning

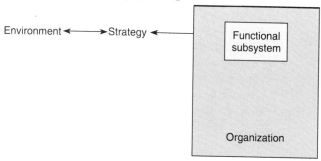

Design a strategy to link
environment and functional subsystem

TABLE 8.1   **Linkage to Systems Concepts**

Concept	Operationalization
Environment	Industries and competitive markets
Open systems	Strategy as the match between environment and organization
Subsystem	Functional subsystem
Level	Levels of strategy
Interdependence	Strategy as the basis for coordination
Equifinality	There is more than one feasible strategy at any time
Stability versus change	Focus on change
Emergent behavior	Environment is a source of emergent behavior

strategic planning, the functional subsystem is considered to be the primary instrument by which the organization engages the environment. The elements of the organization's functional subsystem (organization structure, rewards, and the like) are to be designed primarily for implementing the strategies. In this sense, the functional subsystem is considered to be determined by the strategy of the firm.

The linkages that strategic planning makes to the other internal subsystems of an organization are implicit:

Political Subsystem. Two critical though implicit assumptions about the political subsystem underlie the strategic planning approach. (1) Top management, the major architect of organizational strategies, is considered to be a consensual entity. Thus, there are few disagreements about goals in this group. The differences with respect to goals and specific action alternatives are easily resolved since the top managers are assumed to be predominantly rational. (2) Top managers, by virtue of their position, are assumed to have sufficient power to direct their subordinates toward execution of strategies.

Social Subsystem. The social subsystem is considered to be a derivative of requirements of the functional subsystem. Morale and cooperation are necessary only for strategy implementation. Further, three assumptions about the social subsystem are implicit: (1) human capabilities when absent can be acquired by recruitment. Thus, for example, when a business investment strategy shifts from growth (market share acquisition) to stability (share maintenance), it is necessary to recruit and appoint the right individual to manage the business unit; (2) the individuals are flexible and malleable so that changes in strategic direction can be easily accomplished; and (3) a sufficient level of trust is present in the organization such that internal information—so vital to strategy formulation—is not systematically distorted.

TABLE 8.2   **Strategic Planning: Subsystem-Related Assumptions**

Subsystem	Assumptions
Functional	Explicit dominant subsystem
Social	Supportive social subsystem: Cooperation can be achieved
Political	Top management has sufficient power. Consensus among top managers
Informational	Data acquisition is easy
Cultural	Norms of rationality

Informational Subsystem. Strategy analysis requires abundant data about the environment and internal operations of the organization. It is assumed that information is available so that rational decision making is ensured.

Cultural Subsystem. The cultural subsystem is assumed to be a derivative of strategic requirements. The notion that much of culture is unarticulated and invisible is not relevant within this framework.

Table 8.2 lists how various subsystems are viewed in strategic planning. Strategic planning thus becomes an important step in the rational approaches to planned change in organizations. It is related to environmental analysis, presented in the previous chapter, as assessments of macro and industry environments become the basis of strategy formulation. Strategy becomes the basis of organization design, which we will take up in the next chapter.

In this chapter, we discuss strategic planning from the perspective of the systems model. The scheme of this chapter is as follows: first, we summarize the philosophical, historical, and theoretical underpinnings of strategic planning; second, we present some of the key concepts necessary to understand this field; third, we outline some of the frameworks for strategy formulation; and finally, we sketch its strengths and limitations.

Underpinnings

Philosophical Underpinnings

As we noted in the first chapter, notions of strategy and planning can be traced as far back as the ancients, for example, the Chinese civilization. Strategy has its roots in the art of warfare or the military sciences. The success of a general or an army commander was often attributed to his ability to outwit the enemy and his skills in formulating a superior strategy. The accent on rationality prevalent in the contemporary theory and practice of strategic planning is visible in the writings of Sun Tzu, the legendary

Chinese general. In his *The Art of War,* translated into English in 1905 and popularized recently, Sun Tzu cites the reasons for a general's success:

> The General who wins a battle makes many calculations in his temple before the battle is fought. The general who loses a battle makes but few calculations beforehand. Thus do many calculations lead to victory, and few calculations to defeat; how much more no calculation at all! It is by attention to this point that I can foresee who is likely to win or lose.[2]

Many of the principles of competitive strategy have been distilled from the art of warfare. The military historian Liddell Hart, for example, presents several principles of war, many of which correspond to those in strategic planning:

> The true aim is not so much to seek battle as to seek a strategic situation so advantageous that if it does not of itself produce the decision, its continuation by a battle is sure to achieve this.
>
> But we can at least crystallize the lessons into two simple maxims—one negative, the other positive. The first is that, in the face of the overwhelming evidence of history, no general is justified in launching his troops to a direct attack upon an enemy firmly in position. The second, that instead of seeking to upset the enemy's equilibrium by one's attack, it must be upset before a real attack is, or can be successfully launched.
>
> The principles of war, not merely one principle, can be condensed into a single work—"concentration." But for truth this needs to be amplified as the "concentration of strength against weakness."[3]

It is strongly emphasized in strategic planning that an organization's strategy should take into account other organizations that are competing for its customers. Since different organizations have differing strengths and weaknesses, planners should base their strategy and the allocation of resources on the firm's strengths, but seek to exploit the competitors' weaknesses. In addition, the adopted strategy should, to the extent possible, defend the firm's position in the market from the attacks of competitors. These ideas, prevalent in business strategy are all borrowed from military science.

Liddell Hart also notes that the prime objective of warfare is not only to win the war but also to prepare for peace. In this connection, he introduces the term *grand strategy* which embraces plans of action during both *war* and *peace.* The military analogy is applied to business in this sense: The objective of the strategy is interpreted as achieving a *better state of equilibrium* or peace with the competitors rather than *only* annihilating the competition.

The philosophical assumptions underlying strategic planning can thus be traced to its military science heritage. Three crucial assumptions are worthy of mention. First, strategic planning visualizes environments as pools of scarce resources, for which there is *intense competition.* The resources may be raw materials, customers, finances, or the like. Many organizations seek these resources; since these resources are limited, there is intense competition among organizations. Under these conditions, something like the law of survival of the fittest operates: some organizations fare better while others lose ground. Competitors make moves and countermoves to gain ascendancy in the environment. This assumption of environments as consisting of competitors in dynamic interaction with each other for scarce resources lies at the core of strategic planning.

Second, strategic planning emphasizes the *degree of discretion* available to an organization. Key decision makers are seen as proactive; they have the power to chart the course of their organizations in competitive environments. Organizations are not passive entities shaped by the forces of natural competition. Environments set constraints (which must be overcome or adapted to), but do not determine the destiny of organizations. Bruce Henderson, one of the major figures in contemporary strategic planning, makes this abundantly clear:

> Natural competition in the strict sense, as it is defined by Darwinian natural selection and evolution, contains no elements of strategy. It is pure expediency—almost mindless at some stages. Instinctive needs that are urgent serve as the motivation. Day-to-day survival and cyclical procreation are the ultimate objectives.
>
> This kind of competition by natural selection is glacially slow. It is trial and error: more mistakes than improvements will prove to be fatal. Over time, the more successful patterns must be immortalized and multiplied by the genes, while the mistakes must be diminished in the future generations by the same process. It must be a slow process to succeed at all. . . .
>
> By contrast, strategic competition is revolutionary, not just evolutionary. It is capable of extreme time compression. However, to accomplish this revolution, the preparation must be conservative, careful, precise, and all-inclusive. The environment must itself be well understood. The competitors who are critical or even important to the change must be equally identified and understood. The uncertainties in the environment must be carefully assessed and evaluated. . . .
>
> The wild expediency of natural competition leads to glacial evolution. The meticulous conservatism of strategic competition leads to time compression and revolutionary change because strategy is *management of natural competition.* (Emphasis added.)[4]

Management of natural competition explicitly specifies the zone of discretion available to key decision makers.

Third, this approach portrays the key decision makers in an organization as *rational actors.* For strategic planning to be possible, it is necessary to be able to imagine and evaluate alternative courses of action. But imagination and reasoning power are not sufficient. There must also be knowledge of competition and environment, which must be integrated to allow decision makers to see the patterns of unfolding consequences. It is this knowledge that enables strategists to intervene in a complex (competitive) system with only limited input and yet produce a predictable and desired change in the system's equilibrium. The rationality assumption is manifest in such values espoused by the field as consistency with the environment, logical coordination of plans, or internal consistency.

The rationality assumptions of strategic planning are derived from an open systems view of the organization, *not* from the closed systems perspective of the classicists. As we have seen in Chapter 4, general systems theory distinguishes between two criteria of organizational success: effectiveness and efficiency. To repeat, effectiveness is concerned with the degree to which system outputs correspond to desired outputs, whereas efficiency refers to the ratio of actual outputs to inputs. Rationality of the strategic planning field is concerned with effectiveness rather than efficiency. Strategic planners assert that although much of management's attention is geared toward efficiency, an organization's long-term success and survival hinges on improvements in effectiveness; hence, top managers are rational to the degree they adapt to changes in the environment. Peter Drucker stated this most eloquently when he suggested that it is more important to do the *right things* (improve effectiveness) rather than to do *things right* (improve efficiency).[5]

In summary, strategic planning focuses primarily on industry/competitive environments; that is, markets that are competitive in varying degrees. Top management's key task is to devise the mechanisms by which an organization competes with other organizations in its markets. Top managers are expected to be rational, striving for the long-term survival and success of their organizations.

Historical Underpinnings

Organizations have always practiced some form of planning. Planning practice has evolved over the years; we can broadly identify four phases of evolution.[6]

Phase I: Basic Financial Planning

The beginnings of planning can be traced to the annual budgeting process, where procedures are developed to forecast revenue, costs, and capital needs and to identify limits for expense budgets on an annual basis. As long as environments were relatively simple, and a key decision maker, usually the chief executive officer, could comprehend the environment, budgeting served as an effective mechanism for strategy implementation.

The phenomenal changes in the post-World War II business environment, however, brought about new challenges for many firms: The number of products and markets served, the degree of technological sophistication required, and the complex economic systems involved far exceeded the intellectual grasp of any one manager. The budgeting phase became irrelevant for planning purposes.

Phase II: Forecast-Based Planning

Long-range or forecast-based planning replaced budgeting as a tool to confront the new business realities. As treasurers struggled to estimate capital needs and trade off among alternate financing plans, they began to extrapolate past trends and tried to foresee the future impact of political, economic, and social forces. This resulted in the use of forecasting tools. In addition, managers began to confront the long-term implications of decisions, and the time frames for assessing the consequences of decisions became longer than the annual budgeting phase.

Long-range planning improved organizational decisions (for example, productivity improvement or better capital utilization) as long as the markets were growing predictably. Two forces detracted from its efficacy. First, as organizations gained familiarity with long-range planning, it deteriorated into a mechanical routine: Managers simply copied the previous year's plans, made some performance short-fall adjustments, and extrapolated the historical trends far into the future. Instead of bringing key issues to the surface, the long-range plans buried them in masses of data. This robbed long-range planning of much of its utility.

Secondly, as competition intensified, and as the growth of traditional markets slowed, environments turned hostile and uncertain. Long-range forecasts became irrelevant, as most of them relied on techniques that assumed some predictability of environments. In the face of rapid change, events rendered market forecasts obsolete. After repeated experience of such frustrations, planners discarded long-range planning and tried to understand the dynamics of competition. This led to the next phase.

Phase III: Externally Oriented Planning

The focus during this phase shifted from predicting the future to understanding the key determinants of success in an industry, and concentrating a firm's resources to achieve a competitive advantage, sustainable for some period of time. The planners began to search for opportunities by defining new business capabilities or by redefining the market to better fit their companies' strengths. Additionally, the planners began to look at their companies' and their competitors' product offerings from the vantage point of an outsider; that is, from an outside-in perspective. They came to believe that since the key to survival is the fit with the environment, an organization needs to be capable of judging itself as the key environmental entities judge the organization.

Three characteristics distinguish this phase from previous ones. The first reflected the futility of prediction—a lesson learned from the failure of long-range planning and the resulting attention to industry and competitive dynamics. The planners came to realize that the characteristics of an industry set certain limits to a firm's performance; in addition, a firm's success is jointly determined by its *and* its competitors' actions. Second, since competitive dynamics is a rapidly changing game, planning came to be regarded as an ongoing activity instead of an annual ritual. Finally, planning emphasized the need for seeking opportunities, as the markets became saturated and growth opportunities had to be created.

Much of what we know as strategic planning reflects the insights of this phase. Strategic planning certainly led to improved strategy formulation by honing an organization's capacity to take a hard look at itself and its competitors. However, it was continually plagued by two problems. First, much of the formulation work was done by an elite corp of strategic planners, who often ignored the inputs of those who had to implement the strategies. As strategic planners put their conceptual skills into action, the operating organization came to be alienated from the planning process. This led to problems in strategy implementation. Second, the variety of opportunities generated during this phase posed a heavy burden for top management. Top managers began to realize that explicit choices were being made without top-level participation by planners and managers deep down in the organization, and that these decisions could significantly affect long-term competitive strength and well-being. This knowledge unsettled top management and pushed it into a heavy involvement in the planning process.

Phase IV: Strategic Management
Some organizations have reportedly been able to solve the implementation problem that plagues the strategic planning phase by joining strategic planning and management into a single process. This has prompted some to suggest a fourth phase, whose characteristics we can portray only hazily. The companies that may be considered to be in this phase are some multinational, diversified manufacturing corporations. The challenge of planning for the needs of hundreds of different and rapidly evolving businesses, serving thousands of product markets in dozens of distinct national environments, has pushed them to generate sophisticated approaches to planning. These firms are characterized by the thoroughness with which management links strategic planning to operational decision making. As noted in the McKinsey & Company study, headed by one of its directors, Bill Gluck, this is accomplished by three mechanisms. First, the planning is decentralized, thus enhancing the participation of lower levels of managers including operating managers. Second, the process is made much more flexible, thus encouraging entrepreneurial thinking widely within the organization. Third, an organizational culture is developed and sustained, a process that begins at the top. (See Box 8.1.) It is too early to comment on the efficacy of this final phase, but we will return to some of its themes in the concluding sections of this book.

Table 8.3 summarizes the characteristics of the four planning phases. As seen from the table, the planning process has become increasingly complex, reflecting the complexity of the environments and organizations. The first two phases are not truly strategic, since the idea of competition was not

---

Box 8.1

Strategic Management

Based on a study of formal planning systems in 120 companies worldwide, Frederick Gluck, Stephen Kaufman, and Steven Walleck, a group of consultants working at McKinsey & Co. (an East Coast–based consulting firm), concluded that only a few companies had managed to join strategic planing and management. These firms were characterized not so much by the sophistication of techniques employed as by the thoroughness with which management links strategic planning to operational decision making. This is accomplished by three mechanisms: a planning framework, a planning process, and a corporate value system.

Planning framework: There are many levels at which strategically important decisions must be made; moreover, today's organizational structure may not be the ideal framework within which to plan for tomorrow's business. This recognition leads a firm in the strategic management phase to arrange its planning on as many as five distinct planning levels: (1) product/market planning, the lowest level at which strategic planning takes place, where product, price, sales, and service are planned and the competitors identified; (2) business-unit planning, where the bulk of the planning effort in most diversified make-and-sell companies is done. These self-contained businesses control their own market position and cost structure, and their plans become building blocks for the corporate plan; (3) shared resource planning, to achieve economies of scale or to avoid the problem of subcritical mass; (4) shared concern planning, to devise strategies that meet the unique needs of certain industry or geographic groups or to plan for technologies; and (5) corporate level planning, to identify world-wide technical and market trends not picked up by business-unit planners, set objectives, and mar-

shall the financial and human resources to meet those objectives. The selection of the framework influences the range of alternatives proposed; the definition of the framework is thus a top-level responsibility.

Planning process: Strategically managed companies try to keep their planning process flexible and creative. Unlike the long-range planning phase, which deteriorated to a mechanical routine, firms here recognize that few processes can be institutionalized without attendant loss of creativity. Hence, these firms stimulate their manager's thinking by (1) stressing competitiveness, with top management attending planning meetings to bore in on a few key issues or events; (2) focusing on a theme, whereby some firms reinvigorate their planning processes by asking their managers to key their plans to a specified theme such as international business, new technology, and the like; (3) negotiating strategically consistent objectives between corporate headquarters and business-unit general management; and (4) demanding strategic insights to avoid competition by an innovative strategy.

Corporate value system: Shared by the company's top and middle management is a third, often invisible, mechanism to establish linkages between planning and action. Most firms in the strategic management phase appear to nurture: (1) the value of teamwork; (2) entrepreneurial drive, or the commitment to making things happen; (3) open communications rather than preservation of confidentiality; and (4) a shared belief in the firm's ability to chart its own course amid environmental changes.

Source: Adapted from Frederick W. Gluck, Stephen P. Kaufman, and A. Steven Walleck, "The Evolution of Strategic Management," *McKinsey Staff Paper*, October 1978.

TABLE 8.3 **Four Phases in the Evolution of Formal Strategic Planning**

	Phase I Basic financial planning	**Phase II** Forecast-based planning	**Phase III** Externally oriented planning	**Phase IV** Strategic management
Effectiveness of formal business planning				Orchestration of all resources to create competitive advantage
				Strategically chosen planning framework
			Increasing response to markets and competition	Creative, flexible planning processes
			Thorough situation analysis and competitive assessment	Supportive value system and climate
			Evaluation of strategic alternatives	
		More effective planning for growth	Dynamic allocations of resources	
		Environmental analysis		
	Operational control	Multi-year forecasts		
	Annual budget	Static allocation of resources		
	Functional focus			
Value system	**Meet budget**	**Predict the future**	**Think strategically**	**Create the future**

Source: Frederick W. Gluck, Stephen P. Kaufman, and A. Steven Walleck, "The Evolution of Strategic Management," *McKinsey Staff Paper,* October 1978.

254

Box 8.2

Alfred P. Sloan

Alfred P. Sloan was the chief executive officer and later the chairman of General Motors. When he became CEO, Ford was the leader in the automobile industry. Ford followed a simple strategy of mass production of a single model of car.

Sloan adopted a strategy of product differentiation to combat Ford. GM was then going to produce different models of cars to suit the tastes of different customers. The models varied in terms of quality and price.

To carry out this strategy, Sloan adopted a divisionalized structure. Different models would be produced by different divisions. The divisions would be judged by return on investment or market-related criteria. However, in order to ensure that the divisions did not infringe upon each other's territory, Sloan also centralized policy making.

The main principle upon which the divisional organization worked was the principle of centralized policy making and decentralized operations. The divisions had operating autonomy, but worked under the policy constraints imposed by the corporate office.

central to the planning process. More importantly, each planning phase invokes a unique value system in the day-to-day operations of organizations. The most advanced phase, strategic management, recognizes the need to reconcile the debate between proponents of rational and social perspectives of organizations.

Theoretical Underpinnings

Perhaps no field in business developed with as much close collaboration with practice as the field of strategic planning. Especially in the formative years of the field, it was the top managers of corporations who articulated the key concepts of strategy. Thus, Pierre S. Du Pont, the chief architect of Du Pont corporation, and Alfred P. Sloan, the chief executive officer and later the chairman of General Motors, orchestrated conceptual innovations that marked the beginnings of the field. Sloan, for example, summarized the conceptual underpinnings of his strategy to combat Ford's Model T in his autobiography *My Years with General Motors*[7] (see Box 8.2).

The Concept of Strategy

It was, however, left to the economic historian Alfred Chandler to synthesize the experience of several business organizations and to explicitly articulate the notions of strategy in the scholarly circles.[8] Chandler formally defined strategy as:

The determination of the basic long-term goals and objectives of an enterprise, and the adoption of courses of action and the allocation of resources necessary to carry out these goals.[9]

Chandler's definition is noteworthy for three reasons. First, Chandler espoused the view that strategy formulation is a key responsibility of top management, whereas lower levels of the organization are primarily responsible for execution and operations. Second, he emphasized the long-term orientation of strategic planning, thus distinguishing it from short-term actions characteristic of operating management. Third, Chandler implied that strategy ensures rational allocation of resources, and hence, is the major mechanism for coordination of the enterprise.

Strategy in Single Industries

Meanwhile, scholars such as C. Roland Christensen and Kenneth Andrews at the Harvard Business School had begun formal teaching of business policy, with strategy as a unifying theme. They primarily focused on the strategy of *single-industry firms,* unlike the broader canvas of Chandler. In addition, the Harvard Business School was interested in developing conceptual frameworks for managerial decision making, rather than historical analysis.

The Harvard Business School's efforts mirrored two intellectual influences. First, their concept of strategy was influenced by the ideas of Drucker and Chandler. Thus, for Andrews, strategy is the pattern of long-term objectives and plans (Chandler) stated in such a way as to define what business the company is in or is to be in, and the kind of company it is or is to be (Drucker). Second, these scholars inherited the legacy of the human relations school—a legacy left by Mayo and nurtured by Roethlichsberger at Harvard. Thus, for these scholars, the human issues that come up during execution cannot be isolated from strategy issues. This school thus mounted a valiant effort to integrate the economic and human dimensions of an organization.

The Harvard Business School left a lasting legacy to the strategy area:

1. They conceptualized strategy as the appropriate domain of *general managers;* that is, managers who have multifunctional responsibilities, as opposed to functional managers in charge of marketing, finance, or production.

2. They focused strategy—long-term objectives and plans—on linking an organization with its *environment* and providing *functional integration,* or coordination of such functions as marketing, production, and the like.

3. They distinguished between strategy *formulation and implementation* as two sequentially related phases in top-management decision making.

4. They emphasized the influence of *human* and *economic* considerations during both phases. Such factors as

top-management values influence formulation, whereas implementation is concerned with motivation and control of human (subordinates') behavior.

5. They viewed the strategy of an organization as something *unique* to itself; hence, their focus was on providing analytical frameworks to arrive at strategy rather than deriving generalizations.[10]

As firms began to pursue diversification, they faced choices that could not be addressed by concepts suited for single-industry firms. They needed answers to additional questions: Should we diversify, and if so, to what industries? In what way should we diversify, by acquisition or by internal development? How should we allocate our limited resources among a set of businesses or industries?

Diversification

Igor Ansoff provided the first set of answers to these questions. Ansoff identified two phases in strategic decisions—setting goals and formulating strategies—although he primarily addressed the latter. He distinguished between strategic, administrative, and operating decisions and postulated the major components of strategy[11] (see Box 8.3).

Ansoff argued that strategic decisions are nonrepetitive and are made under partial ignorance. If alternatives cannot be fully enumerated, consequences cannot be fully known in advance; therefore, strategic decisions do not lend themselves to conventional decision theoretic ideas that require computation of the expected utility based on an exhaustive identification of alternatives and consequences. However, Ansoff noted some frameworks are useful guides for thinking about strategic decisions. Diversification is a strategic decision and he presented the first framework for this set of decisions.

Ansoff noted that firms diversify

1. when their objectives can no longer be met by expansion within the existing product-market scope,

2. in the presence of excess cash,

3. when divestment opportunities are more attractive than current expansion plans, or

4. under conditions of unreliable information, which renders trade-offs difficult to make.

Ansoff presented a matrix of alternative diversification routes, presented in Figure 8.2. As shown in the figure, Ansoff identified *two* key dimensions to diversification—*customer missions* and *product technologies*—to summarize four types of diversification:

1. *Horizontal diversification,* when new products that involve related or unrelated technology are targeted to the same type of customers as the ones served by the firm currently, for example,

---
Box 8.3

Key Elements of Ansoff's Framework

Igor Ansoff, a Russian by birth and a mathematician by training, was one of the first scholars to view strategy in a thoroughly analytical manner. After a stint at Lockheed Aircraft Corporation in the 50's, he joined Carnegie Institute of Technology, where he wrote his now classic *Corporate Strategy*. Ansoff distinguished three types of decisions: operating, strategic, and administrative.

Operating decisions absorb the bulk of a firm's energy and attention, and aim to maximize the efficiency of the conversion process: they involve pricing, marketing, production scheduling, or, in general, functional area management.

Strategic decisions are primarily concerned with external, rather than internal, problems of the firm and specifically with selection of the product mix that the firm will produce and the markets to which it will sell. The decision areas embrace the firm's objectives and goals, diversification paths, and means of exploiting current product-market position.

Administrative decisions are concerned with structuring a firm's resources in such a way as to create maximum performance potential. Organization, acquisition, and development of resources are the critical decision areas.

Ansoff noted that strategic decisions set the premises (assumptions and constraints) for operating and administrative decisions. Further, these (strategic) decisions are centralized at the top-management level.

In addition, Ansoff provided a framework to capture the *components* of strategy, and patterns of diversification and related these to the notion of *synergy*. Ansoff distinguished between objectives and strategy, and noted that top management has to make choices about not only objectives but also various components of strategy.

Components of strategy. The four components of strategy postulated by Ansoff are:

1. *Product-market scope,* which specifies the particular industries to which the firm confines its product-market position.
2. *Growth vector,* which indicates the direction in which the firm is moving with respect to its current product-market posture. On the whole, there are four components to growth vector: (*a*) market penetration, denoting a direction of increased market share for the present product-markets; (*b*) product development, whereby new products are created to replace current ones; (*c*) market development, where new missions are sought for the firm's products; and (*d*) diversification, distinctive in that both products and missions are new to the firm.
3. *Competitive advantage,* which seeks to identify particular properties of individual product-markets that will give the firm a strong competitive position (i.e., against its competitors).
4. *Synergy,* wherein a business firm produces a combined return larger than the sum of its parts. A firm may derive synergy from sales, operations, investment, or management arenas.

Ansoff specifically addressed the different paths available to firms for diversification. His contention that a firm is more likely to reap the benefits of synergy if it pursues related diversification—enters those industries that are closely related to its core business on the marketing or production side—is hotly debated even today.

Source: Adapted from Igor H. Ansoff, *Corporate Strategy: An Analytic Approach to Business Policy for Growth and Expansion* (New York: McGraw-Hill, 1965).

FIGURE 8.2

Ansoff's typology of diversification paths

		Product Technology	
		Related	*Unrelated*
Customer Missions	Same type Firm its own customer	Horizontal diversification Vertical integration	
	Similar type New type	Concentric diversification Concentric diversification	Conglomerate diversification

when an automobile manufacturer decides to market motorcycles or lawn mowers.

2. *Vertical integration,* when the firm extends its operations either on the input or the output side and thus serves as its own customer; for example, when the auto firm begins production of wheels or tires.

3. *Concentric diversification,* where a firm enters product-market arenas with similar customers or related technologies so that it can reap synergies on the marketing or technology side; for example, the auto firm starts producing farm tractors (related technology) or computers for small businesses (similar type of customers).

4. *Conglomerate diversification* where a firm enters a totally new market with technologies unrelated to its present ones; for example, the automobile manufacturer enters petrochemicals.

Ansoff also noted that conglomerate diversification offered no potential for synergy, a condition where the diversified entity produces an outcome better than the sum of individual units being acquired or developed. However, an overwhelming number of firms undertake this strategy due to absence of any strategy, lack of synergistic potential or in-depth competence in some firms, or the preferences of top management. Further, foreshadowing the developments of the late 1960s, Ansoff noted that although under normal conditions a conglomerate firm has the potential advantage of better access to capital and better stability of earnings, under abnormal conditions such as recession they have less staying power.

During the 60s, the above three streams—Chandler, Harvard Business School and Ansoff—fueled much of the conceptual development of the field. We should note, in passing, that two other sets of scholars made contributions relevant to strategy during the early period. Morgenstern and von Neumann's[12] studies of game theory and Jay Forrester's[13] studies of feedback loops yielded substantial insights into modeling of competitive interactions. However, these scholars were somewhat ahead of their time in terms of being integrated with other concepts.

Theoretical and empirical developments during the last decades provided answers to several related questions: Are there predictable patterns to an organization's growth? What are the determinants of effective strategy? How do top managers actually formulate and implement strategies? Is formal planning useful? We will deal with each one of these questions in turn.

Patterns of Growth

Scholars pursuing this line of work have traced predictable patterns of growth in U.S. businesses over the years. Chandler pioneered the study of this topic, and others followed his lead.

Based on his study of U.S. enterprises up to 1930, Chandler posited four stages of growth:

Volume Expansion: In the beginning, an owner-manager starts a company selling a product or service. The strategy of growth during this stage is volume expansion, where the owner focuses on increasing the sales of the product or service. During this stage, the entrepreneur remained in the same geographic markets that were initially entered with the same product/service.

Geographic Expansion: In the second stage, the firm begins to look for geographic markets other than the one it initially entered. For example, a shoe manufacturer who started selling shoes in the Midwest, but who decided to expand geographically to the West and/or East Coasts will fit this stage. Geographic expansion enhances the market diversity facing a firm; thus, the shoe manufacturer would have to respond to a more diverse group of customers and competitors as it expands its operations.

Vertical Integration: The next step in the growth of the firm takes place when it begins to integrate vertically by acquiring or creating other functions. For example, manufacturing plants created their own warehouses or wholesaling operations and their own sales force. This further enhanced the environmental complexity the firms faced.

Diversification: In the fourth stage, firms begin to pursue a strategy of diversification by moving into new industries to employ existing resources as their primary markets declined or were saturated. Diversification still further increased the product-market diversity of firms.[14]

A synopsis of Chandler's work pertaining to diversification is provided in Box 8.4.

Although Chandler's four stages rightly characterized the evolution of U.S. businesses up to 1950, Chandler could not foresee the conglomerate diversification that swept U.S. industry during the 1960s and the international expansion it undertook. It was left to other scholars to extend his work, incorporating later developments.

Box 8.4

Chandler on Strategy and Structure

Alfred Chandler's classic work on strategy and structure was based on his in-depth research on four giant firms: General Motors, Du Pont, Standard Oil of New Jersey, and Sears & Roebuck. Chandler divided his analysis of the evolution of strategy and structure of U.S. firms into two periods: pre-1900 and post-1900.

During the pre-1900 period, firms embarked on a strategy of horizontal consolidation of markets and vertical functional integration of the stages of production. Imbalances created by supplies in excess of demand led firms toward a frantic search for market share. In Chandler's own words:

> Each firm expanded because its executives hoped, particularly during the boom periods after the Civil War and again after the depression of the 1870's, to profit thereby from the new markets. Then as the market became glutted and prices dropped, many manufactures became more and more willing to combine in order to control or limit competition by setting price and production schedules. So from the mid-1870's on, many small producers of leather, salt, sugar, whiskey, and other products made from corn, linseed and cotton oil, fertilizer, petroleum, explosives, rope and rubber joined in large horizontal combinations.

Such horizontal expansion of markets created accompanying pressures for vertical consolidation of the stages of production, whereby firms could achieve better control of supplies flowing into and products flowing out of plant facilities. The larger scale of business and vertical integration of functional activities were the typical growth strategies of U.S. firms in this period.

After 1900, the growth of large firms rested fundamentally on basic population and technological changes. Having emerged from an era of consolidation, large firms pursued three basic growth strategies: (1) extending geographic markets and supply sources by expanding overseas, (2) extending product lines mainly to existing customers, and (3) developing new products for different customers. The first two strategies were a continuation of the themes from the pre-1900 period. The strategy of new product introduction brought in a new avenue of diversified growth through technology. To quote Chandler:

> Diversification came when leading companies in these technologically advanced industries realized that their facilities and the scientific know-how of their personnel could be easily transferred into the production of new goods for new markets. . . . The application of science to the development of new products through institutionalized research brought the same strategies of diversification in the electrical, electronics, and to a somewhat lesser extent, the power machinery and automobile industries.

Diversification increased the administrative complexities of running organizations and led to the decentralized and divisionalized organizational structure. While overseas expansion contributed to the need for such organizational restructuring, diversification was responsible to a far greater degree for the move to decentralized administration of separate product lines. Similarly, Chandler noted that each preceding strategy exerted an influence on organizational structure. Chandler is often associated with the by now widely accepted dictum that *structure follows strategy.*

Chandler published his early work in 1962; his research ended before the high point of conglomerate acquisitions of the late 1960s. Although he did not foresee the degree of conglomerate diversification that was to prevail, he had laid the foundation of the strategy field.

Source: Adapted from Alfred D. Chandler, *Strategy and Structure: Chapters in the History of American Industrial Enterprise* (Cambridge, Mass.: MIT Press, 1962).

Conglomerate mergers, in Ansoff's terms, meant that firms were acquiring businesses that were unrelated to their primary businesses. Figure 8.3 illustrates the growing importance of this form of diversification. Chandler had suggested that internal diversification into related product lines, primarily through research and development, was the ultimate stage of growth of a firm. Conglomerate acquisitions represented a different form of diversification. It was left to Leonard Wrigley to postulate a *fifth* stage of evolution and to hypothesize that the trend toward diversification had extended beyond Chandler's original perception.[15] Wrigley's hypothesis was verified by Richard Rumelt, whose work is summarized in Box 8.5. Rumelt discovered that from 1949 to 1959, there was a decided shift away from the single-business category into the related-business category, whereas in the ensuing decade, there was a drastic jump in the number of companies that had moved into the unrelated-business category.[16] Conglomerate diversification was here to stay, and represented a further stage in the evolution of American business.

By the 1970s, it also became clear that many U.S. firms had expanded their businesses overseas. For many businesses, international expansion offered a viable opportunity to expand their volume, since the domestic markets for their products were becoming saturated. Further, locating production

FIGURE 8.3

Percentage of distribution of large mergers by type and period, 1951–1955 to 1975.

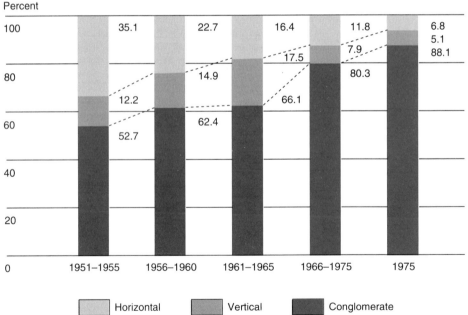

Source: Federal Trade Commission, Bureau of Economics, "Summary of Economic Report on Corporate Mergers," *Economic Papers 1966–69,* in the *Hearings Before the Subcommittee on Antitrust and Monopoly,* 1969.

Box 8.5

Rumelt's Categorization of Diversification Patterns

Richard Rumelt built his typology of businesses based on the earlier work of Wrigley. His focus was classifying the firms based on their diversification strategies. He identified four broad classes of firms; he also discovered several subclasses within each. The four major classes of Rumelt are as follows:

Single product firms are characterized by their core business, which contributes over 95 percent of their sales, although they may be in some other business in a marginal way. They grow only through expansion in their scale of operations.

Dominant product firms have core businesses that contribute between 70 and 95 percent of their sales. Such firms are diversified to a small degree but are still quite dependent upon and characterized by their product-market diversity. Rumelt also identified four subclasses within this category: dominant-vertical, dominant-constrained, dominant-linked, and dominant-unrelated.

Related product firms have begun to diversify by adding new activities that are tangibly related to the collective skills and strengths possessed by the firms. This is evidenced by the fact that the core businesses contribute less than 70 percent of their sales. The two subclasses within these are related-linked and related-constrained.

Unrelated product firms have diversified into areas that are unrelated to the original skills and strengths (other than financial). Within this class, Rumelt identified two types: unrelated-passive and acquisitive-conglomerate. The latter has adopted acquisitions and diversifications as a way of life. These are also sometimes called *holding companies*.

The single- and multibusiness categories represent two distinct philosophies of managing. In single-business firms, the emphasis will be on business strategy and hence, operating problems, as growth is expected to come from the expansion of current operations. In multibusiness firms, the focus shifts from operating efficiencies to a combination of internal and external opportunities for growth. Rumelt's finding was that in the United States, there is a general pattern to the domain expansion activities of a firm, as represented by the move from single to dominant to related and finally to unrelated business. The first three stages were already established by Chandler. Rumelt updated Chandler and confirmed the tendency toward conglomerate forms of organization.

Source: Adapted from Richard Rumelt, *Strategy, Structure and Economic Performance* (Cambridge, Mass.: Harvard University Press, 1974).

---

facilities in newly developing countries provided access to cheap labor and sometimes raw materials.

Some viewed international expansion as a variant of the geographic expansion strategy of Chandler. However, there were major differences. The international expansion increased a firm's diversity of markets. Differences in cultural, legal, economic, and other relevant environments necessitated that a firm's strategies be responsive to local pressures of other countries. At the same time, firms also had to be focused on efficiency derived from economic factors such as economies of scale.

Firms adopted two different directions of multinational expansion. One group adopted country–specific strategies that focused on local responsiveness. This was termed *growth through regional strategy.* The other adopted global product strategies that maximized efficiencies derived from standardization of products across countries. In recent years, partly due to the pressures of foreign competition, most firms have recognized the need to combine both regional and product strategies. This may yet represent a third stage in multinational expansion, leading to what some have called *global strategies.*

From a strategic planning perspective, each stage of growth increased the complexity in strategy formulation relative to the previous stage. Thus, volume expansion necessitated tight operations planning, geographic expansion increased the diversity of customers and competition, and vertical integration further increased the complexity of operations. With diversification, related and later conglomerate, strategic planning had to tackle diversity not only in operations but products and markets. The international expansion still further exacerbated the complexity of strategic planning.

Determinants of Effective Strategy
The first project that set out systematically to discover the determinants of effective strategy originated at General Electric. Sidney Schoeffler, then at General Electric, and Robert Buzzell, of the Harvard Business School, succeeded in using computerized data from multiple sources to correlate the relationship between various factors and the profitability of GE's various businesses. This later came to be known as the PIMS project, an acronym for Profit Impact of Market Strategy.[17] The PIMS project yielded many interesting insights and was the basis for a number of hypotheses (see Box 8.6).

The empirical stream represented by PIMS moved toward industry-specific generalizations. In the strategic planning field, this helped the move *away* from the then dominant school of thought, which held that effective strategies are unique to an organization. The PIMS database pointed to the conclusion that the types of strategies that produce the best results differ in different industries, but that there are broad generic patterns to such variations. A contingency perspective in the strategy area was a move away from a case approach toward drawing some generalizations.

The most popular finding from the PIMS project was the positive relationship between market share and profitability; that is, the larger the market share of business, the higher its profitability. This rationalized the basis of *portfolio models* already being used by a number of consulting firms such as BCG (Boston Consulting Group) and McKinsey & Company for helping diversified firms allocate financial resources among various businesses.

The fascination with diversification as an easy means to growth that characterized the late 1960s gave way to disenchantment, and many ill-conceived mergers came unraveled in the first half of the 70s. Also, many firms abused the portfolio models and began to view their businesses from a remote analytical perspective, to the neglect of base businesses. This led to efforts at refocusing management attention on industry fundamentals.

Building on the work of PIMS, but mostly drawing upon the work of industrial economists, Michael Porter presented a coherent theoretical framework to assess the determinants of effective business strategy. Porter identified two major factors: (1) structure of the industry and (2) the specific business's position relative to the competition.

Porter argued that the characteristics of the industry determine the average profit potential of a business, reminding top managers that competitive battles are fought and won not in analytical ivory towers but in industrial trenches.[18] We have already presented Porter's model of industry structure in the previous chapter and will not repeat it here.

Porter's second factor was a business's relative position. According to Porter, an effective strategy should distinguish a business from its competitors by offering the customers either a lower price or some unique quality. Firms that predominantly copy others or a strategy that is not distinctive would yield below average profits.

Strategy Formulation and Implementation Processes

A second stream of theoretical and empirical work adopted a *descriptive* stance, seeking to identify patterns of strategy formulation and implementation. This was unlike the prescriptive focus of the previous theoretical stream, which sought the determinants of effective strategies. The second stream focused on behavioral processes unlike the economic factors that were the object of prescriptive theorists.

Strategy Formulation.   Do top managers exhibit stable patterns in strategy formulation? Based on their research, Ray Miles and Charles Snow, two behaviorally oriented strategy researchers, answered the question in the affirmative.[19] They argued that strategy formulation is driven by two behavioral factors:

1. Managers' characteristic modes of perceiving environments.
2. Managers' values with respect to the internal characteristics of the organization.

Since these two factors are relatively stable, managers exhibit stable patterns in strategy formulation.

Based on the two factors, Miles and Snow provided a typology of the strategy formulation process, which consisted of four strategic types: defenders, prospectors, analyzers, and reactors.

> *Defenders* perceive a stable environment; for example, mature markets. They continually attempt to protect their market share, value internal efficiency, and undertake tight control of operations.

Box 8.6

Profit Impact of Market Strategy (PIMS)

The PIMS program originated at General Electric under Sidney Schoeffler. Professor Robert Buzzell of the Harvard Business School and Dr. Schoeffler succeeded in using computerized data to discover the relationship between business factors and profitability. Currently, the PIMS program is being operated by The Strategic Planning Institute, based in Boston, Massachusetts. At present, over 200 companies participate in PIMS, including about 125 large U.S. corporations drawn mostly from the top 500 companies on the *Fortune* list, a growing group of large European companies, and many medium-sized companies in manufacturing and service businesses.

The unit of observation in PIMS is a strategic business unit (SBU); that is, a division, product line, or other profit center within its parent company selling a distinct set of products and/or services to an identifiable group of customers. An SBU is in competition with a well-defined set of competitors, for whom meaningful separation can be made in terms of revenues, operating costs, investments, and strategic plans.

Currently, the database consists of more than 2,000 businesses, covering a 4–8 year period. Data is collected for nearly 100 variables pertaining to the *market environment,* the state of *competition,* the *strategy* pursued by the business, and the *operating results* obtained.

PIMS has generated a number of conclusions, some of them controversial. Schoeffler, however, notes that the data clearly establish the following nine propositions:

1. Business situations generally behave in a regular and predictable manner. The operating results achieved by a particular business, its profit, cash flow, growth, and so on, are determined in a rather regular and predictable fashion by the "laws of nature" that operate in business situations.

2. All business situations are basically alike in obeying the same laws of the marketplace.

3. The laws of the marketplace determine about 80 percent of the observed variance in operating results across different businesses. Thus, the characteristics of a business constitute about 80 percent of the reasons for its success or failure, whereas the operating skill or luck of management constitutes about 20 percent. In other words, doing the right thing is more important than doing it well.

4. There are nine major strategic influences on profitability and net cash flow: (a) *investment intensity* (fixed and working capital required to produce a dollar of sales, dictated by the technology utilized by a firm), (b) *cost push* (rate of increase in costs), (c) *productivity* (value added per employee), (d) *market share,* (e) *product quality,* (f) *innovation* and *differentiation* (extensive actions undertaken by a firm in new product innovations,

Box 8.6 continued

R&D, and marketing, and applicable only to firms with dominant market position) (*g*) *vertical integration,* (*h*) *growth* of the served market, and (*i*) *current strategic effort.*

5. The operation of the nine influences in (4) is complex. Sometime the influences offset each other. In that case, it is the net effect that matters. In systems theoretic terms, the nine influences behave *nonlinearly.*

6. Product characteristics do not matter. What matters are the *characteristics* of the business, such as the nine influences in (4).

7. The expected impacts of strategic business characteristics tend to assert themselves over time. When the business changes over time, its profitability and net cash flow will move in the direction of the norm for the new position. The observed deviations in actual performance will even out in time.

8. Business strategies are good if their fundamentals are good, unsuccessful if they are unsound.

9. Most clear strategy signals are robust. When a particular strategic move is clearly indicated to be a good idea, moderate-sized errors in analysis do not render the conclusions invalid.

The data from PIMS is still being analyzed, to build not only generalizations across industries but also to pinpoint industry-specific conclusions, as well as to discover the conditions under which specific strategies (such as building market share, vertical integration, investing in research and development, and the like) are likely to be effective in terms of profitability or return on investment.

PIMS has had its critics. These fall into three groups. One group, wedded to an idiographic stance, critiqued the nomothetic stance of PIMS and disavowed that generalizations are possible in the strategy field. Another group pointed to methodological problems with the database, arguing that many of the critical variables (e.g., share of the served market) are not unambiguously defined and that some are measured using perceptions of the managers (which are subject to distortion). This group also noted that some critical variables (e.g., intentions of the management) are not represented in the data. Still another group critiqued the theoretical generalizations, noting that the conclusions are derivable from classical economic theory.

In spite of these criticisms, PIMS has been the major database on which the empirical foundations of strategic planning have been built during the last decade. Till then, the predominant orientation of scholars in the field was to describe the uniqueness of each firm's strategy problem through case studies. With PIMS and the large sample research it brought with it, it was possible to build some generalizations. *Contingency* formulations in strategic planning were thus made possible. In this sense, PIMS marked the coming of age of the strategic planning field.

Source: Sidney Schoeffler, "The PIMS Program," *Strategic Management Handbook,* Kenneth J. Albert ed. (New York, McGraw-Hill, 1983), pp. 23–1 to 23–10.

Prospectors habitually interpret the environment as dynamic and continue to explore new market opportunities. They are risk-prone, and value innovation and flexibility. Growth is emphasized over stability.

Analyzers adopt an intermediate position between defenders and prospectors. They view the environment in a differentiated fashion: some aspects are changing, others are relatively stable. They value rationality and analysis.

Reactors adopt a closed system perspective and react to environmental contingencies as and when they arise. They are not strategists, and they tend to be crisis ridden except in regulated environments.

Table 8.4 presents a comparison of the four strategic types.

In contrast to the prescriptive theorists, whose determinants of effective strategies were primarily economic, Miles and Snow argued that the actual strategy formulation process is determined by behavioral factors.

Strategy Implementation.   In the strategic planning field, Edward Wrapp[20] pioneered the behavioral study of strategy implementation. Based on his experience with top managers, he identified a number of principles they employed to manage the implementation process. Wrapp's ideas are summarized in Box 8.7.

Wrapp pointed out that mechanisms of implementation (organization design, reward, or control systems, etc.) highlighted in strategy are in practice augmented by other behavioral ploys by top managers.

TABLE 8.4   **Miles and Snow's Typology of Strategies**

	Strategic Type			
Dimension	*Defender*	*Analyzer*	*Prospector*	*Reactor*
1. Perception of environment	Stable	Moderately changing	Dynamic and growing	None
2. Strategy	Maintain market	Maintain, but selectively innovate	Find and exploit new opportunities	No coherent strategy
	Protect turf	Selectively identify opportunities	Aggressively identify opportunities	React to environment
3. Underlying values	Efficiency	Mix of efficiency and flexibility	Flexibility	No defined values
4. Operating focus	Cost control, mechanistic organization	Cost control and innovation	Innovation, expansion, and organic organization	Depends on immediate circumstances

Source: Developed from Ray E. Miles and Charles C. Snow, *Organizational Strategy, Structure and Process* (New York: McGraw-Hill, 1978).

Box 8.7

Edward Wrapp on Politics of Strategy Formulation

Edward Wrapp, who served as the director of the executive program, professor, and associate dean for the Management Program at the University of Chicago's Graduate School of Business, wrote the provocative piece "Good Managers Don't Make Policy Decisions." He was concerned with the overly rational emphasis in the 1960s strategic planning literature. He noted that the rational perspective is incomplete; it needs to be augmented by a political perspective to account for what successful managers did. He notes that successful general managers possess five important skills:

1. Keeping open many channels of communication. Managers develop an enormous network of contacts within and outside the organization, and do not confine themselves to the formal channels for keeping informed.

2. Focusing on a limited number of significant issues. Unlike the grand design notions of the strategy field, managers cannot focus on all the issues, but they should attend to the few key ones.

3. Playing the power game. General managers are power brokers. For any change effort, they know that there are supporters, antagonists, and those who are indifferent. Their success lies

in identifying *the corridors of indifference* and converting them to their own point of view incrementally.

4. Direction with open-ended objectives. Successful top-level general managers are experts at the *art of imprecision*. They do not specify clear goals, but only provide a sense of direction so that as opportunities arise, they can pounce on them and rationalize them to their advantage.

5. Spotting opportunities and relationships in the stream of operating problems and decisions. Good general managers know that the power of a good strategic plan is not obvious to everyone, and the implementation is not automatic. Even if the plan is sound and imaginative, the job has only begun. The long painful task of implementation will depend on the manager's *skill,* not that of the planner.

Wrapp wrote his piece as early as 1967. It may sound as if he were forecasting the failures in strategy implementation that led to the strategic management phase of the late 70s.

Source: Adapted from Edward H. Wrapp, "Good Managers Don't Make Policy Decisions," *Harvard Business Review* 45, no. 5, 1967.

The major conceptualization of behavioral processes during implementation was provided by James Brian Quinn when he discovered that actual strategy implementation in organizations follows a pattern of *logical incrementalism:*

> Successful executives link together a series of strategic processes and decisions spanning years. At the beginning of the process, when it is impossible to predict all events that will shape the future of a firm, the best the executives can do is

to forecast the most likely forces, and attempt to build a resource base and a corporate posture.

They then proceed incrementally to handle urgent matters, start longer terms sequences whose specific future branches are murky, respond to unforeseen events as they occur, build on successes and brace up or cut losses on failures. The process is dynamic, with neither a real beginning nor end.[21]

Logical incrementalism, as the term signifies, stresses both logic and an incremental approach to implementation. The implementation context is one where decisions could not simultaneously be aggregated into a comprehensive decision matrix. Many of the events influencing the firm are unknown, and there are limits to how much information top managers can assimilate. This necessitates an incremental, step-by-step approach to implementation. As Quinn comments:

Logic dictates that one proceed flexibly and experimentally from broad concepts toward specific commitments, making the latter concrete as late as possible in order to narrow the bands of uncertainty and to benefit from the best available information. This is the process of *logical incrementalism*. (Emphasis added.)[22]

The major conclusions of Quinn are presented in Box 8.8.

Effectiveness of Strategic Planning

Concurrent with the adoption of planning systems in organizations have been attempts to assess their effectiveness to organizations. Consistent with the focus of planning, effectiveness is defined in economic terms: profitability, return on investment, or shareholders' wealth.

The first set of efforts rapidly led to the conclusion that strategic planning yields financial results. Stanley Thune and Robert House, in the first study to validate the effectiveness of strategic planning, concluded that formal planners outperformed nonplanners in return on investment, return on equity, and earnings per share. The highlights of their study are presented in Box 8.9.

Later studies, however, showed that strategic planning is not equally effective in all industries. For example, Leslie Rue and Robert Fulmer[23] based their study of 432 firms in consumer durables, nondurables, and services industries. They concluded that while planning yielded results for firms in the manufacturing sector, in the service sector the nonplanners outperformed the planners. Why are the findings inconsistent? Jack Pearce, Elizabeth Freeman, and Richard Robinson,[24] after reviewing the results of 18 research projects, conclude:

Several shortcomings of the methodologies employed in the previous research may have contributed to the inconsistent findings reported for the FSP (formal planning system)-performance link, and these shortcomings may be responsible for the perception that the link is tenuous.

Box 8.8

Quinn and Logical Incrementalism

Based on his study of strategic planning practice in 10 major companies, Quinn argues that successful practice relies on incremental approaches to strategic management rather than on the normative ideal of grand strategy.

Quinn discovered that successful CEOs did not pay much attention to formal planning processes. Rather, the CEOs kept their views submerged till their subordinates had a chance to articulate their own views. They often subtly shaped discussions to help the group come to the same conclusions they themselves had reached. Also, the CEOs sometimes acted not to eliminate differences but to prevent the differences from creating too many difficulties.

Quinn identified four important features of the logical incremental approach:

1. Begin the planning process with broad goals and policies that accommodate a variety of views.
2. Provide the conditions under which different views can attract supporters. This would lead to (3).
3. Work for a less politically charged climate, in which there is enough time to discuss the proposals.
4. Use this climate to create conditions that encourage innovation or kill off unwanted alternatives with less political exposure.

Quinn did not negate the value of comprehensive planning. Rather he complements the analytic with a political process that, in his view, reduces unintended consequences.

Other scholars are picking up where Quinn left off. They have suggested how organizational strategy is determined by the existing power structure of an organization and how coalitions are formed around formulation and implementation issues. Since their ideas are in the embryonic stage, we will have to wait awhile before these ideas can be translated into action.

Source: Adapted from James Brian Quinn, *Strategies for Change: Logical Incrementalism* (Homewood, Ill.: Richard D. Irwin, 1980.)

Thus, although there is some support for the proposition that formal planning contributes to financial performance, we cannot generalize about the utility of planning to all organizations. Given some evidence to the contrary, recent studies have adopted a contingency stance; that is, they have tried to understand the conditions under which formal planning will be successful. These studies are in the embryonic stages, but offer the prospects of a sharpened understanding of the utility of formal planning in organizations.

Summary

Over the years, U.S. firms elaborated their businesses through predictable stages: volume expansion, geographic expansion, vertical integration,

Box 8.9

Thune and House: Effectiveness of Strategic Planning

Stanley Thune and Robert House compared the performance of 18 matched pairs of medium- and large-scale organizations in the food, drug, oil, steel, chemical, and machinery industries over a period of seven years. The sales of each firm exceeded $75 million. Each pair consisted of one firm that undertook formal planning and one that did not. The study continued for seven years.

Thune and House used five financial performance measures: sales, stock prices, earnings per share (EPS), return on equity (ROE), and return on investment (ROI).

Based on their study, Thune and House concluded:

Formal planners significantly outperformed informal planners on ROI, ROE, and EPS; they equaled or slightly surpassed the nonplanners on sales growth.

Formal planners in the drugs, chemicals and machinery industries consistently outperformed the nonplanners whereas no clear associations could be established in the food, oil, and steel industries.

The relationship between economic performance and formal planning was stronger among medium-sized companies in rapidly changing markets.

After adoption of formal planning systems, the formal planners performed significantly better than nonplanners on financial measures.

Herold extended this study, tracking the performance of five matched pairs of firms used by Thune and House for an additional five years. Three pairs were in the drug industry and the remaining two in the chemical industry. Herold discovered that the formal planners not only continued to outperform the nonplanners, but they also extended their margin of difference.

The Thune and House study was the first to validate the effectiveness of strategic planning. Although their conclusions have been modified or challenged by others, many still point to this study as demonstrating the utility of strategic planning.

Source: Adapted from Stanley Thune and Robert House, "Where Long-Range Planning Pays Off," *Business Horizons,* August 1970.

diversification, and international expansion. The effectiveness of any business strategy depends on two factors: (1) the structure of its industry and (2) the business's position relative to its competitors. Organizations have unique preferences for strategy: defenders prefer to stay in their markets and protect their market share; prospectors try to explore new market opportunities, whereas analyzers try to seek a balance between the two approaches. Strategy is implemented incrementally but logically. Research evidence suggests that formal strategic planning contributes to financial performance, although we cannot say this for all organizations.

Thus, the problems of competitive strategy, patterns of growth and diversification, and long-term survival of organizations are typically the domain of strategic planning. Also, rationality and adaptation to environment constitute the central ideology of this field. There have been other voices such as the creative metaphor of Ackoff and the logical incremental perspective of Quinn; but these have not yet occupied the center stage of strategic planning.

Key Concepts

We define six key concepts to set the stage for the main frameworks currently utilized in strategic planning.

Hierarchy or Levels of Strategy

Strategy in the broadest sense refers to the means by which ends are accomplished. Although in the abstract one could talk about *the* strategy of an organization, actually an organization may employ a number of means or strategies to accomplish its goals. For example, in a diversified organization, there may be separate strategies for each one of the major product lines. Even in a single-product organization, there may be separate marketing, production, and finance strategies. Needless to say, strategy is a complex idea when applied to actual organizations.

To capture the complexity of the strategy concept, we distinguish between three levels of strategy: *corporate, business,* and *functional.*

Corporate strategy is concerned with the question: What set of businesses should a firm be in? It is thus concerned with determining the industries that a firm should stay in, enter into, or exit from, and allocation of scarce financial resources among its various businesses. Corporate strategy leads to such decisions as acquisition (buying another firm or a subsidiary), divestiture (selling part of a firm), or joint venture (forming a partnership with another firm).

Business strategy focuses on how to compete in a particular industry or product/market segment. It is thus concerned with the mode of competing within a specific industry and coordination of marketing, production, and other relevant functional areas to implement the chosen mode of competition.

Functional strategy focuses on the maximization of resource productivity *within* each functional area (production, marketing, research and development, etc.).

Corporate strategy represents the highest level of strategies, as it aims to accomplish broad shareholder objectives. Once adopted, it sets some of the major objectives and constraints of business strategies. In a similar sense, a business strategy sets some of the objectives and constraints for functional area strategies. In this sense, the strategies form a hierarchy, with each higher level subsuming lower level strategies. Just as the levels of a system form a hierarchy, so do the three levels of strategy.

The concept of hierarchy helps us to dispel some of the confusion between goals and strategies. Often in organizations managers at different (hierarchic) levels talk about strategies and goals in a way that is confusing to the outsider. For example, a marketing executive in a division may talk about increased consumer awareness of the company's product as a goal, and increased advertising as a strategy. The next higher level, the divisional manager, may talk about higher market share as the goal, with increased consumer awareness as a strategy. Still higher up, a corporate level manager, for example, the CEO, may talk about portfolio strategy where increased market share of the division is only a strategy, not a goal.

Which is strategy and which is goal? The concept of hierarchy reminds us that the distinction between strategy and goals is a function of the level of strategy. What is a strategy at one level often is an objective for a lower level. Thus, the above example is not confusing if we note that the marketing executive, the divisional manager, and the CEO are talking about different levels of strategy.

The distinction among business and corporate levels is not visible in all firms. In single-business firms, corporate and business strategies are closely tied together. However, in diversified firms, with multiple businesses, the distinction becomes pronounced. These firms may have as many business strategies as there are businesses, but a single corporate strategy.

Model of Decision Making

In our discussion of philosophical assumptions, we noted that norms of rationality undergird much of strategic planning. The flow of decision making implied in much of strategic planning has its anchors in rational models, which order the decision-making phases in a logical and sequential manner. A typical sequence of phases is presented in Figure 8.4.[25]

Diagnosis. Diagnosis involves environmental analysis and an assessment of the current performance of the firm. This leads to the detection of strategic problems and opportunities. It also leads to comprehensive and integrated mapping of cause-effect relationships among strategies (means) and goals (ends).

Strategic Alternative Development. Based on the systematic and comprehensive diagnosis, decision makers develop a broad set of alternatives to tackle problems and opportunities.

Evaluation of Alternatives and Choice. Here the consequences of each alternative are evaluated in terms of the goals of top management. The alternative that most satisfactorily accomplishes the goals is finally chosen.

Implementation. Implementation of the alternative logically follows choice. Organizational structures are redesigned, resources are allocated, reward and incentive systems are installed to motivate desired behaviors, and control and evaluation systems are established to monitor performance.

Evaluation of Results. Control systems monitor the performance. This helps to pinpoint operating problems so that any deviations from expected results during the implementation stage are corrected. This phase also provides firm-related data for diagnosis at a later date.

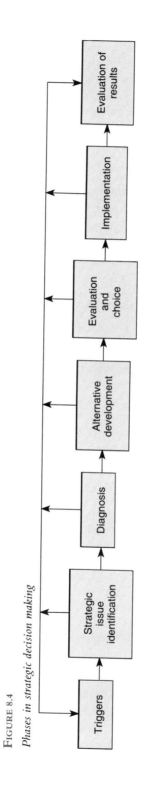

FIGURE 8.4

Phases in strategic decision making

275

According to this model of decision making, strategy formulation consists of diagnosis, alternative development, and choice phases. Formulation is, thus, conceptually separable from the implementation phase, during which the strategic plans are executed. As we saw earlier, the idea that formulation and implementation are sequentially related stages has been a contribution of the Harvard Business School scholars.

Content and Process

It is useful to distinguish between two *interrelated* facets of strategic planning: content and process.

> *Content* refers to the substantive issues tackled in strategic planning—the specific means and plans by which corporate, business, or functional goals will be achieved. For example, portfolio strategy, competitive advantage, or specific mode of competition are the content elements of strategic planning.

> *Process* refers to the specific steps through which strategic plans are formulated and implemented. Environmental analysis and evaluation of alternatives are examples of specific steps in strategic planning.

We note that levels of strategy typically refer to the content of strategies, whereas phases refer to the process. Content and process are *intertwined*. Thus, we may talk of the phases in corporate, business, or functional strategy formulation and implementation. When we summarize the action frameworks in the next section, we will focus on both content and process of strategy formulation at different levels.

Criteria for Evaluating Strategy

How does one recognize an effective strategy? One approach is to execute the strategy and find out what happens. However, that approach is of no help to organizations, since they want to choose a strategy for execution that will result in favorable outcomes. Since strategic plans are made in partial ignorance, it is nearly impossible to make definite predictions about the outcomes of strategy. Therefore, instead of evaluating strategies only on predicted outcomes, strategic planners focus on a comprehensive set of criteria by which to judge a particular strategic alternative.

At all levels of strategy evaluation and choice, a set of five criteria are considered:

> *Environmental fit* examines the degree to which the goals and strategies exploit the attractive opportunities and the significant threats posed by the environment.

> *Internal consistency* addresses the mutual compatibility of goals and strategies at various levels. For example, the chosen strategy should

accomplish the goals of top management. Similarly, functional strategies should support business strategy; and business strategy, in turn, must be consistent with corporate strategy.

Resource and capability fit considers whether the firm has the financial and human resources and operating capabilities to execute the strategies.

Values of key decision makers covers the degree to which risk-return trade-offs underlying the chosen strategies are congruent with the disposition of the key decision makers.

Implementability is the extent to which the chosen strategy is acceptable to the rest of the organization during execution.

Conceptually, therefore, strategy should be judged not only on financial criteria, but also on those related to environment, internal organization, and the dominant values of top management.

Thus, strategic planning emphasizes that strategies should be *congruent* with environmental and intraorganizational factors. This is consistent with the prescriptions of systems theory. In real life, complete congruence is not likely to be achieved, and decision makers will have to make trade-offs among the criteria.

Time Horizons

As seen from the model of decision making, the process of strategy formulation is an ongoing process. This means that the process is cyclical—it gets repeated over time as circumstances change. The time period over which the cycles get repeated depends upon the nature of the firm and its relationship to the environment. Production and demand cycles in one specific industry are of primary concern in an integrated single-industry firm because they dictate the allocation of financial resources between working capital and fixed investment and influence the rate of capacity changes in that industry. The diversified firm, in contrast, must balance over time the sometimes interdependent economic demands of numerous business units that operate in different industry sectors. Actually, therefore, there may be a number of strategic planning cycles in organizations.

Further, although strategic planning focuses primarily on the long-term effectiveness of an organization, three time horizons are typically considered for actual plans. They are short, medium and long term, corresponding to the levels of strategy. As we move from corporate to business to functional levels, the time horizon considered for strategy formulation typically shrinks from long to short term.[26]

Contingency Planning

We noted earlier that strategic decisions are made in partial ignorance (a point underscored by Ansoff). In effect, most of the strategies make assumptions about environments, and sometimes about a firm's capacity to compete. Of course, as the time frame gets longer, decisions will have to be made in an increasing degree of ignorance.

Since changes in the environment often render the assumptions invalid, contingency plans are often made to account for such occurrences.

> *Contingency plans* are plans prepared by a firm for execution if and when some of the assumptions on which its chosen strategies are based prove to be invalid.

Contingency plans form a special subset of the content of strategy. They may be pitched at *any of the three* levels and may include formulation and implementation.

Summary

Two major levels of strategy are addressed in strategic planning: corporate and business. At each level, strategic planning involves a set of sequentially linked steps: diagnosis, strategic alternative development, evaluation of alternatives and choice, and implementation. Typically, strategic plans are evaluated along five criteria: environmental fit, internal consistency, resource fit, consistency with the values of top-level managers, and implementability. Three time periods are typically considered in strategic planning: short, medium, and long term. In addition, firms usually develop contingency plans to be employed if their major assumptions are proven wrong.

Action Strategies

In our discussion of strategy frameworks, we will primarily focus on corporate and business levels. We will not consider functional strategies for two reasons. First, as Ansoff has reminded us (see the section Theoretical Underpinnings), functional strategies represent operating, not strategic decisions. Second, functional strategies are the primary focus of other management disciplines: marketing, finance, production, and the like.

We will deal with (1) corporate level strategies, (2) business level strategies, and (3) the interrelationships between them, in that sequence. In both levels of strategies, we will summarize the process of decision making, key models, and specific criteria of evaluating strategies.

Corporate Level Strategy

The focus of corporate level strategy is the determination of industries in which a firm should operate. The primary goal driving corporate strategy decisions is maximization of shareholders' wealth, stated in such terms as value of the stock or return on investment.

Content

The major content of corporate strategy is the portfolio of businesses:

Portfolio, as the term is used here, refers to the set of specific industries in which the firm decides to operate.

A firm develops a portfolio strategy to concentrate its resources on selected opportunities or industries. Due to resource limitations, a firm cannot pursue every attractive industry to accomplish its goals. Instead, it channels available resources to a select set of industries where the firm is able to realize the best possible return from resources.

The portfolio strategy has three major elements: acquisitions, divestment, and investment levels.

Acquisition refers to purchase of another firm or subsidiary. This may mean entry into an industry or augmenting the scope of an existing business.

Divestment means selling off some currently owned businesses or subsidiaries to release financial resources toward more attractive industries or opportunities.

Investment levels refers to the allocation of financial resources among the portfolio of businesses.

Through these decisions, the firm allocates its limited financial resources to maximize shareholder wealth.

Process

The process of corporate strategy formulation is sketched in Figure 8.5. Here, we will summarize the process according to the phases identified in the model of strategic decision making.

Diagnosis consists of macroenvironmental and industry analyses, as well as the financial capabilities of the firm. Diagnosis involves forecasting of future portfolio positions and performance (in light of macroenvironmental and industry level changes) and comparing the expected performance with corporate objectives. Based on the comparison, a firm can identify problems and opportunities.

Alternative development consists of creating feasible future portfolios.

Evaluation and choice consists of selecting a portfolio from among the alternatives, based on its ability to meet corporate objectives subject to cash flow constraints. The chosen portfolio points toward the businesses to be divested and those to be acquired, as well as the objectives and investment patterns for retained businesses.

Implementation and evaluation of results typically involves organization design (to be covered in the next chapter) and feeding the results back into the diagnosis during the next planning cycle.

FIGURE 8.5

Corporate level strategy formulation process

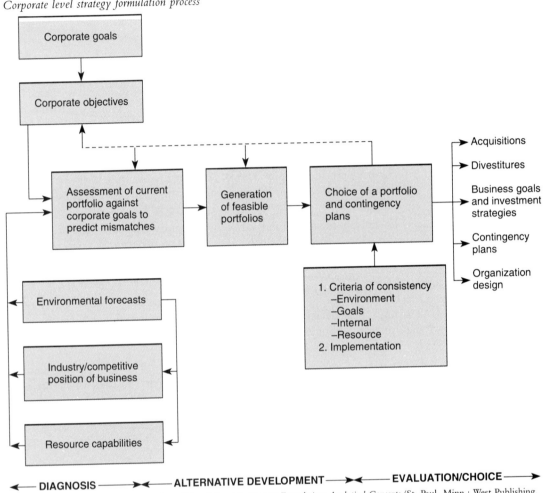

Source: Adapted from Charles W. Hofer and Dan Schendel, *Strategy Formulation: Analytical Concepts* (St. Paul, Minn.: West Publishing, 1978).

In the last two decades, specific portfolio models have been developed to facilitate the diagnosis and evaluation phases. The models represent the major content frameworks for corporate level strategy.

Portfolio Models

We will consider two of the more popular portfolio models: Boston Consulting Group (BCG)'s growth-share matrix, and the General Electric business screen.[27]

Growth-Share Matrix. In this model, the existing or potential businesses of a firm are arrayed on a two-dimensional matrix, with one dimension representing the long-run (typically three to five years) market growth rate of the respective industries, and the other representing the market share position of the firm's businesses.

The rationale for this matrix presentation lies in four crucial assumptions made by BCG:

1. Due to experience curve effects, market share has a direct effect on profitability. As a firm gains greater experience in a particular line of business, its cost of doing business (production, marketing, etc.) declines. Market share is a proxy for experience. As costs go down, it can earn higher profits relative to competitors due to cost advantages.

2. Cash flow of a business is related to the *nature of the market* and its *relative market share*. In the early stages of the product life cycle, a business consumes cash, whereas in later stages, when market growth slows, it begins to generate cash. Dominant businesses throw off more cash in mature markets (given their higher profitability).

3. Gaining share in mature markets or maintaining (and, of course, gaining) share in high-growth markets will consume cash.

4. The relationships among businesses are primarily financial; that is, limited to the generation and use of cash.

Based on these assumptions, BCG uses market growth rate and market share as proxies for cash requirements and generation, respectively. Using the growth-share matrix, BCG displays the cash needs and generation of a firm's various businesses. Specifically, BCG divides industries into high- or low-growth markets, using 10 percent as a cutoff point. Similarly, a firm's position in the market is categorized as high or low, depending on whether or not it is a market leader. A typical growth-share matrix is shown in Figure 8.6A.

The matrix display enables the BCG model to categorize a firm's businesses into four types: *stars, cash cows, question marks,* and *dogs.*

Stars are a set of businesses where the firm currently has a dominant position and the markets are growing. For a firm to maintain its share, it has to plow more cash into these.

Cash cows are dominant businesses in stable or low-growth industries and will generate cash over and beyond their own needs for share maintenance.

Dogs are nondominant businesses in low-growth markets and are cash losers.

Question marks are prospective stars, but require a heavy influx of cash for share gains.

FIGURE 8.6

Portfolio models

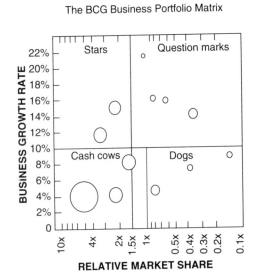

A

The BCG Business Portfolio Matrix

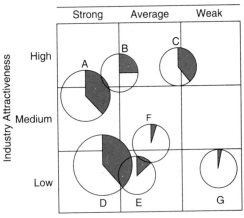

B

General Electric's Business Screen
Competitive Position

According to BCG, the objective of portfolio management is to match the cash requirements of various businesses with available cash. This has relevance for the diagnosis and evaluation phases in strategy formulation. At the diagnosis and evaluation phase, BCG model makes four recommendations for balancing the portfolio:

1. Dogs are candidates for prospective divestment since they are cash losers.
2. Cash cows should support stars and question marks with their cash, since they do not require as much as they generate.
3. Stars should be supported so that the firm at least maintains its market share position in these markets—but since the markets are growing, they require further infusions of cash.
4. Question marks should be carefully analyzed: some should be heavily supported, whereas others should be divested.

Also during the alternative evaluation phase, each feasible portfolio could be evaluated to determine the extent to which cash balancing is achieved.

General Electric's Business Screen.   This model starts with the premise that market or industry attractiveness should reflect differences in the average long-run profit potential for all participants in the market, while differences in competitive position determine the profitability of a specific business relative to its competition. Much like the previous model, the GE screen arrays a firm's businesses along two dimensions, in this case *market attractiveness* and *competitive position*. The variables are assessed on high, medium, and low categories. The resulting array and the investment strategies are displayed in Figure 8.6B.

Unlike the BCG model, however, the GE screen does not specify factors making up market attractiveness and competitive position. Instead, it suggests that since factors may vary from industry to industry, each industry and firm's business position within it should be assessed separately. Since many of the factors cannot be quantified, the assessments should represent the best judgment of well-informed managers.

A Comparison.   Both models—the growth-share and the business screen—are similar, since they attempt to classify and display the present and prospective positions of businesses according to *the attractiveness of the market* and *the ability of the business to compete* within the market. In the case of the BCG model, market growth serves as an indicator of market attractiveness, whereas relative market share corresponds to market position. In GE's screen, multiple factors determine these characteristics.

The models differ in their precision, specificity, and degree of detail. The BCG model is relatively precise, but not very detailed; the GE screen is more detailed with respect to the assessment of each variable and the investment strategies, however, many of the variables are subjectively derived. Further, specificity necessitates greater effort to create the GE screen. Most normative prescriptions argue for joint usage of the models.

In the illustrative example in Box 8.10, the use of portfolio models is described for Zales corporation, a major jewelry store. As can be seen from the case, the cash requirements of various businesses exceed cash generation. Zales divested most of its nonjewelry businesses by 1984 and decided to become a single-industry firm.

Business Level Strategy

After a firm has decided which industries to operate in—its corporate strategy—it then has to address the nature of competition in each industry. Business strategy formulation addresses the question: How should a business compete in an industry?

In a multiindustry firm, as many business strategies exist as there are industries. Here, the amount of financial resources allocated to a business are limited by corporate level strategy. The resources are also limited in an integrated single-industry firm where there is little distinction between business and corporate level strategies. In either case, the focus of business strategy formulation is to utilize its resources to gain the highest possible profitability in its industry.

Box 8.10

Zales: Portfolio Models

Zales Corporation is the world's leading retailer of jewelry merchandise. Its origins can be traced to 1924, when Morris and William Zale opened Zales jewelers in Wichita Falls, Texas. The company experienced a steady 36-year growth in sales volume following a strategy focused on jewelry and related items.

In 1960, when General Electric announced the discovery of a process for manufacturing synthetic diamonds, Zales was faced with the possibility of a market glutted with synthetic diamonds. In response to this threat, in the 1960s Zales undertook a program of diversification aimed at acquiring firms engaged in specialized retailing in other fields.

In 1980, Zales had four primary lines of business: (1) jewelry, (2) footwear, (3) drugs, and (4) sporting goods. It operated 1,845 retail stores in 49 states, Washington, Puerto Rico, Guam, and the United Kingdom. Zales exceeded $1 billion in sales and achieved record earnings of $50 million. Also by the late 1970s Zales began to experience financial constraints. One indicator was that its total debt was beginning to be equal to its equity. It was time to pay attention to its portfolio strategy.

In 1979, it undertook a major corporate strategy audit, including the competitive position of each of its major lines of business:

Jewelry: The jewelry business produced sales of over $600 million, or nearly two thirds of Zale's total sales. The annual sales growth had been impressive (nearly over 16 percent), and operating profit in 1980 was over $100 million. Zales had different stores for high- and medium-priced *goods,* and also operated a catalog division. Industry sales were expected to grow and Zales's competitive position was strong. However, Zales's further growth would require sizable cash outlays.

Drugs: The drug business produced sales of over $140 million and represented 14 percent of total sales. Although the sales growth had been impressive, the business reported an operating loss in 1980. Although industry sales were expected to grow, there were several strong competitors relative to Zales. Zales did not have a leadership position in the industry and it appeared that Zales's strengths did not lie in managing a low-margin business. Also, the changing nature of the retail drug industry called for a further infusion of capital, if Zales were to turn this business around.

Footwear: The footwear business constituted 13 percent of sales ($136 million) and was very profitable. Zales was not a market leader and a number of trends indicated that to become a leader, Zales would have to make major investments.

Sporting goods: The smallest division in Zales generated a sale of slightly over $60 million (6.1 percent of Zales sales). Zales did not have any unique strengths in this business, and there were other strong regional leaders in the industry. A change here would also require capital outlays.

Box 8.10 continued

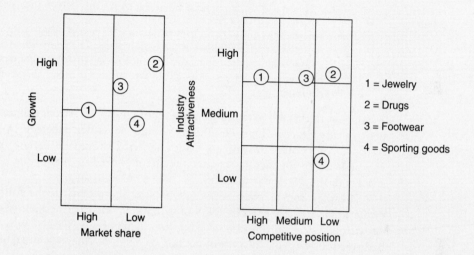

Based on the audit, one could portray Zales's businesses on the BCG growth-share matrix as well as on the GE screen above:

Although there are slight differences between the two portfolio models, the general conclusions seem to be the same. Thus, Zales is very well positioned in its traditional line of business, jewelry; and probably in the footwear business as well. However, if it wants to continue to be a strong player in any of the other businesses it will have to make significant dollar investments to overcome its current competitive disadvantages.

Zales entered the drug, footwear, and sporting goods businesses through acquisitions. Partly as a result of the acquisitions, its debt level had risen over the years. It was not prudent to add to this debt burden by continued investment in weak lines of business.

Despite strong performance in jewelry and footwear, it was clear that capital constraints prevented Zales from being a leader in both simultaneously.

Following the corporate strategy audit, Zales's management decided to concentrate on its traditional business—jewelry. In the 1980s, it began a major program to divest the other businesses. The drug business was sold to Revco, the sporting goods business to Oshman's, and footwear to Sears holdings (a U.K.-based company). The sales generated well over $150 million cash, which was used to retire debt. Zales believes that as a result of its new corporate strategy, it is in a much better competitive position today.

Source: Adapted from Roger A. Kerin and Robert A. Peterson, *Strategic Marketing Problems* (Boston: Allyn & Bacon, 1987).

Content

Whereas portfolio balancing was the main focus of corporate level strategy, business strategy formulation is concerned with achieving a sustainable competitive advantage for a specific business in its respective industry.

> *Competitive advantage* refers to a business's unique strengths *relative* to its competitors, strengths that are valued in the marketplace. The competitive advantages are sustainable to the extent they are not easily copied by competitors. Sustainable competitive advantages allow the business to reap above-average profits in an industry.

According to the above definition, not all of a business' strengths are competitive advantages. Two conditions should be satisfied before calling a factor a competitive advantage. First, the firm should be better than its competitors on the factor. Second, the factor should be one of the keys to success in the particular industry.

The meaning of competitive advantage is captured in the following quote attributed to Marcus Sieff of Marks & Spencer, perhaps the best department store in the United Kingdom, when he was asked why M&S had not followed the successful actions of Sears & Roebuck in selling insurance in their stores:

> We of course study Sears operations, just as they study ours, and we have seriously considered mounting a similar insurance business. . . . But our research convinced us that we could not do a better job than our best English insurance companies are now doing. And, as you know, we believe that *in the long run* the company's interests are best served if we *only do for our customers what we can do better than others.* (Emphasis added.)[28]

Finally, some factors yield temporary advantages but are easily copied by the competitors. Advantages that are not sustainable are not useful for business strategy. For example, in the late 1970s, many banks introduced automatic teller machines, believing that by doing so the banks could outwit their competitors. As many of them later found out, most other banks copied the move, and the advantage could not be sustained.

A typical business strategy has four elements: (1) mission or business definition, (2) strategic thrust of the business, (3) supporting strategic actions, and (4) an integrated set of operating plans.

> *Business definition* or mission statement, as it is sometimes called, specifies the boundaries of the business or the present and prospective scope of a business's activities. The scope includes the breadth of the product line (e.g., full versus limited line), and the type of customers (e.g., price-sensitive versus quaiity conscious), and geographic regions (e.g., regional, national, or global) that will be served by the business.
>
> *Strategic thrust* specifies the route to competitive advantage by which the business expects to outperform its competitors.

Strategic moves specify the guidelines for action to be consistent with the defined scope and strategic thrust of the business. The guidelines may include: (1) level of growth (e.g., market share maintenance, market penetration or development), (2) defensive and offensive tactics to prevent competitors from eroding one's position and to wean the market away from them, and (3) objectives and guidelines for functional areas (marketing, production, etc.).

A set of operating plans for coordinating the functional area strategies, setting the crucial objectives and patterns of resource allocation among them.

An abbreviated real-world example of these components, drawn from secondary sources, is presented in Box 8.11.

As can be seen from the example, there is greater specificity in action steps as we move from business definition to operating plans. However, business definition and strategic thrust are the most important elements since they set the direction for strategic moves and operating plans. Given their importance, most business strategy frameworks deal with business definition and strategic thrust.

Process

The focus of business strategy formulation is on orchestrating the various strategy elements so as to be *consistent* with each other and the realities of the industry. The process is sketched in Figure 8.7.

Diagnosis. This phase is often called *situational analysis,* and draws upon macroenvironmental and industry forecasts and the current position of the business to identify the discrepancy between business goals (as directed by corporate level strategies in the case of multiindustry firms) and expected future performance.

Alternative development. During this phase, alternative business strategies are generated to address the problems and opportunities identified during diagnosis. The primary focus at this stage is to define the scope and strategic thrust of business. Although strategic moves and operating plans are not completely ignored, they are often detailed only after a specific alternative is chosen.

Evaluation and choice. The alternatives are evaluated in the light of objectives and resource constraints established at the corporate level. Key questions are: Does the alternative yield sustainable competitive advantage? Do we have the resources to implement it? Is it consistent with the objectives set at the corporate level?

Implementation and evaluation of results. The business strategy sets the stage for operational issues in the organization. Strategic moves and operating plans are charted out, and business units may be reorganized for implementation. The results from implementation are fed back into the diagnosis phase during the next planning cycle.

Box 8.11

Federal Express: An Example of Business Strategy

Recently, *Forbes* reported that the sales of Federal Express reached the $2 billion mark in fiscal year 1985. It stood 21st in profitability among 1,000 public companies. Then *Forbes* reported:

But right now Memphis-based Federal Express is enduring a fearsome drenching from its 16-month-old ZapMail venture, a network of facsimile machines capable of shooting instant mail—words or graphics—across the country. Overnight express profits, though continuing to gush, didn't grow enough to make ZapMail's $125 million operating loss. Federal's fiscal 1985 earnings dropped $39 million, $1.61 per share in the first annual earnings decline since Federal broke into black in 1976.

Yet the company remains committed to Zap-Mail, an advance it hopes will outstrip its now famous Overnight Letter. Federal this year will sink up to $200 million more into ZapMail capital expenditures. Rather than resting on its success—and risking stagnation—it is wisely pouring profits into new related areas. Federal's founder and chairman, 41-year-old Frederick W. Smith, a man with certifiable long-range vision and $185 million in Federal stock to prove it, explains:

ZapMail is not only an offensive move, but a defensive move as well. In recent years the demand for rapid transmission of information has begun to outpace the demand for rapid movement of freight . . . It became clear that eventually some form of electronic mail would displace much of the overnight document business.

Smith sees the business he founded in the broadest of terms. Federal isn't in the parcel post business or even air transport, but in the evolving field of information movement.

Federal is building a central facsimile network that it hopes will become the standard for facsimile transmissions. But why is ZapMail producing so much more red ink than expected? Clearly, it is a concept that has not been widely accepted. Only about 4,500 machines have been leased so far. Tom Oliver, Federal's senior vice president of electronic products, argues that use will eventually pick up. Oliver figures that in 10 years, a million ZapMail machines will be in place.

But it is hard for Federal to hurry the pace. Earlier this year, Federal tried to flood the market by leasing ZapMail machines for as little as $75 a month. But that only encouraged marginal accounts that really hadn't much use for the machines. Now Federal is trying to earn acceptance the old-fashioned way, with sales representatives bird-dogging customers to get them to use the machines.

In the meantime, overnight express is rolling along, with Federal dominating the market. In their last two quarters, three leading players—Federal, Emery Air Freight, and Airborne Freight—have seen their collective revenues rise by $383 million. Federal gets 63 percent. But Federal is grabbing 86 percent of the gains, even though its rivals are discounting heavily. In the last two quarters, Emery and Airborne showed operating margins under 4 percent. Federal's was 10 percent. Keeping margins up isn't easy in a business where big shippers are demanding discounts. So Federal is dropping costs faster than prices. Four years ago, it cost Federal $22 to handle a package. Now it's close to $18 because of Federal's investment in electronics and automation. Trucking costs about one sixth what

Box 8.11 continued

flying does, and Federal figures to move 25 percent of its volume by truck within a few years.

Meantime, Federal, competitive to the point of pugnaciousness, is on the attack. Federal figures Emery is using its high-margin (9.5 percent) international business to subsidize its lower margin (2.4 percent) domestic battle against Federal. So Federal is jumping into the international fray, hoping in part to bash Emery where it hurts most. Federal's pugnaciousness shows right through in its advertising. To counter United Parcel Service, which entered the overnight business three years ago, Federal is hitting the airwaves with ads boasting of its on-call pickup service and vaunted package-tracking system, neither of which UPS offers. Federal also privately shows focus-group tape of shippers who are complaining about UPS's overnight unreliability.

Although sketchy, the above write up enables us to piece together some of the elements of the Federal Express strategy.

Business Level: The corporate goal of growth is clearly visible. This is to come from the growth of the existing overnight express and from Zap-Mail. The firm is obviously undertaking (1) product development, via ZapMail, and (2) market development, via international expansion. This translates into its investment strategy: invest heavily in ZapMail and use overnight express to provide some cash for the investment. We may further note that Federal Express is a single-business firm (in the Rumelt sense), as most of the revenues are coming from overnight express. Hence, the distinction between corporate and business level is not clear.

Business Definition: We see a redefinition of business from a sole focus on consumer functions to include technology, in this case from air/trucking to electronic transmission. This leads Smith to define his business as information movement.

Strategic Thrust: Two related thrusts are visible. First, in its traditional overnight express business, its route to competitive advantage is via its low-cost position. In ZapMail, it is too early to say, but it still may be the same due to experience and scale effects initially.

Strategic Actions: We noted the dual growth vector as both product and market development earlier. Smith views ZapMail as both a defensive and an offensive move. *Offensive* actions are clearly visible in overnight express; aggressive share acquisitions in international freight to counter the threat from Emery, and discrediting UPS in the eyes of consumer. *Supporting functional area thrusts* include building a central facsimile network for standard setting and aggressive sales calls to promote sales of ZapMail, and changing the operations partly to trucking and investment in electronics and automation to promote the low-cost position, with advertising to counter competitive attacks.

We do not see operating plans here, as the degree of detail in these precludes their inclusion in a write up in the popular press, but we can be sure they exist in some form. Finally, we also see the tentative form of this firm's contingency plans, as we hear Smith talking about "unless the current situation worsens," suggesting a radical revision of plans is likely to be triggered only by a decline in performance.

Source: *Forbes,* 1985.

FIGURE 8.7

Business level strategy formulation process

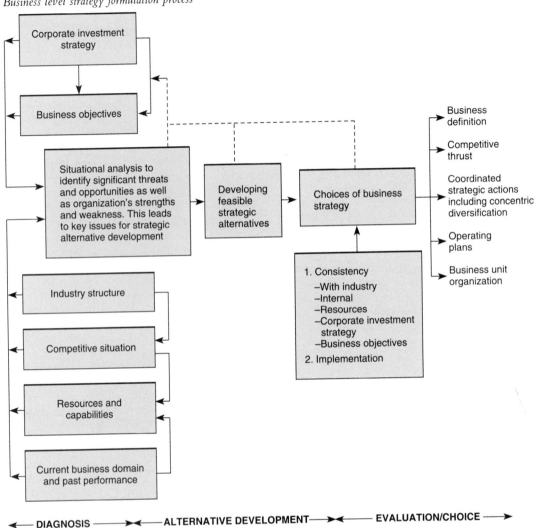

Strategy Models

As we have noted earlier, since business definition and strategic thrust are the most important elements of business strategy, the models primarily deal with these two elements. The most significant strategy model was formulated by Michael Porter,[29] based on his work on industry structure (see the previous chapter on environmental analysis).

Porter's model focuses on two factors: competitive advantage (strategic thrust) and scope of the business (business definition).

Competitive Advantage.   According to Porter, there are two generic routes to competitive advantage: *low-cost position* and *differentiation:*

> *Low-cost position* is one route where a firm is able to achieve costs of delivering product/service so low that its competitors in the market cannot match it. Cost advantages may be derived from many factors, for example, scale or size of operations as in the case of Japanese auto manufacturers, sourcing parts from low-wage areas such as Taiwan and Korea, or tight control of costs and overhead as was the case of People Express airlines.
>
> *Differentiation* is the route by which a business favorably distinguishes its products in the eyes of customers by offering what is perceived to be a *superior* product, service, or the like relative to its competitors.

Business Scope.   The scope of the business (defined either in terms of product line breadth, variety of customer types, or simply geographically) may be broadly classified into two: broad and narrow. When the scope is broad, the firm produces a full line of products and serves almost all customers or regions. When the scope is narrow, it offers only a select product line and serves a selected set of customers or regions.

The two basic types of competitive advantage may be combined with the scope of the activities to yield three *generic strategies* for achieving above-average performance in the industry: cost leadership, differentiation, and focus. The focus strategy has two variants, cost focus and differentiation focus. The generic strategies are shown in Figure 8.8.

> *Cost leadership.* Here, a firm sets out to become the low-cost producer in its industry. The firm has a broad scope and serves many industry segments; the breadth is important to its cost advantage. Low-cost producers often sell a standard or no-frills product and must find and exploit all sources of cost advantage.
>
> *Differentiation.* Here, a firm seeks to be unique in its industry along some factors that are widely valued by customers. It selects one or more attributes that many buyers in an industry perceive to be

FIGURE 8.8

Generic strategies

		Competitive Advantage	
		Low Cost	Differentiation
Competitive Scope	Broad	Cost leadership	Differentiation
	Narrow	Cost focus	Differentiation focus

important, and uniquely positions itself to meet those needs. It is rewarded for its uniqueness with a premium price.

Focus. This strategy rests on a narrow competitive scope within an industry. The focuser selects a segment or group of segments in an industry and tailors its strategy to serve them to the exclusion of others. In cost focus, a firm seeks a cost advantage in its target segments, while differentiation focus exploits the special needs of customers in certain segments.

What factors determine the choice of a strategy? Porter argued that an effective strategy should take into account two factors: (1) characteristics of the industry and (2) the specific capabilities of the business. In some industries—for example, distribution of electronic components—where there are no significant cost reductions possible and distribution cannot be differentiated at the present state of technology, cost leadership and differentiation are perhaps not possible. The firms in this industry are forced to adopt focus strategies. However, in other industries such as automobiles (e.g., BMW), where significant differentiation and cost differentials are possible, one could adopt a cost leadership position or differentiation. Here, the choice depends on the financial resources and capabilities of the specific firm.

Interrelationships among Levels of Strategy

Corporate, business, and functional strategies are *interdependent,* not independent of each other. They are tied together cyclically, as show in Figure 8.9. Once formulated, the corporate level constrains the business level, which, in turn, constrains the functional level. During the formulation stage, the corporate level uses the business level performance (feedback) as input to its diagnosis; similarly, functional level assessments form a crucial input to business strategy formulation.

The three levels differ along the key concepts mentioned earlier (see Table 8.5). To repeat, strategy formulation becomes increasingly *constrained* as we move from corporate level to functional levels. In other words, the scope of formulation is broad at corporate level, relatively narrow at business level, and much more so at functional level. At the implementation stage, corporate strategy requires setting the framework of coordination between headquarters and business units, which may include changes in organization design, reward and incentive schemes, planning, information, and control systems. At the business level, changes in organization design may ensue, and the traditional management process for coordinating operations becomes important. At the functional level, the distinction between strategy and operations breaks down.

In addition, as indicated earlier, the *time frames* considered for the three strategies differ considerably. The corporate level typically addresses longer

FIGURE 8.9

Linkages among strategy levels

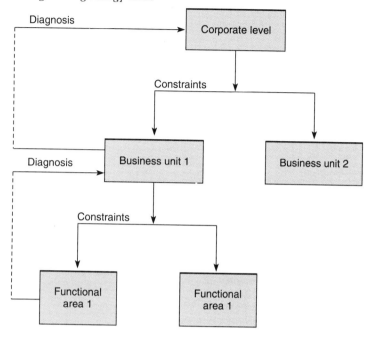

term horizons, whereas functional levels typically address the short term. Business strategies fall somewhere in between. Similarly, *contingency plans* at the corporate level address the whole organization, at the business unit level the respective industries, and at functional levels operational issues. At all levels, plans address a few crucial contingencies, though their focus differs from one another.

Summary

Typical strategic planning frameworks address questions at the (1) corporate and (2) business levels. At the corporate level, portfolio models enable managers to make choices about the industries in which they want to operate. These decisions allocate scarce capital across a select set of industries in such a way as to balance growth and profitability. At the business level, organizations are urged to seek a competitive advantage over other organizations operating in the same markets. There are two ways to competitive advantage: (1) low-cost position or (2) differentiation.

TABLE 8.5   **A Comparison of Strategies by Levels**

Dimensions	Corporate	Business	Functional
	Level of Strategy		
1. Formulation			
Content	1. Entry, exit, portfolio	1. Competitive strategy	1. Operations: managing functional areas
	2. Resource allocation across industries	2. Resource allocation across functional areas	2. Resources allocation within functional areas
Process	1. Unconstrained	1. Relatively constrained	1. Very constrained
	2. Guided by corporate goals, resource availability, environmental realities	2. Guided by corporate investment strategy and market conditions	2. Guided by business strategy and allocated resources
2. Implementation			
Content	Corporate-divisional relations, rewards and control system	Business unit organization design	Management in the traditional sense
Process	Monitoring strategic control	Monitoring management control	Monitoring budgetary control
3. Focus of contingency plans	Macroenvironmental and industry level variables	Industry and Competitor actions	Operational contingencies
4. Time frame of decision impact	Long and medium term	Medium term	Short term

Strengths and Limitations: The Role of Emergent Behaviors

It is now recognized that even well-conceived strategies are often not realized in practice. Although in strategic planning this recognition is relatively recent, the emergent quality of organizational behavior is not a new idea to system theorists.

The recognition of emergent behaviors has prompted strategy scholars to distinguish between deliberate (intended) and emergent strategies. Henry Mintzberg, a major strategy scholar explains:

> As shown in [Figure 8.10], *deliberate* strategies (intentions realized) can be distinguished from *emergent* strategies (patterns realized despite or in the absence of intentions). . . .
>   The concept of emergent strategy may . . . seem controversial—the notion that organizations can pursue "strategies" without intending them. After all, the term strategy has always been associated with voluntarism and free

FIGURE 8.10

Emergent and deliberate strategies

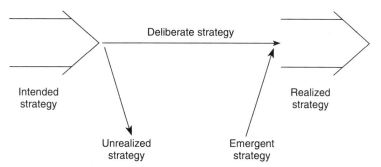

Source: Henry Mintzberg and James Brian Quinn, *The Strategy Process* (Englewood Cliffs, N.J.: Prentice Hall, 1991), p. 14.

will. . . . Were "deliberate" and "emergent" strategies two distinct phenomena in practice, then there might be merit in applying the label strategy only to the former. We contend, however, that the two represent the end points of a continuum, indeed that there may be no such thing as a purely deliberate strategy (intentions realized precisely) or a purely emergent one (total absence of intention, despite pattern in action). . . .

[T]o the extent that ostensibly deliberate strategies contain emergent elements, the two concepts deserve the same label, if only to force practitioners and researchers alike to recognize them as part of the same phenomenon.[30]

Why do emergent strategies depart from deliberate ones? What causes lead to emergence? The strategy field draws our attention to the role of the environment in emergent behaviors; that is, competitor actions or changes in the industry and the macroenvironment may require abandoning formulated strategies even in the midst of implementation. The normative prescription that strategy formulation should be an ongoing process is firmly anchored in this view: Competitors' actions and other environmental changes need to be continuously monitored, and strategy should be updated as often as necessary. The diagnosis phase in strategic decision making focuses on detecting and *anticipating* the need for such changes. Strategic planning tries to control the emergence fueled by external forces.

Emergent behaviors may also ensue from internal subsystem interdependencies, a fact not recognized in strategic planning. We illustrate this idea with the example of the Corning Glass Works (see Box 8.12). The case describes Corning's introduction of portfolio planning approaches.

As can be seen from the Corning Glass Works case, *internal* subsystem-related factors led to emergent behaviors. Corning's top management makes a number of assumptions that reflect the rational emphasis in strateguc

Box 8.12

The Case of Corning Glass Works

The case of Corning Glass Works illustrates corporate-divisional relationships in a decentralized organization, as it relates to the application of portfolio models. This was accomplished by a structural change, the introduction of a resource allocation committee (RAC). The management structure was designed to make it possible for divisional managers to watch over their own areas of responsibility, yet not become so driven by strict organizational lines that they were unable to share with each other and the chairman the total responsibility for the corporation.

The RAC was responsible for recommending priorities and funding levels for developmental projects. The review process was composed of some of the most senior officers of the company. The company's strategic planner described his role as "keeping the process on a strategic level so we don't get lost in the numbers." Performance measurement and rewards were in place because the president said, "People don't do extraordinary things for money, but it sure improves hearing."

At the end of the allocation process, a meeting was usually held where the divisions' financial plans were discussed with all the divisional heads to gain everybody's commitment to the new goals. The president wanted the division managers to see the resource allocation process from the corporate point of view as well as their own. He thought this should

lead them to internalize the goals and eliminate the we/they view.

In the first such meeting ever held, all projects were listed by priority and opened up for discussion. The president felt that it took too much time. Moreover, having to reject so many projects after they were discussed in the meeting caused a lot of pain. In the second meeting, therefore, one-on-one meetings were held with managers whose projects were cut or rejected. Therefore, when people went into the meeting, they knew what to expect. According to the president, "Things went much more smoothly than last year."

The president then described the case of Lee Wilson, who had asked for 12 engineers of a scarce and expensive variety. Wilson did a good deal of politicking before the meeting. Also, the president got together with Wilson before the meeting and prepared him for the fact that he would only get six engineers. He was therefore not only prepared to lose but also, when he appeared in the large meeting, to act as if this was not the case. The president felt that Lee understood and that he would play the role well. It appears that Lee acted as a good soldier and accepted the news with magnanimity. He acted as if he was not upset but that he understood. Wilson reported privately, however, that the negative decision was earthshaking. He believed that it was important to get 12 full-time engineers to build continuity

planning. First, the president believes that social harmony can be attained by participation of subordinates, but on a strictly *rational* basis, to the exclusion of behavioral forces. Second, top management dictates with respect to resource allocation will be followed by subordinates as good soldiers. Finally, the president of Corning Glass Works upholds the norm that open discussions should not cause pain even when resources are scarce.

Box 8.12 continued

and involvement for his projects. Like his president, Lee realized the importance of commitment.

Wilson, however, found a way to get around the turndown. He decided to go outside to get six engineers on a temporary basis so that they would not be charged on his operating budget. According to the assistant controller, this tactic was understandable but not acceptable. The controller believed that Wilson's original request for 12 engineers was probably part of an opening bid in an administrative game. "They got 6, which is probably less than what they wanted, but they went outside and hired some temporary engineers." The controller then asked, "So how have we allocated resources? How have we limited the dollars spent for development? What has the process really accomplished?" The solution the controller proposed was first a top-level determination of firm limits on capital resources and engineer head counts. The limits should not be subject to horse trading. Second, there should be more frequent allocation meetings for tighter monitoring.

The product and planning manager under Wilson was also disappointed and frustrated. He made several presentations into which he and his colleagues put a lot of time and energy. The response in all the pre meetings was very positive, but not when it came to allocating dollars. He noted, "I think they're saying yes to a lot of projects that add up to more time than they can spend. They cause wasted time and expense."

Chris Argyris, a Harvard professor, although working from a different theoretical perspective, comments:

He [the president] wanted to create a spirit of corporate-divisional community in which we/they views were eliminated. However, Wilson and his planning manager used "they" when talking about corporate. Thus we have a cure that made the illness worse.

The same consequences spread to the allocation process. The controller pointed out that if these games continued, the resource allocation process would be seriously undermined. His solutions are important because they represent a typical and automatic response: Tighten up. He wanted the top to develop firm levels of expenditures that were not negotiable. He also wanted more frequent meetings to monitor and control more effectively what divisions were doing.

If these recommendations were implemented, the divisional managers would feel that their space of movement and their autonomy was eroded. Decentralization as a concept and policy would become less credible, and the feelings of mistrust would increase. Again, we have a cure that is likely to make the illness worse.

This case illustrates some of the problems associated with the adoption of the strategic planning process when the thrust of the process is almost *exclusively* at the functional subsystem.

Source: Adapted from Chris Argyris, *Strategy, Change and Defensive Routines* (Boston, Mass.: Pitman Publishing, 1985).

However, as the case unfolds, we see that these assumptions are not *realized* in this organization. The subordinate, Lee Wilson, covertly refused to accept top-management goals, and the trust level declined, leading to administrative games. Further, the controller believed that Wilson's initial bid was not rational but a political ploy, indicating that some at the corporate level did not trust the subordinate in the first place. Predictably, lack of trust led to lowered motivation at the divisional levels. This case also indicates how perception of scarce resources activates the political subsystem (for example, refer to Wilson's politicking before resource allocation). Culture dictates that painful issues should not be discussed in public, but this detracts from the rational discourse so necessary in strategy formulation. In the presence of such emergent behaviors, the intended allocation never gets realized—an unanticipated consequence. Stated differently, operating *within* the cultural framework, the political and social subsystems modify the strategy formulation and implementation.

The major limitation of the strategic planning approach is the lack of recognition of emergent behaviors due to internal interdependencies in the organization.

Chapter Summary

Perhaps no other management approach focuses on the organization-environment interface as explicitly or as comprehensively as strategic planning. Organizations are seen as open systems in competitive equilibrium in industrial markets. Organizational boundaries are constantly shifting, sometimes by competitors' actions, and sometimes by the decisions of top managers (corporate and business strategy decisions). Change is thus a characteristic of most organizations.

Strategy becomes the mechanism of managing internal and external interdependence. It sets the premises for organization design as well as resource allocation. The notion of levels is invoked to bound the uncertainties at lower levels, as well as to make the formulation process manageable.

In the abstract, strategic planning emphasizes survival in competitive environments as the primary criterion of effectiveness. In concrete terms, however, effectiveness is judged by financial indicators such as sales growth, profitability, or return on shareholders' investment. Different constituencies are addressed by different levels of strategy. The corporate level primarily emphasizes shareholders as the primary constituency. At business levels, customers are a major if not the only constituency; for example, such concepts as competitive advantage underscore the need to satisfy customers, if only to survive in an industry.

Three *unique* aspects of this field also deserve mention. First, the organization-environment interface is managed either by choice of environments or internal adaptation. A third alternative, "creating the future" or "redesigning the environment," has not been characteristic of the field. For example, strategic planning is silent on the notion of alternative futures (developed in environmental analysis). Second, since strategists adhere to the norms of rationality in their prescriptions for managing internal interdependence, they highlight the interdependence *within the functional subsystem* to the neglect of other subsystems. Finally, the field arrived at contingency formulations, having started from a case study approach. Unlike management theory, which originated with the search for universal principles and was disenchanted with that search, the strategy field grew out of the belief that every organization is unique.

Specialized Terms

Effectiveness versus efficiency
Stages of growth of a firm
Types of decisions
• Strategic
• Administrative
• Operating
Diversification
• Related
• Conglomerate
Strategy formulation
Strategy implementation
Levels of strategy
• Corporate
• Business
• Functional
Contingency plan

Portfolio models
Competitive advantage
• Low cost
• Differentiation
• Protected niche
Elements of corporate strategy
Elements of business strategy
Criteria for strategy evaluation
Intended, realized, and emergent strategy
Logical incrementalism
Strategic types
• Analyzer
• Prospector
• Defender
• Reactor

Discussion Questions

Theoretical

1. Recently, an organization theorist commented, "Strategic planning is a new buzzword for classical principles of management." Do you agree? State your reasons.

2. Why are budgeting and long-range planning phases not considered to be truly strategic? Clue: refer to assumptions.

3. Outline Chandlers' model of stages of growth of American enterprise. How is conglomerate diversification different from Chandler's third stage?

4. Which are the routes to competitive advantage? Give examples.

5. What are the elements of corporate level strategy? Business strategy?

6. Which causes of emergent strategy are recognized in strategic planning?

7. Distinguish between logical incrementalism and synoptic planning.

8. Identify the system theoretic assumptions in strategic planning. What assumptions does strategic planning make about various subsystems?

★9. Are there any similarities between Emery and Trist's environmental types and the four types of planning systems that the consultants from McKinsey & Co. discovered?

★10. Strategic management phase is considered by McKinsey consultants as an improvement on strategic planning. Draw the major distinctions between the two phases. Comment on McKinsey conclusions from the perspective of the systems model.

★11. Distinguish between strategic, administrative, and operating decisions. In a conglomerate organization, which of the three types of decisions—corporate, business, and functional levels of strategy—will be strategic, administrative, and operating?

★12. How does cultural orientation influence strategy formulation?

Applied

1. Outline an approach to strategic planning for your university. Your business school. Your own firm.

★2. How does strategic planning in a profit-making organization differ from that in a nonprofit organization (e.g., a hospital)?

★3. An economist recently noted, "The so-called approaches to strategic planning either at the corporate or business level should be declared illegal since they resurrect illegal practices such as interfirm collusion and dumping in a more subtle fashion." Comment.

End Notes

1. Adapted from Brenton R. Schlender, "Yet Another Strategy for Apple," *Fortune*, October 22, 1990, pp. 81–82.

2. Sun Tzu, *The Art of War*, ed. James Clavell (New York: Delacorte Press, 1983).

3. B. H. Liddell Hart, *Strategy* (New York: Praeger Publishers, 1954), pp. 164, 347–65.

4. Bruce Henderson, "The Concept of Strategy," in *The Strategic Management Handbook*, (New York: McGraw-Hill, 1983), ed. Kenneth Albert pp. 1-3 to 1-25.

5. Peter Drucker was among the first to address the strategy issue, but he did so only implicitly. To him, an organization's stategy was the answer to the dual questions: "What is our business?" and "What should it be?" See

---

★This is an advanced-level question.

Drucker, *The Practice of Management* (New York: Harper & Row, 1954). See also Charles W. Hofer and Dan Schendel, *Strategy Formulation: Analytical Concepts* (St. Paul, Minn.: West Publishing, 1978).

6. Frederick W. Gluck, Stephen P. Kaufman, and Steven Wallack, "The Evolution of Strategic Management," *McKinsey Staff Paper*, October 1978.

7. Alfred P. Sloan, Jr., *My Years with General Motors* (Garden City, N.Y.: Doubleday Publishing, 1964).

8. Alfred Chandler, *Strategy and Structure: Chapters in the History of American Industrial Enterprise* (Cambridge, Mass.: MIT Press, 1962).

9. Ibid.

10. For a detailed discussion of this perspective see (1) Kenneth Andrews, Edmund Learned, C. Roland Christensen, and William Guth, *Business Policy: Texts and Cases* (Homewood, Ill.: Richard D. Irwin, 1965); (2) Kenneth Andrews, *The Concept of Corporate Strategy* (Homewood, Ill. Richard D. Irwin, 1971).

11. Igor H. Ansoff, *Corporate Strategy: An Analytic Approach to Business Policy for Growth and Expansion* (New York: McGraw-Hill, 1965).

12. See, for example, Oskar Morgenstern and John von Neumann, *Theory of Games and Economic Behavior* (Princeton: Princeton University Press, 1953).

13. For example, see Jay W. Forrester, *Industrial Dynamics* (Cambridge, Mass.: MIT Press, 1961).

14. Alfred Chandler, *Strategy and Structure*.

15. Leonard Wrigley, "Divisional Autonomy and Diversification," unpublished Ph.D. dissertation, Harvard Business School, 1970. See also Richard Rumelt, *Strategy, Structure and Economic Performance* (Cambridge, Mass.: Harvard University Press, 1974).

16. This observation is based not only on available data but on the interesting work in the area by Milton Leontiades, *Strategies for Diversification and Change* (Boston: Little, Brown, 1980).

17. See, for example, Sidney Schoeffler, Robert Buzzell, and Donald Heany, "The Impact of Strategic Planning on Profit Performance, "*Harvard Business Review* 52, no. 2 (March/April 1974).

18. This observation was brought to us by Bruce Herald then of Dart & Kraft during an executive roundtable session held at the University of Kansas, 1984. Porter's work on industry structure was summarized in the previous chapter. See Michael Porter, *Competitive Strategy* (New York: Free Press, 1980).

19. Ray E. Miles and Charles C. Snow, *Organizational Strategy, Structure and Process* (New York: McGraw-Hill, 1978).

20. Edward H. Wrapp, "Good Managers Don't Make Policy Decisions," *Harvard Business Review* 45, no. 5, (1967).

21. James Brian Quinn, *Strategies for Change: Logical Incrementalism* (Homewood, Ill.: Richard D. Irwin, 1980).

22. Ibid.

23. Leslie W. Rue and Robert M. Fulmer, "Is Long Range Planning Profitable?" *Academy of Management Proceedings* (Boston, August 1973).

24. John Pearce II, Elizabeth B. Freeman, and Richard R. Robinson, "The Tenuous Link between Formal Strategic Planning and Financial Performance," *Academy of Management Review* 12, no. 4, pp. 658-75.

25. Authors often differ in terms of the specificity and elaborateness with which they describe the model. Mintzberg, along with his colleagues Raisinghani

and Theoret has described very detailed models whereas Kenneth Andrews has given us simple models. The model presented here leans toward the simple and is drawn from Liam Fahey and V. K. Narayanan, "Politics of Strategic Decision Making," in *The Strategic Management Handbook,* ed. Kenneth J. Albert (New York: McGraw-Hill, 1983).

26. John Camillus and John Grant, at the Katz Graduate School of Business, underscored this when they note that strategic planning cycles usually have a time horizon of 3–15 years whereas operational planning cycles occur with 1–3 year frequency. As we move from corporate and functional levels the activities tend to be increasingly operational.

27. See Gerald B. Allan and John S. Hammond, "A Note on the Boston Consulting Group Concept of Competitive Analysis and Corporate Strategy," no. 9-175-175 (Boston: Intercollegiate Case Clearing House, 1975). See also Derek F. Abell and John S. Hammond, *Strategic Market Planning* (Englewood Cliffs, N.J.: Prentice Hall, 1979).

28. Marcus Seiff as quoted in George Day, *Analysis of Strategic Marketing Decisions* (St. Paul, Minn.: West Publishing, 1986).

29. Michael Porter, *Competitive Strategy.*

30. See (1) Henry Mintzberg, "Of Strategies, Deliberate and Emergent," *Strategic Management Journal,* 1985, pp. 257–72; (2) Henry Mintzberg and James A. Waters, "Tracking Strategy in an Entrepreneurial Firm," *Academy of Management Journal,* 1982, pp. 465–99.

9 ORGANIZATION DESIGN

Chapter Outline

Texas Instruments is reaping the payoff for changes it launched in the mid-80s and carried out methodologically. The goals it set for itself were torn from unremarkable pages in the management playbook: pare staff, pursue total quality management and get close to the customer, and focus on customized products rather than commodities. But CEO Jerry Jenkins runs an outfit whose strong suit is execution. Says the 33-year Texas Instruments veteran, "We never had a problem in this company doing something once we decided we were going to go do it." People's attention also was focused on change, he allows, because, "we were getting our heads kicked in."

The troubles at Texas Instruments centered on nothing less than its main business—semiconductors. Market share had fallen precipitously as Texas Instruments plunged from a race for first place with Motorola to number five. The division's ills were basic: The company that invented the integrated circuit had failed to keep up to date. Five years ago, only 7 percent of TI's chip business was in CMOS (complementary metal oxide semiconductor) technology, which accounted for 20 percent of the market and was clearly the business of the future.

Switching technologies required heavy spending—$1.8 billion over the past three years—when outlays peaked, accounting for 75 percent of Texas Instruments' total capital budget. To cut the cost of those billions, Texas Instruments took advantage of Asia's lower interest rates and hotter stock markets. It has set up joint ventures with partners as diverse as Kobe Steel in Japan and PC manufacturer Acer in Taiwan; they provide money and Texas Instruments contributes technology. Texas Instruments typically takes about a 25 percent stake.

Once decried for its arrogance as a supplier, Texas Instruments took especially the challenge of focusing on the customer. In the 35-member group that makes custom semiconductors for the auto market, engineers who designed a chip used to oversee its progress into a product almost as an afterthought. Three years ago General Motors' Delco Remy division, a customer, approached Texas Instruments to suggest a better way. The result: Today the group puts a single product engineer in charge of each new product from beginning to end.[1]

Even a firm such as HP, which is regarded as an excellent company, sometimes runs into problems of implementation. Some of these problems are attributable to improper or unwieldy organization structure. When that happens, organizations redesign their organization structure.

How should we arrive at an organization chart? How should we group people into departments or divisions? When should we appoint a committee? When should we abolish one? How many levels should there be in an organization? In general, how should an organization be structured? The answers to these questions form the subject matter of organization design.

Organization design has perhaps had the longest history in organization theory. Scholars drawn from sociology, economics, strategic management, and various other disciplines have contributed to our understanding of organization design. Almost all the work that led up to the contingency perspective that we reviewed in Chapter 4 focused on organization design.

What Is Organization Design?

Organization design is primarily concerned with determining an organization's structure. Typically, structure is reflected in the organization chart. Formally, we can identify four major components of the organization's structure:

1. It describes the *allocation of tasks and responsibilities* to individuals and departments throughout the organization.
2. It designates formal *reporting relationships,* including the number of levels in the hierarchy and the span of control of managers and supervisors.
3. It identifies the *grouping together of individuals* into departments and the grouping of departments into the total organization.
4. It includes the *mechanisms of coordination* and integration of effort.

Viewed from an organization design perspective, an organization is a pyramid of superior-subordinate relations. This pyramid is referred to as a *hierarchy.* The higher up in the hierarchy individuals or departments are, the higher their authority. Organizations may be tall or flat depending on the number of levels in the hierarchy: the more levels, the taller the organization. The organization structure determines the span of control of a manager. *Span of control* is the number of immediate subordinates that a supervisor or manager manages. In a flat organization the span of control is wide, whereas in a tall organization, it is narrow. See Box 9.1 for an example of an organization chart.

Organization design, then, refers to the process of arriving at the appropriate organizational form, bases of departmentation, and coordination. This process is based on three key ideas:

1. Organization design is a critical factor in the *long-term* success of an organization. The long term is emphasized because the influence of design is best felt over a number of years rather than in the short run.
2. Organization design is a *continuing* process. As the environment or the strategy of the organization changes, new organization designs will have to be phased in. There is a need to continually assess the suitability of the organization design.
3. Flowing from (1) and (2), there are no designs universally applicable to all organizations for all times. The appropriateness of a particular design depends on the context of the organization. As the context changes, newer designs will have to be invented.

Because of its impact on the long-term performance of the organization, organization design is considered to be a major function of any management.

Box 9.1

Organization Chart for a Printing Company

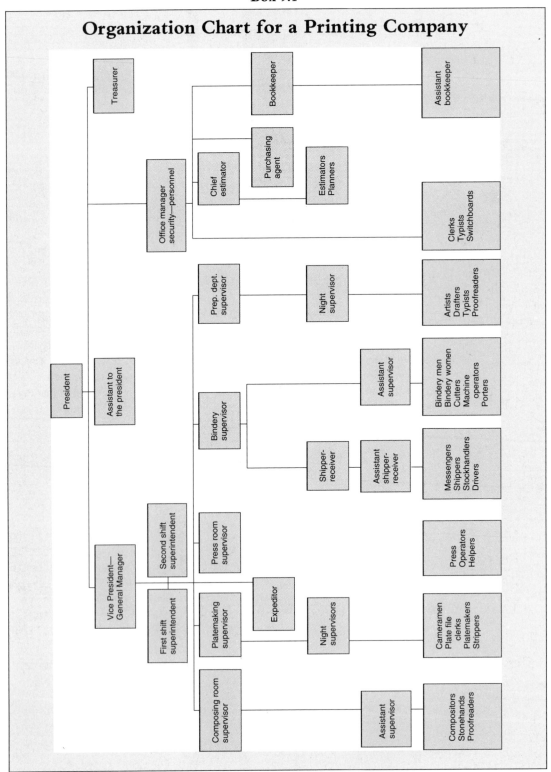

Box 9.1 continued

The organization chart may be used to describe several of the organization's structural characteristics:

1. It describes the organization as a network of superior-subordinate relations. For example, the cameramen report to the night supervisor, the purchasing agent reports to the office manager, and so on.
2. It displays the hierarchy of the organization. The printing company is organized vertically into six levels.
3. It displays the span of control of each manager. The president's span is four; the general manager's is eight; the night supervisor's is still larger, as this manager supervises many cameramen, plate file clerks, plate makers, and strippers.

4. It displays the organizational bases of specialization. From the vantage point of the president, the subunits are based on functions: manufacturing, finance (treasurer), and purchasing and cost control. From the vantage point of the general manager, they are based on time (shift supervisors) and activities (represented by the lowest level of the hierarchy).

We may also note that at the lowest level, the organization structure is likely to be controlled by the technology, whereas from the vantage point of the president, the structure will be dictated by environmental and strategic considerations.

Although many organization design decisions are usually made at the very top levels of the organization, these decisions are also made at the level of divisional managers and in some cases, departmental managers.

Linkage to the Systems Model

As seen from the above definition, organization design deals with some of the internal characteristics of an organization. As shown in Figure 9.1, it

FIGURE 9.1

Focus of organization design

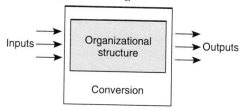

FIGURE 9.2

Logic of organization design

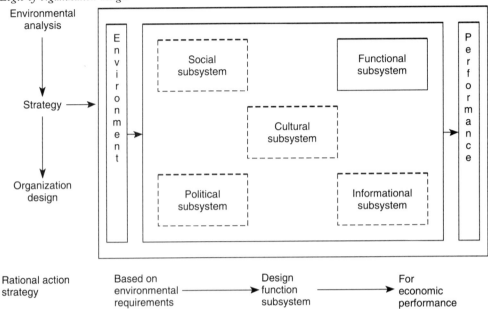

focuses on the conversion process of an organization, and does not attempt to prescribe the outputs or inputs of an organization. As we saw in the previous chapter, design of inputs and outputs is primarily done by strategic planning processes. Organization design only attempts to create an internal organizational system most suited for the optimal delivery of the outputs. Thus, in any rational model of managing, organization design follows environmental analysis and strategic planning.

However, organization design does not address all the internal characteristics of an organization. Given its focus on tasks, it deals primarily with the *functional* subsystem of an organization. As shown in Figure 9.2, thefunctional subsystem is seen as an instrument of the organization's adaptation to the environment. Although modern organization design theorists acknowledge the role of social and political factors, their primary focus is on the formal aspects of an organization.

Contemporary organization design theorists argue that the functional subsystem of an organization should be matched to its strategy and environment. In this sense, they subscribe to the major tenet of the systems theory that organizations are open systems. As we will see later, they have also noted how design takes place at many levels: the corporate level in diversified organizations, the divisional level in diversified and single-business corporations, and even the design of project teams. The interdependence among divisions and departments within an organization is man-

TABLE 9.1   Linkage to systems Concepts

Concept	Operationalization
1. Open systems	Design functional subsystem to match a strategy and environment
2. Levels	Organization design takes place at many levels
3. Interdependence	Manage functional subsystem through departmentation and coordination
4. Equifinality and Multifinality	Alternative organization designs may implement strategy
5. Structure and process	Structure drives long-run performance
6. Dynamic equilibrium	Design is a continual process

aged by installing appropriate coordination mechanisms. Contemporary organization theorists have moved away from universal principles of organization and have adopted a contingency perspective. Finally, they stress the need to redesign an organization as its environment and strategy change over time; design is thus viewed as a continual process.

Table 9.1 summarizes how key systems concepts are operationalized in organization design.

In this chapter, we discuss the field of organization design. The scheme of this chapter is as follows: First, we will summarize the historical, philosophical, and theoretical underpinnings of the field. Second, we will describescribe the key concepts necessary for understanding the design issues. Third, we will discuss the key frameworks for organization design. Finally, we will review the chapter, highlighting the key points.

Underpinnings

Historical Underpinnings

Prior to the 20th century, the church, government, and military had provided us with models of organization structure, specifying the overall form of the organization. These models were conceptualized as bureaucracy by Max Weber. According to him, bureaucracy is a framework of administrative characteristics that would make large organizations rational and efficient.[2]

Weber was interested in answering the following question: What form of organization would serve the increasingly industrialized society he observed in Europe at the turn of the century? In the early days of the Industrial Revolution, personal subjugation, nepotism, cruelty, and subjective judgment passed for managerial practices. The Weberian model was developed partly to deal with these problems. According to Weber, the capitalist market economy demanded that the official business of administration be discharged precisely, unambiguously, continuously, and with as much speed as possible. Weber proposed a set of bureaucratic characteristics that would ensure efficient organizational functioning in both government and business settings. Bureaucracies, as Weber envisioned them, would facilitate the allocation of scarce resources in an increasingly complex society. Weber maintained that a bureaucratic organization is technically superior to any other form of organization. Weber commented:

> The fully developed bureaucratic mechanism compares with other organizations exactly as does the machine with the non-mechanical modes of production . . . precision, speed, unambiguity, continuity, discretion, unity . . . these are raised to the optimum point in a strictly bureaucratic administration.[3]

As we saw in Chapter 4, bureaucracy is characterized by a high degree of formalization, standardization, and specialization. The primary coordination mechanisms that Weber identified were rules and hierarchy. However, Weber had little to say about such issues as appropriate span of control, number of levels in the hierarchy, or the bases of departmentation.

To a large extent, modern day organizations display many of the characteristics of bureaucracies, so that these may sound obvious. In the context of the time, however, the idea made good sense. The codified rules, predictable relationships, and specified job descriptions permitted organizations during the early phase of the Industrial Revolution to make faster decisions than before. Bureaucracy was an ideal weapon to harness and routinize the human energy that fueled the Industrial Revolution.

Institutional innovations over the past decades have provided us with a number of different models for organization design. Most of these innovations have come from business enterprises as they grappled with the appropriate bases of departmentation and coordination.

At the turn of this century, the critical problem of organization was to harness the potential of mass production made available by the Industrial Revolution. Mass production demanded high volume and stability in raw materials, labor, and production techniques for its very existence. Mass production technologies were associated with significant economies of scale; thus, larger organizations enjoyed significant cost advantages over smaller ones.

In order to reap the benefits of mass production, the *functional* form of organization was adopted. In this form of organization, the basis of departmentation is function—marketing, production, research and development, and so on. The organization emphasized efficiency, and the organizational form focused on exploiting the advantages of specialization. Employees developed in-depth skills through focusing on specific functions; this enabled speedy production and lower costs.

Viewed from the perspective of top management, therefore, the departments focused on functional goals: the marketing department focused on selling, the production departments on production goals, and so forth. Within these departments, further division of tasks may take place, again based on function. Thus, the production department may be further divided up into maintenance, manufacturing, and quality control.

Functional Organization

The functional organization is highly *centralized*. The primary coordination mechanism is hierarchy of levels, and the functional heads are inherently dependent upon a central head for coordinating their work. The top level is primarily responsible for strategic direction and coordination of operations; middle management is responsible for the operating organization, and lower levels carry out such activities as selling and welding. The organization is keyed to reaping the benefits of *specialization* and *standardization* for efficiency. See Box 9.2 for an illustration of a functional organization.

The functional organization served well for companies that operated in a single industry or dealt with only a few products and functioned in a relatively stable environment. As long as the environment remained stable, and tasks could be standardized, the organization could be controlled by this form of organization. Further, departmentation by function enabled the organization to reap the benefits of economies of scale. For example, even when there were only a few product lines, constructing one manufacturing facility instead of separate facilities for different product lines reduces duplication and waste. This, in turn, reduced the cost of operations.

However, a functional organization was associated with a number of disadvantages. Given the functional focus, the responsibility for overall coordination is vested at the top. As the environment becomes unstable, or as product lines proliferate, the top of the hierarchy becomes overloaded with decisions and pressures for coordination. Since the lower levels have a restricted view of the goals, there is little opportunity provided to managers to develop an overall view of the organization. As a result, the organization is slow to respond to market changes.

Divisional Organization

As organizations began to extend their product lines, the functional organization created problems of coordination for top management. The *divisional* form of organization was an institutional innovation of the 1930s, by such organizations as General Motors and Du Pont. Viewed from the top, in the divisional organization, the primary base of departmentation was the customer group, or the product line catering to the customer group. Top management oversaw divisional managers; divisional managers were responsible for the overall performance of their respective divisions. The structure of each division often resembled a functional organization, and consisted of such departments as production, marketing, accounting, finance, and personnel. For each product line, all the necessary functions are grouped within the division, and the divisional manager had the authority and responsibility for all these functions.

In a divisional form, top management is relieved of some of the coordination functions by *decentralizing* such functions to divisional managers. Coordination of functions within each product line is delegated to divisional managers. Top levels are responsible for the strategic function of the organization and coordination among divisions; the division managerial level is

Box 9.2

Functional Organization

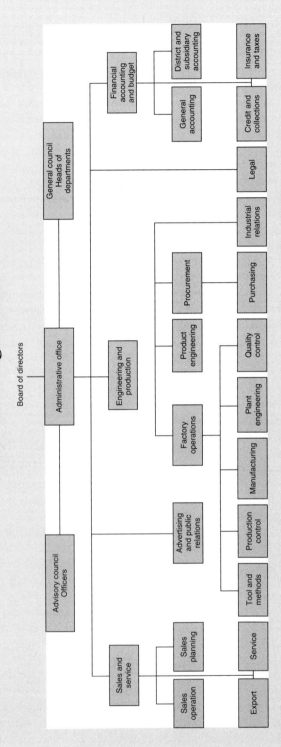

As can be seen from the organization chart, the Administrative Office, (the office of the CEO) oversees and coordinates three main departments: Sales and Service, Engineering and Production, and Financial Accounting and Budget. These departments look after specific functions, whereas the CEO is responsible for product lines. This form of departmentation is called a *functional organization*.

Source: From Joseph A. Litterer, *Organizations: Structure and Behavior.* Copyright © 1963 by John Wiley & Sons, Inc. Reprinted by permission of John Wiley & Sons. Inc.

often entrusted with product line strategic responsibility and functional coordination within the divisions. Hence, standardization across product lines is *not* needed. The organization may lose some of the benefits of specialization of the functional organization, as the various divisions may duplicate some of these functions.

Each division is a more or less self-contained unit, incorporating most of the functions necessary for its respective product line. Employees tend to identify with their product line rather than their functions. Budgeting and planning are on a profit basis because each product line can be run as a separate business. Managers who head the product divisions have considerable influence.

In one sense, a divisional structure is an innovation created to handle product, and therefore, market diversity. Since each division is more or less self-contained, and divisional managers are free to pursue their own product line strategies, the organization offers greater flexibility and responsiveness to distinctive markets. The divisional structure works best in large organizations that have multiple product lines or services and enough personnel to staff separate functional units. What the divisional structure gains in market responsiveness, it loses in efficiency. Thus, the organization may lose the advantages of economies of scale. For example, instead of 50 research engineers sharing a common facility in a functional structure, the research engineers may be distributed among a number of divisions, thus dissipating the research talent. Box 9.3 gives an illustration of a divisional organization.

Matrix Organization

In the last three decades, many organizations have had to grapple with the dual pressures of market responsiveness *and* operating efficiency. We noted earlier that a functional organization optimizes efficiency, whereas the divisional structure is more responsive to markets. In an effort to reap the advantages of both forms of organization, many business enterprises adopted another institutional innovation called the *matrix* form of organization. The unique feature of the matrix organization is that both product and functional structures are implemented simultaneously in the organization. See Box 9.4 for an example of the matrix.

The matrix organization is usually implemented at the top of the organization. Unlike in other organization forms, in a matrix form, some employees have two bosses, which violates classical principles of management. There are two command structures: one follows the functional structure and the other the divisional structure. Top management is the head of the two structures and retains the coordinative responsibility of maintaining the power balance between the two structures. If either command structure dominates, the matrix will evolve into a functional or divisional structure, and the benefits of the matrix will be lost.

Matrix bosses, in charge of the functional or divisional structure, do not have complete control of their subordinates. They must work with each

Box 9.3

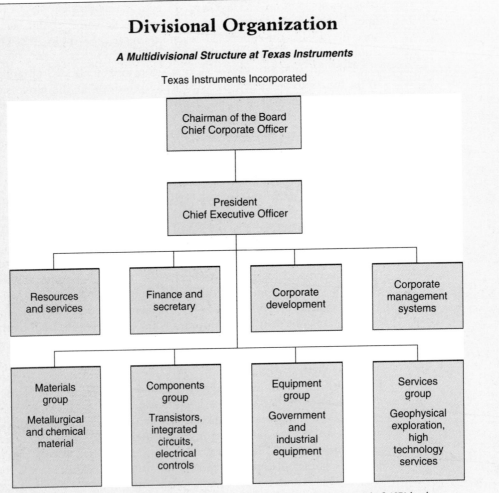

Divisional Organization

A Multidivisional Structure at Texas Instruments

Texas Instruments Incorporated

Chairman of the Board
Chief Corporate Officer

President
Chief Executive Officer

Resources and services

Finance and secretary

Corporate development

Corporate management systems

Materials group

Metallurgical and chemical material

Components group

Transistors, integrated circuits, electrical controls

Equipment group

Government and industrial equipment

Services group

Geophysical exploration, high technology services

Source: This figure appears in the case Innovation at Texas Instruments. 9-672-036. Copyright © 1971 by the President and Fellows of Harvard College. Reproduced by permission.

Unlike the Dictaphone Corporation, the president of Texas Instruments oversees four divisions: materials group, components group, equipment group, and services group. Each division has district markets and products. The corporate level is responsible for the portfolio of business, whereas the divisions are responsible for their individual businesses.

<hr />

Box 9.4

Matrix Organization

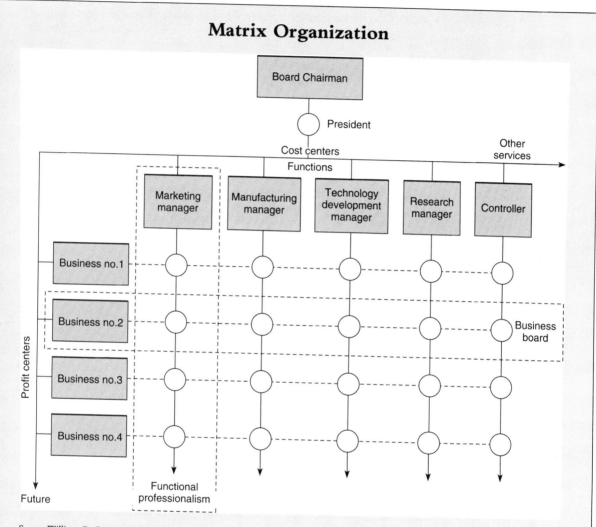

Here, there are two simultaneous hierarchies. Thus, in one hierarchy, the individual reports to a functional manager, (e.g., marketing manager); in the other hierarchy, the same individual reports to a profit center manager (e.g., Bus. No. 2). The individual has two bosses; this is true in all matrix organizations.

other to delineate activities over which they are responsible. They must also collaborate on such matters as performance reviews, promotions, and salary increases, since subordinates report to both of them. These activities require a great deal of time, communication, patience, and skill at working with people.

Managers in the matrix have two bosses—the functional and the divisional. Both the bosses may place legitimate demands on their managers that may be contradictory to each other. Thus, these managers may often experience a great deal of conflict. They face dual pressures—from their function and from their product lines.

The matrix organization no longer resembles a pyramid because there are two bases of departmentation operating simultaneously. The conflicting demands of dual authority structure are resolved at the matrix boss levels so that top managers are not overloaded with decisions. This requires a lot of meetings and effort at communication. The conflict built into the matrix forces discussion and coordination to resolve issues that pertain to both function and product lines.

Thus, over the years, organizations have employed three basic models of organizational design—functional, divisional, and matrix. There are many variations of these three models of organization design reflecting refinements tailored to the unique needs of specific organizations.

Philosophical Underpinnings

Three critical assumptions underlie approaches to organization design.

The first critical assumption is that organization structure—how individuals and work units are grouped together—makes a difference in organizational performance. Thus, it is worth managers' while to expend some effort arriving at appropriate organization design. This assumption may appear obvious to many; however, in the beginning of the century, prevailing economic wisdom failed to address the issues of the internal organization of a firm. Although Adam Smith talked about division of labor in the society as a whole, its implications for organizations was not addressed in traditional economics. It was left to the classical management school to highlight the influence of *the internal organization* of a firm on its economic performance.

The second critical assumption is that organization design influences individual behavior in organizations, and hence, is a *mechanism for control* in the hands of managers. Consider:

> It is possible to identify three distinct ways in which the structure of an organization affects the behavior of individuals and groups.
>
> First and perhaps most obvious, the organization's structure can affect the expectancies that individuals have, and thus influence behavior through a *motivational* effect. . . .
>
> Second, the organization structure may make it difficult to translate intentions or effort into actual performance. Although the individual may want to

perform in a certain way, that person may not have the necessary information, access to appropriate individuals, or authority to do so. In such cases the organization serves to *constrain* behavior. . . .

Third, the organization structure can aid people in translating intentions and effort into action. In such cases the organization serves to *facilitate* the behavior that has been motivated.[4]

The third critical assumption is that organization design is inherently concerned with issues of *efficiency*; that is, structuring of task activities to reduce the costs of transforming the inputs into outputs. Thus, if you utilize the appropriate basis of division of labor and mechanisms of coordination, you can build an efficient organization. This emphasis on efficiency has predictable consequences. The focus of organization design is on the functional subsystem; the social, political, and informational subsystems are viewed here as derivatives of the functional subsystem.

In the field of organization design, these assumptions are treated not as normative or value laden statements, but as empirical descriptions of the world. Thus, considerable theoretical work over the last decade has investigated the validity of these assumptions.

Theoretical Underpinnings

As we have seen in Chapter 4, (Contingency Perspective on Organizations), based on the empirically established relationships between organization structure and contextual variables such as size, technology, and environment, sociologists refuted the belief that there are universal principles of management. However, given their sociological origins, their relevance for organization design was not immediately apparent. As economists and management scholars began to pay attention to the internal structure of organizations, a greater understanding of organization design principles emerged.

Over time, several questions were answered in the literature. What prompts an organization to redesign its structure? What is the relationship between an organization's strategy and its structure? Does the organization design make an economic difference? What is the linkage between organization design and environment? What are some of the principles of organization design? We will take up each of these questions in turn.

Process of Organization Design

Alfred Chandler provided the first set of answers to questions concerning what prompts an organization to redesign its structure. We have already summarized Chandler's contributions to our understanding of strategy formulation in our chapter on strategic planning. In this and the next section, we will focus only on his contribution to the organization design field.

Chandler's essential thesis can be succinctly stated:

> *Structure follows strategy* and the most complex type of structure is the result of concatenation of several basic strategies.[5]

Chandler noted that in the face of changing technologies, demographics, and markets, organizations reformulated their strategies to deploy their resources more profitably. In the absence of changes in the administrative structure, the new strategy meets with administrative problems during implementation. Economic inefficiency results; organizational performance (profits, etc.) suffers. The organization then refashions its administrative structure to *fit* the new strategy. This enables the firm to recover its levels of profitability. This cycle of events portrayed by Chandler is schematically presented in Figure 9.3.

Chandler based his conclusions on his study of U.S. firms. His followers replicated his analysis in the United Kingdom, France, and Japan. If structure follows strategy in the United States, why not in Europe and Japan also? These followers qualified Chandler's thesis: Strategic change alone is not sufficient to bring about changes in structure; it must be *matched by competitive pressures.* That is why the United Kingdom has gone further in implementing the divisional structure than its continental neighbors. The decline of tariff barriers in the Common Market is now causing competition on the continent. In Japan, also, diversified firms did not adopt the divisional form quickly due to similar competitive reasons.

Thus, as organizations reshape their strategies, competitive pressures push them to undertake structural changes.

Relationship between Strategy and Structure

As described in the previous chapter, Chandler noted a *stage-wise* development of strategies. In addition, he also posited the structures that went with

Figure 9.3

Chandler's model of studies change

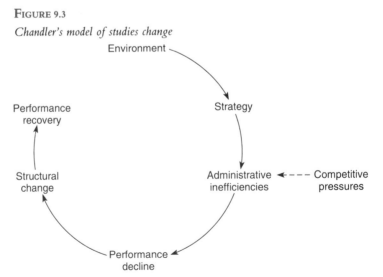

Source: Adapted from Alfred D. Chandler, *Strategy and Structure.* (Cambridge, Mass.: MIT Press, 1962).

each stage of strategy development. For Chandler, the starting point of a firm was an entrepreneur; he suggested four stages of growth:

1. *Volume expansion.* Initial growth was simply by volume expansion. This created the need for an *administrative office* that assisted the entrepreneur in some of the administrative duties.

2. *Geographic expansion.* This second stage took place as firms decided to expand geographically to other locations. This led them to create *multiple field units* in the same function and industry but in different locations. Administrative problems of interunit coordination, specialization, and standardization arose, and the *functional departmental office* was created to handle these problems. Bureaucratic characteristics were thus embedded in the organization structure.

3. *Vertical integration.* The next step in the development of strategies took place when firms began to integrate vertically by acquiring or creating other functions. Manufacturing plants created their own warehouses and wholesaling operations and their own sales forces. The ensuing interdependence among the functions led to the *functional* form of organization. Forecasting, scheduling, and capacity planning techniques came to be employed as administrative mechanisms of coordination.

4. *Diversification.* Firms began to pursue a strategy of diversification by moving into new industries to employ existing resources as their primary markets declined. Diversification led to new problems in administration: appraisal and evaluation of product markets and alternative investment proposals. The functional form was inadequate to handle the problems of managing the capital resource allocation in the face of product market diversity created by diversification. This led to the *multidivisional* structure.[6]

This correspondence is schematically presented in Figure 9.4. Chandler thus proposed that *fit* with strategy is the test of a good structure.

In the ensuing years, two major extensions of Chandler's ideas have taken place: the conglomerate form and the multinational expansion.

Conglomerate Organization

Chandler's work emphasizing the relation between strategy and structure was completed in the beginning of the 1960s. The divisional structure he observed was the outgrowth of a growth strategy of diversification into related products. As we saw in the previous chapter, the 1960s witnessed the trend toward conglomerate diversification.

Scholars picking up the logic of strategy-structure fit extended Chandler's work and identified the *holding company model* as the appropriate structure for managing conglomerate diversification.[7] These scholars argued that

FIGURE 9.4

Chandler's stages of growth in organizational structure

Stage of growth	Organizational structure
Entrepreneur	
↓	
Volume expansion	Administrative office
↓	↓
Geographic expansion	Multiple field centers
	↓
↓	Functional department office
	↓
Vertical integration	Functional form of organization
↓	↓
Diversification	Multidivisional structure

Source: Adapted from Alfred D. Chandler, *Strategy and Structure* (Cambridge, Mass.: MIT Press, 1962).

structures for related and conglomerate forms differed primarily in the degree of *decentralization:* Conglomerate diversification required a greater degree of decentralization than related diversification, as the former managed a greater degree of diversity. In Chandler's multidivisional form, the corporate office actively coordinated divisional activity through strategic direction and corporate policies. In contrast, in the conglomerate organization based on the holding company model, all functions were placed in the division and corporate interests were coordinated through appropriate reward systems.

Thus, the holding company form resembled the divisional form in many respects, but differed primarily in the degree of decentralization. The corporate office exercised relatively little strategic direction. This resulted in a reduction in the size of the corporate staff. Central corporate functions such as engineering, research and development, or marketing are unnecessary: As the divisions are unrelated, it would be difficult to establish functions such as these on a basis meaningful to the whole firm.

Multinational Expansion

Multinational expansion, a second growth strategy not analyzed by Chandler, also came under the scrutiny of scholars interested in issues of strategy-structure fit.[8] Their works suggest that movement into international markets brings with it its own structural imperatives. Although international expansion is at one level similar to geographic expansion, given the differences in cultural, legal, and sometimes economic environments of different countries, it brings in its wake far greater diversity than domestic geographic expansion.

Figure 9.5

Evolution of multinational organizations

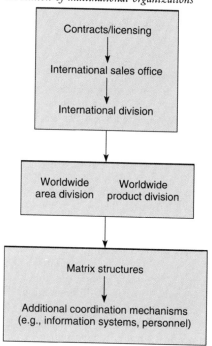

The evolution of the multinational structure takes place in stages. In the first stage, the firms typically form an *international* division. Later, as international penetration proceeds, the division is disbanded and the firm adopts a worldwide product or area structure. Product structure is adopted when there is high product diversity; area divisions come into being when product diversity is low but there are significant area differences. This second stage is called *global* structure and often comes about over an extended period of time.

Finally, firms confronted with the pressures of both product and geographic diversity begin to adopt matrix structures. Over time, changing patterns of global competition, host government demands, and more complex business arrangements such as joint ventures render strategic control of overseas offices by the head office of the multinational corporation (MNC) difficult. Few MNCs have the privilege of adopting simple strategic postures as pure as area or product forms of organization. Confronted with multiple environmental pressures, the MNC head office begins to use matrix structures (with a structure built around both areas and products) and sophisticated information systems to manage the multinational enterprise. See Figure 9.5 for the evolution of the multinational enterprise.

Box 9.5

Lawrence & Lorsch

Paul Lawrence and Jay Lorsch, both at Harvard Business School, investigated the relationship between the structural characteristics of complex organizations and the environmental conditions these organizations face. They framed their question as follows: What kind of organization does it take to deal with various economic and market conditions?

To find answers to this question, Lawrence and Lorsch made a comparative study of competing organizations. Their work was carried out in two distinct but related phases. The first was a detailed study of a number of firms in one industry. This gave them an opportunity to sharpen their questions and find some answers about how the internal organizational states of differentiation and integration were related to each other and to effective performance in meeting the demands of a single industrial environment. The second phase was a study of a highly effective organization and a less effective competitor in each of two other industries.

Lawrence and Lorsch studied organizations in three industries: six in plastics, two in containers, and two in food industries. In the plastics industry the dominant competitive issue was the development of new and revised products and processes. In the container business, industry conditions were more certain in all parts of the environment, while in the food industry, the scientific and market parts of the environment were less certain, but product innovations were quite certain.

To gather this information on internal organizational functioning, Lawrence and Lorsch used both questionnaires and interviews that were given to 30-50 upper- and middle-level managers in each organization. Data on industrial environments in which the companies operated were also gathered by means of both interviews and questionnaires, but the information was selected from only the top executive in each organization.

What did Lawrence and Lorsch conclude? First, the high performing plastics organization, which functioned in the most dynamic and diverse of the three environments, was the most highly differentiated of the three high-performing organizations. In contrast, the container organization, which was in a relatively stable and homogenous environment had little differentiation. The food organization was in many ways like the plastics, the major difference being that the plastics organization appeared to be devoting more of its managerial manpower to devices that facilitated the restriction of conflict.

Lawrence and Lorsch noted, however:

Each of these organizations had developed characteristics that were in tune with the demand of its *present* environment. Whether these same characteristics will provide long run viability depends, of course, on whether the environmental demands change in the future. Given their widely observed tendency toward greater scientific, technological and market change, the plastics and food organizations would seem to be in a more favorable position to maintain their high performance.

Source: Adapted from Paul Lawrence and Jay Lorsch, *Organization and Environment* (Boston: Division of Research, Harvard University Press, 1967).

Linkage between Environment, Organization Design, and Economic Performance

Unlike Chandler, the contingency theorists studied organization design at the divisional level. Taking inspiration from the sociologically oriented contingency theorists, Paul Lawrence and Jay Lorsch linked organization design, environment, and economic performance.[9] Their work is summarized in Box 9.5. Lawrence and Lorsch developed their arguments in five steps:

1. Organizations must formulate their structure so that each department or unit is assigned a task commensurate with its strategy and environment.

2. Each department faces a different subenvironment, and hence, internally each department must be organized to be consistent with its own environment. Thus, where environments are stable and certain, the department must be organized along Burns and Stalker's mechanistic type, whereas those in dynamic environments must follow organic types.

3. Departmentation brings in its wake the need for coordination, and the design must integrate those departments around key interdependencies, as determined by the competitive environments. Where new product introduction is the key, marketing and research and development must be coordinated; where delivery and schedule are important, marketing and production must be coordinated.

4. To be effective, the greater the degree of differentiation, the greater the degree of integration required.

5. The most effective firms are those that have differentiated their structures to the extent needed to adapt to various subenvironments and that simultaneously use mechanisms to integrate those differentiated structures to deal with the competitive issues of the overall corporate environment.

These arguments are presented pictorially in Figure 9.6.

Principles of Organization Design

James Thompson, a renowned sociologist, was the first to articulate some critical principles of organization design. Thompson based his principles on his classification scheme for interdependence.[10] For Thompson, interdependence meant the degree to which departments of an organization had to depend on each other for resources and work flow. Low interdependence means that departments can do their work independently of each other and have little need for interaction, consultation, or exchange of materials; high interdependence necessitates closer coordination. Thompson identified three levels of interdependence:

Lawrence and Lorsch model of organization design

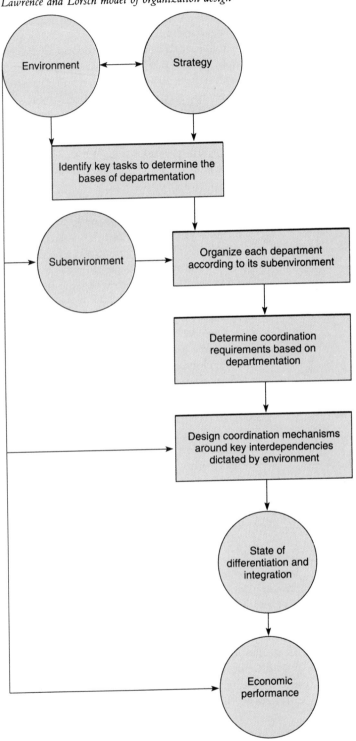

Source: Adapted from Paul Lawrence and Jay Lorsch, *Organization and Environment,*
(Boston: Division of Research, Harvard University Press, 1967).

Pooled interdependence. This is the lowest form of interdependence among departments, wherein the departments work independently of each other. The departments are connected only to the extent that they share financial resources from a common pool, although they contribute to the common good of the organization. Branches of a bank or McDonald's franchises are examples of departments of an organization in pooled interdependence.

Sequential interdependence. This is a higher form of interdependence and exists when the parts produced by one department become inputs to another. Here, the first department must perform correctly on multiple dimensions—quality, quantity, time schedules, etc.—for the second department to perform well. This form of interdependence exists in vertically integrated firms or in assembly lines.

Reciprocal interdependence. This is the highest form of interdependence identified by Thompson. This exists when the outputs of one department form inputs to another *and* when the outputs of the second become inputs of the first. This form of interdependence exists, for example, in hospitals, where a patient may move back and forth between X ray, surgery, and physical therapy as needed to be cured.

Thompson noted that as the interdependence increases, it makes greater demands on managerial coordination, communication, and decision making across departments. In pooled interdependence, managers could employ standardization, rules, and procedures for interdepartmental coordination. In sequential interdependence, coordination of linked departments is necessary. Therefore, in addition to rules, extensive planning and scheduling are required to coordinate the one-way flow of materials. Under reciprocal interdependence, plans alone will not anticipate or solve all problems. Therefore, continuous interaction and mutual adjustment are required and managers will need to be involved in face-to-face communication and decision making (see Table 9.2).

Building on these ideas, Thompson articulated his principles of organization design. The optimal organization design, Thompson argued, should minimize the costs of coordination *across* departments. Accordingly, he suggested that in forming departments, the higher level interdependence should be given priority. The reciprocal interdependence should be contained within a single department. Next, to the extent possible, the departments should contain sequential interdependence. Since the pooled interdependence is the easiest to coordinate, they should be given the lowest priority. Designing departments to contain the reciprocal and sequential interdependence would reduce the need for interdepartmental coordination.

Thompson's principles paralleled the findings of Lawrence and Lorsch. Thus, when a division or single-industry firm departmentalizes according to function—production, marketing, and research and development—this

TABLE 9.2   **Thompson's Categories of Interdependence**

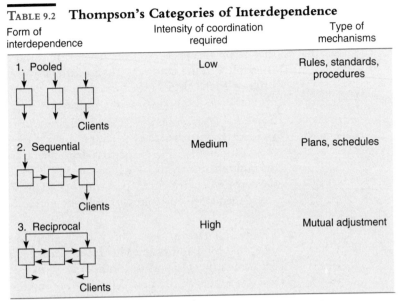

Form of interdependence	Intensity of coordination required	Type of mechanisms
1. Pooled	Low	Rules, standards, procedures
2. Sequential	Medium	Plans, schedules
3. Reciprocal	High	Mutual adjustment

Source: Adapted from James D. Thompson, *Organizations in Action.* (New York: McGraw-Hill, 1967).

creates sequential interdependence: mostly from R&D to production and then to marketing. In stable environments, this can be managed by schedules and planning. As the environment becomes more dynamic, the interdependence among research and development, production, and marketing becomes reciprocal. This requires that additional mechanisms, what Thompson called *mutual adjustment,* must be instituted. All the horizontal coordination mechanisms Lawrence and Lorsch discovered were examples of mutual adjustment.

Finally, as product lines proliferated, costs of coordination would further escalate. Then Thompson would argue that to reduce the costs of coordination among the three departments, the division should be departmentalized according to product lines, when many of the reciprocal and sequential interdependence among the functions is contained within product departments; the product lines are themselves in pooled interdependence. This sequence is presented in Figure 9.7.

Summary

Over the years, many scholars have refined our ideas about organization design. Their work suggests that organization design takes place at many levels; further, they have identified two major contingencies: strategy and environment. Thus, as firms become diversified, they adopt a divisional structure for

FIGURE 9.7

Thomson's logic of organization design

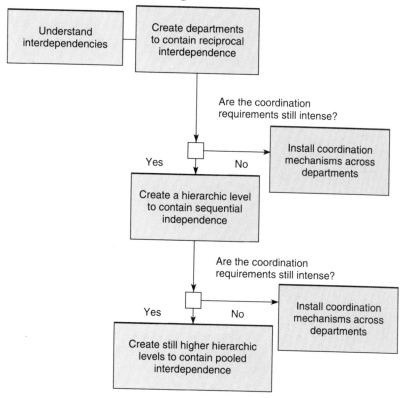

Source: Adapted from James D. Thompson's *Organizations in Action,* (New York: McGraw-Hill, 1967).

related diversification and a holding company model for conglomerate diversification. When they go multinational, they may be based on product or area divisions or, in some cases, employ matrix designs. At the divisional level, a firm may departmentalize according to functional structure; in stable environments, the coordination requirements are lower, whereas in dynamic environments, it may employ a large number of mechanisms.

Key Concepts

To help us understand the major approaches to organization design, we distill five key ideas from organization theory: (1) levels of design, (2) bases of departmentation, (3) bases of coordination, (4) the concept of congruence, and (5) the process of organization design.

Levels of Organization Design

In an organization, the design frequently takes place at different levels. For example, in a diversified corporation, several levels of design occur: at the corporate level, at the divisional level and even at the functional level. In addition, separate organization structures are often created for specific projects (e.g., new product introduction or introducing change); these structures will coexist with other structures.

Similarly, the power to make decisions pertaining to organization design may be vested at different hierarchic levels. For example, corporate headquarters may be involved in designing the overall form of the organization; divisional managers may be empowered to design the internal structure of divisions and so on. However, as we have seen in the case of strategy levels, the higher level organization design decisions constrain lower levels. For example, corporate level actions affect divisional levels. Since this is consistent with systems theory, by now all readers must find this idea familiar.

Bases of Departmentation

In reality, there are many ways in which groupings within an organization can be created:

1. By *knowledge and skill,* as in a hospital that puts surgeons in one department and anesthetists in another.
2. By *work process and function,* as in the grouping of a manufacturing firm into production, marketing, engineering, and so on.
3. By *time,* as in shifts in a factory.
4. By *output,* as in a corporation establishing different divisions for different product lines.
5. By *client,* as in an insurance firm that sets up one marketing department to sell individual policies, another to sell group policies.
6. By *place,* as in the supermarket chain that establishes one division in New York and another in Los Angeles.[11]

Although there are thus many groupings within an organization, they all can be reduced to two fundamental ones:

1. By *function* (including knowledge, skill, work process and function, and time).
2. By *market* (output, client, and place).

In the first, we have groupings by *means,* by the intermediate functions the organization uses for the production of its final outputs. In the second, we have a grouping by *ends*, by the features of the markets served by the organization.

Since organization design takes place at many levels, different bases of departmentation may be employed at different levels.

Bases of Coordination

Broadly, there are three types of coordination mechanisms: (1) bureaucratic mechanisms, (2) vertical coordination mechanisms, and (3) horizontal coordination mechanisms.

Bureaucratic Mechanisms

Almost all organizations employ several bureaucratic mechanisms of coordination. These include *rules, regulations, and standard operating procedures.* In general, bureaucratic mechanisms try to standardize the behavior of employees. Henry Mintzberg has described how bureaucratic mechanisms encourage standardization of behavior; his examples are presented in Box 9.6.

Just how are the rules, regulations, and standard operating procedures crafted? Some organizations at any point in time have inherited them from their own past. In some cases, superiors within departments craft the rules for their employees. In still others, there are separate departments within an organization that create these rules or standard operating procedures. For example, the industrial engineering department in a manufacturing firm often creates standard operating procedures for its workers.

Vertical Coordination Mechanisms

In vertical coordination mechanisms, some form of direct supervision is employed for coordination of activities. There are a number of vertical coordination mechanisms:

> *Direct referral.* In this device, if a problem arises that employees cannot solve, it is referred to the supervisor.
>
> *Plans and schedule.* A plan or schedule provides standing information to the employee. The most widely used plan is the budget. With carefully designed plans and schedules, employees can be left on their own to perform activities within their resource allocation.
>
> *Adding levels to the hierarchy.* Additional levels or positions in the direct line of authority may be added to increase coordination. Such additions reduce the span of control and provide closer communication and control.
>
> *Vertical information systems.* These include periodic reports, written information, and computerized data summaries. Many corporations computerize the information system and provide reports on a weekly

Box 9.6

Mintzberg on Standardization

Coordination can be achieved by *standardization,* in effect, automatically—by virtue of standards that predetermine what people do and so ensure that their work is coordinated. We can consider four forms—the standardization of the work processes themselves, the outputs of the work, the knowledge and skills that serve as inputs to the work, or the norms that more generally guide the work.

1. *Standardization of work processes* means the specification—that is, the programming—of the content of the work directly, the procedures to be followed, as in the case of the assembly instructions that come with many children's toys. It is typically the job of the analysts to so program the work of different people in order to coordinate it tightly.

2. *Standardization of outputs* means the specification not of what is to be done, but of its results. In that way, the interfaces between jobs are predetermined, as when a machinist is told to drill holes in a certain place on a fender so that they will fit the bolts being welded by someone else, or a division manager is told to achieve a sales growth of 10 percent so that the corporation can meet some overall sales target.

3. *Standardization of skills,* as well as knowledge, is another, though looser way to achieve coordination. Here, it

is the workers rather than the work or the outputs that are standardized. Workers are taught a body of knowledge and a set of skills that are subsequently applied to the work. Such standardization typically takes place outside the organization, for example, in a professional school of a university before workers take their first job. In effect, the standards do not come from the analyst; they are internalized by the workers as inputs to the jobs they take. Coordination is then achieved by virtue of various operators' having learned what to expect of each other. When an anesthetist and a surgeon meet in the operating room to remove an appendix, they need hardly communicate (that is, use mutual adjustment, let alone direct supervision); each knows exactly what the other will do and can coordinate accordingly.

4. *Standardization of norms* means that the workers share a common set of beliefs and can achieve coordination based on it. For example, if every member of a religious order shares a belief in the importance of attracting converts, then all will work together to achieve this aim.

Source: Adapted from Henry Mintzberg, "Structuring of Organizations" in *The Strategy Process,* ed. Henry Mintzberg and James Brian Quinn (Englewood Cliffs, N.J.: Prentice Hall, 1991).

or even daily basis to link top management to activities at lower levels.[12]

These mechanisms have different capacities for coordination. Direct referral is the weakest, whereas vertical information systems supposedly have the highest capacity. Figure 9.8 displays the relationship between the vertical coordination mechanisms and their capacity for coordination.

Horizontal Coordination Mechanisms

Whereas vertical mechanisms rely on some variant of direct supervision for coordination, horizontal mechanisms depend on mutual adjustment by departments. Horizontal mechanisms are not often found on the organization chart, although they are very important. There are a number of horizontal coordination mechanisms:

Paperwork or memos. Here, the departments exchange paperwork about a decision or problem or put other departments on a mailing list so they will be informed about activities.

Direct contact. Direct contact between managers affected by a problem offers a higher level of coordination than just paperwork exchanges.

Liaison roles. A liaison person is located in one department but has the responsibility for communicating and achieving coordination with another department. For example, a production control person is often required to coordinate manufacturing and sales.

Task forces. Direct contact and liaison roles usually link only two departments. When linkage involves several departments, a task force is created. A task force is a temporary committee composed of representatives from each department affected by a problem. Typically, task forces are disbanded after the problem is solved.

Full-time integrator. Sometimes individuals are appointed to be integrators solely for the purpose of coordination. Titles include product manager, program manager, or brand manager. Such managers are located outside the department, and have responsibility for coordinating several departments. Unlike adding levels in the hierarchy, integrators have a lot of responsibility but little authority. Persuasion is the primary means of influence at their disposal.

FIGURE 9.8

Vertical coordination mechanisms capacity for coordination

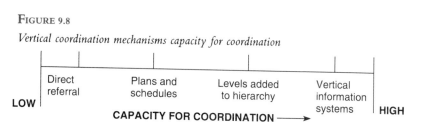

Teams. Project teams are permanent task forces and are employed when activities between departments require strong coordination over a long period of time.[13]

Horizontal mechanisms differ in their capacity for coordination. Paperwork has the least capacity and teams have the highest. Figure 9.9 arrays the different mechanisms on a continuum ranging from lowest capacity to highest.

Organizations use bureaucratic, vertical, and horizontal coordination mechanisms to varying degrees. Dynamic environments force organizations to employ horizontal mechanisms more frequently; whereas in stable environments, organizations may employ bureaucratic and vertical mechanisms. As organizations rely on bureaucratic and vertical mechanisms, they resemble Burns and Stalker's *mechanistic* systems, whereas organizations employing horizontal mechanisms tend to be *organic* in nature. This relationship is sketched in Figure 9.10.

The Concept of Congruence

The test of a good organization design depends primarily on the answers to three questions:

1. Is the organization design suited for carrying out the strategy of the organization?
2. Does the design enable the organization to function adequately in its environments?
3. Do the various elements of organization design—bases of departmentation and coordination—fit together?

Congruence with the strategy and environment is the key determinant of a good organization design. Thus, the bases of departmentation and coordination must fit the strategy and the environment; additionally, the elements must be internally consistent as well.

Since organization design takes place at different levels, the concept of congruence is operationalized differently at different levels. In a single-industry firm, since the distinction between corporate and business strategy is not apparent, divisional and corporate organization designs are the same. However, in diversified firms, there may be as many divisional level orga-

FIGURE 9.9

Horizontal coordination mechanisms

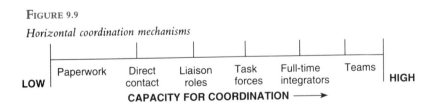

FIGURE 9.10

Linkage between coordination mechanisms and organic-mechanistic systems

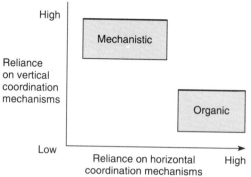

nization designs as there are industries. In these firms, congruence will be operationalized one way at the corporate level, and in quite different ways at divisional levels.

The Process of Organization Design

The general process of organization design is presented in Figure 9.11. As can be seen from the figure, the starting point of organization design is an understanding of the environment and formulation of organizational strategy. This is consistent with the rational approaches to management. Once the environment is analyzed and the strategies are formulated, organization design consists of generating the bases of departmentation and the requisite coordination mechanisms. The alternative organization designs are evaluated in terms of:

1. Congruence with the environment.
2. Congruence with the strategy.
3. Costs of organization design.
4. Value systems of the top managers.

Theoretically, the most important criteria are congruence with the environment and the strategy. Costs and fit with the value systems are pragmatic criteria, and should not be the overriding reasons for the choice of a particular organization design.

Summary

Organization design takes place at several levels: corporate, divisional, and functional. Design decisions involve two elements: departmentation and

FIGURE 9.11

Process of organization design

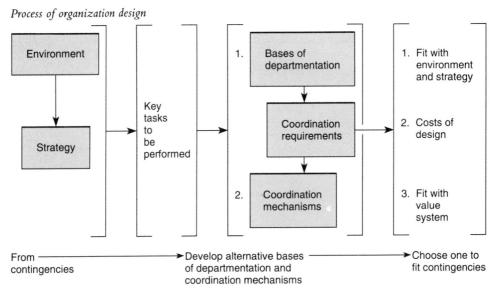

coordination. There are two major bases of departmentation: market and function; and three types of coordination mechanisms: bureaucratic, vertical and horizontal. The more an organization employs vertical mechanisms, the more mechanistic it tends to be, whereas horizontal mechanisms shift an organization in the organic direction. Congruence with environment and strategy are the primary criteria by which organization design should be judged.

Action Strategies

As we have pointed out above, organization design takes place at different levels; consequently, several frameworks for organization design have been formulated, each appropriate for a specific level. In this section, we will summarize four different frameworks: (1) corporate level, (2) divisional level, (3) specific projects (e.g., new product introduction), and (4) sociotechnical systems.

Corporate Level

The design frameworks developed for the corporate level are particularly suitable for managing diversified corporations and multinational firms. For single-industry firms, the distinction between corporate and divisional levels is blurred; hence, divisional level frameworks are more relevant for arriving at organization designs.

Diversified Corporations

Organization design at the corporate level is based on two principles:

1. The basis of departmentation at lower levels is markets—or more precisely, *industries.*
2. The patterns of coordination should be consistent with the *strategy of diversification* (related versus unrelated).

The first principle captures the notion that for diversified corporations, the appropriate organization structure is the *divisional form* of organization. Indeed, this is what Chandler and his followers unearthed during their investigations. In other words, all diversified firms should adopt a divisional structure.

The organization of the corporate office should be consistent with the critical macroenvironmental segments faced by the firm. Thus, all diversified organizations will have a finance and accounting department (separate or together) to cater to the investment community (economic sector), and a legal department to keep track of the legal environment. Additional departments may also be created to cater to other segments. Thus, lobbying for preferred regulation or keeping track of technology may be done by the corporate office in some firms. The organization of the structure within each division should be consistent with business strategy and environment, and this will be taken up in the next section.

In a divisional form of organization, the corporate office retains the responsibility for the decisions pertaining to the form of diversification. The second principle, the one about coordination mechanisms, ensures that organization structure is congruent with the form of diversification, that the firm has undertaken. In firms undertaking unrelated diversification there are no relationships or synergies across businesses, and hence, the demands of coordination are fewer than in the case of related diversifiers. Thus, there will be greater use of vertical and horizontal mechanisms for related diversifiers than is the case for unrelated diversifiers.

The division of responsibility between corporate office and divisions, and the coordination mechanisms—both vertical and horizontal—in related and unrelated diversifiers are presented in Table 9.3.

In both related and unrelated diversifiers, as the number of divisions becomes large, the corporate office may become overloaded with decisions. In such a case, a new hierarchic layer called *group executive* is often created to reduce the span of control of the corporate office. In the case of related diversifiers, highly related businesses should be organized into groups; when synergies are possible within such groups, the appropriate location for staff influence and decision making is at the group level, with a lesser role for corporate staff. In unrelated diversifiers, group executives have a minimum of staff, if any, and oversee each division directly without any attempt at interdivisional activity.[14]

TABLE 9.3   **A Comparison of Corporate Level Designs: Related versus Unrelated**

Dimension	Related Diversifier	Unrelated Diversifier
Strategy of growth	Internal development and acquisition	Acquisition
Key strategic decisions	Resource allocation: Realization of synergy Diversification opportunities	Resource allocation: Entry and exit from industries
Form of organization	Divisional form	
Corporate office size	Relatively large	Relatively small
Centralization (corporate versus division)	Centralized key functions	No centralized line functions
	Shared responsibility for strategies Delegated responsibility for operations	Almost complete delegation of operations/ strategies
Coordination mechanisms		
Vertical	Planning, budgets, and vertical information systems As divisions increase, add hierarchic levels	
Horizontal	Integrators, task forces, teams	None

Source: Adapted from Jay R. Galbraith and Robert K. Kazanjian, *Strategy Implementation* (St. Paul, Minn.: West Publishing, 1986).

The logic of corporate level organization design—how consistency with environment and strategy is ensured—is pictorially presented in Figure 9.12.

Multinational Organizations

In multinational organizations, the forces from global competitors, global customers, universal products, technology investments, and world-scale factories all require global integration. However, the countervailing forces from local governments are also strong. The strategic choices reflect a trade-off between pressures toward globalization and responsiveness to local pressures. Depending on the strategy of the organization, the firm may adopt a divisional structure based either on regions or on product or may locate somewhere in between the two. Figure 9.13 describes these choices.

Divisional Level

At the divisional level, or in the case of a single-industry firm, consistency with the environment and strategy also become the test of good organiza-

FIGURE 9.12

Logic of corporate level design

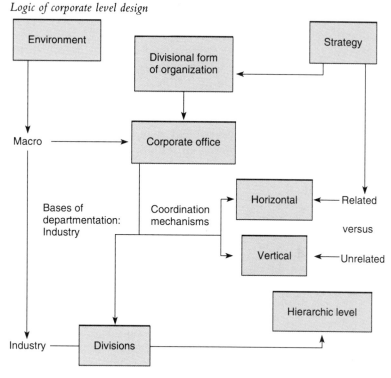

FIGURE 9.13

Multinational organization

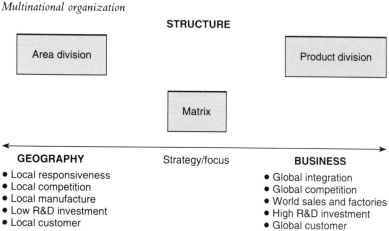

tion design. The primary environment is the industry environment, whereas by strategy we mean business strategy to use the terms we have employed in the previous chapter. There are two principles that drive design choice in this case:

1. The characteristics of the industry, whether it is dynamic or stable, influence the nature and extent of coordination mechanisms. *The more dynamic the environment, the greater the use of horizontal mechanisms.*

2. As product lines proliferate within a single industry, the focus of business strategy may be either on efficiency (i.e., being a low cost player) or responding to customer groups (i.e., maintaining differentiation). In the first case, the firm will adopt a functional structure; in the second, it will adopt a product structure. If both are important, then it will adopt a matrix structure.

The logic of organization design at the divisional level is presented in Figure 9.14, and a comparison of the functional, product, and matrix structures is presented in Table 9.4.

In Box 9.7, we have described the case of Apple Computer's reorganization. As can be seen from the case, Apple, which is a single-industry firm, decided to reorganize from a purely functional organization to product form, although the three area divisions—Apple USA, Apple Education and Apple Pacific, and Apple Europe—are sales divisions, not really responsible for product development and manufacturing. Sculley thus reduced his burden of coordination.

FIGURE 9.14

Logic of divisional level design

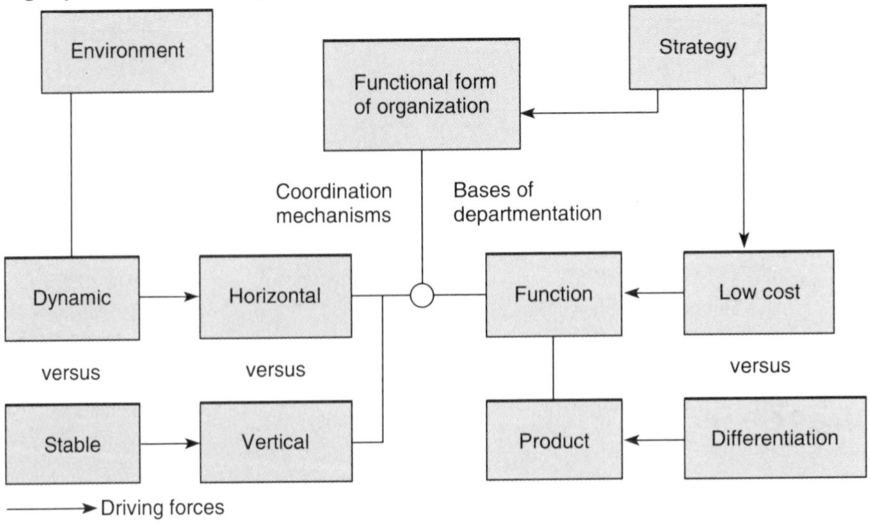

Driving forces

TABLE 9.4   **A Comparison of Divisional Level Designs: Product versus Function versus Matrix**

Dimension	Product	Function	Matrix
Environment	Dynamic	Stable	Dynamic
strategy	Differentiation	Low cost	Differentiation
Number of lines	Many	Few	Intermediate
Goals	Customer satisfaction	Efficiency	Both
Organization design			
Bases of departmentatiom	Product line	Function	Both
Intensity of coordination	Intermediate	Lowest	Highest
Weakness	Loss of economies of scale	Slow to respond to environment	Difficult to implement

Source: Adapted from Robert Duncan, "What is the Right Organization Structure: Decision Tree Provides the Answer," *Organizational Dynamics* (New York: AMACOM), Winter 1979.

Box 9.7

Apple Computer

In 1988, Apple Computer, Inc., announced a reorganization designed to allow the company to double in size by the early 1990s. John Sculley left the presidency to become chairman and chief executive officer. The presidency was to be shared by the heads of four new divisions:

Apple Products—responsible for all product development, manufacturing operations, and product marketing efforts.

Apple USA—responsible for U.S. sales and business marketing, service and support, and Apple's internal information systems operations.

Apple Education and Apple Pacific—responsible for Apple's sales and marketing efforts to education and in the Pacific region.

Apple Europe—responsible for European sales and marketing operations.

With these moves Apple maintained its focus on product development, but increased focus on marketing and service in different geographical areas. It also separated the focus on educational computing, which had been responsible for about 40 percent of Apple's revenue, from the focus on business, which Apple hoped would grow.

Source: Adapted from Brenton R. Schlender, "Apple Sets Plan to Reorganize into 4 Divisions," *The Wall Street Journal*, August 23, 1989, p. 2.

Specific Projects: New Product Introduction

Unlike the corporate and divisional levels, where design involves implementing strategies for a firm's current product-markets, firms may undertake new product introduction projects to create a new industry or differentiation by capturing a new or hitherto untapped market segment. These projects have a finite duration: from the conception to the initial commercialization of the product.

New product introductions are inherently risky: on an average, seven out of eight new products fail during commercialization.[15] What distinguishes successful from unsuccessful introductions? Three factors seem to account for the success of some introductions:

1. Successful companies have a much better understanding of customer needs, and paid greater attention to marketing.
2. Successful companies make greater use of outside technology and advice, and they do more work in-house.
3. Successful new products have one or more senior managers who support and champion their cause.

Thus, although environment (buyers, competitors, etc.) and strategy (new product strategy) play crucial roles, sometimes the organization designs employed for these projects contribute to their success. Organization theorists have argued that new product introductions are facilitated by an organizational form called the *horizontal linkage model.*

In the horizontal linkage model, a temporary organization is created where the functions of research and development, manufacturing, and marketing are brought together in *parallel* rather than sequential fashion, as in ongoing organizations. This may be accomplished through new product teams or task forces that may be designed for a short duration of time. Thus, flow of information during the projects across functions is higher, so that each function takes into account the concerns of the other in designing the product. This not only cuts down developmental time, but ensures a greater degree of success. The horizontal linkage model has three components[16]:

1. *Specialization:* The key departments in new product development are R&D, marketing, and production. The personnel from all the three areas are expected to be highly competent in their tasks.
2. *Environmental scanning:* The three functions are expected to create linkages with the external environment in their respective sector. Thus, R&D personnel should be linked to professional associations and to colleagues in other R&D departments; they are aware of recent scientific developments and can apply new techniques to new product design. Similarly, marketing personnel should listen to what customers have to say, and analyze competitor's products and suggestions by distributors.

3. *Horizontal linkages:* Horizontal coordination mechanisms are designed among R&D, marketing and manufacturing personnel to share ideas and information and to influence the new product introduction decisions. The decision to launch a new product is ultimately a joint decision among the three groups of people.

The horizontal linkage model is pictorially represented in Figure 9.15. Box 9.8 illustrates the popularity of the horizontal linkage model.

Sociotechnical Systems

The corporate and divisional level designs focused on organization structures at the highest levels of the organization. The sociotechnical systems approach is applicable to the functional levels, especially to the manufacturing departments. As we know from contingency theorists (see Chapter 4), lower levels of an organization are determined by the nature of technology. The sociotechnical systems approach is one of the few approaches to utilize this principle.

The sociotechnical approach combines the needs of the people with the needs of technical efficiency. The socio portion of the approach refers to

FIGURE 9.15

Horizontal linkage model

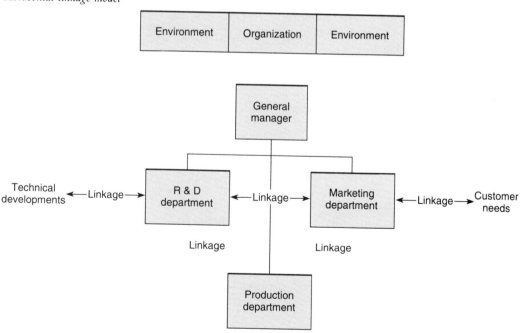

Source: Richard Daft, *Organization Theory,* (St. Paul, Minn.: West Publishing, 1988).

Box 9.8

Horizontal Linkage Model

A Dutch consumer electronics giant, N. V. Philips, marketed the first practical VCR in 1972, three years ahead of the Japanese. By 1979, when Philips launched a major VCR improvement, the company's market share was a trifling 2 percent, and the Japanese manufacturers had already launched three succeeding generations of new VCRs.

Phillips's method of bringing new products to market, called the *phased approach,* is no longer adequate. The phased approach is like a relay race, with the baton passed from product designers to manufacturing and finally to marketing. Phased development allows for careful planning, but it is too slow in the international battleground of consumer electronics. The challenge facing most companies is how to get new and improved products to market faster. Rapid new product cycles are the next great battlefield in industries ranging from electronic components to automobiles and steel.

Sprinting to market with the next-generation product requires a *parallel approach,* or simultaneous coupling among departments. This is similar to a rugby match, wherein players run together, passing the ball back and forth as they move downfield together. Honeywell traditionally required four years to design and build a new thermostat. A major customer refused to wait, so Honeywell set up a special "tiger team" of marketing, design, and engineering employees. The tiger team was told to break all the rules but get the new thermostat out in 12 months. The team succeeded.

The parallel approach is the wave of the future, with companies discovering that rugby-style new product development is the best way to sprint to the new product goal line. Coordination among departments is so important that companies find innovative ways to cooperate.

Source: Adapted from John Bussey and Douglas R. Sease, "Manufacturers Strive to Slice Time Needed to Develop Products," *The Wall Street Journal,* February 23, 1988, pp. 1 and 13; and Bro Uttal, "Speeding New Ideas to Market," *Fortune,* March 2, 1987, pp. 62–66.

individuals and groups who work in organizations. The technical part refers to the tools and machines used in work processes. This approach tries to *jointly optimize* the social and technical aspects of an organization.

The principles of sociotechnical systems were developed during the 1950s and 1960s by Tavistock Institute, a research organization in England. The principles originated with the Institute's work with coal mines. Coal miners had worked in small groups, and this social structure provided mutual support in the dark, hazardous coal mines. The work was difficult, but since it was done by hand, the group members could see the completion of the work, set their own pace, and take breaks when necessary. However, the coal mines introduced mechanical coal cutters that made higher efficiency possible. This broke up the groups and led to a decrease in productivity. The Tavistock researchers studied the problem. They made small adjustments to the technology, defined small groups, and gave members the freedom to redefine their jobs and increase their social interaction. The new job design fit the needs of the employees and the demands of technology. Absenteeism dropped by one half, productivity increased by 95 percent and fewer conflicts and labor disputes occurred.

Ever since then, sociotechnical systems have occurred in such diverse departments as a railway maintenance depot, textile mills, a pet food plant, and new computer integrated manufacturing plants.[17] In practice, the approach leads to the creation of *autonomous work groups.* In these work groups, responsibility for planning, operating, and controlling the work is given to a group of employees. The tasks within a group are highly interdependent and the group structure facilitates coordination among tasks. The need for supervision is reduced. In this sense, by utilizing horizontal mechanisms instead of direct supervision, the manufacturing systems move from mechanistic to organic forms. An example of an autonomous work group in confectionery plants is presented in Box 9.9.

Summary

In this section we have described four organization design frameworks to be employed at different levels. As we have shown, strategy and environment are the primary driving forces for corporate and divisional levels, whereas technology drives the design at lower levels. This is consistent with the contingency principles described in Chapter 4.

Table 9.5 summarizes the applicability of the four levels of designs.

Limitations and Utility of Organization Design

As we have seen, organization design focuses on structuring the organization for implementing its strategy. In this section, we will briefly review the limitations and utility of the approach.

Limitations

In the rational approaches to management, organization design is viewed as the major mechanism to implement strategy, and hence, it is antecedent to strategic planning. Thus, taken by itself, design has no independent standing as an action strategy. Beyond this, however, the organization design approaches suffer from two related limitations.

1. Organization design focuses on the functional subsystem, and considers the human elements of an organization as dependent on the functional subsystem. Thus, the social subsystem—the system of interpersonal relations—depends on formal groupings, and cultural elements—norms, values, and so on—to support the formal structure. In addition, the design focuses on authority—derived from

Box 9.9

Sociotechnical Systems

A large, nonunionized British confectionery (candy) company conducted an experiment on the effects of autonomous work groups in their production facilities. The purpose of the autonomous work groups was to provide shop-floor employees with substantial autonomy in carrying out day-to-day production along with a high level of involvement in operational decision making.

The new design had production employees work in groups of 8 to 12 people, all of whom were expected to carry out each of eight types of jobs. Group members were collectively responsible for allocating jobs among themselves, reaching production targets, meeting quality and hygiene standards, solving local production problems, recording production data for information systems, organizing breaks, ordering and collecting support, and selecting and training new recruits. Each production group was responsible for one product line, and individuals had considerable control over the amount of variety they experienced by rotating their tasks. Group members interacted informally throughout the working day and held formal weekly group meetings to allocate jobs and discuss performance.

Since nearly all the functions typically carried out by supervisors were the responsibility of shop-floor employees, the position of supervisor was eliminated. Groups reported directly to a support manager who had overall responsibility for 40 to 70 employees and whose role was to provide guidance necessary for the development of both social and technical skills within the work groups. Support managers were responsible for providing facilities, creating conditions within which groups could operate, and maintaining disciplinary procedures.

Researchers studying the changes concluded that the autonomous work groups had a substantial and lasting effect on employees' job satisfaction but no consequences for work motivation or performance. At the organizational level, however, improvements in productivity were realized through the elimination of supervisory positions.

Source: Adapted from Toby D. Wall, Nigel J. Kemp, Paul R. Jackson, and Chris W. Clegg, "Outcome of Autonomous Groups: A Long-Term Field Experiment," *Academy of Management Journal* 29 (1986), pp. 280–304.

one's individual position in the hierarchy—as the primary source of power in an organization. As we have seen in the strategic planning chapter, these assumptions are often violated in organizations.

2. The design field focuses on the theoretically *ideal* structure; it does not provide a plan for implementation.

Since the organization design field originated from contingency theory, these limitations are an outgrowth of the theoretical lineage of the field.

What do these limitations imply? First, when a new design is implemented, there are likely to be forces of resistance from the social, cultural, and political subsystems within the organization. For example, people may not have the interpersonal skills crucial for horizontal coordination mech-

TABLE 9.5   **Applicability of Design Concepts**

Levels	Contingencies	Logic
Corporate	Macroenvironment, diversification strategy	Divisional form of organization
Divisional	Industry, business strategy	Product versus function versus matrix
New product introduction	Parallel phasing of functions	Horizontal linkage model
Manufacturing	Social and technical subsystems	Sociotechnical system

anisms to work. They may not be able to make the cultural shift from function focus to market focus as demanded by the divisional structure. And they may not have the negotiation skills required to resolve conflicts that erupt in a matrix. The example in Box 9.10 shows how a matrix introduction in an organization ran into problems. Second, we need to look at other approaches such as organization development for the implementing of organization designs. The example in Box 9.10 illustrates how this was done in one organization.

Applicability

Despite these limitations, organization design focuses on the design of the functional subsystem as a crucial factor in the long-term effectiveness of an organization. It provides some of the ideal configurations of tasks and co-ordination mechanisms for implementing organizational strategies. These ideals, although rarely realized in practice, are rallying points for bringing about organizational change. Organization design affects the day-to-day life of all the employees in an organization. Thus, in rational approaches to management, organization design occupies a prominent place.

Chapter Summary

Organization design involves structuring the functional subsystem to match the strategy and environment of an organization. In the short run, the design influences the behavior of employees; also, it is a long-run determinant of economic performance.

As organizations change their strategies, they change their structures. If they retain their previous structure, they decline in performance; the decline then serves as a stimulus to redesign. The redesign first involves a buildup of subunits and second, devising coordination among the subunits. As organizations diversify and grow, the organization design takes place at many levels: corporate, divisional, and functional.

Box 9.10

Case of Matrix Introduction

A billion dollar manufacturing concern experienced problems staying cost competitive and introducing new products rapidly. Market share and return on investment declined over a period of a decade.

External consultants were called in to diagnose the problem. They recommended a matrix organization. Management accepted the diagnosis as essentially accurate but needed time to discuss matrix and test alternatives. During one meeting, three subgroups were asked to analyze the benefits and costs of three alternative organizational forms—functional, decentralized product divisions, and matrix. The general manager's leadership style and shared manufacturing facilities by all product lines convinced management that matrix was the right choice.

Top management met many more times with and without the consultant to plan the transition to new structures. At these meetings, the specifics of the new organization were discussed. A dual performance appraisal procedure was developed. A decision was made to pay bonuses to business team members based on team performance. Business team managers and members were identified as was the need for new financial information,

particularly cost and return on investment information by business.

About a year later the transition to matrix management was announced to the top 100 people. A one-day orientation program was organized. An internal consultant was hired to help in the transition. Similarly, a steering committee composed of managers was appointed to help in continual monitoring of progress and in recommending improvements. Many meetings were held with individuals and groups to identify problems. Each business team held a special meeting to define roles and work on team building.

By the end of one-and-a-half years, the matrix design was in place. Two functional managers were replaced and a number of issues were unresolved. Furthermore, new concerns emerged about the effectiveness of one business manager in managing his team.

As can be seen from this example, phasing in new structures requires attention to the issues generated in the social and political subsystems. The design literature has traditionally not addressed such issues.

Source: Adapted from Michael Beer, *Organization Development and Change* (Santa Monica, Calif.: Goodyear, 1986).

Organization theorists discovered that when an organization builds up specialized units, this necessitates greater coordination. There are three types of coordination mechanisms: bureaucratic, vertical, and horizontal. However, the coordination requirements are lower in stable environments than in dynamic environments. Indeed, dynamic environments require organizations to employ horizontal coordination mechanisms.

For diversified corporations, organization design at the corporate level consists of a corporate office and creation of divisions based on industries. The design of the corporate office corresponds to macroenvironments, whereas divisional structures respond to their respective industries. In unrelated diversification, the corporate office is leaner and may incorporate only legal and financial markets. In related diversification, the corporate office responds in addition to such environments as technology or markets (depending on the nature of relatedness). As the number of divisions increases, vertical mechanisms such as a new hierarchical level, called the *group executive,* are added. In addition, horizontal mechanisms are also employed in the case of related diversifiers.

In single-industry firms, organization design is based on function or product. If the strategy is to be a low-cost player, and hence, focus on efficiency, the functional structure is adopted; whereas a strategy of differentiation and responsiveness to markets requires a product form of organization. Environment, in addition, influences the coordination mechanisms; as industries become dynamic, there will be greater reliance on horizontal mechanisms.

Organization design for special projects such as new product introduction requires that firms develop horizontal linkages between marketing, manufacturing, and research and development. Sometimes autonomous work group designs are employed in manufacturing organizations to enhance productivity.

Specialized Terms

Hierarchy
Span of control
Functional organization
Divisional organization
Matrix organization
Conglomerate organization
Holding company model
Multinational expansion
  International expansion
  Global strategy
Interdependence
  Pooled
  Sequential

Reciprocal
Levels of design
Bases of departmentation
Bases of coordination
  Bureaucratic mechanisms
  Vertical coordination mechanisms
  Horizontal coordination
    mechanisms
The concept of congruence
Liaison role
Integrator
Horizontal linkage model

Discussion Questions

Theoretical

1. What is organization design? What role does it play in rational action strategies?
2. How is organization design viewed from the systems model?

3. Sketch the linkage between the strategy of growth and organization structure identified by Chandler.

4. Distinguish between the optimal structures in related and unrelated diversification.

5. How is the principle of congruence operationalized in organization design?

6. Point out the limitations and utility of organization design.

★7. Sketch the relationship between the works of (1) Burns and Stalker on the one hand and Lawrence and Lorsch on the other; and (2) Lawrence and Lorsch and Thompson.

★8. How are the works of (1) Lawrence and Lorsch and (2) Thompson reflected in the action strategies presented in the chapter?

Applied

1. You have been invited by the head of a toy manufacturer to help her design an organization structure. The toy manufacturer manufactures and sells two types of toys: (1) some like trucks are standard, and (2) some are highly trendy with life spans less than two years. How would you go about addressing the structure issue?

2. You have been retained by a major conglomerate to help the corporate office establish a meaningful structure linking itself with its divisions. How would you proceed?

End Notes

1. Alison Rogers, "It's the Execution that Counts," *Fortune,* November 30, 1992, p. 80.
2. Max Weber, *The Theory of Social and Economic Organizations,* trans. A. M. Henderson and T. Parsons (New York: Free Press, 1947).
3. Ibid.
4. David A. Nadler, J. Richard Hackman, and Edward E. Lawler III, *Managing Organizational Behavior* (Boston: Little, Brown, 1979). pp. 183–84.
5. Alfred Chandler, *Strategy and Structure: Chapters in the History of American Industrial Enterprise* (Cambridge, Mass.: MIT Press, 1962). See also for elaboration of his conclusions (1) Derek Channon, *The Strategy and Structure of British Enterprise* (London: MacMillan, 1973); (2) Gareth Pooley-Dyas, "Strategy and Structure of French Enterprise," Ph.D. dissertation, Harvard Business School, 1972; (3) Yoshiro Suzuki, "The Strategy and Structure of Top 100 Japanese Industrial Enterprises 1950–1970," *Strategic Management Journal* 1 (1980), pp. 265–91.

★This is an advanced-level question.

6. Ibid.

7. See Richard Rumelt, *Strategy, Structure and Economic Performance* (Cambridge, Mass.: Harvard University Press, 1974).

8. See (1) Larry Fouraker and John Stopford, "Organization Structure and Multinational Strategy," *Administrative Science Quarterly* 13 (June 1968), pp. 57–60; (2) C. K.Prahalad and Yves Doz, "An Approach to Strategic Control," *Sloan Management Review,* Summer 1981, pp. 5–13.

9. Paul Lawrence and Jay Lorsch, *Organization and Environment* (Homewood, Ill.: Richard D. Irwin, 1969).

10. James D. Thompson, *Organizations in Action* (New York: McGraw-Hill, 1967).

11. Drawn from Henry Mintzberg, "The Structuring of Organizations," in *The Strategy Process* ed. Quinn, Mintzberg, and Waters (Englewood Cliffs, N.J.: Prentice Hall, 1988).

12. Jay R. Galbraith, *Designing Complex Orginazitions* (Reading, Mass: Addison-Wesley, 1973). See also his *Organization Design* (Reading, Mass.: Addison-Wesley, 1977).

13. Ibid.

14. See Jay R. Galbraith and Robert K. Kazanjian, *Strategy Implementation* (St. Paul, Minn.: West Publishing, 1986).

15. Edwin Mansfield et al., *Research and Innovation in Modern Organization* (New York: W. W. Norton, 1971), p. 57.

16. This section is drawn from Richard Daft, *Organization Theory* (St. Paul, Minn.: West Publishing, 1988).

17. William Passmore, Carol E. Francis, and Jeffrey Haldeman, "Socio-Technical Systems: A North American Reflection on the Empirical Studies of the 70s," *Human Relations* 35 (1982) pp. 1179–204.

10 ORGANIZATIONAL INFORMATION AND CONTROL SYSTEMS

Chapter Outline

The time is the mid-1990s. You are crawling down the interstate (traffic hasn't improved over the past five years) after a long business dinner with your field service managers. Your car phone rings and its display shows that one of your company's most important customers in Japan is on the line. Your office communications system has prescreened the call, found it to be one you are willing to accept at any time, and automatically forwarded it to your car phone.

You answer the call–it is the president himself, whom you met on your visit to Tokyo last year when you signed the deal to be their primary supplier. He tells you that fire has struck his largest plant, knocking it out of commission. He needs all of the parts that were scheduled to be shipped to that facility diverted to another. He also needs an additional emergency shipment sent to the working plant to make up for the parts destroyed in the fire.

Pulling over to the side of the road, you open your briefcase and use the computer inside to access your corporate database through a cellular radio link. You identify yourself to the system with your key-card and PIN number. The system then knows exactly what information you may access and what changes you are permitted to make.

You order the system to redirect the scheduled shipments (even the ones already enroute) and to send out the needed emergency parts to the customer's plant by the fastest means possible. Within seconds the system replies with the expected shipment and delivery times. It informs you that some of the needed parts are stocked in Europe and asks if you want them shipped by international courier. It quotes the extra cost for this service.

You pass the information on to your customer and ask if he wants to pay the costs for next-day delivery. He agrees, and at the same time expresses a great deal of appreciation and admiration for the speed with which you are able to help him. He asks for a fax confirmation of the new delivery quantities, destinations and time, which you immediately transmit from your briefcase-computer.

On the road to home again, you feel good about the help that you have been able to give to a good customer. You feel even better a few weeks later when this customer increases the percentage of parts that he buys from your company by more than 10 percent because of the excellent service that you are able to provide.

Science fiction? No! The technology exists today to allow you to do what was just described. But most companies have not integrated their internal systems sufficiently—nor established external links to their outside suppliers and other business partners—to permit field personnel or executives on the road to access information and take the immediate action to meet the customer's needs.

The Integrated Information System (IIS), the coming systems structure of the mid-1990s, will turn into reality what is now just technologically feasible. IIS is the name that we give to the integration of all of a company's computing and communications resources (yes, even those PCs and LANs—Local Area Networks—which are springing up like weeds and are just as hard to control) into a unified structure. This single system will allow all of the information and computing resources of a company to be accessed and utilized by every employee in an organization, to the extent that he or she is authorized to do so. In most cases, a company's IIS will be linked to its equivalent in principal customers, suppliers, and other business partners.[1]

As described in the above predictions of some consultants from Arthur D. Little, Inc., an East Coast consulting firm, advances in information technology have made it possible for an organization to control its operations more efficiently as well as to design advanced information systems. What are the functions that information serves? How should an organization design its information and control system? What are the differences in control systems across organizational levels? What role has technology played in the design of information systems? We will explore the answers to these questions that organization theorists have provided in recent years.

In many ways, information is the life-blood of an organization. Managers at all levels—low, middle, and top levels—deal primarily with information. We need information to make decisions, or even to control the operations. Indeed even the diagnosis of an organization requires information.

What Is Organizational Information and Control?

By information and control we refer to the gathering of information for decision making and use of information to control the strategies and operations of an organization.

In any organization, decision makers and operational personnel need information to work effectively. Decision makers need accurate information on the resources available to them, so they can organize and allocate these resources, as and when needed, to the appropriate organizational tasks. For example, a chemical factory must ensure a continuous availability of the chemicals needed to manufacture its products. Therefore, it needs to maintain information on raw material stocks in its warehouses, on the estimated need for more raw materials in the future, on orders placed by the factory with its raw materials suppliers, as well as on the suppliers themselves. Similarly, to ensure smooth functioning, the factory must also possess information about its other resources such as its equipment, its labor force, its sales force, and its cash flow.

Apart from information on resource availability, organizational decision makers may also need other kinds of information such as information on the demand for the organization's products/services, on the organization's competitors, on regulatory agencies, and on consumer characteristics. Thus, organizations must monitor their environment carefully. Finally, organizations also need to be aware of the effectiveness of their internal functioning so that they can determine whether their goals are being achieved.

Linkage to the Systems Model

The information and control primarily addresses the informational subsystem in the systems model. According to this view, the information subsystem within an organization should be so designed as to support its strategies and structures. This logic is displayed in Figure 10.1.

According to the rational strategies of management, the information subsystem design follows environmental analysis, strategic planning, and

FIGURE 10.1

Logic of information and control system

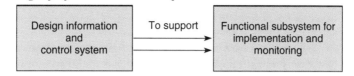

organization design. The information subsystem, thus designed, ensures that managers can track the implementation of strategy and take corrective action when necessary. In this sense, information systems ensures that *negative feedbacks* exist in organizations.

Although the information subsystem intersects all other subsystems—social, political, and cultural, in addition to the functional subsystem—most action models have typically viewed the information subsystem as a support to the functional subsystem. Within the rational strategies, the information subsystem primarily focuses on the technical elements of an organization. In the later chapters that deal with organization development, organizational politics, and organization culture, we will see how communication about human elements actually takes place.

The emphasis on the intersection with an organization's functional subsystem, and thus on its technical elements, is partly due to the fact that the information subsystem has in recent years benefitted greatly from technological developments of the kind described in the chapter introduction case. These developments have primarily been able to capture technical elements more so than human elements. No other subsystem has been so much influenced by technological advances as the informational subsystem.

In this section, we summarize organization theorists' views about information and control. We will eschew the large body of writing describing the technical developments; instead, we will focus almost exclusively on the role information and control play in organizational dynamics. The scheme of this chapter is as follows. First, we will sketch the historical, philosophical, and theoretical underpinnings of this subfield. Next, we will introduce the major concepts that we employ to summarize the action models. Third, we will discuss the major models of information and control. Fourth, we will provide a systems theoretic review. We will conclude with a summary.

Underpinnings

Historical Underpinnings

The earliest forms of information and control systems employed in organizations were the accounting and budgeting systems. With the advent of technology, enormous changes took place in the information systems in organizations.

The modern history of data processing/information management can be divided into three phases:[2]

The First Phase

The first phase began during the latter part of the 19th century, with the mechanization of manual clerical tasks, and an emphasis on data which was indistinguishable from the procedures that manipulate the data. Thus, software (coded instructions that enable a computer to perform various tasks) had not yet been invented and data manipulation procedures were often built into the hardware (the physical components of the computer) in the form of wired control panels. We may call this the "first information revolution." It was a revolution because it enabled the quick and efficient manipulation of huge amounts of data.

The Second Phase

The "second information revolution" came in the mid-1940s when the memory capacity of newer, larger machines increased to allow the inclusion of the "addresses" of data located in the machine memory, within the programs (sequences of instructions) designed for the purpose of manipulating that data. This enabled data to be stored independently of the programs that used them, thus providing flexibility of operation. Soon, the concept of dynamically variable addresses was born whereby variables did not have to be stored permanently at a fixed memory location but could be moved around as and when needed. The "stored programming" era was thus born. Both data and their manipulation procedures (programs) could now be stored inside the machines, to be retrieved or run as many times as and when desired. Software development took off; the concepts of subroutines (frequently used and independently stored routines or programs that can be "called" by master programs when needed), and compilers (programs that translate high-level user languages into a lower-level language that the computer can understand) were enunciated in this period. There was a shift in emphasis from the mechanization of routine clerical activities to the support of scientific (and later, management) activities. In other words, programs came to overshadow data. The programs that were written were independent of the data they used and data sharing among programs was rare.

During this era, computers were primarily applied to routine computations such as transaction-processing. Day-to-day transaction data was speedily and accurately processed by enormous machines with their capacity for performing arithmetic manipulations on tons of data. There was no recognition by top management of the potential uses of transaction data when they are appropriately summarized and presented in an easily understandable form to the organizational decision-maker.

The Third Phase

The third phase began in the mid-1970s when business analysts and operations researchers wanted data to support their business models. Suddenly transaction data acquired immense importance as it was realized that such data, when processed and presented in an appropriate format, could provide a wealth of detail and information on the business functions. Many new technological developments also occurred during this period. Database technology (the ability to store, organize, manipulate, and retrieve data) was introduced and put to extensive use in businesses. Non procedural languages (which enable the user to simply tell the system what to do rather than having to specify how to do it) such as SQL and INGRES were invented and put to use in database management systems. The concepts of artificial intelligence (AI) and expert systems (ES) which were also enunciated in this period were used to simulate complex human problem solving behavior in specific problem situations. Indeed this phase was the "third information revolution". One may add here that this was the age that witnessed the birth of true *Management Information Systems* (MIS). However, the drawback of this phase was that data processing (DP) departments in organizations were in complete control of the design, implementation, and even the day-to-day operations of information systems. As a result organizational decision makers were totally dependent on them for their information needs. Organizational effectiveness suffered because information needed was not always readily available to the appropriate people.

Decision Support Systems

MIS evolved out of the third phase during the mid- and late 70s when a new concept called Decision Support System (DSS) was introduced. DSSs were supposed to be able to provide decision makers with answers to "what-if" type questions. For example, decision makers in a specific decision context were supposed to be assisted by a DSS in identifying and evaluating different decision alternatives. Two notions: prototyping and user involvement came to be developed:

> *The prototype approach* to the design of information systems may be described as follows. First, a simple model of the proposed system is constructed. This model may only consist of a few of the features desired for the final system. These few features incorporated in the model, namely the prototype, are typically in the form of menus that help the user move from one screen to another. The user is encouraged to get a feel for the prototype and to make suggestions for improving the prototype. Based on the user's suggestions, a few more features may be added to the prototype. At this stage the prototype is merely a skeletal version of the eventual system. Design details are avoided on purpose so that it can first be decided what the

structure of the system should be. With the addition of new features, the user reevaluates the system and may suggest further additions/improvements. This process can continue for several iterations. After the user is completely satisfied with the structure of the system, a detailed design of the system is undertaken.

User involvement means encouraging the eventual user of an information system to participate in its design. It has been found that information systems designed with user involvement are more easily accepted by users.

The notions of prototyping and user involvement assisted in the propagation of the DSS concept because these encouraged users to participate in the development of systems meant for their own eventual use.

In the early 1980s, a revolution in hardware technology saw the widespread introduction of personal computers in business organizations. Hardware prices dropped, and popular and user-friendly word-processing, database, and spreadsheet software flooded the market. This phenomenon may be called the "fourth information revolution" because it took away the mystique of computers and brought them to millions of homes and offices of even the most nontechnically oriented business professionals. The proliferation of "end-user computing" saw users of computerized applications undertake development and maintenance of their own applications on a large scale. Thus, users were no longer completely dependent on their data processing (DP) departments to provide them with computerized applications relevant to their functions. As more and more end-users took computing into their own hands, MIS/DP professionals began to recognize the need for assisting these users in their computing activities. Many organizations set up organizational units or physical facilities called "information centers" where end-users would be provided with the full range of training, consulting, and education that they needed to be able to carry on their computing activities.

End-user computing continues to proliferate; however, a fifth information revolution now seems to be in the offing, with increased sophistication of communications technologies. Integrated Services Digital Networks (ISDNs) hold promise for transmission of voice, data, and images on the same lines; optical fiber networks will soon replace existing communication lines, and the cost of transmission will drop. Computers will be networked extensively and inexpensively. Physical location of data will become irrelevant as any user will be able to access any data that is needed, without worrying about where it is stored. That, then, will truly be an information age.

Such an information age holds great potential for the enhancement of organizational effectiveness, specifically with reference to decision-making contexts. Increased sophistication in the gathering, processing, dissemination, and use of information will ensure improvements in the quality and timeliness of decisions. This, in turn, will assist decision makers in the better attainment of organizational goals.

Philosophical Underpinnings

The scholars who studied organizational information and control were concerned with primarily the needs of the "technical system," and, therefore, their models were inherently rational. Early systems designers also held implicit assumptions such as (1) "people are poor information processors," and (2) "information flow downward must be controlled." There was no recognition in these assumptions of the political processes involved in the selection, design, and use of information systems.[3]

This kind of thinking began to change in the late 1960s and early 1970s. Philosophically-oriented scholars in the field such as Russell Ackoff[4] and Chris Argyris[5] raised questions about the implicit, unchallenged assumptions of information system professionals. Argyris argued that if management information systems were to achieve their designers' highest level of aspiration (rationality!), they would create a world for the local decision maker where his daily goals would be defined for him, the actions to achieve these goals would be specified, the level of aspiration would be determined, and the performance evaluated, by a system that is external to him. This would lead to conditions where executives would experience reduction of space of free movement, psychological failure, leadership based more on formal power than on competence, and decreased feelings of essentiality. These would, in turn, create hostility towards the information system expert; the latter's deliberately rational response to this hostility would only exacerbate the situation. Thus, Argyris had made an important point—that the rationality assumption with respect to information and control was an erroneous one.

Contemporary theorists in the MIS area have begun to recognize and even appreciate the nonrational processes at work. This work is still in its embryonic stages, and its applications are not yet clear.

Theoretical Underpinnings

Scholars from diverse disciplines have contributed to our understanding of information and control. These include accounting, human behavior, organization theory, computer science, management science and operations research, microeconomics, cognitive psychology, and strategic planning. We will limit our discussion to the contributions of organization theorists.

Over the years organization theorists have provided answers to several questions: What is information and what are its uses? What are the elements of an information system? What factors determine the design of an information system? How to design a reward system to control executive behavior? What is the problem of control? What are the mechanisms of control?

Information and Its Uses
Information is needed for decision making at various levels in the organization. Broadly, organizations use information for four purposes: For

1. Managing the day-to-day operations of the organization.
2. Management control.
3. Strategic planning.
4. Achieving a competitive advantage.

At the operational level, for example, organizations use information to keep track of orders received for products or services, to monitor inventory stocks of raw materials and finished goods, to schedule personnel shifts, to coordinate equipment usage, and so on. Since decision making at this level is very structured, such information systems frequently have simple models built into them, providing a high degree of automation in decision making.

Information systems for management control typically provide reports of deviations from normal performance of personnel as well as machines or equipment. These systems essentially act as feedback loops for decision makers so that they can ensure the implementation of their decisions. Based on this feedback, decision makers may take appropriate action where they perceive the need for doing so.

At the strategic planning level, information systems help an organization in assessing its strengths and weaknesses, in studying environmental trends, and in setting long-term goals and strategies. The kind of information provided by these information systems for strategic planning is of a very aggregate nature. Decision making at this level is extremely unstructured and, therefore, the role of these information systems is confined to providing such aggregated information to strategic planners in the organization.

In the last few years, organizations have found a new use for both information and information technology. This is popularly known as "Information Technology for Competitive Advantage." This concept implies a direct, visible relationship between the use of information technology (or information) by an organization and the consequent advantage generated for the organization over its competitors.

Elements of an Information System
All elements of an information and control system consist of essentially four elements:

1. The *Sender* is the point where the information contained in the system originates. This source may be an automated system, a person, or a group of persons.

2. The *Channel* is the medium through which the information is communicated. This medium may be a computer, a file, or a person.

3. The *Receiver,* like the sender, may be a person, a group of people, or an automatic process or system.

4. The *Feedback* refers to the *Receiver's* evaluation of the information.

Although more elaborate descriptions of an information system have been suggested by various scholars, all descriptions contain the above four elements: sender, channel, receiver, and feedback.

Factors that Drive an Information System

The early work in management accounting concentrated on ascertaining the characteristics of information that promote effective decision making. Over the years this line work has abandoned the search for universal solutions—the characteristics of information that is appropriate under all conditions—in favor of contingency formulations. Increasingly it was realized that the type of information deemed appropriate should be viewed as contingent on the organizational context.

Although scholars pursued different contingency factors, two major contingency variables stood out: (1) environment, and (2) structure. To quote one authority in the field:

> . . . . then nature of organizational control is dependent on the type of organizational structure which, in turn, is contingent on . . . environment; the implication is that management accounting systems will need to be designed to meet the specific control requirements of specific organizational units . . . [6]

It was suggested that:

1. When environments are stable or when organizations are bureaucratically organized, they would demand internal, financial (quantitative), and ex post type information;

2. When environments become dynamic or when the organizations are structured along organic lines, they would *in addition* demand external, nonfinancial (qualitative) and ex ante type information.

Recently Larry Gordon and V. K. Narayanan verified these ideas; their study is summarized in Box 10.1.

Reward Systems as a Means of Control

The control function of reward systems—how rewards influence behavior—was well understood by management theorists. Although this knowledge underpinned many of the human resource practices in organizations, most

Box 10.1

Gordon and Narayanan's Contingency Model of Information

Two researchers, Larry Gordon, an accounting professor, and V. K. Narayanan, an organization theorist, set out to test the contingency formulations in accounting. At the time of the study, both were based at the University of Kansas, and had access to top-level decision makers in the Midwest. Indeed their study was conducted at 34 profit-oriented, medium-sized firms with sales ranging from $50 million to $200 million. They were all independent firms, i.e., they were not subsidiaries of other firms.

In searching the literature, Gordon and Narayanan discovered that there was strong agreement among scholars that organization structure and environments influenced the characteristics of information used by decision makers. However, whereas the direction of the relationships were clear with respect to environment, less clear was the relationship between the characteristics of an information system and organization structure. Further, the two researchers were intrigued by the differences in strategies advocated by various others; some were arguing that organization structure followed environment and information system followed organization structure whereas others were arguing that structure and information system together formed a package to deal with environment.

The two scholars measured environment by using the construct of environmental uncertainty, similar to the one advanced by Duncan (refer to Chapter 7). They divided organization structures along a continuum from organic to mechanistic similar to the classification of Burns and Stalker (refer to Chapter 4).

With respect to information system, the authors argued that almost all firms paid attention to internally generated, financial and ex post information. Instead they focused on three other characteristics of information system:

(1) external (whether the firm focused on environmental information in addition to internal information);

(2) non-financial (whether the firm focused on market related and qualitative information in addition to financial); and

(3) ex ante (whether the firm focused on forecasts in addition to the results of the past).

What did they find? First as hypothesized, they discovered that as environments became more dynamic, or organization structures became organic, the firms focused increasingly on external, nonfinancial and ex ante type information. This was not a surprise, since by then contingency formulations had become popular in literature.

Second, however, they discovered that almost all the relationships between structure and information system were explained by the fact that organic structures existed primarily in dynamic environments.

Taken together, they argued that:

These results further suggest that organizational structuring and characteristics of information sought by decision makers are complementary strategies in responding to their perception of the environment. Stated differently, as decision makers perceive greater environmental uncertainty, they tend to seek external, non-financial and ex ante information in addition to other types of, information *and* increasingly move toward an organic form of organization (p. 42).

It appears that organization structure and information system formed a decision package to deal with environmental uncertainty. According to Gordon and Narayanan, this raises the intriguing possibility that information technology may be employed to bring about changes in organization structure—a possibility that is underdeveloped in literature.

Source: Adapted from Lawrence A. Gordon and V. K. Narayanan, "Management Accounting Systems: An Empirical Investigation," *Accounting, Organizations and Society* 9, no. 1, (1984), pp. 33–47.

practices typically addressed lower-level employees. It was only in the last two decades scholars began to investigate the role of incentives in channeling executive behavior.

As early as 1973, Malcolm Salter underscored the need to tailor incentive compensation of executives to an organization's strategy. He identified four major dimensions of strategy:

1. *Short run versus long run:* whether the strategy required short-term or long-term orientation.

2. *Risk aversion versus risk taking:* whether the strategy required the executives to take calculated risks or to be conservative in their decisions.

3. *Interdivisional relationships:* especially in large corporations, whether the strategy focused on synergies among business units as in the case of related diversification.

4. *Company divisional relationships:* whether, especially in large companies, strategy hinges on effective corporate divisional relationships.

Salter identified six factors within incentive mechanism that influence behavior along various dimensions:

1. Financial instruments: current bonus versus stock options.

2. Performance measures: qualitative versus quantitative.

3. Degree of discretion in allocation of rewards: nondiscretionary, formula based bonuses versus completely discretionary highly personalized approaches.

4. Size and frequency of awards.

5. Degree of uniformity among divisions.

6. Source of funding: funding from divisional versus corporate bonus pools.

Salter suggested that different strategy choices necessitated different combinations of factors. He argued that current bonuses (stock options), quantitative (qualitative) measures of performance, and formula based (discretionary) and frequent incentives were appropriate for short-(long) term strategies; similarly, he noted that uniformity among divisions encouraged cooperation and enhanced the control of the corporate office whereas funding from divisional bonus pools tended to reduce the influence of the corporate office.

Salter's ideas are summarized in Table 10.1.

Agency theorists were among the first to theoretically conceptualize the problem of control; they incorporated both mechanisms of monitoring and rewards in the discussions of control.

TABLE 10.1   **Salter's Model of Incentives**

TIME HORIZON

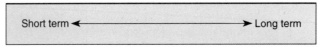

1. Current bonus	Stock options
2. Quantitative	Qualitative
3. Nondiscretionary, formula	Discretionary
4. Frequent	Infrequent

RISK TAKING

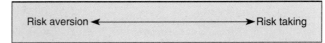

1. Completely discretionary, highly personalized	Current bonus
2. Quantitative	Qualitative

INTERDIVISIONAL RELATIONSHIPS

1. Discretionary	Nondiscretionary Formula based
2. Uniform	Nonuniform
3. Basis of Bonus Pools:	
Mix of corporate and division performance	Division performance

CORPORATE-DIVISIONAL RELATIONSHIPS

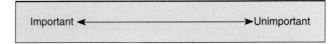

1. Stock option plans	
2. Discretionary measures	Objective measures
3. Uniformity among divisions	Nonuniform
4. Bonus pools based on	
Corporate profits	Division profits

Source: Malcolm S. Salter. "Tailor Incentive Compensation to Strategy." *Harvard Business Review,* March–April 1973, pp. 94–102.

Problem of Control

When we summarized the history of management thought (see Chapter 2), we noted that as modern industrial enterprises came into existence, increasingly the ownership was separated from management. In other words, people who owned the firm—the shareholders—were far removed from the day to day operations of the corporations. This led many to wonder how owners indeed ensure that managers are not pursuing their own self-interests at the expense of the interests of the shareholders. *Agency theorists* formulated the question as one of principal-agent contract, the principal being the owners or the shareholders and the agents being the managers.

Agency theorists argued that in almost all public corporations, the nature of the contract between the principal—shareholders—and the agent—managers—determined the degree to which managers will engage in self-serving behavior. There are two major mechanisms by which the agency problem is contained: (1) monitoring, and (2) bonding.

> *Monitoring* involves keeping track of the behavior of the managers. Financial accounting statements, board of directors, labor markets—all of these are mechanisms of monitoring the behavior of top level managers to ensure they serve the best interests of the shareholders.

> *Bonding* involves structuring the reward systems in such a way that managers' self-interests are aligned with those of the shareholders. Thus when managers act in their own self-interests, they automatically enhance the interests of the shareholders as well.

Agency theorists clearly recognized that managers typically have more information than the shareholders and that they need not act in the shareholders' best interests. To reduce this agency problem, they suggested that the information asymmetry between managers and the shareholders should be reduced through the design of (1) control mechanisms to monitor managers' behavior, and/or (2) rewards and incentive schemes to align managers' interests are with those of the owners.

Mechanisms of Control

Whereas the agency theorists referred to the problem of control at the very top levels of organization, others identified a similar problem in many diversified corporations: How does the top management of a corporation ensure that divisional managers can be made to behave in ways consistent with corporate level strategies?

In a multibusiness firm, it is difficult for top management to play the strategist in all the firm's diverse businesses. Often individual managers are expert at this.[7] Moreover, the bulk of the information required by top management to evaluate the strategies proposed by the firm's business managers is typically provided by the evaluees. This information asymmetry is a potential problem, unless the firms' administrative context encourages the open and full sharing of all business information across its managerial hierarchy.

Also, the multiple strategists in a diversified firm can disagree on the goals that should be pursued. For example, the relative emphasis that should be placed on short-term profitability versus long-term growth can be a bone of contention; or in a multinational corporation, the corporate need for global integration can be in conflict with the more parochial interests of country managers. Goal incongruence is another serious problem for top management in a multibusiness firm.

Although administrative context can be shaped by organization structure, control theorists focus on the process by which top managers seek to reduce information asymmetry and induce goal congruence. Figure 10.2

FIGURE 10.2

Elements of strategic control

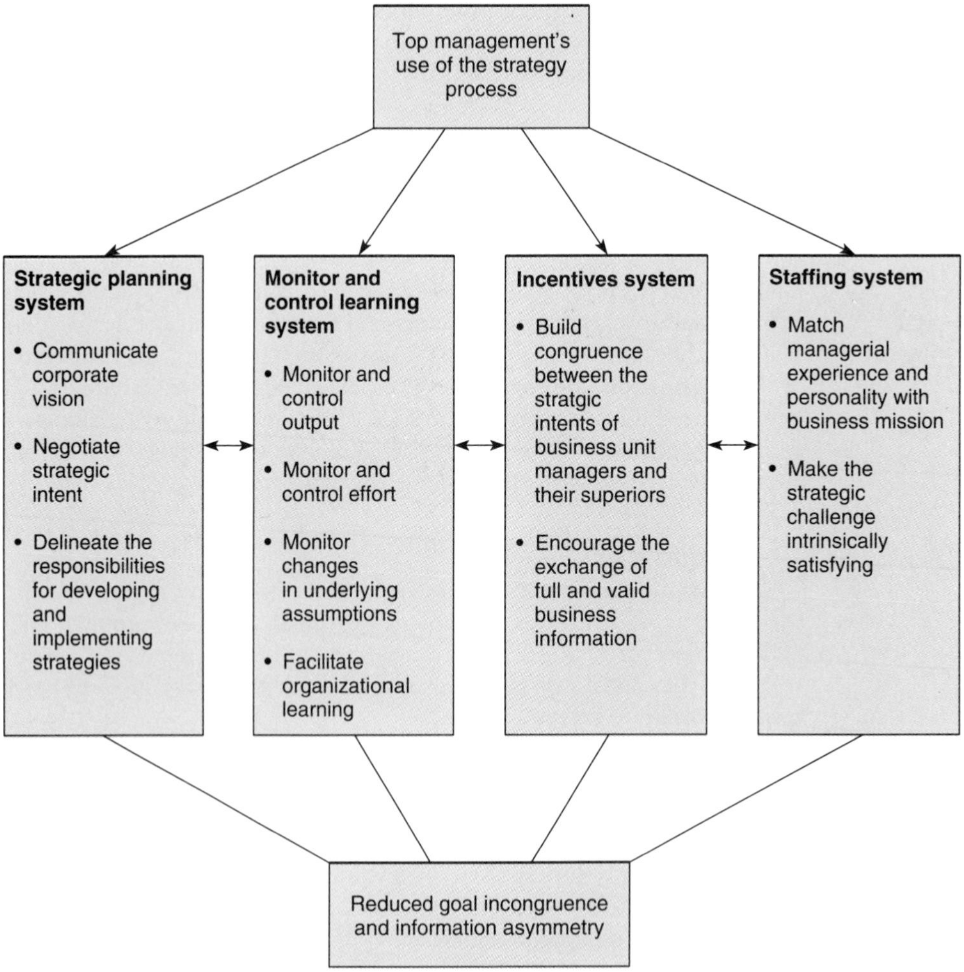

Source: Balaji S. Chakravarthy and Peter Lorange, *Managing the Strategy Process: A Framework for a Multibusiness Firm* (Englewood Cliffs, N. J.: Prentice Hall, 1991).

presents this model. As shown in the figure there are four major processes by which the control is achieved:

1. *Strategic planning system* attempts to negotiate a common understanding among firm's managers of the intended strategy for each of the firm's business, and to help delineate the manager's responsibilities in developing and implementing firm's intended strategies.

2. *Monitoring, control, and learning system* assists in monitoring the actual implementation of the chosen strategies and in sensitizing the firm to changes in the underlying assumptions behind these strategies. Thus these systems help to validate and implement the chosen strategies.

3. *Incentive system* attempts to encourage the exchange of full and valid information within the firm, aligning managers' incentives with strategic direction of the firm.

4. *Staffing system* seeks to reduce goal incongruence by staffing the firm with managers whose experience and personality are consistent with the intended strategies of the firm.

Thus top managers work to reduce the information asymmetry between divisional managers and themselves by designing planning and information systems, while at the same time trying to align the divisional goals with corporate goals through appropriate incentives and staffing.

Summary

In recent years, advances in information technology have brought about a revolution in information and control systems. Information serves several purposes: to inform, to control, and to plan; in recent years, information has been understood to yield competitive advantages. An information system has four major elements: sender, medium, message and receiver. Two major contingencies—environment and organization structure—drive the design of an information system. Organizational reward systems influence executive behavior. In modern organizations agency problem exists between (1) shareholders and top management, and (2) top managers and divisional managers. The agency problem at the second level is resolved by managing the control process through the design of planning systems, monitoring and controlling systems, incentive schemes and staffing.

Key Concepts

In this section we will summarize two major concepts to anchor the discussion of the key models of information and control systems. The two concepts are: (1) levels of information and control, and (2) formal versus informal systems.

Levels of Information and Control

The information and control systems in organizations serve different functions at different hierarchic levels of an organization. Broadly we may identify three levels: (1) operating level, (2) management level, and (3) strategic level.[8]

Operating Level

At the operating level, the role of the information and control system is to ensure that specific tasks are carried out effectively and efficiently. Control can be thought of as near-term blueprints for the activities in the firm—dealing with today's activities to achieve both near-term and long-term success of the firm.

Operating control resembles the process of negative feedback loop illustrated in our discussion of the systems model (refer to Figure 3.7). In practice, the primary component of operating control system is the design of an information system that enables the individuals to make operating decisions, as well as to detect and correct deviations from the plan when they occur.

Management Control

Management control is the process by which management ensures that its strategies are carried out effectively and efficiently. Thus it deals with how one implements strategies within the context of a strategic plan.

Management control differs from operational control in terms of the issues each addresses, the time frames, and the level of detail. Whereas operating control deals with day-to-day activities, management control deals with implementation in general. Thus management control may focus on assessing how the environment reacts to one's plans as they unfold by monitoring competitor or customer reactions in addition to seeing how well one is doing on such output measures as milestones, productivity, and so forth. Indeed control at this level inevitably is oriented toward longer time horizons than in the case of operating control.

Strategic Control

Control at this level deals primarily with setting basic strategic direction within the environmental contexts in which the firm finds itself. Often this implies heavy emphasis on understanding how critical environmental factors might impact an initial strategic direction. In such a case, strategic control deals with the follow-up of critical environmental assumptions and changes in these, thus sensitizing the organization to anticipate the discontinuities.

As shown in Figure 10.3, these three levels cannot be separated by sharp boundaries and each blends into the other. However, strategic control sets the guidelines for management control, and management control sets

FIGURE 10.3

Levels of information and control

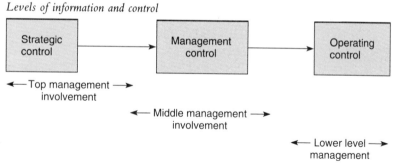

the guidelines for operational control. Top management typically gets involved in the design of strategic and management control systems whereas lower-level management is primarily involved in the design of information systems.

Formal versus Informal Control Process

The degree of formality in the control process may vary from highly formalized to highly informal. When the control is highly formalized, quantification is emphasized, data is collected routinely, and indeed there is greater reliance on information technology. When the control is informal, human channels are increasingly engaged, quantification is less emphasized and technology recedes to the background.

Formal systems are emphasized at the operational level. Since the goals are prespecified, and the activities should conform to plans, quantitative measurement is easy to develop. Management control, which tracks strategy implementation, incorporates both formal and informal processes. The third level, strategic control which involves reducing information asymmetry and goal incongruence, almost always focuses on informal processes.

Summary

Information and control systems are developed at three levels: operating, management and strategic levels. At the operating levels, information systems are designed to support day-to-day decision making as well as to measure activities against plan. At the management level, a combination of formal and informal systems are developed to monitor and control strategy implementation. Finally, at the strategic level, informal processes are designed to align goals and information to support the strategic direction.

We now turn to the action strategies that have been proposed by organization theorists to design information and control systems.

Action Strategies

Under Theoretical Underpinnings we identified four major uses and benefits of information; for (1) making operating decisions, (2) management control, (3) strategic control, as well as (4) as a source of competitive advantage. In this section we present the four action strategies that have been formulated by organization theorists to accomplish the various functions of information. The discussion that follows is summarized in Figure 10.4. We will discuss each one of the four strategies in turn.

Information System Design

What type of information should be provided for different types of operating activities? Organization theorists have struggled with this question over the years. Similar to other developments in organization theory, scholars have abandoned the search for universal solutions in favor of contingency approaches. According to contingency theorists, there are no universally applicable information system designs, but the design should ensure that characteristics of information (provided by an information system) are congruent with the demands of particular tasks. Recently, Richard Daft and Norman Macintosh[9] summarized this principle of congruence in their contingency model of an information system. Their model explicitly identifies the characteristics of both information and tasks so that congruence can be ensured.

FIGURE 10.4

Overview of action strategies

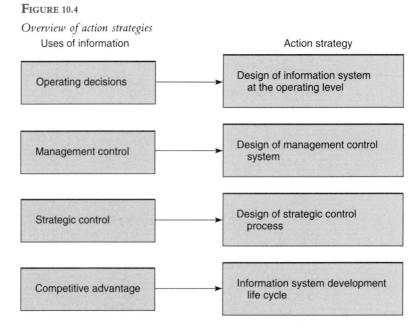

Uses of information	Action strategy
Operating decisions	Design of information system at the operating level
Management control	Design of management control system
Strategic control	Design of strategic control process
Competitive advantage	Information system development life cycle

Characteristics of Information

Two characteristics of information are important in the design of an information system: (1) amount and (2) richness.

Information amount refers to the volume of data about activities that is gathered and interpreted by organizational members. Amount of information is important because employees work under conditions of uncertainty. When things are uncertain, there is greater need for information transmission.

Information richness pertains to the information-carrying capacity of data. Some data are highly informative while other cues provide limited understanding. Different media have different carrying capacity. Face-to-face communication is the richest medium because it conveys several information cues simultaneously—spoken message, body language, and facial expression. By contrast, written reports are lean, because they can communicate limited information.

Characteristics of Tasks

Similar to information, various tasks performed in an organization can also be captured by two dimensions: (1) variety and (2) analyzability.

Variety. Task variety refers to the frequency of unexpected and novel events that occur during the performance of the task. When an individual encounters a large number of unexpected situations, with frequent problems, variety is considered to be high. When there are few problems and when day-to-day job requirements are repetitious, tasks contain little variety.

Analyzability. When a task is analyzable, work can be reduced to mechanical steps, and participants can follow an objective computational procedure to solve problems. Problem solution may involve the use of standard procedures such as instructions and manuals, or technical knowledge such as in a textbook or handbook. For other problems, there is no store of techniques or procedures to tell a person exactly what to do; so employees rely on experience, intuition, and judgment.

Principle of Congruence

The principle of congruence is operationalized by mapping information amount into task variety and information richness into task analyzability. This is presented schematically in Figure 10.5. The figure identifies the two relationships that determine information requirements based upon the type of task performed by a department:

1. When the task variety is high, problems are frequent and unpredictable. So the amount of information required is greater. When variety is low, the amount of information processed is low.

For example, the many problems associated with basic research require vastly greater amounts of information than do routine technical and drafting activities.

2. When tasks are not analyzable, employees need rich information. Face-to-face discussions and telephone conversations transmit multiple information cues in a short time. When the tasks are analyzable, managers use lean media. For example finance work tends to be more routine and better understood than general management, where many problems are unique and hard to analyze.[10]

The implications of the framework are presented in Figure 10.5. *Routine activities* have only a few problems and these are well understood. They require small amounts of clear information. *Engineering* tasks have high variety, which increase the demand for information; they require lean but large information. *Craft* departments require a different form of information. Here task variety is not high, but the problems are not easily analyzable. The managers need rich information. For example, in a psychiatric care unit, when the process of therapeutic change is not well understood, therapists, discuss things face-to-face among themselves to reach a solution. Finally, *nonroutine* departments, such as strategic planning units or basic research departments, require large amounts of rich information; managers spend a lot of time in both scheduled and unscheduled meetings.

FIGURE 10.5

Design of information system

INFORMATION AMOUNT = Task variety	Task analyzability: Low	Task analyzability: High
High	NONROUTINE Frequent face-to-face meetings; group meetings Unscheduled meetings MIS, DSS support	ENGINEERING Large computer bases Written and technical materials Frequent statistical reports MIS support
Low	CRAFT Personal observation Occasional face-to-face; group meetings Telephone	ROUTINE Written reports Rules and procedures Some statistical data MIS support

Task analyzability = INFORMATION RICHNESS

Source: Richard L. Daft, *Organization Theory and Design* (St. Paul, Minn.: West Publishing, 1989), p. 315.

The Daft and Macintosh model assumes that tasks are already defined, that is, an appropriate organization structure is already in place. This assumption, and hence the model, is most applicable to lower levels of organization where tasks are already determined, and the information system designers have only to ensure that appropriate information is provided to individuals for the performance of their respective tasks.

Process of Design

Consistent with the rational strategies of management, the process of design involves four key steps:

1. Identify the key tasks dictated by the organization structure.
2. Identify the characteristics of the tasks.
3. Identify the characteristics of information that are congruent with the characteristics of the tasks.
4. Design the appropriate information system.

These steps are summarized in Figure 10.6. Box 10.2 presents the story of Ingersoll Milling Machine Co., which achieved congruence between the information system and the key tasks—engineering design and drafting—embedded in its organization structure. The company utilized computer technology to provide large amounts of precise, quantitative information for its key tasks which, according to Daft and Macintosh, can be labeled "engineering." The company thus became efficient and outperformed its competitors.

Management Control Strategies

Managers can adopt one of three control strategies to ensure the proper implementation of strategies: (1) market control, (2) bureaucratic control, and (3) clan control.[11]

FIGURE 10.6

Information system: Process of design

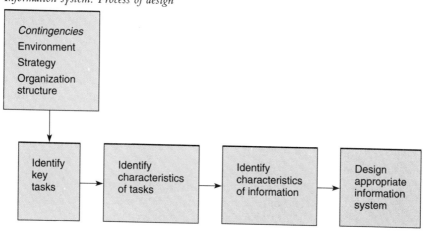

Box 10.2

Ingersoll Milling Machine Co.

Ingersoll Milling Machine Co. is an extraordinarily successful machine tool builder. Ingersoll builds some of the most sophisticated production lines in the world, including highly computerized systems for GE and Ford, and makes large-scale custom machines and machining systems for special applications, such as a $50 million system for computer-controlled auto assembly recently ordered by General Motors.

Ingersoll was first in the industry to use computers; it got rid of drafting tables and everything else that could be computerized. Designers draw blueprints on computer screens rather than on drafting tables. Programmers write instructions to accompany a blueprint, and the computer generates a tape with those instructions. The tape is used to control machinery that shapes the metal to build the machine.

Everyone at Ingersoll speaks the same computer language. All three U.S. divisions are linked to a common computer database. Every department—accounting, engineering, shipping, purchasing—in each division exchanges design, product, and financial information. When an engineer designs a cutting tool, the computer generates a list of materials needed, which goes to purchasing.

The next step was to computerize Ingersoll's tool sales force. Salespeople will use briefcase terminals to call in specifications from the field. The central computer will then instruct the machinery to turn out an order.

Ingersoll's computer technology is so sophisticated that other machine tool builders are barely able to compete. Boeing and other aerospace companies prefer Ingersoll because the company is efficient and accurate. The specialty orders that carry big profits come Ingersoll's way.

The key tasks in Ingersoll were engineering design and drafting—tasks which can be labeled "engineering", according to the terminology of Daft and Macintosh. These tasks are high in terms of the amount of information and low in terms of information richness; i.e., they require large amounts of analyzable information. Ingersoll's huge but highly quantified information system is perfectly tailored to the very complicated yet analyzable task of designing sophisticated machine tool systems.

Source: Adapted from Michael McFadden, "The Master Builder of Mammoth Tools," *Fortune*, September 3, 1986.

Market Control

The concept of market control was discovered by economists. It is used when price competition is employed to evaluate the output and productivity of an organization. A dollar price is an efficient form of control because managers can compare prices and profits to evaluate the efficiency of their corporation. Several conditions have to be met for the use of market control:

1. The outputs must be sufficiently explicit, competition should exist, and we must be able to assign a price. Without competition, we will not be able to assign an accurate price.

2. Market control can be exercised at the level of a whole organization or a self-contained unit within it—for example, a division within a diversified corporation. Profit centers commonly employ market control.

Thus, typically, market control cannot be used in a functional department, such as strategic planning since the outputs are often intangible and competitive bidding will tend to be very expensive. An organization has no way of assigning a price or of comparing the services of such a department with those in the marketplace. On the other hand, a division within a diversified corporation, or to some extent, a self-contained product division within a single industry firm, can employ market control successfully.

Bureaucratic Control

Bureaucratic control is the use of rules, policies, hierarchy of authority, written documentation, standardization, and other bureaucratic mechanisms to standardize behavior and assess behavior. Indeed, this form of control is used virtually in all organizations. These mechanisms are particularly useful in not-for-profit organizations where prices and competitive markets do not exist. However, these mechanisms—as we have discussed in our chapter on organization structure—are useful when the environments are stable and predictable.

Clan Control

This form of control employs values, commitment, traditions, and shared beliefs to control behavior. This mechanism requires trust and sharing among employees, and is appropriate when ambiguity and uncertainty are high—conditions under which market and bureaucratic mechanisms fail. In several departments, e.g. strategic planning and research and development, uncertainty is high and clan control is the only mechanism of control. Despite the absence of written rules and regulations, clan control is invisible but powerful.

Table 10.2 summarizes the requirements of each control mechanism. As shown in the table, when the outputs of a unit can be priced and there is competition, market control is appropriate. When the output is not tangible or when there is no market, other forms of control are necessary. Bureaucratic control is used when the environment is relatively certain and clan control is appropriate when environment is uncertain. Organizations, in reality may employ these mechanisms in combination.

Process of Design

The design process for management control takes place in two steps.

1. In the first step, the general form of control—whether to use market, bureaucratic or clan control is determined. This step is

TABLE 10.2   **Management Control Strategies**

Type of Control	Requirements
Market	Prices
	Competition
Bureaucracy	Rules
	Standards
	Hierarchy
	Legitimate authority
Clan	Tradition
	Shared values
	Shared beliefs
	Trust

Source: William G. Ouchi, "A Conceptual Framework for the Design of Organizational Control Mechanism," *Management Science* 25 (1979), pp. 833–48.

accomplished by identifying the crucial contingency—environment—and determining the characteristics of environment.

2. In the second, the specific form of control is determined, contingent upon the strategy and the structure of the organization.

In Figure 10.7 we have summarized this process.

In Box 10.3 we have described how the installation of a bureaucratic control system in a business school led to heavy turnover of top talent. As can be seen from the example, the business school was an institution reputed to be a research leader, and its environment was characterized by high uncertainty. The specific bureaucratic mechanisms were inappropriate for this environment. Indeed the clan mechanisms that had been in place—self-

FIGURE 10.7

Management control: Process of design

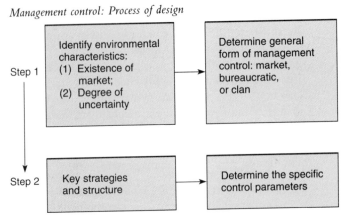

Box 10.3

The Case of the New Dean

Baldridge School of Business was a nationally prominent graduate school of business, situated in the midwestern United States. Many of the faculty members were world renowned for their state-of-the-art research work, and were sought after by many large firms the world over for their advice.

There was intense pressure in the school among faculty members; many of them were prima donnas in their field. However, the faculty members had a high degree of autonomy—they chose their work hours, determined the curriculum and in general had a lot of voice in the running of the school. They even ran the classes according to how they thought fit. The graduate students, however, were very satisfied, since they were greatly in demand—the reputation of the faculty ensured that businesses sought after their students.

Upon retirement of the school's dean, the board of regents appointed someone from outside to head up the school. When the new dean arrived, he was upset by the behavior of the faculty. Few paid him any respect, and some did not even show up when he called a meeting. They let him know that since they would be away on business or research, they could not attend the meeting. He thought that the school was in total anarchy.

One of his first acts as the new dean was to send a memo instructing the faculty that they were expected to be in their offices by 8:30 in the morning, and that they should be available until 5:00 P.M. for meetings upon demand, except when they had to attend classes. It was also made known, that absence from classes—for whatever reasons—would not be tolerated. Also he instituted strict rules for business and research travel.

Many faculty revolted at what they considered to be a totalitarian leader. They pointed out that the system monitored itself, that the entire business school prided itself in being a world class institution and that such meddling was unhealthy. Since the new dean did not budge, senior faculty—especially the superstars—started looking for jobs elsewhere. Over a period of five years, many of them left. Some years later, a business periodical ranking showed that the school had lost its preeminent place among academic institutions.

Source: This is a disguised case developed from the personal experience of the authors. All names are withheld to protect the anonymity of the individuals.

---

monitoring and the intense pressure for recognition and achievement—would have been more appropriate for this situation.

Strategic Process Control

At the strategic level, the focus shifts to designing a process to control the strategic thrusts of an organization. Bala Chakravarthy and Peter Lorange provide us with the most comprehensive model by which these processes can be orchestrated. They primarily address the problem of how to design a strategic control system that top managers in a multibusiness firm can employ when they deal with their individual divisions. Chakravarthy and Lorange argue that the strategic process control should be tailored to the corporate strategy of a multibusiness firm. We will describe their model in some detail;[12] it has three major anchors: (1) elements of strategic control process; (2) a classification of corporate strategies or strategic thrusts; and (3) principle of congruence.

Elements of Strategic Control Process

As we have seen under Theoretical Underpinnings, this design embraces four major elements. Chakravarthy and Lorange spell out their characteristics:

1. *A planning system:* whether it fosters responsiveness to environment or encourages efficiency. If responsiveness is to be encouraged, there is wide participation and the budget discipline is not emphasized whereas when efficiency is to be encouraged, the decision making is to be top down and budgets are tightly controlled.

2. *Monitoring, control, and learning system:* the frequency of monitoring and the degree to which it encourages learning.

3. *Incentive system:* whether it emphasizes short-term or long-term results. When short term is emphasized, incentives are tailored to operating results, and when long-term is important, incentives are tailored to accomplishment of strategic targets.

4. *Staffing system:* Different kinds of leadership styles and experience are important for the strategic control process.

The reader may want to refer back to Figure 10.2 where we have provided detailed descriptions of these elements.

Classification of Corporate Strategies

Chakravarthy and Lorange identify four different corporate strategies: pioneer, expand, dominate, and reorient.

Pioneer: Here the primary planning challenge is for the business unit manager to carve a niche in which the unit can thrive despite its limited resources, i.e. *pioneer.* This is the situation in high growth markets when the firm has low market share. This is a most risky situation, since pioneers typically face an uncertain environment and have limited resources to operate.

Expand: Businesses that try to expand typically have a relatively large amount of resources, although they will face complex environments. Typically "stars" (high growth markets with leading market share) face this kind of situation. They face a less risky situation, since the business unit manager should have no difficulty in identifying a viable niche because the business has many resources.

Reorient: Businesses that try to reorient need to refocus their resources. In other words, the managers should reconfigure the unit's competencies, strengthening those that are relevant to the more focused strategy. This context is only moderately risky, and the challenge is to participate in only the more simple subsegments of its industry niche.

Dominate: Only businesses such as "cash cows" (low growth markets and leading market share firms) which have lots of resources can adopt this strategy. The primary task of the manager in this context is to exploit opportunities so that the business unit dominates the chosen niche by growing aggressively and profitably. This is the least risky of all the contexts.

According to strategic control theorists, these strategies form the basis for designing the control process.

Principle of Congruence

The principle of congruence states that strategic process control should match the strategic thrust of the corporation. To operationalize this, Chakravarthy and Lorange provide descriptions of the control process suited for each strategic thrust.

Pioneer: In this context, the planning system should emphasize adaptation to environment to assist the business unit to discover and consolidate new niches in its chosen environment. A formal monitoring may not be cost effective, and top management may have to rely instead on the shared perceptions of managers based on their day to day contacts with their stakeholders. The incentives should be based on the quality of pioneering effort. Performance against budget and contributions of managers toward ensuring the relevance of the strategy are important criteria for determining incentives. Managers with marketing and research and development experience, and with charismatic leadership qualities, are most suited for this context.

Expand: Here, the planning system should emphasize both adaptation and efficiency, whereas the control system should emphasize contingency planning; the expectation is for the business manager to make appropriate adjustments to the plan during implementation. Unlike the previous context, in measuring performance, there is greater reliance on meeting predetermined profit targets. Finally, general management experience is important in the choice of the manager and the need is for someone with administrative capabilities more than for visionary leadership.

Reorient: In this setting, the planning system may emphasize either an efficiency focus if the business unit is targeted for divestment, or an adaptive focus if it tries to reposition itself in its markets. Its competitive position must be monitored frequently, and a prudent approach to control is for the top management to negotiate in *advance* performance thresholds with the business unit manager thresholds below which reorientation is unlikely and divestment should be seriously considered. Turnaround artists with general management experience are most qualified for this kind of situation.

Dominate: Here the planning system should emphasize efficiency, and top-down management. The budgets and variances from the budgets are sufficient to monitor implementation. Performance against budget becomes the basis of incentives. Finally, individuals with operations and financial experience and administrative skills are appropriate for this situation.

Chakravarthy and Lorange's prescriptions are summarized in Table 10.3.

The process of designing strategic control is sketched in Figure 10.8. Box 10.4 describes the transformation in information and control systems at ITT over the several years. As illustrated in the box, when ITT changed its strategy from growth through acquisitions under Geneen to one of focused diversification under Hamilton and Araskog, the organization was restructured and its planning and control systems had to be modified.

TABLE 10.3   **Chakravarthy and Lorange Model**

	Type of Context			
	Pioneer	*Expand*	*Reorient*	*Dominate*
A. *Planning system*				
1. Focus	Adaptation	Adaptation & efficiency	Selective adaption	Efficiency
2. Decision making	Participative	Mix of top-down & participative	Somewhat participative	Mostly top-down
3. Linkage between plan and budgets	Loose	Less loose	Loose & tight	Tight
B. *Control system* Frequency of monitoring				
1. Environment	Frequently	Frequently	Periodically	Periodically
2. Competitive position	Frequently	Periodically	Frequently	Periodically
C. *Incentive system* Bases of incentives	Strategies	Strategy and operations	Strategy & operations	Operations
D. *Staffing system*				
1. Experience	Marketing; R&D	General management	General management	Operations; finance
2. Leadership style	Charismatic	Administrator	Turnaround expert	Administrator

Adapted from: Balaji S. Chakravarthy and Peter Lorange, *Managing the Strategy Process: A Framework for a Multibusiness Firm* (Englewood Cliffs, N.J.: Prentice Hall 1991).

FIGURE 10.8

Process of designing strategic control process

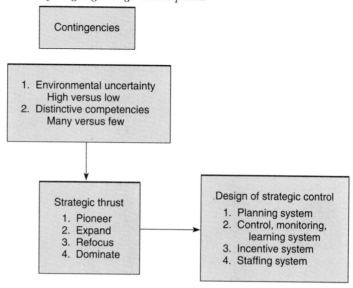

Information System Development Life Cycle

As we illustrated in the chapter introduction case, technological advances have transformed our ways of thinking about information technology. Information is nowadays viewed as a resource, and both business executives and organization theorists now agree that an information system could be a source of competitive advantage. As a result many organizations have on-going information system development efforts. Although almost all efforts require some degree of technology development, they closely resemble organizational change activities.

Are there predictable stages in the successful development of information systems? This question has fascinated several information system theorists. Over the years, they have identified a nine step methodology for information system development. These stages are:

1. *Preliminary proposal.* This stage represents a proposal which suggests a potential business opportunity via information systems. Such an opportunity could be faster invoicing, better inventory control, or faster and more accurate tracking as in the case of Federal Express.

2. *Cost-benefit study.* This stage includes an analysis of gains achievable by the proposed system as well as the development costs.

Box 10.4

The Transformation at ITT

Spanning the last several decades, ITT has witnessed a major transformation from the centralized planning style of Hal Geneen to a more decentralized style by his successors, first Lyman Hamilton and later Rand Araskog.

The Geneen era. When Hal Geneen took over as the chairman of ITT, nearly all of company's operations were abroad. To counteract potential threats abroad, he undertook to develop the United States operations of ITT. He started in 1960 with the acquisition of Aetna Finance Corporation. In 1965 alone, he acquired Avis, followed by Sheraton, Levitt, Canteen, Continental Baking, and Hartford Fire Insurance. During this era ITT acquired over 275 firms.

A challenging task for Geneen was to assimilate the acquired companies into the corporate fold, helping them to make the transition from being a subsidiary into being an integrated division of ITT. He delegated the responsibility for managing ITT's diverse businesses, numbering over 200, to the business unit managers, organized into product groups which were in turn organized into two sectors: Manufacturing, and Consumer and Business Services. He managed the implementation process through a number of information and control mechanisms.

Geneen established a very detailed central planning and control system to manage ITT's portfolio. The business plan was the primary standard for evaluating the performance of business unit managers. Every business unit had to submit periodic reports according to a fixed calendar. The reporting system was the same for all units, and identical forms and charts of accounts were used by all units regardless of their size. An important feature of the system was the monthly meeting, where the business unit managers were scrutinized in detail regarding their operations. For those who could respond to his stringent demands, Geneen supplied top pay, sizable bonuses tied directly to performance, and plenty of excitement. It was expected that some would not stand the pressure and would leave, but the high turnover did not hurt ITT. Talented managers were hired as replacements or came with the acquisitions. Geneen had a strong orientation for short term results. He also stressed the importance of the proper use of numbers.

The financial performance of ITT under Geneen was matched by very few companies of his era.

Hamilton era. When Geneen stepped down in 1977, Lyman Hamilton assumed the post of CEO in January, 1978. He began to divest

3. *Analysis of the existing system.* This stage involves the study and evaluation of current procedures and requirements.

4. *Design of the new system.* In this stage, detailed plans of the proposed system's functioning (with outputs and database) are developed.

5. *Computer programming.* In this stage, the new computer programs—that the system will comprise—are coded.

6. *Testing.* The computer programs and the database are tested for their correctness in this stage.

Box 10.4 continued

weak subsidiaries and attempted to build more profitable ones. Hamilton saw his role as that of a 'fine-tuner' and a consolidator. He reorganized ITT's nearly 1,000 product lines into 5 fairly homogenous business groups. He also restructured management meetings, cutting monthly meetings from three days to one, renamed them Corporate Management Meetings and reduced the number of people required to attend. Unlike his predecessor he was genuinely friendly, although few knew him well since he never got intimate with people. On July 11, 1979, he was asked to resign and Rand Araskog became the CEO.

Araskog era. Araskog followed Hamilton's strategy and refined it further with his own initiatives. He felt that ITT's environment had changed since the Geneen era as exemplified by high interest rates. Continuing the divestiture, Araskog sold off 63 companies, and in 1983 reorganized the five business groups that Hamilton had instituted into four management corporations, in order to take account of either market or technological synergies.

The business unit managers had to ensure in their plans that there was a proper balance between long-term and short-term performance and that R&D spending was justified. Araskog modified Geneen's emphasis on short-term results giving projects time to prove themselves. Disruptions in profits were

tolerated when necessary. He sought to delegate more authority to the business units and to instill an entrepreneurial spirit in the organization by returning the decision making power to line managers and to the heads of large European subsidiaries. His attempt to move ITT from an exclusively top-down, centralized organization to a more decentralized entity resulted in tensions between the old top-down planning system and the new bottom-up process.

The decentralization did not, however, affect ITT's unique financial control organization. The controller of each business group still reported to both the President of the group and the corporate Controller.

Under Geneen, when ITT undertook diversification, he ran a tightly controlled planning system, with frequent meetings, based his incentives on current performance, and selected general managers oriented to short-term performance. As ITT moved to consolidate, Hamilton and then Araskog, began to redesign first the structure, but later the planning system, and incentives. As we leave ITT, the transformation is incomplete, since the question of control systems and staffing patterns are still being formulated.

Source: Adapted from Balaji Chakravarthy, "The ITT Corporation," The Carlson School of Management, University of Minnesota, 1986.

7. *Cut-over.* This seventh stage accomplishes conversion from existing procedures and methods to those of the new system.

8. *Maintenance.* Maintenance, which is an ongoing activity, is needed to modify the new system to correct errors and add necessary new features.

9. *Audit.* In this stage the actual achievements of the new system are compared to the original objectives for corrective action.[13]

Whereas information system theorists focused on the technical elements, organization theorists have argued that effective development of information systems requires the alignment of technical and human (social, political, and cultural) elements. When managers don't focus on the alignment, troubles are likely to develop. An example of such problems is presented in Box 10.5. As can be seen from the example, when the design of the new system did not take into account organizational human factors (in this case the user's needs), it was doomed to failure. Indeed effective system development requires paying attention to both technical and human factors. And effective system development is a definite source of competitive advantage, as illustrated in the chapter introduction case.

Summary

At the operating level, information should be provided to meet the characteristics of the tasks performed by an individual: information richness

---

Box 10.5

Information Systems Development

A firm neared the completion of development of a huge, new computer-based information system which was to retrieve data from its large database via computer terminals on the desks of its employees. When these employees first began to test the system, the developer discovered that the response time (that is, the delay between typing a command and receiving a reply) for simple queries was several minutes—much too long for the workers. The computer technicians attributed the problem to "database design" errors and made many efforts to reduce the response time. Ultimately they gave up. Several hundred thousand dollars had been sunk into the project and were lost. A cursory examination of the events suggested that a technical failure had taken place.

However, a closer examination revealed something different. Months earlier, the computer technicians had attempted to learn about the user's application in great detail. However, they had failed. Perhaps the users had not been sufficiently committed to the new system and had not provided enough time to make clear

explanations. Perhaps the computer technicians had conflicting priorities and had not given sufficient effort. Regardless of the party at fault, the communication between the two groups had been egregious.

Hence, when the computer experts organized the user's data into databases on computer disks they did so erroneously, because they did not understand the user's applications, and did not know how the users would eventually access the data. As the technicians began to test the system, they learned more about the application. At that time, they rearranged the data repeatedly to more appropriately fit the user's needs. The slow response time, apparently due to the convoluted arrangement and repeated rearrangement of data, was in fact due to the initial communication failure between computer technicians and users.

Source: Albert L. Lederer and Raghu Nath, "Making Strategic Information Systems Happen," *Academy of Management Executive* 4, no. 3 (1990), pp. 76–83.

should match analyzability of tasks, and information amount should match task variety. Broadly, a management control system could be based on three mechanisms: market, bureaucratic, or clan. At the strategic level, the task is to match the four elements of the control system—planning, monitoring, control, and learning; incentive and staffing systems—to two major characteristics of the business unit, i.e., complexity of the environment and the distinctive competencies of the firm. Recently, a team of information and organization theorists have proposed a socio-technical approach to the nine-step methodology for developing effective information systems.

A Systems Theoretic Review

As we have seen, information and control embrace the informational subsystem of the systems model. The rational approaches to the design of information and control assume that strategy and organization structure are already in place; hence the purpose of information and control is to ensure that appropriate information is provided to individuals for performance of their tasks according to the demands of the organization structure or to make sure that information asymmetry and goal incongruence between top and middle management are reduced. Since strategic control subsumes incentives and staffing, it becomes vital to the implementation process.

There are three limitations to the above approaches:

1. They do not account for their impact on and the influence of social and political subsystems within organizations. When we discussed strategic planning, we described the case of Corning Glass Works, and in our treatment of organization structure we focused on the example of matrix implementation in one organization. The limitations described in those chapters, which are generic to all rational approaches, are equally applicable to information and control systems as well.

2. The manner in which the information and control system is utilized may generate unintended consequences. For example, if stringent controls are developed—as in the case of ITT under Geneen—it may stifle creativity, result in executive burnouts, and in some instances—as in the case of ITT—may induce employees toward unethical behaviors.

3. Developments in information technology have made possible designs of leaner organization structures, whereby an information subsystem may be used to bring about changes in the functional subsystem, and even in organizational strategies. This possibility is still not fully developed in current treatments of information and control systems.

As we have demonstrated, to a large extent information and control systems drive the actual behavior of individuals in an organization. The systems should, therefore, be clearly linked to organizational strategies and structures. Also they are one important means by which organizations are alerted in response to changes in their environments. They thus aid an organization's adaptation to its environments.

Chapter Summary

In many ways, information is the life-blood of an organization. Managers at all levels—low, middle, and top levels—deal primarily with information. We need information to make decisions, and to control the operations. Indeed even the diagnosis of an organization requires information. Over the years, we have seen a lot of development in information technology and its applications in organizations. Most developments have enabled processing and dissemination of information faster than before.

Information has several uses. It is necessary for (1) day-to-day decision making, (2) controlling operations of an organization, and (3) strategic planning. Recently, as a result of developments in information technology, many organizations are discovering that the information system is a source of competitive advantage. Both organization structure and environment drive the characteristics of an information system. All organizations employ internal financial information. Organically structured organizations in dynamic environments use, in addition, qualitative, external and ex ante information.

Control is necessary for correcting deviations, and also to ensure that managers act in the best interests of the shareholders. There are two major mechanisms of control: monitoring and bonding. In reality, top level managers use four mechanisms: planning systems, control systems, incentive schemes, and staffing to control the operations of divisional and middle managers.

Information and control systems take different forms at three different levels: operating, management control, and strategic. At the operating level, an information system should be designed to match the characteristic of the tasks. In the case of routine tasks, systems such as computer based MIS are useful; whereas in the case of nonroutine tasks, frequent face-to-face meetings and group meetings are needed.

There are three management control strategies: market, bureaucratic, and clan control. Market control is useful when there is competition and when price data is available. Bureaucratic control is useful when the environments are certain and stable. Clan control is necessary when the environments are uncertain and dynamic.

Strategic control is needed to reduce the information asymmetry and goal incongruence between top level managers and their subordinates, especially those who head up various divisions. The key factors that determine the strategic control system are complexity of environment (simple versus complex) and the nature of distinctive competencies of the firm (many versus few).

Information and control systems ensure the implementation of strategies and hence are an important step in the rational strategies of management. When properly designed, they alert an organization to changes in the environment.

Specialized Terms

Uses of information
Elements of information system
  • Sender
  • Medium
  • Receiver
  • Message
Agency problem
  • Monitoring
  • Bonding
Mechanisms of control
  • Planning system
  • Monitoring, control, and
     learning system
  • Incentive system
  • Staffing system
Goal incongruence
Information asymmetry
Levels of information and control

  • Operating level
  • Management control
  • Strategic control
Formal versus informal control
  process
Characteristics of tasks
  • Analyzability
  • Variety
Characteristics of information
  • Richness
  • Amount
Market control
Bureaucratic control
Clan control
Complexity of environment
Distinctive competencies
Systems development

Discussion Questions

Theoretical

1. What is the role of organizational information and control systems in rational action strategies?

2. Sketch the major milestones in the evolution of information system technology. What do the terms—"prototype approach" and "end-user involvement" mean?

3. What are the uses of information? List the elements of an information system?

4. What are the factors that drive an information system?

5. How do reward systems control behavior?

6. Sketch the major arguments of agency theorists. What do they imply for the management of contemporary organizations?

7. Discuss the Chakravarthy and Lorange model. How is it linked to agency arguments?

8. Outline a process for designing (1) an information system, (2) a management control system, (3) a strategic control system.

★9. Distinguish between operating, management, and strategic control systems.

Applied

1. You have been invited to design an information system for the manufacturing manager of Xenon Corporation. Xenon is a publicly traded corporation that operates in a low growth stable industry, where attention to cost control is important. The manufacturing plant employs an assembly line technology. What would be the general recommendations you will make?

2. You have been invited by the Board of Directors of Xenon for a business lunch. The main agenda is to help them devise a control system for its chief executive officer. You know that Xenon has widely dispersed ownership and that the board is mostly composed of outsiders, who also have numerous other responsibilities. What would you advise the board?

End Notes

1. Norman Weizer, *The Arthur D. Little Forecast on Information Technology and Productivity* (New York: John Wiley & Sons, 1991), pp. xv–xvi.

2. F. Edelman, "The Management of Information Resources: A Challenge for American Business," *MIS Quarterly* 5, no. 1 (March 1981), pp. 17–27.

3. See R. P. Bostrom and J. S. Heinen, "MIS Problems and Failures: A Socio-Technical Perspective. Part I: The Causes," *MIS Quarterly* 1, no. 3 (September 1977), pp. 17–32; R. P Bostrom and J. S. Heinen, "MIS Problems and Failures: A Socio-Technical Perspective. Part II: The Application of Socio-Technical Theory," *MIS Quarterly* 1, no. 4 (December 1977), pp. 11–28.

4. R. L. Ackoff, "Management Misinformation Systems," *Management Science* 14, no. 4 (December 1967), pp. B147–B156.

★This is an advanced-level question.

5. C. Argyris, "Management Information Systems: The Challenge to Rationality and Emotionality," *Management Science* 17, no. 6 (February 1971), pp. B275–B292.

6. J. Waterhouse and P. Tiessen, "A Contingency Framework for Management Accounting Systems Research," *Accounting, Organizations and Society,* 1978, pp. 65–76.

7. This section is drawn from the insightful work by Balaji S. Chakravarthy and Peter Lorange, *Managing the Strategy Process: A Framework for a Multibusiness Firm* (Englewood Cliffs, N.J.: Prentice Hall, 1991).

8. This section is based on the ideas developed by Robert N. Anthony, *Planning and Control Systems: A Framework for Analysis* (Boston: Division of Research, Graduate School of Business Administration, Harvard University, 1965).

9. Richard L. Daft and Norman B. Macintosh, "A New Approach to Design and Use of Management Information," *California Management Review* 21 (1978) pp. 89–92.

10. Richard L. Daft, *Organization Theory and Design* (St. Paul, Minn.: West Publishing, 1989), p. 314.

11. William G. Ouchi, "A Conceptual Framework for the Design of Organizational Control Mechanism," *Management Science* 25 (1979), pp. 833–48.

12. Chakravarthy and Lorange, *Managing the Strategy Process.*

13. Albert L. Lederer and Raghu Nath, "Making Strategic Information Systems Happen," *Academy of Management Executive* 4, no.3 (1990), pp. 76–83.

11 ORGANIZATION DEVELOPMENT

Chapter Outline

Metal Containers Inc., a medium-sized company situated in the midwestern United States, was experiencing numerous customer complaints, delayed shipments, and subsequent canceled orders at a time when it was also faced with some aggressive competitors. The president of the company called in a reputed organization development (OD) consultant to help him resolve the problems underlying the situation. The consultant interviewed several individuals, both at the head office as well as in the field. These interviews led him to diagnose the problem as follows. The company was organized functionally which was appropriate for its size and markets, but its manufacturing plant and regional sales district were locked in an intergroup conflict that caused problems in customer relations. The plant perceived sales as concerned only about volume and pleasing the customer, not about the plant's costs. The district sales manager and his salespeople saw the plant as unresponsive to customers, conservative, and overly concerned about costs and long manufacturing runs. As a consequence of the intergroup conflict, the quality of decision making had deteriorated: the functional departments focused their energies on blaming each other rather than on customer satisfaction or cost control.

The OD consultant met with the plant manager and district sales manager to determine their interest in working to improve relations. They both agreed to an intergroup laboratory as a means of improving integration. The plant manager and his staff, and the district sales manager and his salespeople, came together at a motel for two days to work on the problems in their relationship. Each group met separately to develop a list of what bothered them about the other group and what they thought the other group was writing about them. Later, they presented to each other their separate lists. Each group was surprised by what the other group said. As a result of a successful perception exchange, a number of factors that were triggering poor relations and coordination surfaced. During the second day, subgroups composed of plant and salespeople developed action plans for solving these problems. For example, the plant manager and district sales manager agreed to visit customers to determine why erratic demands were being made and what to do about them. Over the next year, relationships and coordination improved and there were more frequent meetings between the two groups to solve problems. Coordination between the groups had improved, and with it the quality of decision making. Customer complaints also became less frequent.[1]

How should an organization improve the communication and cooperation among departments, groups, and individuals? How can it ensure that high-quality decisions are made regularly? How can it manage the coordination problems that inevitably crop up during day-to-day activities so that it can be responsive to its customers, suppliers, and in general its stakeholders? As the chapter introduction case illustrates, many organizations employ consultants to help them answer these questions. Many of these consultants are practitioners of organization development (OD).

As a subfield within management, organization development has shown considerable growth during the past 20 years, and it has attracted a large following of practitioners and clients, scholars and students. Thus, many organizations have ongoing organization development efforts, and some have institutionalized such efforts. There is an increasingly broad knowledge base built around OD as seen in the proliferation of textbooks, papers, and articles published in the area. A number of respectable universities offer programs in organization development. In short, organization development has been accepted as a major change strategy by organizations and scholars. Let us first define OD and distinguish it from other approaches.

What Is Organization Development (OD)?

If we adhere to the commonly accepted meaning of the term *organization development,* it refers to almost all actions that improve an organization's functioning. However, in management literature, organization development refers to a specific change strategy with unique characteristics. Hence, our use of the term *OD* here should not be confused with the commonly accepted meaning of the term. To dispel the potential confusion, we need to answer several questions. What is OD? What is not OD? What characteristics differentiate OD from other change programs?

Definition

Scholars and practitioners of OD have offered various definitions of organization development. To quote a few:

> Organization development (OD) is a response to change, a complex educational strategy intended to change the beliefs, attitudes, values, and structure of organizations so that they can better adapt to new technologies, markets, and challenges and the dizzying rate of change itself.[2]

> Organization development is an effort (1) planned, (2) organizationwide, and (3) managed from the top, to (4) increase organizational effectiveness and health through (5) planned interventions in the organization's "processes" using behavioral science knowledge.[3]

> Organization development is the strengthening of those human processes in organizations that improve the functioning of the organic system so as to achieve its objectives.[4]

> Organization development is a long-range effort to improve an organization's problem-solving and renewal processes, particularly through a more effective and collaborative management of organization culture—with special emphasis on the culture of formal work teams—with the assistance of a change agent, or catalyst, and the use of the theory and technology of applied behavioral science including action research.[5]

Table 11.1 categorizes the definitions according to the nature of OD, characteristics of change activity, target of change, and desired outcomes.

As shown in Table 11.1, the sample of definitions converge on the (1) objectives, (2) targets, and (3) nature of organization development:

> *Objectives:* The desired outcomes of OD are changes in individual, group, and organizational processes that cause the *organization to be better able to adapt,* cope, solve its problems, and renew itself.

TABLE 11.1   **Selected Set of Definitions for Organization Development**

Author	Nature and Scope of the Effort	Characterization of the Change Activity	Target of Change	Disciplines Referred to	Ideals/Values
Bennis	Response to change	Educational strategy	Beliefs, attitudes, values, and structures	Unspecified	Adaptability to environment
Beckhard	Planned organization change	Planned intervention in organizational processes	Total organization	Behavioral science	Organizational effectiveness and health
Lippit	A process	Designed to strengthen human processes	Those processes that tend to move toward organic system	Behavioral sciences (implicit)	Viability Adaptability Problem solving
French and Bell	Long-range effort	Collaboration, management of organization culture	Culture of work teams	Behavioral science	Problem solving Skills and renewal processes

Sources: Adapted from Warren G. Bennis, *Organization Development: Its Nature, Origins and Prospects* (Reading, Mass.: Addison-Wesley Publishing, 1969). Richard Beckhard. *Organization Development: Strategies and Models* (Reading, Mass.: Addison-Wesley, 1969). Gordon L. Lippitt, *Organization Renewal* (New York: Appleton-Century-Crofts, 1969). Wendell L. French and Cecil H. Bell, Jr., *Organization Development: Behavioral Science Interventions for Organization Development* (Englewood Cliffs, N.J.: Prentice Hall, 1973).

Targets: The change is directed toward the *human and social processes* of organizations, especially individual's beliefs, attitudes, and values; the processes of work groups; and the processes of the organization.

Nature: With respect to the nature of the effort, first, OD is a *long-range, planned, systemwide process.* Second the change activities utilize behavioral science interventions of an educational, self-examining, do-it-yourself nature. "A basic belief of OD theorists and practitioners is that for effective lasting change to take place, system members must grow in competence to master their own fate."[6]

Thus, in OD, attempts are made to marshal the individual and group level forces to bring about organizationwide changes. The underlying premise is that if the social subsystem of an organization is allowed to blossom fully, then the forces unleashed will be powerful enough to bring about needed changes in the functioning of the organization. Thus, OD theorists argue that if appropriate conditions are created, individuals and organizations can renew themselves. The challenge of OD programs is to establish the appropriate conditions.

What Is Not OD
A different way of highlighting the uniqueness of OD is to distinguish it from other planned change strategies. We may draw relevant distinctions in both theoretical and practical ways.

Theoretically, Chin and Benne distinguished among three types of change strategies: rational-empirical, normative-reeducative, and power-coercive.

Rational-empirical strategies assume that human beings are rational and that they will follow their rational self-interest once it is revealed to them. A change is proposed by some individual or group that knows the change is desirable and in line with the self-interest of those affected by the change. If the proposed change can be rationally justified and if the proposer can demonstrate that the affected parties gain, then the change (it is assumed) will be accepted.

Normative-reeducative strategies assume that human motivation stems from not merely rational commitments to sociocultural norms, but also that individuals' values and attitudes—their normative outlooks—undergird their commitments. Changes can be accomplished only if individuals adopt different normative orientations. This means that changes should be brought about in individuals' values, attitudes, skills, and significant relationships, not just in their information, knowledge, and intellectual rationales.

Power-coercive strategies rely on the application of power, legitimate or otherwise, to bring about changes. The influence process involves compliance by those who are less powerful with the plans, direction, and leadership of the more powerful.[7]

According to this classification scheme, organization development is neither a rational-empirical nor a power-coercive strategy, but a normative-reeducative strategy of change. The target of change activities are the human processes in the organization (values, attitudes, and beliefs of individuals' group and organizational processes); change activity recognizes the complex nature of human motivation (through application of behavioral science knowledge); and, as we will see later, OD places great value on democracy in the workplace and typically eschews coercive tactics.

In *practical terms,* Tichy and Hornstein distinguish OD from some familiar forms of changes instituted in organizations. They note that change can be brought about in organizations in four ways:

Outside pressure, directed toward the total organization, can comprise a wide variety of tactics including mass demonstrations and civil disobedience.

Analysis from the top, directed toward the total organization, emphasizes achieving technological and structural change by persuading top managers to implement a proposal.

People change, directed toward the individual, not the organization, including some of the techniques in organization development.

Organization development, directed toward the total organization, including such techniques as team development and confrontation meetings.[8]

Organization development may be distinguished from the four action strategies—environmental analysis, strategic planning, organization design and organizational information and control systems—that we outlined in the preceding chapters. In Chin and Benne's terms, the earlier four strategies are predominantly rational-empirical and may, sometimes, involve power-coercive elements; whereas, as we have suggested, organization development is predominantly a normative-reeducative strategy. Similarly, according to Tichy and Hornstein's scheme, unlike organization development, the previous change strategies flow out of analyses from the top and in some cases are brought about by outside pressure.

Distinguishing Characteristics of OD

We may now list several characteristics of organization development that distinguish it from other change strategies. Organization development:

1. Emphasizes group and organizational processes, in contrast to substantive content.
2. Emphasizes the work team as a key unit of learning more effective modes of organization behavior.
3. Emphasizes collaborative management of work teams.
4. Emphasizes total (organizational) system ramifications.
5. Makes use of a behavioral scientist, consultant, change agent, or catalyst.
6. Offers a view of the change effort as an ongoing process.[9]

These characteristics enable us to discuss OD from the vantage point of the systems model.

Linkage to the Systems Model

Cast within the systems model, organization development explicitly focuses on improving the internal organizational processes: decision making, communication, or problem solving; it does not explicitly address the inputs and outputs of an organization. It has no explicit ways of addressing the environment (as in environmental analysis), nor the inputs and outputs of an organization (as in strategic planning). Unlike organization design approaches, it does not focus on the structural features or reward systems within an organization. As shown in Figure 11.1, the focus of OD is internal system processes.

FIGURE 11.1

Focus of organization development

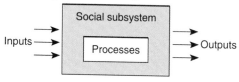

Most OD practitioners adhere to the systems views of organization; hence, it is important to appreciate the logic that permeates their efforts. This is graphically presented in Figure 11.2. The target of OD is the social subsystem—the human and social processes that occur regularly on a day-to-day basis within an organization. It is expected that by improving the quality of these processes, appropriate changes will be brought about in the functional and informational subsystems. In turn, this will enhance the adaptability of the organization to its environment. Viewed this way, OD addresses the social subsystem within an organization.

Unlike the more rational approaches we have seen so far, organization development is not anchored in the view that organizations can be engineered. Rather, it invokes a *biological* image of an organization; that is, the image of an organism that tries to survive in a changing environment. To quote Morgan:

> For the problems of mechanistic visions of organization have led many organization theorists away from mechanical science and toward biology as way of thinking about organization. In the process, organization theory has become a kind of biology in which the distinctions and relations among *molecules, cells, complex organisms, species,* and *ecology* are paralleled in those between *individuals, groups, organizations.*[10]

The architect of change looks less like an engineer and more like a farmer who tries to grow trees and plants by daily attending to them. As a con-

FIGURE 11.2

Systems logic behind organization development

| Intervene in social subsystem: human and social processes | To produce changes in functional/ informational subsystems | To enhance adaptability to environment |

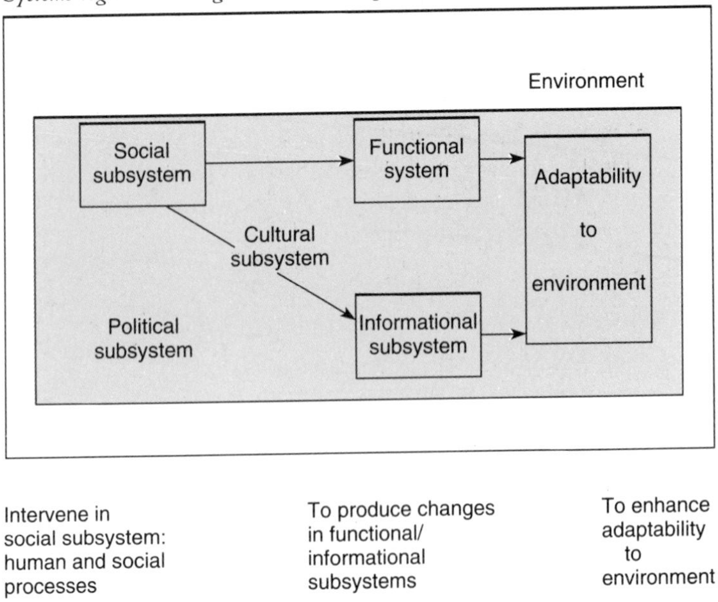

sequence, the OD approach is evolutionary rather than synoptic, as is the case of strategic planning or organization design.

Survival in an environmental context is a recurring theme in organization development. Most OD *practice* assumes that the environments facing the organization are increasingly turbulent. When Bennis articulated the need for organization development in 1969, he explicitly based his arguments on his belief that the rate of environmental change confronting organizations is far outstripping the adaptive capabilities of organizations. He implied that most organizations should move *from mechanistic to organic forms.*

The view of environments as turbulent is shared by others in the profession. As a consequence, OD practitioners espouse two criteria of organizational effectiveness:

1. Adaptability of the organization to the environment. Unlike in rational approaches, where effectiveness is defined as appropriateness of environment and efficiency of operations, OD focuses on enhancing the *adaptive capabilities* of an organization.

2. Development of individuals and groups within organizations. Flowing from the belief that the existing social system is the instrument of organizational adaptation, OD strives to enhance the capabilities of individuals and groups to function effectively and develop over time.

Consequently, the primary organizational stakeholders recognized in OD are the managers (including top-level managers) and employees of an organization. OD is *silent* with respect to other stakeholders: owners, customers, society, and others. Since most OD consultants are process-oriented and typically leave the substantive content of organizational decisions to the organization, they do not strive to be advocates of shareholders, customers, or others who may have a stake in organizational performance or who may be affected by organizational decisions. Such a stance is entirely consistent with the major premise of OD: If the social subsystem in an organization is developed, it will be able to incorporate the concerns of various stakeholders.

Moreover, the OD field has succeeded in operationalizing abstract systems concepts in practical terms. Table 11.2 summarizes this correspondence.

The objective of this chapter is to provide the reader with a bird's-eye view of the organization development field. The scheme of the chapter is as follows: First, we will summarize the historical, philosophical, and theoretical underpinnings of the field. Second, we will discuss the key principles underlying the practice of OD. Third, we will summarize the various interventions practiced in OD. Finally, we will critique the approach from the vantage point of the systems model.

TABLE 11.2   **Operationalization of Selected Systems Concepts in OD**

Systems Concepts	Operationalizations
1. Open systems	Organizations should enhance their capabilities for adapting to the environment
2. Levels	Interventions should focus on multiple levels: individuals, groups, intergroups, and organizations
3. Interdependence	Interventions in one subsystem have organizationwide implications
4. Principle of equifinality and multifinality	Interventions should adopt an evolutionary collaborative stance; this allows for organizations to express their uniqueness
5. Structure and process	Interventions focus on ongoing processes
6. Feedback	Use of action research model (see Theoretical Underpinnings)

Underpinnings

Historical Underpinnings

Historically, the field of organization development grew out of developments that took place in the United States and Great Britain. The most significant of these were: (1) the laboratory training movement pioneered by National Training Laboratories (NTL), (2) the development of the survey research and feedback methodology developed at the University of Michigan, and (3) the practices that were refined at the Tavistock Institute of Human Relations in Great Britain.

Laboratory Training

Developed about 1946, laboratory training is the use of unstructured small-group situations in which participants learn about group processes from their own interactions. In a very real way, Kurt Lewin may be thought of as the spiritual father of the method.[11] He created the field of group dynamics and action research that emphasized the need to base decisions on information from relevant and well-analyzed data. He discovered the laboratory method or *T*-group (Training group) quite by accident, as described in Box 11.1.

Typical T-groups were composed of strangers—individual members of the groups did not know each other before they arrived for the group session. This led to the problem of skill transfer to "back home situations." Skills learned during the T-groups were not necessarily transferred to organizational settings once the participants returned to their home ground. As trainers in the group dynamics movement began to work with systems of larger complexity than T-groups, they began to discover the inadequacy of this training technique. The idea of stranger groups was rejected and attention shifted to working with ongoing work groups in organizations. Thus, the focus of intervention shifted from the interpersonal to the organizational level.

One of the earliest proponents of organization development was the late Douglas McGregor. McGregor, in collaboration with John Paul Jones, established a small internal consulting group in Union Carbide in 1957. The consulting group tried to impart laboratory training skills to employees, thus transferring behavioral science knowledge to them.

During the early 60s, Herbert Shepard initiated a series of organization development efforts at three refineries of ESSO: Bayonne, Baton Rouge, and Bayway. At Bayonne, Shepard and Paul Buchanan started by interviewing the top management. This was followed by a series of three-day laboratories for all members of management. At Baton Rouge, Robert Blake and Shepard initiated a series of two-week laboratories attended by all members of "middle management." Typically, these sessions emphasized T-groups. One innovation in this training program was an emphasis on *intergroup* as well as interpersonal relations. Although working on interpersonal problems affecting work performance was clearly an organizational effort, intergroup problem solving had even greater organizational implications, as a broader and more complex segment of the organization was involved. Bayway, the third of the refineries, witnessed two further innovations. First, Shepard, Blake, and Murray Horwitz utilized the *instrumented laboratory* developed by Blake and Jane Srygley Mouton. An essential characteristic of the instrumented lab is the use of feedback based on the measurement of individual behavior during sessions. Second, at Bayway, more resources were devoted to team development, consultation, and *intergroup conflict resolution* than to laboratory training.[12]

In interpreting the historical evolution of organization development, it is worth summarizing three of the lessons learned during these experiments:

1. As seen in the work of McGregor, organization development efforts should explicitly consider the issue of transfer of learning to the work situation from laboratory experiences. This arose from the discovery of the limited usefulness of stranger laboratories.

2. In the ESSO experiments, it was discovered that management commitment is an important precondition for the success of OD efforts. For example, in Baton Rouge, where such commitment was lacking, follow-up resources for implementing organization development efforts were not made available.

3. The complexity of organizations necessitates that activities should be taken at multiple levels—individual, interpersonal, group, intergroup, and beyond. This was a direct outgrowth of the ESSO experiences.

Box 11.1

Historical Origins of the T-Group

The idea of laboratory groups or T-groups came into existence almost by accident during a workshop that focused on helping community leaders to implement the Fair Employment Practices Act. The workshop was held in Connecticut in 1946 under the direction of the Research Center for Group Dynamics at MIT. Kenneth D. Benne, Leland P. Bradford, and Ronald Lippit were in charge of training, while the research on the conference was being directed by Kurt Lewin and Ronald Lippit. The conference itself began with a series of discussions about how to comply with the Act, and various participants brought in experiences that had caused them problems in dealing with its provisions.

The concept of the T-group developed not in the context of the conference but rather grew serendipitously out of the evening meetings that were originally planned for staff members to discuss the observations that the researchers had made during the conference. Several participants who had free time in the evenings asked if they might attend these staff conferences. They were permitted to do so. It was an unusual circumstance for the staff to discuss observations of conference participants in their presence. The result was a number of arguments between the participants and staff about the accuracy of the research staff's observations. Although the discussion was acrimonious, it was also educational. In an unexpected way, the training staff hit upon the idea for an extremely useful educational tool: the now widely known method of learning about group process and one's impact on others through observing one's own behavior in a group session and receiving feedback about that behavior from others. Until that time, Lewin's research on group process had not *directly* involved group participants in examining the data of their own experience. The two activities had previously been kept separate: the participants had engaged in their group task activities and the researchers gathered data on how group process variables affected the work

In all these experiments, some of the characteristics of OD that we enumerated in the previous section are clearly visible; for example, the conscious utilization of behavioral science knowledge, an emphasis on work teams, collaboration between change agent and organizational participants during planning and diagnosis, and multiple levels of intervention.

Survey Feedback
Survey feedback refers to attitude surveys and data feedback in workshop sessions and constitutes a second major thrust in the history of organization development. The influence of Kurt Lewin is evident in this approach as well, since most of the survey feedback method was developed by his staff. The Research Center for Group Dynamics at MIT (which we referred to in Box 11.1) was founded by Lewin in 1945. After Lewin's demise in 1947, his

---

Box 11.1 continued

of the group. The laboratory (T) group brought these activities together in a strikingly unique way. The participants not only produced data but processed and examined the data in an effort to learn about group dynamics from their own experience. An entirely new way of studying group dynamics was discovered.

The laboratory movement contributed two of the major principles of organization development:

1. One of the primary targets of change in organization development is groups, not merely individuals—an idea directly traceable to its lineage to group dynamics.

2. Organization development emphasizes collaboration between change agent and client system during diagnosis and planning of change activities. This, of course, is directly traceable to the discovery that participants in the group sessions can learn about group process by examining the data of their own experience.

From the serendipitous beginnings emerged a three-week session during the summer of 1947 in Bethel, Maine. The work of that summer later evolved into the National Training Laboratories for group development and T-group training.

The T-group concept during the early conferences emphasized *interpersonal* learning. This emphasis partly reflected the desire to make large-scale bureaucratic organizations more humane and thereby more productive. While it is true that over a period of time, many T-groups continued to focus on effective and creative functioning within large-scale organizations, they tended more and more to emphasize interpersonal interaction in its own right, divorced it from its role in the improvement of organizational functioning. This, of course, was a major departure from the original action research and social change orientation of Kurt Lewin and his group.

Source: Adapted from Leland P. Bradford, Jack R. Gibb, and Kenneth D. Benne, *T-Group Theory and Laboratory Method* (New York: John Wiley & Sons, 1964).

---

staff moved to the Survey Research Center at Michigan, which later became the Institute for Social Research (ISR). Survey feedback was refined at ISR.

In one of the earlier experiments, Mann reported success in administering a companywide survey of management and employee opinions and attitudes. The study was conducted at Detroit Edison beginning in 1948. Over a period of two years, three different sets of data were collected and fed back to the organization: data regarding the viewpoints of nonsupervisory employees toward their supervision, promotion opportunities, work satisfaction, and other facets of their work situation; similar reactions from first- and second-line employees; and information from higher levels of management. Mann called the process that finally evolved an "interlocking chain of conferences." The major findings of the survey were first reported to top management and then progressed down through the organization. The feedback sessions were conducted in task groups, with each supervisor and his or her immediate subordinates discussing the data together. Later, eight accounting departments asked for a repeat of the survey. This generated a new cycle of feedback meetings. Following a third follow-up study, two major conclusions were drawn. The researchers concluded that:

1. An intensive group discussion procedure for utilizing the results of the employee questionnaire can be an effective tool for introducing positive change in organizations.
2. The effectiveness partly hinged on the fact that the procedure focused on the system of human relationships as a whole and that it dealt with employees and managers in the context of their own jobs, their own problems, and their own work relationships.

Survey feedback thus exhibited many of the characteristics of OD: its accent on intact groups, diagnosis of the data by the members of the work group themselves, and its focus on organizationally relevant issues.[13]

Tavistock Model

As early as 1950, planned organizational change efforts that displayed many of the characteristics of organization development were undertaken in the United Kingdom. One of the relatively well-documented pieces of work is the project undertaken at Glazier Metal Company. The project witnessed the collaboration of Wilfred Brown, the managing director of the company, and Elliott Jacques, a behavioral scientist. The Glazier project viewed organizations as a microcosm of the political structure of the society, with three interacting subsystems: judicial, executive, and legislative. The project papers suggest that the change agents adopted a systems view of the organization, as opposed to the merely interpersonal and group levels of interventions that were so characteristic of early efforts in the United States.[14]

In Great Britain, the most significant contributions to planned organizational change flowed out of the Tavistock Institute of Human Relations.[15] There were two related contributions from this school. The first is the *sociotechnical systems* concept, which viewed work settings as composed of both social and technical subsystems. Typically, this led to a structural redesign of the workplace. We touched upon this in the organization design chapter.

The second contribution of Tavistock was its contribution to *group dynamic* approaches. The group dynamic models developed at Tavistock owe much to Lewin's field theoretic notions, but these Lewinian notions were augmented by concepts from psychoanalysis. The unique blending of the two resulted in the development of the Tavistock conferences. These conferences attracted relatively healthy people wishing to learn more about group dynamics, especially as they involved problems of leadership within bureaucratic organizations.

Box 11.2

Bion's Theory of Groups

Bion's intensive work with groups had begun during World War II when, as a British army officer, he was given the responsibility for selecting candidates for officer training and for heading a hospital unit of psychiatric patients. In connection with this latter function, he became heavily involved in group treatment and soon was impressed with its therapeutic potential. For him, its value lay not so much in its efficiency as in the way in which the group situation repeated in microcosmic form the individuals' difficulty in becoming integrated into the larger society.

Bion's fascination lay with the ways in which groups continually form resistances to the reality demands of the task at hand. These resistances take the form of basic assumption matrices wherein the group regressively looks for magical solutions to the hard work before it. While such resistances were observable in therapy groups, Bion's thinking was that of a generalizer who saw the specific phenomena before him as instances of considerably broader and more universal principles. Hence, the ways in which the therapy group resisted its essential task was but a concrete example of the general tendency for all groups to engage in similar avoidances. Not many more steps were needed before Bion was to arrive at the

idea of a small study group, whose primary task was to study its own behavior. The role of the leader or the consultant would be to interpret at selected moments the latent meanings of the group's behavior.

Prominently involved in the organization and direction of these conferences was A. K. Rice, an Englishman who had been associated with Bion's first civilian training group, and whose background included many years as a government administrator in both Africa and India. It was this latter work that had initially led to Rice's interest in organizational psychology and to his wish to learn more about the psychodynamics of leader-follower relationships.

Bion's unique contribution to the Tavistock conference was the original small study group. The gradual elaboration of the conference to intergroup events and others represents the contribution of A. K. Rice. Rice was also involved in sociotechnical systems that we have already described in Chapter 9 on organization design.

Source: Adapted from John B. P. Shaffer and M. David Galinsky, *Models of Group Therapy and Sensitivity Training* (Englewood Cliffs, N.J.: Prentice Hall, 1974), pp. 165–66.

From a conceptual point of view, the credit for developing the Tavistock group goes to Wilfred Bion, whose theory of small-group processes provided the model's basic foundation and led to the development of the small study group. Later, A. K. Rice and Margaret Kirsch were to become prominently involved in the design and administration of Tavistock conferences, which were constructed around the core experience of the small study group initially created by Bion. Bion's key ideas about group dynamics are presented in Box 11.2.

Sociocultural Milieu

We should note that many societal trends facilitated the entry of the behaviorally oriented consultants into organizations. Two of these trends deserve special mention. First, the environments facing organizations were becoming increasingly turbulent. The turbulence of the postindustrial society has had its effects on social institutions and the attitudes and behaviors of individuals. Bennis and Slater noted that postindustrial societies can increasingly be characterized as temporary systems.[16] In such systems, job situations shift, sometimes precipitously; there is greater reliance on temporary problem-solving groups and projects that are dissolved quickly. This transience leads to two conditions: first, it necessitates quick and constructive responses to the increased instability of life; second, it outstrips adaptive capacities of the bureaucratic structures of organizations. Hence, there was a pressing need for alternative ways of managing organizations.

Second, in the United States, the era during which OD emerged witnessed an unparalleled affluence in the society. The expectations of individuals began to increase. Many expected more out of work than a mere employment contract. Individuals began to be concerned with the meaning of work in personal terms to a greater degree than in previous decades. This, in turn, led many to conceive of human issues in organizations on a scale far more intense than in the previous eras.

We suspect that the emergence of organization development as a field during the late 50s and 60s was not accidental; nor was it due solely to the individual scholars involved in the process. The sociocultural milieu supported the emergence of this change strategy: The leading practitioners and authors probably articulated the undercurrents in society in a manner that is both intelligible and pragmatic.

Summary

Organization development grew out of experiments that utilized principles of group dynamics: the T-group training at National Training Laboratories and survey feedback at Michigan in the United States, and the group dynamics work pioneered by Bion in the Tavistock Institute in the United Kingdom. Unlike strategic planning, where practitioners led academics in developing the field, the credit for developing the field of OD goes to academicians and social thinkers like Kurt Lewin and Douglas McGregor. These intellectuals demonstrated persuasively that effectiveness of organizational action can be enhanced by systematic application of behavioral science knowledge.

Philosophical Underpinnings

No other change strategy or approach pays as much explicit attention to the normative and philosophical bases of action as organization development. The early proponents shared a passion for social reform. Thus, Lewin was interested in reversing the dehumanizing tendencies of bureaucracies. Mc-Gregor was an ardent proponent of Theory Y approaches (to be discussed shortly). Similarly, Argyris is normatively oriented, and continues to emphasize the humanization of the workplace.

The full flowering of the field began to take place as practitioners made a shift in perspective from solely individual concerns to joint optimization of individual and organizational performance. Social thinkers had generally been prone to highlight the alienating influence of organizations on individuals. They typically believed that for human and individual development to take place, organizational performance would have to be sacrificed, or vice versa. OD theorists, however, reject this either/or reasoning and share a vision that under appropriate conditions individual development and organizational success can be mutually supportive. This belief is anchored in existential assumptions about human beings and organizations, utilitarian assumptions about research, and pragmatic assumptions about power sharing and democratic processes.

Concept of Human Behavior

Most organization development practitioners share an enlightened concept of human beings. Drawing upon the writings of Maslow, McGregor presented his Theory X-Theory Y dichotomy to describe two differing conceptions of human behavior.[17] Theory X assumptions held that people are inherently lazy, that they dislike work, and that they will avoid it whenever possible. Leaders who act on Theory X premises are prone to controlling their subordinates through coercion, punishment, and the use of financial rewards; the use of external controls is necessary, as most human beings are thought to be incapable of self-direction and assuming responsibility. In contrast, Theory Y is based on the assumption that work can be enjoyable and that people will work hard and assume responsibility if they are given the opportunity to achieve their personal goals and needs while achieving organizational goals at the same time. McGregor noted that the assumptions that managers hold about human beings get reflected in their actions or decisions. McGregor further noted that Theory X assumptions may be increasingly obsolete and that Theory Y assumptions are appropriate for managing modern organizations. Theory Y assumptions undergird most organization development efforts.

Further light on the value bases in organization development is shed by Robert Tannenbaum and Sheldon Davis. Working from existential premises, these scholars suggested that "man perhaps to a greater extent than ever before is becoming alive; he is ceasing to be an object to be used and is increasingly asserting himself, his complexity and his importance."[18] A brief summary of this shift is presented in Table 11.3. The values espoused by Tannenbaum and Davis are similar to McGregor's Theory Y; their description is much more complex and elaborate than the one presented by McGregor.

TABLE 11.3   **Changes in the Underlying Conception of Man Represented by OD**

		From	*To*
Human nature		1. Unchanging	In process
		2. Bad	Good
Attitude toward interpersonal relations		1. Competitive	Collaborative
		2. Distrusting people	Trusting
		3. Avoid facing others	Making appropriate confrontation
		4. Maskmanship	Authentic behavior
Relation to organization		1. Primarily in terms of job description	As a whole person
		2. Feelings not legitimate	Feelings are legitimate
View of process work		1. As being unproductive work	Essential for effective task accomplishment

Source: Adapted from Robert Tannenbaum and Sheldon A. Davis, "Values, Man and Organizations," *Industrial Management Review* 10, no. 2 (Winter 1969), pp. 67–83.

Assumptions about Organizations

Assumptions in organization development extend beyond the level of the individual to the levels of group and organization. Edgar Huse provided an extensive catalog of assumptions OD makes about various levels in organizations. Box 11.3 presents these assumptions.

As can be seen from Box 11.3, most OD practitioners believe in the systemic nature of organizations, although they focus on the social subsystem. Second, they assume that bureaucratic structures are dysfunctional since they create Theory X conditions and stifle the creative capabilities of individuals. For example, in his critique of bureaucracy, Argyris argued that organizational characteristics such as division of labor, unity of command, and hierarchy of management stifle the individual's need for growth, self-control, variety, and autonomy.[19] Third, OD assumes that since most contemporary organizations are to a large extent bureaucratic, there is considerable room for improvement in organizational effectiveness.

In organization development, these value bases are viewed pragmatically—they do not exist except as ideals worth striving for. Most practitioners recognize that in organizations there are constraints on the degree to which individual fulfillment and organizational performance can be integrated. The existential perspective is often criticized as utopian; but most OD practitioners recognize the pragmatic limitation on realizing the values in an absolute sense.

Power Sharing and Democracy

Most organization development practitioners take a positive view toward power sharing and democracy in organizations. They take the view that authoritarian structures stifle productivity and reduce acceptance of needed changes. To counteract these authoritarian tendencies of organizations, an emphasis is placed on democratic values. To some, democracy is even inevitable. Such values are more or less inherited from group dynamics, for example, Lewin's research supporting the superiority of democratic decision making in groups, which showed that the degree of acceptance of changes could be enhanced if the amount of participation by group members increased.

Research as a Basis for Action

An important aim of organization development activity is to introduce ideas from behavioral science into the day-to-day thinking of individuals in organizations. Allowing oneself to utilize all relevant information during decision making—including social psychological data and being aware of how one's own values might influence the way in which one views a situation—are all seen as aspects of the scientific approach. The underlying hope is that a greater knowledge of the behavioral sciences will result in a more rational approach to organization development and a greater openness to inquiry.

Summary

Three philosophical themes underlie organization development:

1. An existential theme, the set of assumptions about the nature of the individual and his or her relationship to the organization. Human beings were assumed to be self-actualizers who contributed toward organizational effectiveness if managers created the proper conditions.
2. A rational theme, focusing on the value of scientific inquiry, especially of a behavioral nature in managing organizations.
3. A pragmatic theme, translating abstract ideals and rigorous scientific findings into concrete actions to improve organizational effectiveness.

Organization development is an attempt at a grand synthesis of the three themes.[20]

Theoretical Underpinnings

In our discussion of the historical underpinnings of the field, we have traced the origins of organization development to group dynamics and social psychology. Theoretical contributions from other social science disciplines such as clinical psychology, anthropology, and even organizational sociology have also enriched the field. However, in this section, we do not enumerate the contributions of each discipline. Instead, we focus on theoretical underpinnings directly identified with the field.

Box 11.3

Some Principles Underlying Organization Development

Principles Regarding Individuals

1. Individuals have needs for personal growth and development. These needs are most likely to be satisfied in a supportive and challenging environment.

2. Most workers are underutilized and are capable of taking on more responsibility for their own actions and of making a greater contribution to organizational goals than is permitted in most organizational environments. Therefore, the job design, managerial assumptions, or other factors frequently demotivate individuals in formal organizations.

Principles Regarding People in Groups

1. Groups are highly important to people, and most people satisfy their needs within groups, especially the work group. The work group includes both peers and the supervisor and is highly influential for individuals within the group.

2. Work groups, as such, are essentially neutral. Depending on their nature, work groups can be either helpful or harmful to the organization.

3. Work groups can greatly increase their effectiveness in attaining individual needs and organizational requirements by working together collaboratively. In order for a group to increase its effectiveness, the formal leader cannot exercise all of the leadership functions at all times and in all circumstances. Group members can become more effective in assisting one another.

Three theoretical questions have been of central importance in the field: How do we conceptualize the stages of planned change in organization? What is the science of action? What is the role of a behavioral science consultant in organization development? We deal with each question in turn.

Stages of Planned Change: Lewin-Schein Model

Judging by the frequency of its use by OD practitioners and the research it has stimulated, the Lewin-Schein model is the most fruitful and simplest conception of the change process. It was originated by Kurt Lewin and elaborated by Edgar Schein. Lewin, who borrowed ideas from physics, visualized the social system as a field of forces. Thus, Lewin argued that the current or existing state of any social system is maintained by certain con-

Box 11.3 continued

Principles Regarding People in Organizations

1. Since the organization is a system, changes in one part of an organization will affect other parts of the organization.

2. Most people have feelings and attitudes that affect their behavior, but the culture of the organization tends to suppress the expression of these feelings and attitudes. When feelings are suppressed, problem solving, job satisfaction, and personal growth are adversely affected.

3. In most organizations, the level of interpersonal support, trust, and cooperation is much lower than is desirable and necessary.

4. Although win-lose strategies can be appropriate in some situations, many win-lose situations are dysfunctional to both employees and the organization.

5. Many personality clashes between individuals or groups are functions of organizational design rather than of the individuals involved.

6. When feelings are seen as important data, additional avenues for improved leadership, communications, goal setting, intergroup collaboration, and job satisfaction are opened up.

7. Shifting the emphasis of conflict resolution from edicting or smoothing to open discussion of ideas facilitates both personal growth and the accomplishment of organization goals.

8. Organizational structure and the design of jobs can be modified to more effectively meet the needs of the individual, the group, and the organization.

Source: E. F. Huse, *Organization Development and Change* (St. Paul, Minn.: West Publishing, 1980), pp. 29–30.

ditions or forces, and sought to identify the conditions that need to be changed to bring about a given result. Since Lewin was interested in groups, his primary concerns related to changing groups. To quote Lewin:

> Group habits can (not) be understood sufficiently by a theory which limits its consideration to the processes themselves. . . . Instead habits will have to be conceived of as a result of forces in the organism *and* its life space, in the group *and* its setting.
>
> Therefore, to predict which changes in conditions will have what result we have to conceive of the life of the group as the result of specific constellations of forces within a larger setting. In other words, scientific predictions or advice for methods of change should be based on an analysis of the field as a whole including both its psychological and nonpsychological aspects.[21]

The Lewin-Schein model conceptualizes organizational change as a three-stage process. The three stages are: (1) unfreezing the system that is operating in a given fashion, (2) moving to a new pattern, and (3) refreezing to a new pattern. The model is presented graphically in Figure 11.3.

Figure 11.3

Lewin-Schein model of planned change

Unfreezing	Movement	Refreezing

1. *Unfreezing.* According to Lewin, the first step in a planned change effort is unlocking or unfreezing the social system from its present field of forces. For successful initiation of change, there ought to exist a sense of tension or a felt need for change among those who are targets of influence. Thus, during the unfreezing stage, the forces for change represented by tension and the desire for change must be harnessed, mobilized, and given direction; while forces resisting change must be overcome, neutralized, or defused. In any organization, someone must gain the acceptance and support of individuals not seeking change and even those who feel threatened by it.

2. *Movement.* The second stage is when behavioral movement takes place in the direction of desired change. Activities should be planned to take the system from its original mode of operation to a new level.

3. *Refreezing.* Lewin further noted that for any change to be permanent, a new force field needs to be created and made secure; hence, the need for refreezing. Otherwise, a change toward a higher level of performance will likely be short-lived. After a shot in the arm, life returns to normal.[22]

Although the model is abstract, it serves as a tool for planning change interventions.

First, it is a sequential model: it provides a dimension along which to order events. For example, unfreezing activity should occur before movement or refreezing.

Second, it suggests the type of activity that needs to be adopted during each stage. For example, the unfreezing step may involve participation in T-groups, management training seminars, or feedback from a survey. The movement stage may involve organizational restructuring, team development, or other similar interventions. Finally, the refreezing step may consist of new policies or norms, or even a new reward system.

Third, the model is simple to explicate. We suspect that this simplicity has primarily been responsible for its popularity.

Science of Action: Action Research

The action research model emphasizes the process of intervening in a client system by a change agent. Kurt Lewin formulated this model as well. The model has evolved due to refinement and elaboration by others.

Action research is a *cyclical* process that focuses on seven main steps:

1. *Problem identification.* This stage usually begins when a key executive in the organization or someone with power and influence senses that the organization has one or more problems that might be alleviated by a change agent.

2. *Consultation with a behavioral science expert.* The behavioral science expert is typically called a *change agent* or consultant. The consultant may be either external to the system or an employee of the organization. During the initial contact, the change agent and the client system carefully assess each other. The change agent attempts to establish openness and collaboration from the beginning, typically sharing his or her own set of assumptions and values with the client system.

3. *Data gathering and preliminary diagnosis.* This stage is usually done by the change agent, typically relying on questionnaires, interviews, observations, and organizational performance data for data gathering.

4. *Feedback to client group.* Since action research is a collaborative activity, the data collected by the consultant is fed back to the client usually in a group or work-team meeting. The feedback step is concerned with helping the client determine the strengths and weaknesses of the organization. The consultant provides the client with all the data that are relevant and useful to the client, though sources of information may be protected.

5. *Joint diagnosis of problems.* During this stage, the group discusses the feedback with the change agent and the question centers upon whether this is a problem the group intends to work on.

6. *Action planning.* If the group decides to work on the problem, the consultant and the client jointly agree on further action to be taken.

7. *Data gathering after action.* Since action research is a cyclical process, data must also be gathered after the action has been taken in order to monitor, measure, and determine the effects of the action and to feed back the results to the client system, which in turn leads to rediagnosis and further action.[23]

Figure 11.4 pictorially presents the action research model.

Two characteristics of the action research model deserve repetition. First, the model emphasizes joint *collaboration* between the client and the consultant. Throughout the process, especially during diagnosis and action planning, there is close collaboration between the two. Further, during each step, the change agent is open about the data and conclusions and encourages the client to be so as well. Second, there is heavy emphasis on *data gathering and diagnosis* prior to action planning and implementation and careful evaluation of results after interventions before further action is taken.

FIGURE 11.4

Action research model

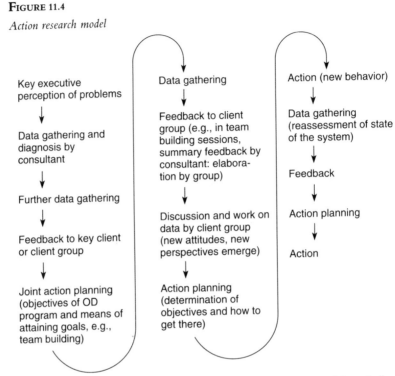

Source: W. L. French, "Organization Development: Objectives, Assumptions, and Strategies,"
California Management Review 12, no. 2 (1969), p. 26.

Role of the Consultant: Intervention Theory

Since much of OD involves a behavioral science consultant, we should ask
two related questions: What is the role of the consultant in OD activity? Are
there characteristics of effective intervention irrespective of the specific
technique employed? These questions are the domain of intervention theory, formulated by Argyris. Argyris maintains that change is not an adequate measure of the effectiveness of an intervention. Instead, he focuses on
the basic or necessary processes that must be fulfilled regardless of the
substantive issues involved if the interventionist is to be helpful with any
level of client system, be it the individual, group, or organization. Argyris
suggests that there are three primary tasks of intervention activity: to produce (1) valid information, (2) free choice, and (3) internal commitment:

1. *Valid information.* Intervention should produce valid and useful
   information. Valid information describes the factors and their
   interrelationships that create problems for the client system.
   Information is valid to the extent that *it is publically verifiable and
   enables prediction and control of client system behavior.* Thus, the

diagnostic activities engaged in by the consultant should represent the total client system; otherwise the consultant's predictions are likely to be based on inaccurate information. The consultant may start with a subset of the system but should not restrict his or her diagnosis to its wishes. Further, usefulness dictates that diagnostic activities focus on variables that can be controlled by the system.

2. *Free choice.* The client system should have free choice. Free choice implies voluntary, not automatic, choice and places the locus of decision making in the client system and makes the system responsible for its destiny. This implies first that the change agent resists attempts by the client system to elicit quick answers to the system problems, an attempt that is likely to occur when the system is experiencing failure. Second, in order for the client to have free choice, valid useful information must have been generated. A freely chosen course of action means that the action must be based on an accurate analysis of the situation, not on the defenses of decision makers.

3. *Internal commitment.* Third, intervention is successful to the extent that the client system is committed to the chosen solution. Internal commitment implies that the client system experiences a high degree of ownership and has a feeling of responsibility about the choice and its implications. Certainly the previous two conditions should have been met for internal commitment to ensue. Argyris notes that under these conditions, the client system's commitment will remain strong over time, under stress, or when challenged by others.[24]

Argyris's focus on valid information, free choice, and internal commitment reflects his belief that the change agent should not advocate change for change's sake. Thus, based on valid information, a client system may sometimes decide that the status quo is best suited to its situation.

Argyris underscores the point that for the interventionist, the primary tasks have major implications. The interventionist's process of intervening is as important as the content of specific interventions. Stated differently, how one intervenes should be congruent with the end state that is being strived for. Since much of OD espouses organic systems, the processes of intervention should themselves be organic.

Summary

The three theoretical models shed light on different aspects of OD efforts. The Lewin-Schein model conceptualizes any change effort as unfolding in three stages: unfreezing, moving, and refreezing; the model serves to plan OD activities. The action research model is more down-to-earth and describes the concrete steps involved in each intervention. Intervention theory is oriented to the behavioral science consultant and serves as a model for his or her behavior.

Central Themes

We distill six key themes that lie at the core of organization development.

Organizations as Systems

OD practitioners take the systems view we have summarized in Chapter 3 to be *the* appropriate perspective from which to observe and plan changes in organizations. The reader may refresh the central systems concepts by referring to the earlier chapter. The systems concepts assume a unique set of meanings in the concept of OD practice.

First, OD focuses on an organization's dynamics rather than its structural complement. The emphasis is on such processes as decision making, problem solving, and communication that permeate the entire organization, instead of the structural properties such as hierarchy, span of control, division of labor, and so on.

Second, the issues, events, forces, and incidents that constitute organizational dynamics are viewed not as isolated phenomena but in relation to other phenomena. OD theorists ascribe greater significance to relations than to the individual phenomenon.

Third, OD theorists ascribe multiple rather than single causes to events. This is a restatement of the complexity of organizations underscored by systems concepts.

Fourth, the analysis takes on a *here-and-now* focus. The levers of change are expected to reside in the *field of forces* at the time of the event. French and Bell emphasize this point:

> This dictum moves the practitioner away from an analysis of historical events and forces to examination of the contemporary events and forces—to a more existential vantage point.[25]

Fifth, since organizational dynamics are interdependent, OD practitioners strive to anticipate multiple impacts of events in order to predict potential dysfunctional consequences. Thus, a conscious effort is made to anticipate and avert unintended consequences of action.

Emphasis on Social Subsystem

The primary focus of OD interventions is what we have called the *social subsystem* in organizations. Since practitioners uphold an enlightened view of human beings (see the earlier discussion of the concept of human behavior), they believe that if the social forces are appropriately mobilized, the organization itself can bring about the necessary changes. Unlocking the social forces is done by three mechanisms.

First, the intact work group is considered to be the target of change rather than individuals alone. Thus, an organization is viewed as a network of overlapping groups, and systemic change is achieved by working with these groups.

Second, OD practitioners share an underlying belief that people learn how to do things by doing them. This is referred to as *experience-based learning*. Experience-based learning is a departure from conventional educational methods, which emphasize cognitive abstract learning often isolated from the context of ongoing organizations. OD tries to build theories inductively from the experience of a specific organization. This allows members to examine organizational dynamics from the data of their own experience.

Third, and flowing from the above, OD adopts an evolutionary stance to the design of change activities. Since different organizations are in different stages and face different types of problems, there is no attempt to prefix the timing, sequencing, and choice of activities into a program. To quote French and Bell again:

> People learn new skills and forget old ones; the structure of the organization changes, and then another change is put on top of that; problems are solved and new ones develop; a sick subsystem gets well and a heretofore healthy one develops bad symptoms. There are good and bad days for OD.[26]

The accent on social process is perhaps the most central theme in OD. The remaining themes are an elaboration of it.

Emotions as Data

The emphasis on the social subsystem in OD is reflected in the importance attached to attitudes and emotions. OD practitioners believe that although attitudes and emotions are often not directly dealt with in an organization, they represent important influences on the actual decision-making and problem-solving processes. They constitute the covert part of the "organizational iceberg." Thus, although the formal decision process often focuses on the overt part of the organization such as policies, structure, goals, technology, and the like, the process is actually guided by the suppressed attitudes and feelings of members. As a consequence, an organization fails to examine the real reasons behind its decisions. OD strives to make them overt in order to examine their influence on actual decisions.

This has important ramifications. First, attitudes and feelings become part of the diagnostic data sought out by OD practitioners. It is believed that this type of data gives important clues to the actual state of the organization. Second, working with them is considered to be important in bringing about lasting changes in organizations. For example, if the autocratic behavior of the manager of an intact work team has led to suppressed anger among subordinates, OD practitioners attempt to unearth the anger as a first step in their effort to enhance the team's problem-solving effectiveness. Third, OD tries to improve the capability of individuals to handle their feelings and channel them in constructive directions.

Climate of Trust and Authenticity

According to OD, healthy social subsystems, where decision making and problem solving tend to be rational, have typically developed an internal climate of trust and authenticity. Such a climate is a necessary precondition for genuine examination of feelings, which are, as we have noted above, important influences on decisions.

OD practitioners acknowledge that a genuine expression of (negative) attitudes and feelings is potentially explosive and often harmful to individuals in organizations. Further, individuals should feel "safe" to be open to authentic expression. If they are punished for genuine expression, then real feelings submerge into the organizational iceberg.

This has an important ramification. Much of the focus of OD activity is on nurturing a climate of trust and authenticity in organizations. This is a prerequisite to meeting the standards of effective intervention—the valid information, free choice, and internal commitment that we outlined in the previous section.

Collaboration as a Strategy

The collaborative stance of OD effort is guided not merely by philosophical assumptions but pragmatic reasons. As we have noted, in OD activity, diagnosis, problem identification, planning, and implementation are all conducted in collaboration with the client system. This has strategic value.

First, collaboration enhances the probability that a climate of trust and authenticity will be built in the organization. Since a collaborative process typically induces a sense of ownership among individuals, they are likely to feel secure and ready to engage in genuine examination of data including attitudes and feelings. Second, collaboration results in comprehensive diagnosis, especially in detecting unintended consequences of a proposed change effort. Finally, implementation is facilitated if the affected individuals had occasion to participate in the design of the change.

Multiple Levels of Intervention

More than any other action strategy, OD is open with respect to the level of intervention. Despite its organizationwide focus, specific change activity may focus on some or all of the individual, group, intergroup, and organizational levels. In fact, in the next section, we will discuss interventions at many levels.

This multiple focus of intervention is derived from the recognition that organizations are systems. One aspect of the systemic character is the interdependence among levels that we summarized in Chapter 3. Hence, for truly systemic change to occur, almost all levels of analysis should be influenced. This may mean training at the individual level, developing teams at the group level, resolving conflicts among groups, or changing organizational processes. Social systems are complex, and no single intervention is likely to be effective in bringing about systemic change.

Further, since OD is an evolving process, there is no predefined sequence in the choice of intervention level. As problems come up and issues are identified, appropriate interventions are adopted. In this sense, OD is open with respect to the level of intervention.

Summary

Similar to other action strategies discussed in this book, OD adopts a systems perspective on organizational change. In operationalizing the perspective, OD has evolved six distinctive themes: (1) here and now focus, (2) experience-based learning and evolutionary character, (3) emotions as data, (4) an internal climate of trust and authenticity, (5) strategy of collaboration, and (6) emphasis on multiple levels of intervention.

Interventions

In OD, it is useful to distinguish strategy from interventions. *Strategy* in OD refers *not* to the product-market strategy of the firm, as in strategic planning, but to the selection, timing, and sequencing of intervention activities to move an organization from its present to a desired state. Strategy ties individual interventions together into a coherent, directed thrust. In practice, since OD is evolutionary, an initial strategy will be formulated, which will be modified and changed as events and experience suggest different directions. Unlike strategy, interventions are specific activities undertaken at various times during organization development.

> By *intervention*, we refer to a specific activity or *tactic* designed to accomplish a specified purpose. For example, during the OD process, a specific activity may focus on improving communication within the top-management group. We would term that a *team-building* intervention.

Interventions are discrete activities with a relatively short-term focus. In contrast, strategy focuses on the interrelationships among the interventions and thus maintains the systemic and long-term focus of the OD process.

Earlier (see Theoretical Underpinnings) we suggested that the Lewin-Schein model is useful for visualizing the change process, whereas the action research model is more down-to-earth and useful for taking concrete actions in the present. That is another way of saying that the Lewin-Schein model has a strategic focus, whereas action research has tactical value. Thus, OD strategy visualizes the total organizational change as unfolding in three broad stages—unfreezing, moving, and refreezing. Although the stage of change guides the choice of interventions, within each stage specific interventions should be chosen to realize specific objectives. Action research describes the process by which such choices are made.

Since diagnostic activity is pervasive during the OD process and is not confined to the initial stages (as in the case of previous action strategies), in OD it is useful to distinguish between diagnostic and change interventions:

> *Diagnostic interventions* aim to gather and analyze data, unearth underlying causes of problems, and plan appropriate change.
> *Change interventions* typically move the organizations in the direction planned during the diagnosis stage.

We label diagnostic efforts interventions for two reasons. First, given the collaborative nature of OD practice, diagnosis involves not merely the designated interventionist but others in the organization who are likely to be affected by the change. Second, diagnosis often starts the change process. For example, convergence of opinion regarding organizational problems may itself cause the change process to unfold. In this sense, the distinction between diagnostic and change interventions is often blurred. We adhere to the distinction for discursive convenience.

As can be seen from the above discussion diagnostic and change interventions, the interventions span the three Lewin-Schein stages. Thus, major diagnostic interventions help unfreeze the system, whereas change interventions are appropriate for the movement stage. The refreezing stage typically involves institutionalization of OD processes, and specific structural (change) interventions typically associated with OD. This stage may also include other design or strategy interventions we have already discussed in previous chapters, although they are not identified with classical OD practice.

Further since OD is an open evolutionary process, some interventions may be applicable to many stages. For example, diagnostic activity pervades all stages and hence, diagnostic interventions may be useful at different times in an OD program. Similarly, some change interventions may be potent forces in unfreezing the system. For example, T-groups often help to unfreeze the system.

Diagnostic Interventions

Organizational diagnosis pervades all stages of the OD process. It involves a systematic collection of data from a wide variety of people and parts of an organization and environment so that a clear understanding of the organizational system can be developed among individuals. Although all action strategies—including strategic planning and organization design—include this activity, in OD, diagnosis is considered an intervention since diagnostic activities can themselves change the behavior and attitudes of people, create enthusiasm and commitment among top management, and thus generate forces for change. In other words, it is an important mechanism for unfreezing the system.

All diagnostic interventions have two major components: (1) the diagnostic model, and (2) data collection techniques. We will discuss these components first before we present the major diagnostic interventions.

Diagnostic Model

Diagnostic interventions use organizational models to focus data collection and analysis. Broadly, there are three types of diagnostic models: (1) theoretical models of social systems, (2) idealized models of organizations, and (3) eclectic models.

1. *Theoretical models of social systems* explicitly specify the variables of organizational systems to focus data collection. Dysfunctions in organizations are brought to the surface during the feedback sessions between consultant and the organization. These models are flexible with respect to analysis, but not with respect to data.

2. *Idealized models* specify not only the variables but the ideal state for the organization as well. Dysfunctions are related to the deviation of the organization from the ideal state. Here, neither the data nor the analysis is flexible.

3. *Eclectic* models are flexible with respect to both data and diagnosis.[27]

Although there are many models of each type, we will discuss three important ones to highlight their diversity: (1) Nadler and Tushman's contingency model, a theoretical model of the social system; (2) Likert's normative model, an idealized model; and (3) Tichy and Hornstein's eclectic model.

Nadler and Tushman's Contingency Model.   David Nadler and Michael Tushman developed a contingency model of social systems to diagnose an organization during OD efforts. They viewed the internal organization as being made up of four components:

1. *Task component:* Consists of the jobs to be done and the inherent characteristics of the work itself.

2. *Individual component:* Consists of all the differences and similarities among employees, particularly demographic data, skills, professional levels, and personality-attitudinal variables.

3. *Organizational arrangements:* Includes all managerial and operational structures of the organization, work flow and design, the reward system, management information system, and the like.

4. *Informal organization:* The social structure within the organization, including the grapevine, the organization's internal politics, and the informal authority-information structure—whom you see for what.

The OD consultant must concentrate on the degree to which the key components are congruent with one another. Nadler and Tushman identified six levels of fit:[28]

1. *Individual-organization:* To what extent are individual needs met by the organization? To what extent do individuals hold clear or distorted perceptions of the organizational structures?
2. *Individual-task:* To what extent are the needs of individuals met by the tasks? To what extent do individuals have skills and abilities to meet task demands?
3. *Individual-informal organization:* To what extent does the informal organization make use of individual resources, consistent with informal goals?
4. *Task-organization:* Are the organizational arrangements adequate to meet the demands of the task?
5. *Task-informal organization:* Does the informal organization facilitate the task performance?
6. *Formal-informal organization:* Are the goals, rewards, and structures of the informal organization consistent with those of the formal organization?

Nadler and Tushman contend that inconsistent fits between any pair will result in less than optimal organizational and individual performance. Their hypothesis is that the better the fit, the more effective the organization will be.

Likert's Normative Model.   According to the normative model, there is a *best direction* for organizational change.[29] In order to specify the direction, Likert categorizes organizations into four types of systems:

System 1: Autocratic, top-down, exploitative management.
System 2: Benevolent bureaucracy.
System 3: Consultative (where employees are consulted but the top person makes the final decision).
System 4: Participative (key decisions are made in groups by consensus).

Each system is described by six characteristics: leadership, motivation, communication, decision making, goals, and control. Table 11.4 provides a summary of these characteristics. Likert argues that System 4 is inherently superior to the other three systems.

The organization is diagnosed by a questionnaire that is administered to employees at all levels, and the extent to which it corresponds to System 4 characteristics is established. The discrepancy between the ideal and the existing state sets the direction for change. Thus, this approach is structured (by questionnaire) and directional (by comparison with System 4 characteristics). This also forms the underpinnings of the survey feedback intervention.

TABLE 11.4   **Likert's Idealized System Types**

Characteristics	System Types			
	System 1	System 2	System 3	System 4
Leadership style	Autocratic	Manipulative	Consultative	Participative
Bases of motivation	Threats and punishment	Rewards	Rewards	Involvement and rewards
Communication patterns	Downward	Mostly downward	Up and down	Up and down, sideways
Locus of decision making	At the top	Mostly at the top	Greater delegation	All levels involved
Goals setting	Orders	Orders, comments invited	After discussion, orders	By group action
Control mechanism	Formal surveillance from the top	Formal surveillance from the top	Surveillance and self-guidance	Informal self-guidance

Source: Adapted from Rensis Likert, *New Patterns of Management* (New York: McGraw-Hill, 1961).

Tichy and Hornstein's Procedure.   Noel Tichy and Harvey Hornstein provide an *emergent pragmatic* model of diagnosis, where the model is neither as specific as in Nadler and Tushman's nor normative as in Likert's models. Their procedure is so termed because the model *emerges* from an exploration of both the consultant's and client's assumptions about behavior and organizations and their *experiences,* as well as on the empirical and theoretical work in the field. Tichy and Hornstein argue that instead of using a specific theoretical model, which may not be appropriate for the organization, interventionists must utilize a collaborative approach between themselves and an organization. Hence, this is more an eclectic procedure than a specific diagnostic model. There are four steps in the procedure:

1. Members of the organization work independently to generate a list of organizational items that represent, in their individual views, keys to organizational diagnosis.
2. Members agree on a common list by eliminating overlapping labels and arriving at a final list that represents all individuals' selections.
3. Categories of organizational components are developed as a group activity.
4. The model is made dynamic. For this activity, group members first imagine how the change in every one of the components affects others. The resulting matrix shows which components the group members believe are the most and least significant in terms

of impacts on other components. This, then, becomes the basis for action planning.[30]

The systems model that we presented in Chapter 3 can also be used as a diagnostic model.

As can be seen from the above discussion, diagnostic models differ in terms of flexibility. The eclectic models are very flexible but their use requires high levels of skill and expertise; the idealized models require the least amount of skill and expertise; and the theoretical models fall somewhere in between.

Data Collection Techniques

As we have seen, some theoretical models (e.g., Likert) use questionnaires, whereas others use interviews to collect data. However, these are not the only data collection techniques. In general, there are four types of techniques:

1. Interviews
2. Questionnaires
3. Observations
4. Secondary data and unobtrusive measures

Since these techniques are well known, we will not discuss them. Table 11.5 presents the advantages and disadvantages of each technique. Since none of them is ideal, typically in OD many techniques are utilized in tandem.

TABLE 11.5   Comparison of Data Collections Methods

| | Data Collection Technique | | | |
Characteristics	Interview	Questionnaire	Observations	Secondary Data
1. Flexibility	Allows data collection on a range of topics	Predetermined questions may miss issues	Adaptive	Not very adaptive
2. Richness of data	Rich, qualitative data	Quantifiable data, not very rich	Can be rich	Easily quantified; not very rich
3. Biases	Self-report bias; Interviewer can bias responses	Self-report bias		
4. Ease of interpretation	Could be problematic	Easy	Difficult	May pose problems
5. Cost	Can be expensive	Less expensive, especially a large sample	Expensive	Least expensive
6. Other benefits	Interviewing can build rapport	Can obtain large volume of data	Real-time data	High face validity

In Summary

Diagnostic interventions differ in terms of the two components: diagnostic model and data collection technique. We now turn to the major diagnostic interventions that are popular in OD and then suggest some contextual factors that guide the choice of the specific intervention.

Major Diagnostic Interventions

We discuss three major diagnostic interventions: (1) open systems planning, (2) survey feedback, and (3) stream analysis. Another intervention—confrontation meeting—combines both diagnosis and change interventions and hence will be described later. These interventions invoke different models and data collection techniques and require somewhat different consultant skills. We will first describe the interventions and then summarize the differences.

Open Systems Planning.   Open systems planning is a process by which managers distance themselves from their organization and systematically examine the relationship between their organization and its environment. Following a definition of the environment and their strategy in it, managers can specify the demands of the environment and its implications for human outputs, people, structure, and so on. By comparing the actual state of the system with the required state, a plan for organizational improvement can be developed.

A model such as Nadler and Tushman's concept of fit can be used to help managers diagnose and plan improvements in their organization. Managers may generate data from their own experience or a more structured data collection may be conducted. Since the model alone cannot ensure that management will have the open dialogue that causes feelings and problems needed to complete the diagnosis to surface, a consultant may be needed to guide management to a consensus. An example of open systems planning is presented in Box 11.4.

Survey Feedback.   We have already pointed to the influence of survey feedback on the origins of OD (see Historical Underpinnings). Survey feedback combines both diagnostic and organizational intervention activity. In this diagnostic phase of the intervention, a change agent, working collaboratively with organizational members, obtains data about the organization and its problems. The consultant relies heavily on questionnaires but also may use other techniques of data collection. Typically, some idealized model such as Likert's guides the consultant's diagnosis. The degree of congruences of the actual organizational system with the idealized model reflects the level of organizational effectiveness. This process is summarized in Figure 11.5.

Box 11.4

Example of Open Systems Planning

A medium-sized manufacturing plant located in the midwestern United States was experiencing high turnover among its salaried employees. The plant manager invited a team of consultants to help him uncover the fundamental reasons for the morale problem. The consultants chose open systems planning to diagnose the plant's problems.

The plant manager and his staff met with the consultants in an off-site meeting. They were presented with concepts of open systems planning. This was followed by a lecture and discussion about social systems. The open systems model guided a diagnosis of the plant's organization. The group started by discussing organizational outcomes. Turnover among salaried employees was identified as a problem, while satisfaction was expressed with the plant's gross margin. With the help of the consultants, the plant's top management began to push back into the causal variables that might explain the turnover problem. They agreed that concern about job security was of foremost concern. Following a discussion of several process and structural variables that might account for the feelings of insecurity, they discovered to their surprise that there were several causes of insecurity that they had not previously considered.

The plant manager had strong beliefs about the need for a systematic objective setting and review process. Thus, he had introduced a new objective setting and training program (OSTP) into the plant. In fact, he served as the instructor himself to demonstrate the importance of objectives. In the year that followed, clearer and much better documented goals emerged. However, when the diagnosis turned to environment, the group realized that they had introduced the OSTP at a time when the plant's orders were dropping. Therefore, the goals set at the time of OSTP were less valid. In addition, the better and more explicit measurement system associated with OSTP and the tough tone that the plant manager conveyed was causing the insecurity and turnover.

This analysis allowed the group to plan specific steps aimed at reassuring people and making the OSTP system less threatening. The plant manager in particular gained significant insights into how his assumptions about the need for OSTP had to be modified in light of current business conditions and the climate in the plant.

Source: Adapted from Michael Beer, *Organization Development and Change: A Systems Approach* (Santa Monica, Calif.: Goodyear Publishing, 1980).

Stream Analysis.   Stream analysis, pioneered by Jerry Porras at Stanford University, is a more recent diagnostic intervention.[31] Porras builds his work on what he considers to be four major streams in organizations: (1) organizing arrangements (structure, rewards), (2) social factors (attitudes, values), (3) technology (job design, work flow), and (4) physical settings. According to Porras, organizational problems can be traced to poor alignment between any or all of these streams.

The specific steps in stream analysis are as follows:

FIGURE 11.5

Basis of diagnosis in survey feedback

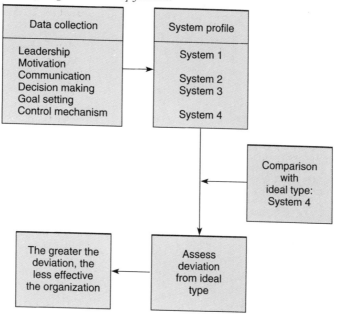

Diagnosis

1. Put together a change management team (CMT) composed of members drawn from several levels within an organization.
2. Collect information about the malfunctioning of the organization and make a list of all the problems identified.
3. Present the information to the CMT, and have the team consensually assign each problem into one of the four streams.
4. Identify the interconnections among the streams.
5. CMT identifies core problems, creates an action plan, and implements the plan. CMT tracks the implementation over time.

As can be inferred from the above discussion, the three diagnostic interventions involve somewhat different data collection techniques, models, and intervention skills. Table 11.6 summarizes the distinctions which are key to understanding the appropriateness of each intervention, a topic to which we now turn.

Factors in the Choice of Diagnostic Intervention
In large-scale OD efforts, diagnosis may take place at a number of times. This leads to the obvious question: How should one pick an intervention

TABLE 11.6   A Comparison of Diagnostic Interventions

	Diagnostic Interventions		
Characteristics	*Open Systems Model*	*Survey Feedback*	*Stream Analysis*
Diagnostic model	Theoretical model	Idealized model	Theoretical categories Could be eclectic
Data collection techniques	Interviews, secondary sources	Questionnaire	Could involve many techniques
Client participation in data collection	Low	Low	High
Client participation in diagnosis	Medium	Low	High
Intervention skills	1. Interviewing 2. Qualitative data analysis 3. Facilitation	1. Quantitative data analysis 2. Some facilitation	1. Facilitation skills 2. Familiarity with various data collection methods

in a specific situation? OD practitioners identify three major factors: (1) scope of diagnosis, (2) extent of client involvement required, and (3) sophistication of the client with respect to OD and the social subsystem in the organization.

Scope of diagnosis. Different diagnostic interventions have different foci.[32] For example, open systems planning focuses on organization-environment relations, survey feedback and stream analysis on internal characteristics of the organization.

Extent of client involvement. Where the focus is attitude and behavior, the required degree of client involvement necessary for subsequent change interventions to be successful is higher than when the focus is structures and systems. In all cases, however, there is some client involvement as well as an expert role by a consultant.

Sophistication of client.[33] Some organizations are sophisticated with respect to their knowledge of the social subsystem. As OD unfolds, most organizations gain some degree of sophistication. Interventions involving simple diagnostic models such as Likert's may be appropriate for relatively unsophisticated systems.

In real OD processes, other factors such as time and cost may also weigh in the choice of intervention.

Change Interventions

As we have pointed out before, change interventions in OD focus on different levels in organizations: individual, interpersonal, group, intergroup, and organizational. We now briefly describe the major interventions at each level.

Individual Level

There is widespread recognition in OD that for organizational change to be sustaining, individuals should acquire new attitudes, skills, and behavior. Individual level interventions aim to facilitate individuals' adaptation to organizationwide changes. Although there are a large number of interventions that range from conventional training programs to highly intensive therapeutic techniques, we will summarize three major interventions traditionally associated with OD: laboratory training, coaching and counseling, and career planning.

Laboratory Training. As we have shown earlier, laboratory methods are one of the historical anchors of OD. Their major *goals* are to enhance the interpersonal effectiveness of individuals by developing (1) self-awareness, (2) sensitivity to group and intergroup processes, and (3) new skills in handling social situations.

The core technique in laboratory training is called the *T*-group (T stands for training). A typical T-group is composed of strangers—that is, people who have not previously known one another—and a trainer. The group has no set agenda, and what goes on in the group becomes the "here and now" data for the learning experience. The trainer abdicates his or her traditional role as a teacher and instead adopts the role of facilitator. Usually, the trainer encourages the individuals to understand what is going on in the group, their own feelings and behaviors, and the impact their behavior has on others and themselves.

Many studies have investigated the effectiveness of T-groups. Most studies suggest that as a result of the training, individuals develop flexibility in role behavior, more openness, better listening skills, less dependence on others, and in general greater interpersonal effectiveness. *Just like any other training program,* the effectiveness of T-groups for organizations has been mixed. If a T-group is the only intervention utilized—that is, it is not coupled to other OD efforts—then organizations are not likely to benefit from the learning of the individuals.

Coaching and Counseling. Coaching and counseling are ongoing organizational activities that help individuals adapt to shifting organizational realities, especially during the OD process. The goal of this intervention is to help them understand the reality of the situation and assess their own attitudes and capacity to deal with it. During the counseling sessions, the

---

Box 11.5

Career Planning Program at Mobil Oil Corporation

An individualized career planning and development process has been applied at Mobil Oil Corporation. The process involves a number of interrelated procedures that ensure uniformity throughout the company in career planning practices. Additionally, the process is closely linked with management practices in other aspects of human resource planning.

The following are the principal components of the process:

- *Human resource objectives:* This document continues to be a five-year manpower forecast of both human resource needs and their costs. It starts from the smallest organizational unit and works its way upward.
- *Management by objectives (MBO):* Individualized employee performance objectives, standards, and action plans are developed within the framework of a results-oriented MBO system. Long-range organizational

objectives cascade downward to ultimately become individual job goals.

- *Coaching and counseling:* The process of setting objectives within the MBO system, the monitoring of performance with respect to objectives, and the feedback of results all revolve around the supervisor's coaching and counseling abilities.
- *Performance appraisal:* The performance appraisal process is an annual multipurpose procedure that focuses on the evaluation of results in terms of the objectives and standards developed through the MBO system. It is also used to establish a basis for individual salary administration.
- *Forecast of potential:* This evaluation also occurs annually. Assessments are made about employees' strengths and weaknesses as well as their likely effectiveness in higher-level positions or

counselor first helps the individual to get in touch with the reality of the situation. The next step is to help the person plan actions that will lead to further diagnosis, change effort, or change of jobs. The self-diagnosis often enables an individual to make informed choices and develop a program of personal relearning to increase the degree of "fit" between self and organization.

Career Planning. Career planning interventions aim to incorporate the career and growth aspirations of individuals in organizational change activity. It is now well recognized that many individual career decisions occur after the individual takes the first job. The goal of this intervention is to help an individual's movement within an organization over time: lateral, upward, and sometimes even downward, but *consistent* with organizational realities.

Box 11.5 *continued*

with increased responsibilities. Individualized developmental action plans are then developed.

- *Career development workshops:* Two- and three-day workshops are conducted that focus on how to develop a personal career within the system. They cover personal needs, career interests and goals, and the development of specific career plans.
- *Personnel development coordinators:* In all cases, the burden of career development is placed on the individual, and all supervisors are evaluated on their development of subordinates. In addition, coordinators work to facilitate the growth and movement of employees at lower organizational levels.
- *Placement summaries:* These documents describe current and future staffing needs in terms of incumbents, ready replacements, and forward replacements.
- *Career development review meetings:* These meetings provide a forum for organizational evaluation and for review

of an organization's requirements during the coming year and its ability to meet them. The review cycle begins with the smaller organizational units, which supply the next higher level of management with information necessary for human resource planning, and so on. The placement summaries act as the basic input document. The purpose of these reviews is to ensure that adequate backup personnel exist for all key positions, both in numbers and in quality, and that appropriate plans for meeting individual development and organizational needs are formulated and pursued.

Mobil employees are expected to assume primary responsibility for their continuing growth and adjustment to organizational changes and opportunities. Developmental plans should be formulated by employees and their supervisors during objective-setting discussions and performance and career development discussions.

Source: J. Walker, *Human Resource Planning* (New York: McGraw-Hill, 1980), pp. 346–48.

Specific activities may include career planning sessions; open job posting, whereby job openings within the organization are potentially made available to interested individuals; explicit socialization during recruitment; and exit planning sessions for individuals leaving the organization. An example of career planning program is presented in Box 11.5.

We described the above three interventions to illustrate the range of variation in individual interventions. They differ in terms of their aims, activities, and time horizon. These differences are summarized in Table 11.7. Laboratory methods involve discrete training programs, focus on interpersonal skill development, and are independent of the organization. Coaching and counseling are typically ongoing activities and facilitate individual adaptation to ongoing organizational changes. Career planning, as the name implies, focuses on an individual's career within an organization, and incorporates a future dimension. There is thus increasing focus

TABLE 11.7   **A Comparison of Individual Level Interventions**

	Intervention		
Dimension	Laboratory Training	Coaching and Counseling	Career Planning
Aims	Improve interpersonal skills	Improve job-related skills	Plan individual's career
Degree of specificity of skills	General	Specific topics	Specific to an organization
Activities	Primarily off-site in a stranger group	Ongoing conducted by superiors	Conducted by human resource specialist
Linkage to organization	None	Focus on specific jobs	Focus on life in organization
Time focus	Present	Present	Future

on organizational factors as we move from laboratory methods to career planning.

Group Level

As described earlier, OD considers the work group as the primary unit of organization and most appropriate medium of organizational change. Consequently, group level interventions constitute the core of most OD efforts. The two key group level interventions are process consultation and team building.

Process Consultation.   At higher levels of management in large organizations, managers may spend a considerable amount of time in meetings. Such meetings touch many facets of an organization's functioning, since meetings are used to share information, coordinate the activities of diverse functions, and diagnose and solve problems. Meetings have behavioral and attitudinal consequences: they could, for example, lead to high-quality problem solving or lead to poor morale.

OD practitioners assume that a meeting's outcome is determined by the process of the meeting itself. Process consultation involves an OD consultant helping the group develop more effectiveness in meetings by examining the meeting's dynamics and the underlying interpersonal or organizational issues that may be affecting its process. The consultant does this in many ways: by observing and gaining impressions, then, when the time is ripe, stopping the meeting and feeding it back; by asking questions at critical junctures of the meeting; and by requesting that formal critique periods be set aside.

Process consultation enables consultants to become tied to an organization's daily life. It may trigger major changes in the organization by uncovering and solving key problems. It will result in increased problem-solving capabilities of the group over time.

Team Building.   Team building is one of the most advanced and frequently used interventions in OD. Its purpose is to increase the effectiveness of working groups.

In team building, members of a group diagnose how they work together and plan changes that will improve their effectiveness. It begins with a contracting process during which the consultant assesses a manager's and group's readiness for change. Initial meetings are held with the manager (and later with the team) where the consultant explains the role of team building in the larger OD program and the demands it will place on the manager and the group. The consultant also explains the ground rules for constructive exchanges during team building. After the contracting phase, three steps are involved:

1. *Data gathering by the consultant:* In the first step, the consultant interviews group members in advance of the meeting. Group members are told that the data will be fed back in the meeting and are urged to specify the parts of the interview that they want to keep out of the meeting. The data include perceptions of each other; relationships among members; and group problems associated with goals, roles, meetings, decision making, and planning.

2. *Off-site team-building sessions:* Shortly after the data collection, the work group meets away from the workplace in order to avoid interruptions and work pressures. The meeting usually lasts for two to three days. During the meeting, the consultant feeds back the data to the group. With the help of the consultant, the group identifies various problems and categorizes them. Then the group sets the agenda for the rest of the meeting. The meeting itself consists of a systematic discussion of the problems and the data associated with it. An action plan is developed and implemented by the group, with some help from the consultant.

3. *Follow up:* The results of the implementation are assessed and reviewed at the follow-up meeting.

If problems are complex, it may take a number of team-building sessions to develop an appropriate action plan.

As can be seen from the above, process consultation involves monitoring naturally occurring meetings within an organization, whereas in team building, the group meetings are typically held outside. The focus of process consultation is any group that meets on a regular basis to coordinate within an organization, whereas team building focuses on a primary work group with a common task (project teams, task forces, etc.). Process consultation takes place over a protracted period of time, whereas team-building sessions are chunked together in two- or three-day sessions. These two interventions are often used in tandem.

Interpersonal and Intergroup Interventions

In organizations, conflicts frequently arise between individuals and groups. Consistent with OD practice, interpersonal and intergroup interventions are designed to work out these conflicts. In the beginning of this chapter, we described the example of an intergroup intervention. OD consultants have also developed interventions at the interpersonal level. An example of this is the *third-party intervention.*

Third-party intervention involves a neutral third party, in addition to the two individuals in conflict. Third-party consultants distinguish between substantive issues such as work methods, and interpersonal issues such as misperceptions. Substantive issues require mediation by a third party and bargaining and problem solving between individuals in conflict. When the conflict is interpersonal and emotional, the feelings must be worked through to change the perceptions of the individuals involved. Here, third-party interventions must focus more on changing people's attitudes and feelings.

Organizationwide Interventions

Unlike individual and group level interventions, organizationwide interventions focus on some or all aspects involving the whole organization as the target for change. We will describe four organizationwide interventions: (1) survey feedback, (2) confrontation meeting, (3) managerial grid, and (4) Quality of Working Life (QWL) interventions.

Survey Feedback.   we noted earlier, survey feedback incorporates both diagnostic and change interventions. During diagnosis, a consultant evaluates the discrepancy between the actual state of the organization or work group and the ideal state prescribed by Likert. This evaluation is fed back to the work group consisting of a superior and subordinates, who then identify the problems, work out a plan to address them, and then implement the plan. Most plans focus on implementing Likert's System 4. An example from the experience of General Motors is presented in Box 11.6.

Confrontation Meeting.   This intervention is often employed when major organizationwide changes are required quickly.

In a confrontation meeting, a large group of people from several levels in an organization are brought together for a short period of time, usually a day or two. Although the process may differ somewhat from one setting to another, most contain the following steps:

Box 11.6

System 4 at General Motors' Lakewood Plant

In a collaborative experiment with the Institute of Social Research at the University of Michigan, General Motors (GM) surveyed its assembly plant in the Atlanta area: Lakewood, an ineffective operation run by authoritative methods. Top management, after consulting with Likert, decided to undertake a bold experiment. It would first appoint Frank Schotters, a System 4 plant manager, to Lakewood and then try to change the ineffective plant by implementing System 4.

Schotters had the assistance of two internal consultants, as well as corporate OD specialists and experts from the Institute of Social Research. Also, some of his line managers had received special training in System 4 at the General Motors Institute. Schotters set out to gain support of Lakewood's management team for a more participatory approach to employee relations. Training sessions emphasizing mutual understanding, trust, and teamwork were conducted for the top-management team and then for the rest of the supervisory force. Initial resistance from supervisors gave way to strong support once the program began to gain momentum. Training was eventually extended to the entire work force including more than 20,000 hours of classroom training during the first year of the program.

A major feature of the System 4 program was to provide employees with information on a wide range of subjects such as future products, organizational changes, and productivity measures. Hourly workers were given feedback on a regular basis on how their labor costs compared with those of other GM plants. Before new automobile model changes, employees were told about projected modifications in product and facilities and were encouraged to participate in planning the changes.

Results of the System 4 program at Lakewood were impressive. Within eight months, the plant had moved significantly toward System 4 scores on survey data. Temporary setbacks in labor costs and productivity during the program start-up gave way to sizable gains in efficiency and a lessening of employee grievances. Likert cautions that the fast results at Lakewood are atypical; two- and three-year lags before improvements show are not uncommon.

Source: Thomas G. Cummings and Edgar F. Huse, *Organization Development and Change*, 3rd ed. (St. Paul, Minn.: West Publishing, 1985).

1. Opening session: The total group meets. Although a consultant is present, the general manager opens the sessions describing the purpose of the meeting and attempting to create a supportive climate.

2. Formation of subgroups: Participants are divided into subgroups representing different organizational levels and units. Bosses and subordinates are not placed in the same group. Each subgroup is assigned the responsibility of generating a list of problems in the organization that prevent the organization from becoming more effective.

3. Total group meeting: Each of the various subgroups presents its list of problems to the total group. Leaders draft broad categories of change and the total group sorts the proposed changes into categories.

4. The subgroups meet with their managers to select their action items and develop action plans, recommend priorities to top management, and plan for communicating.

5. The total group convenes and the subgroups report each action item discussed. Managers make decisions to implement.

Although the confrontation meeting ends here, sometimes a follow-up meeting is planned for the future to review the progress toward goals developed during the confrontation meeting. Both follow up and positive action on the results of the meeting are critical; otherwise, a loss in credibility and trust is likely to result.

A confrontation meeting mobilizes an organization toward an action plan in a relatively short time. However, given its short duration, it is likely to provide nonoptimal solutions. Further, the problems that may require an atmosphere of trust and risk taking may not surface in such a short duration. Crisis situations that create modest pressures and can stimulate a willingness to take personal risks are perhaps the best environment for a confrontation meeting.

Managerial Grid.   A preprogrammed sequence of interventions for developing an organization was developed by Blake and Mouton. Six developmental phases, each featuring one type of intervention, spread over a three- to five-year period are specified as the change strategy. The following are the developmental phases:

Phase 1: One week of laboratory training for all organizational members in which they study the managerial grid concepts and use these concepts to learn about their managerial style, group decision making, and organizational development. People at the top of the organization are expected to attend first.

Phase 2: Team development for all groups in the organization starting at the top. Each management team examines its own functioning and the behavior of its members using managerial grid concepts. The procedure for a two-day meeting is specified in great detail.

Phase 3: All major functional groups that must coordinate their activities are brought together in an intergroup laboratory. Using managerial concepts and predeveloped instruments, groups examine their relationships and develop plans for improved coordination.

Phase 4: Using an agenda specified by Blake and Mouton, the top-management group meets for several days to develop an ideal model of the organization. A plan for organizational development is developed.

Phase 5: Temporary task forces and project teams are formed to implement the organizational changes specified in the plan. These task forces are made up of people throughout the organization who have knowledge or influence in the task force's target area.

Phase 6: A program to measure changes that have occurred and to stabilize the achievements of all previous phases is activated. New goals for organizational development are set.[34]

The grid program combines a variety of interventions described earlier. It begins with individual changes, moves through to group development, then intergroup methods, and ends with total organizational diagnosis and change. The process starts at the top, moves down through the whole organization, comes back to the top for the development of a change plan, and again moves down into the organization for the implementation of the plan.

Quality of Working Life (QWL) Approaches.   QWL approaches represent a relatively new addition to the family of OD interventions. Most of them include several if not all of the following elements:

Participative problem solving: This concerns increasing employee involvement in decision making at various levels. Techniques include quality circles, labor-management problem-solving groups, and the like.

Work design: This involves restructuring the work that people and groups perform to better match employee needs and technological requirements. Techniques include job enrichment, creation of autonomous work groups, and the like.

Innovative reward system: This involves creating reward systems that promote a participative, high-performance climate. It includes employee stock ownership plans (ESOPs), Scanlon plans, which share the benefits of cost savings among employees, and so on.

Work environment improvements: This involves changing the physical or tangible conditions of work by such mechanisms as flexible working hours, or by modifying the placement of equipment and machinery to facilitate new work designs.

In Box 11.7 we summarize the results of one experiment measuring the effects of flexible working hours.

Factors in the Choice of Change Intervention

Given the wide array of change interventions, the question naturally arises: What type of intervention should a behavioral consultant choose? At the current state of development, we can posit three factors that determine the choice of intervention: (1) level of intervention, (2) depth of intervention, and (3) sequencing of interventions. Since we classified the various

Box 11.7

Flexible Working Hours

During the 1970s, the authors of *Organization Theory: A Strategic Approach,* V. K. Narayanan and Raghu Nath, then at the University of Pittsburgh, studied the effects of the installation of a flextime program in the nuclear division of the Westinghouse Corporation. The program was introduced as part of a long-standing OD program within the division.

The flextime program allowed employees some freedom in their work site arrival and leaving times. Previously, employees were expected to clock in and out at fixed times, using a punch card system. Under flextime, employees were expected to be at the work site for a core period of time during the day, but the program allowed them flexibility in arrival and leaving times. In addition, they could bank work hours; that is, they could work less one day and make up for it during another day in the week.

Narayanan and Nath tracked the effects of the program for over a year and compared the flextime division with another comparable division on a number of effectiveness measures such as attitudes, absenteeism, and productivity. They reported the following:

1. There was significant improvement in attitudinal measures: Flextime employees reported better relationships with their superiors, compared to their comparison group.
2. There was a significant reduction of absenteeism in flextime.
3. Although flextime was supported by nonexempt employees, technicians, secretarial, and clerical staff, the engineers resented it. Managers were indifferent to it.
4. Significant productivity gains occurred only in groups where there was great cohesiveness.

Narayanan and Nath went on to add that flextime programs yielded the greatest benefits only when they were introduced as part of a major OD program.

Source: V. K. Narayanan and Raghu Nath, "A Field Test of Some Attitudinal and Behavioral Consequences of Flextime," *Journal of Applied Psychology* 67, no. 2 (1982), pp. 214–18; "Hierarchical Level and the Impact of Flextime," *Industrial Relations* 21 (1982), pp. 216–30; "The Influence of Group Cohesiveness on the Impact of Flextime," *Journal of Applied Behavioral Science* 20, no. 3 (1984), pp. 265–76.

interventions according to level, we will not dwell on this topic. Suffice it to say, the choice of intervention depends on the focus of desired change: individual, group, intergroup, or organizational.

Depth of Intervention.   Roger Harrison developed the notion of the *depth of intervention* to provide guidelines for the choice of intervention.[35]

> *Depth of intervention* refers to the degree of the individual's emotional involvement in the change process. Strategies that touch the deeper, personal, private, and central aspects of the individual fall toward the deeper end of the contin-

uum, whereas strategies that deal with the more external aspects of the individual and focus upon the more formal and public aspects of role behavior fall toward the surface end of the depth dimension.

According to Harrison, interventions such as T-groups (an individual level intervention), which focus on personalization of relationships, the development of trust and openness, and the exchange of feelings are deeper than interventions such as job design, which focus on how individuals like to organize their work. Table 11.8 presents the interventions arrayed according to Harrison's criteria.

Harrison makes two points regarding the depth of intervention. First, he argues that at the surface end of the continuum, the method of intervention is easily communicated and made public. The organization may reasonably expect to learn something of the change agent's skills to improve its own practice, whereas this becomes increasingly difficult at deeper levels of intervention. Concomitantly, the degree of transferability of the benefits of an intervention to members of an organization not originally participating in the process varies depending on the depth of intervention. At the surface levels, the effects are institutionalized and may have considerable permanence beyond the tenure of individuals; whereas at deeper levels, the individual becomes the target and the carrier of change.

Second, the depth of intervention is correlated with the accessibility of data for diagnosis. As the level of intervention becomes deeper, the information needed to intervene becomes less available. At the surface level, data

TABLE 11.8   **Topology of Change Interventions Arrayed according to Depth of Intervention**

Degree of Depth	Specific Intervention	Intervention Type
High ↑ ... ↓ Low	Laboratory training Career planning Stress management Process consultation Team building Interpersonal and intergroup interventions Coaching and counseling Survey feedback Confrontation meeting QWL approaches	1. Individual interventions that focus on intrapersonal analysis and relationships 2. Group level interventions that deal with work style 3. Individual organizational interfaces 4. Systemwide approaches ↓
	Managerial grid cuts across all categories	

Source: Adapted from Roger Harrison, "Choosing the Depth of Organizational Intervention," *Journal of Applied Behavioral Sciences* 6 (1970), pp. 181–202.

are often a matter of public record, whereas at the deepest level important information may not be available even to the individual. Further, at deeper levels, the outcomes of interventions become relatively unpredictable. The need for clinical sensitivity and skill on the part of change agent thus increases. Together, inaccessibility of data and the greater skills demanded of the change agent suggest that the costs of intervention are likely to be higher at deeper levels of intervention.

Harrison puts forth two major criteria for interventions:

1. One should intervene at a level no deeper than required to produce enduring solutions to the problem at hand.
2. One should intervene at a level no deeper than that at which the energy and resources of the client can be committed to problem solving and to change.

Harrison thus suggests depth of intervention as the major criterion for choosing intervention.

Sequencing of Interventions   In large-scale OD efforts, just as in the case of diagnostic interventions, several change interventions will have to be made. Hence, OD strategy will have to focus on the sequencing of interventions over time. Michael Beer has provided a list of criteria for sequencing the interventions:

> *Maximize diagnostic data:* "In general, interventions that will provide data needed to make subsequent interventions should come first."
> *Maximize effectiveness:* "Interventions should be sequenced so that early interventions enhance the effectiveness of subsequent interventions."
> *Maximize efficiency:* "Interventions should be sequenced to conserve organizational resources such as time, energy and money."
> *Maximize speed:* "Interventions should be sequenced to maximize the speed with which ultimate organizational improvement is attained."
> *Maximize relevance:* "Interventions that management sees as most relevant to immediate problems should come first."
> *Minimize psychological and organizational strain:* "A sequence of interventions should be chosen that is unlikely to create side-effects such as anxiety, insecurity, distrust, dashed expectations, psychological damage to people, and unanticipated and unwanted effects on organizational performance."[36]

We should note that the criteria often make conflicting demands on the choice of intervention. Therefore, *in practice,* the change agent often makes complex trade-offs in the selection of interventions and their sequencing.

A Critical Appraisal

Cast within the systems model, organization development primarily addresses the social subsystem within an organization, a point we have emphasized throughout this chapter. This exclusive social subsystem focus limits the potential of this action strategy. We will first discuss the major limitations before we summarize its applicability.

Limitations

The limitations of OD can be summarized along the components of the systems model: environment and the five internal subsystems of an organization.

Environment

As we have shown, the primary aim of OD is to enhance the *internal* adaptive capabilities of an organization to cope with turbulent environments. This aim limits the variety in approaches to managing the organization–environment interface in three ways.

First, OD may be applicable only in environments that offer organizations some room to maneuver and where successful adaptation is possible. Its applicability to organizations confronted with hostile environments and conflicting demands by strident stakeholders is yet to be demonstrated. In such difficult environments, drastic and swift action is necessary, *survival* may be a prime concern, and organizations may not have the time required to enjoy the fruits of OD.

Second, OD eschews *cognitive* approaches to managing the interface. As the rational strategists (environmental analysis and strategic planning) have demonstrated, effective organizational responses need not be confined to functioning within existing environments. Current environments could be abandoned; new ones could be created; turbulence could be anticipated to give organizations time for adaptation. But such approaches require revision of beliefs and cognitions of organizational members. OD is typically silent with respect to management of the cognitive aspects of organizations.

Third, an exclusive focus on the internal organizational system precludes OD from the possibility that the best outcome for an organization may be its dissolution. The proponents of large-scale restructuring that is taking place in the United States have emphasized that *viewed from the perspective of the society at large,* resources need to be channeled from unproductive sectors to productive sectors. Sometimes, this necessitates dissolution of ongoing organizations. Concerns of stakeholders other than those internal to the organization cannot be addressed within the framework of OD.

Internal Subsystems

An exclusive focus on the social subsystem is limited also from the vantage point of the total organizational system. OD assumes that (1) there is sufficient functional expertise in the system, and that (2) the power structure is aligned with the underlying philosophy, and is (3) largely silent with respect to the potential of emerging information technologies.

The process orientation of OD consultants is anchored in the belief that sufficient functional expertise exists among organizational members. This limits the applicability of the technology to a narrow range of organizations. When individuals lack technical and functional skills, they cannot be relied on to make "rational" decisions. This is often the case in many nonprofit organizations and small businesses. At the current state of the art, OD technology is useful to improve the functioning of relatively normal organizations.

Of greater significance is the role of the political subsystem in organizations. As the ESSO experiments demonstrated (see Historical Underpinnings), top-management commitment is a necessary prerequisite to success, a belief held by most OD practitioners. This is a pragmatic necessity, since most consultants derive some of their power and influence from the top management who has hired them. Although from the perspective of the consulting profession, top-level commitment is a harbinger of consulting effectiveness, this limits the potential of the action strategy from the viewpoint of an organization. Major organizational change often requires political realignment, which the current OD technology cannot accomplish.

Finally, OD conceptualizes the informational subsystem in social and human terms to the exclusion of the technological. Recent technological developments in the information sector augment the human information processing capability, opening up the potential for transferring human energies from repetitive jobs to creative tasks and in general exerting pressures on organizations to move toward flatter, nonpyramidal—in general, organic—forms. Most OD practitioners, given their social science heritage, are ambivalent toward technology, an attitude that often spills over into the field. Consequently, they have not been able to harness technological potential toward their own humanistic goals. This further limits the potential of OD.

Level of Applicability

In spite of the above limitations, OD is the most *fully developed* social technology of organizations. It has had a fair degree of success in moving organizations toward organic forms. The evolving dynamic approach to organizational change, characteristic of OD, makes it applicable to situations that demand an *incremental* approach to organizations. This has two implications.

First, OD is useful as a technology for implementing organizational strategies. Once the major directional thrust of the organization—its strategy—is chosen, implementation should follow, but it is often thwarted by pressures of resistance, often emanating from the social subsystem. As we have seen in our discussion of strategic planning, to counteract the resistances, logical incrementalism is offered as a preferred mode for strategy implementation. Since this mode is characteristic of OD, OD technology may be utilized during implementation.

Second, and related to the above, OD is appropriate when an organization is functioning more or less normally but needs some degree of *fine tuning*, which requires an evolutionary approach. We will take up this theme again in our discussion of organization culture, a field that is evolving to address the demands of transformational and discontinuous changes as opposed to incremental changes.

Chapter Summary

Organization development originated from the experiments on group dynamics conducted by social scientists. Over the years, OD consultants have developed an evolutionary change strategy by focusing on the social subsystem of an organization. The strategy uses organizational experience to enhance its learning by developing an internal climate of trust and authenticity. Consultants typically adopt a strategy of collaboration and intervene at many levels within an organization. In organization development, diagnosis itself is considered to be an intervention.

Different diagnostic interventions utilize different diagnostic models and data collection approaches. Open systems planning requires the use of contingency models such as the one developed by Nadler and Tushman, and typically data collection is done through interviews and secondary sources. Survey feedback invokes Likert's normative model and employs questionnaires. Still others such as stream analysis employ eclectic models, and data may be collected through questionnaires, interviews, observation, and archival records. Consultants may choose the appropriate diagnostic intervention based on several criteria: scope of diagnosis, degree of client involvement, and client sophistication.

Change interventions focus on different organizational levels: individual, group, intergroup relations, and organizational levels. Individual interventions focus on interpersonal skills such as in T-groups, work performance as in coaching and counseling, and long-term approaches such as career planning. Team building and process interventions focus on group development. Team building is typically done off-site, whereas process consultation focuses on ongoing meetings. At the organizational level, confrontation meetings focus on immediate problem solving, whereas a managerial grid is a set of preprogrammed sequences of interventions designed to ensure the long-term health of an organization.

Organization development is particularly useful for solving problems during the implementation of strategy or structure. In this sense, it is an evolutionary approach that fine tunes an organization. It is also the most fully developed approach to dealing with the human elements in organizations. In the next chapter, we will focus on some radical approaches to designing the human elements in an organization.

Specialized Terms

Laboratory training
Survey feedback
Action research
Intervention theory
Diagnostic interventions
Diagnostic models
  • Models of social system
  • Idealized models
  • Eclectic models
Process consultation

Quality of Working Life
Depth of intervention
  • Sequencing of interventions
  • Open systems planning
Stream analysis
Coaching and counseling
  • Career planning
  • Team building
  • Confrontation meeting
  • Managerial grid

Discussion Questions

Theoretical
1. Identify the assumptions underlying organization development.
2. Describe (1) Lewin-Schein model of change, (2) action research, and (3) intervention theory.
3. Discuss the major themes underlying OD interventions.
4. Distinguish between diagnostic and change interventions. How does OD treat diagnostic interventions?
5. Summarize the major differences between diagnostic interventions. Under what conditions is each type most appropriate?
6. What are the major differences among T-group training, coaching and counseling, and career planning?
7. Describe the major steps in (1) managerial grid, (2) stream analysis, (3) survey feedback, (4) team building, (5) process consultation, and (6) confrontation meeting.

★8. How does the Lewin–Schein model compare with the stages of planned change (see Chapter 5)?

★9. Discuss the tactical and strategic implications of interventions.

Applied

1. You have been approached by the human resource manager of a medium sized company to help him design an OD program for his firm. The human resource manager reports to the CEO of the company. The firm is organized into functional units. Recently, there has erupted a lot of conflict between marketing and manufacturing. The human resource manager is concerned that this may lead to poor performance.

   Design a data collection strategy for diagnosing the problems of this company.

2. You have been approached by the CEO of a rapidly growing firm to help him design a management development program for his company. How will you proceed?

End Notes

1. This is an example drawn from the experiences of the authors and several other OD consultants known to the authors. See also Michael Beer, *Organization Development and Change: A Systems Approach* (Santa Monica, Calif.: Goodyear Publishing, 1980).
2. Warren Bennis, *Organization Development: Its Nature, Origins, and Prospects* (Reading, Mass.: Addison-Wesley Publishing, 1969).
3. Richard Bekhard, *Organization Development: Strategies and Models* (Reading, Mass.: Addison-Wesley Publishing, 1969).
4. Gordon Lippit, *Organization Renewal* (New York: Appleton-Century-Crofts, 1969).
5. Wendell L. French and Cecil H. Bell, Jr., *Organization Development* (Englewood Cliffs, N.J.: Prentice Hall, 1973).
6. W. L. French, C. H. Bell, and R. A. Zawacki (eds.), *Organization Development: Theory, Practice and Research* (Plano, Tex.: Business Publications, 1983), p. 7.
7. R. Chin and K. D. Benne, "General Strategies for Effecting Changes in Human Systems," in *The Planning of Change*, ed. W. G. Bennis, K. D. Benne, R. Chin, and K. E. Corey (New York: Holt, Rinehart & Winston, 1976).
8. N. Tichy and H. Hornstein, "Stand When Your Number Is Called: An Empirical Attempt to Classify Types of Social Change Agents," Graduate School of Business, Columbia University, undated manuscript.

★This is an advanced-level question.

9. Adapted from French and Bell, *Organization Development,* pp. 19–20.

10. Gareth Morgan, *Images of Organization* (Beverly Hills, Calif.: Sage Publications, 1986), pp. 39–40.

11. French and Bell, *Organization Development.*

12. Ibid.

13. Floyd C. Mann, "Studying and Creating Change," in *The Planning of Change,* ed. W. Bennis, K. Benne, and R. Chin (New York: Holt, Rinehart & Winston, 1961), pp. 605–13.

14. See Wilfred Brown and Elliott Jacques, *Glazier Project Papers.* Also Elliott Jacques, *The Changing Culture of a Factory* (London: Tavistock, 1951).

15. There are a large number of works detailing Tavistock work: (1) E. J. Miller and A. K. Rice, *Systems of Organizations* (London: Tavistock, 1967); W. R. Bion, *Experiences in Groups* (London: Tavistock, 1961); (3) Gouranga Chattopadhyay et al., *When the Twain Meet* (Bombay: A. H. Wheeler & Co., 1986).

16. Philip Slater and Warren G. Bennis, "Democracy is Inevitable," *Harvard Business Review* 52 (1964), pp. 51–59.

17. Douglas McGregor, *The Human Side of Enterprise* (New York: McGraw-Hill, 1960).

18. Robert Tannenbaum and Sheldon A. Davis, "Values, Man and Organizations," *Industrial Management Review* 10, no. 2 (Winter 1969), pp. 67–83.

19. Chris Argyris, *Personality and Organization* (New York: Harper & Row, 1957).

20. Frank Friedlander, "OD Reaches Adolescence: An Exploration of its Underlying Values," *Journal of Applied Behavioral Science* 12, no. 1 (1976), pp. 7–21.

21. K. Lewin, *Field Theory in Social Science* (New York: Harper & Row, 1951), pp. 172–74.

22. Ibid.

23. French and Bell, *Organization Development.*

24. Chris Argyris, *Intervention Theory and Method* (Reading, Mass.: Addison-Wesley Publishing, 1970).

25. French and Bell, *Organization Development,* p. 55.

26. Ibid.

27. This classification is based on Warner Burke, *Organization Development* (Boston: Little, Brown, 1982).

28. David A. Nadler and Michael L. Tushman, "A Diagnostic Model of Organizational Behavior," in *Perspectives on Behavior in Organizations,* ed. J. R. Hackman et al. (New York: McGraw-Hill, 1977).

29. Rensis Likert, *New Patterns of Management* (New York: McGraw-Hill, 1961).

30. Noel Tichy, Harvey A. Hornstein, and J. N. Nisberg. "Organization Diagnosis and Intervention Strategies: Developing Emergent Pragmatic Theories of Change," in *Current Issues and Strategies in Organization Development,* ed. W. W. Burke (New York: Human Sciences Press, 1977).

31. Jerry I. Porras, *Stream Analysis: A Powerful Way to Diagnose and Manage Organizational Change* (Reading, Mass.: Addison-Wesley Publishing, 1987).

32. Beer, *Organization Development and Change*.
33. Burke, *Organization Development*.
34. Robert Blake and Jane S. Mouton, *Corporate Excellence through Grid Organization Development* (Houston: Gulf Publishing, 1968).
35. Roger Harrison, "Choosing the Depth of Organizational Intervention," *Journal of Applied Behavioral Sciences* 6 (1970), pp. 181–202.
36. Beer, *Organization Development and Change*.

12   ORGANIZATIONAL CULTURE

Chapter Outline

It was with some urgency that Robert F. Daniell, the newly appointed CEO of United Technologies Corporation, summoned his top executives. Just weeks after taking the reins from Harry J. Gray, Daniell called a management pow-wow at the Jupiter Beach Hilton in Florida. The subject? UTC's shaky future. Customers of its Pratt & Whitney jet engines, outraged by lousy service, were defecting in droves to archrival General Electric Company. Market shares at UTC's once dominant Otis elevator unit and Carrier air-conditioning company were evaporating. Profits had hit a 13-year low. "Things had to change," says Daniell.

Unlike the iron-fisted Gray, however, Daniell did not lecture at management meetings. Instead, a Boston consultant moderated a rolling discussion in which managers put forth their remedies: dump divisions wholesale, diversify, pump up research and development spending. "Just the fact that we went through all of that yelling and screaming was unusual," says one executive who attended. After two days, Daniell and his team decided to remake UTC—to level its autocratic structure and bring more of its 186,800 employees into the decision-making process. The ultimate goal: to get UTC's haughty culture to take marching orders from its customers.

Worker empowerment. Team building. Getting close to your customer. While a lot of companies are just starting to talk about such methods, Bob Daniell is already proving that they can work wonders on the bottom line. The changes are nowhere more apparent than at jet engine maker Pratt & Whitney, which pulls in more than half of UTC's operating profit. Orders have increased eightfold, to nearly $8 billion, since 1987.

When Daniell finally became CEO, he inherited a divided, argumentative management. Executives were too frightened to admit mistakes, and they directed their staffs like armies. All the way down the line, staffers refused to take responsibility for errors.

At the same time, Daniell was working on a long-term goal: changing Pratt's by-the-book structure. Dictatorial management and a Byzantine approval process made employees feel powerless. Take the case of an airplane builder who wants to mount an engine a fraction of a millimeter closer to the wing than the blueprint specifies. Normally, a good engineer at Pratt could just eyeball the blueprint and give the customer the nod for such a change. But until Pratt changed the system in February 1988, the request would wind through nine departments, including a committee that met only once a week.

Now the design engineer makes the decision and only needs to get three signatures. Says Garvey: "It's all part of quality-taking responsibility." As a result, average response time has gone from 82 days to 10, and the request backlog has shrunk from 1,900 cases to fewer than 100.

Daniell went further with this campaign to improve service. He increased the number of service representatives in the field by nearly 70 percent—despite 30 percent staff cuts in the rest of the company.[1]

Robert Daniell revamped the way United Technologies did business. Thus, field representatives could now make multimillion-dollar decisions that previously took several levels of approval, top engineers spend time with customers, some 5,000 managers get a week's worth of training, and so on. Daniell cut the levels of hierarchy from eight to four, and instilled some new values: empower the workers, get close to your customer, and continually improve. Daniell is engaged in cultural change.

What are the values that drive an organization? What are the beliefs, or norms, shared by employees? What assumptions drive the decision-making process? How do we change the values, beliefs, norms, or assumptions? These questions are the domain of an emerging subfield within organization theory called organization culture.

It is only recently that organization theorists discovered the role of organizational culture. Although some of the early proponents of organization development (OD) had implicitly taken cultural factors into account, the concept was not very well developed, since their focus was on interventions rather than theory building. "Culture" was something studied by anthropologists, or it was a term associated with the intellectuals and elite in the society. In the 1980s, however, organization theorists began to pay serious attention to the value of the concept for explaining some aspects of organizational functioning.

What Is Culture and Organizational Culture?

Definitions of organizational culture in organization theory and in popular business literature are derived from their anthropological counterparts. Anthropologists are concerned with larger societal patterns rather than corporate culture per se. According to one anthropological definition:

> The culture of a people consists of their distinctive modal patterns of behavior and the underlying beliefs, values, norms, and premises. Culture is learned and shared by the members of a society and has a compelling influence on their behaviors. Thus culture provides solutions to problems that all societies must solve if they are to remain viable.[2]

We emphasize five elements of the above definition:

1. Culture is *learned*. Culture is a human creation, not something that humans are endowed with at birth. The notions of needs and instincts (e.g., Maslow's need hierarchy) are often seen as innate to human personality. These notions refer to biological programming: Human beings are endowed with them. Culture, on the other hand, is learned: Human beings learn, construct, and transmit among themselves elements of culture.

2. Culture is *shared* among a collectivity. We talk of culture when there is overlap among the behaviors and beliefs of individuals within a society. Culture can thus be communicated to others. In this sense, culture makes coordination among individuals within a society possible: It is the glue that holds society together.

3. Culture *influences* behavior. This is how culture serves as a mechanism of coordination in organizations. In weak cultures, however, such influence is not felt keenly.

4. Cultural symbols and meanings are interrelated; thus, we talk of *patterns of culture.* A change in one element will initiate changes in related elements.

5. Culture incorporates *instrumental* and *expressive* elements. In the instrumental sense, it standardizes the behavior of individuals of a society; in the expressive sense, it focuses on the spontaneous elements of a society (e.g., plan, fantasy, art forms).

Levels of Culture

It is useful to distinguish three levels of culture in order to link the anthropological definition with its counterpart in organizational studies[3]:

> *Culture,* in the sense anthropologists use it, refers to the shared understandings among individuals *in a society* to allow adequately predictable, coordinated, social activity.

> *Business culture* comprises the effective rules of professional behavior, the boundaries between competitive and unethical behavior, and the codes of conduct in business dealings. In this sense, this refers to (occupational) subcultures such as the legal or medical culture.

> *Organizational or corporate culture* refers to the allowable codes of behavior within an organization. As in the case of business culture, organizational level is constrained by both general and business levels of culture.

We draw the distinction between levels to highlight the significant problems involved in nurturing and maintaining corporate cultures. The process by which individuals learn culture is often called *socialization.* Socialization proceeds in stages:

> *Primary* socialization takes place in the family and during an individual's participation in wider society. This cultural socialization is not homogeneous: knowledge is socially distributed by gender, ethnicity, region, social class, and religion.

> During *secondary* socialization, individuals learn additional cultural knowledge relevant to their participation in the wider socioeconomic world. In the United States, for example, lawyers learn the legal culture, doctors the medical culture, and managers are increasingly trained in business schools.

> What takes place in an organization is *tertiary* socialization, where individuals learn the allowable codes of conduct within a specific organization.

The impact of earlier stages of socialization does not decay with time. One may say that individuals go through a progressive specification of codes for allowable behavior during various stages of socialization. For example, IBM engages in extensive selection and training procedures to inculcate a shared set of values and beliefs among its managers and other employees. Yet even this process does not "deprogram" the original socialization of its personnel. A study of IBM personnel in subsidiaries in 50 countries found extensive differences in work-related values. (See the Hofstede study summarized in Chapter 4.)

Corporate Culture

We define corporate culture as the pattern of artifacts, beliefs, norms, values, and premises held by an organization:

> *Artifacts.* Artifacts are the visible manifestations of cultures. These include observable behaviors of members as well as structures, systems, procedures, rules, and the physical aspects of the organization. The 24-hour hot line at IBM is a cultural manifestation of the norms, values, and assumptions about customers at the company.

> *Beliefs.* Organizations generally share assumptions, including all cognitions—ideas, knowledge, lore, superstitions, and legends. In the sense in which we use the term here, beliefs are assumptions that are at the surface, beliefs about oneself or about one's competitors. For example, a firm may believe that it is superior to competitors in technological leadership.

> *Norms.* Cultural norms regulate behavior. They are the rules or standards accepted by an organization; they specify the details of appropriate or inappropriate behavior. Norms may also specify the reward for appropriate behavior and the punishment for inappropriate behavior.

> *Values.* Values are a special class of beliefs held by members of an organization that pertain to what is "desirable" or "good" or what ought to be. Values are both positive and negative: positive values are the desirables, whereas negative values are the undesirables. For example, an organization may value customer relations or shareholder wealth maximization.

> *Premises.* Organizational cultures contain many premises about the world that remain *unverbalized*. They are likely to be revealed by analytic work or intuitive speculation of an outside observer. One may term this the organizational unconscious.

Taken together, artifacts, beliefs, norms, values, and premises constitute the culture of an organization.

Linkage to the Systems Model

Organizational culture refers to the cultural subsystem within the systems model. Organizational culture displays two types of elements:

1. Elements that are *visible* to organization members (such as beliefs, values, and norms).

2. Elements that are unarticulated and *invisible* to organization members (such as premises).

The visible elements comprise "how we do things around here," whereas the invisible elements constitute the organizational unconscious. Together, they form the internal environment of an organization, which, to some extent, provides the glue that holds an organization and its other subsystems together (see Figure 12.1).

Table 12.1 shows how some key systems concepts are operationalized in this subfield. As shown in the table, culture theorists argue that cultural premises filter data about the environment, allowing only selective information into organizations. Thus, organizations tend to see what they already believe; theorists, therefore, argue that an organization's interpretation of the environment is colored by its cultural premises. Since culture is shared among organizational members, it acts as a powerful integrating force, standardizing the behavior of individuals. This subsystem influences all other subsystems. It focuses on the distinctiveness of an organization—what separates it from other organizations. Finally, the primary focus here is on process—how culture permeates an organization's functioning—rather than structure.

Unlike strategic planning or organization design, culture change does not belong to the rational school of management. This type of change tries

FIGURE 12.1

Focus of organizational culture

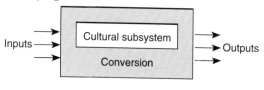

Environment

TABLE 12.1   Organization Cultures: Operationalization of System Concepts

System Concepts	*Operationalization*
Open systems	Premises influence organizational interpretation of environment
Interdependence	Culture is a major integrating force
Subsystem	Cultural subsystem influences all other subsystems
Equifinality/multifinality	Organizational cultures are unique
Structure and process	Primary focus on process

FIGURE 12.2

Logic of cultural change

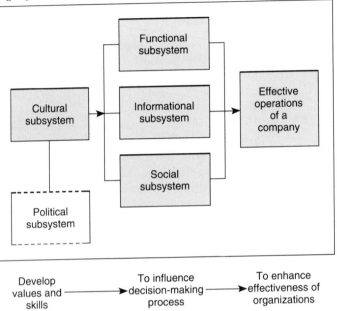

Develop values and skills → To influence decision-making process → To enhance effectiveness of organizations

to influence the values and beliefs of individuals within an organization to bring about changes in the functional, informational, and social subsystems. Most culture change proponents expect that the change is led by the senior executives, and hence supported by the power structure of the organization. Figure 12.2 displays the logic underlying culture change approaches.

It is useful to distinguish culture change from other types of change along two dimensions: (1) scope of change and (2) temporal positioning of the change in relation to external events:[4]

> *Scope of change:* could be incremental or strategic. Incremental change or piecemeal changes are made within the current frame or context of the organization's strategy; its aim is to make the organizational components fit better with each other. Strategic change is aimed at breaking out of the current strategy and forming an entirely new alignment among the components to support the new strategic thrust.
>
> *Temporal positioning:* If the change occurs in advance of expected external changes, it is *anticipatory*; it is reactive if it involves a response to events that have already occurred.

Using these dimensions, we can identify four types of change. As shown in Table 12.2, the two dimensions combine to illustrate four types of organization change:

TABLE 12.2 **Types of Change**

SCOPE OF CHANGE

	Incremental	Strategic	
Anticipatory	Examples: Organization Development	Examples: Strategic planning	Organization Culture
Reactive		Examples: Crisis management	

(left axis: TIMING)

Source: Based on D. Nadler and M. Tushman, *Managing Strategic Organizational Change: Frame Binding and Frame Breaking* (New York: Delta Consulting Group, 1986).

1. *Fine tuning.* Fine tuning involves making incremental changes in anticipation of external events. For example, organizations may expect changes in work force demographics and may redesign jobs to better fit the needs of a changing work force. Many of the OD interventions presented in the previous chapter can be used to tune the organization so that it operates more smoothly and efficiently.

2. *Adaptation.* When incremental changes occur in reaction to external forces such as increased competition and changing customer demands, they are called *adaptation.* The responses are limited to selected parts or features of the organization and the changes are intended to enhance responsiveness to external events. OD also has frequently been used to remedy adaptation problems; for example, to make staff groups more responsive to customers and to resolve conflicts across organizational boundaries.

3. *Reorientation.* This form of planned change involves fundamentally changing the organization in anticipation of future events. Because there is lead time before external changes occur, emphasis is placed on the process of transition from the present organization design and strategy, rather than breaking sharply from them. A growing number of organizations are undertaking major reorientations in anticipation of changing environments. They are seeking to maintain their competitive advantage in the face of future events.

4. *Re-creation.* This is the most drastic form of change and involves significantly modifying the organization design and strategy to

respond to major external disruptions such as deregulation, global competition, and technological innovation. Because external events frequently threaten the survival of the firm, these changes require radical departures from existing practices. Many of the dramatic changes reported in the popular press represent organization re-creations, such as those involving Chrysler, Bank of America, and Burroughs.

The four types of change help to distinguish cultural change from more traditional forms of planned change. Fine tuning and adaptation involve making the existing organization operate more smoothly and efficiently. OD has historically been associated with these types of change. Reorientation and re-creation, on the other hand, involve fundamental changes in the organization. Corporate strategy is usually altered to fit changing external events. The different components of the organization are modified to support the new strategy and to fit with each other. These kinds of changes represent significant transformations of the organization. They result in an entirely new way of operating and relating to the environment. Also, according to this classification, the rational approaches to management, especially strategic planning, are predominantly anticipatory, whereas organization development and culture change could be either anticipatory or reactive.

There are additional ways in which cultural change departs from OD:

1. Culture changes incorporate strong *analytical and conceptual* elements in addition to the social relationships among individuals so characteristic of OD.

2. Culture changes are *not always developmental* in nature. Some organizations have drastically altered their culture, strategic direction, and way of operating without significantly developing their capacity to solve problems. For example, Lee Iacocca's transformation of Chrysler from the verge of bankruptcy was not accomplished by developing human potential but by drastic actions that included bringing managers from outside.

3. The humanistic values that pervade OD are not always present in culture change.

Since the formal study of organizational culture is less than a decade old, action strategies for changing culture are in their experimental stage. Also, the concept itself is in its early stages of development. Hence, we will sometimes adopt a speculative stance in our discussion. The scheme of this chapter is as follows: first, we will trace the historical, philosophical, and theoretical underpinnings of the field; second, we will present the major themes in the management of organizational culture; third, we will summarize the major frameworks for diagnosing and changing a specific organization's culture; and finally, we will review the culture-related ideas from the vantage point of the systems model.

Underpinnings

Historical Underpinnings

Unlike the case of other subsystems, interest in organizational culture was not kindled among practicing managers and organization leaders until the second half of the 20th century. In Chapter 2, we noted how during the first half of the 20th century, managers were influenced by the universal principles of management. Max Weber thought that the principles of bureaucracy were universally applicable. In the same vein, Taylor and Fayol were proponents of a universal theory of management. By the 1930s, the Anglo-American tradition of economics had largely ceased to be interested in the effects of cultural and institutional factors on economic activity. The apparent practical success of U.S. management methods in the post-World War II period further strengthened the belief in universal applicability of the practices developed in the United States.

The importance of culture first came to the attention of practitioners when U.S.-based organizations began to export management practices abroad.[5] Multinational corporations operating in several countries started experiencing difficulty in applying U.S. management practices to other countries. The technical assistance programs of the American Institute of Development (AID) ran into difficulty due to the failure to take into account local values during the administration of the programs. Practitioners in government as well as business started questioning the applicability of U.S. management practices to overseas locations. This awareness led to several cross-cultural training programs for managers and administrators in overseas assignments. At this stage, culture was considered something synonymous with nations, an *external* contingency variable that influenced the choice of appropriate management practice. The notion of culture as a factor *internal* to an organization, over which managers have some influence, had to wait until the late 70s for recognition.

The precipitating event that finally brought the role of organizational culture to the forefront of managerial consciousness was the rise of the Japanese management system during the late 1960s and early 1970s. By this time, it had become clear that the performance of Japanese corporations in many industries was far ahead of typical American and European companies. It was also becoming clear that the Japanese had not copied the American system of management. In fact, they had evolved a management system particularly suited to their cultural and ecological environment, and this system was much more successful than the Anglo-American system of management.

By now, practicing managers in the United States had also become disenchanted with the methods of management that focused only on the objective side of an organization. In the wake of technological changes and forces of deregulation that took shape in the United States and swept through many of the traditional established industries, conventional assumptions about how to do business were becoming obsolete. For example, until recently, AT&T had been a regulated monopoly. As technological advances opened up opportunities and deregulation swept through the telecommunications industry, AT&T began to function in a competitive environment—an experience that was totally new to it. AT&T conceptualized its task not merely as a strategic change but as a cultural transition.

The discovery of culture focused attention on the "soft" side of an organization. A number of consulting organizations—for example, East Coast-based Management Analysis Center—began to offer services to fine-tune organizational culture. In turn, management theorists began to address culture-related issues in organizations.

Philosophical Underpinnings

The field of organizational culture grew out of anthropology and psychoanalysis. Hence, the assumptions that undergird the field are varied and can often be traced to these two disciplines. We will focus on three sets of assumptions: about (1) organizations, (2) relations between individuals and organizations, and (3) organizational change.

Organizations

Four assumptions about organizations permeate different discussions of organizational culture.

The first assumption is drawn from anthropology. According to anthropologists, the culture of a society consists, in part, of a particular set of arrangements for solving the problems of the society. The problems may be special ones peculiar to members of a society, or universal problems common to all societies—for example, meeting the biological needs of the members, training the young, and caring for the old and the sick. Of course, there are many different possible arrangements for solving these problems. From among the possible arrangements, one society adopts one set; a second society a different set. This is another way of saying that no two cultures are identical. When applied to organizations, this assumption suggests that *organizational cultures are unique.*

The second assumption, also drawn from anthropology, suggests that *organizations are symbolic entities,* and highlights the role of language, myths, and shared codes of meaning in organizations.

In anthropology, cultures are often viewed as systems of knowledge. Ward Goodenough clarifies this idea:

> A society's culture consists of whatever it is one has to know or to believe in, in order to operate in a manner acceptable to its members. Culture is not a material phenomenon; it does not consist of things, people, behavior, or emotions. It is rather an *organization* of these things. It is the form of things that people have in mind, their models of perceiving, relating, and otherwise interpreting them.

> . . . Culture consists of *standards* for deciding what *is,* . . . for deciding what *can be,* for deciding what one feels about it, for deciding what to do about it, and for deciding how to go about it.[6]

As shared symbolic systems, organizational cultures manifest themselves in stories, myths, and language. Cultural aspects thus include codes of meaning shared among individuals in an organization.

The third assumption, drawn from psychoanalysis, is the idea that *organizational cultures have an unconscious component;* that is, a component of which the individuals within the organization are unaware.

Ever since the days of Sigmund Freud, clinically oriented psychoanalysts have been concerned with the human unconscious. Freud began to understand the unconscious motivation of individuals through studying the personal histories of his patients. So-called unconscious phenomena are usually unrecognized by the person affected by them. If they obtrude into consciousness—for instance, in the form of an emotional outburst that is out of proportion to its apparent cause—they are largely inexplicable to anyone who is unaware of the nature of the unconscious motivation. When that happens, we may even say, "I don't know what came over me."

The evidence for the existence of the unconscious is now extensive. It is based on the study of the results of association tests, the psychoanalytic technique of free association, material derived from hypnosis, dream analysis, the study of such phenomena as dual personality, functional disturbances, and the dissociation of mental and nervous disorders.

It was left to Jung, Freud's student and colleague, to formulate the notion of collective unconscious. He considered that the study of the way our society had developed illuminated individual history; in fact, he went so far as to say that without history, there can be no psychology of the unconscious:

> I had grown up in the intensely historical atmosphere of Basel at the end of the nineteenth century and had acquired, thanks to the reading of the old philosophers, some knowledge of the history of psychology. When I thought about the dreams and the contents of the unconscious, I never did so without making historical comparisons.[7]

In Jung's view, the conscious mind grows out of an unconscious psyche that is older than it and that goes on functioning in spite of it.

Some cultural elements such as premises are considered to be unconscious dimensions of organizational culture. Few organization scholars have developed theories about the unconscious elements of organizational culture.

Relations between Individuals and Organizations

Anthropologists have long understood that in human beings, unlike in other life forms, the relationship between environment and behavior is a reciprocal one: human beings shape and are shaped by their cultures. In passing, we may note here that we highlighted this reciprocal relationship when we sketched the historical development of management theory.

In tracing the reciprocal relationship between the individual and society, anthropologists identify four central roles played by individuals. Each of us is:

1. A *creature* of culture, which strongly motivates the individual to behave appropriately in every situation and thus display conformity.
2. A *carrier* of culture, where the individual strives to exemplify the desirability of sanctioned ways and to teach them to others.
3. A *manipulator* of culture, who uses common attitudes, values, and patterns of behavior to advance individual interests.
4. A *creator* of culture, wherein the individual serves as a vehicle for cultural change by being able to challenge the *status quo* and bring about innovations.

These four roles further emphasize the give-and-take relation between individual and culture.[8]

This assumption is transported to organizational culture. Thus the relationship between individual and organization is considered to be reciprocal, each influencing the other.

Assumptions about Organizational Change

The final assumption pertaining to organizational change was also provided by anthropologists. According to them, there are many ways in which culture changes occur. Some changes can be anticipated, others come as surprises, and still others are transported from other cultures. Thus, *organizational culture continually evolves through trials.* Indeed, a system has some power to self-determine its own evolution and to find its temporary stability under given conditions.

Table 12.3 summarizes the key philosophical assumptions underlying the organizational culture field.

TABLE 12.3   **Summary of Philosophical Assumptions**

Type of Assumption	*Descriptions*
1. Organizations	Cultures are unique
	Organizations are symbolic entities
	Cultures have unconscious components
2. Relations between individual and organizations	Reciprocal, not unidirectional influence
3. Organizational change	Culture evolves through trials

Theoretical Underpinnings

In organization theory, comparative management scholars were among the first to embrace the concept of culture. They derived their inspiration from the work of anthropologists. Although early anthropological studies focused on tribal cultures (as exemplified by the work of Margaret Mead), during World War II Ruth Benedict demonstrated the utilitarian value of anthropology in her study of the Japanese culture for the State Department. Her work, published later under the title *The Chrysanthemum and the Sword,* not only provided an anthropological analysis of the Japanese society, but alluded to the military moves that the Japanese were likely to make during the war.[9] These national character studies, as they were then called, were followed by systematic studies investigating the differences among cultures.

In the wake of such studies, the *cross-cultural* method was born. This was designed to discover the similarities and differences among cultural patterns in a sizable sample of societies. The potentialities of this method were augmented by the creation of Human Relations Area Files, a cooperative enterprise among a number of universities to collect and process ethnographic data on a worldwide sample of societies.

The cross-cultural method got a boost from multinational corporations and government agencies when they confronted problems in transplanting U.S. management techniques to other countries (as we described in historical underpinnings). Comparative management scholars conceptualized culture as an important *environmental variable* over which an organization had very little control. Economists, international business scholars, and behaviorists all participated in the ensuing research programs. The primary practical outcome of these efforts was sensitizing the managers in overseas assignments to the role culture played in modifying the organizational practices transplanted from the United States.

Early glimpses of culture as an *internal* organizational variable that may offer opportunities for control and change were evident in the work of OD scholars. They formulated the concept of *organizational climate,* a summary measure of how people perceived an organization. In perhaps the first conference exploring the concept of climate, held at Harvard, the conceptual distinction between climate and culture was diffuse. Over time, however climate took a rather restrictive meaning. The climate theorists measured "How does it feel around here?" within an organizational context.

Organizational culture, as we understand it today, arrived as scholars began to contrast the inner workings of Japanese and American enterprises. Through their comparative studies, William Ouchi and the team of Anthony Athos and Richard Pascale brought to light the importance of organizational culture; they went on to assert that culture accounted for the success of an organization to a degree greater than other facets of the organizational system.[10]

During the last decade, scholars have studied and speculated on the role of organizational culture. How does culture influence organizational functioning? What is the relationship between culture and effectiveness? What are the cultural characteristics of effective organizations? How do leaders create cultures? How are cultures maintained and transmitted from generation to generation of employees? We will take up each one of these questions in turn.

Influence on Organizational Functioning: Strategy Implementation

The current interest in organizational culture derives from its presumed impact on strategy implementation. In our earlier chapter on strategic planning, we presented Miles and Snow's strategy types as modes by which organizations implement strategies.[11] Miles and Snow described characteristics of organizational culture that correlated with various strategy types. Ever since their work, there has been considerable research, theorizing, and even speculation that corporate culture can block or improve an organization's ability to implement new strategies.

Journalistic accounts suggest that efforts to implement a new strategy can fail because a company's culture is unsuited to the new business:

> A corporate culture that was once a source of strength for a company can become a major liability in successfully implementing a new strategy. For example, two major oil companies attempted to diversify because the current business would not support long-term growth and faced political threats. They announced new long-range strategies and developed elaborate strategies to implement them. Five years later, both firms had abandoned their plans and gone back to the oil business. Each company failed to implement its new strategy because the values and traditions of being an oil business were so strong and entrenched that employees resisted and even sabotaged the new strategy. Oil operations required long-term investments for long-range rewards, while the new business required short-term orientations and a focus on current returns. Success in the oil business came from wildcatting, while the new businesses based success on such abstractions as "market share" and "numbers growth." These changes violated employees' basic assumptions, values, and norms about their role in the firm and the traditions underlying the company's culture.[12]

The growing appreciation that corporate culture can play a significant role in implementing a new strategy has caused many firms to adopt culture change approaches. For example, hit with deregulation, AT&T has been attempting to change from a service-oriented telephone company to a market-oriented communications company (see Box 12.1).

Relationship to Organizational Effectiveness

Both theoretical and empirical works have examined the linkage between organizational culture and effectiveness.

Box 12.1

Cultural Change at AT&T

Over many years, AT&T developed a strong culture, characterized by lifetime careers, employee loyalty, fair treatment, up-from-the-ranks career ladders, and dedication to service. Then AT&T signed a divestiture agreement with the Department of Justice. Each of the 22 operating companies was to be spun off, and AT&T had to form a separate subsidiary to sell communications equipment. These changes required a complete overhaul of AT&T's way of doing business.

According to W. Brooke Tunstall of AT&T, top management believed culture could be changed, and it proceeded to take the following steps.

1. Set an example. Top managers began acting in a risk-oriented fashion. The chairman gave a speech suggesting that the label Ma Bell no longer fit the culture, and asked the audience to pass the word that "Ma Bell doesn't live here anymore."

2. Transform the system of management. Implementation of a new competitive strategy involved changes in management control systems, organization structure, and reward systems.

3. Articulate a new value system explicitly. AT&T developed a statement of policy setting forth the corporation's new goals and how it would do business in the future. New values were also articulated. The values—to act creatively, be adaptive,

and maximize new opportunities—shaped behavioral norms within AT&T.

4. Provide training to support cultural values. The human resource department developed training programs to modify behavior in support of the desired corporate culture. One program was geared for 2,000 subsidiary managers, and the Bell Advanced Management Program was used to train senior and middle management within AT&T.

5. Revise recruiting aims and methods. The company was to hire individuals who had values, personalities, and educational backgrounds in harmony with AT&T's new culture. Doing so would avoid potential problems of culture clash.

6. Modify symbols. Dropping the label Ma Bell indicated a break from the protective environment of the past. In addition, the traditional logo (a bell within a circle) was replaced with a globe symbolically girdled by electronic communications. The new symbol suggested the dimensions of the new business.

AT&T's managers believed they could redesign culture to fit the new competitive environment.

Source: Adapted from W. Brooke Turnstall, "Cultural Transition at AT&T," *Sloan Management Review* 25 (1983), pp. 15–26.

Theoretically, Jay Barney has suggested that organizational culture leads to higher economic performance when it is a source of competitive advantage. He identifies three conditions that must be satisfied for this to happen:

1. The culture must be *valuable;* it must enable a firm to do things and behave in ways that lead to high sales, low costs, high margins, or in other ways add financial value to the firm.

2. The culture must be *rare;* it must have attributes and characteristics that are not common to the cultures of a large number of firms.

3. A culture must be *imperfectly imitable;* firms without these cultures cannot engage in activities that will change their cultures to include the required characteristics, and if they try to imitate these cultures, they will be at some disadvantage (of reputation, experience, etc.) compared to the firm they are trying to imitate.[13]

Barney noted that if a firm's culture enables it to behave in ways that are inconsistent with its competitive situation, then that culture cannot be a source of competitive advantage. Further, if many firms have similar cultures none will possess a culturally based competitive advantage and one cannot expect above average economic performance. Finally, perfectly imitable cultures, even if rare and valuable, are subject to imitation that dissipates any advantage. These theoretical arguments are new and have never been put to empirical scrutiny.

Empirical efforts, however, do suggest that strong cultures contribute to economic performance. For example, comparative studies of Japanese and U.S. management done during the late 1970s conclude that the strong cultures in Japanese companies, which emphasize employee participation, open communication, security, and equality, at least partly contribute to their relative superiority. A more recent study of U.S. firms came to similar conclusions (see Box 12.2).

These theoretical and empirical studies indicate that organizational culture is a source of competitive advantage and hence has an influence on the long-term (sustained) performance of a firm.

Characteristics of Excellent Companies

The search for cultural characteristics of excellent companies has evolved over the years. Perhaps the first step in the search was initiated by Thomas Peters and Robert Waterman, both consultants with McKinsey Company. Based on their study of several large companies in the Untied States, Peters and Waterman listed eight cultural characteristics of excellent companies:

1. A *bias for action,* for getting on with it. Even though these companies may be analytical in their approach, they are not

Box 12.2

Influence of Organizational Culture on Performance

Denison, then a student at the University of Michigan, examined the linkage between organizational culture and financial performance in his Ph.D dissertation. This was among the first works to systematically investigate the topic.

Denison studied the performance over a five-year period of 34 large U.S. firms representing 25 different industries. To measure culture, he utilized a survey instrument that was completed by over 43,000 people. He utilized Standard & Poor's financial ratios as indicators of organizational effectiveness.

Based on his data, Denison drew three major conclusions:

1. Firms whose cultures support employee participation in decision making, flexible work methods, sensible job designs, and clear and reasonable goals, performed on average *twice* as high as companies scoring low on these factors.

2. The employee participation element of corporate culture only showed differences in effectiveness among firms after three years.

3. Other measures of culture showed differences in all five years.

This led Denison to suggest that such cultural characteristics as employee participation should be considered as long-term investments.

Source: D. Denison, "The Climate, Culture, and Effectiveness of Work Organizations: A Study of Organizational Behavior and Financial Performance," Ph.D. dissertation, University of Michigan, 1982.

---

paralyzed by such an orientation. In many of these companies, the standard motto is, "Do it, fix it, try it."

2. *Close to the customer.* These companies learn from the people they serve. They provide unparalled quality, service, and reliability.

3. *Autonomy and entrepreneurship.* Innovative companies foster many leaders and many innovators throughout the organization.

4. *Productivity through people.* Excellent companies treat the rank and file as the root source of quality and productivity gain.

5. *Hands-on, value driven.* Excellent companies ascribe the greatest importance to values in explaining their success; all levels of management spend considerable time down where the action is, walking the floors and assessing where the action is.

6. *Stick to the knitting.* The companies stay close to the businesses they know without dissipating their energies in acquiring unrelated businesses.

7. *Simple form, lean staff.* The structural forms and systems in these companies are simple, not complex as in matrix structures.

Box 12.3

Peters and Waterman's Study

Thomas J. Peters and Robert H. Waterman based their conclusions on an initial sample of 75 companies. Thirteen European companies were later dropped from analysis since they did not represent a fair cross-section of European companies. The remaining 62 companies, although not perfectly representative of the U.S. industry as a whole, captured a fairly broad spectrum. The companies in three samples were considered to be innovative and excellent by an informed group of observers of the business scene—businesspeople, consultants, members of the business press, and business academics.

The companies were grouped into various categories according to industries. The industry categories included:

1. High-technology companies such as Digital Equipment, Hewlett-Packard, Intel, and Texas Instruments.

2. Consumer goods companies, such as Procter & Gamble, Cheseborough-Pond's, and Johnson & Johnson.

3. Service companies such as Delta Airlines, Marriott, McDonald's, and Disney Productions.

4. Project management companies such as Bechtel and Fluor.

5. Resource-based companies such as Atlantic Richfield, Dow Chemical, and Exxon.

6. General industrial goods companies of interest, including Caterpillar, Dana, and 3M.

Some industries were not in the sample: financial institutions, chemical and drug companies, or small companies. Few firms in the sample had sales of less than $1 billion. Peters and Waterman used three screens to reduce the sample. First, financial performance should support reputation. They used six measures of long-term superiority: three measures of growth over a 20-year period (compound asset growth from 1961 through 1980; compound equity growth over the same period, and the ratio of market value to book value), and three measures of return on capital and sales (average return on total capital, 1961 through 1980; average return on equity, 1961 through 1980; average return on sales, 1961 through 1980). In order to qualify as a top performer, a company must have been in the top half of its industry in at least four

8. *Simultaneous loose-tight properties.* Excellent companies were both centralized and decentralized. Thus they have pushed autonomy down to the shop floor, but they are fanatic centralists around the core values they hold dear.[14]

Their study and some of the criticisms against their conclusions are presented in Box 12.3.

From our perspective, Peters and Waterman were advocating a *universal* approach to managing culture, an approach that flies in the face of all that we know about organizations. Later attempts have explicitly adopted a *contingency* perspective. For example, Terrence E. Deal and Allan A.

Box 12.3 continued

out of six of these measures over the full 20-year period.

Second, they explored a measure of innovativeness per se. They selected industry experts to rate the companies' 20-year records of innovation.

When these criteria were imposed, 19 companies dropped out of the original 62. Of the remaining 43, Peters and Waterman interviewed 21 in depth. They conducted less extensive interviews at 12 companies they had put in a "?" category; these were ones that did not pass all the screens but had just barely missed. Further, they followed all 62 closely in the literature for the 25 years preceding the study.

The Peters and Waterman study has several flaws. Certain methodological weaknesses and recent follow-up studies render interpretation of the results questionable:

1. The authors mainly studied successful companies and did not examine unsuccessful ones to see whether the cultural attributes were *absent* in those poor performers.

2. Measures of performance were confined to financial performance of the firms, and did not include economic measures such as return to shareholders. In fact, one replication

study concluded, "P&W's excellent firms have not demonstrated consistently superior stock market earnings performance over those same years."

3. Several of the companies have experienced financial difficulties in recent years, such as Dana, Johnson & Johnson, and 3M.

4. Another study, comparing P&W's excellent firms with a sample for the *Fortune* 1,000 list, strongly suggests that the excellent companies may not have excellence attributes to any greater extent than the general population of firms.

5. Not all excellence attributes were correlated with performance; only those features having to do with innovation, autonomy, and entrepreneurship had any appreciable relation to performance measures.

Source: Thomas J. Peters and Robert H. Waterman, Jr., *In Search of Excellence* (New York: Harper & Row, 1982). See also D. Carroll, "A Disappointing Search for Excellence," *Harvard Business Review*, December 1983, pp. 78–88; B. Johnson, A. Nakarajan, and A. Rappaport, "Shareholder Returns and Corporate Excellence," *Journal of Business Strategy*, Fall 1985, p. 61; "Who's Excellent Now?" *Business Week* 5 (November 1984), pp. 76–88; and Michael Hitt and R. Ireland, "Peters and Waterman Revisited: The Unended Quest for Excellence," *Academy of Management Executive*, May 1987, pp. 91–98.

Kennedy discovered that strong cultures reflect the characteristics of the marketplace. They identify two major market characteristics:

1. *Degree of risk* associated with the firms' activities.
2. *Speed of feedback:* the speed at which companies—and their employees—get feedback on whether decisions or strategies are successful.

Based on the market characteristics, they identified four corporate cultures, and provided examples of firms in each type. Deal and Kennedy's study is summarized in Box 12.4 and the culture types are presented in Figure 12.3.

Box 12.4

Deal and Kennedy's Study

Terrence E. Deal, then a professor at the Harvard Graduate School of Education, and Allan E. Kennedy, a principal at McKinsey & Company, teamed up to study corporate cultures. They conducted an informal survey by interviewing McKinsey consultants about organizations they were familiar with on a first-hand basis. Deal and Kennedy asked them several questions:

- Does Company X have one or more visible beliefs?
- If so, what are they?
- Do people in the organization know these beliefs? If so, who? and how many?
- How do these beliefs affect day-to-day business?
- How are the beliefs communicated to the organization?
- Are the beliefs reinforced—by formal personnel processes, recognition, rewards?
- How would you characterize the performance of the company?

In total, over a period of about six months, Deal and Kennedy developed profiles of nearly 80 companies. Here's what they found out:

- Over all the companies surveyed, only about one-third (25) had clearly articulated beliefs.

- Of this third, a surprising two-thirds had qualitative beliefs, or values, such as "IBM means service." The other third had financial oriented goals that were widely understood.
- Of the 18 companies with qualitative beliefs, all were uniformly outstanding performers; there were no correlations of any relevance among the other companies—some did okay; some poorly; most had their ups and downs. The consistently high performers were characterized as strong culture companies.

Deal and Kennedy concluded that people are a company's greatest resource, and the way to manage them is not directly by computer reports but by the subtle cues of a culture. A strong culture is a powerful mill for grinding behavior; it helps employees do their jobs a little better, especially in two ways:

1. A strong culture is a system of informal rules that spells out how people are to behave most of the time.
2. A strong culture enables people to feel better about what they do, so they are more likely to work harder.

Source: Terrence E. Deal and Allan A. Kennedy, *Corporate Cultures* (Reading, Mass.: Addison-Wesley Publishing, 1982).

The contingency perspective on organizational culture holds that there should be a match between culture and the market environment or business strategy of an organization. This perspective lies at the core of most culture change strategies that we will describe later.

FIGURE 12.3

Environmental characteristics and cultural types

DEGREE OF RISK

		High	Low
SPEED OF FEEDBACK	Fast	"Macho" tough-guy culture Example: Consulting organizations	Work hard/play hard culture Example: McDonald's
	Slow	Bet your company Example: NASA	Process culture Example: University

Leadership and Culture

How are cultures built? How do they change? These questions have led some scholars and researchers to the conclusion that strong leaders are the force behind creation or change of organizational culture.

Entrepreneurs or organizational founders influence the culture of an organization. They infuse their organizations with the values that they had inherited from prior socialization as well as from their past experiences. Due to their role as leader at a critical juncture of an organization, they are in a position to develop an organization's culture in unique ways. Consider the following example:

> Ewing Marion Kaufman is the founder of Marion Laboratories, a pharmaceutical firm, now termed Marion Dow. Prior to founding the firm, Kaufman used to work as a salesman for another pharmaceutical company. In that job he was highly successful. However, the first time he exceeded his sales quota, his sales territory was cut, thereby reducing his potential market and bonuses. Undaunted, he repeated the feat twice, only to be met with the same response from the organization he was working for. In disgust, he left the firm and started his own firm. Marion Labs is a marketing-driven firm reputed to be at the forefront of humanistic management. "We don't lay off people here; we will reward them for performance." These attitudes are part of the corporate philosophy of Marion.

Strong organizational cultures often exhibit the stamp of powerful founders: Tom Watson in the case of IBM, Ross Perot in the case of EDS, and Akio Morita in the case of Sony, the Japanese firm.

Just as in the case of creation, leaders also play a key role in changing organizational cultures. For example, Jack Welch at General Electric is credited with bringing about a major transformation of the giant company. These executives play three major roles:

Envisioning: This involves articulating a clear and credible vision of the new strategy and of the organization to support it.

Energizing: Executives must personally demonstrate excitement for the changes and model the behaviors that are expected of others. They must communicate examples of early success to mobilize energy for change.

Enabling: This role involves providing the resources necessary for undertaking significant change, and using rewards to reinforce new behaviors.[15]

Leaders who bring about cultural changes are often termed *transformational leaders.* Rosabeth Moss Kanter termed them *change masters.* According to her, change masters are "the right people in the right place at the right time."[16] The right people are the ones with the ideas that move beyond the organization's established practice (envisioning). The right places are the environments that encourage the building of coalitions and teams to support and implement visions (energizing). The right times are those moments in the flow of organizational history when it is possible to reconstruct reality on the basis of accumulated innovations to shape a more productive and successful future (enabling). Her account of leaders who bring about cultural change is presented in Box 12.5.

Maintenance and Transmission of Cultures

Just how does an organization maintain its culture? We have gained a renewed understanding of the mechanisms of maintenance in recent years. We can postulate three major mechanisms: (1) human resource management, (2) socialization practices, and (3) settings and media.

From a human resource management perspective, the processes of maintenance focus on recruitment and selection. Recently, Benjamin Schneider summarized this perspective. According to Schneider, strong cultures are maintained by systematic corporate recruitment.[17] For example, many U.S. firms, such as IBM and Hewlett-Packard, carefully screen their job candidates so that they take in people who will be comfortable with the existing corporate culture. Of course, there will be some mistakes; in such cases, the organization will let go of their mismatches. The process of recruitment and attrition are systematic; this fact enhances the likelihood that the remaining members will share in and reinforce the corporate culture.

Alternatively, the new members undergo a period of heavy *socialization* into the corporate culture. Learning the rules of the organizational game, the ropes to skip and the ropes to jump, are judged to be important keys to individuals' success in an organization. In turn, the organization develops mentors and sponsors to conduct such socialization. We will refer to these roles more fully when we deal with the development of general mangers.

The anthropological influence on organizational studies focused our attention on the *settings* and the *media* by which culture is transmitted and reinforced in organizations. The leaders of an organization institute cere-

Box 12.5

Rosabeth Moss Kanter on Change Masters

The art and architecture of change works through a different medium than the management of the ongoing, routinized side of an organization's affairs. Most of the rational, analytic tools measure what already is (or make forecasts as a logical extrapolation from data on what is). But change efforts have to mobilize people around what is not yet known, not yet experienced. They require a leap of imagination that cannot be replaced by references to all the "architect's sketches," "planner's blueprints," or examples of similar buildings that can be mustered. They require a leap of faith that cannot be eliminated by presentation of all the forecasts, figures, and advance guarantees that can be accumulated.

The tools of change masters are creative and interactive; they have an intellectual, a conceptual, and a cultural aspect. Change masters deal in symbols and visions and shared understandings as well as the techniques and trappings of their own specialties.

Change masters are—literally—the right people in the right place at the right time. The right people are the ones with the ideas that move beyond the organization's established practice, ideas they can form to visions. The right places are the integrative environments that support innovation, encourage the building of coalitions and teams to support and implement visions. The right times are those moments in the flow of organizational history when it is possible to reconstruct reality on the basis of accumulated innovations to shape a more productive and successful future.

The concepts and visions that drive change must be both inspiring and realistic, based on an assessment of that particular corporation's strengths and traditions. Clearly there is no "organizational alchemy" capable of transmuting an auto company into an electronics firm; there is only the hard work of searching for those innovations that fit the life stage and thrust of each company. But all companies can create more of the internal conditions that empower their people to carry out the search for those appropriate innovations. And in that search might lie the hope of the American economic future.

Source: Rosabeth Moss Kanter, "Change Masters and the Intricate Architecture of Corporate Culture Change," *Management Review* 72, no. 10 (October 1983), pp. 18–28.

monies and rituals where the dominant values and beliefs of the organizationare reinforced and propagated; stories, slogans, and symbols become the media by which such propagation is accomplished.

Ceremonies and *rites* are the elaborate planned activities that make up a special event. These create a special bond among people, help foster common understanding, and reinforce core values. Annual award ceremonies, Monday morning workout sessions, and election of key officers are ceremonies instituted in many organizations.

Stories, slogans, and *symbols* serve as the media by which culture is transmitted. Stories are narratives of events that took place in organizations that people recount *repeatedly,* thus transmitting cultural components to new individuals. Such stories are often about how an organization handled a problematic situation or about the "heroes" who made things happen in the organization—things that are judged, in retrospect, to have been important to the organization. Slogans are simpler than stories and represent the corporate credo. IBM's famous "Think" slogan is an example. In a sense, both stories and slogans are symbols, but when we talk of symbols, we include physical artifacts as well.

Deal and Kennedy gave us a glimpse of these rituals through which such socialization processes occur as well as creation of settings for reinforcing and transmission of central values (see Box 12.6 for some examples).

Summary

Organization theorists began to pay attention to culture when confronted by global competition, especially Japanese successes. They borrowed from the key assumptions of anthropologists and psychoanalysts: organizations are unique, they contain symbolic and unconscious elements, change is evolutionary, and individuals influence and are influenced by culture. Theoretical developments have suggested five aspects of culture: (1) culture needs to be aligned to strategy during implementation; (2) culture may be a source of competitive advantage; (3) the market environment influences an organization's culture; (4) transformational leaders establish and change an organization's culture; and (5) culture is maintained by recruitment and selection as well as socialization practices, and transmitted through ceremonies, stories, slogans, and symbols.

Key Themes

We distill four key themes that underlie many of the culture change activities: (1) objective of cultural interventions, (2) requirements of change, (3) levers of cultural change, and (4) process of change.

Objective: Building Strong Cultures

Corporate cultures vary in the degree to which they are integrated. In some organizations, which we will term *strong cultures,* the patterns are interwoven tightly and the culture of the organization is very strong and cohesive; everyone knows the goals of the organization and these goals set the pattern for people's activities, opinions, and actions. Organizations such as IBM or Hewlett-Packard reportedly have strong cultures. Employees within the organization take pride in proclaiming their identity (e.g., I'm with IBM).

Box 12.6

Examples of Cultural Elements

Tough-Guy, Macho Culture

A world of individualists who regularly like high risks and get quick feedback on whether their actions are right or wrong. Example: consulting firms.

Slogans: "Make great ads"

Heroes: Temperamental outlaw heroes

Value: Winning high stakes

Rituals: Superstition to protect people from mistakes

Work Hard/Play Hard Culture

Benign and hyperactive world of sales organizations. Examples: real estate, computer companies, retailers such as McDonald's.

Slogans: "Try it, fix it, do it"

Heroes: Super salespeople

Value: Volume

Rituals: Tupperware's rallies, Mary Kay's conventions

Bet Your Company Culture

A world of high risk but slow feedback. Example: NASA.

Slogans: "Progress is our most important product"

Heroes: Hunker down heroes who kept working on a project until it became a reality

Value: Invest in future

Rituals: Business meeting, well run, analytical

Process Culture

Low risk, slow-feedback corner of the world. Examples; banks, government, utilities.

Slogans: "Underevaluating excellence"

Heroes: Job may make the hero, not individual

Value: Technical perfection

Rituals: Slow rambling meetings

Source: Adapted from Terrence E. Deal and Allan A. Kennedy, *Corporate Cultures* (Reading, Mass.: Addison-Wesley Publishing, 1982).

Sometimes, however, the patterns are fragmented and difficult to read from the outside—some people are loyal to their bosses, others are loyal to the union, still others care only about their colleagues who work in the sales territories, and so on.

As we noted earlier, culture influences behavior; strong cultures exert a strong influence on organizational behavior. They informally standardize behavior by communicating to employees codes of acceptable behavior and thus act as a control mechanism.

The objective of most cultural change interventions is to build a *strong desirable* culture within an organization. By *desirable* we mean a culture that is appropriate for the strategy and the environment of an organization. By *strong* we mean a culture whose patterns are tightly interwoven and fully communicated and understood by employees, with severe sanctions against violating expectations.

Characteristics of Culture Change

We can identify five major characteristics of cultural change:[18]

1. *Change triggered by environmental and internal disruptions.* Cultural change is initiated only when there are strong reasons to do so. Since there are strong vested interests in any organization—that is, political subsystems that try to preserve the status quo—organizations are likely to fine tune structures rather than undertake major cultural change. Only when internal and external factors render organizational strategies and structures obsolete would organizations undertake cultural change.

Change typically occurs in response to three types of disruptions:

   a. *Industry discontinuities:* changes in legal, political, economic, and technological conditions that shift the basis for competition within industries.
   b. *Product life-cycle shifts:* stages in business growth rates, which require different strategies.
   c. *Internal company dynamics:* changes in size, corporate portfolio, executive turnover, and the like.[19]

These disruptions severely jolt the organization into undertaking cultural change.

2. *Revolutionary change.* Cultural change involves abrupt shifts in most parts and components of an organization. Since different features of an organization—for example, strategy and structure—tend to reinforce each other, it is difficult to change them in a piecemeal fashion. Cultural change requires that they be changed simultaneously to support a new strategic direction.

Studies of organizational growth point to the benefits of implementing cultural change as rapidly as possible. The faster an organization can respond to disruptions, the quicker it can attain the benefits of operating in a new way.

3. *New organizing paradigm.* Organizations undertaking cultural change have devised entirely new ways of organizing and behaving. Although the changes are tailored to specific environments, the following general features capture the new organizing paradigm: (a) *leaner, more flexible structures;* (b) *information and decision making pushed down to the lowest levels;* (c) *decentralized teams and business units* accountable for specific products, services, or

customers; and (d) *participative management and teamwork,* which helps to promote commitment to the organization.

4. *Driven by senior executives and line management.* A key feature of cultural change is the active role of senior executives and line managers in all phases of the change process. They are responsible for the strategic direction and operation of the organization and should actively lead the transformation. However, since existing executives may lack the talent, energy, and commitment to undertake these tasks, outsiders may have to be recruited to lead the change. Research on cultural change has documented that externally recruited executives are three times more likely to initiate such change than intact executive teams.[20]

5. *Continuous learning and change.* Since cultural change is uncertain and risky, it requires more innovation and learning. Organizational members must learn how to enact the new behaviors required to implement the new directions. Because members must usually learn qualitatively different ways of perceiving, thinking, and behaving, the learning process is likely to be substantial and occurs at all levels of the organization, from executives to lower-level employees.[21]

Taken together, these characteristics of organizational change set it apart from many incremental change efforts such as organization development.

Levers of Cultural Change

Earlier, we identified five elements of organizational culture: artifacts, beliefs, norms, values, and premises. As can be seen from Figure 12.4, these may be arrayed along a continuum from surface to deeper elements. Artifacts are on the surface and hence, more easily changed, whereas deeper elements such as premises are quite difficult to change. Most cultural change approaches initially focus on the surface (thus, relatively easily changed) elements of culture such as artifacts, beliefs, or norms.

The levers of changing the surface elements are rites and ceremonies, stories, and language and symbols. We have already seen the impact of these levers on the maintenance and propagation of culture. The same levers are used to bring about changes in culture as well. Table 12.4 presents examples of how rites, ceremonies, stories, language, and symbols are used to implement culture.

FIGURE 12.4

Levers of cultural change

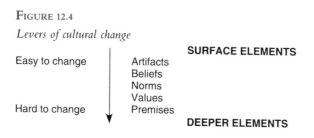

TABLE 12.4 **Implementation of Culture**

Underlying Culture	Surface Techniques for Implementing Culture

Shared values
    Customer service at any cost
    Employees are part of family
    Attain sales targets
	Ceremonies
	    Annual awards for meritorious customer
	        service
	    Monthly meetings to acknowledge people
	        who attain 100% of sales targets

Guiding beliefs
    Customers deserve special treatment
    We like this company
    The company cares about us
	Stories
	    Founder's difficulty establishing company
	        over many obstacles without ever laying
	        off anyone
	    Heroic efforts to please customers by
	        legendary salespeople
	Language and symbols
	    "Build bridges" (to be in touch with
	        customers)
	    "We don't stand on rank" (equality of
	        family)
	    Open offices for easy communication
	    Special plaques for customer service and sales
	        leaders

Source: Adapted and modified from Vijay Sathe, "Implications of Corporate Culture: A Manager's Guide to Action," *Organizational Dynamics,* Autumn 1983, pp. 5–23.

Process of Cultural Change

There are two broad stages in *planned* culture change efforts: (1) diagnosis and (2) change.

1. *Diagnosis.* Culture change interventions generally start by diagnosing an organization's existing culture to assess its fit with current and proposed strategy. The degree of "misfit" is assessed and this assessment serves as the basis of initiating change efforts.

2. *Change.* Those advocating culture change generally focus on the more surface elements of culture such as norms. Since culture change is risky, however, most practitioners in this area suggest that changes in corporate culture should be considered only after other less difficult and less costly solutions have been ruled out.

Summary

The objective of culture change activities is to build strong cultures. They are undertaken when there are significant environmental and internal shifts, and are led by senior line managers. Cultural changes involve continuous learning and innovation. Most culture change efforts focus on the surface elements: artifacts, beliefs, and norms. The process of change involves the two steps of diagnosis and change.

We will now present the currently popular approaches for diagnosis and changing culture.

Methods for Diagnosing Culture

As we saw in the preceding section, culture change interventions start by diagnosing the organization's existing culture to assess its fit with current or proposed business strategy. This requires uncovering and understanding people's basic assumptions, values, norms, beliefs, and artifacts. Collecting such information poses at least three difficult problems:

1. People take cultural assumptions for granted and rarely speak of them directly. Rather, a company's culture is implied in concrete behavioral examples such as daily routines, stories, rituals, and language. This means that considerable time and effort must be spent observing, sifting through, and asking people about cultural outcroppings in order to understand their significance for organization members.

2. Some values and beliefs that people say they espouse have little to do with the ones they really hold and follow. People are reluctant to admit this discrepancy, yet somehow the real assumptions underlying idealized portrayals of culture must be discovered.

3. Large, diverse cultures are likely to have several subcultures, including countercultures going against the grain of the wider corporate culture. This means that focusing on limited parts of the organization or on a few select individuals may provide a distorted view of the organization's culture and subcultures.

To address these problems, practitioners have developed several techniques to diagnose various aspects of culture. We present three major approaches: (1) assumption analysis, (2) culture gap survey, and (3) managerial behavior approach.

Assumption Analysis

Assumption analysis was developed by Richard Mason and Ian Mitroff to bring to the surface and test an organization's *beliefs,* which, as we have seen, are a component of culture.[22] Mason and Mitroff argue that much of the strategic analysis actually taking place in organizations is built on hidden beliefs or assumptions held by individuals. As a result, the strategy analyses are superficial and often degenerate into a politically charged drama where the participants push their preferred alternatives instead of engaging in rational analysis.

The objective of assumption analysis is to bring to the surface the hidden beliefs for scrutiny so that *integrative* solutions can be forged. Assumption analysis is founded on the philosophical method called the *dialectical inquiring system.*

> *Dialectical Inquiring System.* A system is dialectical if it examines a situation completely and logically from two opposing points of view.

Most strategy analyses in organizations center on data and conclusions. This assumes that different individuals hold similar beliefs and reasoning, a condition that is not often realized in practice. Nevertheless, it is difficult for individuals to articulate their own beliefs and reasoning because these assumptions lie below their levels of awareness. To enable such articulation, a dialectical inquiring system is necessary. In assumptional analysis this system is created through structured debate:

> Structured debate consists of the most forceful presentation possible of the two opposing plans under the constraint that each side must interpret the same data.

The strategy maker comes to understand a decision's fundamental assumptions by observing the conflict that emerges between a plan and a counterplan.

Mason and Mitroff note that the collision among assumptions that takes place in a structured dialectical debate helps unearth the beliefs in an organizational setting and thus leads to a comprehensive analysis of strategy issues. However, they also note that the approach is applicable only when supported by other norms within the organization, such as the willingness of individuals to lay bare their fundamental assumptions, or receptiveness in the organization to bringing conflicts to the surface and dealing with them.

We may note that in practice, this approach deals with the surface elements of organizational culture and does not concern itself with deeper levels such as values and premises. However, assumption analysis suggests that beliefs about the environment that undergird most strategic decisions are never fully validated by data. Box 12.7 presents the example of the use of assumption analysis in a pharmaceutical company.

Culture Gap Survey

A second method uses standard surveys to uncover corporate culture. An example is the Kilmann and Saxton Culture-Gap survey, which is used to detect the gap between the existing culture and what it should be.[23] This survey measures culture at the norm level just below the surface of member behaviors. Organizational members are asked to respond to 28 standard norm pairs in terms of both actual norms and desired norms to achieve high performance. The differences between the actual and desired norms represent culture gaps in four major areas: (1) task support norms, (2) task

Box 12.7

Pharmaceutical Company Pricing Issue

This case involves a drug company that was faced with a major pricing policy decision on an important product. The decision would have vast impact on the economic structure of the entire company. As a result, the decision required analyses of the entire internal financial structure of the company, as well as market considerations.

When the problem surfaced, there were already three existent and significant groups of managers within the drug company, each of which had a significantly different policy with respect to the pricing of the drug: the high-price group, unbeknownst to themselves and to the others, held very different macroassumptions regarding important stakeholders and had very different detailed microassumptions about the problem. These three natural groups were formed into SAST groups. Stakeholder analysis was used to identify the assumptions of each group. The groups were asked to consider all the parties who might affect or be affected by an important decision. They listed as many parties or interest groups as they could who had a stake in the policy under consideration. For the most part, drug company categories are generic and, with little modification, apply to many business situations. As it turned out, it was important to differentiate between large-scale chain retailers and small-scale, singly owned pharmaceutical outlets.

Pricing policy is greatly affected by what is assumed about each of the stakeholder categories. For instance, it is difficult to support a policy of raising the price of the drug if it is assumed that the physician is price sensitive to the needs of patients. In fact, the whole point of getting managers to identify important stakeholders is to help them confront the question: What is it that you have been assuming about stakeholders or that you have had to assume about them so that starting from these assumptions as premises you are able to derive your policy? In response to this question, the high-price group assumed that "the physician prescribed the best quality drug for the patient." The low-price group assumed that "the physician prescribes the lowest price drug that will serve the patient's needs." Finally, the mid-price group assumed that: "The physician was satisfied with the current price, since it represented a good trade-off between price and quality." The controversy underlying these differences in assumptions among groups led to the stakeholder "physician" being rated as very important but also as very uncertain by each group. This became a major issue in the debate.

As a result of the SAST process two critical issues emerged that were significant for the choice of a pricing policy. These were:

1. How does the price of the drug affect physicians' prescription behavior?
2. Will the parent company (of which the drug company was a subsidiary) provide the finances, advertising, and general administrative support necessary for the company to execute such a strategy?

The second issue was resolved when the parent company indicated a preference for supporting a high-price, lower volume business. The first was resolved through a careful analysis of the regret involved in choosing each option. The group finally coalesced on the assumption that if the price were raised and then subsequently lowered for market reasons, the physician would still prescribe the drug. However, once the price of the drug was lowered, the company could not raise the price and still expect the physician to prescribe it. As a result of this debate, the company decided to raise the price.

Source: Richard O. Mason and Ian I. Mitroff, *Challenging Strategic Planning Assumptions* (New York: John Wiley & Sons, 1981), pp. 76–78.

innovation norms, (3) social relationship norms, and (4) personal freedom norms. The survey is usually administered as part of a larger effort to detect and close culture gaps in organizations.

Managerial Behavior Approach

A third approach to cultural diagnosis involves describing culture in terms of key managerial behaviors. This method provides specific normative statements about how managerial tasks are performed and how relationships are managed in an organization. The data provide clues to the *cultural risk* of trying to implement organizational changes needed to support a new strategy. If the new strategy requires behaviors that are drastically different from the prevalent ones, then managers will find it difficult to implement it. Based on the risks, managers can decide whether the implementation plan should be changed to manage around the existing culture, whether culture should be changed, or whether the strategy itself should be abandoned.

H. Schwartz and S. Davis describe the three steps in this approach:[24]

1. *Identify the existing culture.* In the first step, an organization's culture is described: how managerial tasks are performed and how organizational relationships are usually managed. Data is usually obtained from a series of individual and group interviews asking managers to describe "the way the game is played," as if they were coaching a new member. Four key relationships—companywide, boss-subordinate, peer, and interdepartment—and six managerial tasks—innovating, decision making, communicating, organizing, monitoring, and rewarding—are studied. This results in a number of implicit norms; see, for example, the corporate culture of an international banking division in Box 12.8.

2. *List organizational changes needed to implement strategy.* In this step, changes needed to implement a new strategy are identified: changes in organization structure, systems, people, reward systems, and so on. Thus, a strategic decision to diversify may require the following supporting changes; change from functional to product division, development of a profit-center accounting system, and development of autonomous managers.

3. *Assess cultural risks.* The final step involves assessing the degree to which the needed changes (step 2) fit with the organization's culture (step 1). Modifications that are incompatible with the culture are likely to be resisted. Because some of the proposed changes are more central to the new strategy than others, the degree of cultural risk depends on two issues:

   a. The degree of importance to the strategy.

   b. Compatibility with the existing culture.

The risks can be arrayed on a matrix, as shown in Figure 12.5. The greatest risks are those where the changes are highly important to the strategy but highly incompatible with the existing culture.

Box 12.8

Summary of Corporate Culture at an International Banking Division

Relationships	*Culture Summary*
Companywide	Preserve employee autonomy.
	Allow area managers to run the business as long as they meet the profit budget.
Boss–subordinate	Avoid confrontations.
	Smooth over disagreements.
	Support the boss.
Peer	Guard information; it is power.
	Be a gentleman or a lady.
Interdepartment	Protect your department's bottom line.
	Form alliances around specific issues.
	Guard your turf.

Tasks	*Culture Summary*
Innovating	Consider it risky.
	Be a quick second.
Decision making	Handle each deal on its own merits.
	Gain consensus.
	Require many sign-offs.
	Involve the right people.
	Seize the opportunity.
Communicating	Withhold information to control adversaries.
	Avoid confrontations.
	Be a gentleman or lady.
Organizing	Centralize power.
	Be autocratic.
Monitoring	Meet short-term profit goals.
Appraising and rewarding	Reward the faithful.
	Choose the best bankers as managers.
	Seek safe jobs.

Source: Reproduced by permission of the publisher from H. Schwartz and S. Davis, "Matching Corporate Culture and Business Strategy," *Organizational Dynamics* 10 (Summer 1981), p. 38.

FIGURE 12.5

Cultural change: Assessment of risk

DEGREE OF IMPORTANCE OF STRATEGY

	High	Low
High	Moderate riskiness	Not risky
Low	Very risky	Moderate riskiness

COMPATIBILITY WITHIN EXISTING CULTURE

TABLE 12.5   **Comparison of Diagnostic Methods**

Dimension	*Assumption Analysis*	*Culture Gap Survey*	*Managerial Behavioral Approach*
Elements of culture focused	Beliefs	Norms	Beliefs/norms/values
Method	Dialectical debate	Survey	Individual and group interviews
Type of activity	Behavioral process	Analytical	Analytical
Primary utility	Strategy formulation	Strategy implementation	Assessment of risks of change
Time frame	Short	Relatively short	Short to medium
Intrusiveness into organization	Low	Medium	Relatively high

Summary

The four methods differ in terms of elements, data, and intrusiveness. In general, the greater the focus on the surface elements, the quicker the diagnosis. Table 12.5 summarizes these differences.

Culture Change Approaches

Culture change is risky and difficult to implement. Based on the cultural diagnosis, an organization may decide not to undertake culture change. However, large-scale cultural change is necessary in certain conditions: if the firm's culture does not fit with the environment, if the industry is very competitive, if the company is mediocre, or if the company is about to become very large. Culture change approaches have originated in response to this need for culture change.

Culture change approaches are in the formative stage; hence, their effectiveness is not known with certainty. As a result several practical guidelines have been suggested by culture change advocates to avoid major pit-falls. We may identify six guidelines for all culture change approaches:

1. *Clear strategic vision.* Effective cultural change should start from a clear vision of the firm's new strategy and of the shared values and behaviors needed to make it work. A useful approach to providing clear strategic vision is development of a statement of corporate purpose, listing in straightforward terms the basic values the organization believes in.

2. *Top-management commitment.* Cultural change should be managed from the top of the organization. Senior managers and administrators need to be strongly committed to the new values and need to create constant pressures for change. They also must have the staying power to see the changes through.

3. *Symbolic leadership.* Senior executives must communicate the new culture through their own actions. Their behaviors need to symbolize the kinds of values and behaviors being sought.

4. *Supporting organizational changes.* Culture change must be accompanied by supporting modifications in organizational structure, human resource systems, information and control systems, and management styles.

5. *Selection and socialization of newcomers.* One of the most effective methods for changing corporate culture is to change organizational membership. People can be selected and terminated in terms of their fit with their new culture.

6. *Ethical and legal sensitivity.* Cultural change can raise significant tensions between organization and individual interests, resulting in ethical and legal problems for practitioners. Recommendations for reducing the chances of such problems include: setting realistic values for culture change and not promising what the organization cannot deliver; encouraging input from throughout the organization in setting cultural values; providing mechanisms for member dissent and diversity, such as internal review procedures; and educating managers about legal and ethical pitfalls inherent in cultural change and helping them to develop guidelines for resolving such issues.

We will now describe two major culture change approaches: (1) Tichy's approach to strategic change, and (2) Mohrman and Cummings' self-design strategy.

Tichy's Strategic Change Approach[25]

Noel Tichy's approach is premised on the idea that to bring about major strategic change, cultural, technical, and political systems of an organization should all be managed so that each supports the other. For example, if environmental forces push banks to offer a wider range of financial services, then organization structures might change from functional departments to product groups. This would require corresponding changes in the political systems—for example, budgets or promotions—and in cultural systems—for example, values to support the product structure. Otherwise, the three systems would become misaligned and banks would have severe difficulties in implementing and taking advantage of the new structure.

Tichy presents three basic sets of managerial tools for aligning the technical, political, and cultural systems: (1) mission and strategy of the organization, (2) the organization's structure, including administrative procedures, and (3) human resource management practices. Figure 12.6 displays the tools proposed by Tichy. These tools can be used to adjust any or all of the three systems.

Figure 12.6

Tichy's model: Tools for culture change

Managerial areas	**Managerial tools**		
	Mission and strategy	Organization structure	Human resource management
Technical system	• Assessment of environment • Assessment of organization • Definition of mission and fit of resources	• Differentiation • Integration • Alignment of structure to strategy	• Fitting of people to roles • Specification of performance criteria • Measurement of performance • Staffing and development
Political system	• Determination of those who influence mission and strategy • Management of coalitional behavior around strategic decisions	• Distribution of power • Balance of power across groups of roles	• Management of succession politics • Design and administration of reward system • Management of appraisal politics
Cultural system	• Management of influence of values and philosophy on mission and strategy • Development of culture aligned with mission and strategy	• Development of a managerial style aligned with structure • Development of subcultures to support roles • Integration of subcultures to form company culture	• Selection of people to build or reinforce culture • Development to mold organization culture • Management of rewards to shape the culture

Source: Noel Tichy, *Managing Strategic Change: Technical, Political, and Cultural Strands* (New York: John Wiley & Sons, 1983).

Tichy suggests the following three steps to change an organization from its present condition to some desired future state:

1. *Develop a vision.* Change must start with some vision of a revised organizational state. This image must include a view of technical, political, and cultural systems, as well as a view of what the organization will look like when these are aligned.

2. *Uncouple, intervene separately.* During this step, the three systems—technical, political and cultural—are unhooked from each other, and interventions are made *separately* in each system. Managers and employees are thus allowed to experiment with new designs without having to worry about rules, or measurement and reward systems.

3. *Plan for recoupling the three systems.* Once appropriate interventions have occurred in one or more of the three systems separately, it is necessary to plan how they will be recoupled with one another.

In using the tools for change, Tichy points out that managers must recognize that the nine cells represent a jigsaw puzzle with the different parts needing to be aligned with one another. An effective organization possesses a reasonable fit or congruence among the parts.

Mohrman and Cummings' Self-Design Strategy[26]

In turbulent environments, organizations need to develop the capacity for self-designing; that is, ability to transform themselves without assistance from external sources to achieve high performance. Susan Mohrman and Thomas Cummings have developed a self-design strategy that involves an ongoing series of designing and implementing activities carried out by managers and employees at all levels of the firm. The approach helps members to translate corporate values and general prescriptions for change into specific structures, processes, and behaviors suited to their situations.

Mohrman and Cummings identify five conditions that require the self-design strategy:

1. There is the need for a *systemic* change process that involves altering most features of the organization and achieving a fit among them.

2. In situations experiencing heavy change and uncertainty, changing is never totally finished, as new structures and processes will continually have to be modified to fit emerging conditions. The change process needs to be *dynamic and iterative,* with organizations continually changing themselves.

3. Since current knowledge about transforming organizations provides only general prescriptions for change, organizations need

to translate that information into specific structures, processes, and behaviors appropriate to their situations. This requires considerable innovation; self-design strategies should facilitate this *organizational learning*.

4. Since systemic change affects many organizational stakeholders, the change process must attend to the interests of *multiple stakeholders*.

5. Transformational change needs to occur at *multiple levels of the organization* if new strategies are to result in changed behaviors throughout the firm. Top executives must formulate a corporate strategy and clarify a vision of what the organization needs to look like to support it. Middle- and lower-level managers need to operationalize those broad parameters by creating structures, procedures, and behaviors to implement the strategy.

The self-design strategy is presented schematically in Figure 12.7. It consists of three stages: (1) laying the foundation, (2) designing, and (3) implementing and assessing.

Laying the Foundation
The first step provides organizational members with the basic knowledge and information to get started with the change effort. It involves three types of activities: (1) acquiring knowledge, (2) valuing, and (3) diagnosing.

1. *Acquiring knowledge.* This involves knowledge about how organizations function, principles for achieving high performance, and the self-design process. This information is generally gained through reading relevant material, attending in-house workshops, and visiting other organizations that have successfully transformed themselves.

FIGURE 12.7

Mohrman and Cummings' model

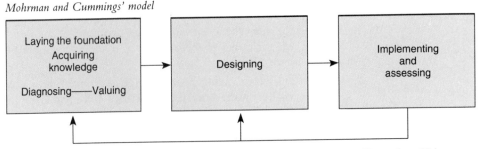

Source: Susan Mohrman and Thomas G. Cummings, *Self-designing Organizations: Learning How to Create High Performance* (Reading, Mass.: Addison-Wesley Publishing).

2. *Valuing* or determining the corporate values that will guide the transformation process. These values represent those performance outcomes and organizational conditions that will be needed to implement the corporate strategy. They are typically written in a values statement that is discussed and negotiated among the multiple stakeholders at all levels of the organization.

3. *Diagnosing* the current organization to determine what needs to be changed to enact the corporate strategy and values. Organizational members typically look for incongruities between the organization's functioning and its valued performance and conditions.

Designing

This second stage of self-design involves generating organization designs and innovations to support corporate strategy and values. Organizational members pay attention to specifying the broad features of a new organization while leaving the specifics to be tailored to the different levels and groupings within the organization. Referred to as *minimum specification design,* this process recognizes that designs need to undergo considerable refinement and modification as they are implemented throughout the firm.

Implementing and Assessing

This last stage involves implementing the organization changes designed above. It includes an ongoing cycle of changing structures and behaviors, assessing progress, and making necessary modifications. Information about the progress of implementation is collected and used to clarify design and implementation issues and to make necessary adjustments.

According to Mohrman and Cummings, although the steps are presented sequentially, there is considerable iteration among them. As shown in Figure 12.7, the feedback loops suggest that the implementation and assessment activities may lead back to affect subsequent designing, diagnosing, valuing, and acquiring knowledge activities. This iterative sequence of activities provides organizations with the capacity to transform and improve themselves continually. Box 12.9 presents the story of a glassmaking company that used the self-design strategy.

Systems Theoretic Review

As we have seen, organization culture interventions have espoused fundamental organizational changes, in contrast to the incremental approaches advocated by organization development consultants. They also emphasize the interrelationship between the culture and the strategy of an organization.

Box 12.9

Self-Design at Mega Glass Company

In the mid-1980s, Mega Glass Company was one of the fastest growing and most successful firms in the United States. Started only a few years earlier by a group of entrepreneurs and experienced glassmakers, Mega had grown rapidly into the nation's fourth-largest glass company through selected acquisitions, innovative products and production methods, and skillful financial management. In the face of this success, two key problems were emerging. First, senior executives were uncertain about how to maintain this entrepreneurial spirit as Mega grew older and larger. They feared that the company would become bureaucratized. Second, management felt that they had already reaped most of the benefits that could be obtained from cost cutting and reducing slack resources, and they sought other means of achieving performance gains.

A company task force was put together to recommend solutions to these problems. After reading, visiting other firms, and consulting with experts, the task force recommended to senior management the need to move toward a corporate culture promoting involvement and innovation at all levels of the firm. It argued that Mega's rapid growth had primarily been managed from the top of the company and that middle managers and employees had been left out of the decision-making and growth process. They would need to be more involved in the future if Mega hoped to continue to improve and to innovate in the competitive glassmaking industry. After considerable discussion and debate, senior management decided to initiate a companywide change process aimed at enhancing involvement, innovation, and performance, and at keeping the entrepreneurial spirit alive as the company continued to expand and grow.

As a first step toward change, senior executives met for several days to discuss Mega's strategic direction and to clarify the kinds of values and norms that would be needed to implement it. The outcome of this meeting was the first draft of a vision statement for Mega. It laid out the firm's dynamic, flexible approach to business and identified a number of corporate values, including participative decision making, management by continuous dialogue, employee growth and learning, attractive rewards, customer service, and ethical and legal behaviors. The key issue now was to translate these abstractions into concrete structures, processes, and behaviors throughout the firm.

Senior executives decided to get professional help to manage the change process and contacted university-based action researchers with experience in transformational change. After initial discussion and contracting, the researchers suggested that the top three levels of management at Mega should meet for a series of intense workshops to gain knowledge about organization change, to review the values statement, and to assess preliminarily how well those values were being enacted at Mega. The initial workshop took place at corporate headquarters and included about 45 senior executives, from the president and his staff down to managers of production plants and distribution centers. Participants gained knowledge of how organizations function, innovations to achieve high performance, and a self-design strategy to manage transformational change.

Against this conceptual background, the second workshop addressed the values statement and assessed how well the values were currently being enacted at Mega. Participants had a spirited debate about the practicality of the values and whether they were realistic for a

Box 12.9 continued

company that had grown rapidly with a firm management hand and a history of cost cutting and pruning of slack resources. Members were asked to assess how consistently Mega operated on each of the separate value statements. They identified five major areas of inconsistency, including rewards based on skills and achievement, the continual upgrading of employee skills, open feedback and information exchange, flexible approaches to problem solving, and identification with the customer. Members formed corporatewide task forces around each of these inconsistencies in order to assess further why these values were not being implemented and to suggest ways to reduce the inconsistencies. A similar process of clarifying and assessing company values was initiated at lower levels of Mega, down through the production plants.

Over the next two years, the task forces designed a number of organizational changes aimed at promoting the corporate values. Included among these were greater information sharing between headquarters and plant personnel, a more development-oriented performance appraisal system, open job posting, performance-based reward structures, and employee involvement methods such as self-managing teams and employee-management committees. At the plant levels, similar suggestions for improvement were initiated. For example, one plant that had been experiencing labor problems started an employee-involvement program jointly managed by union officials and managers. This effort did much to turn around the poor labor climate and productivity of the plant. Also, a new plant was designed and implemented using high-involvement concepts such as self-managing teams, a flat hierarchy, skill-based play, gain sharing, and realistic job previews. All of these changes took place with the guidance of the

company's values and strategic direction.

When implementing these changes throughout Mega, periodic measures were taken of how well the changes were progressing and whether they were achieving expected results. This information was collected by the various task forces and plant-level design teams through surveys, company records, and selected interviews. The data pointed out areas where the implementation process was having difficulty and enabled members to make necessary modifications. For example, methods for communicating between headquarters staff and plant personnel were revised based on members' reactions to initial communication efforts. Similarly, the team structures in the new plant were modified based on early experience with the initial designs. This feedback and adjustment process did not always go smoothly, as members sometimes denied the feedback data and failed to make necessary alterations in organizational improvement. This was part of the learning process, however, and members of Mega gradually came to realize the benefits of assessing and altering the improvements.

At this time, Mega is still in the process of implementing its strategic direction and enacting its corporate values to support that direction. There have been some dramatic successes, such as the turnaround of the unionized plant, and some initial disappointments, such as the technical start-up of the new plant. The company is continuing to grow rapidly through additional acquisitions, productivity improvements, and innovative products. Perhaps equally important, Mega is building—in the capacity to change and improve itself continually at all levels of the firm.

Source: Susan Mohrman and Thomas G. Cummings, *Self-Designing Organizations: Learning How to Create High Performance* (Reading, Mass.: Addison-Wesley Publishing).

However, there are two areas where culture change theorists have not developed their approach to incorporate organizational realities:

1. While culture theorists acknowledge the influence of cultural elements such as premises on how organizations interpret their environments, they have not provided mechanisms by which organizations may understand environments unfettered by existing premises.
2. They have not accommodated the implications of information technologies for cultural characteristics.

Additionally, it is not clear whether organizations can change their cultures fast enough to survive major environmental jolts. Thus, viewed from the vantage point of the systems model, prevalent culture change approaches are not systemic enough since they do not address either the environment or all the subsystems in an organization. However, culture change approaches offer a promising set of strategies for radical changes in the human elements of an organization.

Chapter Summary

Organizational culture refers to the pattern of artifacts, beliefs, norms, values, and premises held by an organization. Culture is shared among large groups of organizational members, and it is transmitted through a process of socialization whereby new members learn the culturally appropriate ways of behaving in an organization. Culture incorporates instrumental and expressive elements: instrumental elements standardize behavior, and expressive elements focus on the spontaneous elements of the organization.

The organizational culture field draws five major assumptions from psychoanalysis and anthropology: (1) organizational cultures are unique; (2) organizations have symbolic elements: language, myths, and shared codes of meaning; (3) culture incorporates unconscious elements that are invisible to the members of an organization; (4) the relation between individuals and culture is reciprocal, each influencing the other; and (5) cultural changes take place in many ways.

Culture theorists have emphasized five ideas. First, they have noted that culture influences strategy implementation. Second, imitable cultures may be a source of competitive advantage. Third, there should be a match between culture and the market environment or business strategy of an organization. Fourth, leadership plays a major role in establishing and changing culture; culture leaders play three major roles; envisioning, energizing, and enabling. Finally, culture is transmitted and maintained through human resource management, socialization practices, and through ceremonies, rites, stories, slogans, and symbols.

The objective of culture change is to build a strong culture. Culture change is typically triggered by environmental and internal disruptions; to be successful, it has to be led by senior executives and line management. Although all the elements of culture—artifacts, beliefs, norms, values, and premises—provide levers of change, surface elements like artifacts or beliefs are easier to change than deeper elements like values and premises.

There are two broad stages to culture change: diagnosis and change. Three approaches to diagnosing culture are currently available: (1) assumption analysis is useful to examine and change the beliefs that undergird strategy formulation, (2) culture gap surveys focus on diagnosing the organizational norms through a survey, and (3) the managerial behavior approach is useful for assessing the risk of culture change.

Noel Tichy, Susan Mohrman and Thomas Cummings have proposed ways of managing culture change. Tichy has proposed a strategy of culture change that incorporates three major elements: (1) mission and strategy of an organization, (2) its structure and administrative procedures, and (3) human resource management practices. He identifies three stages: (1) develop a vision, (2) uncouple the three elements, and (3) recouple the three elements. Mohrman and Cummings' self-design strategy also proposes a three-stage strategy: (1) laying the foundation, (2) designing, and (3) implementing and assessing.

Both approaches are experimental and we are in no position to assess their efficacy. However, from an open systems model, we can suggest that both approaches underplay the environment and the information subsystem within an organization.

Specialized Terms

Levels of culture
- Business culture
- Corporate culture

Socialization
- Primary
- Secondary
- Tertiary

Artifacts
Beliefs
Norms
Values
Premises

Types of change
- Fine tuning
- Adaptation

- Reorientation
- Re-creation

Leadership roles
- Envisioning
- Energizing
- Enabling

Maintenance
Transmission
- Ceremonies
- Rites
- Stories
- Slogans
- Symbols

Assumption analysis
Culture gap survey

Managerial behavior approach   Self-design strategy
Tichy's culture change approach

Discussion Questions

  1. What are the elements of culture? How does corporate culture differ from national culture?

  2. Describe the systems logic underlying culture change approaches.

  3. How are systems concepts operationalized in organizational culture? What are the major philosophical assumptions behind the field?

★4. How does culture affect strategy implementation? Should one fit culture to strategy or fit strategy to culture?

  5. What are the links between culture and organizational effectiveness?

  6. What are the cultural traits of excellent companies?

★7. What are the major problems with Peters and Waterman's study and their conclusions?

  8. What is the role of leaders in shaping culture? What do they actually do?

  9. How are cultures maintained and transmitted?

10. What is the objective of culture change? What are the characteristics of successful culture change?

11. How does culture change differ from (1) strategic planning, (2) organization development, and (3) organization design?

12. What are the levers of cultural change?

13. What is (1) dialectical inquiring system, (2) self-design strategy, and (3) managerial behavior strategy?

★14. "Cultural change in organizations can only be incremental. It has to be preceded by national change." Comment.

Applied

  1. A chief executive officer of an electronics business received two competing product development plans from his marketing and R&D departments. He has invited you as culture change expert to sort out the plans so that he can maximize his profitability. How would you proceed?

  2. Prepare a proposal outlining a culture change approach for the division of a large *Fortune* 500 company.

End Notes

1. "Changes at United Technologies," *Forbes,* August 28, 1989, pp. 42–46.
2. Vern Terpstra and Kenneth David, *The Cultural Environment of International Business,* 2nd ed. (Cincinnati, Ohio: South-Western Publishing, 1985).
3. Ibid.
4. David Nadler and Michael Tushman, *Managing Strategic Organizational Change: Frame Binding and Frame Breaking* (New York: Delta Consulting Group, 1986).
5. This section is based on the talk given by Raghu Nath to the Academy of Management in its annual meeting, 1985. See Raghu Nath, "The Role of Culture in Cross-Cultural and Organizational Research," paper presented at the National Meeting of the Academy of Management, San Diego, August 11–14, 1985.
6. See, for example, Ward Goodenough, *Cutlture, Language and Society* (Menlo Park, Calif.: Benjamin Cummins, 1981.
7. Carl Jung as quoted in Frieda Fordham, *An Introduction to Jung's Psychology* (Middlesex, England: Penquin Books Ltd., 1977), pp. 132–33.
8. David Kretch, Richard S. Crutchfield and Egerton L. Ballachey, *Individual in Society* (New York: McGraw-Hill, 1962).
9. Ruth Benedict, *The Chrysanthemum and the Sword* (New York: New American Library, 1974).
10. Richard Pascale and Anthony Athos, *The Art of Japanese Management* (New York: Warner Books, 1981).
11. Raymond Miles and Charles Snow, *Organization Strategy, Structure and Process* (New York: McGraw-Hill, 1977).
12. "Corporate Culture: The Hard-to-Change Values That Spell Success or Failure," *Business Week,* October 27, 1980, p. 148, as abstracted in Thomas G. Cummings and Edgar F. Huse, *Organization Development and Change,* 4th ed. (1989), p. 423.
13. Jay B. Barney, "Organizational Culture: Can It Be a Source of Sustained Competitive Advantage?" *Academy of Management Review* 11, no. 3 (1986), pp. 656–65.
14. Thomas J. Peters and Robert H. Waterman, Jr., *In Search of Excellence: Lessons from America's Best-Run Companies* (New York: Harper & Row, 1982).
15. M. Tushman, W. Newman, and D. Nadler, "Executive Leadership and Organizational Evolution: Managing Incremental and Discontinuous Change," in *Corporate Transformation: Revitalizing Organization for a Competitive World,* ed. R. Kilmann and T. Covin (San Francisco: Jossey-Bass, 1988).
16. Rosabeth Moss Kanter, "Change Masters and the Intricate Architecture of Corporate Culture Change," *Management Review* 72, no.10 (October 1983), pp. 18–28.
17. Benjamin Schneider as quoted in Vern Terpstra and Kenneth David, *The Cultural Environment of International Business.*
18. This discussion is drawn from Cummings and Huse, *Organization Development and Change.*
19. Michael Tushman, William Newman, and Elaine Romanelli, "Managing the Unsteady Pace of Organizational Revolution," *California Management Review,* Fall 1986, pp. 29–44.

20. M. Tushman and Virany, "Changing Characteristics of Executive Teams in an Emerging Industry," *Journal of Business Venturing,* 1986, pp. 37–49.

21. Cummings and Huse, *Organization Development and Change.*

22. Richard O. Mason and Ian I. Mitroff, *Challenging Strategic Planning Assumptions* (New York: John Wiley & Sons, 1981) pp. 76–78.

23. See, for example, Ralph Kilmann, Mary Jane Saxton, and Roy Serpa, *Gaining Control of the Corporate Culture* (San Francisco: Jossey-Bass, 1985).

24. Howard Schwartz and Stanley Davis, "Matching Corporate Culture and Business Strategy," *Organizational Dynamics* 10 (Summer 1981).

25. Noel Tichy, *Managing Strategic Change: Technical, Political and Cultural Strands* (New York: John Wiley & Sons, 1983).

26. Susan Mohrman and Thomas G. Cummings, *Self-Designing Organizations: Learning How to Create High Performance* (Reading, Mass.: Addison-Wesley Publishing).

13 ORGANIZATIONAL POLITICS

Chapter Outline

Mr. Horner—who had led the world's largest accounting firm through six years of tumult, growth, and change—was moving out of his corner office at KPMG Peat Marwick a few weeks ago, vacating it for his successor. A partners' revolt, arousing passions rarely seen in the staid world of accountancy, had forced him out even though he may have been the best man to lead Peat through the treacherous times it now faces. The players could have been lifted straight out of a board game or Greek tragedy: a charismatic but stubborn protagonist, too proud to bend to the wishes of those who elected him; a group of young, impatient partners who believe they should be making more than their already-six-figure incomes; an agitator preoccupied with a personal grudge, and a loyal but ambitious underling maneuvering to win center stage if his mentor stumbles. . . .

The latest sparks of unrest began flashing in January, when compensation figures at four competing accounting firms were reported in the press. Partners at three of those firms had averaged $228,100 or more in the previous year, the reports said. Peat had long told its partners that they were at, or near, the top of the industry in terms of compensation. So the press reports "hit Peat Marwick like a thunderbolt," said a former tax partner, who contends that Peat partners averaged less than $200,000 in fiscal 1989. . . .

Younger partners, in particular, started questioning Peat's pyramid-like pay system. Mr. Horner was making $1.2 million by the end of his term as chairman, roughly 10 times what the lowest-level Peat partner earns. And there were 12 rather well-paid vice chairmen, three added during the Horner days. The younger partners were irritated, and their political clout made their voices important. The numbers are telling: of the 1,850 current Peat partners, 751 got their spots in just the last six years, giving the younger group more votes than usually mandated by seniority and performance. . . .

To blunt criticism, Mr. Horner named a task force to study the firm's governance structure, including its possibly bloated upper management. But he put several of the controversial vice chairmen on it. In April, when it recommended keeping the prevailing structure, many partners were outraged. "The committee was too beholden to Larry," said one. . . .

If all this was like a cauldron waiting to boil over, it was Charles T. Smith who turned up the heat. Mr. Smith, a retired partner in Greenville, South Carolina, served on Peat's board from 1984 to 1986. At that time, Mr. Smith asked Peat to consider his 13 years with the firm prior to 1967 in calculating his pension. "The plan was clear," said Mr. Hanson, who, as chairman of the firm, first handled the complaint. "He knew when he came back that he had no right to an extended pension." Fueling Mr. Smith's bitterness, partners say, was that he retired in December 1986, 10 months before changes in the partners' pension plan would have provided fatter benefits. . . .

Mr. Smith's complaints, detailed in a 1-inch-thick, double-sided letter sent to all 1,850 Peat partners at his own expense in June, found a wide audience. The letter, an abridged version of a roughly 300-page tome he had sent to the Board, saved its most pointed barbs for Mr. Horner, according to several current and former partners who read it. "I don't think there was any question that he intended to put Larry in a bad light," said D. Edward Martin, a former Peat partner. . . .

The timing of the letter proved to be as vexing as its contents. It came just a few weeks before Mr. Horner and K. Dane Brooksher, his hand-picked running mate, started visiting partners in six cities to discuss their candidacies for chairman and deputy chairman. Both men were already endorsed by the board but it was the partners who would have the final say. . . .

Mr. Horner's choice of Mr. Brooksher had been troubled from the beginning. Months before going on the campaign trail, Mr. Horner faced growing support for another running mate—and rejected it. With the 56-year-old Mr. Horner nearing the firm's age-60 retirement date, the partners wanted an heir apparent who was young, charismatic, and responsive to partner needs. Mr. Madonna, 47, fit the bill. But Mr. Horner, in fact, chose Mr. Brooksher, 51, who seemed far less promising and certainly not as charismatic, or so the partners said. And he compounded the error by refusing to switch running mates even after the partners told him, in meetings around the country, that Mr. Brooksher would not do. Mr. Horner said he did not want to drop Mr. Brooksher because it might cost Mr. Brooksher the respect of his clients and that could hurt the firm. . . .

The decision did not sit well in-house, and on Aug. 7, at the Plaza Hotel in New York, Mr. Horner called a special meeting of the board to announce that he would pull out of the race for chairman. He said he was doing it "for the benefit of the firm." He wanted to move on. The new chairman, he said, would need more than three years to wrestle with the long-term problems facing Peat, such as the viability of the partnership issue. "He made his case so convincingly that there wasn't a lot of room left for discussion," said J. Neal Purcell, who was present at the meeting. "It was irreversible."[1]

Mr. Horner, the top man in the accounting firm, was overthrown in a rebellion that he could not squelch. He represented the old guard in the firm that was under attack from the "young turks." He did not have enough power to stop his opponents, each of whom had something to gain from his resignation. He was a victim of organizational politics.

How does one diagnose the power of organizational actors in a situation? How do they exercise their power and to what ends? How do political behaviors influence organizational functioning? What are some of the approaches to managing various facets of politics? The field of organizational politics tries to provide some answers to such questions.

The political subsystem in organizations is perhaps the most dynamic of all the subsystems. This subsystem deals with issues of control, governance, and distribution of rewards in an organization. Although the study of politics has had a long history—philosophers, political scientists, and sociologists have studied politics—only recently have organization theorists begun to pay systematic attention to this topic.

What Is Organizational Politics?

We present a simple definition of power and politics:

Power is the capability of a social actor to overcome resistance to achieve desired objectives in a given social situation. The social actor may be an individual, subunit, or organization.

Politics, or political behavior, is behavior undertaken by the social actor to enhance or exercise power in organizations.

The above definitions emphasize four characteristics of power and politics. First, power is a *relation;* it is not an attribute of the actors. When we speak of the power of an individual, we are assuming a situation and a set of interdependent actors. Thus, a person is not "powerful" or "power-less" in general, but only with respect to other social actors in a specific relationship.

Second, power is *context-specific:* an actor's power varies with the specific situation at hand. An example provided by Crozier will illustrate this point:

> Mr. Dupont, a prominent and well-to-do resident of a small provincial city, asks Mr. Durand, a craftsman with a small business, to make some repairs on his house. Thus, by this request, a relation of power is established between them. The price which Dupont will ultimately agree to pay will be a function of the balance of power which prevails. If Durand is the only one in town capable of undertaking the necessary repairs, if he has all the work he needs, and if, for various reasons, Dupont cannot take his business out of town, the zone of uncertainty which Durand controls by his behavior alone is maximal; his client has, in fact, no choice. The balance of power is clearly tilted in his favor. Dupont, however, is not completely empty-handed. He can, in fact, refuse to have the repairs done at all if Durand's conditions seem exorbitant. He can even tip the balance in his favor if he is able to call on competing craftsmen. This is true, at least, unless these competitors can agree among themselves and thus eliminate Dupont's freedom to choose, which would put us back *mutatis mutandis,* in the original situation.[2]

Third, and as illustrated by the above example, power relations in a situation are *dynamic;* they could change over time as individuals take action to shift the balance of power in their favor. Political behavior is intended not only to exercise but to enhance the power position of the players. The thrust and parry of political behavior is manifest in the bargaining and negotiations that ensue as Durand and Dupont attempt to reach an agreement.

Fourth, *not all relations in an organization are characterized by power.* It should be apparent that individuals in a power relationship are pursuing divergent objectives (as in the example above). In organizations, many day-to-day interactions are controlled by rules, technology, or structure. Individuals who are technologically or structurally interdependent, or who follow rules, may not necessarily have divergent objectives, and, therefore, may not encounter any resistance to their activities. In such cases, power is *not* an explanation for their behavior.

Although it is simple to define, it is not easy to recognize the power of social actors in a situation. There are always clever individuals in any organization who may want to give the appearance of being powerful. For example, some individuals, who may be adept at reading a situation and the preferences of the powerful, may advocate positions that they know will be supported by the powerful. Alternately, there are individuals who always come down on the side of the powerful. These individuals are not necessarily powerful, although, on the surface, it is difficult to distinguish them from those who have power in the situation.

Linkages to the Systems Model

Viewed from the perspective of the political subsystem, organizations are *negotiated entities.* Organization-environment relationships, as well as intraorganizational relationships, are neither constant nor given, but they emerge from interactions and negotiations among various individuals. The individuals are not passive; rather, they continually strive for autonomy and dominance. They seek to advance their own self-interests, which are often different from those of others. Hence, organizations are continually evolving due to the push and pull of the self-interests of various individuals. Equilibrium, when achieved, lasts only for a short duration.

The description of organizations as political systems leads to several predictions. First, since individuals' self-interests are divergent, *commitment to organizational goals does not automatically evolve,* but has to be orchestrated by management. Second, interdependence leads to conflict. Since individual striving for autonomy and independence is thwarted by interdependent others, *conflict is pervasive in organizations.* Third, exercise of power is required to stabilize a system as well as to bring about changes. Thus, when an organization pursues a set of goals, it implies a stable set of powerful actors whose self-interests coincide with the goals of the organization. Similarly, changes in strategies, structure, or goals will not happen if powerful actors are not aligned with the change.

Table 13.1 summarizes the above discussion of the manner in which key systems notions are operationalized in organizational politics.

TABLE 13.1   **Linkage to Systems Concepts**

Systems Concept	*Operationalization*
Open systems	Organization-environment relations are negotiated among individuals within and outside organizations
Interdependence	Interdependence creates conflict
Dynamic equilibrium	Push and pull of divergent interests leads to short-lived equilibrium
Stability and change	Exercise of power is necessary, both for stability and for bringing about change
Subsystems	Political subsystem interacts with all other subsystems

The political subsystem in an organization influences all the other internal subsystems.

Functional Subsystem
Critical aspects of the functional subsystem are shaped by organizational politics. Thus, *goals* of the organization that drive the functional subsystem are determined by politics. The strategies of an organization and the dominant organization design are not merely the outputs of rational decision making; they are determined in the political arena, where various factions vie for dominance. The relationship between functional and political subsystems is not, however, unidirectional. Some factions in an organization derive power from the functional subsystem. For example, functional expertise or task interdependence empowers some individuals and subunits. However, individuals in an organization invoke sources of power over and beyond expertise and structural location to shape strategies and organization design. Horner's exit was engineered by discontented individuals working in unison, not because they were in any technical sense superior to Horner. Indeed, from a purely rational perspective, Horner may have been the ideal leader for the accounting firm.

The capability to influence the functional subsystem is unequally dispersed within the organization. As the Peat Marwick case illustrates, in many organizations, top management does not have unilateral power to influence the functional subsystem. Thus, Horner could not have his candidate elected to the top-management position. Indeed, different hierarchic levels in an organization exert power in different forms. In many cases, the primary source of top-management power is *not* its ability to make technical and even product-market–related strategic decisions, but its ability to set the premises of the organization.

Informational Subsystem
Politics influences and is influenced by the informational subsystem. Of course, information is a source of power; individuals wield it strategically to further their interests. Hence, during decision making, they withhold, distort, and selectively present information. When the goals of two parties are not necessarily congruent (as in the case of intergroup conflict), information flow is likely to be problematic. Such incongruence is present to some degree in superior-subordinate relations. Thus, for top management, *feedback from the organization for monitoring goal attainment is questionable;* it will not ensue smoothly and spontaneously.

Cultural Subsystem
Concepts such as decision premises and symbolic tactics describe the connection between political and cultural subsystems. Individuals in their political roles manipulate (organizational) cultural symbols to their benefit. Cultural assumptions determine the rules of fair exercise of power; in turn,

cultural changes are associated with political dynamics. Individuals bring to their organizations different assumptions and beliefs. This enhances the potential for conflict.

Social Subsystem
Both political and social subsystems deal with the informal elements of an organization. Despite this similarity, politics hinges on alliances, the social subsystem on friendships and affiliation. Whereas the political subsystem is conflict filled, the social subsystem seeks harmony. To some extent, the two subsystems are antagonistic to each other. Where the social subsystem is dominant, politics is underplayed; where politics is dominant, the social subsystem is placed under great tension. The two subsystems represent contradictory tendencies in organizations.

The organizational politics field recognizes a large number of contingencies that influence the functioning of an organization. The environment, specifically the power of environmental actors, is a major contingency. Various subunits within an organization derive power from technological factors and structural location. In addition, other contingencies related to the human elements in an organization, such as values and belief systems, drive organizational politics.

The discussion of contingencies in organizational politics is distinctive in two ways. The field recognizes that:

1. Individuals' actions may alter the nature of the contingencies that influence their power bases—an idea we illustrated earlier by describing how the negotiations evolved between Dupont and Durand. This is quite different from the traditional (contingency) theories, which viewed contingencies as given and more or less uncontrollable.

2. Relevant contingencies may change over time due to both the environmental influences and the internal dynamics of organizations. Just as in the case of organization development, politics emphasizes the dynamic character of organizational contingencies.

Political action differs markedly from other action strategies. The organizational politics field emphasizes that disagreement over goals is a pervasive fact of life in organizations. The action strategies, therefore, depart from rational approaches characteristic of strategic planning or organization design (which assume some degree of consensus over goals). Unlike organization development, politics rejects the idea that collaboration will eventually lead to consensus or compromise over goals.

From the vantage point of politics, there is a degree of coercion in goal-setting processes in organizations. When power is relatively concentrated in the hands of top management, goal setting involves first, compromises among the top management and secondly, the imposition of the goals on the rest of the organization. When power is dispersed within an organization, the process is often protracted and organizations may not be able to establish clear goals. In either case, exercise of power is inevitable in important organizational decisions.

Since the goals are problematic, the field does not espouse any concrete set of organizational effectiveness criteria. The criteria may evolve partly in response to top-management goals, but also in response to the push and pull of interest groups in organizations and environments. In the abstract, however, politics emphasizes feasibility as the guiding principle of organizational action. "The decisions should be workable." The test of feasibility is whether the decision makers have enough power to enforce their decision.

Further, organizational politics reminds us that espousal of effectiveness criteria is a political act, and therefore, sometimes a ruse by the espousers to gain their covert ends. This has two implications:

1. Students of organizations should be skeptical of publically articulated criteria because the real criteria may be very different from the public ones.
2. Decision makers may often choose to hide the criteria of effectiveness if premature disclosure may jeopardize their decisions.

In this chapter, we will summarize the field of organizational politics. Our exposition of organizational politics will take place in four stages. First, we will consider the historical, philosophical, and theoretical underpinnings of power and politics. Second, we will consider some of the key constructs related to power and politics and frameworks for diagnosing the political dynamics of organizations. Third, we will summarize the action strategies revealed by this field, and some of the methods of managing politics. Fourth, we will review the political subsystem from the vantage point of the systems model.

Underpinnings

Before we discuss the key concepts and frameworks, we will briefly sketch the historical and theoretical developments and philosophical assumptions that undergird the writings in the organizational politics field.

Historical Underpinnings

Political behaviors have always been prevalent in organizations. However, unlike in the case of previous action strategies, systematic technologies for managing politics have never been applied in organizations, nor do such technologies currently exist. The historical anchors of the field of organizational politics lie not so much in organizational practice but in the writings of scholars and practitioners that dealt with the politics of nation states and economies. Three different scholarly traditions are evident in these works: (1) the philosophical method, (2) the empirical method, and (3) the pragmatic method.

Although politics is as old as the human race, serious study of politics had its origins in ancient Greece. The subject of politics was central to the work of Plato and Aristotle. Plato initiated the tradition of the *philosophical method,* which focused on developing, through rational argumentation, a description of the ideal nation state. In his *Republic,* Plato illustrated the method by examining the concept of justice through the depiction of the ideal state. The method has survived over the years in the works of futurists who attempted to extrapolate from the social and physical sciences to a future vision of society, and in the works of such sociologists as Mannheim, who chose utopias as a subject of study. Modern day political philosophers such as Rawls also utilized the method in their examination of the concept of justice.

Similarly, Aristotle started the tradition of the *empirical method.* This method focused on describing alternate forms of government that actually existed, rather than depiction of the ideal form.

Ever since the Roman empire, and up until recently, the predominant form of government had been monarchy. Management in some form or other was practiced even during the ancient civilizations when kings and emperors confronted the problem of controlling the populace. In their efforts to control the populace, they were supported by other individuals—lords, military generals, and officials—who often supported the emperors for their own purposes. The kings and emperors had enormous wealth and property, which they enhanced through taxation. This enabled them to exercise power inside the state with a blending of punishment and reward systems. Changes in power took place when the crown passed to others through inheritance or by conquest.

In many cases, elaborate rationalizations were built up to legitimize the power of the kings and emperors. For example, the *divine right* theory of kings, developed in England, proposed that the king was vested with the right to rule by God. This theory thus rationalized the exercise of power by the monarchy. In many ways, such rationalizations enabled the king to maintain the myth that the existing power hierarchy was the "natural order" of affairs, which human beings could not alter: How could humans undo what has been ordained by divine will?

The *pragmatic* examination of political behavior had to wait until a change in philosophical outlook took place—the shift away from viewing the events of the world as predetermined toward one where human beings began to attribute some power over events to their own behavior. As early as the third century B.C., Chanakya, a minister in the court of an Indian king, Chandragupta Maurya, wrote the *Arthasastra*—a treatise that set forth his principles of how to govern the state. However, many point to Machiavelli's *The Prince,* written in the early 16th century, as the starting point for a pragmatic examination of politics. Machiavelli set forth management precepts for the successful operation of a *state,* not for organizations as we know them today. Yet he replaced theology, metaphysics, and in general the sanctimonious quality of the traditional treatises on rulers to reveal instead the inner machinations of power.[3]

The study of political phenomena in its earlier days was confined to the study of alternate forms of government. This is the primary domain of political scientists. Many use as a benchmark for the origin of modern political science the establishment of a separate chair of political science at Columbia University in 1856, occupied by the German émigré Francis Lieber.[4] Although the American Academy of Political and Social Science was started in 1899, the American Political Science Association, founded in 1903, signaled the arrival of political science as a separate academic discipline.

Although initial interest in politics was kindled by political scientists, economists and sociologists all have contributed to our understanding of politics in varying degrees. The technological advances during the Industrial Revolution that resulted in a concentration of productive resources led a number of economists to pay attention to the question: Who is in *control of such productive resources?* These economists, headed by Karl Marx, viewed power as being derived from the control of productive resources. In the concept of *class society* that lies at the heart of Marxist analysis, Marx proposed a scheme for stratifying society based on the degree of control of productive resources enjoyed by various groups in the society.

According to Marx's theory, a class society is the product of a determinate sequence of historical changes. The most primitive forms of human society are not class systems. In tribal societies, there is only a very low division of labor, and property is owned in common by the members of the community. The expansion of division of labor, together with the increased level of wealth that this generates, is accompanied by the growth of private property. This involves the creation of a surplus product that is appropriated by a minority of nonproducers who consequently stand in an exploitative relation vis-à-vis the majority of producers.

Although orthodox Marxist ideas were later refuted by historical events as well as theoretical analysis, two legacies remained. First, the idea that *conflict* is an endemic characteristic of societies began to receive serious academic attention since Marx's seminal writings. Marx had suggested that when the relation between two classes of a society is characterized by dependence and domination, it sets in motion a cycle of exploitation of one class over another, leading to perennial conflict. To paraphrase this idea in the language of systems theory, when two subsystems are in a relation of dependence and domination, the situation is inherently conflict-filled. Stability, equilibrium, and homeostasis are only one aspect of system functioning; the other, the more dynamic aspect, is best characterized as conflict.

Second, the notion that political actions have a *symbolic* component is traceable to the works of Marx:

> The ideas of the ruling class are in every epoch the ruling ideas: i.e., the class which is the ruling *material* force of society is at the same time its ruling *intellectual* force. The class which has the means of material production at its disposal, has control at the same time over the means of mental production, so that thereby, generally speaking, the ideas of those who lack the means of mental production are subject to it.[5]

Just as in the case of the divine right theory of kings, these "ruling ideas" serve to legitimize the use of power in the interests of the power holder.

Marxist ideas had not merely theoretical flavor, but pragmatic significance as well. Marx himself linked his ideas to a process and strategy of fundamental social change. Since Marx was morally committed to a classless society in which political coercion would disappear, he looked for a counterforce in society to challenge and eventually overcome the power of the ruling class. He found this in the economically dispossessed workers. As this new class gained consciousness of its historic mission and its power increased, the class struggle could be effectively joined. The outcome of this struggle was victory for those best able to organize—for Marx this meant the dispossessed workers. In capitalist economies, the Marxist idea that there is power in organizing was reflected in the emergence of trade unions, which organized the workers and demanded additional benefits from owners and management by the threat and sometimes by the act of strikes. The power to be derived from organizing is also visible in the successes of nonviolent strategists like Thoreau, Gandhi, and Martin Luther King, who advocated such tactics as public demonstrations and moral suasion to change what they saw as an oppressive social order.

Unlike economists, political sociologists focused on the stratification of society along sociological lines. Although they took their initial cues from Marx, sociologists paid greater attention to the role of social class in political differences among various groups. In 1957, C. Wright Mills suggested that a power elite existed in the United States that shaped the major policy decisions of the society.[6] Mills saw a remarkable homogeneity and harmony among the higher circles and implied that the unbroken consensus of the higher circles is tantamount to a "conspiracy" against the rest of the society.

Arrayed against these conspiracy theorists were conflict theorists who saw conflict among groups as a fundamental characteristic of society. The conflict theories received support from empirical works that examined the *decision-making processes* at work in political institutions such as the legislature. In one of the prominent early works, Robert Dahl examined the role of power and influence in the decisions made in the political system in New Haven, Connecticut.[7] He concluded that political decision making at the local level was characterized by shifting coalitions composed of members from diverse backgrounds and approximated a pluralistic model.

Most of the writings of economists and sociologists on power pertained to issues at the societal level rather than at the organizational level. Up until recently, discussions of power in organizations were implicit or infrequent, and sometimes discouraged. Jeffrey Pfeffer, one of the major scholars in the field of organizational politics notes:

> Power and politics are not neglected because they lack relevance in explaining what occurs in organizations—Power has been neglected for several reasons. First, the concept of power itself is problematic in much of the social science literature. In the second place, while power is something it is not everything. And third, *the concept of power is troublesome to the socialization of managers and the practice of management because of its implications and connotations.* (Emphasis added.)[8]

The recent developments in the field of organizational politics owe much to the early works of economists, sociologists, and political scientists. Organization theorists such as March focused on developing political models of decision making, whereas others such as Pfeffer addressed the politics of organization-environment relationships. Contingencies that determine the bases of power were also elaborated. Before we address the theoretical underpinnings of the emerging field of organizational politics, we will consider some of the fundamental philosophical assumptions regarding organizations and their functioning embedded in these works.

Philosophical Underpinnings

Although writings on power and politics differ widely with respect to the perspectives adopted and the values represented by the scholars, they share some common assumptions and foci. The assumptions pertain to the nature of both organizations and human actors; the typical foci are governance, control, and justice. We will touch upon each of these assumptions and foci in this section.

Assumptions about Organizations

The first and most important set of assumptions pertains to organizations as open dynamic systems. The political perspective, perhaps more than any other, views organizations as negotiated, continually evolving entities. The relationships between the organization and its environment, as well as the relationships within subunits of the organization, are continually negotiated by its members. The negotiations are characterized by political tactics; the outcomes are influenced by the relative power of the actors in the situation.

Since the members bring different objectives to the situation, the negotiations are filled with conflict; *conflict is endemic to organized life.*

The characterization of organizations as arenas of conflict has important implications. Much of organization theory (e.g., strategic planning, design) assumes the existence of consensually shared goals among members of an organization. In a sense, therefore, the problem of goals is assumed away.[9] Under the political perspective, goals are deemed problematic: Individuals and subunits pursue different, sometimes conflicting goals, which renders the concept of organizational goals an obscure and sometimes vacuous idea. Although some degree of cooperation occurs in an organization, consensus on goals is never fully achieved.

Since the organization continually negotiates with its environment, its boundaries are shifting continuously. This further obscures the goals of the organizations. The shifting nature of goals due to the push and pull of internal and external forces renders the very existence of organizations problematic. This point is forcefully brought to light by Crozier:

> The vision of the organization which emerges from this reasoning is far more complex, "incoherent," and conflictual than what appears in the "spontaneous" view of the phenomenon. Clearly the functioning of an organization no longer corresponds to the Taylorist image of an arrangement of cogs set in motion by a single rationality. Nor can it be understood as the expression of impersonal mechanisms or functional requirements which are supposed to assure the "spontaneous" satisfaction of the "needs" of integration and adaptation of a system whose structure is given at the outset. In the present view, *the organization is in the end nothing more than a universe of conflict,* and its functioning is seen as the outcome of confrontation between contingent, multiple, and divergent rationalities employed by relatively free actors using the sources of power available to them. The resulting conflicts of interest, incoherences, and "structural inertia" are not manifestations of some sort of "organizational dysfunction." *They are rather the price which an organization must pay for its existence,* the condition of its being able to mobilize the contributions of its members and to obtain their "goodwill," without which it could not function properly. . . .
>
> If it is true that an organization is a theater of confrontation and conflict such as we have described, then its very existence as a setting for collective action becomes problematic. Contrary to what certain proponents of "systems analysis" seem to believe when they abusively compare organizations to self-regulated "organic" or "cybernetic" systems, neither the integration, the cohesion, nor *a fortiori,* the endurance of an organization come about naturally and automatically.
>
> In fact, the organization's stability is under constant threat from the centrifugal tendencies stemming from the deliberate actions of its members. In pursuing their personal strategies—always divergent, if not contradictory—the members of the organizations naturally seek to protect or perhaps to enlarge their zones of freedom by reducing their dependence on others, or, in other words, by limiting their interdependent relationship to the other parties involved. *It might even be said that an organization exists not so much because of as in spite of the action of its members.* (Emphasis added.)[10]

Assumptions about Individuals

Embedded in the view of organizations is a set of assumptions about human actors and their linkage to the organization. The political perspective views individuals as *autonomy-seeking* entities, making choices and trying to manipulate and change the organization to their benefit. The relationship between individuals and the organization is a reciprocal one: each influences the other. Certainly, the organization largely determines the context of individuals' actions, and hence the resources of the actors; at the same time, the organization is equally influenced and "corrupted" by the pressures and manipulations of the actors. Human actors make choices, and their actions are contingent but never determined. The political perspective, thus, views humans as *strategic actors*—autonomous agents, who can exercise their freedom, are capable of calculation and manipulation, and can adapt to their environments and invent responses depending on the circumstances and the maneuvers of their partners.

The active role ascribed to human beings in this perspective is not based on an absolute sense of freedom. An individual's actions are anchored in the political context, which is riddled with inequalities: individuals differ in terms of the social, economic, cultural, and individual resources they can marshal. Of course, over time, the resources change: To quote Crozier again:

> Two preconditions—are the existence of (1) an *opportunity* and (2) a *capacity*. Passive groups have neither. Erratic groups have opportunities but have a great deal of trouble taking advantage of them, because their membership is too large and the characteristics of the relationships among the members are such as to make the establishment of continuous, organized coalitions very difficult. Strategic and conservative groups, on the other hand, with relatively fewer members and relatively greater capacities for taking an active role are able over a period of time to acquire considerable capacities. They are not only capable of taking advantage of existing opportunities but may also succeed in creating new ones. Erratic groups may eventually, however, learn to organize themselves so as to make better use of their opportunities. Even passive groups may develop capacities by discovering an opportunity. Here nothing is predetermined for all time.[11]

The power of different individuals changes over time as conditions change or by the collective action of the actors.

Foci

Typically, organizational politics focuses on issues of governance, control, and, less frequently, justice. Governance addresses how a minimal agreement on goals needs to be achieved, particularly how conflict among groups has to be negotiated. Top management's role is then one of governance and negotiation of conflict among groups. Control issues deal with the bases of power, mechanisms of control, and tactics for employing and enhancing power, or in Crozier's terms, the problem of capacities and resources and strategic actions to exploit opportunities and create new resources. Organizational politics typically deals with the distributive aspects of justice as in the case of the structuring of reward systems.

Theoretical Underpinnings

As we noted earlier, in management literature and organization theory, systematic attention to organizational politics is a recent development. Many of the earlier theorists like Frederick Taylor took for granted the right of management to manage. Thus, management's position in the organizational hierarchy gave it authority and hence power to make decisions, which the employees then obediently accepted. Similarly, Weberian Bureaucracy recognized only rational-legal authority as the source of power in organizations. Even Elton Mayo, the leader of the research team in the Hawthorne studies, accepted the existence of a "managerial elite" and only paid attention to the social needs—the need for belonging and recognition of the employees.[12]

However, this acceptance of managerial authority was never complete in real organizations—as demonstrated by the rise of the union movement, whereby lower-level employees coalesced to exert power over management and owners.

In the late 30s, Chester Barnard noted that acceptance of authority is not absolute.[13] He pointed out that there are zones within which employees allow management to exercise authority. Employees do not accept authority outside of these zones. This idea was, of course, earlier postulated by Machiavelli, who had talked about how rulers governed with the consent of the governed. Unlike Machiavelli, Barnard was talking about organizations. Thus, Barnard emphasized that although organizations are, by definition, cooperative systems, cooperation cannot be taken for granted by executives.

Later, Selznick, in his pioneering study, *TVA and the Grass Roots,* identified sources of power other than authority (derived from organizational position).[14] Lower-level employees could invoke several sources of power to influence management. Thus, Selznick elaborated the notion that organizations are political systems.

At this stage, power and politics had a *negative* connotation. Politics led to conflict; both, therefore, were bad. With increased scholarly attention to the topic, organizational theorists began to argue that *in organizations, politics is inevitable.* In some ways, exercise of power is necessary to get things done; under some conditions, it is "functional" and, therefore, necessary.

Theoretically, scholars began to answer several questions: How does one describe organizational decision making from a political perspective? What contingencies contribute to the power of various departments? How does one describe organization-environment relations?

Organizational Decision Making

At the organizational level, Carnegie Mellon University undertook the first major effort at modeling organizational decision making as a political process. This culminated in *The Behavioral Theory of the Firm* by Richard Cyert and James March.[15] This work, which built upon the ideas of Chester Barnard and Herbert Simon, represented a unique collaboration between an economist and a sociologist. Just as Dahl had done in the case of the polity at New Haven (see Historical Underpinnings), the Carnegie school revealed the role of power in organizational decision making (see Box 13.1).

The Carnegie school challenged the assumptions of the prevalent rational models of decision making rooted in classical economics. The rational models assumed that organizations have a consistent set of goals, and there is general agreement on priorities among goals. Secondly, decision making is orderly and logical. Thus, the alternative chosen optimized the accomplishment of goals. Third, the information search is extensive and as a result, cause-effect relationships are known with some degree of accuracy. The rational models thus focused on decisions that can be characterized as routine.

Cyert and March departed from the (then) conventional rational models in major ways. See Table 13.2 for a comparison between the assumptions of the rational and political models of decision making.

TABLE 13.2   **Differences Between Rational and Political Models**

Organizational Characteristic	Rational Model	Political Model
Goals, preferences	Consistent across participants	Inconsistent; pluralistic within the organization
Power and control	Centralized	Decentralized, shifting coalitions and interest groups
Decision process	Orderly, logical, rational	Disorderly, characterized by push and pull of interest
Rules and norms	Norm of optimization	Free play of market forces, conflict is legitimate and expected
Information	Extensive, systematic, accurate	Ambiguous, information used and withheld strategically
Beliefs about cause-effect relationships	Known, at least to a probability estimate	Disagreements about causes and effects
Decisions	Based on outcome-maximizing choice	Result of bargaining and interplay among interests
Ideology	Efficiency and effectiveness	Struggle, conflict, winners and losers

Source: Based on Jeffrey Pfeffer, *Power in Organizations* (Marshfield, Mass.: Pitman Publishing, 1981), p. 31.

Box 13.1

Cyert and March and a Behavioral Theory of the Firm

Richard Cyert, an economist, and James March, a sociologist, were both associated with Carnegie Mellon University. They were among the first group of scholars who studied organizational decision making from a political perspective. Until their work, the rational decision-making models—like the ones currently prevalent in strategic planning—which viewed an organization as a single entity trying to optimize its objectives, were dominant.

Cyert and March's investigations led them to conclude that organizational decisions are not made by single individuals—many individuals are involved in major decisions. Thus, they challenged the foundations of rational decision-making models. The key idea they introduced was that of a *dominant coalition,* an alliance among top managers powerful enough to bring about a decision.

Cyert and March partly based their decision-making models on the earlier work of one of their colleagues, Herbert Simon. Simon had suggested that human beings may be characterized as intendedly rational; that is, they intend to be rational, but they have limited information processing abilities. Cognitive limitations prevent them from being rational in the objective sense of the term.

A dominant coalition comes to dictate decisions in organizations for two reasons. First, major decisions are made under conditions of severe uncertainty. There is limited information and on top of that, all managers suffer from cognitive limitations. Second, most organizational level goals are ambiguous and sometimes the goals of subunits are inconsistent. Managers disagree about their priorities.

Under the twin conditions of uncertainty and disagreement, decision making is not characterized by rational deliberations but by bargaining and negotiations. Managers coalesce around a set of goals and priorities to accomplish with limited resources. They build temporary alliances or coalitions through a number of mechanisms. They engage in joint discussion of goals and problems, share opinions, make trades and side payments ("I'll support you on A if you support me on B") in order to reach agreement on the problems to be solved.

Because of the dynamics of coalition, managers will be concerned with immediate problems. The search for alternatives is not exhaustive; what takes place is a *problemistic search;* that is, looking around in the immediate environment for a way to quickly resolve the problem. They accept a satisfactory solution—not an optimal one. The decision behavior *satisfices,* not optimizes.

Cyert and March note that in the case of nonprogrammed decisions of major importance—decisions for which there are no established precedents or procedures—the coalition model of decision making is a more appropriate model than the rational model.

The behavioral theory of the firm laid the foundations of a political theory of organizational decision making. Most of the current works in politics acknowledge the influence of Cyert and March. As we will see later, these two scholars also identified two of the important conditions for the exercise of power: uncertainty and disagreement about goals.

Source: Adapted from Richard M. Cyert and James G. March, *A Behavioral Theory of the Firm* (Englewood Cliffs, N.J.: Prentice Hall, 1963).

Three departures from the rational model deserve special attention:

1. Unlike the rational views in economics, whereby the firm decision making was approximated by individual decision making, Cyert and March emphasized that in organizations, decisions involved many managers.

2. They argued that since managers hold different goals as important, agreement on goals is problematic.

3. Most managers have only limited bits of information at their disposal; further, they are handicapped by a limited information processing capability, an idea drawn from Simon.

Under these conditions, the process of decision making is characterized by bargaining and negotiations, and a *dominant coalition* emerges to determine goals and make decisions. A coalition is an alliance among a set of managers who agree about goals and priorities. A coalition is dominant when it has sufficient power to impose its decision on the rest of the organization.

Cyert and March emphasized the need for bargaining and negotiations to build some agreement on goals and priorities. Their model is applicable to situations Thompson and Tuden described as having no agreement on goals.

Graham Allison, a political scientist, illustrated these ideas with the case study of the Cuban Missile Crisis.[16] His study is presented in Box 13.2.

Box 13.2

Graham Allison and the Cuban Missile Crisis

Graham Allison, a political scientist, examined the role of politics in decision making at the executive branch of the federal government. In his book, *The Cuban Missile Crisis,* he examined the decision made by President Kennedy to avert the crisis generated by the Soviet Union's missile installation in Cuba.

The facts of the case are rather simple. After the United States' disaster at the Bay of Pigs — where Fidel Castro exposed a CIA plot to assassinate him — the Soviet Union decided to press their advantage by installing missiles in Cuba. Belatedly, the United States discovered the scope of the operation. The executive committee of the National Security Council (NSC) convened an emergency session, and at the end of its deliberations, President Kennedy ordered the naval blockade of Cuba. In the resulting test of strength, Khrushchev was forced to yield and hurriedly withdrew Soviet missiles. The case is a spectacular one involving the confrontation between two superpowers with real risk of a global war. It was unambiguously resolved with the Soviet Union backing off, yielding Kennedy a major victory.

Allison examined the decision process in some detail. He found that seven solutions were discussed:

1. Do nothing, which would have increased the Soviet striking force by 50 percent and shifted the balance of power in their favor.

Box 13.2 continued

2. A diplomatic offensive with no risk of war, but which would have resulted in delays that would have enabled the Soviet Union to wield their new found power.

3. Negotiation with Castro, which was, upon examination, found to be unrealistic since the Soviet Union, not Castro, controlled the operation.

4. Exchange of Soviet installations in Cuba for the U.S. installations in Italy and Turkey, a low-cost alternative (the secretary of Defense had shown that nuclear submarines in the Mediterranean were more effective than missiles) but one that would have planted seeds of doubt in the minds of the European allies regarding the U.S. commitment.

5. Invasion, favored by hawks, entailed the risk of war and escalation into Turkey.

6. A precision air strike, which was immediate and radical, but which the military experts were not sure of bringing off with technical precision.

7. A naval blockade, which, although illegal and involving delays, would give the Soviet Union time to decide. All things considered, this last solution was the most acceptable once the global objective was clear: to compel the Soviet Union to withdraw their missiles without bringing on world war.

Allison noted that on the surface, the decision process appeared rational, with careful evaluation of alternatives and the choice of the alternative based on rational deliberations. However, Allison contended that the *actual* decision process was far from rational. Although he gave numerous reasons, we focus only on the major ones. First, Allison noted that the decision process was not one of optimization; it was similar to the *satisficing* put forth by Simon: the first solution that satisfied the President's minimum criteria was the one chosen. In fact, the naval blockade solution was not put forward until late in the deliberations. Second,

the solutions advanced were not the inventions of decision makers, but rather programs previously elaborated in the context of comprehensive planning by the various administrative agencies; the range of possible solutions was rather limited, and each option was structured in advance. Third, information was often delayed and structured in advance. Bureaucratic information processing procedures inevitably slowed down its preparation in usable form; for example, from the time an agent was first able to identify the profile of a missile to the time the director of the CIA could obtain reliable information, 13 days had elapsed. This was also due to the necessary precautions involved in classifying and verifying intelligence data, resulting from, among other things, internal CIA problems, rivalries between the agency and the air force, and so on. Finally, the point of view of the specialists was far from neutral. Since the air force preferred a massive strike, an option that it had carefully studied and prepared and an action for which it was ready, they argued that a limited operation was uncertain, although later studies showed that their fears were grossly exaggerated.

Allison argued that, based on the evidence, the rational model was a caricature of the actual decision-making process. He further argued that decisions were shaped by a political process. He even demonstrated how skillfully Kennedy got the group to go with his favored solution: naval blockade. The hawks wanted an invasion. Kennedy wanted to maintain the appearance of neutrality and appease the hawks. So he put forward the solution favored by Stevenson: the exchange of bases. The hawks were very vehement in their criticism of this option. Kennedy rallied to their side and gave them a symbolic victory, which made it possible to paint the solution he favored as a middle-of-the-road solution.

Allison's study, which has now become a classic, gave very clear evidence of the influence of political processes in decision making.

Source: Adapted from Graham T. Allison, *Essence of Decision* (Boston: Little, Brown, 1971).

Cyert and March's dominant coalition approximated the top management in many organizations, where power is concentrated at the top of the organizational hierarchy. However, in some large organizations, as in the case of universities, power is not heavily concentrated at the top; instead, it is dispersed throughout the organization. There it is difficult to see a single dominant coalition. It was left to Cohen, March, and Olsen, to formulate models of decision making in organizations characterized by a low concentration of power. Very provocatively, they characterized the decision making using a *garbage can* metaphor. Cohen, March, and Olsen also suggested several ploys administrators used to tackle difficult issues.[17] What they witnessed was neither a rational nor a humanistic administrator, but what can be best characterized as a mini-Machiavellian one.[18] A summary of the work is presented in Box 13.3.

Cohen, March, and Olsen noted that in open systems, political processes are the key mechanism of decision making. Although it took several years for the ideas of Carnegie Mellon University to take hold, they had changed the landscape of organizational theory.

Structural Contingency Model of Interdepartmental Power

Meanwhile, scholars interested in the structural properties of organizations began to address the issue of political differences among departments of organizations. They argued that certain departments in an organization are more powerful because of the *contextual factors* involved. Structural contingency theorists viewed interdepartmental power as a stable phenomenon upset only by shifting circumstances. The Aston group scholars (refer to Chapter 9 on Organization Design) were among the first to identify the sources of interdepartment power. Building on their work, Pfeffer and Salancik provided a comprehensive answer to the question: What makes some departments in an organization more powerful than others?[19]

Pfeffer and Salancik identified five factors that influenced the power relationships among departments:

Dependency. If one department is dependent on another for material, resources, or information, then the second department can exert some degree of influence on the first. In many organizations, data processing departments often derived their power from the dependency of other departments for information.

Financial resources. Control over financial resources is an important source of power. If a department generates a large amount of income for the organization, then it may become powerful.

Centrality. This reflects the significance of a department in the organization's primary tasks. If the work of a department significantly affects the final output of an organization, then it is said to be central. The greater the centrality, the greater the power.

Box 13.3

Cohen, March, Olsen, and the Garbage Can Model of Decision Making

Extending the earlier work at Carnegie Mellon University (see Box 13.1), James March, along with his colleagues Cohen and Olsen, developed the garbage can model of decision making to describe the decision making they observed in organizations much more complex than typical business firms.

According to Cohen, March, and Olsen (CMO), universities typified very complex organizations. They called these very complex organizations *organized anarchies*. Such organizations are characterized by rapid change and a collegial nonbureaucratic (internal) environment. The major feature of organized anarchies is the extreme degree of uncertainty. In an organized anarchy, administrative decisions can be described as a process with a single individual or even a small coalition unable to influence the course of decisions. Organized anarchies display three characteristics. First, just like in the case of the behavioral theory of the firm, problems, alternatives, solutions, and goals are not at all clear. CMO called this *problematic preferences*. Second, unlike in the case of behavioral theory, the knowledge base that applies to decisions is not clear. It is difficult to intuit what causes what. This is termed the characteristic of *unclear poorly understood technology*. Third, participants of the decision process turn over; employees are busy and have limited time to devote to any one problem. CMO called this the characteristic of *fluid participation*.

CMO found that in organized anarchies, decision making cannot be characterized by a sequence of steps starting with a problem and ending with a solution; in fact, problems and solutions may not have any connections at all. Some problems may never be solved; sometimes a solution may be adopted when there was no problem to start with. CMO noted

that it is accurate to describe solutions and problems as independent streams of activities.

CMO identified four streams relevant to organizational decision making: (1) *problems* or points of dissatisfaction with current activities; (2) *solutions,* or alternatives, which are somebody's products; (3) *participants,* who come and go through the organization; and (4) *choice opportunities,* which are occasions when an organization may make a decision.

CMO note that these streams are independent and the pattern of decision making takes on a random character. Hence, the metaphor of an organization as a garbage can in which these streams are stirred. When a problem, solution, participant, and choice happen to connect, a problem may be solved. This does not mean, however, that the solution will fit the problem.

Simulation studies suggest four consequences of garbage can decision processes. First, solutions are proposed even when problems do not exist. Thus, an employee may be sold on an idea and may try to sell it to the organization. In universities, programmed instruction often has been thus sold, often creating problems of its own. Second, choices are often made without solving problems. Many choices just happen. Third, problems may persist without being solved. Some problems just don't go away even though administrators want to solve them. Finally, some problems are solved so that the organization moves in the direction of problem reduction on the whole.

As the garbage can model suggests, under extreme uncertainty, politics becomes an organizational phenomenon not amenable to manipulation by individuals.

Source: Adapted from Michael D. Cohen, James G. March, and Johan P. Olsen, "A Garbage Can Model of Organizational Choice," *Administrative Science Quarterly* 17 (March 1972) pp. 1–25.

Substitutability. This refers to the extent to which a department's function can be substituted by other readily available resources. Substitutability reduces power. For example, the availability of outside contractors reduces the power of staff departments.

Capacity to cope with uncertainty. Departments that are able to cope with the significant uncertainty facing an organization emerge powerful. For example, in many organizations facing significant market uncertainties, the marketing department is more powerful than the production department.

Pfeffer and Salancik thus provided a model for diagnosing the power relations among departments in an organization. They also noted that as environments change, power bases shift, and hence, the power of the departments also changes over time.

Politics of Organization-Environment Relations

A final seam in the fabric of political theory was sown when scholars began to address how organizations exercised power in relation to the environment. Whereas the strategy theorists viewed the environment as product markets or in economic terms, political theorists began to address how managers shaped their environments. Just like intraorganizational relations, organization-environmental relations are negotiated; managers employ political tactics to ensure favorable environments.

From a political perspective, organization-environment relations are characterized by power and dependence. First, organizations are dependent on the environment for resources. To survive, they have to get raw materials, financial resources, customers, and the like, all of whom are outside the realm of direct control. Second, if the dependencies are of some size, they pose a threat to organizational survival. For example, an accreditation agency could close down a hospital, or a bank could withhold loans from a small firm unless it conforms to some of the banks' wishes. Third, the dependence requires that managers actively manage the dependence, either expanding the organization's influence or conforming to the demands of the environment.

Political strategies for managing the environment began to get serious attention, a topic we will deal with later in this chapter. These complement the analyses presented in environmental analysis and strategic planning, which adopt a rational perspective on organization-environment relations.

Summary

From a political perspective, individuals in organizations act strategically; that is, to further their self-interests. Therefore, organizations are negotiated systems and conflict is natural to organized life. Organization theorists have identified three ways in which politics gets played out in organizations.

First is the political process by which important decisions are made in organizations—how a dominant coalition, an alliance of powerful managers, generally sets organizational goals and bargains over major decisions. Second, five factors influence the power relations among departments: (1) dependence, (2) financial resources, (3) centrality, (4) substitutability, and (5) capacity to cope with uncertainty. Third is how organizations manage their dependence on the environment.

Key Concepts and Frameworks

We have organized the various concepts useful for understanding organizational politics in the framework shown in Figure 13.1. The framework consists of four building blocks: (1) conditions, (2) power bases, (3) decision arenas, and (4) political tactics.

According to the framework, certain *conditions* must be present before power can be exercised by social actors to affect outcomes of decisions. Under opportune conditions, various actors bring to bear the *power bases* available to them in *decision arenas* to influence the outcomes of the decisions in their favor. The outcomes ensue from the bargaining and negotiations that take place among various social actors. The actors employ various *political tactics* in the thrust and parry of organizational politics; such tactics may be oriented toward a specific decision outcome, to enhance the power base of the actor, or even to modify the conditions facing the organization.

The framework is built on the ideas developed by the two theoretical streams (see the previous section), which focused on structural bases of power and on the politics of decision making. Thus, structural contingency theorists identified the conditions for the exercise of power and the features of the organization that bestow power on individuals and departments. Similarly, decision theorists refined the notions of political tactics and decision arenas.

Conditions for the Exercise of Power

Not every aspect of organizational functioning is subject to political explanation. Three conditions need to be present for politics to ensue: (1) conflict, (2) importance of the decision, and (3) power distribution.

The primary condition for politics is conflict. Three characteristics of organizations promote conflict: interdependence, heterogeneous goals and beliefs about technology, and scarcity of resources.

> *Interdependence.* The first condition for the exercise of power in organizations is interdependence among actors whereby what happens to one affects another. For example, what one subunit does

FIGURE 13.1

Framework for organizing concepts

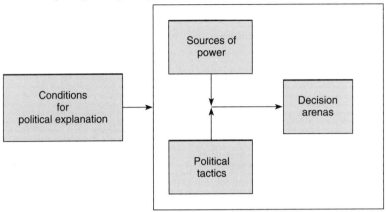

may affect another, as Thompson informed us in our discussion of organization design. Such interdependence may be at the level of work flow, information, or sharing of resources; it ties the organizational participants together. In the absence of interdependence, there is no need for any relation between them; hence, conflict and exercise of power are unnecessary.

Heterogeneous goals and beliefs about technology. The second condition is that the actors hold goals that are inconsistent with each other. Structural features of organizations—differentiation as Lawrence and Lorsch told us—create conditions where different departments pursue different goals. A similar condition is beliefs about the cause-effect relations; that is, the linkage between decisions and outcomes. Under conditions of uncertainty, cause-effect relations cannot be derived with any degree of confidence. Hence, the beliefs of individuals play an important role. Reasonable actors may differ in their beliefs, another condition necessary for conflict.

Scarcity of resources. A third additional condition that promotes conflict is the scarcity of resources. To the extent that resources are insufficient to meet the various demands of organizational participants, choices have to be made concerning the allocation of these scarce resources. For example, the pyramidal structure of an organization always ensures that there is a scarcity of positions at the top relative to the number of individuals at the bottom. The greater the scarcity relative to the demand, the greater the conflict.

The conditions leading to conflict and exercise of power are presented schematically in Figure 13.2. As shown in the figure, the conditions of inter-

FIGURE 13.2

Conditions for the exercise of power

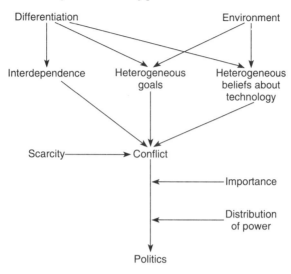

Source: This model is taken from Jeffrey Pfeffer, *Power in Organizations* (Marshfield, Mass.: Pitman Publishing, 1981).

dependence, heterogeneity of goals and beliefs, and scarcity of resources promote conflict in organizations.

For this conflict to eventuate in politics, two further conditions are necessary. One is the *importance of the decision issue* or the resource. If an issue is too trivial, individuals may not use power plays to resolve the issue.

The other condition is the *distribution* of power. Political activity, bargaining, and coalition formation occur when power is dispersed. When power is highly centralized, the centralized authority can make decisions using its own rules and values. Organizational politics gets played out over a protracted length of time, when there is some dispersion of power.

The above discussion implies two things. First, at the level of top management, goals and directions of the organization are always debatable, and most of the (strategic) decisions are very important to the survival of the organization. One would, therefore, expect the political side to be dominant. Second, in many decisions—especially those that are *routine*—politics is not a likely explanation for organizational behavior.

When conditions promote the use of power, the decision calculus is not dictated by rational considerations alone, but by the relative power positions of the players. Stated differently, the concerns and the preferred solutions of the relatively more powerful tend to prevail. This leads us to consider the bases of power in organizations.

Bases of Power in Organizations

Individuals and subunits in organizations have access to various bases of power. Although power is contingent on the situation, there are some general guideposts that enable us to assess the power bases of the players involved in any situation. We will consider four sources of power: (1) control of resources, (2) control of uncertainty, (3) irreplaceability, and (4) strength of numbers.

Control of Resources

Resource control is the most talked about source of power in organizations. As open systems, organizations require a continuing provision of resources—personnel, money, legitimacy, customers, and various material and technological inputs—to function. Some of these resources are more critical to an organization's mission than others. Those individuals and subunits that can provide the most critical and difficult to obtain resources come to have power in the organization.

Players often try to create dependencies around them by controlling the resources that are critical to other individuals or subunits. It is not sufficient to merely provide valued resources to the organization; the individual or the subunit must necessarily control the flow of resources—it must be able to exercise discretionary increases or decreases in the flow of resources. Pfeffer illustrates how, with a relatively small amount of resources, resource dependence can be created:

> The mechanism works as follows. Consider a situation in which there are two components to some organization's budget. There is a large, relatively fixed, component that is based, perhaps, on last year's budget plus some increment. . . . The second component of the budget represents a small, discretionary allocation of resources which is not based on statute, formula, previous experience, or any other such stable foundation. Rather, this allocation is based on the decisions made by some other social actor with respect to either providing or not providing some amount of these incremental resources. Initially, the organization is offered the additional budgetary resources with few or no constraints or strings attached. . . . The incremental resources appear to be quite appealing, as they permit change adaptation, and new activities can be more easily undertaken; they provide the margin for excellence, the incremental resources that will make it possible for the organization to perform and operate at a more satisfactory level. Thus, in almost every case, the incremental resources will be accepted. . . .
>
> Very quickly what was slack becomes necessity. If at this point the social actor with discretionary control over the incremental funds comes back and threatens to withdraw the resources if the organization fails to comply with a request, the organization is likely to comply.[20]

Thus, whereas the control of resources gives the individual power, the strategy of deployment is crucial to exercising the power.

Control of Uncertainty

As pointed out by the strategic contingency theorists on power, individuals and subunits may derive power from their structural position in the organization. For a subunit to derive power over another from its structural location, three conditions must be satisfied. First, the two subunits must be interdependent. Second, one subunit must be in a position to cope with uncertainty for the other. Finally, there are no substitutes to the subunit's coping abilities. When substitutable, the second subunit can rely on another for coping with uncertainty. This in itself reduces the power of the first subunit.

The shifting power base of different functions in organizations reflects how uncertainties facing organizations have changed over time. In the 50s, technological and manufacturing functions were important, since most of the uncertainties concerned the reliability of the product. At that time, a large proportion of chief executive officers had an engineering background. As time went on, markets presented the critical uncertainty, and individuals with a marketing background came to be the leaders. Later, in the 70s, the critical uncertainties centered on the financial and legal sectors. This was reflected in the rise of people with finance and legal backgrounds to the helm of affairs.

Irreplaceability

Individuals and subunits may derive power from being irreplaceable or nonsubstitutable. Access to specialized skills, knowledge, and capabilities crucial to the organization enable an individual or a subunit to gain power. Expert power is a base only when it is crucial to the organization, and when individuals with expertise are not easily replaceable.

A number of political ploys get played out in organizations to create and destroy irreplaceability of actors. For example, people with unique knowledge tend to keep the knowledge secret. Organizations often bring in outside expertise (e.g., consultants) to counterbalance that already in the organization. This, of course, is resisted by the "experts" in the organization, who see their power bases eroding.

Most of the above sources may be employed by individuals and subunits. The final source of power, the strength of numbers, is a collective source of power.

Strength of Numbers

Individuals may often band together for the purpose of winning their objectives. There is strength in numbers. Typically, lower level members in an organization form unions to exert pressure on management. Of course, strength of numbers is not confined to union activity.

Mere numbers, by itself, does not guarantee power: *The strength from numbers depends on the strength of internal consensus.* Subunits are comprised of many individual actors who, at one time or another, may be in a position to affect decisions relevant to the subunit. Subunits have the advantage in a political struggle if they have a consensually shared, easily articulated and understood position and perspective. If the subunit members are not agreed among themselves on their goals and tactics and display dissension, their power is considerably reduced. If there is no consensus within the subunit, then outsiders will be able to "buy" some of their members through side payments, various inducements (e.g., promotions), and even bribes. Many rulers in the olden days used to practice the tactic of "divide and rule" to control some of their rebelling subjects.

Decision Arenas for the Exercise of Power

Power and politics play a key role in decision making and resource allocation in organizations. We noted that under conditions of conflict and scarce resources, important decisions are influenced by the relative power positions of the social actors. Individuals and subunits attempt to influence resource allocation patterns, personnel changes (recruitment and succession), structural changes, and even organizational strategies.

Resource Allocation
Resource allocation is one arena where the influence of politics is likely to be acute. Although many have studied the influence of power on resource allocation over the years, in recent times, the work of Pfeffer and his colleagues has provided systematic evidence of such influences.

> The initial study of the effects of power on resource allocation was conducted at the University of Illinois at Urbana-Champaign. The study focused on 29 departments, and the budget data was collected over a 13 year period. The researchers focused on discretionary funds—the portion of the funds not committed by contract or bequest; they wanted to explain the allocation of such funds by such factors are the proportion of total credits hours taught by each department, the representation of each department on the University's Research Board committee, as well as on the University's executive committees. They noted that if the allocation reflected the demands of the task alone, funds would be allocated according to the total number of credit hours. However, the evidence indicated that although instructional hours played an important role, other "political factors" such as committee representation influenced the resource allocation. Those departments which were better represented got more dollars. Similar findings were also reported from the Universities of California, Berkeley; and Minnesota.[21]

The influence of power on resource allocation has also been observed in government, voluntary, and business organizations.

Personnel Changes
Executive recruitment and succession is another area where power plays a very important role. Individuals and subunits try to sponsor their own

candidates for organizational positions. Managers' influence with their subordinates depends to some extent on their upward influence; that is, influence with their superiors. As these managers try to get their candidates promoted, or hire more individuals, they are, in a sense, competing with other subunits for a limited number of openings in the higher levels of the organizational hierarchy. Inevitably, power plays a role in promotion decisions just as in the case of resource allocation decisions.

Especially at the top levels, developing alliances throughout the organization is important if an individual wants to get things done. Hiring and promotion can be used to strengthen network alliances and coalitions by putting one's own people in prominent positions. This is true even in the case of senior executives, especially if they are brought from outside. As Helmich and Brown observed:

> The replacement of persons in the executive role constellation enables the outsider (1) to get rid of those lieutenants who appear to be shirking their duties, (2) to quiet those in the surrounding work team who might oppose the leader's new policies, and (3) to bring new lieutenants who are loyal to the successor. In short, the use of strategic replacements empowers the outside manager to form a new informal social circle which revolves around himself and supports his own status and policies.[22]

Structural Changes

Organizational restructuring and interdepartmental coordination are also permeated by politics. Almost all structural reorganizations redistribute power. We noted how, as an organization moves from functional to divisional, there is greater decentralization. Similarly, in matrix systems, coordination between matrix bosses is filled with uncertainty and conflict. Under these conditions, politics plays a major role in decisions related to organizational structure and patterns of coordination.

Organizational Strategies

Organizational strategies are formulated under conditions where politics is an important determinant of the choices made by the organization. The environment is not fully known, there are competing goals and cause–effect explanations, and there is a scarcity of resources. Although strategic planning primarily looks at the rational elements of choice, the values and beliefs of the powerful sectors of the organization inevitably shape the decision process.

Political Tactics

Individuals and subunits in an organization employ a number of political tactics in order to obtain their objectives in organizations. We may distinguish between two sets of tactics: (1) substantive and (2) symbolic. Figure 13.3 presents a tree diagram summarizing the political tactics.

FIGURE 13.3

Tree diagram for describing political tactics

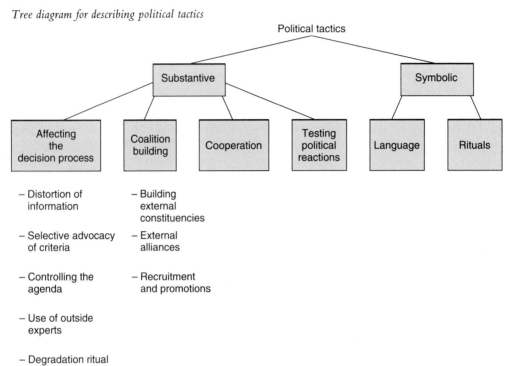

- Distortion of
  information

- Selective advocacy
  of criteria

- Controlling the
  agenda

- Use of outside
  experts

- Degradation ritual

- Building
  external
  constituencies

- External
  alliances

- Recruitment
  and promotions

Substantive

Substantive tactics involve issues when redistribution of power or resources in organizations is likely to take place. Individuals try to skew decisions in their favor through a number of tactics.

Affecting the Decision Process Directly.   Individuals may try to influence the decision process directly through a variety of political tactics. This may involve intentional distortion of information, selective advocacy of objective criteria, controlling the agenda, use of outside experts, attempts to discredit opposing camps, and so on. Such ploys may also be called *gambits.*[23]

> *Distortion of information.* In politics, individuals *intentionally* distort information. This is not to be confused with unintended distortions that ensue from the universal psychological characteristics of individuals (e.g., selective perception). There are many ways in which individuals distort information. They may withhold from others valuable bits of evidence, especially those damaging to their own position. They may reinterpret past events inventing a new

explanation for such events. Outright lying is not common but may also occur. In government agencies, when projects are put forth, subunits typically portray their preferred alternative in most favorable terms.

Selective advocacy of criteria. Individuals and subunits try to control decision premises by selectively advocating those criteria that favor their preferred alternative. Objectives and criteria are to a large extent subjective. Thus a marketing department may advocate market share growth as a means of justifying more salespeople, whereas a manufacturing department may talk of technological leadership for investing in new equipment. The point to note is that almost all objectives and criteria tend to reflect the interests of the actor.

Controlling the agenda. A more subtle type of political ploy is to control which decisions come up for resolution. In many instances, the more powerful individuals ensure that issues not to their liking do not come up for resolution. They could get decisions postponed, delete them from the agenda, or even affect the order of consideration such that certain issues are not paid attention by decision makers.

Use of outside experts. Sometimes individuals use outsiders such as consultants to lend credence to their preferred alternatives. There are a number of advantages to using an outsider: outsiders are typically perceived as objective, and if the outsider is an expert, additional weight may be placed on the alternative.

Degradation ritual. Sometimes individuals may attempt to discredit others in the organization. Although such norms as teamwork, harmony, and so on may prevent the very frequent use of such tactics, nevertheless the tactic is employed in protracted political battles. It may also be used to "cover up" or get over an embarrassing situation. In the latter case, a scapegoat is found, discredited as the cause of the malfunctions in the organization, and is occasionally transferred, demoted, or fired.

A frequently quoted example of how an individual affected the decision-making process is provided by Pettigrew (see Box 13.4).

Success in affecting the decision process depends on the degree of uncertainty facing the organization and the relative power positions of the actors, a point we elaborated earlier.

Coalition Building.   Individuals and subunits not only exercise their power during decision making, they also attempt to enhance their power bases. One of the most important tactics to enhance the power base is coalition formation. Coalitions come about when actors join their efforts to

Box 13.4

Andrew Pettigrew and Information as a Source of Power

Andrew Pettigrew is a British scholar who has written extensively on the role of power in decision making and organizational change. His book, *Politics of Organizational Decision-Making,* describes political processes in the organizations he studied. We focus here only on the role of information in decision making.

Pettigrew describes the case of a senior manager who controlled information given to the board of directors and thereby influenced the decision to purchase a large computer system. The board of directors had formal authority to decide from which company the computer should be purchased. The board asked a staff department to recommend which of the six computer manufacturers should receive the order.

Mr. Jim Kenney was in charge of the staff department. There were other managers who also had a stake in the decision, such as those in charge of programmers and systems analysts. The latter would be affected by the computer purchased because it determined the type of work they performed.

Kenney disagreed with the recommendations of others. However, he had one great advantage: all the information going to the board went through him; he controlled the flow of information to the board members who would make the final decision. Other viewpoints reached the board only through Kenney. Kenney shaped the decision premises

of the board by discussion of his preferred computer manufacturer more often than other manufacturers. Also, his comments about other manufacturers tended to be negative. The board eventually decided in favor of his preferred computer manufacturer.

The data presented above does not permit us to read the intentions of Kenney. On the one hand, Kenney may have been motivated to stamp out opposition to his plans and thus kept the board deliberately uninformed of the positive aspects of alternate proposals. If so, his intentions are highly questionable on ethical grounds. On the other hand, he may have genuinely believed that his proposal was the better of the two. In such a case, we cannot characterize his proposal as unethical. Organization theorists would argue that irrespective of his intentions, Kenney's behaviors may be viewed as an attempt to influence the board members.

All decisions are made with information. By controlling the information, the decision premises can be controlled. By doing so, the decisions can be shaped in one's favor, even though that individual may not have the authority to make the decision.

Sources: Adapted from Andrew M. Pettigrew, "Information Control as a Power Resource," *Sociology* 6 (1972), pp. 187–204; *The Politics of Organizational Decision-Making* (London: Tavistock, 1973).

gain political objectives. When actors realize that there is insufficient power to enact a decision, and they expect resistance, they form coalitions. There are a number of ways of building coalitions.

> *Building external constituencies.* Individuals build external constituencies to exert power on the organization in a direction desired by them. In a sense, hiring a consultant is an example of this. For example, the deans of business schools routinely cultivate important business people to exert pressure on the university for gaining important ends.
>
> *Internal alliances* are equally visible and important. Although different groups may have different objectives, where common positions can be staked out, alliances are possible.
>
> *Alliances through recruitment and promotion.* Senior executives often realize that hiring their own is a way of building coalitions. Thus, typically outsiders try to bring their coterie of people from the outside. By recruitment and promotions, key individuals may be placed in strategic locations to assist in times of need.

Coalitions are usually unstable in the long run. As the saying goes, politics makes strange bedfellows. As long as there is some commonality of interest, the alliance will probably remain; otherwise it will dissipate.

Co-optation. Co-optation involves giving a representative of the organization, group, or subunit whose position is sought a position on the decision-making group; it tries to diffuse the opposition before decisions are made. Co-optation is useful for dealing with external constituencies (this will be elaborated upon later in our discussion of action frameworks) as well as internal subunits of the organization. Internally, people may be invited to sit on committees, to act as advisors to projects, and the like. The assumption is that exposing them to information or subjecting them to group pressures may change their minds.

Testing Political Reactions. Senior executives often test political reactions before making decisions to see if the organization will go along with a decision. This may be done through "kite-flying," whereby an alternative is leaked by someone invisible. If there is considerable negative reaction, the senior officers may decide to choose another alternative and "squelch" the rumors about the alternative by denying it. This often occurs in the personnel arena when an individual is being considered for a powerful position. It may also occur in major policy decisions: thus, the Treasury department in the federal government routinely tests public reaction by leaking proposed budgets before making recommendations.[24]

Symbolic Tactics

Whereas substantive tactics come to play in an attempt to enhance and exercise power, powerful actors also employ symbolic elements to mobilize support and quiet opposition. They invoke evocative language, use symbols, engage in rituals, and conduct ceremonies in organizations to lull individuals into going along with them. This area is discussed at length in our discussion of organization culture; here, we merely point out that political actors try to manipulate cultural symbols in order to gain acceptance of their power position and their activities by others in organizations. Symbolic tactics do not redistribute power, they merely affect feelings, attitudes, and perceptions of people.[25] We give two examples of symbolic tactics from presidential politics:

> *Language.* In 1980, after much debate, lobbying, and hue and cry, the congress passed and President Carter signed into law the windfall profits tax on oil, which at the time was estimated to raise about $227 billion over the next 10 years. A year before, a tax increase of similar magnitude had been approved to provide funds for the Social Security System. The oil tax was *ostensibly* designed to return to the government some of the money oil companies would receive through decontrol of prices on domestically produced oil. How could anyone object to taxing the profits of the big oil companies if the profits are *windfall,* as contrasted with *hard earned* or *deserved* profits? In fact, virtually every analyst pointed out that the tax had nothing to do with profits. It was a form of excise tax, as it was based on the price of oil. . . .It could have been called an excise tax on gasoline, or the Oil Products Sales Tax, or the Oil Price Increase Tax, any of which might have been of equal accuracy. The labeling of the tax as a tax on windfall profits, even when most of the people involved knew it was no such thing, had a powerful effect. It helped create an atmosphere in which the tax could be passed, in spite of substantial industry opposition.
>
> *Rituals.* Consider the Reagan administration tax policy as related in *Newsweek* (March 2, 1981, p. 29). The tax policies were based on the White House forecast of rapid economic growth, a plunging inflation rate, and a balanced budget. The forecast was the product of an internal debate reflecting conflicting views:
>
> "Supply-siders," led by David Stockman, insisted that the tax-cut program would provide powerful incentives for work and investment, and consultant John Rutledge maintained that Reagan's unorthodox policies would revolutionize public expectations and allow inflation to fall far faster than conventional analysis would indicate. Treasury Undersecretary Beryl Sprinkel, a monetarist, warned that a stimulative fiscal policy risked a recessionary collision with the tight monetary policies of the Federal Reserve, but he was appeased with assurances that the Fed would be supported regardless of the economic cost.
>
> Meanwhile, Murray Weidenbaum, the chairman of the Council of Economic Advisers, attempted to keep the forecast within limits that conventional economists might accept. "You must understand," says one insider "that the final bargain on the forecast was struck by Stockman, who had to produce a balanced budget in some way by 1984, and Weidenbaum, who had to defend the forecast whatever it was." The final compromise amounted to a curious

---

Box 13.5

The Case of the Over-Productive Crew

This case illustrates some of the political dynamics that evolve at the operating levels of organizations.

In an electronics company, a small group of women involved in production was found to be contributing 120 percent toward the profit of the firm. Because of an explicit action experiment by their foreman, these women—most of whom had little formal education in general and none at all in electronics—were solving production and design problems that university professors and members of the company's engineering department could not cope with. Also productivity was constantly increasing in the group, some 300 percent in two years, even though they were not on an incentive system.

As might be expected, the women had considerable freedom in their jobs. They designed and operated their own equipment, their maintenanceman made and supervised their expense and supplies budget, which constantly showed a lower and lower percentage in relation to volume, they moved around a lot, traded their jobs, and so forth.

After this had been going on for over a year, higher ups could stand it no longer, and instituted proceedings to break up the activity. The foreman was promoted away from the group and a new engineer was imported from Europe to "straighten up the confusion in the department." An engineering executive remarked:

"Dollar wise they're doing a pretty good job in here as far as it goes, but they have got one overriding weakness in the way they are presently set up. Do you realize that girls do all their own testing in here? The same girls that make the tubes test them. It just isn't logical. Human nature isn't that way. You can't trust the same people who make something to also test it. It's not healthy.

"We've got plans in the works for taking on this place and really making it over. And when we do we'll see to it that the testing operations are carried on in a separate department. We'll really whip this operation into shape. I'd like to make this a model showplace for the company. Right now it's the worst in the company.

"The place has never been *under engineering control*. That's the trouble with it. . . . Most of the product design changes have been developed and put into practice by the production people themselves. That's not good. They design their own products, they alter and maintain their own production equipment and processes, and they are free to go off in all directions at once. The first thing we would do if we could get hold of this room would be *to put every operation under close engineering surveillance*." (Emphasis added.)

Viewed from a purely rational perspective, the management of the electronics firm may be seen as irrational in its behavior when it dismantled the successful production unit that

---

exercise in circular economics: *aides simply assumed that the President's program would work as intended, then came up with the theoretical underpinning to prove they were right.* (Emphasis added.)[26]

One could ask why all the fuss and debate? In the political arena, such rituals as debate, devil's advocacy, planning, and so on are promoted to give the appearance of deliberation, irrespective of whether it is actually necessary from a rational perspective.

In most cases, political exercises involve both substantive and symbolic tactics. The example presented in Box 13.5 describes the political dynamics

---

Box 13.5 continued

contributed 120 percent of its profits. However, the behavior makes sense when we consider that the political dynamic is an *inevitable* part of organizational functioning. It is possible that the success of the production department was felt by the engineers in many ways: as a threat to their knowledge and status, as a threat to the position of the engineering department in the company, as a violation of the status system in the company as a whole, and as Clark notes, "as a violation of the Western European culture's assumption about the authority as flowing from 'up' towards down through the vehicles of role incumbents."

Notice also the conditions promoting political behavior, influence of power bases, political tactics, and the decision arenas where the political dynamics are played out. To begin with, the engineering department and the production unit are *interdependent* at two levels. We can infer that they are hierarchically interdependent. At the work flow level, the engineering department is perhaps in charge of designing both products and (manufacturing) processes, which the production unit then has to execute. Given the history of failure of the engineering department, this has led to the issue of who controls the design process. Although we do not have data about the beliefs of the production unit, as the engineering executive clearly demonstrates, the ensuing behavior of the production unit is at variance

with the *beliefs about technology* held by the firm's engineers. Given the interdependence and variance with the beliefs of engineers, politics becomes inevitable.

The two groups have obviously different *bases of power.* For the production unit, their only "defense" is their demonstrated ability to produce. However, as we have seen in the political arena, this does not give them any real power. The engineering group is perhaps hierarchically superior, and as we see from the case, it could affect the decision premises successfully. It is also likely they have greater control of uncertainty (e.g., new product introduction). Clearly the engineering department has greater power than the production unit.

The engineering department brings to bear its power base on *changing the structure* of the production unit, which among other things ensures their control. They accomplish this through *executive recruitment:* promoting the foreman away from the job and bringing in an engineer from outside. In addition we also see *symbolic* elements of their tactic: use of evocative language suggesting what is good and bad, what is human nature, and articulating the goal of model showplace.

Source: Adapted from Melvin Steckler, *American Radiotronics Corporation (A);* and James V. Clark, "A Healthy Organization," in *Planning of Change,* ed. W. G. Bennis, K. D. Benne, and R. Chin (New York: Holt, Rinehart & Winston, 1961).

---

that got played out in an electronics firm; we also discuss the case from the vantage point of the framework presented in this section.

As illustrated by this case, political tactics modify decision-making processes in organizations away from the idealized descriptions usually found in rational models of decision making. Almost all phases of rational decision making are pervaded by political tactics. In our chapter on strategic planning, a field that adheres to a predominantly rational conception of organizations, we noted how the strategy formulation can be captured by a number of phases—diagnosis, alternative development, choice ande-valuation, implementation, and evaluation of results. Table 13.3 displays some of the common political tactics that individuals employ during the various phases of decision making. As can be seen from the table, the various phases become arenas where different individuals and subunits vie for control by an opportune mixture of symbolic and substantive tactics. An illustration of the idea that strategic decisions are inherently political is provided by Bower in his now classic work on resource allocation patterns in a conglomerate business organization (see Box 13.6).

In this section, we have presented some of the key ideas for understanding how politics gets played out in organizations. Over the years, some action frameworks have emerged whereby politics and some of the conflict emerging from politics may be managed. We will turn to this issue after the summary.

Summary

Politics surfaces in organizations when (1) there is interdependence among individuals/departments within an organization, (2) differing goals and beliefs are held, and (3) resources are scarce. Individuals have or gain power

TABLE 13.3   **Political Tactics across Decision-Making Phases**

Phase of Strategic Decision Making	Focus of Political Action	Example of Political Activity
Issue identification and diagnosis	Control of: 1. Issues 2. Cause-and-effect relationships	Control of agenda Interpretation of past and future trends
Alternative development	Control of alternatives	Mobilization Coalition formation Resource commitment for information search
Choice and evaluation	Control of choice	Selective advocacy of criteria Search and representation of information to justify choice
Implementation	Interaction between winners and losers	Winners attempt to "sell" or co-opt losers Losers attempt to thwart decisions and trigger fresh strategic issues
Evaluation of results	Representing oneself as successful	Selective advocacy of criteria

Source: Liam Fahey and V. K. Narayanan, "The Politics of Strategic Decision-Making," in *The Handbook of Business Strategy*, ed. Ken Albert (New York: McGraw-Hill, 1982).

Box 13.6

Joseph L. Bower and Managing the Resource Allocation Process

Joseph Bower studied a sequence of decisions in a conglomerate—decisions of the kind constantly faced by the management of a large corporation. Bower was able to demonstrate that even in the important but routine decisions—resource allocation patterns where rationality ought to play a major role—political processes were rampant.

Bower examined a firm that employed an extremely well-developed planning system; corporate management put a good deal of time and effort into the design and operation of this system. Plans and goals were coordinated through a participative process involving personnel at all levels. All were allowed to express their opinions. In return, all were expected to make themselves aware of their relationship to the overall picture, which was supposed to insure that the firm's general interest would take precedence over particular interests. The planning system was expected to generate full information and to help top management identify optimal solutions and facilitate their execution. However, Bower was able to demonstrate that *in practice, the plan had no influence on the resource allocation process or the choice of investments.*

Bower explained why. Of course, his study was limited to the influence of three highest echelons of management: the *corporate* level, consisting of the management staff detached from corporate headquarters and assigned to general management roles without operational responsibility; the *divisional* (or business unit) level, which consisted of grouping subsidiary companies on the basis of similarity in technology or markets; and a third level, *the product-market* level, which consisted of unified operations in single markets. (These levels are similar, but not identical to, the levels of planning we identified in the chapter on strategic planning.)

According to the planning model the corporate level set the general objectives on the basis of information received from the subunits. In reality, the decisions were made at the product-market level. Their procedure was to use some economic rationale that varied depending on the necessity to arbitrate among other groups, all of whom were seeking to expand their base of influence. The influence of the division level was on defining the personnel policy. This affected the career mobility of higher management who were thus encouraged to make their decisions to fit in with the wishes of divisional level management.

What was then left to the corporate level, which the textbooks describe as superpowerful? Bower found that its role was to establish the rules of the game by structuring and restructuring the complex collection of companies. It also established the criteria of rationality that the operational decision makers were expected to internalize since it was on this basis their effectiveness would be judged.

What Allison did in the context of presidential decision making, Bower accomplished in the case of profit-seeking enterprises. Strategic planning is not an exercise in rationality; it is inherently political. Bower provided incontrovertible evidence to this fact of organizational decision making.

Source: Adapted from Joseph C. Bower, *Managing the Resource Allocation Process* (New York: Richard D. Irwin, 1972).

when they can control resources, decisions, and uncertainty for others, when they cannot be easily replaced, or when they can band together. They exert their power to influence major decisions: resource allocation, personnel changes (as in the example of Horner in the chapter introduction case at the beginning of this chapter), structural changes, and organizational strategies. They employ both substantive and symbolic tactics. Substantive tactics include directly influencing the decision process, coalition building, co-optation, and testing of political reactions. Symbolic tactics typically use evocative language and rituals.

Action Strategies

The political tactics and strategies that we discussed earlier are specific actions undertaken by individuals and coalitions to exercise and enhance their power. In this section, we present three action strategies for managing organizations as political entities: (1) political strategies for managing the organization's environment, (2) managing interdepartmental conflict, and (3) industrial relations.

Figure 13.4 presents the linkages between theoretical streams and the action strategies.

Political Strategies for Managing Environment

Since organizational politics emphasizes the resource dependence of organizations on environments, political strategies focus on managing the environmental dependence. Logically, there are two ways by which an organization manages its external dependence:

FIGURE 13.4

Linkages among theoretical underpinnings, action strategies, and key concepts

1. An organization can try to reduce demands made by external elements by reducing its dependence on those elements and/or by gaining some countervailing power over them. This can be accomplished by (*a*) the choice of environment, (*b*) the establishment of favorable relationships with external elements, and (*c*) controlling the environmental elements.

2. An organization can try to minimize the cost of complying with the demands made by those external elements. An organization does this by organization design: creating separate subunits to deal with each major source of external dependence; staffing and organizing these units differently so that each is capable of managing its environmental entity; and establishing mechanisms for coordination among the different subunits.[27]

These mechanisms are schematically presented in Figure 13.5.

The choice of environmental domain is typically the focus of discussion in business and corporate level strategy formulation. Whereas strategic planning highlights the role of strategy in the economic performance of the firm, from a political perspective, strategies are merely one way of reducing external dependence. Similarly, organization design is a way of adapting to the external dependence. Since we have looked at these topics in the previous chapters, we will focus on the two strategies that are uniquely polit-

FIGURE 13.5

Strategies for managing organization-environment relations

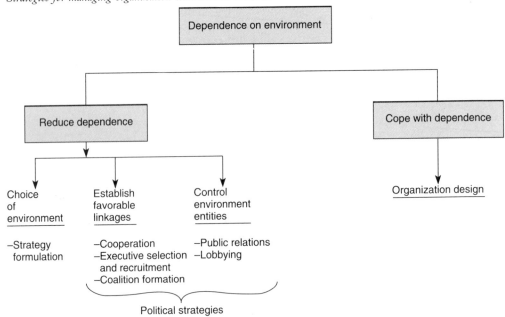

ical in character: (1) establishing favorable linkages with environmental entities, and (2) controlling the elements in the environment.

Establishing Favorable Linkages with Environmental Entities

Organizations manage their dependence with other entities by developing mechanisms for coordinating interorganizational relations. As Pfeffer and Salancik note:

> Social coordination of interdependent actors is possible as a means for managing mutual interdependence. Behavior, in this instance, is not determined by hierarchical mandate but by agreements to behave in certain ways. Some of these agreements may be tacit, taking on the characteristic of social norms. Others may be more or less explicit. The bases for coordinating interorganizational behavior are so numerous that they appear to be a natural part of organizational activity.[28]

Although business strategies such as joint ventures and mergers are mechanisms for coordination of interorganizational behavior, organizations also employ subtle mechanisms for such coordination.

> *Co-optation.* Organizations attempt to coordinate their action with environmental entities by co-opting representatives from environmental groups or organizations on advisory committees or boards of directors. Interlocking directorates facilitate interaction between organizations over time, evolving a stable collective structure of coordinated action through which interdependence is managed. Such co-optation is one of the most *flexible and easiest to implement.* Thus, any organization can create advisory or directing boards and appoint outsiders to them; it has considerable discretion over this activity. However, such co-optation may render the organization susceptible to influence from outsiders in ways not originally intended. For example, in the case of the Tennessee Valley Authority studied by Selznick,[29] local conservative agrarian interests, initially hostile to the project, were co-opted; but in the process many of the New Deal aims and objectives of the program were diverted to benefit these agrarian interests.

> *Executive succession and recruitment* sometimes serve to integrate the organization with its environment and to develop coordinated structures of interorganizational behavior. Recruiting executives from outside gives rise to the flow of information among organizations. Many aerospace companies routinely recruit personnel from the department of defense, thus obtaining up-to-date information about technical specifications, administrative procedures, and so on.

> *Coalition formation.* Whereas interlocking directorates or joint ventures are useful for interorganizational coordination when the number of organizations is relatively few, more formalized coalitions are formed

when there are large number of players. These assume the form of *trade associations* and *cartels*. Many industries have associations whose major purpose is to exchange information and exert political influence for the benefit of the members. Cartels are an even more overt attempt to organize a set of interdependent organizations. In recent years, the most widely known cartel is OPEC, the Organization of Petroleum Exporting Countries.

Coordinating the relationships among interconnected organizations through co-optation, executive recruitment, and coalition formation ensures a stable environment for an organization. In addition, it also enables an organization to meet specific objectives through collective action.

Controlling Environmental Entities

An organization also undertakes individual and collective action to shape its environment. Many organizations do not take the environment as given but continually attempt to shape the environment to their advantage. Thus, individually, the organization tries to portray itself as a good citizen; collectively, organizations try to influence the legislation. At least two tactics are evident.

> *Public relations.* A traditional way of establishing favorable relationships is through advertising. Recently, organizations have also been *taking* a proactive role in shaping public opinion. For example, Mobil Oil used to produce a series of commercials regarding the future of the oil industry. Also, organizations undertake "image advertising," where public relations people cast the organization in a favorable light in speeches, press reports, and television.
>
> *Lobbying.* Organizations, either individually or collectively, try to influence government regulation by lobbying senators and representatives and through the formation of political action committees. Thus, political strategies are employed to prevent foreign companies from gaining a foothold in a local market, to obtain preferred tax treatment, and in general to establish rules of the game favorable to the organizations. Trade associations often undertake collective activity for the benefit of its participants.

The concept of collective action for managing the environment is unique to a political perspective. Collective action enables organizations to pool their resources to advance their common interests at the expense of some autonomy. Political strategies augment the more economically oriented business and corporate level strategies. In Box 13.7, we present the case of the cigarette industry: how the firms in the industry managed to ward off threats to their survival and autonomy successfully by a set of well-orchestrated political strategies.

Box 13.7

The Case of the Cigarette Industry

The cigarette industry provides an interesting illustration of the tactics employed by key decision makers of firms in managing the external dependence of organizations:

Over the years, the firms in the tobacco industry had been incessantly under attack for manufacturing and selling cigarettes, their core business. Prior to 1962, large liability suits had been brought against cigarette firms by the families of alleged victims of cigarette smoking. These suits were settled *in favor of cigarette firms* by the courts. In addition, the Federal Trade Commission (FTC) forbade cigarette firms from making advertising claims that filtered cigarettes reduced tar and nicotine, and forced numerous other adjustments in industry advertising claims. The FTC regulations that directly affected business practices and the dangers inherent in large liability suits led the industry to establish two separate organizations—the Tobacco Research Council and the Tobacco Institute—to interface with groups critical of the industry, to coordinate and present unified cigarette-industry positions, and hence, to ward off potential dangers.

In 1964, the Surgeon General issued a report that was damaging to the tobacco industry. After the publication of the report, new legislation was proposed to strengthen the FTC in setting standards for cigarette advertising and labeling; other proposals surfaced in Congress that were aimed at educating the public as to the hazards of cigarette smoking. The tobacco industry countered through a variety of measures. Prior to the issuance of the Surgeon General's report, the American Medical Association (AMA) had argued against health warnings on cigarette packages and called for more research; the Tobacco Research Institute awarded the AMA $10 million for such studies. In Congress, representatives from tobacco states introduced bills designed to delay and prevent FTC regulation of the cigarette industry. Business associations representing advertising agencies, newspaper publishers, and broadcasters all made statements supporting the cigarette industry. Congressional hearings involving all parties were eventually organized in 1964 and 1965. As a result of the congressional hearings, a uniform weak warning was required to appear on all cigarette packages. Legislation passed in 1965 forbade the FTC or any other legislative bodies from making regulations concerning the cigarette industry for three years, until 1969. Implementation of the new advertising and labeling rules promulgated by the FTC, which had first been delayed, was made irrelevant by this legislation.

Later on, in the period 1966–70, the threats to the tobacco industry increased. The Public Health Service (PHS) created a Clearing House for Smoking and Health to collect and disseminate information and to coordinate governmental antismoking efforts. More health organizations, such as the National Advisory Cancer Council, blamed cigarette smoking for an epidemic of lung cancer. Newly appointed Advisory Task Forces on Smoking and Health concluded that cigarette advertising promoted disease and death. The FTC continued to monitor cigarette advertising and recommended stronger warning labels. In January 1967, a lawyer names John Banzhaf filed a fairness doctrine complaint with FCC in which he claimed that broadcasters carrying cigarette commercials should be required to warn the listeners of the associated health hazards. The court ruling favored Banzhaf. Later Action on Smoking and Health (ASH), organized by Banzhaf, charged the Tobacco Institute with unfair and deceptive trade practices. The ensuing investigation revealed that supposedly impartial prosmoking magazine articles were actually written by the Tobacco Institute's public relations firm. The Tobacco Institute responded, saying the reports were inaccurate, misleading, and biased. The Institute launched an advertising campaign challenging the charges being made about cigarette smoking. In Congress, representatives from tobacco states presented action on proposals directed against the cigarette

Box 13.7 continued

industry. At House hearings, witnesses supported by the cigarette and broadcast industries questioned the medical evidence that cigarettes were harmful. As a result, a house bill ignoring the broadcast issue, banning FTC and FCC regulation for another six years, and strengthening the warning label on cigarette packages was passed and sent to the Senate. Believing that they could not persuade the Senate, the cigarette industry officials decided to compromise and withdraw advertising from radio and television in exchange for legislation protecting their other advertising from FTC's stronger warning labels. In response, the broadcasters withdrew their support for cigarette-industry positions and approached Congress with an offer to relinquish cigarette advertising over a four-year period. Congress enacted legislation prohibiting cigarette advertising on the media, requiring a stronger health warning, and requiring the FTC to give Congress six months' notice before setting up new regulations.

In the period 1971 onward, the FTC required clear and conspicuous warnings in advertising, went to court to obtain rulings against billboard advertising, and forced the industry to report more sales and advertising data. Through petitions to governmental agencies, ASH initiated increasingly successful attacks on the cigarette industry. Through persistent effort, ASH was often successful with its petitions, but the results eventually affected smokers and smoking behavior rather than the cigarette industry. Although successive Surgeon Generals remained critical of the cigarette industry, the government behaved in contradictory ways, and few of the proposals made by the Surgeon General have been acted upon. Members of the Congress from tobacco states continued to support the industry, as did representatives of transportation firms and advertising agencies. As a result, many congressional initiatives to increase cigarette-industry taxes or modify or cancel tobacco price-support pro-grams were defeated. In addition, lawyers for the cigarette industry obtained delays and fa-vorable rulings in cases involving smoking restrictions on airlines and buses; they were also successful in obtaining rulings that both the Consumer Product Safety Commission and the FDA lacked the right to regulate the cigarette industry.

The story of the cigarette industry illustrates many of the political tactics in managing external dependence. Prior to 1962, when external threats were emerging to the core business, the firms *competing in the cigarette industry* formed a *coalition* by establishing the Tobacco Research Council and the Tobacco Institute. Among other things, this degree of organization provided them a stable source of power. Over time, some relatively unstable coalitions were also undertaken: with the AMA in 1964, with broadcasters, advertising agencies, and the news media. These relationships were built on resource exchange: research money for the AMA, advertising revenues for the broadcasters and the news media, and revenues for the ad agencies. These coalitions evaporated when resource exchanges were stopped, as in the case of the broadcasters in the 1970s. All throughout this period, there were persistent attempts at *public relations* to mold public perceptions regarding the hazards of smoking and *lobbying* efforts to influence Congress. As a result of the industry efforts over a very long period, *to a large extent, the antismoking target has tended to be smokers' behavior rather than the cigarette industry itself.* Firms in the industry have been quite successful in warding off many of the threats to their autonomy and survival by a set of carefully orchestrated political strategies.

The values currently prevalent in our society are such that a majority of people view smoking as a social evil. Since tobacco companies are one of the key actors in the propagation of this evil, we could regard their actions at self-preservation as being at variance with the social values and hence, unethical. Although the aims of the tobacco companies are highly

Box 13.7 continued

questionable, we are forced to acknowledge the success of their political strategies.

We make one additional point with this case. Political strategies of the type organization theorists present may be used ethically or unethically. As we noted earlier, the tobacco industry's tactics would be viewed by many as an example of unethical behavior. A student of organizations should not condone such behavior but at the same time cannot deny the existence of such behaviors.

Source: Adapted from R. L. Dunbar and N. Wasilewski, "Regulating External Threats in the Cigarette Industry," *Administrative Science Quarterly* 30 (December 1985), pp. 540–59.

Managing Interdepartmental Conflict

Just as in the broader domain of politics, our views about conflict and management of conflict have undergone a radical revision since the days of classical theorists and the Human Relations school. Classical theorists did not specifically address the issue of conflict management. Thus, for example, in Weber's bureaucracy, conflicts among departments were to be handled at the level of a common superior. Indeed, these were treated as exceptions. Similarly, the Human Relations school regarded organizations as cooperative systems and held that conflict was bad. Both classical theorists and the Human Relations school prescribed the role of management as eliminating conflict.

As the political side of the enterprise began to gain increasing attention, the focus shifted to viewing conflict as *inevitable* in organizations. Contemporary thinkers hold the view that depending on the circumstances, conflict may be productive. The role of management is not so much to eliminate conflict as to *manage* it. From this vantage point, it is not the existence of conflict but the process of managing conflict that contributes to the effectiveness of an organization. With this shift in focus, conflict in organizations began to receive serious theoretical attention.

As early as the 1930s, social psychologists were interested in the phenomenon of intergroup conflict. In one of the earliest studies, Sherif worked with Boy Scouts and discovered how the process of conflict escalated (see Box 13.8). They discovered three outcomes of intergroup conflict:

1. In the face of intergroup conflict, individuals *identified* with their own group more than other groups. Thus, intragroup communication was high, but communication across groups was limited. Similarly, individuals developed a feeling of "we" for their group and of "they" for the other group.

2. Individuals *accentuated* differences among the groups in a predictable fashion. Thus, they attributed all the good qualities to their own group, whereas they saw the "other" group in negative terms.

Box 13.8

Sherif and the Intergroup Conflict

Some of the earlier observations on intergroup conflict were made by Muzafer Sherif when he conducted experiments with Boy Scouts. These experiments are classic and laid the foundations of modern theories of organizational conflict.

In the Boy Scout camp where Sherif was making the observations, there were a number of groups who had different names such as White and Black. These groups participated in various competitive activities such as games. As time went on, Sherif noted that intense feelings were generated among the groups. Amid the competitive activities, each group began to withdraw into itself. The members of each group stuck to themselves and there were strong group feelings. Also, the Boy Scouts in each group were confident about themselves, whereas they derided other group members. Sherif noted that these feelings had no "objective" basis, and intergroup communications broke down as time went on. Each group derided the other, displaying strong "we-they" feelings. "They" were always the bad guys; "we" were always the good guys. Sherif argued that in the competitive situations, there was always a winner; hence, one group could win only at the expense of the other. This led him to believe that goal incompatibility was a major cause of intergroup conflict.

To test his hypothesis, he created a situation where the groups would have to collaborate with one other: he decided to cut off the water supply. In order to provide water for the camp, the groups would have to work to-gether. Water had to be brought from a well far away; no one group could accomplish the task. Under the new situation, the members of various groups started collaborating with each other. The intense antagonistic feelings among them began to decline, and there was now increased communications among the groups.

Sherif had hypothesized that when there was a commonality of goals among the groups, intergroup conflict would evaporate. He coined the term *superordinate goal* to describe goals that are shared by the various groups.

To further test the hypothesis, he restored the water supply. As the water supply was restored, the need for cooperation among the groups was no longer there. Competitive games were still going on; and the situation reverted back to where it had been before the water was cut off—the intense group feelings returned and conflict followed.

Based on these experiments, Sherif provided the outlines of a theory of intergroup conflict. He argued that in the presence of conflict, intragroup communication would increase, whereas intergroup communication would decrease, members would suffer from distorted perception, and we-they feelings would be rampant. Sherif also suggested that creating superordinate goals would alleviate such conflict.

Sources: Adapted from Muzafer Sherif, "Experiments in Intergroup Conflict," in *Intergroup Conflict and Cooperation*, ed. M. Sherif, O. J. Harvey, B. J. White, W. R. Hood, and C. W. Sherif (Norman, Okla.: University of Oklahoma Books Exchange, 1961). Muzafer Sherif and C. W. Sherif, *Social Psychology* (New York, Harper & Row, 1969).

3. *Frustration* occurred where the members of one group saw the members of other groups as interfering with their goal attainment.

When these processes were at work, each group began to advance its position at the expense of others. Thus, conflict began to erupt.

Building on the work of these social psychologists and others, organizational theorists began to study interdepartmental conflict. They noted that interdepartmental conflict—conflict between departments in an organization—is an endemic feature of large organizations. It may occur between departments on the hierarchical level (e.g., marketing and manufacturing departments) due to a variety of reasons. (Readers may want to refer back to the work of Lawrence and Lorsch in our chapter on organization design.) Or it may occur between departments that are related hierarchically, as between corporate headquarters and a division. (For an example, refer to Box 8.12 in the chapter on strategic planning.)

Organization theorists elaborated a model of interdepartmental conflict in organizations and suggested various tactics for managing the conflict.

Model of Intergroup Conflict

The model of intergroup conflict is presented in Figure 13.6. The model has five major elements: (1) antecedent conditions, (2) attributes of intergroup relations, (3) trigger, (4) intergroup conflict, and (5) behavioral consequences. We will discuss each one briefly.

Antecedent Conditions. Enduring organizational and contextual factors determine the potential for conflict in organizations. According to the contingency theorists of organization design, goals, technology, and structure have a profound influence on the internal functioning of an organization. We noted how organizations differentiate into departments to confront environmental uncertainty. As an organization becomes differentiated, each department develops different operative goals. Organization structure also determines the patterns of division of labor, skills and attitudes, and power of various departments. Similarly, technology and work flow influence the pattern of interdependence. Thus, departments in an organization are faced with differences in power, goals, and resources; at the same time, they are dependent on each other for their performance. Under these conditions, *if integrating processes are absent,* there is great potential for conflict.

Attributes of Intergroup Relations. The antecedent conditions translate into a number of attributes of specific intergroup relations that determine the frequency, intensity, and extent of intergroup conflict:

1. Perhaps the most important attribute is *incompatibility among goals* between departments. As a department pursues its goals, it

FIGURE 13.6

Model of intergroup conflict

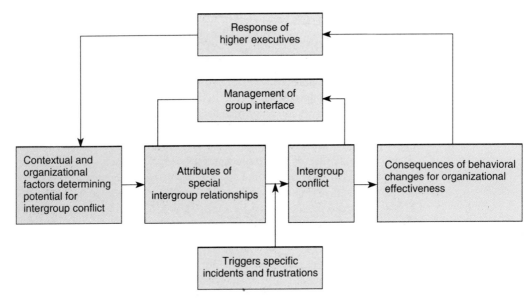

Source: Adapted from Richard E. Walton and John E. Dutton, "The Management of Interdepartmental Conflict, *Administrative Science Quarterly* 14 (1969), pp. 73–84; and Louis R. Pondy, "Organizational Conflict: Concepts and Models," *Administrative Science Quarterly* 12 (1967), pp. 296–320.

discovers that other groups pursuing other goals often interfere with its goal attainment. Thus, for example, the marketing department may be focused on the specific needs of a diverse set of customers for increasing their sales. This may mean that the manufacturing department will have to have short production runs and hence higher costs, which they want to eschew. Goal incompatibility exists among many departments in organizations.

2. The degree of *differentiation* among departments translates into different interpersonal orientations, skills, time frames, and so on between departments. This leads to difficulty of communication and negative attributions about the "other" groups that are perceived as different from "us."

3. *Interdependence* among departments enhances the potential for conflict. As we noted (see Figure 13.2), the higher the interdependence, the higher the degree of conflict.

4. Under conditions of *resource scarcity,* the potential for conflict is enhanced. As we saw earlier in the chapter, power plays are common when resources are scarce.

5. *Differential power distribution* among departments leads to conflict when actual working relations do not reflect perceived power, as when a low-prestige department decides to dictate to another of higher status, though they are at the same hierarchical level.

6. Related to all of the above, *uncertainty* experienced by different departments enhances the potential for conflict. As environments change, newer problems crop up, and departments will have to *renegotiate* their roles and activities. Under certain conditions, departments, often politically motivated, reach out and grab the domains of activity of other departments. This sparks conflicts in the organization.

7. An organization's *reward systems* potentially influence the degree of cooperation among departments. When department managers are rewarded for attainment of the organization's goals, the potential for cooperation is greater. On the other hand, if the reward system is oriented to departmental goals, then potential for cooperation is lessened.

Contextual factors set the stage for the drama of intergroup conflict. The specific attributes provide the script. Such specific attributes need to be diagnosed for managing the conflicts in organizations.

Triggers.   When intergroup relations are characterized by potential conflict, specific events bring the conflict to the surface. These triggers may often seem trivial (e.g. a damaging remark by an individual about another group). The specific triggers, in conjunction with the contextual factors, lead to full-fledged conflict. What was potential or latent now becomes manifest.

Intergroup Conflict.   Consistent with Sherif's predictions, when intergroup conflict erupts, some specific behaviors emerge.

1. Individuals begin to strongly identify with their own group. In other words, they develop and strengthen their group identity. Occasionally, they begin to show signs of "we" feelings.

2. The presence of other groups invites comparisons, and also leads to the "they" feelings about the groups with which they are in conflict. The "other groups" are viewed as the enemy to be overcome.

3. Perceptual distortions creep up among the groups, whereby they overestimate the positive aspects of their group but accentuate the negative aspects of others.

4. As conflict escalates, communication between groups declines; where it exists, it is filled with mutual recriminations and slander.

5. When one group wins in the conflict, the "defeated" group occasionally loses cohesion and may dethrone its leaders.

When organization theorists began to view conflict as inevitable in organizations, they held out the above behaviors as natural outcomes of intergroup conflict and not the psychological defects of the individuals involved.

Behavioral Consequences.   As we noted in the beginning of our discussion of this section, intergroup conflict is endemic to organizational life. It has both negative and positive consequences. Ultimately, it is the degree of conflict that determines whether it is functional or dysfunctional for the organization.

Very low levels of conflict generally signal complacency in an organization. Then, the organization is not goal oriented or has set very low levels of goals; there is little cohesiveness within groups, and poor task orientation. At the same time, when conflict is intense, the members divert their energy from organizational goals; instead, the conflict itself occupies their attention. They suffer from distorted perceptions and judgment. In protracted conflicts, some groups lose, depending on their power and resource position. This leads to dissension, and the organization suffers from the lack of contribution from demoralized loser groups. Thus, there is a zone of intensity within which the conflict is manageable. In this zone, conflict stimulates various groups to be focused on the task; productivity is high and there is balance between departmental and organizational goals.

Strategies for Managing Conflict

What are the alternative ways to manage interdepartmental conflict? According to organization theorists, there are two dimensions along which to array conflict management strategies: (1) short run versus long run, and (2) process versus structure.

1. *Short run versus long run:* Some strategies focus on managing ongoing conflicts. Their impact is transitory and does not extend beyond the specific conflict situation. On the other hand, long-run strategies focus on developing an organization's capability to manage conflicts. Although these strategies are not directly relevant for ongoing conflicts, their impact is enduring.

2. *Process versus structure:* Process strategies intervene in organizational processes, whereas structural strategies redesign an organization. Typically, process strategies resemble organization development interventions, whereas structural approaches draw their inspiration from organization design.

Taken together, the two dimensions yield four major types of strategies. The strategies are summarized in Figure 13.7.

FIGURE 13.7

A typology of conflict management strategies

	Short range	*Long range*
Structure	Bureaucratic authority Limiting interaction Integration devices Separating the parties	Rotation of members
Process	Confrontation and negotiation Third-party consultation	Superordinate goals Intergroup training

Short-Run Structural Approaches.   There are four structural mechanisms to manage conflict in the short run:

> *Bureaucratic authority* may be invoked to resolve conflicts when two departments at the same hierarchical level cannot agree on a solution to a specific problem. Here, a superior invokes legitimate authority to force a resolution to the conflict. The resolution is typically binding on the specific situation only. Hence, the process has to be repeated whenever newer conflicts erupt. This mechanism is effective when the intensity of conflict is low.
>
> *Limiting interaction* and communication among departments reduces the potential for conflicts. Interactions are limited to areas where there is some agreement on goals and means. This strategy is best suited for conditions where the intensity of conflict is low to moderate, and the rules of decision making and interaction are well defined.
>
> *Integration devices,* postulated in the chapter on organization design, offer another mechanism for managing conflicts. The integrators and/or the integrating departments work well when the intensity of conflict is moderate. Integration devices serve as communication channels and build a sense of collaboration among affected groups.
>
> *Separating the departments structurally* so that the two are not interdependent with each other may be necessary; at very intense levels of conflict, none of the above may work.

Short-Run Process Approaches.   Unlike structural approaches, process approaches directly intervene in interdepartmental conflict. There are two major short-run process strategies:

> *Confrontation and negotiation.* In this strategy, the conflicted departments confront one another and negotiate their differences. This strategy is risky since it cannot guarantee a negotiated outcome.

When conflict is intense or when an organization quickly requires a resolution to the conflict, sometimes this is the only feasible strategy. It works well when the groups have some degree of skill in confronting one another, and do indeed work to resolve conflict in a way that will benefit each other. Some call this a "win-win" orientation. If such an orientation does not exist or it cannot be developed, then confrontation will be ineffective and the conflict will escalate.

Third-party consultation. When the conflict is intense and protracted, and the departments are suspicious of each other, a third-party consultant may have to be brought in from outside the organization. The third party should not only have conflict resolution skills but should be credible to the conflicted departments. Also, he or she must be seen as an impartial outsider. A third party typically enables the conflicting parties to focus and define issues, thus getting the departments to work on the "problem" to the exclusion of emotional issues. The third party also establishes communication channels, interprets messages, challenges the stereotypes held by the groups, and builds a group's awareness of the positive actions and intentions of the other group.

The short-run strategies, process or structural, typically do not leave a lasting imprint on organizational memory. Since they address specific conflicts, their effects are fleeting. Rather than focusing on specific conflicts one at a time, organizations may invest in developing their capacity to handle conflicts. This is a long-range effort, and takes place over several years. Such long-range efforts develop individual managers' attitudes and skills so they can handle conflicts with minimal outside intervention. For example, as we noted earlier, confrontation and negotiation require a "win-win" attitude among departments. Organizations may invest in developing such an attitude as an element of its long-range strategy for conflict management. As in the case of short-run strategies, there are both long-range structural and long-range process strategies.

Long-Run Structural Strategies.   A major structural approach to conflict management is *rotation of members*. Rotating individuals among departments on a permanent basis is one way to foster integration by inculcating appropriate attitudes among individuals. As we noted in organization design, differentiation among departments leads to differences in interpersonal, goal, and time orientation among individuals. As individuals move from one department to another, they gain an appreciation of the points of view of different departments. This leads to an accurate exchange of information, enabling resolution of conflicts.

Japanese organizations typically move individuals from production to sales to research and development departments on a continual basis. In

American firms, on the other hand, people are often rotated between line (e.g., operating divisions) and staff departments (e.g., strategic planning) for the same purpose. Rotation of individuals works slowly to reduce conflict, and takes long periods of time to change attitudes.

Long-Run Process Strategies.   There are two major process strategies: building superordinate goals and intergroup training.

> *Superordinate goals.* Top managers may continue to build commitment in organizations to superordinate goals, a term coined by Sherif (see Box 13.8). Superordinate goals subsume departmental goals to generate commitment by departments. In times of crisis, typically such goals are visible to the organization as a whole. That is why departments often come together in a crisis. To a degree, top managers can insure such commitment by highlighting superordinate goals under normal conditions as well. To be effective, the goals must be important, and a significant amount of departmental activity must be devoted to them. They should also be backed up with appropriate structures and rewards.
>
> *Intergroup training.* The most intense long-term strategy, intergroup training, was invented by Blake and Mouton.[30] Here, the focus is on training individuals and groups in the skills of conflict management.

Organizations, therefore, have a variety of strategies available to them for managing conflicts. Indeed, they use mechanisms in numerous combinations. The more mechanistic the organization is, the more likely it is that short-term tactics will be employed. On the other hand, one is likely to find the use of both short- and long-range mechanisms in organic organizations.

The case of Scientific Instruments, presented in Box 13.9, describes the evolution of interdepartmental conflict in the case of a project management team. In the example, the organization had to resort to an integrator to head the project team to manage the intergroup conflict. The integrator was a highly regarded scientist and thus commanded the respect of various departments. One could infer that being an outsider, he was politically credible to the departments. The urgency and importance of the project perhaps necessitated this strategy. However, we could easily see that this was a short-term strategy, intended to solve only the immediate problem. It is doubtful whether, if similar conflicts erupt, the organization would be able to handle them differently. Also, the solution raises an important unresolved question: What is the role of the project leader once the design is completed?

How should one pick one strategy over another? Short-range approaches alone may be sufficient for organizations facing very stable environments. In dynamic environments, exclusive reliance on short-range approaches is likely to be inadequate, as in the case of Scientific Instruments in

Box 13.9

The Case of Scientific Instruments, Inc.

Scientific Instruments, Inc. (SII), is a medium-sized firm in the electronics industry that produced and marketed a broad line of electronic instruments and gauges. The markets included the machine tool industry, government, and aviation industries. Most of the products were in mature markets, and although specifications of the products varied with customers and over time, the design and manufacturing posed no serious challenges. In an attempt to stimulate the growth of the company, recently SII has been looking for attractive opportunities to expand its business.

The firm was organized along functional lines, with R&D, manufacturing, and marketing departments. In addition, there were three separate staff departments: personnel, finance, and legal. Each of the functional departments was headed by a vice president who reported to the President of the company. The R&D department, the focus of this case, consisted of three units: hardware, process design, and systems and control (S&C). The hardware unit primarily dealt with the core of the instruments, process design was in charge of designing the manufacturing setup, whereas S&C was responsible for system integration. Typically, the work flowed from hardware to process design and finally to S&C. These departments were staffed by specialized and highly qualified engineers. The relationships among them were excellent. It was common to find the engineers sharing jokes and stories in the company cafeteria and away from work as well. The president often remarked about the collegiality of the R&D department to outsiders and to other vice presidents.

In its efforts to expand the markets, the firm landed a contract with an aeronautical firm for the design and manufacture of a set of complex instruments. The instruments were to be used for the parts of a space shuttle the client was manufacturing. SII knew that once it got its foot in the lucrative space business, more opportunities were likely to follow; the potential sales that may accrue could well mean manifold growth for the firm. Although the deadlines were stringent, SII felt that the excellent engineering and manufacturing talent that it possessed would enable it to meet such deadlines.

The vice president in charge of R&D was given the responsibility of coming up with a prototype. The manager organized a project team by selecting an engineer from each of the three units and assigned the task of instrument development to them. He noted that although the instrument was more complex than their regular products, he had full confidence in them to carry out the task.

Each engineer worked on his own within his respective unit, as was the practice. The units knew the urgency; they also knew that their work would be lost if another unit produced a design that was markedly superior.

Three months later, the R&D manager discovered that the job had not progressed very much. He was concerned that the firm might not meet the deadlines imposed by the client. The three engineers were closely affiliated with their units, and the relationship among the units had deteriorated to such an extent that they were on the verge of open warfare. Matters came to a head when the systems integration unit "proved" that any design based on the premises of the other two units would be theoretically impossible. Knowing the importance of the project, the manager hired a chief engineer with impeccable credentials who was then on the faculty of MIT to head up the project. He assigned the three engineers to work under him. The chief engineer solved the design problem soon enough, and though the three units initially tried to prove him wrong, they were later satisfied with his direction.

Box 13.9 continued

Although this case may be discussed from several vantage points, we use it here to illustrate the dynamics of intergroup conflict. Before the contract was landed, the organization, especially the R&D unit, was functioning more or less smoothly. The environment was stable, as the firm was dealing with mature markets; and the goals were more or less clear. The work flow was sequential: from hardware through process design to system integration. The organization was functionally organized; the R&D unit was further departmentalized into units with specialized tasks and specialized personnel. Since the environment was stable, one could infer that the level of integration was sufficient to manage the potential conflict inherent in the functional setup and sequential interdependence.

As the firm landed the new contract, the situation changed. There was uncertainty created by the task demands of the new product design: Notice that the task was described as complex and challenging and something the firm had not dealt with before. The R&D manager initially stayed with the existing structure and delegated the design task in the same manner as previously.

In the absence of additional integrating mechanisms, certain attributes of intergroup relations developed. The differentiation among units in the R&D department already existed. The new task brought with it a higher level of uncertainty for the department. We could infer that it resulted in a higher level of interdependence: The sequential approach of the past was not suitable and the units had to collaborate to a greater degree to come up with a design. This necessitated the use of additional integrating mechanisms that were not forthcoming in the early stages. This led to incompatibility in goals among the units: They came to define their situation as one where their own goal attainment could be thwarted by the efforts of other units.

We do not know from the case what the specific triggers were. However, we do know the dynamics of conflict that evolved. First, the engineers assigned to the project began to identify with their unit more than with their project. The units became closely knit; the collegiality that existed among the units evaporated; communications were confined to the specific units; interunit communication decreased.

The observation that the groups were ready to declare open warfare suggests that the conflict had escalated to a level of intensity beyond that which is functional. Specific behavioral outcomes are also visible: energies of one unit were diverted away from the project and toward "proving" that the other units were wrong. Certainly, the task was not being accomplished. We could speculate that the engineers assigned to the project were thoroughly frustrated.

Given the press of time, the R&D vice president adopted a short-term strategy to reduce the level of conflict. He brought in an *integrator* from outside. The fact that he was an outsider and, hence, likely to be a disinterested party to the conflict lent him credibility. So did his reputation. The higher level of integration thus brought about seemed to have worked in this case.

Source: This case is adapted from a number of case histories as well as from the experience of the authors in project management.

Box 13.9. When environments are dynamic, long-range strategies are necessary for developing an organization's conflict-handling capacity without outside assistance. In addition, they create appropriate conditions for the effective application of short-range solutions such as confrontation and negotiation that may be necessary on an ad hoc basis.

Both process and structural strategies are required for managing conflicts. However, their specific sequencing—that is, which should come first—is contingent on the level of trust prevailing in a given organization. In extreme conditions, when the trust level among departments is either very low or very high, it may be appropriate first to implement structural solutions. When the trust level is moderate, process strategies may be a more effective starting point.

Industrial Relations

As we pointed out in the discussion of philosophical underpinnings, one of the major foci of organizational politics is distributive justice: How should the benefits from an organization (e.g., profits) be distributed among stakeholders (e.g., shareholders and workers)?

The answers to questions of distributive justice are often shaped by one's ideology or belief systems. For example, the capitalist ideology gives preeminence to entrepreneurship. Here, shareholders who provide capital are considered to be the owners of an enterprise, and managers are the agents acting in the shareholders' best interests. Labor is viewed as an input to the organization, with labor costs being determined by the (labor) market forces. On the other hand, a socialist ideology gives preeminence to labor, and workers are deemed to be the major stakeholders in an organization. In the capitalist ideology, the questions of distributive justice are resolved in favor of shareholders, whereas in socialist ideology, workers are given preference.

The ideological differences pertaining to distributive justice are most acute between shareholders and managers on the one hand and workers on the other. The differences often disrupt the functioning of an organization (e.g., strikes by unions) and in some cases could threaten its survival (e.g., Eastern Airlines, which, under Frank Lorenzo, had to file for bankruptcy).

Over the years, the field of industrial relations has specifically addressed the question of distributive justice and provided mechanisms for managing the differences between shareholder/managers and workers. The two major mechanisms evolved by the field are: collective bargaining and industrial democracy.

Collective bargaining. Collective bargaining refers to the negotiation between management and workers. This approach acknowledges the incompatibility of goals between management and workers, but contains the intensity of conflict so that it does not totally threaten the survival of the organization. Workers typically rely on a union in the bargaining process. The bargaining itself follows a prescribed format and usually begins with the presentation of demands or proposals by one party that are evaluated by the other. This is followed by counterproposals and concessions. The issues typically focused upon are wages and salaries, working conditions, fringe benefits, and so on. Thus, they center upon distribution of rewards and governance in organizations.

Industrial democracy. This approach attempts to co-opt the workers into management, thus reducing the incompatibility of goals between management and workers. It may assume different forms: electing union leaders to the board of directors, or establishing workers' councils and employee stock options (ESOPs). This approach enhances the degree of participation of workers in the running of the enterprise. Power equalization is viewed as necessary for reducing the incompatibility of goals and the excesses of management. At the same time, it is expected to enhance the productive contribution of the workers to the organization.

The two mechanisms—collective bargaining and industrial democracy—thus invoke different approaches to managing the differences between shareholders and workers. Collective bargaining takes the differences as a fact of life and attempts continually to build compromise between shareholders' and workers' interests. Industrial democracy seeks to reduce the incompatibility between the two groups by giving more power to workers in major organizational decisions.

Although both mechanisms are sometimes concurrently employed, different nations have adopted them to varying degrees. Some socialist European nations such as Sweden have adopted industrial democracy as the primary mechanism for resolving questions of distributive justice. Similarly, nations such as Germany (and of course, Sweden) have enacted into law various facets of industrial democracy such as worker representation on boards of directors, thereby allowing workers to have a voice in major organizational decisions.

Japanese organizations try to integrate workers into the organization to such an extent that the differences between managers and workers are lessened to a great degree. The tight sense of integration fostered among the various groups in Japanese organizations and society has led some to coin the term *Japan Inc.,* meaning that the various groups think and act as if their interests are similar and not divergent. Even in the United States, some Japanese firms have succeeded in coaligning workers' interests with those of the organization. Witness, for example, the fact that workers at the Nissan plant in Alabama rejected the UAW's move to unionize them. This is the third time that a unionization attempt in a Japanese firm in the United States has failed.

In the United States, a few organizations practice industrial democracy to a limited extent. For example, Chrysler's appointment of Mr. Frazer of the United Auto Workers to its board of directors was a move towards industrial democracy. However, in the United States, collective bargaining between union and management has been the primary mechanism for resolving shareholder-worker conflicts. This has been due to historical and ideological reasons. Union-management relations in the United States have been adversarial from the time when the union movement sprang up in response to the power of the Robber Barons. Also, the capitalist ideology prevailing in the United States has prevented the sharing of power with the workers by managers.

Chapter Summary

From a political perspective, managers have three major tasks: (1) negotiate resources with the environment, (2) manage internal conflicts, and (3) reconcile the conflicting demands of shareholders and workers.

Since organizations are dependent on the environment for resources, managers need to negotiate with the environment to ensure a stable flow of resources. They do this by (1) establishing favorable linkages with other organizations through co-optation, recruitment of key people and forming or joining trade associations and cartels; and (2) where possible, controlling environmental actors through public relations and lobbying.

Conflict is pervasive in organizations and managers need to limit it to acceptable levels. In the short run they may do so by (1) structural solutions such as bureaucratic authority, integration devices, limiting interaction among feuding parties, or by separating them altogether, or (2) process solutions such as bargaining and negotiations or third-party consultation. In the long run, they have to enhance the capability of their organizations to deal with conflict through such mechanisms as (1) rotating people through various departments, (2) creating superordinate goals, and (3) intergroup training.

Industrial relations is the major mechanism by which organizations deal with conflicts between shareholders and workers. In the United States, this typically takes the form of collective bargaining. In Europe, industrial democracy is more prevalent.

Specialized Terms

Historical underpinnings
- Philosophical method
- Empirical method

Organizational decision making
- Dominant coalition
- Garbage can model

Structual contingency model of
  power
Politics of organization-
  environment relations
  • Resource dependency
Conditions for the exercise of power
  • Interdependence
  • Heterogeneity of goals and
    beliefs
  • Scarcity of resources
Bases of power
  • Control of resources
  • Control of uncertainty
  • Irreplaceability
  • Affecting the decision process
  • Strength of numbers
Decision arenas for the exercise of
  power

• Resource allocation
• Personnel changes
• Structural change
• Organizational strategy
Political tactics
  • Substantive
  • Symbolic
Political strategies for managing
  environment
  • Favorable linkages
  • Controlling environment
Interdepartmental conflict
  • Model of conflict
  • Strategies for managing conflict
Industrial relations
  • Collective bargaining
  • Industrial democracy

Discussion Questions

Theoretical

1. Define power and politics. When is power an explanation for
   organizational behavior?

2. A prominent journalist recently commented, "Almost all
   government agencies are filled with turf battles. We should strive to
   eliminate the battles." Comment in light of theoretical developments
   in organization theory.

3. How does the political model of decision making differ from the
   rational model depicted in the chapter on strategic planning?

4. What are the bases of power? How does a knowledge of power
   bases help managers in their work?

★5. Discuss the linkage between the structural contingency model of
   interdepartmental power and the model of interdepartmental
   conflict. How are Sherif's findings on intergroup conflict relevant
   for the model of interdepartmental conflict?

6. Distinguish between substantive and symbolic political tactics. Give
   examples.

★7. Sketch the linkage between philosophic assumptions and three action
   strategies described in this chapter.

★This is an advanced-level question.

8. What assumptions about organizations and human beings are made in the field of organizational politics?
9. Review organizational politics from the perspective of the systems model.

Applied

1. The tobacco industry has approached you to devise a strategy in response to the activism of the antismoking lobby. Outline a strategy for the industry.
2. Outline a long-run approach to managing interdepartmental conflict in Scientific Instruments.
★3. How does organizational politics in a business organization differ from such politics in a university?

End Notes

1. Alison Leigh Cowan, "The Partners Revolt at Peat Marwick," *New York Times,* November 18, 1990, pp. F1, F10.
2. Michael Crozier and Erhard Friedberg, *Actors and Systems: the Politics of Collective Action* (Chicago: University of Chicago Press, 1980), p. 4.
3. We use the term employed by Claude George in *The History of Management Thought* (Englewood Cliffs, N.J.: Prentice Hall, 1967).
4. See Albert Somit and Joseph Tanenhaus, *The Development of American Political Science,* for an historical review.
5. Karl Marx and Friedrich Engels, *The German Ideology* (London, 1965).
6. C. Wright Mills, *The Power Elite* (New York: Oxford University Press, 1956).
7. Robert Dahl, *Who Governs? Democracy and Power in an American City* (New Haven: Yale University Press, 1961).
8. Jeffrey Pfeffer, *Power in Organizations* (Marshfield, Mass.: Pitman Publishing, 1981), p. 2.
9. The bureaucratic theorists assumed that goals are reasonably consistent; the rationality assumptions behind the strategy and structure school viewed goals as consistent across actors; the organization development scholars viewed cooperation as possible.
10. Michael Crozier and Erhard Friedberg, *Actors and Systems: The Politics of Collective Action,* pp. 45–47.
11. Ibid.
12. Elton Mayo, *The Social Problems of an Industrial Civilization* (Boston: Division of Research, Harvard Business School, 1945).
13. Chester I. Barnard, *The Functions of the Executive* (Cambridge, Mass.: Harvard University Press, 1938).
14. P. Selznick, *TVA and the Grass Roots* (Berkeley, Calif.: University of California Press, 1949).

15. Richard M. Cyert and James G. March, *A Behavioral Theory of the Firm* (Englewood Cliffs, N.J.: Prentice Hall, 1963).

16. Graham T. Allison, *The Essence of Decision* (Boston, Mass.: Little, Brown, 1971).

17. Michael D. Cohen, James G. March, and Johan Olsen, "A Garbage Can Model of Organizational Choice, " *Administrative Science Quarterly* 17 (March 1982), pp. 1–25.

18. The view that administrative ploys are mini-Machiavellian was a criticism Argyris made against their work [see Chris Argyris, *The Inner Contradictions of Rigorous Research* (New York: Academic Press, 1980)]. We use it here to make the explicit linkage to Machiavelli and political processes.

19. Gerald R. Salancik and Jeffery Pfeffer, "Who Gets Power—And How They Hold Onto It: A Strategic Contingency Model of Power," *Organizational Dynamics,* Winter 1977, pp. 3–21.

20. Pfeffer, *Power in Organizations,* p. 106.

21. Jeffrey Pfeffer and Gerald Salancik, "Organizational Decision-Making As a Political Process: The Case of a University Budget," *Administrative Science Quarterly* 19 (1974), pp. 135–51.

22. Donald L. Helmich and Warren Brown, "Successor Type and Organizational Change in the Corporate Enterprise," *Administrative Science Quarterly* 17 (1972), p. 351.

23. This tactic was termed *temporal gambits* by V. K. Narayanan and Liam Fahey, "The Micro-politics of Strategy Formulation," *Academy of Management Review* 7, no.1 (1982), pp. 25–34.

24. Ibid.

25. Pfeffer, *Power in Organizations,* p. 183.

26. Liam Fahey and V. K. Narayanan, "The Politics of Strategic Decision Making," in *The Handbook of Business Strategy,* ed. Kenneth Albert (New York: McGraw-Hill, 1982).

27. John P. Kotter, "Managing External Dependence," *Academy of Management Review* 4 (1979), pp. 87–92.

28. Jeffrey Pfeffer and Gerald Salancik, *The External Control of Organizations: A Resource Dependence Perspective* (New York: Harper & Row, 1978).

29. Selznik, *TVA and the Grass Roots.*

30. Robert Blake and Jane S. Mouton, *Corporate Excellence through Grid* (Houston: Gulf, 1968).

SUMMARY OF ACTION STRATEGIES

In this section of the book, we have summarized the major action strategies that have been developed by organization theorists over the years. Broadly, we classified these strategies into two classes—rational action and human system strategies.

As we have seen, the rational action strategies consist of a set of sequential steps—environmental analysis, strategic planning, organization design, and design of organization information and control systems. These steps invoked an open systems perspective by their careful and deliberate attention to environment. Internally they focused on the functional and informational subsystems.

Human system strategies—organization development, organization culture, and organization politics—on the other hand, focused respectively on the social, cultural, and political subsystems. They were not as tightly knit as the rational system strategies; this is an acknowledgement of the turbulent nature of human dynamics in organizations.

These two sets of strategies may be compared along three major dimensions: (1) technical versus human focus, (2) content versus process, and (3) rational versus nonrational.

1. *Technical versus human focus:* whether the action strategy undertakes to bring about changes in the functional and informational elements in an organization as opposed to feelings, attitudes, values of power structures of individuals in it.

2. *Content versus process:* whether the focus is on content—changing the visible, easily measurable, and substantive elements of an organization (such as product-market strategies or organization structure) or whether the strategies focus on process or how things are done, events that lead to changing the human and qualitative features of an organization.

3. *Rational and nonrational:* whether strategies are chosen to fulfill predetermined economic goals or whether the goals are noneconomic and/or goal formulation itself is considered problematic.

In our discussion of the strategies in this section, we have illustrated how rational action strategies focused on technical elements, are content-oriented, and primarily pursued economic goals. Human strategies, on the other hand, focused on human elements, are process-oriented, and pursued non-economic goals, and often, as in the case of organizational politics, focused on goal formulation. Table II.2 summarizes the characteristics of various action steps.

From a systems theoretic perspective, whenever an organization contemplates long-term action, both strategies—rational action and human system—must be integrated. However, a comprehensive set of guidelines to

TABLE II.2   Focus of Action Strategies

Action Strategies	Open Systems Framework (Primary Element)	Focus
Rational Action Strategies		
Environmental analysis	Environment	Technical, content, rational
Strategic planning	Organization-environment interface	Technical, content, rational
Organization design	Functional subsystem	Technical, content, rational
Organization information and control systems	Information subsystem	Technical, content, rational
Human System Strategies		
Organization development	Social subsystem	Social, process, nonrational
Organization culture	Cultural subsystem	Social, process, nonrational
Organization politics	Political subsystem	Social, process, nonrational

facilitate this integration has not yet been developed by organization theorists. Further the principle of "equifinality" would suggest that different organizations will achieve integration in different ways. The manner in which different general managers and their organizations achieve this integration will define their uniqueness.

Although not comprehensive, we may suggest three key foci for integration: (1) environmental and subsystem interdependence, (2) process and content, and (3) temporal sequencing.

Environmental and Subsystem Interdependence

Central to the open systems perspective is the notion of interdependence, between an organization and its environment and among an organization's internal subsystems. The values of balance and congruence are inherent in these views. The purpose of action is to bring an organization into congruence with the present and anticipated states of environment as well as to modify internal subsystems so that they are congruent with one another. Action strategies taken to modify one subsystem must take into account the manner in which the planned actions would affect the other subsystems. When necessary, they should be augmented by action strategies oriented to other subsystems.

Process and Content

As we noted earlier, the process component deals with the "how" of actions; the content deals with the "what" of action. We will note that all actions have process and content elements. For example, environmental analysis may focus on understanding the industry in which an organization operates or on the specific behaviors of customers. In this case, we are dealing with the content of analysis: industry in the first case and customers in the second case. The analysis may be conducted by an outside expert or by a task force within the organization. Now we are talking about the process of analysis.

One of the lessons from systems perspective is that both process and content are inextricably intertwined. Jointly they influence the functioning of the organization. In the above example, both the consultant and the task force may bring forth similar recommendations, i.e. the content of action may be similar. Yet the process was different in the two cases. This may influence the implementation of recommendations. In some organizations, the consultant recommendations may be more palatable to general managers; in some others, the internal task force may speed up their acceptance and implementation.

The process-content interconnection portrayed above suggests that while taking action, both process and content must be consciously designed. The relative emphasis of process and content elements may vary from one context to another. Consider two organizations A and B. The top management of company A has recently come to agreement regarding the strategic direction of the company; however, they are not sure how to structure the organization and develop their employees to meet the new strategy. Company B has been floundering for the past few years due to competitive challenges and is not sure what their strategic direction should be. In the case of A, undertaking a strategic planning process is not very useful. In the case of B, strategic planning may indeed be the first phase of the action strategy. In A's case, the process elements may be crucial; in the second case the content may dominate in the beginning. In both cases, however, both process and content elements will need to be interfaced.

Temporal Sequencing

Implicit in the above example, is the role of timing: how does one sequence action strategies so as to achieve congruence among subsystems and between organization and environment? A third focus of integration is the temporal sequencing among actions. It is virtually difficult to bring various elements of an organization to congruence all at once. However, one may accomplish this to a degree *over time*.

As we have seen, rational action strategies start with the functional and informational subsystems, trying to bring them into alignment with the environment. Thus, once environment is analyzed, strategy is formulated, organization structure and information and control system is designed, then implementation can begin. During implementation, an organization may undertake developmental, cultural, and political activities in the service of implementation. In the human system strategies, social, cultural, and political subsystems precede functional and informational elements. Here the specific sequencing of action strategies is not fixed, unlike in the case of rational action strategies.

Which should come first in an organization, rational action or human system? It depends on the specific context of an organization. Thus, a diagnosis is necessary to determine temporal sequencing. To aid the diagnosis, we may postulate two major principles for temporal sequencing:

1. When there is great cohesion among top management or when an organization is in crisis, rational action strategies may be the best starting point. When the top management is cohesive, they can attend to the alignment of functional and informational subsystems easily. When an organization is in crisis, speedy action may be necessary.

2. When there is conflict among top management or major segments of an organization, there is likely to be distortion of information and opportunistic behavior by individuals and various segments of an organization. Here human system strategies may have to precede rational action strategies in order to bring some semblance of order back to the organization.

In either case, all subsystems will have to be eventually tackled, although the starting points are different.

The major goal of general management action is to bring various subsystems of an organization into congruence with one another and with the organization's environment. Neither the rational action nor human system strategies, taken by themselves, are comprehensive enough to account for total organizational phenomena. Both these sets of strategies are complementary and need to be integrated. In this summary we have provided three major foci of integration: interdependence, process-content, and temporal sequencing. We may add that interfacing the various action strategies is still very much an art.

III GENERAL MANAGEMENT AND THE FUTURE

Part Outline

14 THE ROLE OF GENERAL MANAGEMENT

Chapter Outline

If Paul Allaire gets his way, Xerox is in for monumental changes. Says Allaire, "We changed a lot in the 1980s, but in the next five years, we'll have to change so much it will make the last ten look like a practice run." Allaire is 52 years old. He first learned about pleasing the customer when his father, who ran a quarry outside of Worcester, Massachusetts, taught him to hurl a few extra shovelfuls onto every order. After college and business school, he joined Xerox in 1966 as a financial analyst and in 1975 began an eight year stint running Rank Xerox, the company's London-based subsidiary. Allaire's successful restructuring of that operation—he cut staff 40 percent and reduced costs by $200 million—helped him win the CEO job. . . .

Allaire doesn't give a hoot for most CEO perks. He drives himself to work and, when he takes a ski trip, flies coach. Nor is he a workaholic. While his day typically runs from 7 A.M. to 7 P.M., he makes it a rule to work only the occasional Sunday and never on a Saturday. He admires Jack Welch for his toughmindedness, Allaire couldn't have a more different management style. He is a listener who quietly sits in meetings, sizes things up, and then gets people quickly on to the next issue. But don't let the mild manner fool you. Says Leonard Vickers, a Xerox senior VP: "A mild rebuke from Paul is like a tongue-lashing from other people. You immediately get the point."[1]

CEO Paul Allaire has an important task: rebuild Xerox to meet intense competition, which includes formidable global giants, both U.S. and Japanese. So do all CEOs and indeed many other top managers of corporations. But what exactly do they have to do to run and manage their companies? Just how do they come to power? What are the career stages one goes through before one gets to the top-management level? In this chapter, we will sketch some answers organization theory has provided to these questions.

So far in this book, we have presented the major theoretical ideas and action strategies that organization theorists have formulated from extensive research. We focused on the total organizational system for explaining behavior and prescribing action steps. In this chapter, we shift our attention to the key managers entrusted with the overall performance of an organization. We summarize the implications of organization theory for the role and functions of the key managers.

There are two reasons for shifting from the organizational to the individual level of analysis. The first reason is purely pragmatic. When we talk about action steps or strategies, we need to keep in mind that it is individuals who take action, nor organizations. From an action perspective, "organization" is an abstraction. When we say that an organization has taken a particular action, we imply that the key managers have prescribed the action and they and/or their subordinates have carried it out. The second reason is pedagogical. We want to remind the reader of the relevance of organization theory to managerial action. In Part II, we described the major action implications of organization theory. In this chapter, we summarize its implications for the general managers of organizations.

Our focus in this chapter is on key managers, whom we will term *"general managers."* General managers have major influence on the behavior of an organization, and are ultimately entrusted with its overall performance. As we pointed out in the introduction, organization theory is mostly relevant for general managers. For lower-level managers, organization theory is useful for understanding, and perhaps predicting organizational behavior. But it is the general managers who initiate organization-wide actions, and hence, the action implications of organization theory are primarily relevant for them.

But first let us formally define the term *general managers.*

Who Is a General Manager?

By the term *general managers,* we refer to those managers in an organization who are responsible for formulating and implementing strategic direction within an organization. They could be responsible for:

1. an entire organization (e.g., the Chief Executive officer); or
2. a more or less self-contained unit within a major organization (e.g., president of a division); or for
3. integrative functions that cut across divisions (e.g., Vice President of Strategic Planning or Human Resources, Chief Financial officer etc. of a diversified firm).

By this definition, not all managers are general managers. A foreman or plant manager in a manufacturing plant, a sales manager in a marketing division, or a functional manager (e.g., marketing) in a single-industry firm or a division of a diversified firm does not qualify as a general manager, since neither is in charge of a self-contained unit, nor does any one of them perform functions which are truly integrative.

There are three characteristics that set general managers apart from other managers in an organization:

1. They are the *top level* or *senior managers* of an organization.
2. They have *cross-functional* or *cross-divisional* responsibilities; i.e., they perform the major integrative functions in an organization.
3. They are the *powerful actors* in an organization; they allocate resources, make major organizational level decisions, and in general, have a significant impact on the functioning of an organization.

As we said earlier, organization theorists have shed some light on the role and functioning of a general manager. In this chapter, we will summarize our knowledge about general managers. In doing so, we have decided to step away from the large body of literature that has developed under the rubric of organizational behavior. Our focus is exclusively on organizational roles rather than the psychological and social psychological factors that affect the functioning of all individuals.

The scheme of the chapter is as follows. First, we will briefly sketch the historical development of the general management function in organizations. Second, we will summarize the major works that deal with the role and functions of general managers. Third, we will present a systems theoretic review of general managers' roles and functions and some of the new roles general managers are currently fulfilling. Fourth, we will discuss how they are selected. Fifth, we will sketch our knowledge about the career stages of individuals as they enter an organization and evolve into general managers. Finally, we will describe the cross-national differences in the development of general managers.

Historical Development of General Management Function

At the turn of the century as the ownership came to be separated from the control or management of a corporation, general managers began to appear in organizations. Position titles such as the chief executive officer and/or president in the United States or managing director in U.K. firms represented the key general managers of a corporation. Although many of them owned stock in their respective companies, few of them owned controlling interest, and hence could not in any sense be called owners of their companies. Rather, they were "hired hands" who were supposed to run their companies in the best interests of their shareholders, at least in theory. In all but the smallest companies, they reported to the Board of Directors, who performed a watchdog function, i.e., they were the guardians of the shareholders' interests in the corporations.

Alfred P. Chandler, in his landmark study of the managerial revolution in U.S. business, documented the appearance of general management in corporations:

> The practices and procedures of modern top management had their beginnings in the industrial enterprises formed by merger. . . . . The process of merger brought more persons, with more varied backgrounds, into top management. In the new consolidations a family or single group of associates held all voting stock. It was scattered among the owners of the constituent companies and financiers and promoters who assisted the merger. It became even more widely held after the company sold stock to finance the reorganization and consolidation of facilities. . . .
>
> The shift in strategy from horizontal combination to vertical integration first brought the managerial enterprise to American industry. . . . The owners no longer administer the enterprise. The experienced manufacturers, who helped

to carry the merger and who, normally with the advice of one or two financiers rationalized the facilities of a new consolidation, became the core of its top management. Although they were still large stockholders, they rarely controlled the company as did the owners of entrepreneurial firms. Moreover they hired and promoted managers with little or no stock ownership in the company to head the new functional departments and central staff officers.

. . . Once administrative centralization and vertical integration had been achieved, the separation of management and ownership widened. The scattered owners of the widely held stock had little opportunity to take part in management decisions at any level; and only a few managers continued to be holders of large blocks of voting stock.[2]

Over time, in large companies, there began to appear different types of general managers, some in charge of formulating policies and others in charge of executing them. For example, Alfred Sloan, then CEO of General Motors, separated policy making from operations. He instituted a system in General Motors in which the policy making (key strategic decision) was centralized in an executive committee at the headquarters, and operations were decentralized and delegated to managers in charge of divisions (Chevrolet, Buick, etc.). Although the CEO and the executive committee were significantly more powerful, the divisional heads had resource allocation responsibilities, and had significant influence on the decisions pertaining to their divisions. In many ways, their function was integrative: they had to coordinate product development, purchasing, manufacturing, and marketing functions of their respective divisions. In addition, they were assessed on return on investment (ROI), an overall performance measure.

Divisional Managers

As firms undertook diversification as a growth strategy, and adopted the divisional form of organization, general managers began to appear at the *middle levels* in organizations. Divisional general managers or presidents were responsible for self-contained entities, their divisions. Although the primary responsibility for resource allocation among the divisions rested with the headquarters, the divisional managers had significant influence on how they allocated their divisional resources. Also they had the responsibility for coordinating the various functional activities within the divisions.

In the chapter on strategic planning, we summarized two different types of diversification—related and conglomerate. In multidivisional organizations, the divisional level general managers had some responsibility for the strategic direction of their divisions (e.g., what product lines to produce, and where to sell them), although there was strong direction from the corporate headquarters. In conglomerate firms, the divisional managers had greater autonomy in setting the strategic direction of their divisions, since the headquarters controlled only the financial resources. Despite these differences, the job of the divisional chiefs was integrative: they had to coordinate the various functions—marketing, manufacturing, finance, and research and development. They allocated resources, and their units were more or less self-contained. Thus they fit the description of general managers.

To cope with the coordination problems arising from product-market diversity, organizations began to invent other roles: product manager, project manager, integrator, and so on. Thus, in many organizations, product managers focused on specific products or product lines, but had to rely on manufacturing and marketing for getting their work done. A project manager was in charge of a specific project of finite duration. Integrator was a role designed to facilitate coordination in an organization. Although these roles were integrative, they could not be called general management, since many of these roles had no major resource allocation responsibility. Nor were they in charge of a self-contained entity. However, in many organizations, these jobs became training grounds for future general managers.

International Division

As organizations undertook multinational expansion, still more general management roles began to appear. In the early stages of expansion, when a firm established an international division, the head of the international division had to coordinate and oversee the operations and in many cases the strategies in different countries. When a firm adopted world wide product divisions, the presidents of the divisions functioned somewhat analogously to the divisional general managers, except that they had the responsibility for their respective product lines worldwide, not just in one country. Similarly, where country divisions were established, the heads of country divisions were responsible for all the product lines in their respective regions.

Integrative Staff Roles

As organizational environments became increasingly turbulent, and as the need for adaptation became pressing, organizations instituted many *integrative* staff roles. For example, such titles as vice president of strategic planning, organization development, and chief information officer began to appear in diversified firms. They reported to the chief executive officer, and in some cases had membership on the board of directors. Their responsibility cut across divisions. For example, the vice president of strategic planning had to coordinate the strategic planning for the entire corporation: this meant not merely corporate level strategies, but overseeing the strategic planning in divisions, in some cases in conjunction with their planning counterparts in the divisions. The incumbents of these jobs had significant resource capabilities, were responsible in some ways for the performance of the entire organization, although they had no direct authority over the divisions. Rather, they had to influence the divisional heads by various means of persuasion.

In recent years, two further trends have appeared: (1) addition of a new layer of management leading to the role of the sector executive; and (2) the creation of the office of the CEO.

Sector Executive

In divisionalized organizations, when coordination problems become severe, a new level of management is added between product divisions and the chief executive officer. This stratum tends to be composed of product group executives, sometimes called sector executives. Each sector executive is responsible for a number of product divisions. Quite often, this is the result of a consolidation of product divisions into product groups, with sector executives forming a new hierarchic level.

Office of the CEO

A second trend is the creation of the office of the chief executive officer, predominantly in multinational corporations. The office of the CEO may consist of the chairman, vice chairman, president, and sector executives; it oversees a wide range of operations and handles strategic planning. It is also involved in policy matters, major financial decisions, and acquisitions. This trend appears to be a response to the intense coordination needs of complex multinational corporations (MNCs), the time pressures on the CEO, and perhaps the need to prepare individuals to assume the corporations' top leadership positions.

These two trends were the focus of a study by Business International Corporation (BIC); a summary of their findings is presented in Box 14.1.

Summary

As organizations diversified and faced turbulent environments, they also expanded the number of general management positions. General managers began to appear in the middle levels of organizations, general management jobs became numerous, and general managers with different foci of responsibility were created.

Despite such proliferation of general management positions in organizations, our understanding of a general manager's roles and functions is very much in its embryonic stage. There are only a few systematic theoretical and empirical works explicating the role of different general managers. In the next section, we piece together some of the major functions from related theoretical writings.

Box 14.1

Business International Corporation Study

To uncover emerging organizational trends due to globalization of industries, BIC surveyed 74 of the *Fortune* 100 firms. Based on the survey, the BIC group arrived at three major conclusions. First, no new forms for organizing for international business have evolved since 1975. The companies still use worldwide product or regional structures, an international division, a matrix, or a mix of any of these. Second, worldwide product structure is increasingly popular. Third, firms are grappling with the problem of how to account more equitably for product, regional, and functional demands *at the same time*.

BIC found two methods that are being used to deal with this increased interdependence: creation of a new layer of management between the CEO and the product divisions, and establishment of an office of the CEO.

New Layer of Management

Nearly half the companies in the survey that experience change in organizations had added a new layer of management between the chief executive officer and product divisions. This stratum tends to be composed of product group executives, each of whom is responsible for a number of product divisions. Several reasons for this experiment were cited:

To ensure better coordination among divisions manufacturing technologically similar products and/or serving similar markets.

To create a high-level group to handle

long-range strategic planning without having to take on the day-to-day management of product divisions.

To strengthen the corporation's ability to deal with the external environment and to develop an executive cadre sensitive to environmental issues.

To reduce the number of executives reporting directly to the CEO in order to make his span of control more manageable.

BIC study noted that the group executive's job can be ambiguous. He has no single divisional power base. In some cases, the group executives function more in a staff than in a line capacity.

Office of the CEO

Such an office was created in five of the corporations studied to achieve the following goals: to coordinate the diverse goals of an MNC; to relieve time, travel, and management pressures on the CEO; to provide for long-range planning; and to groom executives for leadership positions. In several of the companies studied this development occurred simultaneously with the addition of a very limited new layer of management, as the newly appointed sector managers became members of the office of the CEO.

Source: Adapted from Business International Corporation, *New Directions in Multinational Corporate Organization* (New York: February 1981).

Role and Functions of General Management

Over the years, scholars have described the various roles to be performed by a manager. The early writings were conceptual and normative in nature. They exhorted what an ideal manager should do; they were devoid of empirical content. Further, they did not distinguish between types of managers (e.g., general versus functional, by levels).

Although Kautilya and Machiavelli described the political roles of a leader, management scholars and organization theorists first recognized the roles of a manager in the functional subsystem. Weber, for example, anchored his discussion of bureaucracy on the notion of rational-legal authority. Similarly other classical theorists focused on top manager's activities in the functional subsystem. For example, Fayol distinguished managerial activities from five other industrial activities: technical (production), commercial (buying, selling, and exchange), financial (locating optimum sources and uses of capital), and accounting (including statistics).

Even during the heyday of classical management theory, some scholars ventured to describe managerial activities in the social subsystem. Mary Parker Follet made the concept of *integration* the cornerstone of her description of general manager's functions. Her concept of integration required a different view of authority from the one prevalent in the writings of classical theorists. It required managers and their subordinates to shed their organizational roles to find solutions that satisfied both sides without one side dominating the other. According to Follet, integrative solutions emerge from negotiations among parties rather than the logical or engineering approaches advocated by classical theorists.

The focus on social subsystem dominated the work of Chester Barnard as well. Barnard identified three executive functions:

> . . . first to provide the system of communication; second, to promote the securing of essential efforts; third to formulate and define purpose.[3]

Barnard, thus emphasized that managers have to be communicators to weld individuals into a social system. Further, for the binding to take place, executives continually negotiate with subordinates: they exchange inducements (rewards such as money, status, etc.) in return for appropriate contributions from subordinates.

The social functions of managers received great emphasis from scholars of the Human Relations school. Thus Mayo and the Hawthorne researchers emphasized the interaction between superiors and subordinates; supervisory attention to employees was a prerequisite to the smooth functioning of an organization. The later day human resource theorists, McGregor, Argyris, and Likert, extended this line of reasoning. For them, *integration* served as an organizing metaphor for the discussion of managerial functions.

The emphasis on managers as information processors received serious attention, first from Herbert Simon. Simon argued that the critical problems faced by managers are nonroutine in nature. That is, these problems have typically not been encountered in the same form by the organization before, and they are not susceptible to ready made solutions. For Simon, the essence of managerial work is the solution of non routine problems.

As we noted earlier, these early scholars did not distinguish between general managers from managers in general. Although they have enriched our understanding of one or two specific roles of managers in general, they could not provide us with a holistic description of general manager's work. A focus on general management is perhaps first evident in the works of business policy scholars at the Harvard Business School. Based on intensive case studies, they discarded the view that a general manager's job can be described in simple terms. Rather they focused on the complexities of the job. C. R. Christensen, one of the major figures went on to state that:

> . . . (general managers need the rare ability) to lead effectively organizations whose complexities he can never fully understand, where his capacity to control the human and physical forces comprising that organization is severely limited, and where he must make or review and assume ultimate responsibility for present decisions which commit concretely major resources for a fluid and unknown future.[4]

For such jobs, the Harvard School advocated that individuals develop an administrative point of view. Christensen identified many elements of the administrative point of view:

1. A focus on understanding the specific situation.
2. A focus on the total situation as well as the specific decision.
3. Sensitivity to interrelationships: the connectedness of all organizational functions and processes.
4. Examining and understanding any administrative situation from a multidimensional point of view.
5. Approaching problems as one responsible for the achievements of the organization.
6. An action orientation.[5]

Others at Harvard have refined these notions. An example of a more recent description of the general manager's job developed at Harvard is given in Box 14.2.

The Harvard attempt was perhaps the first major step to grapple with complexities of a general manager's role. The writings were essentially conceptual and in many cases devoid of empirical content. This situation began to change in the late 1960s when researchers turned their attention to the question: What do general managers do? Two sets of scholars gave us two distinct but related views of the role and functions of general managers: (1) Mintzberg and (2) Dalton and Thompson. We will first review their

Box 14.2

The Functions of General Managers: Harvard School

Consistent with the ideas of Christensen, Andrews and others have developed an approach to general management which breaks down the general manager's job into three major categories: *architect of corporate purpose, organization builder,* and *personal leader.* Professor Norman Berg elaborated these three roles further:

1. The general manager is responsible for the establishment of the long term objectives for the company that are challenging and attainable.

2. The general manager is responsible for the development of supporting plans that will contribute to the accomplishment of the overall objectives selected.

3. The general manager is responsible for the resolution of the inevitable conflicts that arise and the trade-offs that must be made in many of the activities of the organization.

4. The general manager is responsible for the selection, development, motivation and fair treatment of its members.

5. Finally the general manager is responsible for the overall performance of the organization.

Source: Adapted from Norman A. Berg, *General Manager: An Analytical Approach* (Homewood, Ill.: Richard D. Irwin, 1984), pp. 6–7.

works, then place them in the context of system model and then point out some newer duties of general managers.

Mintzberg's Study of Managerial Work

The most notable of the empirical works on general managers is that of Henry Mintzberg.[6] Mintzberg took the classical theorists to task by pointing out the paucity of real world (empirical) understanding of managerial work behind their theories. He set himself the task of understanding what managers actually did rather than what the classical theorists prescribed they should do. Although he was interested in understanding managerial work in general, he studied six chief executive officers, hence his focus was on general management. Based on his work he identified three major roles performed by the managers: (1) interpersonal, (2) informational, and (3) decisional.

1. *Interpersonal* roles referred to building and maintaining person-to-person relationships both within and outside the organization.

Box 14.3

Mintzberg's Study of Managerial Work

Professor Henry Mintzberg, currently at McGill University, is one scholar who studied the nature of managerial work in detail. While he was a doctoral student at the Massachusetts Institute of Technology, his curiosity in what a manager does led him to study the activities of managers as part of his doctoral dissertation. Using the method of structured observation, Mintzberg studied five chief executives. Structured observation involved developing a category of activities and then following the managers around on daily basis observing and systematically documenting their activities. As a result of his extensive field observations, he came to some interesting conclusions about managerial work.

First, Mintzberg noted that six characteristics distinguish managerial work from others. These characteristics are:

1. Much work at *unrelenting pace*. The work of managing an organization is taxing: the quantity of work to be done, or that the manager chooses to do is substantial and unrelenting.

2. Activity characterized by *brevity, variety, and fragmentation*. A manager cannot expect a concentration of efforts. Although there may be some seasonal patterns in a manager's job, there were no short-term patterns.

3. Preference for *live action*. Mintzberg discovered that managers gravitated toward work that is current, specific, and well-defined.

4. Attraction to *verbal media*. Managers demonstrate very great attraction to the verbal media.

5. *Network of contacts*. A manager maintains communication relationships with three groups: superiors, subordinates, and outsiders.

6. The manager sometimes controls his work but very often he is *controlled by the situation* as dictated by subordinates, superiors, and outsiders.

Second, perhaps more germane to the role of general managers, Mintzberg discovered ten different roles for the managers he studied. He classified them into three different sets: (1) Interpersonal roles, (2) Informational roles, and (3) Decisional roles.

Mintzberg thus set the stage for discussing the activities of a manager at a concrete level, away from such abstractions as planning and organizing propagated by the classical theorists.

Source: Adapted from H. Mintzberg, *The Nature of Managerial Work* (New York: Harper & Row, 1973).

2. *Informational* roles described how executives received and transmitted information.

3. *Decisional* roles referred to various activities of managers as they made decisions.

Mintzberg also provided a detailed description of the three roles of managers. A summary of his work is presented in Box 14.3.

Interpersonal Roles

The three interpersonal roles identified by Mintzberg are (1) figurehead, (2) leader, and (3) liaison.

1. The most basic of all managerial roles is that of *figurehead*. Because of his formal authority, the manager is a symbol, obliged to perform a number of duties. Some of these are trite; others are of an inspirational nature; all involve interpersonal activity, but none involves significant decision-making activity.

2. In his *leader* role, the manager defines the atmosphere in which the organization will work. Leadership involves interpersonal relationships between the leader and the led. This is the role that has received most attention in popular and scholarly circles.

3. The *liaison* role deals with the significant web of relationships that a manager maintains with numerous individuals and groups outside the organization or the subunit he heads. CEOs build and maintain their status system by joining external boards, performing public service, and attending social events and conferences.

Most of these roles revolve around building and maintaining interpersonal relationships both within and outside the organization.

Informational Roles

A second set of activities that Mintzberg discovered in his study of chief executives relates to receiving and transmitting information. The manager serves as the information nerve center of the organization. Three roles involved here are: (1) monitor, (2) disseminator, and (3) spokesperson.

1. As *monitor*, the manager seeks continually and is continually bombarded with information that enables him to understand what is going on in the organization and its environment. He seeks information in order to detect changes, to identify opportunities, to build up knowledge about his milieu, and to be informed when information must be disseminated and decisions made.

2. As *disseminator* the manager transmits both *factual* information and *values* into his organization and from one subordinate to another. Because of his special access to information, the manager is uniquely positioned to undertake this activity.

3. As *spokesperson*, the manager transmits information out to the environment. The manager may lobby for his organization and may serve as the public relations head.

Decisional Roles

Mintzberg identified four decisional roles: (1) entrepreneur, (2) disturbance handler, (3) resource allocator, and (4) negotiator.

1. As *entrepreneur,* the manager infuses the organization with purpose. He initiates and controls much of the change in the organization. This includes exploiting opportunities and solving nonpressing problems.

2. As *disturbance handler,* the manager deals with involuntary situations that are partly beyond his control. The disturbances are many: departure of a subordinate, feud between subordinates, loss of an important customer, and the like.

3. As *resource allocator,* the manager brings organizational strategies to life. For, it is in the making of choices involving significant resources that strategies are determined. It involves scheduling of time, programming work, authorizing actions, and budgeting.

4. As *negotiator,* the manager participates in negotiation with outside entities: other organizations, individuals and the like. It is frequently the manager who leads the contingent from his organization in such negotiations.

Although Mintzberg studied chief executive officers of small companies, he did not distinguish between general managers, claiming instead that the roles he identified are valid for all managers. More importantly, Mintzberg did not attempt to imbue the roles with any purpose. For example, managers may be engaged in planning or designing an organization, but they may perform several roles to accomplish this. Mintzberg was silent with respect to the purposes behind these activities; he was trying to find out what managers did concretely.

Instead of focusing on the concrete activities of managers, Dalton and Thompson focused on the functions performed by top level managers.

Dalton and Thompson's General Management Functions

A second stream of work by Dalton and Thompson attempted to discover what successful general managers did, and how their work differed from lower level managers.[7] Instead of focusing on concrete work activities like Mintzberg, they set out to categorize the functions performed by the very senior managers. Based on intense case work with a large number of mangers, they identified four major functions performed by senior managers: (1) providing direction, (2) exercising power, (3) representing the organization, and (4) sponsoring key people.

Providing Direction
The senior managers play major roles in providing direction for the whole, or at least a significant part of the organizations to which they belong. They envision for themselves and for others the unique capabilities, and the "distinctive competencies" of their organization. Finally, they articulate and demonstrate in their actions a sense of direction that guides the actions of other members of the organization.

Exercising Power

The successful senior managers are skilled in the exercise of power: they are willing and capable of using the power at their disposal to influence other's decisions toward satisfactory ends for the organization. They initiate, request, review, set agendas, persuade, assign, and design their own and others' time in order to get decisions made and work done that will benefit the whole organization.

Representing Internally and Externally

Top level managers build and maintain complex networks inside and outside the organization in order to gather and share information, contacts, and resources. Formally and informally they represent the organization to its essential publics. They usually work at the interface with critical organizations, whether they are key clients, government agencies, regulatory bodies, scientific communities, or financial sources. They have also developed relationships with a broad cross-section of employees inside the organization with whom they maintain contact as they moved up in the organizational structure.

Sponsoring Key People

A major function of the senior managers is to consciously select and sponsor key individuals who have the capacity to make significant current and future contributions to the organization. The sponsor provides opportunities and experiences of greater responsibility for those individuals who have already proven themselves in the basics.[8]

Although the job of general managers differed substantially from other types of managers, Dalton and Thompson were quick to point out that most organizations they studied had more than one individual who performed general management functions. The four functions are sufficiently complex as to preclude their performance by any one individual except perhaps in some very small organizations.

Summary

Over the years scholars have both theorized and studied general management roles and functions. On the theoretical end, various scholars have highlighted different functions of managers, without necessarily providing a comprehensive view of the nature of the work. Empirically oriented scholars have been comprehensive, although their approaches have been different. Mintzberg focused on the concrete activities of managers; Dalton and Thompson focused on the abstractions that guide managerial work. In the next section, we elaborate and interpret their work from the vantage point of the systems model.

Systems Theoretic Review

In this section we will review the many roles of a general manager from a systems theoretic perspective. Our analysis of managerial roles will stress three major themes: First, we will identify the diversity of managerial roles that need to be performed in an organization. Second, we will review the models of managerial work from the vantage point of the systems model. Third, we will point out some of the emerging roles of the general manager and review them from systems theoretic perspective.

Diversity of Roles

Based on the systems model, we may identify three sets of managerial roles that need to be performed in an organization:

> *Environmental Interface Roles.* Roles that describe how general managers interpret and influence the environment and foster organizational adaptation.
>
> *Subsystem Related Roles.* Managerial roles that pertain to various subsystems in the organization: functional, social, informational, political and cultural.
>
> *Integration.* Set of roles that describe the linking of organization to environment as well as the subsystems.

In Part II of this book, we summarized the key action strategies formulated by organization theorists. We may array the strategies according to the roles prominently featured in each one of them. Table 14.1 displays the key linkages. As can be seen from the table, for the general management function to be executed properly, a diversity of roles will have to be performed in organizations.

In small organizations, many of these roles are performed by a single individual, or the entrepreneur. However, as organizations grow larger, it

TABLE 14.1   **Action Strategies and General Management Roles**

System Theoretic Roles	Action Strategies
Environmental interface	Environmental analysis
Subsystem related roles	
Functional	Strategic planning
	Organization design
Social	Organizational development
Informational	Design of information & control system
Cultural	Build strong culture
Political	Managing conflict
Integrative	Integrator across subsystems and environment

becomes nearly impossible for one individual to perform many, if not all, roles. Then organizations rely on several individuals for their performance. As we have seen in our discussion of the historical underpinnings, in large organizations, there are several general managers, an occurrence that attests to the diversity of general management roles.

Models of Managerial Work

How does the systems model shed light on the empirical findings of Mintzberg and Dalton and Thompson? Refer to Table 14.2. As shown in Table 14.2, Mintzberg's spokesperson, liaison, negotiator, and entrepreneurial roles refer to environmental interface roles, whereas others refer to internal subsystem roles. However, since Mintzberg focused on concrete activities, his research does not focus on integrative roles. On the other hand, Dalton and Thompson focus on abstract categorizations, and hence, their scheme captures the major integrative role: directing the organization.

Some Emerging Trends

Although conceptually the functions of general managers fall under three classes—environmental, subsystem-related, and integrative—in concrete terms new roles are likely to become important, as the environments facing an organization change and bring additional challenges to the running of the organization. Here we highlight two roles that are becoming important for some of today's general managers: (1) lobbying role and (2) cultural role.

TABLE 14.2   **Linkages between Systems Model and Models of Managerial Work**

System Theoretic Roles	Mintzberg's Roles	Dalton & Thompson's General Management Functions
Environmental interface	Spokesperson Liaison, negotiator, and entrepreneur	Representing externally
Subsystem-related		
Functional	Entrepreneur, Resource allocator	Providing direction
Social	Leader	Sponsoring key people
Informational	Monitor	
Cultural	Figurehead, Disseminator	Representing internally
Political	Disturbance handler	Exercising power Sponsoring key people
Integrative		Providing direction

Lobbying Roles

Increasingly, some top managers in the U.S. are discovering that for their organizations to be effective, they have to interface with the regulatory and legislative bodies. In systems theoretic terms, this refers to a specific environmental interface role. In concrete terms, this has come to mean a lobbying role for the chief executive officer. Much of the success of Lee Iacocca, after he took over the role of the chairman of Chrysler Corporation, can be attributed to his effective lobbying with the Congress to release financial resources to his organization, which was in financial distress. In the 1990s, many CEOs are discovering that lobbying is a regular part of their work. For example, a recent *Wall Street Journal* reported on how and why many CEOs are now lobbying Congressmen in earnest (see Box 14.4).

Cultural Roles

As a consequence of the excesses of the 1980s and the wave of deregulation, many have questioned the legitimacy of top level managers. Indeed they clamor for transformational leaders—individuals who, as we have seen in our chapter on organizational culture, can fulfill cultural roles. Leaders are expected not merely to articulate values, but to act those values in their life on a day-to-day basis. Development of cultural skills, in addition to other skills, may be the greatest management challenge of the coming decade.

From a systems theoretic point of view, lobbying is an environmental interface role; its emergence is a reflection of the importance of government as an important environmental element. Clamor for developing cultural roles is an outgrowth of the recognition of the influence of organization culture.

Summary

From a systems theoretic point of view, almost all the functions of general managers can be clustered into three: subsystem related, environmental interface, and integrative roles. The models of managerial work—by Mintzberg and Dalton and Thompson—both are captured by the systems model. In a similar way, the two emerging roles—lobbying and cultural roles—refer to environmental interface roles and subsystem related roles within the systems model.

As we have stressed in this chapter, general managers are the key actors in organizations, since they are responsible for the major decisions in organizations. Hence their selection and development is crucial for the performance of organizations. In the next two sections, we summarize our knowledge about the selection and development of general managers.

Box 14.4

Lobbying Role for Top Level Managers

Organizations such as the Business Round-table and the American Business Conference have long brought top executives to Washington to express business views on major issues. But executives have usually shunned lobbying on narrow issues specifically affecting their own companies. They viewed that as a distasteful task better left to subordinates.

Now, however, many argue that government policy is so intertwined with their companies' welfare that "lobbyist" must be an unwritten part of almost any CEO's job description. And by virtue of their hands on experience in business, the chief executives are usually regarded as the most effective kind of corporate lobbyist, far more potent than the hired guns who usually troll the halls of Congress on their behalf.

The experience of the following CEO exemplifies this emerging trend:

For two difficult days, Mr. Kertzman, the chief executive of a *mid-sized* company called Computer Solutions Inc., and the chairman of the 3,500 member American Electronics Association, and a dozen fellow CEOs from around the country have turned into full time lobbyists. Their mission is to persuade Congress to cut the capital gains tax. Their problem is that they make a lot of money.

Mr. Kertzman primarily visits Democrats, and for good reason. They are the ones he needs to win over for a capital-gains cut to pass, and unlike most other top officers in his industry, the 41-year old entrepreneur is himself a Democrat. He doesn't hesitate to use that fact to curry favor, referring to himself as the "Sandinista in pinstripes."

As the chairman of a major trade association, Mr. Kertzman comes to Washington about 20 times a year, and he believes that the experience benefits not only his industry but his company as well. By focusing on national issues, he says, he has become more aware than he might have been otherwise that the manufacturing economy is weak, and he has trimmed his expansion plans.

But there are plenty of frustrations on the way. Foremost among these is the knowledge that he is just one of many interests vying for attention on Capitol Hill. Another frustration is the relative inexperience of the powerful Congressional staffs. During a meeting with a Ways and Means Committee staffer, Mr. Kertzman recalls talking about the importance of improving corporate productivity. "Productivity is a double-edged sword," the staffer replied. "It also loses jobs." Kertzman says he thought, "I am going to have a tough time." "Washington is being run by kids," he adds. "It is a frustrating experience for a CEO to be lectured by a kid."

Of course, the power of persuasion isn't the only weapon corporate chiefs bring to lobbying. There is also the power of money—especially campaign funds given through corporate and trade association political action committees. It is an issue that is often raised only obliquely in talks with lawmakers, or not raised at all. But the CEOs on the other hand and the lawmakers on the one know it is there all the same.

Source: Adapted from Jeffrey H. Birnbaum, "Chief Executives Head to Washington to Ply the Lobbyist's Trade," *The Wall Street Journal* 71, no. 107 (March 19, 1990).

Selection of General Managers

In the chapter introduction case, we presented Paul Allaire, the newly appointed CEO of Xerox. He had been with Xerox for over 20 years and had been promoted from within. Many organizations select CEOs and indeed general managers, from within their companies. However, some pick their leaders from outside. We will review both types of selection before we point out some implications of the systems model.

Insider Succession

Only rarely do organizations follow the textbook prescriptions, adhered to very frequently at lower levels, near the top of the management pyramid. One of the few academic works that dealt with executive succession concluded:

> Even though there are some common components, the factors affecting the choosing of senior people and the way the decision-making process operates at the top level are different in important respects from the process at the middle range.[9]

How does the top management selection differ from selection of lower-level employees? First, the situation with respect to selection of top-level managers reverts, in a sense, to the *small business context*. At the top, the group of individuals is small. They have highly personal relations, and the members interact as they would in a small company. The individuals know each other very well and they can speak about a candidate from close personal contact or direct observation. Hence there is no need to rely on files or memos.

Second, the *tolerance for individuality increases* at the higher echelons, where the interplay among individuals is intense. The executive appraisal becomes more realistic when a direct need exists to fill identifiable, immediate or prospective vacancies. This evaluation includes not only the next promotion, but positions several steps further ahead. Consequently, executive potential in candidates is often spotted quite early on in their careers.

Third, although the process may sometimes appear arbitrary to an onlooker, a *set of contextual factors* frequently shape the choice of executives. The following set of questions are typically posed:

1. Among the positions open, what appears to be the best allocation of the high-potential people available to the firm?
2. What are the requirements for each position as now constituted and functioning with the present or recent incumbent?
3. Are the requirements for the future the same? What changes in operations and structure can we expect?

4. Do we want to change the way the job is done to meet business objectives? Do we need to accept changes in the way the job is to be done to accommodate the candidate available for the position?

5. How will association with a given group of people in a different situation change the "new" man's behavior?

6. What needs of the organization, including its development of given individuals, must be projected 1, 3, 10 years ahead?

7. What effect will a decision with respect to the appointment of Mr. A have upon the opportunities, motivation, and development of others at levels below, above, or coequal with him?

8. How might a decision with respect to the one or several candidates be read by various segments of the "corporate constituency": Customers, investors, financiers, creditors, employees, unions, and so on?[10]

We note that many of these questions are not raised in the case of lower-level employees, and only rarely among middle-level executives.

Suffice it to say that the top management succession is different from the one we find among other layers of managers.

Outsider Selection

During this decade, many U.S. companies looked outward for their top-level executives. This is partly because of four reasons:

1. Many of these companies had not spent resources to develop internal management talent;

2. The management in place has not performed well;

3. Takeover architects brought new management teams—with whom they were more comfortable—into the targeted companies; and

4. Environmental shifts were so sudden (as in the telecommunication industry) that both insiders and company development programs were obsolete.

Since the corporate searches for outside CEOs are usually conducted in strict secrecy, hardly any academic treatise has studied the process. In one journalistic account, Patricia O'Toole concluded that when it comes to outsider succession, CEOs like Iacocca—who typifies a success story—are exceptions, and that outsiders, in general have not succeeded. Some of her conclusions are presented in Box 14.5.

Review

Organization theorists would argue that, the executive succession must be viewed from an open systems perspective. But just what does this mean?

Box 14.5

The Corporate Messiah

The confusions and strains caused by the sudden collapse of the U.S. industrial economy, the equally sudden rise of the global market, inflation, recession, and high interest rates left many corporate managements feeling that the world was out of control. Not knowing how to adapt to an environment in which change was the only constant, most corporations focused their energies on increasing—or regaining—control over their businesses. For the most part, control meant control over numbers, especially, the sacred bottom line. Management by the numbers became the strategy for survival, and numbers experts were running more corporations than ever before. Bottom lines were fattened by cutting costs, changing accounting procedures, and shifting assets to make the most of corporate tax laws—moves that added little productive value to the enterprise but did create the illusion of higher profits.

At many troubled companies another illusion took hold: the belief that salvation lay in the hands of supremely capable executives, if only they could be found and hired. The quest

for these corporate messiahs played itself out differently in differing companies, but in simplified form, the reasoning went like this: "We've botched it and we need help. Only an outsider can set things right because all of us on the inside have had a hand in causing the problems. Since it will take an extraordinary leader to save us, we're going to have to pay an extraordinary amount to get him to take on this impossible task."

More often than not, the corporate messiah's task *did* prove impossible—but not because the company was beyond redemption. A bigger problem was that the million-dollar compensation contract used to lure a savior set up such unrealistically high hopes for a quick miracle that the savior was usually doomed from the start. As soon as he proved unable to walk on water, his days were numbered.

The situation is fraught with other perils as well. At the top, most executive searches are carried out in secret. Corporate boards want to conceal the fact that they are looking outside for a new president or chairman lest their competitors and Wall Street conclude that the

---

First, technical excellence is only one criterion for picking a CEO. Perhaps more important are the political and cultural skills of an individual, and his/her match with the organization. Second, the response of various influential constituencies should be carefully considered both during the process and choice of executives. Thirdly, the selection should be broad based, and both insiders and outsiders should be included as potential candidates.

Career Development of General Managers

At this stage a question that typically occurs to many students and aspiring general managers is: if there are so many roles to be performed, who performs them all? Where do I fit in? As we noted earlier, since the roles are

Box 14.5 continued

present management is weak. In addition, there is often a need to conceal the search from their own senior executives, whom they have decided to pass over for the job.

On the other side of the transaction, the candidate wants to keep the matter confidential so his current employer won't find out he's considering another job. And although a corporation can guard its anonymity by using an executive search firm to delve discretely into a candidate's background, the candidate is less well positioned to get the inside story on his corporate suitor. He has to be careful not to give himself away, and his best sources of information—other executives in the company—are usually off limits.

A company in need of a messiah is also a company in a hurry. Eager to find a hero, the search committee often puts more energy into persuading the candidate to take the job than into considering how well he will mesh with the company. Because of the need for secrecy, interviews and meetings typically take place away from the office, in restaurants and other social settings. If the candidate's professional credentials are in order, a little charm and goodwill on his part go a long way toward

convincing the company there is no need to look further.

The cost and complexity of a first-class search for a new president or chairman also reinforce the belief that the corporation really is getting a messiah. At large companies, the fee paid to the search firm runs to several hundred thousand dollars. Lawyers and compensation consultants are engaged at great expense to come up with contracts that candidates will find irresistible. A corporate director may be retained at a six-figure sum to oversee the search. Intelligence on the best and brightest is gathered through impressive webs of contacts. No stone is left unturned, no avenue unexplored. All of this plus the secrecy, the size of the messiah's paycheck, and the need for swift change create enormous expectations. As executive recruiter David S. Joys told *The New York Times Magazine,* "The thinking becomes, 'We've scoured the country. We've chosen this guy from dozens. He must be superman.' And when he isn't, things can go sour very quickly."

Source: Patricia, O'Toole, *Corporate Messiah: The Hiring and Firing of Million Dollar Managers* (New York: William Morrow and Company, 1984).

diverse, all except small organizations rely on a number of individuals to perform them. Organizations typically have a number of general management positions, although their responsibility and authority may be vastly different. As we have suggested in the beginning, in addition to CEOs, divisional general managers or presidents, and even some in charge of integrative staff roles, have significant general management responsibility.

What is the typical career progression of an aspiring manager from the day he enters an organization till he becomes a general manager? Dalton and Thompson identified four career stages through which a new entrant passes before that individual assumes general management responsibilities: (1) apprentice, (2) independent contributor, (3) mentor, (4) sponsor:

1. *Apprentice.* During the first stage, employees are expected to work under the supervision and direction of a more senior professional

in the field. His/her work is never entirely his/her own but assignments are given that are part of a large project. The individual is expected to do most of the detailed and routine work on a project.

2. *Independent Contributor.* At this stage, the individual is given independent responsibility for a definable portion of a project, process, or clients. The individual is expected to work on his/her own without too much guidance from supervisors.

3. *Mentor.* During the third stage, the individual is expected to stimulate others through ideas and information. He/she should be involved in developing people by acting as an idea leader, serving as mentor to young professionals, and/or by assuming a supervisory position. He/she also begins to deal with outside to the benefit of the organization, i.e., working out relationships with clients, and developing new business.

4. *Sponsor.* At this level, the individual has 'arrived.' All the general management functions Dalton and Thompson identified earlier: providing direction, exercising power, representing the organization and sponsoring key people and projects are expected at this stage.[11]

According to Dalton and Thompson's categories, only the individuals in the final stage may truly be called general managers. Individuals in the mentor stage perform some of the functions, but are not truly general managers. Neither apprentices nor independent contributors are general managers.

As can be seen from the progression, the lower-level employees are expected to perform roles in the functional subsystem. Middle-level managers, entrusted with implementation, are in addition expected to perform social subsystem—mentor type—roles, whereas political, cultural, integrative, and environmental interface roles are usually reserved for top level managers.

One further observation is in order. Dalton and Thompson studied managers in the United States. In U.S. firms, most of the lower-level managers are expected successfully to fulfill their functional subsystem roles: detail work in the case of apprentice, or project performance in the case of independent contributor, but not roles in other subsystems. However, as they move up the ladder, they are expected to perform environmental interface roles as well as significant political subsystem–related roles. Stated differently, their technical competence or excellence becomes less important for performing general management functions.

We should emphasize that Dalton and Thompson confined their study to the United States. In other countries, especially Japan, we find somewhat differing patterns of career development, a point to which we now turn.

Cross-National Differences among Selection of Managers

As a point of comparison to what takes place in the U.S., we may summarize what little we know about the backgrounds, selection, and development of executives in Japan. There are three major differences in the origins of executives:

1. Although in Japan there is a fair degree of social and occupational mobility, the mobility is, of course, greater in the U.S.

2. (*a*) The proportion of business leaders whose fathers were executives or professional men, is greater in the U.S. and the U.K. than Japan; (*b*) in the U.S., unlike in Japan, few business leaders were sons of government officials; and (*c*) the proportion of business leaders who were sons of farmers were by far the largest in Japan.

3. Higher education plays an extremely important role in the selection of the Japanese business elite, relative to either the U.S. or the U.K.

Japanese general management selection and development depends primarily on training and experience *within* a company.[12] Present day Japanese enterprises have institutionalized ways of selecting top level executives largely on the basis of education, length of service in the company, and career achievement. A typical career begins with entrance examinations on academic subjects right after graduation from a university. For those who are accepted, a lifetime commitment to the company is strongly implied. Men move up step by step in an intricate hierarchy. Promotion is shaped by a special merit system that has customarily been based largely on seniority. However, it is common for large companies to make promotion dependent on systematic performance appraisals often associated with examinations on specialized work and management problems. In short, the qualifications of a chief executive are assessed not merely by his ability to deal with management matters, but also by his loyalty to the organization.[13]

Under the lifetime employment system, training within the company is not only necessary, it also pays. The employees are promoted within the company and their jobs change as the product and the technology change, so education is necessary. This thought is expressed at Hitachi in the following phrase: "The essence of enterprise is people." At Matsushita, a similar phrase is used: "Matsushita produces capable people before it produces products." By people, these Japanese corporations mean not only the higher echelons, but rank and file workers. Recently, as the product and its production process have become more technology intensive, and as the company activity has become more international, the training within the industry has become

Box 14.6

Japanese Emphasis on Training

Trainees can be classified under three headings: (1) the newly hired employees, (2) general employees, and (3) managers.

New employees are trained mostly by lectures and on-the-job training. The indoctrination of company philosophy and teaching of technical skills are important subjects. The length of training varies from company to company, but it is usually from three to eight months. In Matsushita, the orientation and training of employees from universities (about 800 persons) are centralized in the head office and the training is conducted as follows: lectures in the head office, three weeks; training in retail stores, three months; training in the works, one month; lectures on cost accounting, one month; lectures on marketing, two months. After this eight-month training, new graduates are distributed to various departments and subsidiaries.

General employees are trained in functional skills and also in human skills, and for this purpose they undergo (1) on-the-job training, (2) self-development, (3) off-the-job training. Off-the-job training is most emphasized, and this is done with planned instruction by the supervisors. Under the promotion by length of service system the employees are not in competition with one another and the supervisors are willing to pass on the necessary skills.

Job rotation is another means and this is one of the characteristics of training in Japanese corporations. In the USA or in Europe, people will move from company to company in the same profession, but in Japan people will move from department to department doing similar jobs in the same company. Honda has a planned rotation program for the first ten years; Toyota's policy is to rotate employees once every three years; Canon has a policy choosing the head of the section from among those members of staff who have served in at least three different departments. . . .

Self-development is another important aspect of training, and opportunities for frequent promotion and wage increases stimulate the desire for self-development. The company encourages this by distributing reading materials, and lists of recommended books, and subsidizing the cost of buying books. Group activities such as Quality Circles (QC) are widely used, and in successful companies more than 80 percent of the employees participate, the company paying overtime for group activities.

Off-the-job training is conducted in company training centers and in outside institutions and consists of, for example, technical training classes, other functional training classes, and language classes. Hitachi has six training centers in addition to a number of training rooms at plant sites.

Manager training consists mostly of off-the-job training in the company's training centers and its purpose is to improve conceptual skills and human skills.

The amount of money spent on training is not clear; one survey shows the cost at about 15,000 yen per employee per year. This does not include the cost of on-the-job training. At Hitachi about 2.2 days are spent in training each university graduate employee in technical skills every year. This does not include on-the-job training either.

Source: Toyohiro Kono, *Strategy and Structure of Japanese Enterprises* (Armonk, N.Y.: M. E. Sharpe, Inc., 1984), p. 321, 322.

more important. The need for training comes from the necessity of the company, but it also derives from the idea of respect for people. By contrast, United States and European companies tend to think that the necessary human resources can be bought from outside by money.[14] Recently, Toyohiro Kono, a Japanese scholar, summarized the training programs in Japan; we present his findings in Box 14.6.

Suffice it to say that there are significant differences between Japanese and United States firms in terms of selection and development of executives. In relative terms, Japanese firms rely more on insider succession, and pay greater attention to general management development than their U.S. counterparts. For Japanese firms this also makes economic sense since most employees expect to stay with their firms lifelong—again something that is different from the expectations in the United States.

Chapter Summary

By the term, "general managers," we refer to those managers in an organization who are responsible for formulating and implementing strategic direction within an organization. They could be responsible for: (1) an entire organization (e.g., the chief executive officer), (2) a more or less self-contained unit within a major organization (e.g., president of a division), or (3) integrative functions that cut across divisions (e.g., vice president of strategic planning or human resources, chief financial officer etc. of a diversified firm).

There are three characteristics that set general managers apart from other managers in an organization. First, they are the *top level* or *senior managers* of an organization. Second, they have *cross-functional* or *cross-divisional* responsibilities; i.e., they perform the major integrative functions in an organization. Third, they are the *powerful actors* in an organization: they allocate resources, make major organizational level decisions, and in general, have a significant impact on the functioning of an organization.

Over the years, as organizations diversified and faced turbulent environments, they also expanded the number of general management positions. General managers began to appear in the middle levels of organizations, general management jobs became numerous, and general managers with different foci of responsibility were created.

Two groups of scholars have studied general management functions: (1) Henry Mintzberg, and (2) Dalton and Thompson. Mintzberg conducted an observational study and concluded that general managers performed three major roles: interpersonal, informational, and decisional. Interpersonal roles included leading subordinates, serving as a figurehead, and acting as a liaison; informational roles were monitoring, disseminating, and acting as a spokesperson; decisional roles were entrepreneurship, disturbance handling, resource allocation, and negotiations. Dalton and Thompson, after intense clinical work identified four major functions of general managers: providing direction, exercising power during implementation, representing their organizations externally and internally, and sponsoring key people. Two additional roles are becoming important for some of today's general managers: (1) lobbying role, and (2) cultural role (building strong cultures).

In the United States, general managers are often picked up from inside the company. A typical general manager would have evolved through four stages: apprentice, independent contributor, mentor, and then a sponsor. However, in recent times, many U.S. firms have looked for outsiders to save them from disaster. This is quite unlike the firms in Japan where general managers typically come from within the firm, after a long stint with the company.

Specialized Terms

General manager
Divisional manager
Integrative staff role
Sector executive
Office of the CEO
Interpersonal roles
Informational roles
Decisional roles
Figurehead
Leader
Environmental interface roles
Integration

Liaison
Monitor
Disseminator
Spokesperson
Disturbance handler
Resource allocator
Negotiator
Apprentice
Mentor
Sponsor
Subsystem roles
Lobbying

Discussion Questions

Theoretical

1. Who are general managers? How does their job differ from that of middle or lower level managers?
2. Enumerate the different types of general managers in a multinational corporation. Give examples.
3. Review Mintzberg's roles from the perspective of the systems model.
4. Analyze Dalton and Thompson's career stages from the perspective of the systems model.

 5. What are the advantages and disadvantages of insider versus outsider CEO selection?

★6. Based on the notions developed in organizational effectiveness and organizational politics, describe how you would assess the performance of a general manager.

Applied

 7. You are one of the trustees on the board of a major public university. The chancellor of the university will retire in two years. How will you proceed to find a replacement for him?

 8. You own an executive search firm. You are retained by a *Fortune* 500 firm to fill a new position: the head of its international division. How will you proceed?

End Notes

 1. Adapted from *Fortune,* "Can He Make Xerox Rock?" June 17, 1991, p. 38.
 2. Alfred P. Chandler, *The Visible Hand: The Managerial Revolution in American Business* (Cambridge, Mass.: Belknap Press of the Harvard University Press, 1977), pp. 415–16.
 3. Chester I. Barnard, *The Functions of the Executive* (Cambridge, Mass.: Harvard University Press, 1966), p. 217.
 4. C. Roland Christensen, "Education for the General Manager," Harvard Business School, Case No. 9-375-241.
 5. C. Roland Christensen, *Teaching by the Case Method* (Boston: Division of Research, Harvard Business School, 1981).
 6. Henry Mintzberg, *The Nature of Managerial Work* (New York: Harper & Row, 1973).
 7. G. W. Dalton and P. H. Thompson, *Novations: Strategies for Career Management* (Glenview, Ill.: Scott, Foresman, 1986).
 8. Ibid., pp. 121–23.
 9. Albert S. Glickman, Clifford P. Hahn, Edwin A. Fleishman, and Brent Baxter, *Top Management Development and Succession: An Exploratory Study,* Supplementary Paper No. 27, Committee for Economic Development, November 1968, p. 13.
10. Ibid., p. 16.
11. Dalton and Thompson, *Novations.*
12. Hiroshi Mannari, *The Japanese Business Leaders* (Tokyo: University of Tokyo Press, 1974).
13. Toyohiro Kono, *Strategy and Structure of Japanese Enterprises* (Armonk, N.Y.: M. E. Sharpe, Inc., 1984), p. 321.
14. Ibid.

★This is an advanced-level question.

15 FUTURE DIRECTIONS

Chapter Outline

"Millions are already attuning their lives to the rhythms of tomorrow."
Alvin Toffler, *Third Wave*[1]

In our discussion of the history of management thought, we argued that
(1) environments present the major challenges of organizations, and (2) the
management solutions reflect human and social inventions that reflect not
only the environments but the cultural values of the prevailing period. In
this book, we have attempted to synthesize the major currents in contemporary organization theory, which in turn reflect the dominant ethos. As we
have shown, most of the developments—with notable exceptions—took
place in the United States.

Consistent with our argument, we should predict that organization
theory will progress in the future as the environments and cultural shifts
take place. In this chapter, we attempt to paint one scenario of how the
organization theory is likely to evolve. Thus, we enumerate some of the
major environmental trends that are affecting the organizations of today,
and identify their implications for organizations and organization theory.

The scheme of the chapter is as follows. First, we provide a review of
the book, to remind readers of the major themes of the book. Next we
summarize the unique contributions of this book. Third, we identify nine
environmental trends that are changing the ways of managing organizations. Fourth, we point out the key implications for organization theory.
Finally, we conclude with a chapter summary.

Review

This book has been divided into three parts. In Part I we presented various
theoretical developments in the field of Organization Theory. First, we
described the history of development of Organization Theory during the
20th century. Next, we presented in successive chapters, the concepts
of open systems theory, contingency perspective, and organizational
change. Finally, in the last chapter we described how to define and assess
organizational effectiveness.

Having described and discussed various theories in Part I, we turned to
the discussion of applied aspects in Part II. In the beginning of Part II, we
presented an overview of the two major classes of organizational action:
rational action and human system strategies. Rational action strategies consisted of four sequentially ordered steps: environmental analysis, strategic
planning, organization design, and design of organizational information
and control systems. Human system strategies consisted of organization
development, organization culture, and organizational politics. In Part II,
each of the seven strategies was discussed in separate chapters. In each
chapter, we presented an analysis of the given action strategy from the

open systems perspective. This analysis indicated that the areas of environmental analysis, strategic planning, organization design, and organizational information and control systems have been primarily oriented to technical, content, and rational aspects of organizations while the other three areas of organization development, organization culture and organizational politics have emphasized the social, process, and nonrational aspects of organizations.

In the concluding section of Part II, we strongly emphasized the need to integrate rational and human system strategies when general managers undertake any action. Focusing on one strategy to the exclusion of the other is tantamount to doing a quick fix. We believe that this would harm rather than help organizations. We also pointed out how an integrated plan combines social and technical, content and process, rational and nonrational aspects of organizations. Implementation of this plan should not only help organizations but also develop people working in it. In our opinion, such a holistic approach is essential for organizations to be effective in the ever changing complex global environment of today and tomorrow. No short cuts or quick fixes will do the job.

Some Unique Aspects

We now briefly discuss some unique aspects of the book.

1. *Organizational environment:* We have devoted a complete chapter to the description and discussion of the various aspects of the environment. In particular, we have discussed how to assess the environment. In the years to come, environment is going to become more complex, turbulent and uncertain. Therefore, organizations need to monitor the environment and assess it in order to develop meaningful strategies and design appropriate organizations to implement these strategies.

2. *Linkage between theory and action:* Most organization theory books have presented theoretical developments and then discussed applied areas without providing proper linkages between the two. On the other hand, in this book, we have tried to develop a substantive linkage between theory and action by analyzing each action phase in terms of the open systems framework. This linkage between theory and action is very important. Without this linkage, action has very little meaning because it is guided by ad hoc reasoning rather than an integrated theoretical framework. We strongly believe that action plans must be grounded in adequate theory. Physics, which is probably the most developed of the natural sciences, has followed this pattern where developments in the applied side have always been grounded in prior theoretical developments. We believe a similar process needs to be followed

in social and organizational sciences. In this book, we have attempted to do this for the organizational theory field.

3. *Holistic approaches versus quick fixes:* We have emphasized that there are no quick fixes based on a limited action focused on one of the subsystems. Organizations are holistic systems with many interacting subsystems. These organizations in turn interact with their environments. Thus, organizations can be managed effectively only through a systematic action plan that involves all subsystems and the environment.

4. *Integrated action plans:* In Part II, we have emphasized the need to integrate rational and human system strategies. Unfortunately, in some management practice, each action step is treated as if it is independent of the other phases. We believe that both types of action—rational and human system-based strategies—need to be integrated so as to bring about strategic change and develop effective organizations.

Looking to the Future

In this book we have tried to present the state-of-the-art knowledge about how to understand and manage organizations. We would now speculate as to what is likely to happen in the future. Before we undertake this speculation, it is important to mention a point of caution. We believe that it is impossible to forecast or predict any discrete event in the future. At the most, what can be done is to outline some trends. Therefore, we only attempt to outline some of the trends we think are significant and point out their implications.

In our view there are nine trends the study of which may provide some insight into the future: (1) globalization, (2) discontinuity, (3) emergence of networks, (4) computer and communication technologies, (5) information explosion, (6) power sharing, (7) enlightened work force, (8) diversity in the work force, and (9) coexistence of bureaucracy and innovation. We will now briefly discuss these trends.

Globalization

In the early 60s, President Kennedy[2] said in his inaugural address that we are living in an interdependent world. Unfortunately, it has taken humankind several decades to recognize this fact. Today, it has become almost a cliché to say that markets have become global in scope. Buckley defines globalism thus:

"By globalism, I mean that the insular, parochial business world of the past, which was dominated by segmented markets and localized products is gone. It is dead, buried by high speed transportation and modern communications. We have come to the time when there is one global market for quality products."[3]

According to Michael Porter, many industries, such as auto and airlines, have become global industries.[4] **We believe that this trend toward globalization is going to accelerate and, in the coming years, many more industries will become global in scope.**

The trend toward globalization has many important implications for organizations. In order to manage effectively in the global environment, it is important for organizational leaders to develop a global perspective rather than a narrow nationalistic perspective that has prevailed for most of the 20th century. A recent example of the self-defeating nature of the narrow nationalistic perspective was the trip by President Bush and several auto executives to Japan during January 1992. In particular, pronouncements by Lee Iacocca produced resentment in Japan. In return, Japanese responded in a way to frustrate Lee Iacocca who flew back alone to Detroit. Iacocca's behavior was so dysfunctional that even *The Wall Street Journal* wrote in its editorial, "Perhaps the President should hold down the talks to one simple proposition: The U.S. will let in anything that Japan wants to sell, if the Japanese will keep Lee Iacocca."[5] Therefore, it would be a great challenge to develop leaders with the new type of mind–set. This would not be easy but necessary.

This global mind–set would provide the underpinning for the development of appropriate management philosophy for the 21st century. Thus, environmental diagnosis will be done in the global context. Strategies will need to be developed taking into consideration not only local issues but also global issues. Organization design will not only fit the strategy but also will be congruent with the local context. Organization development must be congruent with strategy as well as local culture and environment. Issues of organizational politics and conflict must be managed in such a way that agreed upon strategies can be implemented in a timely and effective manner. And finally, organizational information and control subsystems must make relevant information available to managers and decision makers who are dispersed all over the globe.

The above are exciting challenges. In order to meet these challenges we strongly believe that the field of organization theory has to become multicultural. Thus, there is a need for teams of scholars from different cultures working together to develop knowledge about managing global organizations of the future.

Discontinuity

Most of the organization theory literature today deals with issues of managing incremental changes. Most of the theory in the field has been built through the study of organizations which are experiencing incremental changes. Yet, environments in the future are going to experience drastic and discontinuous changes. A forerunner of what is to come has already happened in 1989 and 1990. Unexpected changes of epoch proportions have happened, such as the dissolution of the Soviet empire. As a result, state-owned enterprises in Eastern Europe are being privatized at unprecedented speed. Who would have imagined even a few years ago that such monumental changes would take place?

Most organizational leaders have still not digested the changes that have taken place in the 1989–1991 period. Thus, their policies, strategies, and resulting organizational structures still reflect the past rather than the present. There is very little knowledge or experience to deal with the changes we are witnessing today. **We predict that changes in the 21st century will be even more momentous and discontinuous than what has been experienced so far.** This decade as well as the next century will be the age of discontinuity.

To deal with and manage discontinuous changes, we need to develop a different kind of organization theory than what we have today. This will require new modes of thinking as well as a lot of research and experimentation. In particular, we will have to learn how to develop early warning signals for detecting discontinuous changes. We will have to develop strategies which are drastically different from the existing ones. New modes of thinking and behaving will need to be developed.

To sum up, present day management techniques will not be adequate to deal with these systemwide discontinuous changes. There is a dire need to develop change technologies which are consistent with the emerging discontinuities.

Emergence of Networks

We are going to witness increasing emergence of networks within as well as among organizations. They will not be shown on any organization charts. Yet, they will exercise tremendous influence and power within organizations and among organizations. Successful managers of the future will have to develop and cultivate these networks.

At the inter-organizational level, many of these networks will cross organizational as well as national boundaries. They will link people and information across various disciplines and nations. **Emergence of these global networks will lend a new qualitative dimension to the organizational environment.**

One example of these networks is the emergence of international strategic alliances. Some of these alliances involve technology sharing or development of new technologies; others involve production sharing; still others involve both the development of technology as well as production and distribution of goods and/or services.

Another example of emerging networks is seen in the crisis management area. In the case of the Three Mile Island nuclear reactor crisis, a large network of organizations got involved. These organizations included the utility; the supplier of the reactor, Babcock-Wilcox; the media; the office of the governor of Pennsylvania; the Federal Emergency Management Agency; the Nuclear Regulatory Commission; and even an expert team from Westinghouse Nuclear, who was the direct competitor of Babcock-Wilcox.

A study of these networks would add a new dimension to organization theory and would greatly enhance our understanding of the global environments in which organizations of the future would be operating. Forming and managing these networks would require further developments in organization and inter-organization theories. To effectively manage such networks would require different management skills and styles than are required in managing hierarchical organizations of today.

Computer and Communication Technologies

Advances in computer and communication sciences as well as the merging of these two technologies to create new products and systems are going to have profound impact on how our organizations are organized and managed in the next century. Computer aided manufacturing has already revolutionized manufacturing. Flexible manufacturing has considerably reduced the lot size and is allowing manufacturing according to the unique demands of customers. In the not too distant future, for example, it will be possible for a customer to walk into an automobile showroom, and design his or her own car, and get it manufactured and delivered according to his or her own unique specifications.

The factory of the future will permit manufacturing of the product without the human hand ever touching the product. The factory will be comprised of a number of computers networked into a Local Area Network (LAN). An experiment was tried by General Motors, and Toyota is already building such a factory in Japan. Early experimentation with this idea indicates that each shift in such a factory would be managed by a team of workers whose job would be to insure that the LAN is operating properly. These workers would be highly educated and possess knowledge of computer technology. They would also have a high level of team skills. **Such a combination of human and technical skills would create a new type of work force which, in turn, would need new type of organization and management system.**

Information Explosion

Great advances have already occurred in information technology in the last few decades. We are already witnessing an increasing information explosion. According to some estimates, 90 percent of the world's knowledge has been generated in the last few decades.

It is becoming increasingly obvious that centralized information gathering and decision-making systems are not likely to work. It is impossible for any single person or single unit to collect, absorb, and process all the relevant information that is needed for decision making in today's fast changing world. Therefore, there is a growing trend towards decentralization of information. The emergence of the concept of "Information Center" in an organization is a recognition of this fact. These centers are "end user" oriented. So, they help other units in the organization to develop their own databases and programs to analyze these data.[6]

Power Sharing

As can be seen, there are decentralization trends in decision making and information processing. These trends have profound implications for organizational design. To be congruent with decentralized decision making, it becomes necessary to distribute power and modify organization structures. This in turn requires the development of new leadership and management styles so as to effectively manage empowered people.

Enlightened Work Force

The last few decades have seen a tremendous increase in the education level of the population. This is not just for some countries but is a worldwide phenomenon.

A well-educated work force has a very different type of motivation than an uneducated work force. For example, an educated person develops an enhanced sense of self-worth and, therefore, likes to exercise a greater degree of control over one's life including the job. Such a person is demotivated, if not frustrated, by controlling type of management.

Existence of an educated work force leads to strong pressures to develop organizational and management systems which enhance the self-worth of their employees and, thus, develop in them a strong motivation for self- and organization development. **Our prediction is that, in the next century, every major corporation will have to attend to these developmental issues by appropriately modifying its control, evaluation, and reward subsystems as well as instituting suitable training, development, and career-planning programs.**

Diversity in the Work Force

Japan, Singapore, Taiwan, and Korea have the great advantage of having a homogeneous work force. It is relatively easy to develop consensus because a homogeneous work force is likely to have shared values. In the continental countries such as the United States and the former USSR, there are many ethnic groups in the work force. A recent study by the labor department indicates that the work force diversity in the United States is going to increase dramatically during the decade of the 1990s. For example, it is predicted that 85 percent of the net increase in the work force is going to come from so-called minority groups in the United States such as women, Blacks, Hispanics, Asian Americans, and others.[7]

Though work force diversity always existed in the United States, there was a myth of the melting pot which assumed that all workers in the United States acquired the same values. Therefore, they could be managed according to the values of the dominant majority.

At the lower levels of the organization, there has been a great cultural diversity in the United States. However, at the management level, minority groups have so far been under-represented. For example, in Hughes Corporation, women comprise 36 percent of the work force and other minorities 33 percent. Yet, in the official and managerial population, the percentages are 16 for women and 19 percent for minorities.[8] The management group in the United States has always been dominated by the white males. As a result, the management system, its culture and values, and resulting strategies and structures, have always been based on the assumption that the work force subscribes to an ethic which is based on the heritage of the white male group.

The study of Yankelovich (1983) indicates that the present generation does not believe in the Protestant work ethic.[9] In fact, the values of the present generation can best be described as hedonistic, i.e., every man for himself. This "me" generation demands that their individual needs be satisfied. In fact, Harry Triandis argues that this individualistic value in the United States has gone too far and it has been totally disassociated from any obligation to family, organization, or society.

Minorities in the American work force have so far been relatively undemanding and passive. **Our prediction is that this is going to change in the coming years.** Minority groups are going to demand that they be treated appropriately, i.e., in the manner which is appropriate to their cultural heritage. Work force diversity, therefore, will offer a great challenge to the American management in the 1990s and beyond.

If properly handled, this could provide a competitive edge to American corporations in the global marketplace. When diversity is properly managed, it leads to "innovation." Research results in the group creativity area indicate that heterogeneous groups, when managed properly, produce much more innovation than homogeneous groups.[10]

On the other hand, if the diversity is not managed, it generates dysfunctional conflict in the organization. Dealing with this conflict channels organizational energies away from productive activities. If this conflict is not managed, it often leads to disastrous consequences for the organization. It is, therefore, imperative that Organization Theory provide some answers as to how to manage the emerging work force diversity. This would involve development of an appropriate organizational culture that values diversity and ways of institutionalizing this culture in the organization.

Bureaucracy and Innovation

Several decades ago, Bennis argued that bureaucracy is dead and will be irrelevant for modern organizations.[11] It is true that bureaucracy has severe limitations. At the best, it can lead to efficiency. Max Weber likened bureaucracy to a frictionless machine—once started it runs smoothly. Weber also predicted that bureaucracy has its inherent logic and momentum. Once established it can continue forever. Thus, bureaucracy is very difficult to change because it is a very stable system. Though Bennis was accurate in his prediction that bureaucracy is not relevant for changing environments, we know that bureaucracy has persisted in most of today's organizations in the United States.

As we mentioned earlier, in the recent past (1989–1991), there was an assault on bureaucracy in the Eastern European nations and the Soviet Union. Yet, even there, the bureaucrats are resisting the change. At this point, no one really knows whether the needed changes will ever be implemented in those nations. Yet, it is clear that bureaucracy is becoming less and less relevant for organizations and nations of today.

The greatest fault of bureaucracy is that it kills innovation and creativity. It also prevents organizations from adapting to changing environments. As we mentioned above, the environment in this decade as well as in the next century is going to become very volatile, discontinuous, and unpredictable. We, therefore, predict that bureaucracy will become less and less viable in the management of both organizations and nations.

What will replace bureaucracy is not clear. In spite of predictions, democracy has not replaced bureaucracy in most organizations.[12] In the short term, one can conjecture that some form of bureaucracy combined with some mechanisms for power sharing is likely to be more practical. At least, the Japanese experience is consistent with this hypothesis. In Japanese organizations, hierarchy exists alongside consensual decision making. Thus, one possible scenario for the future is the emergence of hybrid systems which have, at the same time, some characteristics of bureaucracy but also engage in participative practices. Much more experimentation and research needs to be done to identify future forms of organization.

Implications: A Paradigm Shift

As we have noted above, it is clear that environment is going to become more globalized; there will be increasing emergence of networks particularly of the informal type—developments in computer, communication, and information technologies will create exciting possibilities; environments are going to become more discontinuous and hard to predict—there will be a greater need for power sharing and empowering the employees; bureaucracy will be replaced by hybrid forms of organizations; the work force is going to become more educated and diverse thus requiring major attention to issues such as selection and promotion, management styles, organization structures, and organization cultures.

Taken together, the above trends point to the need for organizational transformation, i.e. a major paradigm shift. According to Kuhn and Beam when major transformations or paradigm shifts occur, there is a need to totally reorient the mind-set and develop new ways of thinking and behaving.[13] It may be worthwhile to cite an example of paradigm shift to illustrate the nature of transformational change that usually accompanies a paradigm shift. In the field of physics, a paradigm shift occurred when Albert Einstein demonstrated the relationship between mass and energy. This new thinking ultimately led to the splitting of the atom and creation of a new source of energy, i.e., nuclear energy.

In our chapter on the history of management thought (Chapter 2) we identified three major epochs in the history of organization theory. In the first epoch, dominant thinkers were classical theorists who expounded the theory of bureaucracy. During the second epoch, modern theorists developed such ideas as participative management, power sharing, and empowerment. In the third epoch, we have seen a full flowering of the open systems perspective.

We believe that organization theory is now entering the fourth epoch. During the fourth epoch, there is an increasing need for experimentation and action research to identify characteristics of effective organizations of the future. We believe that, given the trends discussed above, there is a need for appropriate experimentation and action research which should enrich the field of organization theory.

Ethnocentric, Polycentric, and Geocentric Approaches

For the most part, organization theory has been built upon work and thinking done in the developed nations of the West primarily the United States. Thus, present day organization theory has a very strong ethnocentric bias. What we need is a polycentric perspective whereby frameworks developed in non-western cultures, particularly of the East and developing countries, need to be given equal consideration in the development of models and theories in the organization field. This polycentric approach should lead to the emergence of various frameworks. Then a comparative analysis of these diverse theories and frameworks can be conducted to identify similarities as well as differences among them. Based on this comparative analysis, we might be able to develop truly geocentric models and theories which have worldwide applications.

Collaborative Teams of Scholars and Practitioners

There is a dire need for teams of scholars from diverse cultures and different disciplinary backgrounds to work together to develop new theoretical concepts and test them in the global context. Such teams should not only include social scientists but also physical scientists and technologists. In addition, academic scholars need to work intimately with practitioners so that new theories can be converted into appropriate action plans. In this collaborative way, we would be able to develop not only rigorous but useful organization theories that are implementable.

Chapter Summary

In this chapter we reviewed the main contributions of this book. First we have used the open systems perspective as an integrative framework for organization theory. Second, we have argued that there is a close link between theory and general management action. Third, we have argued for integrating rational action and human system strategies. Finally we have emphasized that there are no quick fixes when it comes to managing organizations.

We outlined nine trends that may influence the functioning of organizations: globalization, prevalence of discontinuity, emergence of networks, widespread use of computer and communication technologies, information explosion, demands for power sharing, development of an enlightened work force, increasing diversity, and the formation of hybrid organizations that foster innovation.

Taken together we have argued that we need models of organizational transformation that require renewed experimentation and theory building. This, in turn, would require organization theory to move from its ethnocentric origins to a truly geocentric perspective. To accomplish this we need teams of scholars and practitioners to discover knowledge and solutions to managerial challenges.

We are living in a global village. One thing we can be sure of is that there will be many more surprises in the coming years, like the ones we witnessed since 1989. We also believe that scholars and practitioners of organizational sciences should get together to develop better theories and action plans to meet the emerging needs of the future.

The 21st century will be an exciting time and we are sure that organization theory will contribute a great deal to make this world a better place to live and work.

Specialized Terms

Linkage between theory and action	Globalization
Holistic approaches versus quick fixes	Discontinuity
	Networks

Computer and communication
  technologies
Factory of the future
Information explosion
Power sharing
Enlightened work force
Work force diversity
Empowerment
Protestant work ethic

Bureaucracy and innovation
Paradigm shift
Hybrid forms of organizations
Organizational transformation
Three epochs of organization
  theory
Ethnocentric, polycentric, and
  geocentric approaches

Discussion Questions

1. Briefly describe what you have learned from the prior chapters.

2. What are the unique aspects of this book? Briefly discuss each unique aspect.

3. Looking to the future, briefly describe various trends and how these are likely to impact on the development of Organization Theory.

4. What do we mean by "Globalization"? Discuss important implications of this trend for organizations.

5. What major events have led to discontinuous environments for organizations? How is this discontinuity likely to effect the development of Organization Theory?

6. What kind of networks have emerged in recent years? Illustrate your answer by some examples. What implications does the emergence of networks have for organizational leaders?

7. How is the "Factory of the future" going to be different from the present factories? What implications has this for the work force?

8. What are some of the organizational implications of the "Information explosion"? In what ways is the concept of "Power sharing" connected with the notion of "Information explosion"?

9. What is "Work force diversity"? How is it likely to impact the American labor force in the decade of the 1990s? Discuss some of the implications of work force diversity for American organizations.

★10. What is the relation between bureaucracy and innovation? Is democracy inevitable? If yes, why? If not, why not? Can bureaucracy and democracy coexist in the workplace?

★11. What is the concept of "Paradigm shift"? What are some of the implications of this concept for organizations of tomorrow?

★This is an advanced-level question.

12. Briefly describe ethnocentric, polycentric, and geocentric approaches. Why is it necessary to develop geocentric models and theories in the organization field? How can these models be developed?

End Notes

1. Alvin Toffler, *The Third Wave* (New York: William Morrow and Company, 1980), p. 25.
2. J. F. Kennedy, Inaugural Address, Washington, D.C., 1961.
3. R. J. Buckley, Highlights of Conference Speeches, *Human Resources Building,* ed. R. Nath (New York: UNDP, 1985).
4. M. E. Porter, *Competitive Advantage: Creating and Sustaining Superior Performance* (New York Free Press, 1985).
5. Editorial, *The Wall Street Journal,* no. 60 p. A10.
6. IBM, *The Management of End User Computing: Support Organization* (White Plains, NY., 1984).
7. W. B. Johnston and A. H. Packer, *Workforce 2000: Work and Workers for the 21st Century* (Indianapolis, Ind.: Hudson Institute, 1987).
8. M. R. Currie, "Workforce Diversity in the 1990s: The Challenge and the Opportunity," Presentation at the first joint meeting of Hughes Employees Networking Organization, Los Angeles, Calif., August 8, 1990.
9. D. Yankelovich, *The World at Work: An International Report of Jobs, Productivity, and Human Values: A Joint Project of the Public Agenda Foundation and the Aspen Institute for Humanistic Studies* (New York: Octagon Books, 1985).
10. A. I. Murray, "Top Management Group Heterogeneity and Firm Performance," *Strategic Management Journal* 10 (1989), pp. 125-41.
11. W. G. Bennis, "The Coming Death of Bureaucracy," *Think,* November-December 1966, pp. 30–35.
12. Ibid.
13. Kuhn and Beam, *The Logic of Organizations* (San Francisco, Calif.: Jossey-Bass, 1982).